This book explores the social position of virtuoso ascetics in two civilizations – traditional Theravada Buddhism and medieval Catholicism – in which they achieved a position of considerable prestige and cultural ascendancy. In both settings, it is argued, virtuoso asceticism was able to give rise not only to prominent monastic institutions, but also to a broader cluster of processes – a "virtuoso complex" – that developed into a major axis of social and cultural organization. Emphasizing the combined impact of religious–ideological premises, institutional features of the monastic organization, selected characteristics of the macrosocietal context, and patterns of virtuoso radicalism in shaping the precise expression of the virtuoso complex in each case, the study exposes historical similarities and differences that have not been given due attention in either Weberian or other macrocomparative accounts. Virtuoso asceticism, in this perspective, emerges as a vital factor not only in the rise of the West, but also in the ideological expansion of the Buddhist East. Moreover, it is shown to entail a range of characteristics clearly distinct from those usually subsumed under the better-known category of religious charisma. Merging Weberian sociology with the Maussian tradition of gift analysis, and criticizing the neglect of meaning in current comparative historical sociology, the author also argues the need for a multidimensional approach capable of better addressing the part played by religious orientations in shaping the institutional strength and ideological power of religious elites in the historical framework of the great traditions.

Virtuosity, charisma, and social order

Cambridge Cultural Social Studies

General Editors

Jeffrey C. Alexander, *Department of Sociology, University of California, Los Angeles*

Steven Seidman, *Department of Sociology, State University of New York, Albany*

Editorial Board

Jean Comaroff, *Department of Anthropology, University of Chicago*

Donna Haraway, *Department of the History of Consciousness, University of California, Santa Cruz*

Michele Lamont, *Department of Sociology, Princeton University*

Thomas Laqueur, *Department of History, University of California, Berkeley*

Cambridge Cultural Social Studies is a forum for the most original and thoughtful work in cultural social studies. This includes theoretical works focusing on conceptual strategies, empirical studies covering specific topics such as gender, sexuality, politics, economics, social movements, and crime, and studies that address broad themes such as the culture of modernity. Although the perspectives of the individual studies will vary, they will all share the same innovative reach and scholarly quality.

Virtuosity, charisma, and social order

A comparative sociological study
of monasticism in Theravada Buddhism
and medieval Catholicism

ILANA FRIEDRICH SILBER
Hebrew University, Jerusalem

CAMBRIDGE
UNIVERSITY PRESS

Published by the Press Syndicate of the University of Cambridge
The Pitt Building, Trumpington Street, Cambridge CB2 1RP
40 West 20th Street, New York, NY 10011-4211, USA
10 Stamford Road, Oakleigh, Melbourne 3166, Australia

First published 1995

Printed in the United States of America

Library of Congress Cataloging-in-Publication Data
Silber, Ilana Friedrich.
Virtuosity, charisma, and social order : a comparative sociological
study of monasticism in Theravada Buddhism and medieval Catholicism
/ Ilana Friedrich Silber.
      p.   cm. – (Cambridge cultural social studies)
Includes bibliographical references and index.
ISBN 0–521–41397–4
1. Monasticism and religious orders, Buddhist.   2. Monasticism
and religious orders – History – Middle Ages, 600–1500.
3. Asceticism – Theravada Buddhism.   4. Asceticism – Catholic Church.
I. Title.   II. Series.
BL631.F75   1995
306.6'91657–dc20   94-2502
                                                                          CIP

A catalog record for this book is available from the British Library.

ISBN 0–521–41397–4 Hardback

In memory of my father
who taught me the reality of ideals
and to my mother
who taught me her love for the world of ideas

Contents

vii

Preface

One of the true rewards in bringing this book to its completion is the opportunity to properly acknowledge intellectual debts incurred along the way. My greatest debt is to Shmuel N. Eisenstadt, who first introduced me to the ambitious horizons of comparative historical sociology in general and to the importance of religious traditions in the dynamics of civilizations in particular. His influence on my work goes much beyond the explicit references to his writings in either the body of the text or the footnotes – although I am well aware that he would have handled the topic in a very different manner. I have also had the privilege of benefiting from the encyclopedic knowledge and prodding guidance of R. J. Zwi Werblowsky, one of the very few true comparativists in the study of religion. Stanley J. Tambiah's rich amalgam of anthropological, historical, and macrosociological traditions of analysis first triggered my interest in Theravada Buddhism. His encouragement at an early stage bolstered my confidence to undertake the dauting task of juggling many different worlds of scholarship. I wish to put on record my deep gratitude to Steven Collins, who commented on two earlier versions of the manuscript and, above all, lent me precious intellectual support at times when the cost of crossing the boundaries of disciplines and fields of expertise seemed to become overwhelming. I also thank Michael Carrithers, as well as an anonymous reader, whose critical comments spurred me on to produce what I hope is a better book. Jessica Kuper's commitment to the book and friendly handling of the publishing process greatly helped me bring the manuscript to its final form.

My thanks to Arnold Eisen for his judicious reading and editing help on the earlier chapters, and to Steven Kalberg for commenting on the dissertation from which this book evolved and, more important, for long-lasting Weberian "elective affinities." Although they may not be aware of it, Erik Cohen, Yaron Ezrahi, Don Handelman, Michael Heyd, and David Shulman all served, each in his own field and in his own way, as exemplars of interdisciplinary and theoretically informed cultural analysis at the Hebrew University of Jerusalem. Last but not least, I want to thank Jeffrey Alexander for his stimulation in sharpening certain aspects of the theoretical argument.

I also wish to acknowledge the support I received from various institutions: a doctoral grant from the Israel Research Foundation that enabled me to complete the dissertation on which the book is based; a Pearlman fellowship from the Faculty of Social Sciences at the Hebrew University that sponsored my postdoctoral work in the department of Anthropology at Harvard University; and the repeated financial support I received as a fellow researcher at the Truman Institute, which also kindly financed editorial work on the manuscript. Many parts of this book have been written in the library of the Van Leer Institute, a unique haven of cultural and intellectual life in Jerusalem, and I am grateful to the institute's director, Yehuda Elkana, for his steady hospitality.

Finally, this book may well not have come to completion without the unfailing confidence of Michael Silber, who shared with me, as both husband and historian, this prolonged experience in academic single-mindedness and asceticism. Romy and Mika lent their precious presence and, luckily, never let me completely submit to the virtuoso imperative.

Introduction

Writing about the ascetic type, Nietzsche observed: "It must be a necessity of the first order that again and again promotes the growth and prosperity of this life-inimical species. It must indeed be in the interest of life itself that such a self-contradictory type does not die out. . . . 'Triumph in the ultimate agony': the ascetic ideal has always fought under this hyperbolic sign."[1] It is the "triumph" of the ascetic that will form the main concern of this book.

Although the social bases and implications of religious ideals have been classic topics of sociological debate, one important and closely related theme has not received its due attention: that minority of "virtuosi," as Max Weber called them, who gear their lives to a superior enactment of religious ideals. I propose to expand upon this neglected strand of Weberian sociology and examine the social position of these religious virtuosi from a comparative and macrosociological perspective. More specifically, I intend to focus on historical settings in which virtuoso elites achieved considerable prestige and ascendancy, or in Nietzsche's apt metaphor, where they attained a paradoxical form of "triumph."

The inquiry will concentrate on a distinct type of religious virtuosi – hermits and monks – in two civilizations in which they became especially prominent: traditional Theravada Buddhism and medieval Catholicism. At one level, therefore, the present work may be read as a comparative sociological study of monasticism. Beyond this, however, it also aims at a more inclusive understanding of religious virtuosity (of which monasticism is only one, if a crucial, form of expression) in its historical interaction with different social orders. Although the notion of virtuosity itself, originally taken from the arts, is frequently encountered in Weber's writings, it seems to have been read as no more than a suggestive metaphor and has been left largely unexplored. Weber's work remains the only sociological treatment of the subject, and there has been little attempt – with the important exception of Michael Hill's study of religious orders in nineteenth-century England[2] – to analyze religious virtuosi as a distinctive sociological type.

This neglect may seem surprising in light of the long-standing socio-

---

[1] F. Nietzsche, *On the Genealogy of Morals* translated and edited by W. Kaufmann (New York: Vintage, 1969), pp. 117–18 (essay 3, section 2).

[2] M. Hill, *The Religious Order: A Study of Virtuoso Religion and its Legitimation in the Nineteenth Century Church of England* (London: Heineman, 1973).

1

logical concern with religious phenomena in general, and religious specialists and institutions in particular.[3] It is less surprising, however, given the natural tendency of social scientists to be drawn to religious figures of more obvious historical and social significance – such as priests, prophets, and charismatic leaders – who often enjoy a widespread appeal, and at times even possess a dramatic potential for effecting far-reaching social transformations. Although religious virtuosity is not without affinities to these forms of religious leadership, it clearly addresses itself only to a restricted minority, a "spiritual aristocracy" in Weber's words. Furthermore, this aristocratic minority has often been associated with a tendency to spiritual inwardness and social withdrawal, seemingly of little interest to all but those specializing in the sociology of religion in the narrow sense of the word.

In this work, however, religious virtuosity will be shown to form not only a specific type of religious orientation – and not merely the characteristic of a religious minority – but also a cultural variable of far-reaching macrosociological significance. I shall first address the overall social position of religious virtuosi as closely related to and shaped by specific features of their macrosocietal context. A second, complementary focus will be the development of a whole cluster of processes – what I term a "virtuoso complex" – that came to form a macrostructure of central importance in traditional Theravada Buddhism and medieval Catholicism, the two historical settings selected for comparison.

Analyzing this "complex," I suggest, may add a new angle to the analysis of the part played by religious ideology and structures in the dynamics of macrosocietal formations. Although this is, of course, an old, classical sociological issue, it has been forcefully revived in a recent flurry of works that have all preoccupied themselves once again with the issue of the emergence of capitalism and the "rise of the West."[4] Symptomatic of a remarkable spurt of revival in historical macrocomparative sociology in which neo-Marxist, world-systemic, and state-theory approaches have been very influential during the last decade or so, these studies have also

---

[3] In the humanities, in contrast, the search for religious rigor and spiritual perfection has received ample and distinguished treatment. For an unsurpassed overview, see J. Passmore, *The Perfectibility of Man* (London: Duckworth, 1970).

[4] See in particular D. Chirot, "The Rise of the West," *American Sociological Review* 56 (1985): 181–95; J. Baechler, "Aux origines de la modernité: castes et féodalités: Europe, Inde, Japon," *Archives Européennes de Sociologie* 27 (1986): 31–57; idem, *The Origins of Capitalism* (Oxford: B. Blackwell, 1975); M. Mann, *The Sources of Social Power*, vol. 1 (Cambridge University Press, 1986); J. Hall, *Powers and Liberties: The Causes and Consequences of the Rise of the West* (Berkeley and Los Angeles: University of California Press, 1985); idem, "Religion and the Rise of Capitalism," *Archives Européennes de Sociologie* 26 (1985): 193–223; R. Collins, *Weberian Sociological Theory* (Cambridge University Press, 1986), chs. 3 and 9 especially.

all explicitly oriented themselves, in one way or another, to Weber.[5] The Weber invoked, however, is the one who emphasized status groups, bureaucratic structures, and patterns of domination – that is, that side of Weber most compatible with conflict theory.[6] Relatedly, it is not the Weber of the *Protestant Ethic* with its well-known (if never exclusive) emphasis on the importance of religious orientations, but rather the one who underscored the role of a specific constellation of economic and institutional conditions (such as markets, bureaucracies, legal systems, and state administrations) in favoring the emergence and expansion of capitalism.[7]

Most relevant to my present purpose is the tendency common to this cluster of works, not so much to overlook religion – which, in fact, is discussed extensively by all and whose role is well emphasized – but rather to systematically bracket out its ideological contents. In this perspective, religious institutions are either addressed as yet another form of economic organization or interest group, or assessed in terms of their contribution to the expansion of economic activity and state structures – be it through some form of social control or the more "Durkheimian" functions of normative integration and the enhancement of social solidarity.[8] (The selective way in which only certain aspects of Durkheim are made use of is here itself significant.)[9] Even

---

[5] See T. Skocpol (ed.), *Vision and Method in Historical Sociology* (Cambridge University Press, 1984); D. Smith, *The Rise of Historical Sociology* (Philadelphia: Temple University Press, 1991); R. Collins, "Maturation of the State-Centered Theory of Revolution and Ideology," *Sociological Theory* 11(1993): 117–28.

[6] There are of course differences between these various authors; the overlap and convergence, however, seem to me the more striking and significant.

[7] See especially Max Weber, *General Economic History*, translated by F. H. Knight (New York, Collier-Macmillan, 1961 [1922]), pp. 207 ff. The conditions listed are technological advance, rational bookkeeping, a rationalized and predictable law system, rationalized modern state structures, a pool of free manpower, and the development of unified, unrestricted markets. The last chapters of the same volume, however, also reassert the importance of Protestantism in a way that does not deviate from his earlier thesis on the Protestant ethic and the spirit of capitalism. Although this is not a topic I can expand upon here, these scholars do not entirely ignore the possible part of Protestantism in early Western modernity, but again, relate to it in ways that underplay Protestantism's doctrinal contents and soteriological orientations.

[8] The word "functions" is used here devoid of its systemic, functionalistic charge. These scholars also share indeed a common opposition to Parsonian functionalism. Paradoxically, however, they do represent a form of functional, if not functionalist, approach to religion.

[9] Durkheim, after all, has also initiated a rich tradition of cultural analysis among symbolic anthropologists in particular. There is a vast development between Durkheim's relative insensitivity to religious contents in *The Elementary Forms of Religious Life* (Glencoe, Ill.: Free Press, 1961), where the emphasis is indeed on the normative and solidary implications or "functions" of religion in general, and his later work on collective systems of classification (in collaboration with Marcel Mauss), predicated on a much more systematic attention to collective representations and the symbolic contents of cultural structures.

when duly noting the importance of monasteries, the analysis is restricted to viewing them as economic, protocapitalistic enterprises, or as crucial links in the economic and bureaucratic statelike network of the medieval Church, furthering the latter's intensive exploitation and extensive canvassing of material and human resources.[10]

Perhaps one way to break out of the endless circle of controversies concerning the social bases and implications of religious–ideological orientations – or more broadly, the perennial culture versus social-structure debate – is simply to acknowledge that the answer to this ever-vexing issue might not always be the same everywhere, at all times, and in all aspects or spheres of social life.[11] Religious–ideological orientations, in short, may be more influential in some contexts or situations than in others, and may even vary in the specific way in which they exert their influence in different circumstances and environments.

In the specific case of virtuosity and the virtuoso "macrocomplex," I shall argue that a failure to give appropriate weight to religious–ideological orientations would deprive the phenomenon of a most essential and necessary dimension. Recognizing the importance of religious orientations does not mean, of course, excluding the impact of other variables. In true Weberian spirit, religious orientations will be considered here as only one – albeit essential – variable, interacting and combining with a range of institutional and structural factors in the process of religious virtuosity's historical development and institutionalization.[12]

Both Buddhism and Christianity belong to that category of great-salvation religions, designated by Karl Jaspers as the "Axial Age" reli-

---

[10] See especially Collins, *Weberian Sociological Theory,* pp. 52 ff.; Mann, *Sources of Social Power,* p. 37; F. Hall, *Powers and Liberties.*

[11] This brings me rather close, I believe, to the (eclectic) position held by Ernst Gellner. See E. Gellner, *Plough, Sword and Book: The Structure of Human History* (London: Paladin, 1991), p. 15. Gellner is also interestingly eclectic in combining a concern with the impact of religious breakthroughs and ideological–cognitive megatrends or mutations in the history of civilization (elaborating, for example, on Karl Jaspers's notion of the Axial Age, also adopted by Bellah and Eisenstadt), with a heavy emphasis on the role of religious specialists in the control of material and ideal resources (such as literacy and symbols of legitimacy) and the enforcement of social control. Also arguing that the relation between culture and social structure may vary across time and situations, see A. Swidler, "Culture in Action: Symbols and Strategies." *American Sociological Review* 5 (1986): 273–86. Within this more flexible and differentiated approach, however, one should recognize the existence of periods and situations where cultural orientations or value ends *do* have a direct and straightforward influence upon action.

[12] The commitment to a form of multicausality acknowledging the impact of religious beliefs and values as part of a full spectrum of patterned action orientations has been most recently and systematically explored as a characteristic of Weber's approach distinguishing it from other schools of comparative-historical sociology, in S. Kalberg, *Max Weber's Comparative-Historical Sociology* (Cambridge, Eng.: Polity, 1994).

gions, that propound the idea of a radical breach between a transcendent ultimate reality and the world of given, mundane reality.[13] As underscored by Ernst Gellner in particular, an important feature of these great scripturalist religions is that they offer a universal and individual, theoretically "context-free" conception of salvation, in sharp contrast with "communal religions," that is, community-oriented and nonscriptural religions primarily concerned with underwriting and fortifying communal organization and the rhythm of communal life.[14] Religions of salvation, however, are not only and purely salvational, and may be expected to display a specific combination of communal and salvational orientations.[15] This underscores the need (as rightly felt indeed by some of the recent macrocomparative approaches already mentioned), to complement Weber's well-known attention to the salvational contents and meaning of religious orientations with a more "Durkheimian" or even "Parsonian" concern with the role of religion (and ritual practices)[16] in the consolidation of communal integration and solidarity.[17]

Conversely, however, the specific nature and context of a religion's "communal" orientations (such as its capacity for normative integration and large-scale solidarity) should also be understood as largely dependent upon its specific doctrinal and salvational contents. Analyzing the virtuoso "complex," I submit, will precisely require that we pay attention to religious virtuosity both as a form of religious salvational orientation and as the nexus of a complex type of "communal" integrative processes. The

13 See R. Bellah, "Religious Evolution," *American Sociological Review* 29 (1964), 358–74; S. N. Eisenstadt, "The Axial Age: The Emergence of Transcendental Visions and the Rise of Clerics," *Archives Européennes de Sociologie* 23 (1982): 294–314; Gellner, *Plough, Sword and Book,* p.81; B. J. Schwartz, "The Age of Transcendence," *Daedalus* 104, no. 2 (1975), 1–7.

14 Gellner, *Plough, Sword and Book,* p. 91.

15 Ibid., p. 92. Gellner, however, bases the persistence of communal orientations on the fact that those processes by which he also explained the success of a message of individual and universal salvation – namely social trends such as accelerated urbanization, which uprooted individuals and dismantled communal frameworks – were never total and pervasive. My emphasis, rather, is on "communal" dimensions related to the emergence of large-scale and differentiated religious and political collectivities, and to the fact that these religions have also become part of collective belief systems and the ideological core of entire civilizations.

16 On Weber's general insensitivity to ritual (in contrast, of course, to Durkheim), associated by him with either the "passivity" of contemplative mysticism, the sacramental traditionalism of Catholicism, or simply primitive "magic," see R. Robertson, "On the Analysis of Mysticism: Pre-Weberian and Post-Weberian Perspectives," *Sociological Analysis* 36, no. 3 (1975): 248.

17 Weber, of course, was also well aware of the conservative potential of religious ideology, but addressed it rather in terms of legitimization of economic and political inequality than in terms of collective integration and solidarity. As for Durkheim, he was not unaware, of course, of the need to study religious symbolic contents as such, although this has not been the distinctive strength and emphasis of his approach taken as a whole.

precise nature of these communal processes, moreover, cannot be understood independently of the salvational orientations involved in and affecting their institutionalization and historical deployment.

To that extent, the present study pursues the trend represented by an older generation of macrosociologists such as Robert Bellah, Peter Berger, S. N. Eisenstadt, Roland Robertson, and Edward Shils, all of whom stressed religious and ideological orientations as *both* structures of meaning and an all-important, constitutive dimension of the social order.[18] In rather eclectic fashion, however, I shall also borrow theoretical insights and concepts from a variety of additional directions, ranging from the Maussian tradition of gift exchange, to Anthony Giddens's theory of structuration, and Michaël Mann's macrohistory of sources of power. As such, I also see my work as coinciding with the emergence of an eclectic and alternative current of historical and theoretical sociologists interested in the autonomous contents, forms, and impact of culture in various senses of that term, while also searching for new and interdisciplinary modes of cultural analysis.[19]

Focusing on Theravada Buddhism and medieval Catholicism has a number of substantive and methodological advantages. In both civilizations, religious virtuosity has given rise to extensive and historically enduring monastic networks. There is indeed a vast difference between virtuosity as a purely individual, occasional, and localized phenomenon, and those few historical instances in which virtuosity became institutionally sustained and reinforced to the point of engendering a specialized "virtuoso institution." Furthermore, as will be explained in Chapter 2, monasticism is a rather complex and precarious institution, predicated on some form of withdrawal from and reversal of ordinary patterns of

---

[18] This group of scholars are all rather systematically shunned (because perceived as overly "Parsonian" and "idealist") in many of the more "materialist" and institutionalist or conflict-theory works in historical macrosociology.

[19] See J. C. Alexander (ed.), *Durkheimian Sociology: Cultural Studies* (Cambridge University Press, 1988); C. Calhoun, "Beyond the Problem of Meaning: Robert Wuthnow's Historical Sociology of Culture," *Theory and Society* 21, no. 3 (1992): 419–44; J. A. Goldstone, "Ideology, Cultural Frameworks, and the Process of Revolution," *Theory and Society* 20 (1991): 405–54; L. Greenfeld, *Nationalism: Five Roads to Modernity* (Cambridge, Mass.: Harvard University Press, 1992); S. Kalberg, "The Origin and Expansion of Kulturpessimismus: The Relationship between Public and Private Spheres in Early Twentieth-Century Germany," *Sociological Theory* 5, no. 2 (1987): 150–64; idem, "Max Weber's Types of Rationality: Cornerstones for the Analysis of Rationalization Processes in History," *American Journal of Sociology* 85, no. 5 (1980): 1145–80; A. Kane, "Cultural Analysis in Historical Sociology: The Analytic and Concrete Forms of the Autonomy of Culture," *Sociological Theory* 53 (1990): 53–70; L. Roniger, *Hierarchy and Trust in Modern Mexico and Brazil* (New York: Praeger, 1990); Swidler, "Culture in Action"; D. Zaret, "Religion, Science and Printing in the Public Spheres in Seventeenth-Century England," in C. Calhoun (ed.), *Habermas and the Public Sphere* (Cambridge, Mass.: MIT Press, 1992), pp. 212–36.

social life. The powerful emergence and historical resilience of this peculiar type of virtuoso institution in these two settings, therefore, formed a major consideration in their selection for comparative study.

The emphasis, however, will be not so much on the monastic institution per se but rather, as already suggested, on the relationship between monasticism and society, and on the location of this relationship within the social structure at large. An important feature was the development of a network of material and symbolic exchange between the virtuoso and other social sectors, epitomized in a gift relationship between monks and laymen that resulted in a massive pouring of wealth into the monastic sector. In both civilizations, monasticism was thus able to establish itself in a position of cultural centrality and relative ascendancy over a nonmonastic audience willing to grant it a status of intrinsic spiritual superiority, as well as to provide it with uncoerced material support. At the same time, though – and in striking contrast to Tibetan monasticism in particular – monks in these two traditions also maintained a distance (both theoretically and practically) from the exercise of political power as commonly understood. Indeed, an essential feature of the gift relationship is that, however well established and routinized it became, it also remained fundamentally voluntary on both sides and supported, at most, by informal sanctions only.[20] In both settings, therefore, we see the case of a virtuoso elite ideologically self-defined as marginal and even opposed to extant forms of social life, and yet sustaining a position of cultural prestige and corporate wealth all the more noteworthy because devoid of the ordinary paraphernalia of political control and power. The result is a kind of "decentered centrality" not found in this precise configuration in any other civilizational setting.[21] Ideologically, the monastic sector exemplified the single-minded dedication to otherworldly ideals that were of central significance for society at large, and yet by definition could apply only to a minority living on the margins of social life. Institutionally, ascetic virtuosi were always defined as withdrawn from the center of secular rule and control, even though they were to become vital, at times, to the center's spiritual concerns, symbolic legitimacy, and even political expansion.

Emphasizing the similarity of the Theravada and Catholic configura-

[20] In both cases, admittedly, there is evidence for the occasional use of, if not actual coercion, at least "coercive persuasion," that is, monks inducing laymen to provide them with specific services or "donations" by threatening to prevent lay access to some crucial economic good – such as irrigation water in the Theravada context, or monastic mills in the Christian one. Such instances do appear, though, as occasional deviations from the dominant pattern of uncoerced donations.

[21] Although monasticism itself is present in Mahayana Buddhism, Tantric Buddhism, Jainism, and Eastern Christianity, it did not become the nexus of a full-fledged virtuoso–society complex in the sense that will be elaborated here (see Chapter 9 especially).

tions in such broad terms obviously poses the risk of oversimplifying what was in fact a rather complex and tension-ridden situation. In each case, the cultural status of the virtuoso sector, however prestigious and central, was rife with ambiguities. Furthermore, there were important fluctuations in the relationship between monasticism and the laity in general, and political centers in particular. Finally, although there were important similarities in the overall power and significance of monasticism in these two settings, there were basic differences as well. Christian monasticism took shape as part of a wider Church, and in subordination to a secular clergy in relation to which it was a controversial and competing historical development. In contrast, the Buddhist monastic order, the Sangha – somtimes said to have acquired "churchlike" characteristics over time – never had to come to terms with a wider ecclesiastical institution. Moreover, although monasticism achieved a pivotal social position in both cases, it also developed very different organizational characteristics and patterns of interaction with society at large. It is precisely these differences that this book describes and analyzes, albeit against the backdrop of an essential similarity that helps throw the differences into relief. Both similarities and differences will be stressed as equally essential to an adequate understanding of the virtuoso phenomenon in its interaction with different sociohistorical contexts.

The Theravada Buddhism–medieval Catholicism axis of comparison has a special and hitherto untapped interest for comparative sociology. Weber himself left us only scattered and unsystematic remarks on medieval Catholicism, to which he meant to devote a full-fledged study on a par with his detailed interpretations of other great traditions.[22] To the extent that Weber did discuss medieval Catholicism, he was rather interested in comparing it with India – mostly, it seems, because of what he saw as a somewhat similar combination of religious otherworldliness with a high degree of stratification and an organic conception of the social order[23] – than with Buddhism, which he tended to treat as merely a heterodox offshoot of Brahmanism. Moreover, whenever he did compare Buddhism to Western religions, he referred to Protestantism rather than to medieval Catholicism.

The Buddhism–Catholicism comparison has also been overlooked in a more recent body of comparative work, that of Louis Dumont, which focuses on the contrast between Indian "hierarchy" and Western "equality," and, more recently, on the "otherworldly" origins of Western indi-

---

[22] See the important collection of essays reexamining Weber's (incomplete) interpretation of Western Christendom by W. Schluchter (ed.), *Max Webers Sicht des okzidentalen Christentums* (Frankfurt: Suhrkampf, 1988).

[23] See W. Schluchter (ed.), *Max Webers Studie über Hinduismus und Buddhismus: Interpretation und Kritik* (Frankfurt: Suhrkampf, 1984), pp. 45 ff.

vidualism and the analogy with the Indian renunciate as an individual out of the world.[24] Whereas Dumont's work loomed large in the genesis of this study, it often tends to conflate Indian and Buddhist renunciation and does not deal with corporate (as distinct from individual) renunciation.[25] Consequently, although his work is undoubtedly a monumental landmark in the comparative study of asceticism and renunciation, it does not really address monasticism proper – the core of our comparison.

A similar preference for a comparison of medieval Europe with India rather than with Southeast Asian Buddhism is to be found in S. N. Eisenstadt's corpus of work on the comparative study of civilizations. On the background of apparent sociostructural similarities (such as a high degree of political pluralism and decentralization), Eisenstadt's dominant concern is to bring into relief some essential differences between medieval Europe and India with regard to their evaluation and construction of the political sphere.[26] To the extent that Eisenstadt did dwell on Buddhism, moreover, he is mostly engaged in assessing, in this specific case as in many others, the overall potential for transformation resulting from a specific configuration of religious orientations and sociopolitical structures. Although religious orientations and religious elites are given systematic weight in this perspective (in this respect probably the most systematic elaboration of the Weberian tradition in historical sociology), monasticism is addressed only with regard to its contributions to religious protest and political change, and is not otherwise given any sustained or distinctive attention.

An important implication of this focus on monasticism and the relationship between monasticism and society is the challenge it poses to the

[24] L. Dumont, *Homo Hierarchicus* (Chicago: University of Chicago Press, 1970); idem, *From Mandeville to Marx: The Genesis and Triumph of Economic Ideology* (Chicago: University of Chicago Press, 1977); idem, "A Modified View of our Origins: The Christian Origins of Modern Individualism," *Religion* 12 (1982): 1–27.

[25] Corporate renunciation was not to flourish, indeed, within the confines of the Brahmanic tradition. It is significant that otherworldliness was able to give rise to various forms of renunciation, and even to maintain elements of renunciation in the conception of the Brahmin priest – as emphasized in J. C. Heesterman, "Brahmin, Ritual and Renouncer," *Wiener Zeitschrift für die Kunde Süd- und Ostasiens* 8 (1964):1–31 – but did not receive monastic institutionalization.

[26] See especially S. N. Eisenstadt, "The Protestant Ethic Thesis in an Analytical and Comparative Framework," in *The Protestant Ethic and Modernization: A Comparative View* (New York: Basic, 1968), pp. 3–45; idem, *European Civilization in Comparative Perspective* (Oslo: Norwegian University Press, 1987); idem, "The Expansion of Religions: Some Comparative Observations on Different Modes," *Comparative Social Research,* 13 (1991): 45–70; idem, "Die Paradoxie von Zivilisationen mit ausserwertlichen Orientierungen: Uberlungen zu Max Webers Studie über Hinduismus und Buddhismus," in Schluchter (ed.), *Max Webers Studie,* pp. 333–62.

common contrast of Buddhist otherworldly "weakness" with Western "power" and "dynamism" in matters of institution building and worldly involvement. This contrast is heavily emphasized in Weber's own work, where it seems to have been rooted, ultimately, in his overriding concern with the unique features of Western rationality. For Weber, only religious orientations inducive of what he designated as active, inner-worldly asceticism could have encouraged a sustained, rationalized involvement in the world of the type which was to become so crucial, in his eyes, to the development of Western modernity. As is more fully developed in Chapter 1, the importance he gave to Protestantism – and more specifically, Puritan Calvinism – in this respect was accompanied by a relative neglect and somewhat ambiguous assessment of medieval monasticism. Although underscoring the latter's conservative implications, he also emphasized it as the ideological matrix from which Protestantism fatefully emerged, and was bent on giving it a part in his overall interpretation of the unique features of Western civilization.

Weber's overall vision of history, in any case, is now easily criticized for its "Western" and even more specifically "Calvinist" bias. As has now been argued by many, Buddhism's potential for economic rationalization and worldly involvement may have been much greater than Weber granted.[27] I shall not deal here, however, with the issue of the differential potential of Christianity and Buddhism for economic dynamism and "modernity," which is now becoming a focus of renewed interest as the leading edge of economic expansion is understood by many to be moving away from the West and into (or even to some minds, back into)[28] the East. Neither do I wish to address the meaningful issue – so salient to Dumont's work and recently insightfully reassessed by Steven Collins – of the legacy of "outworldly" asceticism to the development of individualism and/or Western egalitarianism and other social utopias, all undoubtedly central to our understanding of Western moder-

---

[27] For example, H. S. Alatas, "The Protestant Ethic and Southeast Asia," *Archives de Sociologie des Religions* 15 (1963): 21–34; R. N. Bellah (ed.), *Religion and Progress in Modern Asia* (New York: Free Press, 1965); Eisenstadt, "Protestant Ethic"; idem, "Some Reflections on the Significance of Max Weber's Sociology of Religion for the Analysis of Non-European Modernity," *Archives de Sociologie des Religions* 32 (1971): 29–52; S. J. Tambiah, *World Conqueror and World Renouncer: A Study of Buddhism and Polity in Thailand against Historical Background* (Cambridge University Press, 1973); idem, "Buddhism and This-Worldly Activity," *Modern Asian Studies* 7 (1973): 1–20. Tambiah has especially brought into relief Buddhism's worldly potential in the political sphere.

[28] See the analysis of the rise and temporary nature of Western economic hegemony as building upon a preceding system of world economy in which the "Oriental" powers eventually lost their commercial leadership, in Janet Abu-Lughod, *Before European Hegemony: The World System, A.D. 1250–1350*, (New York: Oxford University Press, 1989).

nity.[29] Finally, I shall not deal here with the more specific issue of Christian monasticism's contribution to Western economic rationalization and expansion – which I have actually broached elsewhere.[30] My present interest, rather, is with the need to turn to comparative analysis with other concerns in mind than the advent of capitalism and rationality or "modernity" in general. However crucial these themes undeniably are, they have tended to divert attention from others that are no less important from an empirical and theoretical point of view.

Shifting away, thus, from the issues that have hitherto dominated the comparative sociological discourse on religious asceticism, I plan to focus here on the differing capacity of virtuoso elites to achieve institutional strength and collective relevance.[31] Although this issue is pertinent to all religious elites, it becomes even more intriguing in the case of virtuoso elites dedicated to otherworldly ideals nominally opposed to worldly involvement and thus irrelevant to the immediate concerns of the average majority.

A major contention of this book is that one needs to distinguish among various criteria of institutional vitality and collective relevance. With regard to such evident criteria of institutionalization as formal organization, institutional autonomy, and political power, Theravada Buddhist monasticism will be shown to have much less institutional strength than its Christian equivalent. In terms of the position of monasticism within the overall social structure, however, Buddhist monasticism will emerge as more solidly institutionalized, maintaining (with only minor variations) an enduring social position and pattern of relationship with wider society. Christian monasticism, in contrast, underwent critical shifts in social position, was the focus of constant uncertainties and controversies, and emerged seriously undermined toward the end of the period under study.

The intriguing problem, therefore, is how to conceptualize the tenor, or basis, of monasticism's institutional strength in the Theravada case. A proper understanding of the Buddhist Sangha, it will appear, must draw not so much on its own organizational and institutional features as on the specific pattern of virtuoso–layman relations that came to form a

---

29 S. Collins, "Monasticism, Utopias and Comparative Social Theory," *Religion* 18 (1988): 101–35.

30 See Silber, "Monasticism and the Protestant Ethic: Asceticism, Ideology and Wealth in the Medieval West," *British Journal of Sociology* 44, no. 1 (1993): 103–23.

31 I do not mean, however, that such an angle of analysis is of no relevance to more "modern" concerns. In fact, it would be intriguing to pursue the analogy with another powerful component of "modernity" left marginal in the studies already mentioned, namely, the advent of intellectual, artistic, and scientific elites, or even of the professions in general, with the element of ascetic discipline and distancing from the masses that this has entailed.

diffuse but enduring and essential axis of societal organization in Theravada countries. This virtuoso–layman relation, moreover, is not a unique and exclusively Theravada phenomenon. It is a major purpose of this book to show that it had a striking, albeit partial and less enduring, equivalent in at least one more civilizational context, that of medieval Catholicism.

This analysis has a number of theoretical implications. First, it implies that institution building can be seen not only in terms of organizational–corporate structures, but also in terms of sets of relationships or relational structures. These two views, to my mind, are to be understood as complementary rather than mutually exclusive perceptions of what society is about. The emphasis on relational structures is not new. Already essential to Simmel's approach, it has reappeared, in widely differing forms, in a variety of current sociological trends, such as network theory or certain brands of structuralism. Relational structures have an even longer lineage of anthropological proponents, perhaps due to anthropology's traditional concern with kinship and systems of exchange.

Rather than just reasserting the importance of relational structures from a purely ontological and theoretical perspective, I propose to consider the two basic modes of institutionalization – organizational–structural versus relational – as empirical and culturally influenced variables. From such a perspective, social groups or even societies may be found to display different aptitudes for and reliance upon two fundamental and possibly complementary strategies of institutionalization, and differentially apply them to various spheres of life. It becomes then the task of comparative sociology to "diagnose" such variations within and between societies, as well as to enquire into their social and cultural sources – a challenge addressed here from the limited perspective of our own specific topic, the institutionalization of religious virtuosity.

Focusing on the interaction between virtuosi and laymen, moreover, has some interesting implications for the perennial dichotomy between micro- and macrosociological traditions of analysis, and the possibility of bridging the gap between them – a prominent and vexing issue in contemporary sociological theory.[32] In line with some recent theoretical treatments of the problem, I regard the micro/macro distinction as refer-

---

[32] See, for example, G. Ritzer, "Micro–Macro Linkage in Sociological Theory: Applying a Metatheoretical Tool," in G. Ritzer (ed.), *Frontiers of Social Theory: The New Syntheses* (New York: Columbia University Press, 1990); R. Wiley, "The Micro–Macro Problem in Social Theory," *Sociological Theory* 6 (1988): 254–61; J. C. Alexander et al. (eds.), *The Micro–Macro Link,* (Berkeley and Los Angeles: University of California Press, 1987); S. N. Eisenstadt and H. J. Helle, "General Introduction to Perspectives on Sociological Theory," in S. N. Eisenstadt and H. J. Helle (eds.), *Macrosociological Theory: Perspectives on Sociological Theory,* vol. 1 (London: Sage, 1985).

ring to different analytical perspectives or emphases rather than "empirically" different realities: One same social process can be analyzed from
either a micro or macro perspective, depending on the analyst's priorities.[33] My own choice here is to stress the macrosociological significance
of a process of interaction and exchange – concretely expressed, as already explained, in the development of a gift relationship – that belongs
essentially to what is traditionally defined as the microsociological plane
of local and even face-to-face relations.[34] In this analysis, the overall
position of religious elites invested with macrosocietal significance as the
prime carriers of central religious ideal emerges as ultimately dependent
upon a microsociological, voluntary, and rather precarious process of
interaction and exchange between these elites and their lay audience.
Judging from the broader and historically more resilient deployment of
the virtuoso–layman interaction at both the local and central level in
traditional Theravada Buddhist countries, Buddhist virtuosi appear to
have been much more "successful" at this process than their Christian
counterparts. A major objective of this book is precisely to delineate the
ideological and institutional configurations that facilitated this major
difference in the sociological implications of virtuoso religion in Western
Europe and Southeast Asia.

To state it a bit provocatively: Alongside the traditional Weberian
account, which inserts virtuoso asceticism in the established narrative of
the "rise of the West," emerges a possible alternative account, one that
inscribes virtuoso asceticism as a dominant aspect of a narrative focusing
on the "tenacity," or even "tenacious expansion" of the East. Shifting
attention to the more solid and successful features of a specific type of
socioreligious structure in the "East," however, does not necessarily
contradict the more conventional Weberian search for the unique features of Western civilization. My interpretation of the medieval West
will in fact confirm in many ways, and complement rather than contradict, those features that a traditional Weberian interpretation emphasizes as typically Western. More essentially, I certainly do not mean to
sketch here any alternative "grand map of history." Nor do I claim to
present a sector of Asian civilization on its own terms. Much more
modestly and strictly within the scope of Western sociological discourse,

---

[33] See especially R. Münch and N. J. Smelser, "Relating the Micro and Macro," in
Alexander et al. (eds.), *Micro–Macro Link,* pp. 356–87.

[34] I shall not refer here to the extensive sociological literature relevant to the
subject, nor shall I elaborate on the precise relation of the type of exchange
characteristic of the virtuoso–layman relation and existing typologies of exchange, none of which seems to me to exactly apply. Overall, my preference will
be to situate my argument in this regard within the tradition of gift analysis. I
have most benefited, however, from R. Paine, "Two Modes of Exchange and
Mediation," in B. Kapferer (ed.), *Transaction and Meaning* (Philadelphia:
ISHI, 1976), pp. 63–86.

it seems to me that concern with the unique dynamics of the West should be matched with an equal concern for the unique dynamics of non-Western civilizations. Moreover, it is precisely this kind of more balanced comparative perspective that might bring into light, because viewed from hitherto unexpected angles, aspects of our own civilization of which we otherwise might not have been aware.

It should be stressed that the focus on "traditional Buddhism" and medieval Catholicism shifts the comparison away from the early, formative phases of each religion (although occasional reference will be made to various characteristics of these initial stages) to the interaction between monasticism and society in its more institutionalized, established stages, when the partial convergence in institutional development that lies at the core of the comparative rationale in this work emerged.[35] This choice, moreover, has the notable advantage of keeping early modern or modern developments, *in either setting,* beyond the pale of our comparison. A great deal of West-versus-East comparative analysis has suffered, precisely, from the tendency to compare "Asian" developments in bulk (conflating both traditional and "modern" periods) with either early or modern Western ones – skipping thus a more differentiated comparison with the premodern West. Dominant comparative conceptions might emerge significantly modified when one compares the traditional medieval West with its Eastern equivalent – that is, before the onset of colonial, Christian, and "modern" influences.

"Traditional Theravada Buddhism," to use Heinz Bechert's definition, refers to the period from the final codification of the canonical scriptures to the onset of the colonial "modern era," and is broadly characterized by the development of formalized state–Sangha relations and the establishment of Buddhism as the dominant "national" religion, first in Sri Lanka and then in a number of Southeast Asian kingdoms.[36] The exact period in which Buddhism may be said to have been dominant differs, however, for each of the three major Theravada Buddhist countries we shall focus upon. It is the longest in the case of Sri Lanka, where it stretches from the arrival of Buddhism from India during the reign and

[35] This may be a particular instance of the observation that "religions, however different they may be in their origins, fundamental insights and doctrinal structures, do tend to become similar." See R. J. Z. Werblowsky, *Beyond Tradition and Modernity* (London: Athlone, 1976), p. 84. The issue of historical connection and mutual influence between Buddhist and Christian monasticism will not be addressed here. Monasticism may have penetrated the West through the mediation of Buddhist monasticism (although other sources of influence have been considered). There can be no doubt, however, that it would not have grown such solid roots into Western soil if not for endogenous cultural forces favoring its development.

[36] H. Bechert, "Sangha, State, Society, 'Nation': Persistence of Traditions in 'Post-Traditional' Buddhist Societies," *Daedalus* 102, no. 1 (1973): 85.

under the sponsorship of Ashoka (mid-third century BCE), to the coming of the Portuguese in 1505 (although some reference will be made to the later Kandyan independent period). In the case of Burma, it roughly spans the era from the Pagan period (ninth to thirteenth centuries)[37] to the end of the nineteenth century, whereas for Thailand, the traditional era may be dated from the mid-thirteenth-century Sukhodaya kingdom to Mongkut's reign (1851–68).[38]

Precolonial, "traditional" Theravada Buddhism has been characterized by many students of the field as exhibiting a rather impressive continuity in cultural and institutional structures,[39] all the more remarkable given the rapid succession of kingdoms, sweeping migratory trends, endemic warfare, and recurrent waves of invasion.[40] This continuity is especially emphasized in contrast with the profound discontinuities introduced by colonial rule and the penetration of Western influences. The issue of structural continuity versus change, however, has by now become a thorny source of controversy.[41] A closely related issue is the extent to which one may choose to emphasize national and regional variations, or rather play up the important similarities between the ma-

[37] There is some disagreement on whether the Pagan period can already be taken to represent the traditional Theravada pattern. M. Aung-Thwin sees basic institutional continuities from the ninth to the nineteenth centuries; see "The Role of *Sasana* Reform in Burmese History: Economic Dimensions of a Religious Purification," *Journal of Asian Studies* 38 (1979): 674; whereas Charles Keyes would tend to date the onset of the traditional pattern from the end of the Pagan period. See "Structure and History in the Study of the Relationship between Theravada Buddhism and Political Order," *Numen* 25 (1978): 167.

[38] Mongkut's reign signals the onset of effective Western influence even if, unlike in Burma and Ceylon, no colonial conquest took place and absolute monarchy came to an end only in 1938.

[39] See for example G. Obeyesekere, "Religion and Polity in Theravada Buddhism: Continuity and Change in a Great Tradition," *Comparative Studies in Society and History* 21, no. 4 (1979): 626–39; Tambiah, *World Conqueror,* especially pp. 516 ff.; Keyes, "Structure and History."

[40] The apparent contradiction between social and political instability and a general sense of cultural continuity has been aptly summed up by Keyes: "Indeed, both socially and politically traditional Theravada Buddhist societies were in constant turmoil. . . . Yet, for all this social and political flux, both peasant and ruler in traditional Theravada Buddhist society lived in meaningful worlds. . . . Rulers and peasants all also knew that underlying the turmoil of existence was a permanent moral order, that which was grounded in Karma. The Buddhist religion thus flourished despite the constantly changing political scene." See *The Golden Peninsula: Culture and Adaptation in Mainland Southeast Asia* (New York: Macmillan, 1977), p. 94.

[41] See, for instance, the polemic intensity of some of the articles discussing S. J. Tambiah's work, in *Contributions to Indian Sociology* n.s. 21, no. 1 (1987). See also (although the author is less preoccupied with the issue of continuity in premodern periods), E. Cohen, "Socio-cultural Change in Thailand: A Reconceptualization," in E. Cohen, M. Lissak, and U. Almagor, *Comparative Social Dynamics: Essays in Honor of S. N. Eisenstadt,* pp. 82–94 (Boulder, Colo.: Westview, 1985).

jor Theravada Buddhist countries and even talk of a global Theravada pattern.

Much of these debates may be reduced to differences in foci of analysis and in theoretical underpinnings, and may well have to remain so, given the nature and paucity of historical data (especially compared to the wealth of material pertinent to the medieval West). It is now clear, however, that in the long span of the "traditional" period, Theravada polities and social structures underwent not merely short-term, marginal, or "cyclical" change, but also more profound and gradual transformations – such as a long-term trend toward increased political centralization, and the steady expansion of intra-Asian trade. It is also evident that the debate on continuity and change has addressed mostly central political and administrative processes – such as the nature of Buddhist kingship and polity – and that greater agreement might have obtained concerning processes at the local, village level.

Be that as it may, it is noteworthy that even those who call for a more differentiated and dynamic picture have also emphasized how distinctly conservative traditional Theravada Buddhism has been,[42] stressed a general sense of cultural continuity in the face of apparently constant social and political turmoil,[43] or tried to "identify those principles in Buddhism and those perennial socio-economic circumstances by which events are replicated in the Theravada realm."[44] Searching for discontinuities thus, in this field as any other, does not necessarily imply denying all continuity. No less crucially, a stress on continuity does not necessarily imply a static analysis. Since these (ever-vexing) issues are cardinal to my comparative argument, I might as well make my own choices fully explicit. For present purposes, I shall give priority to similarities and continuities throughout the period considered and in all parts of the Theravada "complex," if also pointing out significant regional and historical divergences when appropriate. I need to stress, however, that I emphasize continuity in only one dimension, and not with regard to other aspects of Theravada Buddhist history. With regard to the specific object of this inquiry at least – namely, the virtuoso–layman relation – it is the endurance and resilience of certain forms and patterns that begs to be explained, all the more so when contrasted with the fluidity of the picture in the medieval West.

This choice, once again, does not necessarily imply a static analysis. The task, rather, is to define the sociocultural forces and dynamics allow-

---

[42] See R. F. Gombrich, *Theravada Buddhism: A Social History from Ancient Benares to Modern Colombo* (London: Routledge & Kegan Paul, 1988), introduction.

[43] See fn. 19, this chapter.

[44] M. Carrithers, "The Modern Ascetics of Lanka and the Pattern of Change in Buddhism," *Man* 14 (1979): 294.

ing for the production and reproduction of what might have seemed a very fragile and unlikely form of relationship between virtuosi and society. The persistence of that structure cannot be explained away or taken for granted as the mere result of inertia or routine survival; in fact it will be shown to owe a lot to some major developments in the ideological and institutional history of Theravada polities, as especially emphasized in chapters 3 and 4. Continuity then, in this case at least, is to be seen as the result of a complex combination of forces of reproduction and change, and actually becomes all the more intriguing in face of the more recent stress on processes of change in other aspects of Theravada history.

As for the medieval West, we shall focus on the era between the sixth and thirteenth centuries (sometimes called the "Benedictine centuries"), in what corresponds to modern France, Germany, Italy, and England – leaving out Spain and Ireland.[45] This era encompasses a baseline period lasting until roughly the eleventh century, during which we shall see a partial convergence with developments in the Theravada Buddhist context. This is followed by a period of critical changes within the virtuoso sector itself and in the relationship between virtuosi and society: the eremitic revival; the Gregorian period; the apostolic and mendicant movements. This period also witnessed far-reaching social and political changes – all in contrast to Theravada's relative "continuity" – and is now increasingly focused upon as a time of ferment and institution building (very far from the once-dominant conception of that period as a time of "darkness" and immobility). Within the pale of historical sociological literature, the tendency is now to emphasize the importance of this period in setting into motion – much before the Protestant Reformation – a number of dynamics of crucial importance for the understanding of Western modernity.[46] It is now a matter of increasing consensus that the twelfth century in particular represented a momentous turning point in the his-

[45] There is much debate concerning the adequate definition and the internal periodization of the "Middle Ages." I shall be following here, roughly, Southern's distinction between a "primitive age" between ca. 700–ca. 1050; an "age of growth," ca. 1050–ca. 1300; and a time of "inflationary spiral," ca. 1300–ca. 1520. See R. W. Southern, *Western Society and the Church in the Middle Ages,* (Harmondsworth: Pelican Books, 1970). The period addressed here coincides with Southern's first two stages. Le Goff, in contrast, propounds a very long Middle Ages, stretching from the third to the mid-nineteenth century. Forced to look for subphases, however, he sees a prolongation of Late Antiquity until the seventh century, a High Middle Ages until the tenth, followed by a period of growth until the fourteenth century; the period between the mid-twelfth and mid-thirteenth centuries, in his opinion, saw the most decisive mutations. See J. Le Goff, *L'imaginaire médiéval* (Paris: Gallimard, 1985), pp. viii–xviii.

[46] See for example Chirot, "Rise of the West"; Mann, *Sources of Social Power;* Collins, *Weberian Sociological Theory.* I have also approached the issue through the specific angle of monastic economy in "Monasticism and the Protestant Ethic: Asceticism, Ideology and Wealth in the Medieval West," *British Journal of Sociology* 44, no. 1 (1993): 103–23.

tory of Western Europe, and it is not incidental that it will also be emphasized here as an important watershed in the dynamics of the relationship between virtuosi and society.

Admittedly, this emphasis on a general contrast between a relative "continuity" in the virtuoso–layman relation in the Buddhist case and sharp changes in the Christian one, involves some serious methodological problems. The major one, already referred to and often bemoaned by Theravada scholars, is the relative paucity of historical data on social and religious developments in the Theravada Buddhist setting – stemming, at least in part, from the relative lack of interest in historical recordkeeping characteristic of Buddhist, and even more generally, Indian civilization.[47] This problem is compounded by the fact – common to Southeast Asia and medieval Christendom – that sources on monastic history are themselves monastic, since monks were the only ones with the literacy and other scholarly skills necessary for the writing of records and chronicles.

Another severe methodological stricture relates to the nature of virtuoso asceticism itself, and the tendency to radical forms of withdrawal from society with which it seems to have been often associated. Any historical and sociological interpretation of virtuoso asceticism must allow for the fact that we may well know nothing about those virtuoso ascetics who were most successful in maintaining isolation and anonymity, either as individuals or in groups. Furthermore, both clergy and more established monks might have systematically ignored or even suppressed evidence about forms of virtuosity with which they were not in agreement. We may only speculate whether more historical documentation on these issues would have affected, among other things, the understanding of either Theravada Buddhism's relative "continuity" or medieval Catholicism's "change."

The present inquiry belongs to the realm of comparative sociological interpretation, and makes no claim to cover new historical ground. Within these limits, however, I believe I have offered a new perspective on a number of old issues, and have posed a new set of questions to the many specialists in whose fields I have been treading – at the undeniable cost of sacrificing much in historical complexity. One important issue that I was not able to tackle here is that of gender. Although women constituted a significant and increasing element of the virtuoso sector in medieval

---

[47] This is very far, at any rate, from the Judeo-Christian concern with historical processes, and even more, from the well-known passion of the Chinese for record keeping – allowing for superbly documented studies of Buddhist monasticism in China, such as that of J. Gernet, *Les aspects économiques du bouddhisme dans la société chinoise du Ve au Xe siècles* (Saigon: Ecole française d'Extrême-Orient, 1956). The Chinese impact has also facilitated historical documentation on branches of Buddhist monasticism that have flourished in areas tributary to or on the periphery of China.

Christianity (especially after the period of our inquiry) in the Theravada tradition their part quickly dwindled after a brief presence in the early phases. Exploring this and other gender-related differences would no doubt enrich our overall understanding of the interaction between religious virtuosity and social order, a task already much encouraged by the recent increase in historical studies of women's religiosity in general, and of female monasticism in particular in early and medieval Christianity.[48]

Finally, a comparative study limited to only two cases, however broadly defined and carefully selected, can only be tentative in its conclusions. Ideally, it would be desirable to locate this study of monastic virtuoso religion within a broader comparative framework, including Eastern Christian monasticism, early Irish monasticism, Tibetan Lamaism, and Buddhist monasticism in China. India would also constitute an important case, since otherworldliness there gave rise to radical forms of renunciation (although only to a late and relatively weak development of monasticism within the frame of classical Hinduism). A comprehensive comparative analysis should also consider those settings in which only quasi-monastic forms of virtuoso organization evolved (such as the early Muslim monasticism and Sufi orders), or where no monasticism evolved at all (rabbinic Judaism), despite the presence of virtuoso orientations encouraging the voluntary search for some form of above-average religious perfection. Although falling short of such a truly comprehensive project, I do hope to have at least indicated the interest that further work in these various areas holds in terms of its potential significance for the comparative sociological study of civilizations.[49]

The first section of this book, essentially theoretical in character, proposes to define the major ideological and institutional forces shaping the relationship between virtuoso elites and society, and thus to establish the basic frame and parameters of a multidimensional comparative analysis. Chapter 1 is a review and critique of Weber's foundations in this domain, emphasizing not only his vital contributions (in this field as in so many others) but also some of his major biases and limitations. Chapter 2 analyzes monasticism as a specific type of social formation, with distinctive ideological and organizational dynamics that were not attended to in

[48] See C. W. Bynum, *Jesus as Mother: Studies in the Spirituality of the High Middle Ages* (Berkeley and Los Angeles: University of California Press, 1982), ch. 5; S. Helkin, *Holy Women of Twelfth-Century England* (Chapel Hill: University of North Carolina Press, 1988); R. Ruether and E. C. McLaughlin (eds.), *Women of Spirit* (New York: Simon & Schuster, 1979).

[49] For a welcome and recent contribution to the cross-cultural and comparative understanding of monasticism (from a comparative religious rather than comparative sociological perspective), see the recent volume of essays, *Monastic Life in the Christian and Hindu Traditions: A Comparative Study*, edited by Austin B. Creel and V. Narayanan (Lewiston, N.Y.: Mellen, 1990), which I was able to consult only after completion of this manuscript.

the Weberian framework. It starts with a critical survey of the still rather scant sociological literature on the subject and suggests application of a modified form of Victor Turner's well-known notion of antistructure to the understanding of monasticism as a type of "alternative structure." This is followed by a discussion of a number of functionalist or "functionalistlike" interpretations that have the merit of drawing attention to aspects of the relation between monasticism and society understated in the Weberian approach, yet that themselves remain partial and unsatisfactory. This chapter then outlines the comparative rationale of the present research, incorporating elements of both the Weberian and functionalist approaches, while also offering additional dimensions of inquiry.

Sections II and III of the book are detailed analyses of the Theravada and medieval Catholic historical cases respectively in terms of the parameters of comparison elaborated in the first section. I need to stress, with regard to specialist readers who may want to relate to only one or both of these chapters, that they make no claim to fully cover all aspects of the interaction between monks and society in each setting, but rather present and select materials informed by the specific comparative questions and priorities deployed in this Introduction and in Part I.

The fourth and last section is a theoretical and comparative discussion of religious virtuosity as a distinctive sociological phenomenon and cultural variable. The first chapter in this final section aims at clarifying the defining features of virtuosity in relation to charisma – one of Weber's better-known legacies to the social sciences – and at establishing the ideal-typical features of what I call the "virtuoso–society complex." The following chapter maps out, on the basis of the case studies, the major ideological and institutional forces shaping the differential expression of this complex in these and other civilizational settings.

Finally, the conclusion points out some implications of this analysis of religious virtuosity and the virtuoso complex with regard to the place of religious ideology and structures in the context of premodern macrosocietal formations. As already suggested, religious ideological orientations are given systematic and detailed attention here, both as a defining feature of virtuosity itself and as part of the constellation of variables shaping the differential development of the virtuoso macrocomplex in different civilizations. In contrast, a number of important works in comparative historical sociology have simply chosen to deemphasize religious orientations, and rather to focus on the economic and institutional facets of religious organizations. Singling out Mann's contribution in this regard, I wish to both draw upon and criticize his challenging analysis of "ideological power." In the case of virtuoso elites, I argue, "ideological power" is simply, to a large extent, the power of ideology. Seriously relating to religious ideology and ideals, however, does not imply defining them as a set of homogeneous, unequivocal directions or clear-cut answers to problems of meaning. One important lesson of Weber's *Protestant Ethic* is precisely that religious beliefs and orientations do offer soteriological answers, but that these answers themselves engender new sets of existential problems, and may very well end up having unintended and paradoxical effects. Admittedly, this specific tack of analysis was not truly pursued by Weber himself in his studies of non-Western civilizations, or even, for that matter, in the understanding of any aspect or period of Western civilization preceding the Reformation. To some extent, we now stand at a point where neither the classical nor the more contemporary macrosociological approaches to religion provide us with sufficient tools of cultural analysis. What is probably needed (and has already started to arise) is an increasingly interdisciplinary and eclectic approach to the interpretation of collective structures of meaning. Tackling the issue from the very specific angle offered in this book, at any rate, I hope to have addressed the social significance of religious virtuoso orientations in a way that not only builds upon the Weberian tradition but also contributes to the search for new modes of cultural analysis within the expanding boundaries of interpretive sociology.

Part I
Virtuosi and society: elements of a comparative macrosociological approach

1 The Weberian legacy

Weber's typological and comparative framework

In Weber's classic statement,[1] "virtuoso" or "heroic" religiosity is primarily defined in opposition to mass religiosity. Human beings vary in their religious capacities and in the special personal attributes – the "charisma"[2] – necessary to attain the highest religious ends. As a result, a status stratification emerges in which the most qualified come to constitute a kind of "spiritual aristocracy" devoted to the methodical pursuit of salvation. This methodical pursuit usually entails the subjugation of natural drives (as defined in each cultural setting) to some form of rigid discipline, and implies a criticism of the more complacent lifestyle of the masses. (Incidentally, Weber does not seem to have attached to the term virtuosity any of the negative connotations nowadays possibly associated with it – virtuosity in the sense of "merely" technical brilliance and superficial, "soulless" artistic performance.)[3]

The virtuosi's superior religious status is not, however, without ambiguities. Their single-minded and methodical pursuit of the highest religious ends appears to engender a whole range of tensions in their relation with society at large. A first and major source of tension is what Weber sees as a basic antagonism between virtuosi and the religious establishment.[4] In the case of Christianity, for example, there is an inevitable tension between the characteristic tendency of virtuosi to seek sanctification on their own, and the Church's institutional monopoly on mediating the bestowal of religious grace. Furthermore, the Church makes salvation universally accessible, through its sacraments, to people with varying degrees of ethical and religious qualification – a leveling that stands in marked contrast to the elitism of the virtuoso. Such tensions have resulted, historically, in many and varied compromises. We-

---

[1] M. Weber, *The Sociology of Religion* (Boston: Beacon, 1964), pp. 162–5.

[2] This is only one of his many different uses of the word.

[3] The notion of virtuosity appears to have undergone divergent semantic development in the various European languages. In English, the term was first associated in the sixteenth and seventeenth centuries with the pursuit of science and knowledge, and only later with artistic excellence. As reported in German dictionaries of Weber's time, the term mostly applied to the arts in general and to music in particular. Weber's extension of the term to the field of religion brought it closer, in fact, to the Italian usage, which allowed for a much broader semantic scope, first connoting some form of religious and moral excellence, and only second the idea of artistic expertise.

[4] Weber, *Sociology of Religion,* p. 187.

ber especially emphasized the "concessions" that religious virtuosi have made, "adjusting their demands to the possibilities of everyday life religiosity, in order to maintain ideal and material mass patronage."[5]

The precise nature of these concessions determines the virtuosi's actual influence on everyday life. The critical distinction is that between two types of virtuoso religion: the first, "contemplative–orgiastic" in character, best exemplified, in Weber's view, by Buddhism and Jainism; the second, "activist–ascetic," of which Protestantism, and more specifically Calvinism, is taken as the prototype.

In contemplative virtuoso religion, action in the world is perceived as essentially inferior, and an abyss separates the virtuoso's lifestyle from that of the layman. The relation that evolved between them, as Weber sees it, is one of "magical anthropolatry": the layman either worships the virtuoso himself directly, as a saint, or "buys" the virtuoso's blessings or magical powers in order to promote his own mundane interests or religious salvation.[6] The contemplative virtuoso does not exhort the layman to approximate his own way of life. Even when acting as spiritual adviser, his influence lies not in the sphere of ethics, but rather – and in Weber's frame, merely – in that of ritual.[7]

In his discussion of the activist–ascetic model of religious virtuosity, in contrast, Weber does not focus at all on the virtuoso–layman interaction.[8] Instead, his attention is now turned to the virtuoso's orientation to everyday life and the workaday world, and more specifically, to the affinities between activist–ascetic religious virtuosity and economic rationalization, the well-known theme of his thesis in *The Protestant Ethic and the Spirit of Capitalism*.[9] There is in fact a striking imbalance in Weber's treatment of what he had defined as two basic, contrasting types of virtuosity. The bulk of his writing on the subject is concerned with inner-worldly asceticism and its far-reaching implications for Western rationalization and modernization. Contemplative or mystically oriented virtuosity, on the other hand, is consistently downplayed, treated much less extensively, and credited with little sociological significance.[10]

The crucial role that Weber attributed to inner-worldly, activist asceticism in the development of Western rationalization and modernity, at

---

[5] H. H. Gerth and C. Wright Mills (ed. and trans.), *From Max Weber: Essays in Sociology* (New York: Oxford University Press, 1975), p. 288.

[6] Ibid., p. 289.

[7] On Weber's generally pejorative and (sociologically) insufficient treatment of ritual, see this volume, Introduction, fn. 13.

[8] Gerth and Mills (ed. and trans.), *Max Weber*, pp. 290–1.

[9] M. Weber, *The Protestant Ethic and the Spirit of Capitalism* (New York: Scribner, 1958).

[10] For a fuller analysis of Weber's relative neglect of mysticism, see W. R. Garret, "Maligned Mysticism: The Maledicted Career of Troeltsch's Third Type," *Sociological Analysis* 36, no. 3 (1975): 205–23; Robertson, "Analysis of Mysticism."

any rate, clearly establishes that virtuosi constituted much more than just an additional category in his typology of religious specialists. Far from being a marginal theme in his work, virtuosity emerges as a leading motif in his conception of the differential historical development of civilizations.[11] The Protestant ethic itself, in his understanding, represented a transformation and extension of medieval monastic virtuosity. It "carried asceticism out of monastic cells into everyday life"; no less crucially, it transferred the demands of inner-worldly asceticism to all members of the religious community, overthrowing the distinction between virtuosi and nonvirtuosi that underlay the virtuoso's position in the Catholic social order.[12]

In some sense, we see here the notion of virtuosity stretched to its limits, since Protestant virtuoso asceticism entails the repudiation of the very idea of a distinction between virtuosi and nonvirtuosi, of the implied contrast with mass religiosity intrinsic to the very notion of virtuosity itself as defined by Weber himself at the beginning of this chapter.[13] Weber's use of the term virtuosity here may simply reflect his overall assessment of Protestant active asceticism as not only a transformation of traditional forms of virtuosity but also as a form of religiosity entailing a most demanding level of religious strain and ascetic rigor – of a kind otherwise expected of religious elites only.

Be that as it may, the story then becomes, in Weber's narrative of the far-reaching implications of this crucial mutation in the history of Christian virtuosity, not one of repeated conflicts and "compromises" with the world, but rather one of unrelenting, rationalized channeling of one's

[11] For the intertwining of the theme of religious virtuosity with other essential aspects of Weber's comparative sociology of religion, see W. Schluchter, "Weltflüchtiges Erlösungsstreben und organische Sozialethik: Überlegungen zu Max Webers Analysen der indischen Kulturreligionen," in W. Schluchter (ed.), *Max Webers Studie über Hinduismus und Buddhismus: Interpretation und Kritik* (Frankfurt: Suhrkampf, 1984), pp. 11–71. On the centrality of the notions of rationality and rationalization, and their various meanings in Weber's work, see Kalberg, "Max Weber's Types of Rationality"; A. Swidler, "The Concept of Rationality in the Work of Max Weber," *Sociological Enquiry* 43 (1973): 35–42; also directly relevant is W. Schluchter, "The Paradox of Rationalization: On the Relation of Ethics and World," in G. Roth and W. Schluchter, *Max Weber's Vision of History: Ethics and Methods* (Berkeley and Los Angeles: University of California Press, 1979), pp. 11–64.

[12] "The conception of the calling thus brings out that central dogma of all Protestant denominations which the Catholic division of ethical precepts into *praecepta* and *consilia* discards. The only way of living acceptably to God was not to surpass worldly morality in monastic asceticism, but solely through the fulfillment of the obligations imposed upon the individual by his position in the world. That was his calling." Weber, *Protestant Ethic,* p. 80; see also pp. 153–4.

[13] Touching upon this issue, see D. Martin, *Pacifism: An Historical and Sociological Study* (New York: Schocken, 1965), p. 163.

personal drives and religious anxieties in an uncompromising attempt to act as the active vessel of the will of God in the world.

In the Catholic framework, in contrast, Weber stresses again the importance of "concessions" and "compromises" in determining not only the virtuosi's relation to the world, but also the world's, and in particular the Church's, ambivalent relation to them. The compromise solution arrived at was to allow the virtuoso, with his higher ethical achievements, to ensure his own salvation and accumulate good works to the credit of the Chruch, which would in turn redistribute them to the nonvirtuosi. This ideological procedure fitted well into medieval Catholicism's "organic" conception of differences in class and position: "The virtuosi of religion, be they of an ascetic or contemplative type, are also assigned their specific responsibility within such an organic order, just as specific functions have been allocated to princes, warriors, judges, artisans and peasants."[14]

The church's ambivalence toward ascetic virtuosi is discussed again and at greater length in Weber's study of "hierocratic domination"[15] and its relation to monastic asceticism. Here again, no direct reference is made to the basic issue of the virtuoso–layman interaction adumbrated in his discussion of "contemplative" Buddhist virtuosity. Instead, his analysis focuses on the political advantages of monasticism for ecclesiastical and secular rulers. At this point, it should be noted that although modern comparative historical sociologists are now bent on emphasizing the economic dynamism of monasticism in medieval Christendom, Weber himself was in fact much more attentive to monasticism's politicobureaucratic than economic implications.[16] Although monastic asceticism originated as a method of individual salvation only indirectly and spiritually meant to benefit the entire Christian collective, it was eventually transformed into a most useful tool serving the temporal interests of the Church. This transformation corresponded to the evolution of monasticism from its initially asocial, individual orientations into an institution purveying a wide range of social goals and services. Asceticism, moreover, made monks outstandingly efficient, a fact that led Weber to see in them the first "professionals" and which "predestined them to serve as the principal tool of bureaucratic centralization and rationalization in the Church."

Significantly, Weber mainly discusses the usefulness of monasticism in a Caesaropapist framework, where it could help support the ruler's legiti-

---

[14] Weber, *Sociology of Religion,* p. 233.
[15] M. Weber, *Economy and Society: An Outline of Interpretive Sociology* (New York: Bedminster, 1968), vol. 2, ch. 15.
[16] I have dealt with this issue in greater detail in Silber, "Monasticism and the Protestant Ethic."

macy and domesticate his subjects: "If the political ruler wants to create an apparatus of officials and a counter weight against the nobility . . . he cannot wish for a more reliable support than the influence of the monks on the masses."[17] Although "concessions" and "compromises" are not the key notions here any more, the overall picture emerging is that of a rather conservative (in the sense of contributing to the maintainance of the political status quo) relation between monasticism and social order. Somehow qualifying this heavy stress on the political incorporation of monasticism, Weber recognizes that monasticism could readily establish a strong power base of its own in such a context, and even come to a clash with the temporal authorities to safeguard its religious autonomy. Again, moreover, it should be noted that Weber mostly addresses monasticism within the framework of Caesaropapism, and leaves aside the role of monasticism in the much more decentralized context of Western feudalism, which might have received a fuller analysis had Weber lived to complete his planned study of medieval Catholicism.[18]

This emphasis on the "conservative" political implications of monasticism notwithstanding, Weber was nevertheless bent on giving a part to medieval monasticism in his overall interpretation of the unique development of Western rationalization. After all, he did see monasticism as the ideological matrix from which Protestant inner-worldly ascetic virtuosity fatefully emerged. But he also gave it place of pride in his understanding of the medieval West as a uniquely "restless," check-and-balance type of civilization: "All in all, the specific roots of occidental culture must be sought in the tension and peculiar balance, on the one hand, between office charisma and monasticism, and on the other between the contractual character of the feudal state and the autonomous bureaucratic hierocracy. . . . In the Occident, authority was set against authority, legitimacy against legitimacy, one office charisma against the other."[19]

Again, therefore, we see Weber's insistence on Western asceticism as somehow deeply related to and constitutive of the West's uniquely dynamic pattern on rationalization, an interpretation made only more insistent if situated on the backdrop of his contrastive, "mirror image" interpretation of the nature and role of virtuoso asceticism in non-Western, especially Indian and Buddhist, civilizations.

Weber's understanding and categorization of religious virtuosity is intimately related to and confirmed by other aspects of his sociology of religion. Here I shall mention only the significant connection to his discus-

[17] Weber, *Economy and Society*, p. 1171.
[18] Revisiting and aiming at reconstructing Weber's (incomplete) interpretation of Western Christendom, see Schluchter (ed.), *Max Webers Sicht des okzidentalen Christentums* (Frankfurt: Suhrkampf, 1988).
[19] Weber, *Economy and Society*, 1192 We may notice once again, in this oft-quoted passage, Weber's loose assimilation of monasticism with charisma.

sion of types of religious prophecy. As Talcott Parsons has summed it up, "exemplary prophecy tends to produce 'elitist' movements of those who achieve superior religious status, and to leave the others in a state of dubious belongingness, apart from the belongingness they derive from their secular statuses. It is on the basis of ethical prophecy and an order binding on whole categories of persons that anything like a firmly organized 'church' can most readily be built up."[20]

For Weber, thus, not only do religions vary in the status they bestow upon virtuosi, but this varying status is itself intrinsically related to religions' varying capacity to incorporate the laity, to create broader frameworks of "belongingness." The social position of virtuosi is understood to be intimately connected with broader features of their religious and social environment, such as the nature of the religious–ideological matrix from which the virtuosi emerged in the first place (the overriding distinction here being that between exemplary vs. ethical prophecies) and the related structures of collective integration.

This more "structural" and "contextual" approach had already appeared in Weber's analysis of the "functional" incorporation of virtuosi into the Catholic and Caesaropapist social orders. But it was also suggested in a more complex sense in the *Protestant Ethic,* where the virtuoso's momentous "rationalizing" impact stems not from a simplistic model of the influence of religious beliefs on economic behavior, but rather from the historical encounter and consonance – the "elective affinities" – between certain Calvinist religious orientations and the emerging structures of a modern capitalistic system, joining in the formation of a full-fledged and unprecedented capitalistic civilization. A similar tendency to situate virtuosi within the context of broader collective structures was also suggested in Weber's insertion of monasticism as part and parcel of his understanding of the medieval West as a whole, as a check-and-balance type of civilization.

In line, perhaps, with his principled resistance to holistic and systemic interpretations, Weber did not develop this type of global, contextual approach much further. Such an avenue of enquiry, however, might lay bare more persistent, structural factors in the tension-ridden interaction between virtuosi and their social surroundings than conjectural alliances, concessions, and compromises – the recurrent terms of his analysis.[21] As the present study tries to show, it is precisely this kind of more

---

[20] Weber, *Sociology of Religion,* p. xxxvii.

[21] Pierre Bourdieu proposes to systematize this aspect of Weber's sociology of religion dealing with the interactions, tensions, and transactions between the various groups involved in the same religious field: priests, prophets, laity, and sorcerers. See "Une interprétation de la sociologie religieuse de Max Weber," *Archives Européennes de Sociologie* 12 (1971). Bourdieu, however, does not deal with the position of virtuosi in this structure of interactions; more funda-

systematic attention to the broader collective structures from which religious virtuosi emerged, and with which they interacted, that might have modified Weber's relative underassessment of the sociological significance of contemplative virtuoso religion as it developed in the framework of Buddhist civilizations.

Beyond Weber: virtuosity and monasticism

Since Weber's time, there has emerged a wealth of studies (mostly historical) of specific religious figures of various kinds corresponding, by and large, to Weber's definition of virtuosi. Some of these studies are especially helpful in drawing attention to aspects of the interaction between virtuosi and society to which he did not attend. Research on mystics and mysticism,[22] or on sainthood in a variety of cultural settings,[23] in particular, may clarify the sociological implications of the more contemplative and/or individual forms of virtuosity that were systematically underplayed in Weber's approach. Peter Brown's work[24] is one of the most recent and challenging contributions in this respect, and will be referred to at a later point in our discussion. Taken collectively, at any rate, this growing body of literature points to a variability and complexity in virtuosi's ideological orientation and institutional expres-

mentally, he does not address the ideological and institutional structures (be they conceived as shaping forces, resources, or constraints) that may variously shape the overall field of interactions.

[22] See, for example, "Church, Sect and Mysticism" in *Sociological Analysis,* 36 (1975); James L. Peacock, "Mystics and Merchants in Fourteenth-Century Germany: A Speculative Reconstruction of their Psychological Bond and its Implications for Social Change," *Journal for the Scientific Study of Religion* 8 (1969): 47–59.

[23] Works on saints and holy men are too rapidly multiplying to aim here at an inclusive listing. See, for example, J. Wach, *Sociology of Religion* (Chicago: University of Chicago Press, 1971), pp. 357 ff.; J. Mecklin, *The Passing of the Saint: A Study of a Cultural Type* (Chicago: University of Chicago Press, 1941); S. Czarnowski, *Le Culte des héros et sus conditions sociales: St. Patrick, héros national de l'Irlande,* preface by H. Hubert (Paris: Alcan, 1919); P. Brown, *The Cult of the Saints: Its Rise and Function in Latin Christianity* (Chicago: University of Chicago Press, 1981); idem, "The Rise and Function of the Holy Man in Late Antiquity," *Journal of Roman Studies* 61 (1971): 80–101; idem, "The Saint as Examplar," *Representations* 1 (1983): 1–25; E. Gellner, *Saints of the Atlas* (Chicago: University of Chicago Press, 1969); A. Vauchez, *La sainteté en Occident aux derniers siècles du Moyen-Age,* (Ecole Française de Rome, 1981); D. Weinstein and R. M. Bell, *Saints and Society* (Chicago: University of Chicago Press, 1982); J. S. Hawley (ed.), *Saints and Virtues* (Berkeley and Los Angeles: University of California Press, 1987).

[24] See especially Brown, "Rise and Function of the Holy Man"; idem, "Saint as Examplar"; also, idem, *Cult of the Saints;* idem, "Late Antiquity," in P. Veyne (ed.), *A History of Private Life,* translated by Arthur Goldhammer (Cambridge, Mass.: Harvard University Press, 1987), pp. 237–312; idem, *The Body and Society: Men, Women and Sexual Renunciation in Early Christianity* (New York: Columbia University Press, 1988).

sion that can hardly be subsumed under Weber's overly dichotomic and elementary typological categories.[25]

What is needed, however, is not so much a refinement of these categories but rather a more precise analysis of the essential features of virtuosity per se, and of its propensity to become the nexus of a range of highly distinctive, and largely overlooked, sociological processes. Weber's concern with the sharp contrasts between different types of virtuosity – especially its "activist–ascetic–ethical" and orgiastic–contemplative–exemplary" poles – has in fact tended to obscure the common features that led him to identify them as expressions of one same phenomenon in the first place, and to understate their common sociological implications.

Most striking, and not much elaborated upon in Weber's analysis, is the emergence and impressive historical resilience of a specialized virtuoso institution: monasticism. Although many (and perhaps all) human societies have some type of religious specialists – priests, prophets, shamans, diviners, and so forth – not all societies have engendered the phenomenon of religious virtuosity, with the implied split between a virtuoso religiosity and a mass religiosity.[26] Even fewer have engendered the institutionalization of religious virtuosity in the form of monasticism. Weber, as noted, strongly emphasized monasticism's professionallike, rational efficiency and political usefulness. As is shown in the next chapter, however, monasticism is also based on profoundly asocial or even antisocial principles (celibacy, withdrawal from general society) and displays a range of ideological and organizational features that make it into a rather precarious type of social formation. Its emergence and historical persistence in certain civilizational settings only, but not in others, is therefore an issue that calls for greater attention and cannot be taken as self-evident.

Although Weber undoubtedly recognized the historical significance of monasticism and its direct relevance to some of the major themes of his work (such as the development of western "rationalization"),[27] he actually gave it very little conceptual and theoretical attention.[28] It is also a

---

[25] See Schluchter, "Weltflüchtiges Erlösungstreben," especially pp. 35–43.

[26] Weber never uses the term in contexts other than that of the so-called great traditions.

[27] I have examined this aspect of Weber's work in greater detail, although only with respect to the narrower issue of economic rationalization, in Silber, "Monasticism and the Protestant Ethic."

[28] This is perhaps most conspicuous in contrast to his famed typological elaboration of "church" versus "sect." Beyond these two major types of organizations, his attention, like Troeltsch's, rather focused on mysticism. See the issue "Church, Sect and Mysticism" in *Sociological Analysis* 36, no. 3 (1975). This, in conjunction with the fact that he did not clearly articulate the relationship between virtuosity and charisma, reinforces the feeling that there is here a range of religious phenomena that have not received a full and systematic treatment in the Weberian scheme.

further indication of his failure to tackle the issue of virtuosity in a fully systematic fashion that he did not address the distinction (and mutual relation) between virtuosity in its more organized and corporate, monastic form, and in its less organized, more individual, or withdrawn manifestations. Although aware of the withdrawal from normal social relations that tends to accompany the virtuoso's single-minded pursuit of religious ends,[29] he paid no attention to the more radically individual and/or withdrawn, eremitic forms of virtuosity. Nor did he consider the element of voluntary withdrawal remaining present even in organized, monastic forms of virtuosity, or the part that this may play in the interaction between monasticism and society at large. What monopolized his attention, on the contrary, were monasticism's bureaucratic functions and overall political incorporation.

The virtuoso–layman interaction

The analysis to be advanced here will stress the development of an extensive pattern of material and symbolic exchange between virtuosi and laymen, epitomized in a gift relationship (laymen giving, monks receiving) that developed on a massive scale in both Theravada Buddhism and medieval Catholicism. This will mean drawing systematic comparative attention to an axis of interaction with society that, as mentioned, received unequal treatment in Weber's case studies. Noted in the "Buddhist–Jainist" context – but also quickly dismissed as involving a commercialized relation of "magical anthropolatry" of no serious "ethical" impact – it was not systematically followed up in any of the other civilizational settings that Weber addressed. (This unequal treatment, incidentally, is consonant with the fact that processes of exchange do not receive much theoretical weight in Weberian sociology.)[30]

The pattern of exchange between virtuoso and layman, and its reproduction over centuries, I submit, is of crucial significance in understanding both the resilience of monasticism as a specific and far from self-

---

[29] See, for example, Weber, *Sociology of Religion,* p. 166.

[30] A similar emphasis on exchange has been recently developed by Bryan Turner, albeit from a different theoretical perspective and with a different appraisal of Weber's sociology of religion. See B. Turner, *Religion and Social Theory: A Materialist Perspective* (London: Heinemann, 1983) ch. 4. I, of course, fully agree that Weber's typological distinction of virtuoso and mass religiosity has been strangely neglected (p. 89). However, I also believe that Turner tends to inflate the presence, in Weber's sociology of religion, of the assumption of an exchange relationship between virtuosi and the mass, especially one entailing "an implicit parallel between economic and religious systems." Whereas Turner sees the relationship geared to the need of the religious elites "to exchange the benefits of charisma for various forms of payment and tribute in order to maintain their separation from labour and the market place," I prefer to develop a less "economic," more Maussian conception of this exchange as gift relationship.

evident social formation, and its different institutional characteristics in the two cases under study.

Moreover, the existence of a gift relationship as understood since Marcel Mauss,[31] is important in that it signals a very special type of interaction and exchange. On the one hand, the gift is supposed to deny reciprocity and situate itself outside the normal range of transactions and exchange (it is in fact an insult under certain circumstances to return a gift, or return it too quickly). On the other hand, the gift also represents an important mechanism of solidarity and reciprocity in the long range. Mauss himself was interested in the functioning of this mechanism of solidarity as a "total phenomenon," that is, as touching upon many levels of social life in different social settings. Here, the gift relationship between monks and laymen will be shown to form an integral aspect of a broader and complex sociological phenomenon, the virtuoso–society syndrome.

Focusing on the virtuoso–layman axis of interaction and exchange also has the important advantage of mitigating the pervasive elitist orientation of Weber's sociology of religion. Consistently investing religious elites, virtuoso or otherwise, with a dominant, shaping impact in the history of civilizations, Weber typically treated "mass religion" as a residual category, often synonymous to "peasant religion," and usually endowed with heavily depreciative connotations of passivity, irrationality, and reliance on magical, "primitive" ritual and symbolic orientations. Although certainly not contradicting Weber's emphasis on the crucial significance of religious elites, I shall at least underline their lasting involvement in, and dependence upon, a relationship of interaction and exchange in which the laity (still massively, if not solely, rural in character throughout most of the period discussed) emerges as a crucial and active partner.

A more systematic comparative emphasis on the relationship with the laity will also enable us to counteract a pervasive slant in Weber's underestimation of the impact of "otherworldly" religious orientations in general, and of Buddhist virtuosity in particular. This bias is clearly rooted in Weber's overriding concern with the varying potential of different civilizations for rationalization and rationalized activity in the world and with the unique development and features of rationality in the West. In his comparative scheme, Puritan Calvinism often provided the fundamental frame of reference, the epitome and prototype of a religiously anchored, rationalized involvement in the world. I shall not so much focus, however, on the already richly discussed issue of whether Buddhism was or was not able to engender orientations furthering economic and political worldly rationalized and dynamism approximating the modern Western model.[32] More central to my purpose is to bring into relief a very distinctive type of

[31] M. Mauss, *The Gift* (New York: Norton, 1976).
[32] See the Introduction, fn. 18.

Buddhist social construction – deriving at least in part from Buddhist otherworldly orientations – whose far-reaching "worldly" significance has to be understood independently of the approximation to a Western model of economic and political dynamism and/or rationality.

In my view, the virtuoso–laity structure of interaction was a principle of no less, and perhaps even greater, social scope and impact in Theravada Southeast Asia than the better-known mechanisms of institution building derived from more worldly or "rational" cultural orientations in the Christian West. The institutional implications of the virtuoso–laity structure of interaction in Theravada Buddhism must be assessed according to different criteria of social significance and vitality than those used by Weber, and compared, not with late-Christian, Protestant developments, but with the earlier, medieval stages in the history of Christian virtuosity.

The significance of the virtuoso–laity axis of interaction can be understood, however, only within the overall field of social relations. Emphasizing the virtuoso–layman interaction, therefore, is not meant to diminish the importance of the other facets of the interaction between virtuosi and society brought out in Weber's work, such as the relations with the religious establishment and the political center.[33] The intent, rather, is to underline the importance of this interaction as an important and overlooked parameter in the operation of macrosocietal structures, no less and at times even more crucial than the more obvious and better-studied interaction between religious and political establishment – of which the Western church-and-state dynamics provide a major prototype. Last but not least, focusing on the virtuoso–layman relation enables us to clarify the relationship between virtuosity and charisma – one of Weber's best-known legacies to the social sciences.

Virtuosity and charisma

Although Weber did occasionally use the word "charisma" in connection with religious virtuosi, he never tried to articulate the analytical or empirical relationship between the two phenomena.[34] (This is noticeable in

---

[33] On the contrary, this should contribute to the analysis of monasticism as part of a field of interacting as well as competing social groups, including the laity itself. This is in part compatible, once again, with Bourdieu's suggested reading of Weber (see this chapter, fn. 21). Bourdieu, however, emphasizes the competition for power *over* the laity only, in terms of social groups' different capacities to mobilize the laity's resources (material or otherwise). In that specific regard, it seems possible to read Weber as addressing "power" over the laity primarily in terms of ethical impact – albeit also facilitating thereby, in the case of monasticism, a process of "domestication of the masses" ultimately benefiting both ecclesiastical and political rulers.

[34] See, for example, his definition of religious virtuosi at the beginning of this chapter and in fn. 1.

his very definition of religious virtuosi quoted at the beginning of this chapter, and in the later quote, assessing the tense balance of occidental culture, where monasticism is implicitly and loosely credited with charisma.) This relative neglect, moreover, is all the more striking in light of the crucial role attributed to religious virtuosi in his comparative analysis of civilizations in general, and of Western uniqueness in particular.

Religious virtuosi may become, but are not necessarily, charismatic leaders; they are not necessarily connected with especially dramatic, highly emotional movements; and they are not necessarily either especially disruptive or dramatically creative. In short, religious virtuosi are not necessarily a "hot," but rather a cold – or at any rate a cooler – phenomenon. The analogy from the arts and music may be relevant: There the term virtuosity has come to connote an exceptional level of proficiency and technical excellence, not necessarily coincidental with the more "charismatic" notions of artistic creativity or innovative genius. (Weber himself does not develop that contrast, and as already mentioned, does not attach to the term virtuosity any of its possible pejorative contemporary connotations.) Nevertheless, ascetic virtuosi have hardly left society indifferent; their virtuosity, to pursue the artistic metaphor, has not lacked audience. It has had, in fact, a tremendous appeal, and one with an interesting contrast to that usually associated with the idea of genuine charisma – a theme we shall expand upon in Chapter 10. Understanding this appeal, I submit, can add an important and neglected dimension to the general comprehension of cultural–ideological elites and their patterns of impingement upon society at large.

To some extent, admittedly, virtuosity may be understood as anchored in the charismatic impulse in the most extensive sense of that term, pertaining to the quest for a meaningful order and for the sense of a fundamental connection to the realm of ultimate meaning. In that broader sense indeed, as propounded by Edward Shils and S. N. Eisenstadt,[35] religious virtuosity in general and monasticism in particular may be seen as one of the most extreme and most autonomous expressions, both ideologically and institutionally, of the charismatic motif in the history of human civilization. The central concern of virtuoso asceticism, at least in its original impulse, is the single-minded pursuit of ultimate religious ends. It is also that essentially "charismatic" impulse that leads to the effort to systematically pattern the virtuoso's way of life in accordance with these ends, and to the methodical avoidance, through asceticism and withdrawal, of whatever is perceived as apt to

---

[35] See E. Shils, "Charisma, Order and Status," *American Sociological Review* 30 (1965): 199–213; S. N. Eisenstadt (ed.), *Max Weber on Charisma and Institution-Building* (Chicago: University of Chicago Press, 1968), especially pp. ix–lvi.

interfere with that end. However, a closer analysis of monasticism, and of the complex pattern of interaction that has tended to develop between monks and laity, discloses a number of features at variance with those associated with either "pure," "routinized," or "institutional" charisma, at least in Weber's original (albeit not always consistent) usage of those terms – as we shall explain in Chapter 10. If there is charisma in regard to religious virtuosity, it is of a sort that clearly indicates the need for a more refined spectrum of categories to account for the many and contradictory expressions of charisma as an essentially multifaceted and protean phenomenon.

Weber's work, in sum, is of seminal importance in suggesting the distinctiveness of religious virtuosity as a sociological phenomenon, and its significance for the comparative sociological study of civilizations. On the other hand, as we have seen, his approach suffered from important biases and limitations. The next chapter highlights aspects of the relation between virtuosi and society that were understated in the Weberian approach, first by further elucidating the distinctive features of monasticism as a virtuoso institution, and second by reviewing and criticizing a number of interpretations that offer, loosely speaking, a Durkheimian or "functionalist" counterpart to the Weberian approach.

Fundamentally, however, this book remains very much in line with Weber's overall enterprise. Not only does it take Weber's notion and analysis of virtuosity as a starting point, but it also applies a combination of ideal-type analysis and comparative historical research, two distinctly Weberian methodological tools. More important, it is also Weberian, I believe, in adopting a multidimensional and nondeterministic style of explanation that gives much weight to religious–cultural orientations and collective structures of meaning, while also emphasizing the need to take into account a whole constellation of sociostructural variables. Where it perhaps both pursues and goes beyond Weber is in the fuller elaboration of virtuosity, the elaboration of new comparative parameters, and a new (if not necessarily opposed) comparative assessment of the social significance of occidental versus Asian forms of religious virtuosity. Finally, this book expands upon Weber's basic concern with the interpretation of meaning, but also enriches it with other and newer forms of symbolic and cultural analysis, by trying, in the final chapter, to better define the precise significance of religious–ideological orientations as they become a necessary ingredient of the interaction between virtuoso elites and society, and a constitutive dimension of the social order at large.

2 Monasticism and social order: a multidimensional comparative perspective

In line with Weber's general attentiveness to the ideal–typical features of religious institutions, but also compensating for his failure to direct this very same attentiveness to monasticism, the first task of this chapter is to highlight the distinctive features of monasticism as a specific type of religious organization. I shall aim here, in contrast to the existing literature on the topic, at a conceptual approach potentially applicable to "traditional" forms of monasticism in either East or West, and resolutely viewing monastic institutions as partaking of and interacting with broader sociocultural frameworks.

Reaching for a fuller and more contextual understanding of monasticism will throw light on religious virtuosity not only as a specific type of religious orientation giving rise to a specific type of religious elite or institution, but also as a central dimension in the dynamics of the two world religions compared. The result, ultimately, is a modified comparative perception of these two civilizations that uncovers both historical similarities and differences not yet been brought into relief in Weber's or other macrocomparative accounts, and that inscribes virtuoso asceticism as a vital factor not only in the rise of the West, but also in the ideological expansion and tenacity of the Buddhist East.

Monasticism as virtuoso institution and "alternative structure"

A most essential feature of monasticism is its marginal, even antithetical character vis-à-vis society at large. The monastic way of life contradicts normal patterns of behavior in the most basic parameters of ordinary human life such as sex, food, kinship, and property, to mention only the most salient. Adhering to an atypical and in many ways asocial type of behavior, monks voluntarily opt out of social life as commonly defined. This withdrawal can even assume a spatial dimension, leading to seclusion in faraway, unpopulated areas such as deserts and forests, or on the fringes of human settlements.

As such, monks have often been perceived as marginal phenomena of minor social significance. Some attention, however, has been paid to the internal features of monasticism as a type of social formation, and comparisons have been made with modern closed, total institutions or with the various communal experiments of Western counterculture.[1] Monasticism has also been scrutinized for its typological similarities with and differences from the sect type of religious organization.[2] In general, however, the tendency has been to relate to monasticism as a thing in itself rather than as part of a wider sociocultural context. Furthermore, sociological research on the topic has generally been limited to contemporary settings and Christian forms of monasticism.

It is important to underscore, however, some important contributions of this Christian-based body of sociological analysis. To begin with, the similarities to total institutions are suggestive indeed. Monastic daily life is fully scheduled, planned in its smallest details, and rationalized, besides requiring total immersion of the individual in the community and total obedience to authority. The rites of passage upon entrance are also similar, entailing social leveling and the relinquishing of all signs of one's previous life and status. The essential difference remains, obviously, that the entry into monasticism is based on an ideological and fully voluntary individual choice (at least in theory). This very basic difference notwithstanding, it is remarkable that religious opting out, while essentially motivated by a purely individual search for salvation, was able to spawn a communal framework characterized by a tighter, "greedier" structure than most ordinary social frameworks. In a paradox worth underlining, radically asocial and even antisocial orientations gave rise to a remarkably powerful form of social organization: "It is the withdrawal from normal social order and the turning toward a spiritual, supra-mundane world, and not the vision of a new social order, which led to the formation of a new, historically exceptionally enduring and influential form of life."[3]

---

[1] E. Goffman, *Asylums* (Chicago: Aldine, 1961), pp. 4–5; G. A. Hillery, Jr., "The Convent: Community, Prison or Task Force?" *Journal for the Scientific Study of Religion* 8 (1969): 140–51; E. Servais and F. Hambye, "Structure et méthode: problème et méthode en sociologie des organisations claustrales," *Social Compass* 18 (1971): 27–44; G. A. Hillery and P. C. Morrow, "The Monastery as a Commune," *International Review of Modern Sociology* 6 (1976): 139–54; L. Moulin, "Pour une sociologie des ordres religieux," *Social Compass* 10 (1963): 145–70; H. P. M. Goddijn, "The Sociology of Religious Orders and Congregations," *Social Compass* 7 (1960): 431–47; M. Ple (ed.), *La séparation du monde* (Paris: Cerf, 1901); Y. Zerubavel, "The Benedictine Ethic and the Modern Spirit of Scheduling: On Schedules and Social Organization," *Sociological Inquiry* 50 (1980): 157–69.

[2] M. Hill, "Typologie sociologique de l'ordre religieux," *Social Compass* 17 (1971): 45–64; idem, *A Sociology of Religion* (London: Heinemann, 1973), pp. 84–7; idem, *Religious Order* – to which we shall refer again in the last part of this work in relation to a typological definition of religious virtuosity in general.

[3] W. Bergman, "Das frühe Mönchtum als soziale Bewegung," *Kölner Zeitschrift für Soziologie und Sozialpsychologie* 37 (1985): 32. In this respect, monasticism is an extreme expression of the religion/rationality paradox so central to Weber's concerns: Underpinning the formation of a capitalistic civilization was a

Another feature of monasticism emphasized in Christian-based material is its basically conservative nature, for all that it entails elements of potentially subversive criticism of society at large. This is suggested in Joachim Wach's characterization of monasticism as "protest within"[4] and Michael Hill's typological analysis of the religious order (both monastic and nonmonastic) as a "sect within the Church," distinguished from the sect proper by its acceptance of an external, ecclesiastical source of authority.[5] The combination of subversive and conservative elements is even more forcefully emphasized in Jean Seguy's analysis of monasticism as both "utopia" – that is, entailing the model of an alternative, perfect mirror society – and "implicit protest," a form of criticism or dissent remaining within the bounds of the established order of things.[6]

A convenient way to sum up these opposing features of monasticism is to borrow, with some modification, Victor Turner's well-known notions of structure and antistructure.[7] Antistructure, in Turner's work, refers to a property of certain conditions or situations in social life – usually temporary, transitory, and "liminal" – that makes them particularly conducive to solidary, nonhierarchical modes of fellowship. Monasticism may contain a strong element of such antistructure: It definitely entails strong egalitarian aspects, elements of status leveling and destructuration, and many tenets antithetical to ordinary social life and structure. No less

process of increased "practical" rationalization (*Zweckrationalitat*) rooted, in part, in religious motivations – usually taken as arch-irrational but constitutive, for Weber, of "substantive" rationality (*Wertrationalitat*). In monasticism, too, we see a powerful and rationalized organization rooted in religious orientations, and no less paradoxically, in asocial and even antisocial orientations. On Weber's typology of forms of rationality, see Kalberg, "Max Weber's Types of Rationality"; Swidler, "Concept of Rationality."

[4] Wach, *Sociology of Religion*, pp. 156–205.

[5] See this chapter, fn. 2. M. Hill sees many parallels between sects and religious orders: Both are voluntary associations; membership in both is achieved by proof of merit, however defined, be it on the basis only of a high level of commitment; both emphasize exclusiveness, and expulse their deviants; both carry the self-conception of an elect; both have personal perfection as their goal; both have a totalitarian hold over their members (more systematically so in the order than in the sect); finally, both characteristically tend, if in different ways and degrees, to keep apart from "the world." The differences however, as he sees them, are crucial. First, orders, being part of a wider institutional church, rely on a source of authority that is ultimately external, though they may be permitted a considerable degree of organizaional autonomy in their internal arrangements. Sects, on the other hand, are self-legitimating and rely on no external sanctions in regulating their beliefs and structure. Second, sects are very rarely celibate.

[6] J. Seguy, "Une sociologie des sociétés imaginées: monachisme et utopie," *Annales E.S.C.* 26 (1971): 328–54; idem, "Pour une sociologie de l'ordre religieux," *Archives de Sciences Sociales des Religions* 57 (1984): 55–68.

[7] See, for example, V. Turner, *Dramas, Fields and Metaphors: Symbolical Action in Human Society* (Ithaca, N.Y.: Cornell University Press, 1974), especially the chapter, "Metaphors of Anti-Structure in Religious Culture," pp. 272–300.

important, it shares with liminal or antistructural situations the distinctive element of withdrawal from normal social life. At the same time, however, it is not a passing phase in human relationships but a highly institutionalized structure in itself, eventually becoming an integral part of the wider social structure. Hence it might be useful to perceive in monasticism not so much antistructure as a type of "alternative structure," characterized by a tight intermingling of structural and antistructural elements. It is precisely this dense interweaving of structure and antistructure, I submit, that distinguishes monasticism from other social institutions and makes it a kind of "alternative" structure within society at large.[8]

Precariousness of the monastic institution

This leads us to a feature of monasticism that has not received systematic treatment, namely, that its potential for interweaving antistructural and structural elements does not prevent the monastic institution from being a most fragile social formation. Like total institutions, but also like any other type of social organization, monasticism has to meet a variety of common organizational problems, such as the maintenance of internal discipline and commitment; recruitment; material needs (food, clothing, housing, and instruments of the liturgy); management of property; contact with and protection from the outer world; self-perpetuation; and so forth. However, given the need to maintain and weave together both structure and antistructure, some of these ordinary problems are posed in especially acute fashion in the case of monasticism, confronting it with a range of problems and dilemmas that in the long run are apt to undermine its institutional resilience.

To begin with, the problem of regulating the interaction with the external world, admittedly present to some degree in any boundary-maintaining social formation, is made more acute by the ideology of social withdrawal intrinsic to monasticism's self-definition, and by the need to develop insulating mechanisms to that effect. A basic dilemma here is to define and control the degree of insulation versus involvement, and autonomization versus incorporation within the wider social environment. A related problem is that of self-perpetuation: Being based on celibacy, monasticism is deprived of one of the most basic mechanisms of social reproduction and must rely on the external world from which it withdraws for recruitment and continuity. It also lacks the natural or at least explicit exercise of a number of other mechanisms of

---

[8] I have further developed this theme in Silber, "'Opting Out' in Theravada Buddhism and Medieval Christianity: A Comparative Look at Monasticism as Alternative Structure," *Religion* 15 (1988): 251–77.

social integration and regulation, such as the whole range of incentives and sanctions usually associated with an individual's material advancement or family ties.

At the ideological level, a major source of precariousness lies in monasticism's virtuoso dimension itself, that is, its commitment to a rigorous ascetic discipline and search for perfection, the enactment of which is most arduous and problematic by definition. It is important to note, however, that a large share of monasticism's fragility in this regard seems to stem, paradoxically, precisely from the very same ascetic-rationalizatory orientations enhancing its capacity for a powerful, total type of organization. This is most evident in monasticism's tendency to accumulate wealth as a result of the ascetic limits on consumption, and of a rationalized collective management of labor and property – wealth in turn threatening its basic vocation of poverty and asceticism, and constituting a major spur to corruption and decline.

Ascetic rationality and efficiency may also become a source of instability and precariousness by encouraging the increasing "social functionalization" of monasticism, that is, the harnessing of its special efficiency to a variety of social, extramonastic (be they secular or religious) goals. Such a trend, stressed in Weber's analysis of Christian monasticism, cannot but threaten the insulation and segregation deemed necessary to monasticism's special vocation and purity.

Moreover, monasticism may be challenged not only by trends that weaken its insularity or bring about its corruption, but also by the forces of virtuoso "ultracism" or "radicalism"[9] emerging from its own midst. These typically develop as a reaction to what they perceive as corruption and decline, and entail the call for a return to a purer, more rigorous enactment of the monastic vocation. In this respect, monasticism may be said to engender its own criticism and to be susceptible to recurrent waves of reformism. These may be seen, to some extent, as an innate mechanism for revitalizing monasticism as a virtuoso institution. Perhaps more essentially, however, monasticism may have to cope with the

---

[9] The two are present and closely related in each case, but I shall use only "radicalism" from now on simply because it is a more common notion. Ultracism is used here in the sense of "holding of extreme opinions on any question," and connotes the desire to bring religious virtuosity to its maximum possible expression. Radicalism, however, which may be seen as another variant of extremism, adds the notion of "going to the root or origin," and of touching upon what is essential and fundamental (extremism may be displayed on questions of minor importance, although it is only triggered as a rule by issues perceived as fundamental). This is close to the definition of Christian radicalism as "a concern with religious criticism and reform based on the roots of Christianity, especially the New Testament roots" developed by Rosalind and Christopher Brooke in *Popular Religion in the Middle-Ages* (London: Thames & Hudson, 1984).

internal conflict and segmentation resulting from different interpretations of the monastic ideal, and especially with the perennial tension
between more and less radical definitions of withdrawal from the world.
A particular aspect of that problem is the tension between communal
("cenobitic") versus individual and solitary ("eremitic," although the
word has also been applied to some forms of limited cenobitism) forms
of virtuoso renunciation. Challenge may also come, however, from an
altogether different direction: from forms of religious virtuosity that
develop outside, or even against, the monastic framework.

It should be clear at this point that although the institutionalization of
virtuosity could give rise, in the shape of monasticism, to the impressive
phenomenon of "alternative structures" characterized by a tight interweaving of structural and antistructural elements, these alternative structures retain an intrinsic precariousness that makes their very existence
and historical resilience far from self-evident. How, then, are we to
account for the emergence and persistence of such virtuoso alternative
structures and for the place they came to occupy within society as a
whole? To answer this question, we should consider some general interpretations of the relationship between religious virtuosi and the social
order that offer, loosely speaking, a functionalist counterpart to the
Weberian approach. By functionalist, I refer to the tendency to interpret
virtuosi as fulfilling certain functions in answer to certain needs of society (whatever the extent to which the latter is explicitly considered as a
closed and systemic entity – a central feature of rigid forms of functionalism only). Although not devoid of serious inadequacies, these
functionalist interpretations do have the merit of highlighting a number
of aspects of the interaction between religious virtuosi and society that
will have to be taken into account in any attempt at a comprehensive
sociological understanding of the subject.

Virtuosity and social order: the functionalist approach

A first and clear example of functionalist interpretation of the relation
between religious virtuosi and society is found in Emile Durkheim's
work (not too surprisingly, since Durkheim is often noted to have anticipated many features of modern functionalism). Addressing himself to
virtuoso ascetics in general, rather than to monasticism in particular,
Durkheim suggests a rather straightforward connection between virtuosi
and the realm of central social values. Briefly, virtuoso ascetics are said
to represent the extreme expression of values and norms that other
people enact much more moderately and imperfectly, not only in the
religious sphere but in social life in general; virtuoso asceticism constitutes the symbolic form of the basic asceticism inherent in all social life

and fulfills the exemplary function of "keeping norms too high, so that they should not sink too low."[10]

A more complex normative function is attributed to virtuoso ascetics in what may be called the safety-valve model. In this model, societies would assign to monasticism, as a special, insulated sector, roles and orientations whose legitimacy they cannot utterly deny but which entail a subversive, antisocial, or antistructural potential.[11] This type of interpretation has also been advanced for individual forms of virtuoso asceticism, most notably in Louis Dumont's analysis of renunciation in India.[12] A notable variant is to be found in Shils's notion of "segregation of charisma":

All societies seek to make some provision for those persons whose actions are impelled by the possession of charismatic legitimacy. Within religious systems, the cenobitic or anchoritic monastic orders are institutional frameworks for the segregation and control of the charismatically endowed, i.e., those who are prone to experience a sense of direct contact with transcendental powers. . . . By segregation, the custodians of the routine spheres of life show both their apprehension of the disruptive nature of intense and concentrated charisma and appreciation of a virtue requiring acknowledgement. . . . A continuous reinforcement of the barriers against a free movement of charismatic persons is carried on by the custodians of the routine order.[13]

In this approach, virtuosi are still connected to the realm of central values, but a strong element of ambivalence is introduced: Virtuosi represent something that is considered potentially disruptive, yet has a place in the collective set of values. Correspondingly, segregation is the sign of both apprehension and deference on the part of nonvirtuosi. Although the notion of segregation is perhaps unjustifiably loaded with coercive connotations in Shils's formulation, it has the merit of perceiving the monastic institution as to a large extent the result of forces and pressures from the broader environment.

These interpretations have a number of shortcomings. First, they do not address the variability in patterns of interaction between monasti-

[10] E. Durkheim, *The Elementary Forms of Religious Life* (Glencoe, Ill.: Free Press, 1965), especially p. 356.
[11] See, for example, Hill, "Typologie sociologique," 60; E. Troeltsch, *The Social Teachings of the Christian Church* (New York: Allen & Unwin, 1931); E. Shils, *Center and Periphery: Essays in Macrosociology* (Chicago: University of Chicago Press, 1975), pp. 121–34. On Christian monasticism as containing and domesticating potentially anarchic tendencies, see L. Kolakowski, *Chrétiens sans église* (Paris: Gallimard, 1969), especially p. 59.
[12] L. Dumont, "World-Renunciation in Indian Religions," in *Religion, Politics and History in India: Collected Papers in Indian Sociology* (The Hague: Mouton, 1970), p. 46. Also N. Yalman, "The Ascetic Buddhist Monks of Ceylon," *Ethnology* 1 (1962): 315–28; R. J. Z. Werblowsky, *Beyond Tradition and Modernity* (London: Athlone, 1976), p. 89.
[13] Shils, *Center and Periphery*, p. 130.

cism and society in different historical and civilizational settings. Moreover, they tend to see monastics and/or other virtuosi as fulfilling specific
functions and contributing to the overall normative integration and well-
being of the social order. Such an approach overlooks the element of
conflict and competition, of cultural and political power games and compromises between the virtuoso and other social sectors, which was
rightly if excessively emphasized by Weber. It also takes for granted, in a
quasi-mechanistic fashion, the persistence through time of the "safety
valve" or "segregation" process, and relatedly, of the monastic institution. Moreover, these interpretations present an altogether monolithic
image of virtuoso ascetics in general and monasticism in particular, ignoring the inner differentiation and tensions within the virtuoso sector itself. Both the presence of clashing conceptions of the monastic life and
the relation between monasticism and other forms of virtuosity could
introduce a strong element of dynamism into a picture that tends to be
overly conservative and static.

Virtuosity and power

The interpretations offered hitherto have assumed a rather stable relationship between virtuoso ascetics and society, even if they are not necessarily segregated in monastic enclaves. However, it is important to consider another, more dynamic aspect of virtuoso asceticism, stemming
from the potential of systematic asceticism and withdrawal from the
world to generate not only rational efficiency and communal institutions, but also a type of charismatic, supernatural prestige that may in
turn be converted into innovative influence or power in the world.

This "convertible" aspect of virtuoso asceticism is brought into relief in
Peter Brown's famed analysis of the rise and function of the holy man in
late Roman society.[14] The holy men he describes are hermits living either
in the desert or at the edge of villages, "athletes of God" conquering their
body in spectacular feats of mortification, and initially met with hostility
and suspicion. In the wake of economic trends that greatly weakened the
large landowners and their former functions of village patronage, these
usually poorly integrated communities became needful of an external
source of authority that could mediate between them and the outside
world, as well as among the villagers themselves. This need came to focus
on the holy man – the stranger par excellence. Crucial to the holy man's
success as a mediator was "the deep social significance of asceticism as a
long, drawn out, solemn ritual of dissociation" from all social ties, that
lent him the objectivity and certainty men desperately needed in a society

[14] Brown, "Rise and Function of the Holy Man."

marked by the erosion of institutions at every level of life."[15] His rise coincided with institutional decline; hence it is no accident, according to Brown, that his position later deteriorated with the reassertion and renewal of collective institutions. Although this analysis stresses the determinant impact of social–institutional, contextual factors on the rise and decline of this type of holy men, it also recognizes the influence of a certain ideological climate – a widespread need for "certainty." In contrast with the other interpretations already examined, no importance is given to more specific value contents, or to a realm of central ideals. (Brown himself has acknowledged this as a flaw in a later essay in which he starts exploring the symbolic and religious meaning – rather than only the social functions – of the holy man as Christian exemplar.)[16] Be that as it may, Brown's analysis accords with the previous ones in identifying the function of the virtuoso ascetics as rather "conservative" in kind – filling an institutional vacuum, and providing an alternative to functions previously filled by now-eroded institutions.

Virtuosity and change

The convertibility of ascetic prestige into influence and worldly power can also proceed, however, in a less conservative and more innovative direction. This is pointed out in Dumont's seminal analysis of Indian renunciation, already alluded to,[17] which supports the safety-valve model, but combines it with a stress on the dynamic, innovative potential of virtuoso ascetics. The relation between the renouncer and the man in the world, in Dumont's perspective, is one of antithesis and complementarity. The renouncer "dies" to the world and to all caste distinctions and interdependence; moveover, even as he opts out of the world and is overtly striving at total extinction, he becomes invested with (quasi-occidental) individuality, something for which caste society has no room. Significantly, renunciation is often represented as the last and supreme among the four stages of life of the Brahman, an acceptable option only after worldly obligations have been carried out. Dumont sees here a subdued hostility to renunciation itself: Renouncers represent a transcedence and sacredness that are acknowledged as such

---

[15] Ibid., p. 91.

[16] Brown, "Saint as Examplar." Notwithstanding the similarity in terms, it is not clear whether Brown invests the saint as holy exemplar with "exemplary" meaning (or function) in either Durkheim's or Weber's sense; what he explicitly calls for, rather, is a newer, Geertzian style of cultural analysis (although the two, of course, are far from incompatible). I believe a close reading of Brown's other writings all closely relevant to the topic (see Chapter 1, fn. 19), would reveal a more complex and perhaps not altogether consequent conception of the relation between virtuoso ascetics and society.

[17] See this chapter, fn. 11.

by the man in the world, but allowed to develop only outside, or at the limits, of the social order as commonly understood – a conception very close to Shils's "segregation of charisma." Renunciation thereby functions as a safety valve for the Brahmanic order that finds in it a way to reserve a permanent niche for the transcendent without posing a threat to the everyday life in the world. Most significantly for the present discussion, however, renouncers have been, according to Dumont, the major element of development and innovation in Indian religion. They have been at the origin of all sects, which themselves display features characteristic of renunciation, transcending caste without denying it, and superimposing a religion of individual choice upon common religion, rather than negating it.

Dumont's approach is thus double-edged: It relates virtuoso and society in terms of antithesis and complementarity within a global, encompassing structure. With the idea of renunciation as a safety valve, it may seem to lead to just another instance of functionalist interpretation. On the other hand, it also emphasizes the voluntariness and individuality inherent in the virtuoso's extraordinary option, and the subversive and innovative potential that may become attached to it.

Both Brown's and Dumont's studies, therefore, have underlined that ascetic withdrawal may become the basis of power in the world and possess a dynamic, innovative potential. No less crucially, they underline virtuosi's potential mobility or fluidity, not only in the move in social position from marginal to central, from conservative to innovative, or from orthodox to heterodox, but also in the possibility of their decline or deinstitutionalization. No attempt has yet been made, however, to define the conditions facilitating or blocking the emergence of such dynamics in different historical contexts – an issue that we begin to confront, while also extending it to monasticism more particularly, in the framework of the present comparative enquiry.

A multidimensional comparative approach

Coming back, then, to monasticism proper, I propose to approach it as a social formation with its own internal demands and dynamics but standing in a close dialectical relation to the social and cultural environment in which it sustained itself over time. Differences in the ways of coping with the basic dilemmas it faced – segregation versus involvement, autonomization versus social functionalization or incorporation, acceptance or refusal of power (and of what kind of power) in the world – and in the resulting patterns of interaction with society, will be shown to have evolved under the combined impact of different cultural and institutional environments. Monasticism, therefore, may be said to constitute not only a reversal, but also a reflection or reproduction of the social order at large; it may be approached as a cultural variable shaped by a constellation of factors that the comparative analysis should help us to circumscribe.

I shall show, first, that the extraordinary resilience and central social position of so inherently precarious and non–self-reproducing an institution as monasticism relied in these two cases on very different, even contrasting patterns of institutionalization; second, that these variations in patterns of institutionalization were shaped by major ideological and institutional characteristics of the civilizational contexts with which monasticism interacted; third, that partial convergence seems to have obtained for a while, resulting in a rather similar constellation of characteristics in the relation between virtuosi and society.

The presentation of each case study will proceed in three major sections. The first section will deal with the ideological groundings for the emergence of religious virtuosity in general and monasticism in particular, and for a specific pattern of interaction between virtuosi and society. The second section will analyze monasticism and the dynamics of its interaction with society at large at the institutional level, in relation to basic institutional features (economic, social, and political) of the macrosocietal context. The third part will focus on the forces of virtuoso radicalism that emerged from inside or outside the monastic institution in each setting, and will consider their role in maintaining or undermining the dominant pattern of institutionalization described in the second section.

This division into three sections is mostly a matter of exposition, however; a major aim of this work will be to convey the interconnectedness and mutual reinforcement of the various influences involved as these played themselves out in the course of history. Before doing so, though, we must sort out the variables with which each section will be dealing, and that will form the building blocks of our comparative analysis.

A. The ideological groundings

The emergence and resilience of monasticism in these two civilizational settings cannot be understood independently of its relation to the realm of central, ultimate collective values – albeit not the straightforward, "exemplary" relation of the Durkheimian model. More precisely, monasticism should be understood in relation to the inner contradictions of religious systems propounding ideals that are not fully applicable or not incumbent upon all, while also developing into world religions, that is, religions mustering mass allegiance and operating as the central value system of macrosocietal, civilizational entities. Although this type of contradiction is present to some extent in many cultural systems, it has been recognized as particularly salient in "otherworldly" or "outworldly" civilizations.[18] Such is the case of Theravada Buddhism and medieval Catholicism, usually characterized in post-Weberian language as incorporating a strong strand of otherworldly orientations in their central value systems.[19] Both civilizations are geared, at least in part, to cultural orientations inimical to the valorization of society and its mundane concerns,[20] and promoting ideals of perfection and self-transcendance that are obviously not applicable to all.

From this point of view, monasticism may be said to represent the closest embodiment of the otherworldly impulse in both contexts, and to constitute – as intimated in some functionalist models already referred to – a convenient way of maintaining, yet also neutralizing, world-rejecting orientations and their obviously antisocial, anti-institutional implications. No religion, however, can be totally otherworldly: "If it were, it would not survive its founder, let alone succeed in creating social structures, shaping cultures and producing continuities."[21] A crucial factor to be considered, therefore, is not only the prominence of the otherworldly motif in the two religious systems under study, but also its specific mode of coexistence with more worldly motifs. This mode of coexistence will be shown to help account for the varying types of religious virtuosi that emerged in each setting, their orientations toward the social order, and in particular, the different ways in which monasticism coped with the dilemmas posed by its interaction with society at large.

No less fundamental, however, than the relative strength and position of the otherworldly impulse in each case are the ideological structures developed to maintain it as part and parcel of a world religion – a variable hinted at, but not systematically considered, in the classic Weberian framework. Of particular importance here is the extent to which the religious matrix appears to encourage the emergence of a religious double standard distinguishing between an elite search for perfection and a

[18] I use here interchangeably "outworldly" and "otherworldly," although outworldly seems to me preferable to otherworldly, which is of more common usage, and which may be mistaken to connote the belief in a world afterlife, found also in religions that do not devaluate or reject the world here and now.

[19] On this paradox of otherworldly civilizations, see Eisenstadt, "Die Paradoxie."

[20] Detailed discussion of this common feature of Christianity and Theravada Buddhism, although couched in slightly different terms, can be found in F. Reynolds, "Contrasting Modes of Action: A Comparative Study of Buddhist and Christian Ethics," *History of Religion* 20 (1980):128–46. See also the recent debate on Christian (mainly early) vs. Indian and (Buddhist) "outworldliness" in Dumont, "Modified View"; followed by R. N. Bellah, K. Burridge, and R. Robertson, "Responses to Louis Dumont," *Religion* 12 (1982): 83–8, and S. N. Eisenstadt, "Transcendental Visions – Other-Worldliness and its Transformations: Some More Comments on Louis Dumont," *Religion* 13 (1983): 1–19.

[21] Werblowsky, *Beyond Tradition and Modernity*, p. 85.

more average religiosity, and giving legitimacy to a split between virtuoso and mass religiosity – rightly addressed by Wolfgang Schluchter as a strategy of "relativization" in coping with world-renouncing orientations.[22] In itself, however, this basic double standard is not sufficient to account for the emergence of more specific patterns of interaction between virtuosi and society. No less important, we shall also consider the impact of different conceptions of religious authority and of the religious collective, encouraging differing modes of incorporation of virtuoso elites within a wider religious collective. Reaching for a fuller ideological analysis and going beyond fully explicit doctrinal contents will also necessitate, I submit, locating the orientations just described within the cultural field at large, and examining their relation to other, possibly competing, symbolic and ideological orientations.

This detailed attention to doctrinal contents and related principles of ideological organization is very much in line with Weber's concern with granting religious orientations a large measure of autonomy and a central role in shaping the basic premises and historical dynamics of entire civilizations. It also coincides with recent pleas for historical sociologists to both recognize the analytic autonomy of culture and give serious weight to the analysis of culture's internal structures.[23] Arguing for the impact of religious or ideological orientations as such, it should be emphasized, does not necessarily mean adopting an idealist or simplistic consensual model of the role of religious beliefs in social life. Rather, the ideological and institutional dimensions of virtuoso religion in its interaction with society at large will be treated here as deeply intertwined with each other. Moreover, both (as probably all) religious systems may be shown to contain significant tensions or inner contradictions, and thus the potential for divergent interpretations. It is important to recognize, though, that there were some ideological parameters, however equivocal, and that the ideological game was not entirely open-ended.

The specific path taken by the institutionalization of virtuosity will not be presented, therefore, as a direct result of clear-cut religious–cultural premises, but rather as the result of the interaction between ambiguous or multivocal ideological premises and specific institutional societal struc-

---

[22] See Schluchter, "Weltflüchtiges Erlösungsstreben," pp. 41 ff.; also idem, *Max Weber's Vision of History*, p. 32.

[23] See, recently, J. A. Goldstone, "Ideology, Cultural Frameworks, and the Process of Revolution," *Theory and Society* 20 (1991): 405–54; C. Calhoun, "Beyond the Problem of Meaning: Robert Wuthnow's Historical Sociology of Culture," *Theory and Society* 21, no. 3 (1992): 419–44; A. Kane, "Cultural Analysis in Historical Sociology: The Analytic and Concrete forms of the Autonomy of Culture," *Sociological Theory* 53 (1990): 53–70. Kane, however (and unlike Goldstone), sees this as more readily feasible with regard to short-span event analysis than in the context of long-range macrosociological interpretations; S. Kalberg, *Max Weber's Comparative-Historical Sociology*, ch. 2.

tures. In other words, the process of institutionalization should not be seen as the direct expression of potentialities present in the ideological–religious system. Rather, the acting out of internal virtualities combined with and/or was accelerated by major trends in the economic, ideological, and political structures of the broader macrosocietal context, as is brought out in the second chapter of each case study.

B. The interaction between monasticism and its institutional context

In both settings, monasticism seems to have been able to sustain itself over extensive periods of time as a sort of "alternative structure" in the sense defined earlier in this chapter, coping with a range of distinctive dilemmas and with the problem of maintaining its virtuoso withdrawal and renunciation at the same time as it evolved a mainfold relationship to society. The analysis of the major institutional characteristics monasticism developed in the process starts with its internal structures. As already suggested, however, institutionalization should be assessed on the basis not only of organizational structures, but also of monasticism's position within, and interaction with, society at large. Moreover, and in contrast to those models that have emphasized the element of segregation in the interaction between monasticism and society, the present study will draw attention to an aspect of that interaction that none of the interpretations already referred to take into account, namely, the development of an elaborate network of symbolic and material exchange, entailing, among other things, a massive stream of donations to monasteries. Although understood as a contribution to the material support of monasteries, donations could converge with other characteristics of the monastic economy in contributing to the corruption of monastic discipline. Lay donations thus may be seen as adding to the many basic dilemmas facing the monastic institution in its interaction with the environment. However, the gift is also important in that it functions, as already suggested, as an important mechanism of solidarity and reciprocity in the long range. Although the gift relationship played a crucial role in the two cases selected for comparison, it can also be shown to have been founded on different ideological premises and to have given rise to different institutional implications. As such, it will constitute a key factor in our analysis of the different pattern of institutionalization of ascetic virtuosity in these two settings.

Monasticism's social position will be analyzed in terms of institutional autonomy (organizational, economic, and social); social involvement and functionalization, that is, the tendency to provide religious and/or social services to the lay environment; political power; and cultural impact, in the limited sense, for the time being, of diffusion of virtuoso ascetic orientations among lay society. It should be stressed that greater autonomy may not mean lesser involvement, but involvement with different characteristics. Similarly, greater involvement does not necessarily mean greater political power or cultural impact, and these various dimensions in monasticism's social position should be carefully kept apart. Analysis of monasticism's social position in these terms should enable us to assess the effectiveness and scope of the segregation between monasticism and society – the dimension we saw emphasized by Shils – as well as the nature of the pattern of exchange between monasticism and society in each case.

Monastic status and power, furthermore, are to be situated in the context of other foci of spiritual and secular authority with which, as Weber rightly perceived, it sometimes cooperated and sometimes clashed. Although the network of exchange between monks and laymen is a crucial aspect of the relation between the monastic sector and society, it is not the only one. The overall position of religious virtuosi was interrelated with the structure of elites (religious and secular) at large, which may help to explain some of the basic differences in the overall position of the virtuoso sector in our two cases.[24] In addition to differences in economic, organizational, and political resources, we must consider differences in the ideological and symbolic resources that the various elites were able to muster. A major dimension of the analysis at this point will be the relative strength of nobility, and kingship in particular, most apt to shape and control the traffic of wealth and prestige in general, and to impinge upon the position of the monastic sector within this traffic. Another major issue is whether monasticism maintained a closer relation to a specific social group or stratum in terms of recruitment, leadership, or patronage. The impact of economic structures will also be considered, especially the effect of economic trends on the gift relationship. The model applied is one of interaction and competition between various types of elites, promoting alternative principles of organizational and symbolic hierarchization, and capitalizing in the process on a variety of contradictory yet mutually intensifying ideological strands extant in the religious–cultural matrix at large. (One of the little-noted effects of the existence of a monastic sector, indeed, was to raise the pitch of the ideological discourse and articulation of other groups and sectors – themselves influencing, at least in part, monastic discourse and organization.)

[24] For an emphasis on the structure of elites and their relation to broader strata from a comparative macrosociological perspective, see in particular S. N. Eisenstadt, *The Political System of Empires* (New York: Free Press, 1963); S. N. Eisenstadt and S. R. Graubard (eds.), *Intellectuals and Traditions* (New York: Humanities Press, 1973).

The bulk of this discussion will show that the interaction between religious–cultural premises and social–structural factors is crucial to the understanding of the dynamics between virtuosi and society in both cases, although it worked in opposite directions: In Theravada Buddhist societies, it helped solidify a dominant pattern of virtuoso–layman relationship into a major axis of social organization; whereas religious–cultural premises and social–structural contextual factors interacted in the medieval Christian setting so as to ultimately defeat its cultural and social importance.

C. The part of virtuoso radicalism

Further counteracting any overly consensual model of religion will be the importance given, in the third chapter of each case study, to the forces of virtuoso radicalism,[25] implying the criticism of a monasticism perceived as declining or corrupted, as betraying its true virtuoso vocation. Virtuoso radicalism, as such, is a source of tension within the monastic sector and a challenge to the specific pattern of institutionalization that came to prevail in each case; as already suggested, it is both a testimony to the virtuoso sector's ideological vitality, and one of the major sources of the innate precariousness of monasticism. The precise character and impact of virtuoso radicalism, moreover, will be shown to differ very much in each case and to exemplify once again, perhaps even exacerbate, the intertwined impact of ideological orientations and institutional factors in shaping the fate of virtuosity in these two civilizations. I shall consider in particular the impact of eremitic radicalism, that is, of that kind of virtuoso radicalism striving at more extreme (if not necessarily totally solitary) forms of withdrawal and disconnection from society. In both cases, this type of eremitic radicalism can be seen, in Turnerian terms, as the best expression of monastic "antistructure" attempting to disentangle itself from the civilizational double bind of interrelated ideological and institutional structures. However, it will be shown to reproduce and even confirm these structures in some crucial ways, confirming also the increasing divergence between the Theravada and Christian cases. Another major form of virtuoso radicalism – much more developed in the Christian than the Buddhist case – would tend to propound alternative forms of collective virtuoso institutions and alternative (sometimes actually enhanced rather than minimized) patterns of interaction with the laity. I shall try to bring out the contrasting role played by these various forms of virtuoso radicalism and the contrasting overall impact of virtuoso radicalism in general upon virtuosi's social position in each

[25] See this chapter, fn. 8.

setting. Virtuoso radicalism may be said to have been a potent factor in the development of the historical pattern of interaction between monasticism and society in both settings, but with an important difference: It contributed to upholding the centrality of the virtuoso–layman relation in the Theravada Buddhist setting, whereas it converged with a number of macrosocietal trends to shake the foundations of this relation and undermine the very principle of a differentiated virtuoso sector in the Christian case.

Stressing the mutually reinforcing and converging impact of religious–cultural premises, patterns of institutionalization and their sociopolitical context, and patterns of virtuoso radicalism, admittedly entails the danger of a tautological, circular and a posteriori functionalistic type of analysis. This is especially true in the case of Theravada Buddhism, where the convergence is also said to have helped maintain and conserve the overall configuration of the virtuoso–society relation (a problem I shall return to in the following chapter). The comparative method should, however, provide a partial palliative; I hope to confirm, in the move from one case to the other, the significance of the variables involved.

As a heuristic device, the Weberian Western-centered bias will be self-consciously inverted in the order of presentation of our two major case studies. I shall begin by delineating a set of phenomena – summed up here in the notion of the virtuoso–layman "syndrome" – that were especially strong and salient in Theravada Buddhist civilization, and only then assess their equivalents in medieval Catholicism, in an attempt to understand what sustained them over centuries in the first case and prevented their full-fledged development in the second. I cannot claim to have totally avoided Western, ethnocentric biases in this way, if only because comparative analysis is in fact a constant back-and-forth process, but I do hope to have at least introduced an alternative set of questions about the issues at hand.

Part II
Virtuosi and society in Theravada Buddhism

3 Ideological groundings: hierarchy and ritualized exchange

The most remarkable feature of Theravada Buddhism, from the perspective of this study, is that its early scriptures already provided both the notion of a community of virtuosi and a specific model of interaction between virtuosi and laymen. As we shall see, the early doctrinal preoccupation with the relation between virtuosi and laity is itself rooted in a very distinctive mode of coexistence, or "economy," of otherworldly and worldly orientations within the canonical corpus, combining an extreme world-negating definition of salvation on the one hand with a sustained concern with the social order as the inevitable and even necessary *context* of this search for salvation on the other.

Theravada Buddhism is known for its conservative concern with the proper preservation and understanding of its canonical texts,[1] and the Pali scriptures did indeed remain a constant source of reference and ideological inspiration throughout the traditional period. Canonical Buddhism, however, is not the only ideological influence to have been at work. Neither did the interpretation of Buddhist doctrines remain static from the time of their early efflorescence in northeast India, through their spread to what became their bastion in Sri Lanka and later diffu-

---

[1] "Canonical Buddhism" refers to Buddhism as expressed in the texts of the Pali canon. The latter is not historically homogeneous, but was probably codified mainly during the reign of Ashoka (272–232 BC). According to Theravada Buddhism, which claims to be the only true, orthodox Buddhism (the "Doctrine of the Elders"), the canon was established at the three first Buddhist councils, one immediately after the Buddha's death, the second a century later, and the third, under the auspices of Ashoka, in the mid-third century BC, at which point it is believed to have been transmitted, along with commentaries, to Sri Lanka. The canon is said to have been preserved orally up to the first century BC, and to have been "closed," in the sense of being put down into writing, in the second half of the first century BC. It consists of *tripitaka* – three baskets: *Vinaya,* including the rules of discipline; *Sutta,* sermons and discourses by the Buddha and his disciples; *Abhidhamma,* philosophical commentary on the discourses, compiled after the first two, part of it at the third council. Included in the *Sutta-pitaka* is the popular corpus of *jatakas,* 547 tales of previous existences of the Buddha (in a fifth-century Pali version, believed to be a translation of more ancient Singhalese and Pali versions). The fifth-century systematized commentary by Buddhagosa, *Visudhimagga,* is taken to represent the unified, orthodox interpretation of the canon. For a recent reexamination of the formation of the Pali Canon, see S. Collins, "On the Very Idea of the Pali Canon," *Journal of the Pali Text Society* 15 (1990): 89–126.

sion throughout Southeast Asia.[2] Understanding the dynamics of the virtuoso–layman relation on the ideological level will thus also require us to consider a number of later ideological developments that, even if innovative and deviating from canonical premises, became part and parcel of Theravada "orthodoxy."

Very broadly, later ideological developments dramatically accentuated the worldly and political facets of the Theravada tradition. This is most manifest starting with the great monastic chronicles of Sri Lanka, where Buddhism first became a central component of national self-consciousness and kingly legitimacy.[3] However, similar processes, partly after the influence of the Sinhalese model, are also later discerned in the other Theravada countries. Despite its doctrinal conservatism, moreover, Theravada Buddhism has displayed an intriguing capacity to coexist with, and even absorb, heterogeneous cultural influences.

What emerges now from the expanding body of modern scholarship, in fact, is not just plain ideological inertia or dogmatic conservatism, but a rather formidable ideological travail that somehow allowed for the selective retention of canonical premises at the same time as it absorbed variegated cultural influences and accommodated new ideological developments. Throughout (and, to some extent, as a result of) this array of complex developments, I submit, some of the basic canonical guidelines for the interaction between virtuosi and laymen (our central focus of interest) can be said to have been retained basically unmodified – while also obstructing the potential impact of other canonical premises.

The worldly facets of otherworldliness

Buddhism views salvation as the release from *samsara,* the cycle of births and rebirths in a life of impermanence and suffering. The basic condition for such release lies in learning to transcend all desire and thus uproot the very source of all suffering. Only through the appropriate

---

[2] There is actually no secure contemporary evidence on early Buddhism before the time of Emperor Ashoka (third century BC), but only that inferred from texts or other material from later periods.

[3] The *Dipavamsa* and *Mahavamsa* are the two earliest Sinhalese chronicles, written respectively in the fourth and late fifth century. Composed as dynastic chronologies, they are to be read as documents of sacred and even "national" history rather than "objective" historical sources. See B. L. Smith, "The Ideal Social Order as Portrayed in the Chronicles of Ceylon," in G. Obeyesekere, F. E. Reynolds, and B. L. Smith (eds.), *The Two Wheels of Dhamma* (Chambersburg, Pa.: American Academy of Religion, 1972); H. Bechert, "The Beginnings of Buddhist Historiography: Mahavamsa and Political Thinking," in B. L. Smith (ed.), *Religion and Legitimation of Power in Sri Lanka* (Chambersburg, Pa.: Anima, 1978), pp. 1–12. A third major Sinhalese "chronicle," the *Tupavamsa,* was composed in the thirteenth century.

ascetic discipline and the practice of meditation can one hope to ascend the stages leading to perfection and reach *nirvana* – a state of ultimate enlightenment, utter bliss, and total detachment from mundane fetters.

Given such exacting otherworldly premises, Buddhism may seem to be a religion of the elite only, a monastic creed of little relevance to the vast majority who are unable or unwilling to follow the demanding path to enlightenment. By and large, this is indeed how it has been long perceived by many interpreters, including Weber himself. Nevertheless, as is by now increasingly recognized, many characteristics of Buddhist doctrine also dull the edge of its otherworldliness. First, transcending all desire does not imply a discipline of physical or mental mortification. Rather, the way to salvation is conceived as the Middle Way, avoiding both mortification and self-indulgence. The follower of this way is not to be steeped in suffering, but in equanimity, the result of a true asceticism in both body and spirit. Buddhism also implies a certain worldliness "in the very belief that man is perfectible and that perfection can be attained here and now."[4] Buddhahood itself implies a similar belief: The Buddha is only a man, or at most a "superman," (*mahapurusa*) who has perfected himself through innumerable existences. Moreover, his achievement is not unique but accessible to others as well: There were other Buddhas before him, and there will be others after.[5]

However, it is through the notion of *karma* in particular, and the accompanying idea of merit, that Buddhism makes place for worldly orientations. Progress along the path to salvation, according to the law of karma, is the result of the merit one has accumulated during past and present lives. Yet merit also ensures the betterment of one's condition, whether in the present or in future existence, in what are primarily worldly terms such as wealth, health, and power. Although the accumu-

[4] I. B. Horner, *The Early Buddhist Theory of Man Perfected* (London: William & Norgate, 1936). Also, J. Dunnington, *Arahantship* (Kandy: Buddhist Publication Society, 1974). Horner, however, suggests that this may already be a corruption of the original notion of arhatship as a state of infinite becoming. See, however, the alternative interpretation by G. D. Bond, "The Development and Elaboration of the Arahant Ideal in the Theravada Buddhist Tradition," *Journal of the American Academy of Religion* 52, no. 2 (1985): 227–42. Bond would give historical primacy to the idea of an immediate enlightenment achievable here and now, followed by the development of the idea of enlightenment achievable in a very distant future only, and of a gradual path of perfection stretching over many lifetimes. As Dunnington stresses, nirvana can also be taken to occur at the death of the arhat, and not to be followed by any rebirth (p. 14), weakening the notion of nirvana as attained in a worldly here and now.

[5] On the Buddha's "humanity," see A. Bareau, "The Superhuman Personality of the Buddha and its Symbolism in the Mahaparinirvanasutra of the Dharmaguptaka," in J. M. Kitagawa and C. H. Long (eds.), *Myth and Symbols* (Chicago: University of Chicago Press, 1971); W. L. King, *A Thousand Lives Away: Buddhism in Contemporary Burma* (Cambridge, Mass.: Harvard University Press, 1965), ch. 5.

lation of merit in itself does not lead to nirvana, which is altogether beyond the cycle of rebirths, it cannot be dispensed with even in the pursuit of the highest stages of salvation: An advanced stage of spiritual achievement, just like worldly wealth and power, is an indicator of great amounts of past karma. An analogous ambiguity lies in the all-important notion of *dharma,* usually translated as "law" or "order":

> In the earliest Buddhist traditions accessible to us, [dharma] refers, first and foremost, to the sacred reality which the Buddha had discovered at the point of his Enlightenment. In this context, it is recognized both as the law which regulates and governs the totality of existence and at the same time, as the Truth which enables men to break free from the limitations which existence imposes. [Dharma], in other words, was taken to be the source of both order in the world and salvation from it.[6]

These ambiguous premises are further reflected in canonical Buddhism's equivocal orientation to the social order in general and to kingship in particular.[7] Although early Buddhism (not unlike other salvation religions), entailed no elaborate political theory, it did articulate a contractual, elective theory of the origins of kingship. In this account, the very first king (*Mahasammata*) had been elected by humans to overcome anarchy and enforce law and order in return for a share of the produce of each of his subjects. Beyond these rather pragmatic foundations, moreover, the canonical texts repeatedly propound the ideal of the meritorious king (*dharmaraja*), culminating in the figure of the wheel-rolling universal ruler, the *cakkavatti,* able to bring the world under the aegis of dharma.[8]

The image of the meritorious king, as later developed in the greater chronicles of the fourth and fifth centuries, is far from static and mono-

---

[6] F. E. Reynolds, "The Two Wheels of Dhamma: A Study of Early Buddhism," in G. Obeyesekere, F. E. Reynolds, and B. L. Smith (eds.), *Two Wheels of Dhamma,* p. 15.

[7] On early Buddhist conceptions of kingship, see esp. B. G. Gokhale, "Early Buddhist Kingship," *Journal of Asian Studies* 26 (1960):15–22. U. N. Ghoshal, *A History of Indian Political Ideas* (Bombay: Oxford University Press, 1959), ch. 4; R. von Heine-Geldern, *Concepts of State and Kingship,* (Ithaca, N.Y.: Cornell University Press 1957); L. Dumont, "The Conception of Kingship in Ancient India," *Contributions to Indian Sociology* 6 (1962): 48–77; E. Sarkisyanz, *Buddhist Backgrounds of the Burmese Revolution* (The Hague: Nijhoff, 1965), chs. 2, 5, and 7; and Tambiah, *World Conqueror,* chs. 3 and 4.

[8] Stressing their canonical foundation (although not necessarily their actual stature in contemporary political life), it should be emphasized that the loci classici for both the *mahasammata* and *cakkavatti* conceptions are found in the *Digha Nikaya* (The Book of Long Sayings), which is part of the *Sutta-pitaka,* one of the three "baskets" in the Pali canon (see this chapter, fn. 1). For the founding myth of kingship, see the *Agganna Sutta,* (*Digha Nikaya,* ch. 27), in *Dialogues of the Buddha,* translated by Rhys Davids, pp. 85; for the Cakkavatti figure, see the *Mahasudassana Sutta* (*Digha Nikaya,* ch. 17) and *Cakkavattisihanada Sutta* (*Digha Nikaya,* ch. 26).

lithic: compassionate, but also able to handle violence in the name of dharma, and eventually resolving the tension by being both in sequence – a dialectic celebrated in the figure of the great warrior-king Dutthagamani (r. 161–137 BC).[9] The same tension is also already present in the legendary rendering of Emperor Ashoka's "conversion of heart" after a period of bloody conquests and massacres. Be that as it may, the contrast has been often pointed out between the Buddhist idea of an ethical kingship responsible for the welfare of his people and of the Sangha on the one hand, and the Indian *Kautaliaya-Arthasastra* tradition of pragmatic politics on the other (even if the latter never totally disconnects itself from dharmasutric notions of *rajadharma,* i.e., of the king's ethical duties as upholder of the social order).[10]

Kingship, at any rate, was invested with enough positive value to function as an important metaphor in the very conception of the Buddha himself. Although in some sense facing each other as two basically complementary archetypes, images of the Buddha and of the universal king or world ruler have also tended to nurture each other to the point of coalescence.[11] The same amount of merit is necessary to become a Buddha as to become a *cakkavatti,* a world ruler. Gautama Buddha himself, the latest Buddha, is said to have had the choice between these two possible "careers" – one of the most remarkable illustrations of how the ultimate in world renunciation and the ultimate in worldly involvement are both antithetical and yet intimately connected in Buddhist thought. Buddhas and *cakkavattis* are believed to bear the same thirty-two bodily marks characteristic of the *mahapurusa.* The characterization of kings as *bodhisattvas* – or Buddhas-to-be – is a later development (probably reflecting Mahayana influences),[12] further expressing this propensity to a

9 A. Greenwald, "The Relic on the Spear: Historiography and the Saga of Dutthagamani," in Smith (ed.), *Power in Sri Lanka,* pp. 13–35.

10 As Heesterman has pointed out, "Whatever the claims of *artha, dharma* disturbingly keeps hovering over it and even Kautilya's notorious *Arthasastra* does not break with the *dharmasastra* in order to formulate an independent raison d'etat." J. C. Heesterman, *The Inner Conflict of Tradition: Essays in Indian Ritual, Kingship and Society* (Chicago: University of Chicago Press, 1985), p. 111. The tension between *arthasastra* and *rajadharma,* and the contrast between the Indian and Buddhist conceptions of kingship, are extensively discussed in Tambiah, *World Conqueror,* chs. 3 and 4.

11 This has been richly analyzed in Reynolds, "Two Wheels of Dhamma." See also Regina T. Clifford, "The Dhammadipa Tradition of Sri Lanka: Three Models within the Sinhales Chronicles," in Smith (ed.), *Power in Sri Lanka,* p. 46; Tambiah, *World Conqueror.*

12 On the Theravada appropriation and transformation of the bodhisattva figure, see J. C. Holt, *Buddha in the Crown: Avalokitesvara in the Buddhist Traditions of Sri Lanka* (New York: Oxford University Press, 1991), especially pp. 53–62. According to Holt, the characterization of kings as bodhisattvas is fully manifest in Sinhalese materials only from the tenth century on, if already adumbrated as early as the fourth century. Buddhalike status, however, is not an intrinsic

merging of the two images. Such multiplicity of cross-references clearly implies the inclination toward a moral social order infused by and supporting Buddhism. This inclination appears to even border at times upon the outright affirmation of the social order – as long as it is ruled by a proper Buddhist king and in the proper Buddhist way – and goes far in explaining how Buddhism could become the dominant ideology of historical polities.[13]

Nevertheless, this increasing sublimination of kingship does not totally overcome what remains a very basic reticence of the Theravada tradition toward actual kings as at best, in the *Mahavamsa*'s expressive wording, "sweet food mixed with poison."[14] Kings are repeatedly described in the *Vinaya* itself, the book of discipline of the Sangha, as greedy thieves, tyrannical and unpredictable, comparable to the worst calamities.[15] The advisable attitude in the face of such dangerous and unpredictable forces is one of accommodation and opportunistic compliance.[16] The Buddha himself is thought to have modeled the rules of procedure and debate in the Sangha on those of the assemblies in the small republican state communities of ancient India, and seems to have retained a nostalgic inclination for a republican, nonmonarchical form of polity.[17]

Most crucially, kings may come and go, and be better or worse, but never actually supplant the ultimate superiority of the true renouncer. Although taken for granted as part and parcel of an overall understanding of what the "world" is about, they remain of essentially secondary

component of properly Buddhist kingly status (Ashoka, for one, is not known to have referred to himself as a bodhisattva). See Tambiah, *World Conqueror*, p. 73. One also has to take into account the impact of the Indian conception of divine kingship. On the combination of and tension between these various symbolic layers in Burmese kingship, see M. Aung-Thwin, "Divinity, Spirit and Human: Conceptions of Classical Burmese Kingship," in L. Gesick (ed.), *Centers, Symbols and Hierarchies: Essays on the Classical States of Southeast Asia* (New Haven, Conn.: Yale University Press, 1983), pp. 45–86.

[13] One may see a very real messianic potential in canonical Buddhism around these ideas of the true ruler, or the various Buddhalike and kinglike figures of canonical Buddhism. Other ideological premises, however – such as a perception of time stressing both a cyclical movement and ultimately, Buddhism's decline – would appear, on the contrary, to discourage the actualization of this millenarian potential.

[14] *Mahavamsa*, ch. 36, verse 133. See W. Geiger (ed.), *The Mahavamsa* (London: Luzac, 1964), p. 266.

[15] See, for example, I. B. Horner, *Book of the Discipline*, part 1, pp. 73–4 (London: Luzac, for the Pali Text Society, 1938). The label "king," moreover is generalized to a broad category of king-dependent officials, thus implying a negative perception of all representatives of the king's government and administration. See ibid., p. 74.

[16] R. F. Gombrich, *Theravada Buddhism*, pp. 116–17.

[17] E. Sarkisyanz, *Buddhist Backgrounds of the Burmese Revolution* (The Hague: Nijhoff, 1965), ch. 3; Gokhale, "Early Buddhist Kingship,"15.

importance from a soteriological point of view. There is thus a basic tension between those elements "inflating" the king's image as world ruler and Buddhalike, and those confining the king to the status of the most meritorious of all laymen, allowing for a difference of degree only between kings and other laymen on the continuum of accumulated merit. Relatedly, although Buddhism is far from oblivious to its political environment, and deeply aware that its destiny is intertwined with the latter, there seems to be an oscillation between what I choose to call a "maximalist" and a "minimalist" conception of society: between an ideal Buddhist social order supported and ruled by a Buddhalike universal ruler, and a social order as the inevitable, perhaps even necessary, but soteriologically insignificant context of an ascetic path that leads to salvation but away from society – or to use the classic phrase, from "home to homelessness."

The opposition to mortification, the assumption of the perfectibility of man in the here and now, the tension between nirvana and karma, and between renunciation and worldly involvement, as well as the ambiguous attitude to kingship and social order, all indicate that Buddhism entails a certain tolerance, and even affirmation, of worldliness alongside its systematic cultivation of renunciation. Falling somewhere in between Weber's dichotomous otherworldly versus worldly categories, these doctrinal premises do not constitute outright worldly orientations, but rather form the worldly "facets" of Buddhism's truly and essentially otherworldly teachings. Canonical Buddhism does propound a radical detachment from the material and social world, and certainly never sanctifies the latter as the proper locus or vehicle of ultimate salvation; but it also never loses sight of the worldly context in which the search for salvation takes place, if only as the background against which the way to release must define and maintain itself.[18] This distinctive and delicate stance is most manifest, to my mind, in the pains taken to provide a specific model for the relations between virtuoso and layman, a model that was to constitute a crucial link in the development of Buddhism into one of the major historical world religions.

[18] For emphasis on this dialectical necessity within the scriptures of the existence of a lay world and phenomenology – a "conventional truth" – in contradistinction to which the way to salvation – or "ultimate truth" – defines itself, see S. Collins, *Selfless Persons: Imagery and Thought in Theravada Buddhism* (Cambridge University Press, 1982) where it is analyzed with regard to the doctrine of *anatta* in particular but also as a more general principle. Cf. p. 152: "Socially and psychologically, it was and is necessary that there be both effective and cognitive selfishness in order that the doctrine of *anatta* can act, or be thought to act, as an agent of spiritual change. For Buddhist thought, the existence of (for example) enthusiastically self-interested merit-making is socially, psychologically and indeed logically necessary as the raw material which is to be shaped by *anatta*."

The virtuoso–layman relation

The built-in tension between karma and nirvana, between striving for a better rebirth and for the escape from the cycle of rebirths, is mitigated, if not solved, in a striking way: The quest for nirvana remains the realm of the "virtuoso," who is able and willing to engage in the path of renunciation and mediation, whereas merit accumulation, of no immediate soteriological relevance, provides "secondary goals" for the others. What is involved here is clearly and unabashedly a matter of spiritual hierarchy: Those who strive for salvation are held to have chosen the nobler and more difficult option, and to be superior to those who do not wish or are not able to do so.

This has led many students of Buddhism to see it as a "monkish" creed in which the laity was largely neglected and debased, or, in Weber's terms, as a "soteriology of the elite" only.[19] As a dramatic index of the disparate treatment of virtuosi and laymen, the five basic recommendations constituting the lay ethic are often contrasted with the elaborate 227 precepts for monks as laid down in the *Patimokkha* section of the *Vinaya*. Laymen, in most general terms, are simply enjoined to abstain from destroying life, stealing, engaging in illicit sexual relations, telling lies, and drinking intoxicating liquors. Succinct as it may seem, however, the lay ethic is definitely part of the scriptural body. Furthermore (especially when contrasted with Brahmanic ritualism), the Buddhist emphasis on intention as the criterion for the karma value of all human actions has major ethical and spiritual significance. In some sense, the five lay precepts – precisely because they are stated in most general terms – may be understood to be quite demanding, depending on their interpretation and scope of application.[20] Most significantly for our own purposes, the monkish and lay ethics are never really disconnected, and have several points of linkage.

First, anyone can become a monk; one can elect to join or leave the Sangha at will. This open and voluntary access to the highest religious status is especially significant when understood in its historical context as forming a sharp contrast with the Brahmanic emphasis on caste mo-

[19] Other phrases used by Weber that point to the same idea are "soteriology of cultivated intellectuals"; "religious technology of wandering and intellectually schooled mendicant monks"; "religious technology of wandering and intellectual schooled monks," etc. *The Religion of India* (Glencoe, Ill.: Free Press, 1958), pp. 205–6, 215.

[20] The scope of the five precepts for the laity is, for example, much expanded if one accepts that they were not purely negative but also entail a positive amplification. For example, abstaining from destroying life also implies protecting living beings, etc. See M. Wijayaratna, *Buddhist Monastic Life According to the Texts of the Theravada Tradition*. Translated by C. Grangier and S. Collins (Cambridge University Press, 1990), p. 167.

nopoly and exclusiveness.[21] Second, the precepts for the monks can be
seen as a specification and amplification of the basic five injunctions for
laymen – and thus as reinforcing rather than contradicting them.[22] This
is in tune, more generally, with the way Buddhism perceives the relation
among various levels of spiritual achievement, seeing the higher levels as
building upon and encompassing the lower ones. Third, there is an
intermediate stage between the two sets of precepts – the ten precepts
to be observed on *uposatha* days (every half-lunar month) by all laymen
or on a more regular basis by older persons. Involving a greater degree
of renunciation than the five, they enable the layman to take upon
himself, if he so wishes, a discipline closer to that of the monk.

A fourth element linking monk and layman at the doctrinal level is a
basic ambiguity in the very definition of the monastic vocation. If Buddhism were indeed totally otherworldly and exclusively concerned with
the ascetic's personal quest for salvation through withdrawal from the
world, the monk would be exclusively engaged in the quest for nirvana;
his contact with the layman would be reduced to the bare minimum.
However, another major concern is the maintenance of the teachings
themselves: Their correct transmission, and the survival of the monastic
community that is the prerequisite for it, demand a certain degree of
worldly involvement and interaction with the laity (if only to ensure
further recruitment to the Sangha). This tension between the practice of
the doctrine and its transmission and preservation was already felt in the
councils held in the first century BC.[23] Although the Buddha was reported to have stressed practice, the councils opted for the preservation
of his teachings. The basic issue, however, was never conclusively settled. In fact, it intermeshed with another issue: that of "compassion"
versus "selfishness" or, more precisely, "unkind indifference" (since the
very notion of a self is contestable from a Buddhist perspective). A
monk who concentrated exclusively on the quest for nirvana could be
deemed to lack in kindness (a cardinal Buddhist virtue) for refusing to
help others on their slower way to salvation.

Even Buddhas are not immune to these basic dichotomies and tensions,
as witnessed in the distinction between "teaching" Buddhas (deemed
superior) and "silent" Buddhas. Bodhisattvas became central figures in

---

[21] This contrast has often been noted. See, for example, R. Thapar, "Renunciation: The Making of a Counter-Culture?" In R. Thapar, *Ancient Indian Social
History: Some Interpretations* (New Delhi: Orient Longmans, 1987), pp. 84–5.

[22] This point has been fully developed in G. Obeyesekere, "Theodicy, Sin and
Salvation in a Sociology of Buddhism," in E. R. Leach (ed.), *Dialectic in Practical Religion* (Cambridge University Press, 1968), p. 25.

[23] See A. Bareau, *Les premiers conciles bouddhiques* (Paris: Presses Universitaires
de France, 1955); W. Rahula, *History of Buddhism in Ceylon* (Colombo:
Gunasena, 1956), p. 158.

Mahayana Buddhism, where they are believed to voluntarily delay their Buddhahood in order to help others reach salvation. As noted, the bodhisattva ideal was also integrated into Theravada tradition, mainly through its juxtaposition with the idea of the righteous, benevolent king. On the account, Gautama Buddha himself, when contrasted with bodhisattvas as understood in Mahayana, may appear as relatively less compassionate since he did teach the principles of salvation (after a long period of hesitation) but did not assume any role of direct soteriological intervention.[24] On the other hand, the Buddha is believed to have exhorted his very first disciples "to travel for the good of the many . . . out of compassion for the world . . . teach the Dhamma," and thus to have invested the Sangha with a missionary vocation and with the duty to preach to the laity from the very start.[25] Admittedly, there is place, theoretically, for many possible interpretations of the ways and extents of that "teaching" or "preaching." The concern with preaching to the laity, however, and the attempt to somehow combine it with ascetic withdrawal from the world may in fact distinguish early Buddhism from other contemporary world-renouncing movements more exclusively focused upon the ascetic's personal salvation.[26]

The fifth point of contact – perhaps the most crucial for the historical development of the relation between virtuoso and society – is through the articulation of an elaborate gift relationship between monk and layman. Strikingly, the gift relationship is already present in the account of the Buddha receiving the very first offering from his first two lay disciples just after he had reached enlightenment.[27] Begging and dependency upon laymen's material support was a common feature of the ascetic life in the context of the larger milieu of world-renouncing, wandering mendicants when Buddhism first emerged.[28] However, the mutual dependency of monks and laity through the medium of a gift relationship appears to have received an unprece-

---

[24] The Theravada ideal of the arhat is indeed criticized by Mahayana as too self-centered, as not having overcome all attachment to the "I." See E. Conze, *Buddhism: Its Essence and Development* (New York: Harper & Row, 1959), pp. 126–7.

[25] See Wijayaratna, *Buddhist Monastic Life,* p. 132; see also Gombrich, *Theravada Buddhism,* p. 114.

[26] See G. Obeyesekere, "Exemplarische Prophetie oder ethisch geleitete Askese? Uberlegungen zur frühbuddhistischen Reform," in Schluchter (ed.), *Max Webers Studie,* pp. 247–74.

[27] *Mahavagga,* First *Khandaka,* 4:3. "We take our refuge, Lord, in the Blessed One and in the Dhamma. . . . May, O Lord, the Blessed one accept from us these rice cakes and lumps of honey, that that may long be to us for a good and a blessing." *Vinaya Texts,* translated by T. W. Rhys Davids and H. Oldenberg (Delhi: Motilal Banarsidass, 1966), p. 82.

[28] S. Dutt, *Early Buddhist Monachism, 600 BC–100 BC* (London: Kegan Paul, Trench & Trubner, 1924).

dentedly extensive and fastidious ideological elaboration (and regulation) in the Theravada tradition.

Barred by *Vinaya* discipline from providing for their own food and
shelter, monks were thrown into a state of dependency on the laity and
hence prevented from cutting themselves off from society. This dependency is mutual, since on the laity's side the Sangha is said to form a
"field of merit," in the sense that providing monks with material support
through gifts (*dana*) represents the most effective (if not the only) way
for laymen to reap merit. Ideally, the best gift is the one given with a
proper attitude of selflessness and nonattachment, with no expressed
regard for the gift's karmic outcome. Moreover, it is not so much what
and how much is given, but whether it is given in the proper way and
with the proper state of mind that determines the gift's value.[29] Nevertheless, one may also find evidence, in both canonical and paracanonical
texts, of a rather detailed system of correspondences between the types
of gifts given and the eventual benefits and advantages for the donor.[30]

It is important to emphasize, however, against Weber, that the layman
does not "buy" the virtuoso's blessings or magical powers. In theory at
least, the idiom is not that of a "commercial" exchange: No goods or
services are expected from the monk in return for the gift (least of all
"blessings" or "magical powers"). It is the very fact of giving that confers
merit upon the layman; it is not the monk who does so. However, *dana*
are not analogous to a bestowal of gifts between friends or equals.[31] On
the contrary, the transaction involves the donor's acknowledgment of
the recipient's superiority, but at the same time as it implies that the
layman has some form of vested interest in this superiority and is far
from being totally alienated from it.

It must be noted also the *dana* are a far cry from the idea of the
"spontaneous" gift. The manner of receiving the gift is carefully coded
and extremely significant: The monk confers a favor upon the layman by
accepting the gift. He should not express pleasure at its reception or
consumption, nor is he supposed to actively prompt any lay giving, or

[29] See, for example, N. A. Falk, "Exemplary Donors of the Pali Tradition," in
R. F. Sizemore and D. K. Swearer (eds.), *Ethics, Wealth and Salvation: A Study
in Buddhist Social Ethics* (Columbia, S.C.: University of South Carolina, 1990),
pp. 125–43. This volume contains many other invaluable contributions to the
understanding of *dana* in the Theravada tradition.

[30] See *Dasavatthuppakarana,* edited and translated by J. Ver Eecke (Paris: Ecole
française d'Extrême-Orient, 1976), pp. 6–15.

[31] Here I am at variance with Michael Ames who, rightly stressing the non-
reciprocal nature of *dana* in both doctrine and actuality, and looking for correspondences between types of exchange in the secular and the ritual–religious
spheres, sees *dana* as analogous to gifts between equals – as distinct from bribes
to superiors and fines to inferiors. See "Ritual Prestations and the Structure of the
Sinhalese Pantheon," in M. Nash et al., *Anthropological Studies in Theravada
Buddhism* (New Haven, Conn.: Yale University Press, 1966).

express any preference. What gifts may legitimately be given and accepted is, again, carefully defined and categorized.[32] Monks must accept gifts from all, with no distinction of wealth or status (this last is another revolutionary injunction in light of the many restrictions governing the acceptance of gifts in the Brahmanic tradition). Only as an exceptional measure of reprobation did the *Vinaya* provide the possibility of refusing *dana* by overturning the alms bowl.[33] In time, tension would emerge between two conceptions of *dana,* one implying the duty of giving laymen something in exchange (mainly, the teaching of dharma, *dharmadana,* also conceived as the greatest gift of all), the other emphasizing nonreciprocity. Whatever the theory, monks and laymen are undoubtedly thrown, through the medium of *dana,* into a highly ritualized and necessary interaction.

Giving in general, and giving to the sangha in particular, developed into a major dimension of righteous kingship in the Theravada tradition. It is significant that a king, King Bimbisara, figures as a prominent follower and patron of the Buddha soon after the latter's enlightenment. A suggestive theme, in this regard, is that of the king giving in excess, reaching for such a level of liberality that he squanders his kingdom's resources, and forcing others to put checks upon his generosity.[34] This is forcefully illustrated in the *Jataka* tale of Gautama Buddha's penultimate rebirth as King Vessantara: In this most popular Jataka tale, King Vessantara is banished by his subjects for giving away the auspicious royal elephant, symbol of the kingdom's security and welfare.[35] In a subsequent phase, though, and after having gone through the trial of the highest form of offering, the giving away of his own children, Vessantara is fully reincorporated, his children and kingdom restored, and the *dana* ethic fully reasserted in a mood of triumphant apotheosis. A similar theme appears in relation to Emperor Ashoka at the very end of his life, prevented by his own officers from depleting the kingdom's treasures in a last spell of unbounded generosity.[36] Both stories strongly testify to the saliency of *dana* in the

[32] It is noteworthy that *dana,* fundamentally, bear no intrinsic relation to the utility of the gift for the monks on the receiving side. See S. Z. Aung and Rhys Davids (eds.), *Points of Controversy or Subjects of Discourse,* translation of the *Katha-vathu* from the *Abhidamma-Pitaka* (London: Luzac, 1969), ch. 7, verses 4–6.

[33] *Cullavagga* V, 20:2–4, *The Book of the Discipline,* part 5, pp. 173 ff.

[34] This connection between kingship and excessive giving is richly analyzed, and King Vessantara and Ashoka's paradigms of giving compared, in J. S. Strong, "Rich Man, Poor Man, Bhikkhu, King: Asoka's Great Quinquennial Festival and the Nature of Dana," in Sizemore and Swearer (eds.), *Ethics, Wealth and Salvation,* pp. 107–24.

[35] See L. G. McClung, *The Vessantara Jataka: Paradigm for a Buddhist Utopian Ideal* (Princeton, N.J.: Princeton University Press, 1985), p. 151.

[36] E. Lamotte, *Histoire du Bouddhisme Ancien* (Louvain: Publications Universitaires, 1958), p. 271; J. Przyluski, *The Legend of Emperor Ashoka in Indian and Chinese Texts* (Calcutta: K. L. Mukhopadyay, 1967), p. 122.

Theravada tradition and to the central role *dana* came to play in the definition of righteous kingship – incidentally also confirming the latter's oscillation between its "merely" lay status as most prominent among lay donors and its more ambitious Buddhalike dimensions.[37]

Another aspect of canonical Buddhism that plays an important role in preventing a severe polarization between virtuoso and layman is the seemingly paradoxical compatibility between the Buddha's lofty teachings and what is usually viewed as "popular" or even "primitive" beliefs in a pantheon of gods, spirits, and demons, as well as in "animistic" and magical practices.[38] The attitude of the canonical texts toward such beliefs is far from consistent, varying from total rejection to wholesale acceptance.[39] The orthodox position, as understood by many, would seem to accept these beliefs as part of an overall cosmology, while denying them any ultimate soteriological significance: Gods and demons have nothing to do with the quest for nirvana. The situation of the arhat – the true virtuoso, the one who has achieved full enlightenment – in this respect is interesting: In the course of his exceptional mental and spiritual progress, he is also said to attain extraordinary powers as natural by-products of his asceticism and spiritual worth. At the same time, exercise of these powers might hinder the holy man in the attainment of his supreme goal and might also be confused by laymen with vulgar magical practices.[40] At any rate, magical cosmological elements coexist with more strictly soteriological beliefs not only for laymen but for virtuosi as well. There is enough ambiguity in the attitude of the Buddhist canon toward magical beliefs and practices to prevent the issue from becoming a real line of demarcation between virtuosi and laymen. More generally, monks and laymen accepted the same cosmology – where heavens, gods, demons, and kings all had their place. The difference hinged, rather, upon involvement with the forces assumed by that cosmology versus transcending these forces in pursuit of an equally shared soteriological ideal.

Last, the very fact that the Pali canon stipulates meticulous regula-

---

[37] The king's *mahadana* emerge not only as a magnified but also as a more perilous version of lay *dana,* and thus somewhat akin to the Indian tradition of kings' *dana* to brahmins, by which it may well have been influenced in the first place. See especially D. Shulman, "Kingship and Prestation in South Indian Myth and Epic," *Asian and African Studies* 19 (1985): 93–117.

[38] This refers only to the relation between "high" Buddhism and "lower" magico-animistic orientations within canonical Buddhism. Their relation in Theravada Buddhism as a presently operative cultural system will be returned to later in this chapter.

[39] See J. Masson, *La religion populaire dans le canon bouddhique* (Louvain: Museon, 1942).

[40] See S. J. Tambiah, *Buddhism and the Spirit-Cults in North-East Thailand* (Cambridge University Press, 1970), pp. 48–51.

tions for monks' interaction with laymen is significant in itself and indicates the very real importance of the laity in the overall scheme.
Doctrinal Buddhism may be said to be characterized by the existence of
a "segregative–connective" arrangement, instituting a clear-cut distinction between virtuoso and layman, but also avoiding disconnection between the two and establishing what forms in fact a sort of necessary,
interdependent *face à face*. This basic arrangement entails the enforcement of a double standard – here, a term to be taken as a neutral descriptive device devoid of the pejorative connotations it has often acquired in
western axiology.[41] Although unambiguously affirming the superiority of
the virtuoso's pursuit of outworldliness and relegating the layman to a
lower, and some would say negligible, status, this double standard also
provides lay activities with a certain degree of legitimation. The lay
world, moreover, however spiritually inferior, is allowed a significant
degree of autonomy. Crucially, however, it is never conceived as the
locus of salvation, nor is it necessarily expected to model itself after the
highest Buddhist ideals. Admittedly, the many points of linkage between the virtuoso and the lay ethics do corroborate Obeyesekere's
emphasis on a process of "ethicization," whereby social morality becomes inextricably intertwined with religious morality.[42] Nevertheless,
at no point is the principle of renunciation as such expected to govern
laymen in worldly affairs, nor is the renouncer himself supposed to be
directly involved in the supervision and management of the social order.
As a result, the image of the virtuosi emerging from the canonical scriptures is that of a very special type of elite, combining ultimate superiority with a narrowly defined involvement in and lack of control of secular
and collective life on the other.

At the risk of being repetitious, it should be emphasized again that the
virtuoso's spiritual and social position cannot be understood independently of the presumed existence of a laity, from which he arises and
differentiates himself. In fact, the delineation of the opposition and interaction between virtuosi and laymen – which, as has been noted, was
probably much less formalized in the Buddha's own time[43] – acquires
such importance in the canonical texts that it might seem ultimately no
less crucial than the definition of the virtuoso's progress on the way to

[41] Another term, suggested by R. J. Z. Werblowsky and perhaps more neutral
from this point of view, is "two-tiered religiosity." See "Modernism and Modernization in Buddhism," in *The Search for Absolute Values in a Changing World*,
Proceedings of the Sixth International Conference on the Unity of the Sciences
(San Francisco, 1977), p. 126.

[42] Obeyesekere, "Exemplarische Prophetie," p. 250.

[43] H. Bechert, "Contradictions in Sinhalese Buddhism," *Contributions to Asian
Studies* 4 (1973) p. 11; G. Schopen, "Two Problems in the History of Indian
Buddhism: The Layman/monk Distinction and the Doctrines of the Transfer-
ence of Merit," *Studien zur Indologie und Iranistik* 10 (1985): 9–47.

salvation, of which the laity appears to be the natural and necessary audience. The notion of an "audience" happens to accord with the Weberian metaphor of a virtuoso performer (although Weber himself did not at all suggest stretching the metaphor in that specific direction). It is also congruous with Nietzsche's notion of the ascetic's "triumph." As Tambiah notes, renunciation expects to be acclaimed by the world: "It would seem as if the movement set in motion by the Buddha, which attracted the youths of the 'noble families' of his time, was intended to make its point to these same families, the point that the renouncers' life is an exemplary one which had to be respected, admired and supported by the society at large, whose troubles, obsessions and vices it transcended."[44]

The construction of ideological conservatism

Although the virtuoso–layman relation is thus carefully provided for in the canonical scheme, it also entails tensions and contradictions that may well have formed the logical seeds of serious doctrinal divergences. One may argue that on purely doctrinal grounds, the potential for heterodox interpretations was enormous. There is in fact evidence of numerous sects and doctrinal divergences[45] emerging in Buddhism in its first centuries. The formation of a Theravada orthodoxy – in which committing the canon to writing, toward the end of the first century BC, was an important phase – took place in (and perhaps through) contention with heterodox trends that had already surfaced in the very first Buddhist councils.[46] Buddhism did eventually branch out in a variety of directions. The great divide between Theravada and Mahayana, in particular, hinges upon critical differences in the relation of the fully enlightened virtuoso to the rest of mankind, epitomized by the different importance

[44] S. J. Tambiah, "The Renouncer, his Individuality and his Community," in T. N. Madan (ed.), *Way of Life: King, Householder, Renouncer–Essays in Honour of Louis Dumont* (New Delhi: Vikas, 1982), p. 307.

[45] Bareau, for one, counts at least twenty (and perhaps up to thirty) sects and around five hundred points of controversy in Hinayana Buddhism. See A. Bareau, *Les sectes bouddhiques du petit véhicule* (Saigon: Ecole française d'Extrême-Orient, 1955). Some, if only a few, of the five hundred subjects of controversy in Hinayana Buddhism compiled by Bareau do bear directly on the relative position of virtuosi and layman: whether a layman can reach arhatship, whether the Sangha merely receives and/or purifies and/or enjoys the gifts, the nature of the layman, whether he purifies the gift, whether he is impure, etc.

[46] See C. S. Prebish, "A Review of Scholarship on the Buddhist Councils," *Journal of Asian Studies* 33, no. 2 (1974): 239–54; Bareau, *Les premiers conciles bouddhiques*. The historical factuality of the first two, at least, is not beyond doubt. Within Sri Lanka, the Mahavihara "orthodoxy" had to contend with the heterodox, partly Theravadin, partly Mahayanic, tendencies of the Abhayagiri monastery (founded at the end of the first century BC). See also Collins, "Pali Canon."

accorded the arhat versus the bodhisattva or future Buddha.[47] The latter, as already noted, developed into a figure of major intercessory status in Mahayana Buddhism. In Theravada Buddhism, by contrast, it is the arhat, devoid of any role of soteriological intercession with regard to the rest of mankind, who is more central to the monastic ideal. The bodhisattva notion itself, in its Theravada version, is rather seen as a teacher and preacher of salvation with no immediate soteriological significance, albeit receiving increasing and more "proximate" relevance through its intertwining with the notion of the benevolent Buddhist king.[48]

Within Theravada Buddhism, however, it is important to note the overall stability in the very conception of salvation (the escape from samsara and attainment of nirvana) and the contrast between a very real potential for heterodoxy or sectarianism on purely doctrinal grounds, on the one hand, and the rather minimal historical realization and institutional expression of that potential, on the other. Most significant for our own purposes, not only did doctrinal divergences remain within the boundaries and under the umbrella of a relatively uniform conception of salvation, of dharma and nirvana, but they did not feed upon, and did not give any special prominence to, those tenets of scriptural Buddhism that might have undermined the dominant conception of the virtuoso and of the relation between virtuoso and layman.[49]

In particular, the rejection of all mediation (be it personal, divine, or institutional) in the search for salvation, and the reliance upon individual striving only – a combination of well-known explosive potential in Christianity – might have stood against the emphasis on the practice of renunciation within the framework of a community endowed with an elaborate code of discipline. The fact that no institutional authority was ever sanctified as such, and the undermining of individuality and hence individual autonomy by the *anatta* doctrine of "nonexistence of the self," probably blunted what could have become a source of very serious tension.

No less pregnant with subversive implications is the possibility of various applications of the notion of a Sangha, and especially its possible signification – considered by Prebish to be the primary one – of a "spiritual elite," an "*ariya sangha*" (the reference here is to those who have

[47] See Conze, *Buddhism*. Awareness of the distinct emphases of Mahayana probably played an important role in the self-perception of Mahavihara "orthodoxy," although Bareau notes that Theravadin scriptures are astonishingly silent in this respect. Bareau, *Les sectes*, introduction and p. 299.

[48] See Sarkysyanz, *Buddhist Backgrounds*, ch. 7; see also this chapter, fn. 13.

[49] This doctrinal conservatism of Theravada Buddhism has recently been stressed again in contrast with the greater flexibility and complexity of Mahayana in Collins, *Selfless Persons*, pp. 23–5.

realized one or another of the four classical stages of spiritual progress – usually rendered in English as "stream winner", "once returner", "nonreturner", "perfected saint" – posited apart from common people, *prthagjana*.[50] The fact that (as Prebish emphatically states) membership in the Sangha as an ecclesiastical unit was not deemed coterminous with membership in the arya sangha, and that even a layman could become a member of the arya sangha without joining the conventional monastic group, might have contributed to blurring the distinction between virtuosi and laymen. This undoubtedly reminds us of the Christian idea of a "true" or "invisible" Church – superseding, inter alia, the established institutional distinction between priesthood and laity – that had momentous significance for the history of Christian heterodoxy. It is significant that this idea, though present in the early texts and however capable of undermining the division and dominant pattern of interaction between monks and laymen, never received (to my knowledge) any significant expression in subsequent Theravada Buddhist history.

One theory that has been advanced to explain Theravada's general lack of doctrinal fermentation is its stronger concern with "orthopraxy" than dogmatic orthodoxy, its conviction that salvation depends more on right practice (including mental practice, meditation) than right belief. (In a sense, this concern with proper behavior is in continuity with the Indian ritualism against which Buddhism in many other ways reacted.) Although this might have been expected to give free rein to doctrinal creativity, the argument goes, it combined with a general distrust of free rational inquiry, and facilitated doctrinal stagnation.[51] Although this ritualistic, orthopraxic bend might have played a role, there is also much evidence of Theravada conservatism as actually entailing an active labor of construction of tradition: selecting some doctrinal premises, suppressing the potential impact of others (as already suggested), and last but not least, imposing not only specific doctrinal contents but also a specific ideological structure in its interaction with heterogeneous cultural influences. A key feature of this ideological structure, as we shall now see, is the principle of symbolic hierarchization.

[50] See C. S. Prebish, *Buddhist Monastic Discipline: The Sanskirt Pratimoksa Sutras of the Mahasamghikas and Mulasarvastivadins* (University Park: Pennsylvania University Press, 1975), p. 3; the idea of the ariya sangha is seldom commented upon in the literature. See, however, R. I. Heinze, *The Role of the Sangha in Modern Thailand* (Taipei: Chinese Association for Folklore, 1977), pp. 53–62. For a controversial stress on the notion of the arya sangha in the early scriptural corpus, see P. Masefield, *Divine Revelation in Early Buddhism* (Colombo: Sri Lanka Institute of Traditional Studies in conjunction with Allen & Unwin, 1988), ch. 1.

[51] See Peter A. Jackson, *Buddhadasa: A Buddhist Thinker for the Modern World* (Bangkok: Siam Society, 1988), ch. 1. Focusing on Thailand, Jackson also gives much weight to the stifling effect of state control upon the Sangha.

The principle of symbolic hierarchization

Approximation to canonical standards of purity and orthodoxy admittedly remained an important point of reference; this is clearly evidenced in the cycle and discourse of "corruption" and "reform" examined in greater detail in the following chapters. Nevertheless, canonical Buddhism did not constitute the only significant ideological influence. To begin with, one has to stress the strengthening of what may be called the "Ashokan" streak in Buddhism – implying royal supervision of the Sangha (Ashoka is believed to have conducted the first reform of the Sangha with backing of the king) as part of the king's role in promoting the material and spiritual welfare of his subjects, and the infusion of Buddhist symbology into state rituals. Whatever the historical accuracy of the Theravada rendering of Ashoka's patronage of the Sangha as depicted in the Pali chronicles, it came to form a powerful archetype that shaped the interaction between later kings and Sangha, and made Buddhism an integral component of kingly legitimacy. This process, moreover, was further enhanced through what appears as an increasingly symbolic upgrading of kingship to Buddhalike stature.

Another crucial and related ideological development is the incorporation of Buddhism into a central dimension of national self-consciousness – a process first manifest in the great monastic chronicles of Sri Lanka, but also evident in the later Burmese and Thai chronicles, and dramatically accentuating the worldly and political facets of the Theravada tradition. No less important, if easily taken for granted, was the pervasiveness of the ideology of merit itself and the development, beginning in the earliest stages, of extended notions of transfer of merit.[52] As will be further explicated in the next chapter, these notions greatly facilitated the incorporation of monkhood into a wider network of mutual relevance and solidarity.

What is important for the moment is simply that these various ideological developments significantly strengthened Buddhism's "worldlier" sides, and evolved into deeply anchored, "valid" Buddhist orientations whatever their actual relation to pristine canonical Buddhism. Significantly, though, this strengthening of the worldlier sides of Buddhism, however extensive, never led to a more formal and encompassing "church like" definition of the religious collective, or to the articulation

---

[52] On the development of canonically equivocal notions of transfer of merit, see R. F. Gombrich, "Merit Transference in Sinhalese Buddhism," *History of Religions* 11 (1971):203–19; also R. McDermott, "Is there Group Karma in Theravada Buddhism?" *Numen* 23, no. 1 (1985): 67–80; C. F. Keyes, "Merit-Transference in the Karmic Theory of Popular Buddhism," in C. F. Keyes and E. Valentine Daniel (eds.), *Karma: An Anthroplogical Enquiry* (Berkeley and Los Angeles: University of California Press, 1983), pp. 261–86.

of institutional principles of religious authority, within or without the Sangha. Nor did kingship or any worldly social institution ever muster enough ideological autonomy to challenge the classical hierarchy of ultimate values. This is all the more striking in view of the deep intertwining of world-negating and world-affirming premises expressed, as noted, in the canonical images of Buddhahood, kingship, and dharma order.

Hierarchization, in fact, appears to have operated as a major principle in sustaining the relatively peaceful coexistence of heterogenous symbolic orientations. In this specific case, the hierarchization of symbolic layers seems to have worked to isolate the supreme ideal of renunciation, whatever its worldlier "facets," from the lower levels. The availability of lower and worldlier codes did not contest the legitimacy of the higher ones, although it certainly circumscribed the scope of their direct translation into everyday life. On the other hand, the sociocultural centrality of higher Buddhist codes could be maintained only at the cost of allowing alternate, if subordinate, symbolic orientations to thrive alongside them. Thus the very hierarchy that upheld the supremacy of the renunciatory, otherworldly orientations also ensured their segregation from the lower normative levels; enshrined at the very apex of the hierarchy of cultural orientations, the highest Buddhist values could be both revered and kept at bay. An important aspect of the efficacy of this hierarchization (whose significance will be stressed again through comparison with the Christian case) is that no alternative pattern of hierarchization ever coexisted or competed with it.

This may also help us to understand how "high" Buddhism – that is, Buddhism as defined by the Pali canon – has always coexisted rather comfortably with a gamut of "lower," "magico-animistic" beliefs and practices. The ambiguous stance of the canonical texts themselves in this regard has already been noted. The issue here is rather the coexistence of these seemingly divergent orientations within Theravada Buddhism as an operative cultural system – an issue that is a central concern of the sociological and anthropological literature on contemporary Theravada Buddhism.[53] In contemporary settings, the "lower" orientations, what-

---

[53] For example, M. Spiro in *Buddhism and Society: A Great Tradition and its Burmese Vicissitudes* (London: Allen & Unwin, 1971) distinguishes between "nibbanic" (soteriological–normative), "kammatic" (soteriological–nonnormative), and "apotropaic" (nonsoteriological) levels. King, in *A Thousand Lives Away,* distinguishes between "high," "low," and "medium" Buddhism, and going further, between seven cultic layers defined by their distance from the central ideal, nirvana. A general and oft-repeated hypothesis is that of a functional complementarity between doctrinal Buddhism and other, "lower" beliefs, each fulfilling different psychological needs, the former geared to otherworldly and distant goals, the latter catering to worldly and more immediate needs. See for example M. Ames, "Magical-Animism and Buddhism: A Structural Analysis of the Sinhalese System," *Journal of Asian Studies* 23 (1964): 21–52; also Obeyesekere,

ever their tension with the "higher" soteriological doctrines, are shown to be widely shared by both monks and laymen, at least in the case of the ordinary "village monks." They also evidently contribute to pull monks, as either practitioners or consumers, in the direction of magic and apotropaic practices, and to invest monkhood and Buddhist rituals themselves with pervasive "magical" overtones.[54] The latter might even actually supersede their original Buddhist significance.[55] Similar processes, in fact, were most probably at work in the traditional period, merging "higher" and "lower" orientations, for example, in the worship of Gautama Buddha's relics – a well-established and important "orthodox" practice that developed just after his death and equally engaged both monks and laymen – or in the monks' ritual chanting of *paritta,* protective verses invested with some form of worldly "magical" efficacy.

Too little is known, historically, concerning this thriving realm of popular beliefs – often treated as an inchoate residual category – and concerning possible changes in its internal structure and relation to "higher" Buddhist orientations in the various countries where the Theravada tradition became predominant.[56] Although these "lower" symbolic orientations appear to bring monks and laymen closer, they would also appear to deflect the interaction between them from its more strictly otherworldly soteriological purposes. The important point, however, is again that the hierarchy of values itself, as described, remained uncontested.

One major reason for this state of affairs may be the development of an elaborate system of cosmological beliefs that themselves furthered the all-

---

"Theodicy, Sin and Salvation," pp. 7–40. As opposed to this approach, which tends to explain the coexistence of higher and lower cultural–symbolic orientations by stressing their difference and complementarity in function, a number of studies have stressed the blurring of differences between the two types of orientations at the day-to-day motivational level. See, for example, J. Halverson, "Religious and Psychosocial Development in Sinhalese Behavior," *Journal of Asian Studies* 37 (1978): 221–32. Closely related, of course, are the various attempts to apply (and modify) Redfield's distinction between Great and Little Traditions. For a critical survey of that literature, see Terence P. Day, *Great Tradition and Little Tradition in Theravada Buddhist Studies* (Lewiston, N.Y.: Mellen, 1988).

54 There is much evidence that even purely Buddhist symbols and acts can be apprehended in a magical mode. See, in particular, Tambiah's analysis of the magical power attributed to the recitation of Pali sacred verses, in "The Ideology of Merit and the Social Correlates of Buddhism in a Thai Village," in E. R. Leach (ed.), *Dialectic in Practical Religion* (Cambridge University Press, 1968), pp. 41–121. On the magical aspects of the worship of Buddha himself, see King, *A Thousand Lives Away.*

55 This has been argued, in particular, by B. J. Terwiel for contemporary Thailand in "A Model for the Study of Thai Buddhism," *Journal of Asian Studies* 35 (1976): 391–403.

56 For an attempt, or more precisely plea, to confront these difficult issues despite the obvious problem of documentation, see Day, *Great Tradition and Little Tradition.*

embracing principle of a cosmic hierarchy of beings, fully congruent with the ultimate values of canonical Buddhism. In King Lu-Thai's influential fourteenth-century cosmological treatise on the *thraiphum* (the three worlds), for example, the world is divided in three major categories of realms (themselves further subdivided into many further internal categories) distinguished according to their level of detachment from the world of desire and materiality. To this is added a full-blown cosmography with Mount Meru as its central axis, a description of the periodic creation and destruction of the lower cosmic realms, and of the path to the highest goal of final release. In sum, cosmological beliefs contributed to reaffirm a hierarchical arrangement putting gods and spirits in subordinate position, and maintaining "higher," "otherworldly" soteriological Buddhist orientations at the very apex.[57] The result, to use Geertz's terms, is a strong congruence between "ethos" and "worldview," further enforcing the unique "reality" of Buddhism as a religious system providing a sort of overarching umbrella to a rich variety of beliefs and practices. The very same arrangement, moreover, appears to have allowed the recurrent incorporation of new cults and practices as long as they preserved the key reverential attitude to anything directly related to the Buddha and his message.

This does not mean, however, that hierarchization is the only and exhaustive principle of cultural organization, nor that it was always able to ensure a fully peaceful relationship with all heterogeneous cults and practices. It is only with the multiplication of studies into the historical development and local expression of various cults and rituals of the kind initiated by Obeyesekere and Holt[58] that one may hope to reach a fuller and more diversified picture of the pattern of interaction between "high" Buddhism and the various heterogenous cultural orientations that have been thriving in cultural settings where Theravada Buddhism has been traditionally dominant.

Doctrinal orthodoxy and historical continuity

The doctrines and institutions of Theravada Buddhism, however, have not remained unchanged throughout the long history of its diffusion in Southeast Asia. Most obviously, the original outworldliness has been significantly toned down and has undergone a far-reaching process of institutionalization – or even, as often said, "domestication" – the sub-

---

[57] F. Reynolds and M. Reynolds (trans.) *Three Worlds According to King Ruang* (Stanford, Calif.: Stanford University Press, 1978).

[58] G. Obeyesekere, "Gajabahu and the Gajabahu Synchronism: An Inquiry into the Relationship between Myth and History," in Smith (ed.), *Power in Sri Lanka,* pp. 155–76; idem, *The Cult of The Goddess Pattini* (Chicago: University of Chicago Press, 1984); Holt, *Buddha in the Crown.*

ject of the next section. It would be absurd to claim that members of these societies, or even of their monastic communities, behaved in full accordance with the canonical principles, or that the course of Buddhism in these societies was devoid of corruption and decadence. Nevertheless, we shall see that the actual relationship between virtuoso and society, as it evolved in Theravada societies, has not radically diverged from the basic segregative–connective arrangement characterizing the canonical model. From that perspective at least, it does seem true, as Charles Keyes has observed more generally, that "the world as lived in by people in the Theravada Buddhist societies of Southeast Asia was also the world as it was expressed in the teachings of their religion."[59]

What may be most striking (at least for a Western mind accustomed to the anticlerical tendencies that have accompanied the Christian Church from its very inception), is that the basic requisite for such an arrangement – the very distinction and hierarchy between virtuosi and laymen, with the double standard therein entailed – was never, or not until very recently,[60] contested or displaced by any alternative formula. Moreover, the ritualized, necessary interconnection of virtuosi and layman was not only enforced but even amplified. Not only did it prove effective at the local face-to-face level, but it also received extensive endorsement and formal institutionalization in the historical relationship between Sangha and king. Most crucially, the gift relationship between Sangha and laity received forceful endorsement and consolidation through the crucial role that material support of the Sangha came to play in the definition of kingly legitimacy, that is, at the very center of political authority in the societies in question.

At the same time, virtuosi's segregation from mundane, secular spheres of activity, and in particular from formal political involvement and the direct exercise of political power, was on the whole preserved. This segregation reinforced the virtuoso's prestige and ultimate superiority while effectively circumscribing his direct impact upon lay matters – thereby reproducing the disconnection between spiritual prestige and political power found in the canonical segregative arrangement. (I shall leave aside for the moment the issue, raised in Chapter 2, of the virtuoso's "power" in other than strictly political terms.)

This congruity between the doctrinal model of the interaction between virtuosi and laymen and its actual historical course does not mean that behavior was always on a par with doctrine, that no changes occurred at the ideological level, or that one may draw a direct, causal link between ideological orientations and actual behavior. Rather, the basic

---

[59] Keyes, *Golden Peninsula,* p. 93.
[60] See S. E. G. Kemper "Buddhism without Bhikkhus: The Sri Lanka Vinaya Vardena Society," in Smith (ed.), *Power in Sri Lanka,* pp. 212–35.

structure of relations between virtuosi and laymen seems to have been sustained and reproduced to some degree independently of its precise conformity with the canonical model, as long as basically congruous with the latter from the point of view of the segregative–connective arrangement already delineated.

The historically successful maintenance of a hierarchy of values, with the virtuoso's search for otherworldly salvation at its apex, may seem somewhat puzzling given the virtuoso's formal exclusion from access to power in the more ordinary, political sense. (Cultural hegemony, to use Gramscian terms, is more easily expected when combined with political hegemony.) I submit, however, that the virtuoso's symbolic superiority was maintained throughout the centuries, not only through the sheer persuasiveness and "static" impact of otherworldly ideals, but also through the active interaction and mutual reinforcement of a range of ideological and institutional dynamics. The virtuoso–layman relation and the renunciatory, otherworldly ideological hierarchy are to be seen as historically interrelated and mutually reinforcing phenomena. Moreover, certain characteristics of the macrosocietal frameworks in which they unfolded reinforced the resulting congruity between the doctrinal–ideological model and its actual historical embodiment. This congruity among the virtuoso–layman relation, the hierarchy of ideological orientations, and macrosocietal frameworks is based not so much on a rigid, one-to-one correspondence between the various factors, as on the flexibility of the virtuoso–layman relational structure itself and its adaptability to a diversified and unstable environment – the topic of the next chapter.

4 Virtuosity institutionalized: the Sangha in social context

The Sangha's organizational structures

Doctrinal Buddhism may seem to have originally addressed itself to the individual renouncer, emphatically enjoined to rely only on his own efforts in the pursuit of spiritual progress and salvation.[1] The relentless emphasis on transcending family and property ties, on moving from home into homelessness and seeking refuge in none but oneself, "wandering along like the rhinoceros," all seem to point toward an essentially individual, isolated, or even solitary way of life.

Nevertheless, the Buddha never advocated the practice of extreme solitude,[2] and the idea of a Sangha, of a community of ascetics, appears to have been present from the very start, if at first only on a limited basis. The early followers of Gautama Buddha were supposedly enjoined to become wandering mendicants – not an uncommon vocation at the time. At least during the three-month rainy season, however, and following a practice common to other wandering sects as well, *bhikkhus* were supposed to retreat to a common residence. The development of a collective form of asceticism is often traced to this period of restricted mobility, favoring the intensification of communal life and the fulfillment of more lay-oriented duties.[3] Be that as it may, the existence and corporate self-consciousness of a monastic order are already manifest in the *Patimokka,* probably the oldest layer in the *Vinaya* literature, stipulating various categories of offenses to a shared ascetic discipline. In time, the order of monks took on a clearly sedentary and cenobitic complexion, a process reportedly ratified by the Buddha himself. Although the mendicant-eremitic ideal did not totally disappear, the cenobitic-monastic strain clearly became predominant.

This cenobitic trend did not necessarily imply, however, a systematic

---

[1] For a stress on the utter individuality of the renunciatory option, see injunctions such as: "Be you a refuge to yourself, Betake yourself to no external refuge . . . look not for a refuge to anyone besides yourself," *Mahaparinibbana Sutta,* 2:33. In M. Müller (ed.), *Sacred Books of the East,* vol. 11 (Delhi: Motilal Banarsidas, 1965), p. 45; or, "The self is lord of self. Who else could be the lord?" *Dhammapada,* 12:160, in M. Müller (ed.), *Sacred Books of the East,* vol. 10, p. 45.

[2] The basic structure imposed on the renouncer's individuality – however conceived – by the very idea of a virtuoso community is analyzed in Tambiah, "Renouncer," pp. 299–319.

[3] On the swift transition to the cenobitic pattern in the early Sangha, see especially Dutt, *Early Buddhist Monachism.*

effort at formal communal organization. To begin with, the Buddha himself is said to have refused to designate a successor and to have enjoined his disciples to let *Vinaya* and dharma alone guide their behavior.[4] Indeed, no transmitted hierarchy was ever sanctified: Whatever hierarchy there was (and still is) in the Sangha pertains, at least ideally, to relations of respect rather than obedience. The teaching and advice of older monks was to be sought – discipleship to an older monk was a requirement, at least during the novitiate – but did not imply any constraining power. In what forms a major contrast with Christian monasticism, no "vow of obedience" ever accompanied the vows of chastity and poverty. Nor was there any commitment to *stabilitas loci,* that is, to remaining in one and the same monastery, preferably for life. One could join or leave the Sangha at will and freely leave one monastery for another.

The most important principle of continuity in the monastic order was the lineage of ordination – *upasampada* – which required the presence of five fully ordained monks to ordain another one. As such the lineage of ordination constituted the minimal requisite, and necessary warrant, of the Sangha's continuity and purity. Beyond this, the Sangha's major form of internal regulation consisted in the observance of the rules of discipline as contained in the *Patimokkha* and expanded in the *Vinaya.* These rules distinguish between eight levels of transgressions, the gravest – *parajika* – entailing immediate expulsion from the order, the others leading either to suspension and/or some form of expiation.[5] Recital of the *Patimokkha,* which, together with the periodical practice of public confession and pardoning of transgressions, became the main feature of the *uposatha* service held at the end of every lunar half-month, and was expected to periodically reinforce both knowledge and practice of the rules. The fact that schism was ranked among the gravest of offenses, moreover, clearly betrays a sharp concern with monastic discipline and unity. Nevertheless, the correct working of such a system relied nearly exclusively on the internalization and voluntary observance of norms. Not surprisingly, normative compliance was not always up to expectations, and the history of the Sangha has been marred by recurrent decay and relaxation of discipline, as well as by an unabated tendency to segmentation.

The absence of strong principles of hierarchical authority was accompanied by resolutely egalitarian features in the Sangha's communal life. Binding decisions were to be made by majority vote of all members.[6]

---

[4] *Mahaparinibbana Sutta,* 16:108.
[5] The four *parajika* offenses are sexual intercourse; stealing; murder or incitement to suicide; and falsely claiming superior, miraculous powers.
[6] Assessments vary about whether the early Sangha's procedures of communal decision making were "egalitarian" or even "democratic." See, for example,

The order was also supposed to transcend social distinctions and remain open and egalitarian both in its recruitment and it its relation to the laity; in particular, monks were to accept *dana* from all without distinction. Although the Sangha in Thailand and Burma remained true to this principle, recruitment in Sri Lanka began very early to evolve along caste lines.[7] Only members of the highest caste – incidentally, also the largest – could be ordained into the *Syam Nikaya,* the oldest and most influential branch of the Sangha. In all three *nikayas* lower castes were either excluded or grossly underrepresented. Moreover, the succession to the headship of the temple and its property came to be regulated in terms of discipleship. Since pupils tended to be chosen from the teacher's kin group, relations between teacher and pupil became tied to property and family interests.

This penetration of the Sangha by caste principles in Sri Lanka (Burma and Thailand had no caste system) clearly indicates that the order was far from immune to the influence of patterns of social organization and stratification prevalent in wider society.[8] Also significant, in this regard, is the development in Thailand, starting with the end of the Ayutthaya era, of a (state-imposed) system of monastic ranking paralleling secular rankings in the king's service.[9] Nevertheless, the penetration of such external principles of stratification cannot always be equated with, and did not necessarily enhance, the internal organization of the Sangha. In Sri Lanka, in fact, the development of highly

Thapar's conception of Buddhist monasteries as a counterculture of egalitarian sanctuaries in "Renunciation." Others would see them as simply replicating tribal traditions. See de Gokuldas, *Democracy in Early Buddhist Sangha* (Calcutta, n.p., 1955).

[7] On Sri Lanka's caste system, milder than India's (the visible manifestations being less developed, with much less cultural diversity between castes, no category of "untouchables," and its distinctions emphasized chiefly in situations involving home, family, and food), see B. Ryan, *Caste in Modern Ceylon: the Sinhalese System in Transition* (New Brunswick, N.J.: Rutgers University Press, 1953); R. F. Gombrich, *Precept and Practice: Traditional Buddhism in the Rural Highlands of Ceylon,* (Oxford University Press [Clarendon Press], 1971), ch. 8; K. M. Malalgoda, *Buddhism in Sinhalese Society, 1750–1900* (Berkeley and Los Angeles: University of California Press, 1976), part 1.

[8] This may hold for Burma and Thailand as well, where the Sangha might be simply under the influence of a different social environment than in Sri Lanka. Of special significance here is Embree's conception of Thai society, in particular, as "loosely structured." This conception, however, has rightly been under attack. See H. D. Evers (ed.), *Loosely Structured Social Systems: Thailand in Comparative Perspective* (New Haven, Conn.: Yale University Press, 1969), and idem, "The Buddhist Sangha in Ceylon and Thailand," *Sociologus,* n.s. 28 (1968): 20–35. It is in fact in Thailand that the Sangha eventually developed the highest extent of hierarchization and centralization.

[9] See D. K. Wyatt, *The Politics of Reform in Thailand: Education in the Reign of Chulalongkorn* (New Haven, Conn.: Yale University Press, 1969), pp. 9 ff; Tambiah, *World Conqueror,* chs. 10, 11, and 14.

localized forces of monastic landlordism deeply embedded in caste and kinship posed an obstacle to royal attempts at unification and centralization.[10]

In all three Theravada countries, and despite some significant variations in degree of formal organization, the Sangha typically retained the tendency to a relatively amorphous pattern of organization. This was most evident in the low level of centralization and hierarchization both within and between individual monasteries. The very possibility of moving from one monastery to another may be thought to have played an important role in facilitating the access by members of peripheral and small monastic communities to advanced education in the great monastic centers; it may also have favored the development of broader intermonastic networks. Whatever intermonastic relations did develop, however, appear to have remained essentially informal, and did not sustain a shift to more articulated or centralized forms of organization. The same is largely true of *nikayas,* perhaps best translated as monastic "branches," sharing a common lineage of ordination (although the term has also been used to designate other kinds of subgroupings within the Sangha). Although these may seem in some way the closest equivalent of the Western concept of monastic "order," it is not clear what mechanisms connected various monasteries in one *nikaya,* or whether *nikaya* distinctions had any real application beyond the capital centers.[11]

In all three countries, admittedly, the Sangha did at times attain significant degrees of hierarchization and centralization – trends that achieved their most extensive and continuous deployment in Burma, and also thriving in Sri Lanka between the twelfth and fifteenth centuries especially.[12] Organizational structuring of the Sangha would actually culminate much

[10] See H. Bechert, "Theravada Buddhist Sangha: Some General Observations on Historical and Political Factors in its Development," *Journal of Asian Studies* 29 (1970): 769; idem, "The Structure of the Sangha in Burma: A Comparative View," in A. K. Narain (ed.), *Studies in the History of Buddhism* (Delhi: B. R. Publishing, 1980), pp. 32–42.

[11] See Gombrich, *Theravada Buddhism,* p. 158. *Nikaya,* however, is also used for a variety of subgroupings within the Sangha. For a useful discussion of the various uses of *nikayas,* see Bechert, "Structure of the Sangha in Burma," pp. 33–4. Bechert prefers to see *nikayas* as *Vinaya* sects – defined as communities of monks who mutuallly acknowledge their ordination and make use of the same redaction of the *Vinaya* texts – and prefers to talk of *nikayas* within the Theravada Sangha as "subsects." See also R. A. L. H. Gunawardana, "Buddhist Nikayas in Medieval Ceylon," *Ceylon Journal of Historical and Social Studies* 9 (1966): 55–66.

[12] See Bechert, "Theravada Buddhist Sangha"; idem, "Structure of the Sangha in Burma"; D. E. Smith, *Religion and Politics in Burma* (Princeton, N.J.: Princeton University Press, 1965), pp. 3–37; S. J. Tambiah, "A Note on the Hierarchical Structure of the Sangha in Thailand," in *Buddhism and the Spirit-Cults in North-East Thailand,* pp. 77–80; H. Bechert, *Buddhismus, Staat und Gesellschaft* (Frankfurt: Alfred Melzner, 1966), vol. 2, p. 185.

more recently in Thailand (starting with King Chulalongkorn's Sangha
Act of 1902), with the establishment of an elaborate structure fully modeled after, and coinciding with, that of the king's secular administration.[13]
As a rule, however, organizational structures in the earlier, traditional era
proved to be temporary, crumbling as soon as they were not actively
sustained by the secular establishment.[14] Even when they did enjoy external support, these structures did not necessarily imply standardized and
effective enforcement at the village level. Mendelson argues that the
elaborate textual descriptions of a complex monastic hierarchy in Burma,
headed by a *sangharaja* nominated by the king and ruling over the entire
order through local "archbishops," "abbots," and a disciplinary council,
refer to an ideal picture rather than the real situation. The *sangharaja,* in
his view, never formed more than a tenuous bridge between the king and a
largely autonomous order, which at the local level might cooperate or not,
depending on political circumstances.[15] Similar questions arise concerning the actual operation of formal structures of the Sangha in the
Ayutthaya era (1350–1767).[16] As for Sri Lanka, the centralized structures
established by Parakramabahu I (1153–86) undoubtedly established an
unprecedented extent of formal state control of the Sangha that survived
in theory until the fifteenth century; but these structures can hardly have
had much reality, even during this period, once the king's initial and
successful bid at religious and political centralization was challenged by
strong centrifugal reactions or, at times of foreign rule, by invaders, such
as after the Magha invasion (1215–36) – when monasteries were plun-
dered and their wealth confiscated.[17]

Centralization and hierarchization, at any rate, always arose at the initia-

---

[13] The Sangha's administrative matters in Thailand are now entrusted by the state
to the Department of Religious Affairs, specifically established for that purpose. See Wyatt, *Politics of Reform in Thailand,* p. 247; Tambiah, *World Conqueror,* ch. 19.

[14] In both Burma and Sri Lanka, significantly, the organizational structures of the
Sangha were disrupted by the onset of colonial regimes of separation between
state and religion. Only in Sri Lanka can we witness some attempt (although
again under the king's sponsorship) to initiate potentially self-regulating organizational structures. See K. Taylor, "The Devolution of Kingship in Twelfth-
Century Ceylon;" Bechert, "Structure of the Sangha in Burma."

[15] See E. M. Mendelson, "Buddhism and the Burmese Establishment," *Archives
de Sociologie des Religions* 17 (1964): 87. See also Bechert, *Buddhismus, Staat
und Gesellschaft,* vol. 2, p. 17. The authority of such "leaders" of the Sangha,
moreover, cannot but have been rather limited, since they most probably were
not invested with the right to expel or punish any monk, nor make any decision
of a binding legal character. See Wijayaratna, *Buddhist Monastic Life,* p. 155,
fn. 8.

[16] See the ambiguous evidence discussed in Tambiah, *World Conqueror,* pp. 179 ff.

[17] See B. L. Smith, "Polonnaruva as a Ceremonial Complex: Sinhalese Cultural
Identity and the Dilemmas of Pluralism," in Narain, A. K. ed. *Studies in the
History of Buddhism,* pp. 295–320; Taylor, "Devolution of Kingship."

tive of the external political authorities, on whom their enforcement heavily depended. The organizational structures of the Sangha, if at times quite extensive, tended to fluctuate with the vicissitudes of monarchy and state, and were not sustained for long without their active support. Whatever monastic officialdom was appointed by the king had no official guarantee of continuity since, as a rule, the accession of a new king automatically terminated the authority of the hierarchy appointed by his predecessor.[18] Most crucially, neither the monastic hierarchy as such, nor the precise degree of centralization and continuity it implied, were ever perceived as intrinsic requisites of the Sangha's purity and corporate identity.

An important aspect of the general organizational weakness of the Sangha was that it wielded no temporal authority of its own and could not enforce an effective system of sanctions to protect its internal discipline and purity. One major consequence was that the Sangha came to depend on external forces, and especially on the willingness, ability, and even initiative of the political center to ensure its internal cohesion and purity. The role of the king as protector and guardian of the Sangha's adherence to the *Vinaya* was traced back to the historical precedent of Ashoka as depicted in the Pali chronicles and commentaries, and made into the archetype of ideal Buddhist kingship. Monarchs periodically embarked on celebrated "campaigns of purification" of the Sangha, in which a variety of religious, political, and even economic motives seem to have often combined.[19] Although such campaigns theoretically took place on the Sangha's own terms, with its assent and in accordance with the *Vinaya* rules, the boundary between "purification" and interference proved to be a fine one. This is perhaps most clearly illustrated by the centralizing zeal of King Parakramabahu I, which penetrated into the internal management of the Sangha through the imposition of royal supervision and control of the ordination process, and through the enactment of *katikavata* laws that added to, and at times even deviated from, canonical law, even if theoretically in agreement with dharma and *Vinaya*.[20]

Monastic economy

Similar dependence on the external environment was evinced in the monks' nearly total reliance upon the laity for their material support, with

[18] See J. F. Cady, *A History of Modern Burma* (Ithaca, N.Y.: Cornell University Press), p. 54.
[19] See Bechert, "Theravada Buddhist Sangha." Also Tambiah, *World Conqueror,* ch. 9.
[20] See N. Ratnapala, *The Katikavatas, Laws of the Buddhist Order of Ceylon from the Twelfth Century to the Eighteenth Century* (Munich: J. Kitzinger, 1971). See also M. Carrithers, *The Forest-Monks of Sri Lanka: An Anthropological and Historical Study* (Delhi: Oxford University Press, 1983).

the gift relationship, in conformity with the canonical model, playing a central role. Monks were not supposed to farm or handle any money or private property. The *Patimokkha* regulations are quite severe in this respect, forbidding a *bhikkhu* "to dig the earth or have the earth dug,"[21] "receive gold or silver" (the last of the ten precepts taken by novices upon entering the order), "pick up or cause to be picked up or consent to the deposit of gold or silver,"[22] or even "engage in the various kinds of buying and selling."[23] Even when these strict interdictions were transgressed, as they were in a most systematic and permanent manner in Sri Lanka's regime of monastic landlordism, monks usually did not engage in commerce or any kind of sustained economic entrepreneurship.

At the same time, though, the Sangha clearly had tremendous economic implications, if only by receiving a significant share of the population's resources in wealth and manpower through the influx of religious donations. *Dana,* as a result, could become the source of serious tension between Sangha and state. We should note here the structural contradiction (most fully analyzed by Aung-Thwin in the case of Burma)[24] between the role of the king as benefactor and chief donor to the religion on the one hand, but also chief rival of the Sangha over the resources of the kingdom on the other. Monastic ownership of land, in particular, constituted a recurrent source of disputes and legal wrangles between monks and king, monks and laity, or even among monks themselves.[25]

The case of Sri Lanka is especially interesting, since monasteries attained an unparalleled level of economic autonomy – in many ways similar to the Christian situation discussed in the next section. Monastic autonomy, as depicted by Gunawardana,[26] was extensive enough to introduce an element of "feudalism" into the social structure of early medieval Sri Lanka. In this context, autonomy may have been sustained by the fact that monasteries played an important role in the irrigation system until the shift of the political and cultural centers to the "Wet Zone" after the Magha invasion in the thirteenth century.[27] The wealth

[21] *Pakittiya dhamma* 10. *Vinaya Texts,* Part 1, p. 33
[22] *Nissaggiya pakittiya,* 18. *Vinaya Texts,* Part 1, p. 26
[23] *Nissaggiya pakittiya,* 19. See *Vinaya Texts,* p. 26.
[24] Aung-Thwin, "Role of *Sasana* Reform."
[25] See Than Tun, "Religion in Burma, 1000-1300," *Journal of the Burma Research Society* 42, no. 2 (1959): 62.
[26] See R. A. L. H. Gunawardana, *Robe and Plough: Monasticism and Economic Interest in Early Medieval Sri Lanka* (Tucson: University of Arizona Press, 1979). Sri Lanka is also the more consistently "deviant" case, in that monasteries also derived income from a variety of commercial activities. See ibid., pp. 77–8.
[27] R. A. L. H. Gunawardana, "Irrigation and Hydraulic Society in Medieval Ceylon," *Past and Present* 53 (1971): 3–27. Significantly, although it may not necessarily have led to enhanced monastic autonomy, this also seems to have been a period of general prosperity, enabling a rich surplus in wealth and generous endowments to the Sangha.

of the Sangha, at any rate, combined with the transfer to monastic authorities, around the ninth and tenth centuries, not only of fiscal rights but also of the administrative and judicial authority that the king had traditionally enjoyed over the property of the Sangha. Each *nikaya* employed an extensive bureaucratic network – composed at first perhaps of royal delegates, but increasingly replaced by monastic officials – that coordinated its variegated economic interests. Providing land and/ or grain in exchange for various products and services from the laity (such as maintenance or repair work on monastic precincts), the monastery played a "redistributive" role within the economy. This role, however, was not always enacted in a wholly benevolent fashion: For example, monks did not shy from enforcing their property rights and other stipulations by threatening to withhold irrigation water or repossess the land. The Burmese Sangha of the early Pagan and Ava eras seems at some point to have reached a comparable level of economic, if not administrative, autonomy, based in part on hereditary "dedicated" or "slave" manpower. Also important in the Burmese case was the use of lay "liason officers" to deal with the outside world, as well as the direct assignment of certain monks to look after lands and property.[28]

However extensive their holdings, use of gold, and commercial activities (in the management of which all monastic officials were usually seconded by lay agents and overseers), it is crucial that monks in Theravada countries never became directly involved in the creation of capital or actual development of the land. Furthermore, as Carrithers points out, "Even when monks became landlords, as some did very early in Sri Lanka, the actual acquisition and use of goods by landed monks tends to take the same form, that of receiving alms, as among more truly mendicant monks,"[29] thus perpetuating the formal frame of the gift relationship between Sangha and laity.

Finally, whatever economic autonomy was achieved, it was always ultimately threatened and limited by the king's right to confiscate or redistribute the Sangha's wealth as part – or as has been argued, as the major motive – of a legitimate campaign of religious purification.[30] The fate of the Sangha's temporal wealth in times of reformation varied from

---

[28] Than Tun, "Religion in Burma, 1000–1300," 62.

[29] Carrithers, *Forest-Monks of Sri Lanka,* p. 140.

[30] See the debate over this point between Aung-Thwin, "Role of Sasana Reform" and V. L. Lieberman, "The Political Significance of Religious Wealth in Burmese History: Some Further Thoughts," *Journal of Asian Studies* 39 (1980): 753–69, followed by M. Aung-Thwin, "A Reply to Lieberman," ibid. 40 (1980): 87–90. Both Aung-Thwin and Lieberman would agree, as Lieberman puts it, that "in purifying the Order, successful Burmese rulers were strengthening royal control over scarce human and material resources"; but they differ on the importance of this factor in patterns of political decentralization and recentralization, and of dynastic survival or decline.

case to case. In Sri Lanka, autonomy appears to have been more success-fully maintained, and monastic temporal property to have remained better preserved. To some extent, however, this may well be the result of a certain conception of the laity's role in protecting the wealth of the Sangha; the belief that "monastic property belonged to the Buddha himself" and that "he who protects the Buddha's property is even wor-thier than the one who gave property in the first place,"[31] once again emphasizes some form of monastic dependence on the laity.

The Sangha's social incorporation

The Sangha's incorporation in its social environment is most evident, perhaps, in the incorporation of monkhood (in Burma and Thailand but not Sri Lanka) as a temporary stage in the life cycle of most of the male population, usually applying to youth not yet burdened with the duties of an adult member of the community, or elderly persons whose partici-pation in social life is already on the decline. The incorporation entailed cannot be defined as a classical rite of passage, since there was much fluidity. The precise age at which a young man entered the Sangha and the length of time he spent in it varied greatly. Also, participation was far from universal: Not every boy necessarily joined, and only a minority of the elderly, for whom this remained even more clearly a purely volun-tary option.[32] Joining the monkhood for longer periods of time than the average normative requirement was usually a source of increased social prestige and could even be an important channel of upward mobility. The institution of temporary monkhood was supplemented by that of periodic "monachization" of the laity on *uposatha* days, when laymen could observe not five but eight or ten precepts and thus somewhat approximate the life of the monk for at least one day.

This institution of temporary monkhood is a development not pro-vided for in canonical Buddhism, and bears some affinities with the Brahmanical postponement of renunciation to the last stage of the life cycle. Both may be seen as a way to "domesticate" renunciation by

---

[31] S. Kemper, "The Buddhist Monkhood, the Law, and the State in Colonial Sri Lanka," *Comparative Studies in Society and History* 26 (1981): 410.

[32] On the status of those *upasaka* who choose, in old age, to observe ten precepts instead of five, see Obeyesekere, "Theodicy, Sin and Salvation," p. 109. For a comparison with the Indian model of stages in the Brahmin's life, see R. Thapar, "The Householder and the Renouncer in the Brahmanical and Bud-dhist Traditions," in T. N. Madan (ed.), *Way of Life: King, Householder, Re-nouncer: Essays in Honour of Louis Dumont* (New Delhi: Vikas, 1982), pp. 273–98. With regard to the connection to kinship, it may be noted that the *Vinaya* advises the *bhikkhu* to assist his parents when needed, and to maintain a close relationship with them. There are also many instances in Theravada litera-ture, however, of a contrary stance on that issue.

incorporating it as a temporary stage in the life cycle. Moreover, a significant consequence of the Theravada institution of temporary monkhood is that laymen could exert normative control on monks because they were themselves closely acquainted with the status and duties of monkhood. Further underlining the rather weak autonomy of the Theravada Sangha vis-à-vis wider society, it is worth noting that entering the monkhood, although theoretically entailing a disconnection from kinship ties, actually remains symbolically intimately associated with it, since it is understood as the major way of giving merit to one's parents, and to one's mother especially.

A further indication of the weak autonomy of Theravada monasticism was its tendency to maintain a close connection with local units and its failure to develop any kind of trans- or supranational organizational framework. This may be associated with Buddhism's tendency to develop into a central element of national identity, expressed in its intertwining with the "founding myths" of the respective kingdoms as recorded in their great historical chronicles.[33] In the case of Sri Lanka, this intimate connection between Buddhism and national identity began, in the *Mahavamsa* account, with the very arrival of Buddhism on the island and was sustained, together with Mahavihara orthodoxy, by geographical insulation. However, it was also manifest in the other Theravada countries, for example in the Burmese conviction of being Buddhism's chosen nation in the ideal state of Jambudipa.[34] This intertwining of Buddhism with national identity and social order was dramatized in elaborate nationwide cults and state rituals – such as the Tooth Relic festival in Sri Lanka – that helped bridge regional differences and cement a broader identity.[35] Still, and somewhat paradoxically, these coun-

[33] See Smith (ed.), *Power in Sri Lanka,* and especially Bechert, "Beginnings of Buddhist Historiography," pp. 1–12; Clifford, "Dhammadipa Tradition of Sri Lanka," pp. 36–47; and B. L. Smith, "The Ideal Social Order as Portrayed in the Chronicles of Ceylon," pp. 48–72. See also F. E. Reynolds and R. T. Clifford, "Sangha, Society and the Struggle for National Integration: Burma and Thailand," F. E. Reynolds and T. M. Ludwig (eds.), *Transitions and Transformations in the History of Religions: Essays in Honor of Joseph M. Kitagawa* (Leiden: Brill, 1980); F. E. Reynolds, "Civic Religion and National Community in Thailand," *Journal of Asian Studies* 36 (1977): 267–82. This tendency became most evident in times of invasion and during modern colonialism in Sri Lanka and Burma. See Smith, *Religion and Politics in Burma.*

[34] M. Aung-Thwin, "'Jambudipa': Classical Burma's Camelot," *Contributions to Asian Studies* 16 (1981): 38–61.

[35] See Reynolds and Clifford, "Sangha, Society"; Reynolds, "Civic Religion and National Community in Thailand." See also Smith's rich analysis of the use of both Buddhist and Indian cultic and symbolic devices in Polannaruva as a "ceremonial center" coping with the challenges of regional diversity, in "Polonnaruva as a Ceremonial Complex," as well as the rich analysis of the Tooth Relic cult in H. L. Seneviratne, *Rituals of the Kandyan State* (Cambridge University Press, 1978).

tries were also well aware of being a part of a wider, supranational Theravada complex. This was very concretely expressed in the reciprocal transfer of *bhikkhus* of pure monastic lineages between Sri Lanka and Burma. It is noteworthy, however, that this broader Theravada consciousness never generated the formation of a supranational center or churchlike framework.

It should be clear by now that the sangha has become very much a part of the wider structure. On a more routine day-to-day level as well, monks have been drawn, sometimes to a very great extent, into interaction with laymen – although again, always within definite limits. Here, we shall be able to use, with caution, the invaluable contribution of contemporary anthropological studies that clearly picture the monastery as a cardinal institution of communal life at the local, village level.

Monastic involvement in local affairs was expressed, above all, by their participation in lay rituals. This participation mainly limited itself to the delivering of sermons, the recitation of Pali sacred verses (*parittas*), and the acceptance of *dana* on various ceremonial and merit-making occasions. Of all the various rites of transition connected to the life cycle, significantly, *bhikkhus* were present only at funerals. Letting themselves be fed by the laity, and thus offering the possibility of merit being transferred from the donors to the dead, their role in mortuary rites, at least in comparison with the kind of active, sacramental intercession associated with Catholic priesthood, remains largely indirect.

In a broader sense, however, the presence of *bhikkhus* at various lay rituals may be rightly said to have constituted the more "priestly" pole of their interaction with the laity, to the extent that it offered laymen the opportunity to improve their soteriological prospects through the ceremonial services (however "passively" and "indirectly" defined) of specialized intermediaries.

In an even looser sense, *bhikkhus* no doubt became invested with a crucial function of mediation between the day-to-day world and the realm of transcendental, otherworldly values. Central to this "mediating" function is the paradox, illuminated by Tambiah, of monks' chanting and preaching in sacred words that proclaim otherworldly ideals (the conquest of worldly desires and the extinguishing of life in nirvana) and yet are also believed to confer worldly blessings and protection from a variety of mundane evils and misfortunes.[36] What may seem as the superimposing of magical orientations and interpretations upon "purely" Buddhist practices[37] thus clearly contributed to invest

[36] See especially Tambiah, *Buddhism and the Spirit-Cults*, chs. 10, 11, and 12; also, Tambiah, "Ideology of Merit."
[37] On the magical aspects of Buddha himself, see King, *A Thousand Lives Away*. See also Terwiel, "Model for the Study of Thai Buddhism."

bhikkhus' ritual performances with more worldly forms of significance with regard to the laity.

In general, however, that monks coexisted with numerous cults of local deities with their own respective "specialists," as well as with brahmins in the context of court rituals, somewhat lessened the possibility of the Sangha taking the burden, as it were, of all mediating, priestlike functions. At a more essential level, it is crucial to remember (especially with regard to any possible analogy to the Christian priesthood) that whatever mediating ritual significance the Sangha acquired remained a historical development with no explicit doctrinal anchoring, and no later, post factum doctrinal elaboration.

Shifting now to more practical aspects of the Sangha's interaction with the laity, it is important to note that monasteries were the keepers and transmitters not only of the Buddhist written tradition, but more broadly, of literacy itself. Up to the recent establishment of non-monastic schools, local monks were the only ones to provide youth with literacy and other basic skills. Individual monks were also called upon for general advice and counseling, which could vary broadly in nature and scope. In this respect, monks' relative "advantage" as counselers is that they were perceived as "objective" outsiders, as a third party with no personal interests at stake. At its broadest, this advising capacity could address individual as well as communal problems, range from mere advice to therapy, and often include a whole gamut of "magical" and astrological practices not strictly within the frame of reference of "higher" Buddhism.[38] Paradoxically, the widespread belief (actually rooted in canonical doctrine itself) that spiritual progress could be expected to engender extraordinary powers, naturally encouraged the drive to "tap" *bhikkhus* in general, and *bhikkhus* of outstanding holiness in particular, for such supernatural energies. Somewhat lessening the weight of this latter aspect of the monks' interaction with the laity, here again it must be stressed that in all Theravada countries, other "specialists" were available and that Buddhist monks were

[38] The broadest range of services seems to obtain in present-day Thailand, where besides its religious functions, the monastery also serves as a community center, counseling agency, hospital, school, community chest, free hotel, news agency, charity employer, bank (at low or no interest), clock, sports center, morgue, poorhouse, landlord (also at charity rates), home for the aged, reservoir, asylum for the psychotic, music school, and refuge for criminals. See H. J. Kaufman, *Bangkhuad: A Community Study in Thailand* (Locust Valley, N.Y.: Augustin, 1960), pp. 113–15. Thailand's government is trying to use monks as local agents in the implementation of its modernization policies. It is too soon to judge the extent to which such a high level of communal involvement can be sustained without undermining the distinction between monk and layman as traditionally defined. See N. Mulder, *Merit, Monks and Motivation* (De Kalb, Ill.: Northern University Press, 1968).

never the only ones to provide magical, "therapeutic," or astrological services.

Fundamentally, the monks' rather extensive involvement in communal life was not without dilemma: Although their communal activities might contribute to their public status, these same activities could also undermine it by compromising the withdrawal and segregation from society on which their spiritual prestige depended. There have always been *bhikkhus* who condemned too great an involvement in lay life. Laymen themselves, though of course interested in the services provided, could not forget that seclusion from laymen was a condition of monks' special spiritual worth, which in turn enhanced the value of whatever services and counseling the monks may have provided. Most of all, segregation of monkhood and laity was the crucial prerequisite for the Sangha's validity as a "field of merit" enabling laymen to accumulate merit by giving *dana*.

Contemporary anthropological studies of traditional village settings would seem to indicate, however, that the virtuoso–layman relation is able to maintain a momentum of its own, not always dependent on the Sangha's actual conformity to the *Vinaya*. Obviously, laymen would not support monks who were blatantly unworthy, and the laity, as already suggested, may be seen as exerting continual normative control upon the monkhood, even if this control did not take as dramatic a form as the kings' "campaigns of purification." Nevertheless, standards of purity and adhesion to what was supposed to be a monk's role appear to be flexible or, more precisely, to comprise an interesting blend of ritualization and flexibility. Renunciation has perhaps been maintained most stringently and consistently in the sphere of sexual abstinence. On the other hand, material deprivation may not have been so essential. Mortification was never propounded as an end in itself – in line with the Buddha's conception of the Middle Way. Ironically, monks, as a rule, probably lived a life of greater comfort than most villagers. In general, they were allowed significant leeway in the interpretation of their role: Standards of knowledge and spiritual achievement were minimal; monks could engage in various occult arts, even if contrary to doctrine; they had freedom of movement (and in fact were encouraged to travel after the end of the rain season); finally, they could vary in the scope of their involvement with the laity and communal affairs. Most important, monks were more often engaged in the accumulation of merit than in the pursuit of nirvana, or to use Spiro's terms, oriented to the "kammatic" rather than "nibbanic" dimensions of Buddhism,[39] without in any way impairing the basic pattern of their relationship with laymen.

[39] Spiro, *Buddhism and Society.*

At the same time, however, monks had to conform to precise rules of appearance and deportment. This conformity to a highly stylized image and etiquette is crucial in the layman's eyes, even overshadowing (within, of course, certain limits) the precise extent to which monks practice the Middle Way.[40] In other words, monks are not now, and most probably were not in the past, consistently required to adhere to the highest values: It was enough if they symbolized them. An essential point was that the cleavage between monks and laymen be maintained.[41] The maintenance of this cleavage both depended upon, and was a necessary condition for, the monks' potency as symbols or renunciation, or "living reminders of the impossible."[42] This symbolic feature was obviously able to persist, at any rate, independently of the Sangha's actual nibbanic achievements. What is involved here is a kind of "objectification" of the Sangha's charisma, perhaps not altogether dissimilar from that associated by Tambiah with the cult of relics,[43] an important facet of its institutionalization in Theravada countries that already emerged in Buddhism at a very early stage. Not unlike relics, the Sangha appears to have operated to some extent as a symbolic – more precisely iconic – reminder of "high" Buddhism, independently, and despite its many other possible worldly usages and meanings for the laity.

The gift relationship

The gift relationship appears to have played a major role in the Sangha's symbolization of renunciation. Although *dana* are officially intended to provide material support to monks striving for salvation, in fact they generally bore no direct relation to the monk's actual needs; there was

---

[40] At the limit, this allows for the phenomenon of false monks – monks who engage in sinful and corrupt behavior and only pretend to be monks – receiving material support from laymen as long as they are clothed in the yellow robe, symbol of sanctity. Again, however, no layman would keep supporting a monk who is blatantly unworthy, and laymen, on the contrary, prefer to offer their gifts to monks reputed for their higher spiritual standing (even if, doctrinally, the worth of one's gifts is not dependent upon the receiving monk's precise spiritual worth).

[41] A similar conclusion has been reached concerning, specifically, the possible corrupting impact of monastic wealth – considered fully legitimate as long as it does not lead monks to act in ways that would blur the distinction between them and laymen – in Kemper, "Wealth and Reformation in Sinhalese Buddhist Monasticism," in R. F. Sizemore and D. K. Swearer (eds.), *Ethics, Wealth and Salvation*, p. 161.

[42] E. Leach (ed.), *Dialectic in Practical Religion*, (Cambridge University Press, 1968), p. 2.

[43] I am extending here to the Sangha itself the notion of reification of charisma as originally developed by Tambiah in his treatment of the trade of amulets in present-day Thailand. See S. J. Tambiah, *The Buddhist Saints of the Forest and the Cult of Amulets* (Cambridge University Press, 1984), ch. 22.

often a surplus of gifts, sometimes reaching staggering proportions. This surplus itself acquired important meaning for the layman. Not only was the extent of his gift bearing an indicator of his "store of merit," it also became an important component in his social status as a form of "conspicuous consumption":[44] The more luxurious his gifts, the more respect he garnered from his fellow villagers. Theoretically, *bhikkhus* were enjoined not to store unconsumed *dana,* but to discard them after seven days. However, the surplus in gifts seems to have acquired additional meaning, for the monk this time, as a form of "conspicuous nonconsumption." This is most evident in the (extreme) case of monastic buildings built for a monk of outstanding saintliness and left uninhabited. The same seems to apply to the accumulation of *dana* in the public alm halls (*dana-sala*) erected in Anuradhapura, where kings deposited the gifts they regularly bestowed on the Sangha.[45] As long as it is not consumed and remains, as it were, "on display," this surplus in gifts actually testifies to the monk's asceticism and spiritual worth. The gift, then, is an important mechanism in sustaining the monk's symbolization of renunciation, an ongoing process in which the layman plays as important a role as the monk. Furthermore, by continually reaffirming both the connection and disconnection between monks and laymen, the gift relationship epitomizes the segregative/connective process as defined earlier at the interactional, microsociological level.

Yet it cannot be overlooked that donations to the Sangha have developed into something not altogether identical to what was implied by the canonical notion of *dana. Dana* theoretically involve what Tambiah has called a double negation of reciprocity:[46] the monk standing as a model of nonreciprocity, not supposed to return anything in exchange for the gift; the layman for his part theoretically expecting nothing from the monk in direct return for his gift, since the merit attached to gift giving does not derive from the monk himself. The latter, ultimately, is not the bestower of merit, but only the occasion for it. In practice, as often observed, this model appears to be readily displaced by a simple pattern of reciprocity whereby gifts are given to monks in reward for their participation in various merit-making ritual occasions and other services, or even in direct (and most uncanonical) exchange for merit itself. As noted, gift giving was also incorporated as an important parameter in the local status system. (This could easily have been transformed into a

---

[44] At the same time, it has and probably had the indirect effect of diminishing differences of wealth within the community.

[45] See W. Geiger, *Culture of Ceylon in Medieval Times,* p. 56. Edited by H. Bechert (Wiesboden: Harrassowitz, 1960).

[46] Tambiah, *Buddhism and the Spirit Cults,* p. 213.

pattern of competitive destruction of wealth in the potlatch style; it is significant that it never did.) Although the actual *dana* relation is thus a far cry from the canonical model of nonreciprocity, it never relinquished the idiom of nonreciprocity that forms an essential rather than merely surface component of the interaction between monk and layman. As Strenski notes, monks regularly reasserted their independence from reciprocity in a number of ways, and the result was "a style of exchange which both avoids the appearance and substance of reciprocity and expresses more durable and inclusive patterns of relationship."[47]

The *dana* relation evolved into a partly "particularized" and partly generalized form of exchange. On the one hand, it would be mainly a face-to-face local transaction, permeated by local kinship networks and interests. Although the gift was given, in theory, to the "Sangha of the four quarters," in practice it was often given to a specific *bhikkhu,* frequently a friend or relative. On the other hand, through its connection to merit-making, it played a crucial role in a complex and expansive economy of merit in which notions of equivocal canonical status – such as the possibility of sharing in others' merit by rejoicing in their merit making, acquiring merit just before death, transferring merit not only to the gods and the dead but also to the living, and so forth – have converted merit into a reified, fluid, and transferable substance.[48] Merit was sometimes acquired for oneself, sometimes transferred to specific others, and also – and more often than not – transferred in an abstract and universalistic fashion "to all living beings."[49]

Furthermore, gift giving was predominantly a public endeavor, open and visible to all, and nurturing the general interest. Not only did it sustain the overall merit economy, it also contributed to the maintainance and enhancement of monasteries, which in many ways became

[47] I. Strenski, "On Generalized Exchange and the Domestication of the Sangha," *Man* n.s. 18 (1983): 472.

[48] In Keyes's words, "Throughout Buddhist Southeast Asia, although perhaps not to the same extent in Sri Lanka, merit is conceived almost as a substance that can be possessed in variable quantities and that can be translated into this-worldly virtue or power as well as stored up to be used at death to ensure a good rebirth." See Keyes, "Merit-Transference," p. 270; on the development of canonically equivocal notions of transfer of merit, see this volume, Chapter 4, fn. 26. It should be noted that Theravada monkhood never developed the notion of taking upon itself the sins (or "bad karma") of others, whether in exchange for *dana* (as Brahmans did, cf. Thapar, "Householder and the Renouncer," p. 276) or with no reference to gifts, as was conceivable, if not characteristic, of Christian monkhood.

[49] For some typical epigraphic examples, see *Epigraphica Zeylanica,* vol. 4, part 3, pp. 133, 140–1, 145; vol. 4, part 4, p. 169; part 5, p. 260; *Corpus Inscriptionum Indicarum,* vol. 1 (Oxford: Clarendon Press, for the Government of India, 1925), p. 121. See also Schopen, "Transfer of Merit and the Monk-Layman," 33 ff.

the central foci of public life.[50] The munificence of donations of all kinds
also played an important role in publicly attesting to the vitality of the
sasana (the Buddhist religion) as a whole. Most suggestive from this
point of view are numerous epigraphical formulations conveying such
notions as "delight in causing the religion of the Buddha to shine" or
"maintain the religion in splendor."[51] *Dana* could consist in the daily
giving of perishable food, but also in the giving of a much more tangible
and lasting wealth, ranging from the monk's minor personal possessions
allowed (and many not allowed) by the *Vinaya* to the gift of land and
slaves, and the building, repair, or adornment of monastic buildings.
Although all things, and the *sasana* itself, are subject to the law of decay
and impermanence, such tangible, material donations were somehow
believed to ensure the *sasana*'s survival throughout the predicted 5,000
years of its existence and until the coming of Maitreya Buddha, when all
will attain enlightenment.[52]

A related property of *dana* is the extensive and inclusive scope of its
operation, its applicability to all laity, from simplest peasant to king –
chief donor and supporter of the Sangha and chief merit maker for
whom the Sangha functioned as for all laymen as field of merit. As
conveyed in the notion of the king's *mahadana,* gift giving could be
extended with little modification from the local, microsociological to
the central, macrosocietal level. At this central level, indeed, lavish
support of the capital monasteries in particular would come to form a
crucial aspect in royal displays of pomp and legitimacy.[53]

Dana constitutes such a central and powerful phenomenon in Theravada Buddhist countries that some have gone as far as seeing in it the
source of a basic competition between kings and Sangha over the kingdom's material and human resources – the latter perhaps the more crucial in a part of the world where scarcity in manpower, rather than land,
seems to have been the dominant issue – and placing it at the root of
such major macropolitical processes as dynastic cycles, religious and
military polities, and the recurrent emergence and breakdown of poli-

---

[50] This was suggested in M. Moerman, "Ban Ping's Temple: The Center of a
Loosely Structured Society," in M. Nash (ed.), *Anthropological Studies in
Theravada Buddhism* (New Haven, Conn.: Yale University Press, 1966), p.
153. See also A. Brand, "Merit, Hierarchy and Royal Gift-Giving in Traditional Thai Society," *Bijdragen tot de Taal-, Land- en Volkenkunde* 131 (1975):
111–37.

[51] See, for example, *Epigraphica Birmanica,* vol. 3, part 2, pp. 196–8; vol. 4, part
1, p. 48. Closely related is the wish to "increase in prosperity to the great king."

[52] M. Aung-Thwin, "Prophecies, Omens and Dialogue: Tools of the Trade in
Burmese Historiography," in D. K. Wyatt and A. Woodside (eds.), *Moral Or-
der and the Question of Change: Essays on Southest Asian Thought* (New
Haven, Conn.: Yale University Press, 1983), pp. 80–1.

[53] For a rich analysis of this aspect of royal prestations, see Brand, "Merit, Hierarchy and Royal Gift-Giving."

ties.[54] Be that as it may, what strikes me as remarkable is that although the flow of donations could evidently be affected by contextual economic and/or political trends,[55] nothing ever undermined – at least until recently – the basic principle of a gift relationship between monks and laymen.

Sangha, kingship, and political power

The specific mode of incorporation of monks into the social structure, allowing for rather extensive involvement at the same time as maintaining this involvement within bounds – is further reflected in the political domain. Monks undoubtedly became part of the broader political game. To begin with, monastic branches, sects, and even individual monasteries competed among themselves for the patronage of wealthy and powerful laymen, and above all kings, who manipulated them in turn, to some extent, in accordance with their own political ends. That the Sangha could attract not only wealth, but also people evading military service or the burden of heavy duties, could become of the greatest political concern for the king, and a major point of tension between him and the Sangha. However, the Sangha could also represent an important political asset for the ruler by mediating between him and the masses, protecting the people from tyrannical rule but also reconciling them with that rule.[56] Monks might intervene, for example, to prevent capital punishment. Their mediating capacity also comes to the fore in their activities as peace intermediaries or diplomatic emissaries.[57] Not to be dismissed either is the influence acquired by monks who served as tutors and teachers for the king or his family.

Most important, however, monks became a crucial party in the legitimation of kings and an all-important ingredient of capital-city politics. The Sangha, in fact, possessed enormous political clout if only through its close connection with the laity, and inasmuch as it became a crucial point of reference in the definition of the benevolent Buddhist monarchy. Further, in matters of succession, the Sangha represented a force that no prince would wish to antagonize, since kingship depended

[54] M. Aung-Thwin, *Pagan: The Origins of Modern Burma* (Honolulu: University of Hawaii Press, 1985). See, however, Lieberman, "Political Significance of Religious Wealth."

[55] Lieberman, ibid., emphasizes such factors as kingly policies, wars, invasions, but also more structural economic changes such as a shift from landed to cash donations toward the end of the fifteenth century.

[56] See C. Kasetsiri, *The Rise of Ayadhuya: A History of Siam in the Fourteenth and Fifteenth Centuries* (Kuala Lumpur: Oxford University Press, 1976), pp. 136 ff; Spiro, *Buddhism and Society,* pp. 378–82.

[57] See Gunawardana, *Robe and Plough,* pp. 205–7; Cady, *History of Modern Burma.*

upon the recognition of karmic proficiency for its legitimacy and could not rely on merely dynastic, hereditary principles. In general, the Sangha's major motive for political involvement was to oppose usurpers or kings who jeapardized the Sangha's interests and the survival of Buddhism. This did not necessarily imply unanimous or centralized corporate political behavior. Rather than interference, the tactic could be one of "active withdrawal," for example, refusing the king's *dana* or leaving the capital and moving to peripheral monasteries. At such times, monasteries might also provide refuge for the regime's opponents. In tenth-century Sri Lanka, for example, monks left the capital (Tapovana) over a breach of their right of sanctuary, whereupon army and laity rose in protest and forced the king, Udaya III, to ask for forgiveness and have the monks return. This tactic did not always have the same result, however, depending on the issue involved and the monks' popularity.[58]

The relation between Sangha and king, if theoretically one of interdependence and mutual support, was thus never static and free of tensions. Royal power could definitely be either enhanced or limited by the Sangha. This very uncertainty invested the Sangha with a political weight that had to be taken into account. Significantly, however – and in accordance with the doctrine of renunciation and detachment from worldly affairs – the Sangha's political activity never amounted to the autonomous political power wielded by the Catholic Church in Western Europe (omitting for the moment any direct comparison with Christian monasticism). There were numerous exceptions to this attitude of disengagement, but they were usually individual aberrations and were frowned upon by other monks.[59] Although certainly not without political importance, and even if it did try to influence or oppose rulers (especially in matters pertaining to Buddhism itself), the Sangha never vied with kings for authority over worldly and political affairs. Moreover, except for recent developments, it did not try to assert itself as a truly autonomous force in the existing political framework, and even less to propound an alternative form of political structure.

The relation between Sangha and king, for all its tensions, has been often and rightly described as one of interdependence and complementarity. In rare deviation from this pattern, a king might want to be a *bhikkhu* himself, not before his accession or after his abdication (the usual pattern), but while retaining his royal functions – for example, King Lu-Thai in fourteenth-century Sukhodaya – or claim for himself spiritual superiority through inordinate mystical powers – such as King

---

[58] See Gunawardana, *Robe and Plough,* pp. 208, 211.
[59] See, for example, M. Htin Aung, *A History of Burma* (New York: Columbia University Press, 1967), p. 53.

Takhsin at the end of the eighteenth century.[60] Another case, evidently unique in the history of Theravada Buddhist countries, is that of a monk bidding for kingship – Chao Phitsanulok, king of Fang (1767–8).[61] These various attempts at conflating renouncer and ruler into one person, however, can be seen as marginal deviations from the dominant pattern of mutual dependence and complementarity between the two.[62]

It would be a mistake, nevertheless, to overestimate the ultimate symmetry of the relationship. First, the interdependence and complementarity are never total, for the simple reason that there are always other partners available. Kingship had cosmological and ideological resources other than Buddhism proper.[63] Of primary importance here were elaborate court rituals, in which brahmins and not monks played the essential role. Another important resource of Indian origin was the *Kautilya* tradition of pragmatic, secular statecraft. There was also the whole range of cosmological orientations, rituals, and corresponding specialists of so-called popular Buddhism, actually shared by all strata of the population, including monks and kings themselves. The elaboration, especially in Burma, of the notion of the king as *devaraja* – or king of the spirits – is a clear indication of the symbolic consolidation of kingship through ideological resources other than "high" Buddhism.[64]

In the final analysis, though, the king was more heavily dependent on the Sangha than vice versa. First, kings always had to consolidate their position in the face of very strong centrifugal forces, something that

60 See Barbara Watson Andaya, "Statecraft in the Reign of Lu Tai of Sukhodaya (ca. 1347–1374)," in B. L. Smith (ed.), *Religion and Legitimation of Power in Thailand, Laos and Burma* (Chambersburg, Pa.: Anima, 1978) pp. 2–19; L. Gesick, "The Rise and Fall of King Taksin: A Drama of Buddhist Kingship," in Gesick (ed.), *Centers, Symbols and Hierarchies: Essays on the Classical States of Southeast Asia* (New Haven, Conn.: Yale University Press, 1983), pp. 87–105; J. Butt, "Thai Kingship and Religious Reform (18th–19th Centuries)," in Smith (ed.), *Power in Thailand, Laos and Burma,* pp. 34–51. Whatever the use of Buddhism in the legitimation of kingship and polity, it is important to stress that there could be a source of very real "existential" tension between a king's Buddhist inclinations and the pragmatic necessities of his kingly activities, especially with regard to the use of violence. Kings could also become monks for a short time during their reign. See Kasetsiri, *Rise of Ayudhya,* p. 138.

61 See R. Lingat, "La double crise de l'église bouddhique au Siam (1767–1851)," *Cahiers d'Histoire Mondiale* 4 (1958): 402–10. There is also the "border" case of Dhammaceti, a regular monk who became king through a whim of the queen of Pegu (1453–72), who wished to retire in favor of a monk. See N. Ray, *Theravada Buddhism in Burma* (Calcutta: Calcutta University Press, 1946) pp. 182 ff.

62 Confirming this argument in the case of Burma, see J. P. Ferguson, "The Quest for Legitimacy by Burmese Monks and Kings: The Case of the Schwegyin Sect (19th–20th Centuries)," in Smith (ed.), *Power in Thailand, Laos and Burma,* p. 68.

63 This is stressed, for example, in H. Bechert, "The Sangha as a Factor in the Social Life of Sri Lanka and Burma," in *P. E. P. Deraniyagala Commemoration Volume* (Colombo: University of Ceylon Press, 1980), p. 87.

64 See Aung-Thwin, "Divinity, Spirit and Human."

could not but increase their concern with the legitimation of central authority. Second, although kingship could rely on brahmanic, and not exclusively Buddhist, sources of legitimation – and even, as Sarkisyanz states it, on a distinctive "Ashokan" lay Buddhist tradition rather than monastic-canonical Buddhism proper[65] – kingship never mustered sufficient symbolic autonomy and strength of its own to displace, let alone rival, the ultimate superiority of the renouncer at the apex of the social and spiritual hierarchy. It is striking that even though kings were gradually invested with exalted, Buddhalike status (*bodhisattva, cakkavatti,* etc.), they always remained laymen, and as such had to bow down to the simplest *bhikkhu.*

Kingship, thus, was in a situation of relative symbolic weakness vis-à-vis the Sangha. The weakness of Southeast Asian kingship, paradoxically combined with the grand conceptions of the king as *cakkavatti, dharmaraja, devaraja,* or bodhisattva,[66] has been noted by many. Geertz's words are apt here: "Sovereignty, like divinity, was both one and many. The landscape . . . throughout Southeast Asia, and over the course of at least fifteen hundred years, was dotted with universal monarchs, each represented . . . as the core and pivot of the universe, yet each quite aware that he was emphatically not alone in such representation."[67] In Tambiah's view, however, Theravada kingship oscillated between strength and weakness, periodically diplaying a stronger deployment and embodiment of the ideal world ruler – the potential for which is intrinsically implied in the Theravada conception of the relation between Buddhism and polity.[68] Even in its "stronger" phases, though, an important aspect of the relative weakness of Theravada kingship was its disconnection from lawmaking and the fact that laws promulgated by one king were automatically abrogated upon the accession of a new king. The role of the first and foremost of kings, Mahasammata, was "to protect his people and to administer justice with equity, not to proclaim law."[69] Even on purely organizational grounds, the Sangha, however

[65] Sarkisyanz, *Buddhist Backgrounds.*
[66] See this volume, Chapter 3, pp. 60–2.
[67] C. Geertz, *Negara: The Theatre State in Nineteenth-Century Bali* (Princeton, N.J.: Princeton University Press, 1980), p. 125. See also Gesick (ed.), *Centers, Symbols and Hierarchies.*
[68] S. J. Tambiah, "A Reformulation of Geertz's Conception of the Theater State," in S. J. Tambiah, *Culture, Thought and Action: An Anthropological Perspective* (Cambridge, Mass.: Harvard University Press, 1985), pp. 316–38; idem, "The Galactic Polity in Southeast Asia," ibid., pp. 252–86; idem, *World Conqueror.*
[69] See R. Lingat, "Evolution of the Conception of Law in Burma and Siam," *Journal of the Siam Society* 38 (1950): 18. Even in Siam, where the practice developed of connecting royal decisions with *dhammasattham* rules, and decisions of kings could thus become permanent rules, this was not because these decisions emanated from kings, but because they were illustrations of the eternal law and partook of its authority.

"amorphous" it may be relative to the Christian *ecclesia,* was often a better organized and efficient institution than the king's state apparatus. There were periods of enhanced centralization – as in the reign of Parakramabahu I in Sri Lanka, or in the Ayutthaya and especially the Chakkri eras in Thailand. Usually, however, the king's administrative apparatus remained rather inefficient, and was largely limited to the extraction of taxes and labor.

From the point of view of the virtuoso–society relation, therefore, it is important to note both continuity and discontinuity between the local and macrosocietal levels. The continuity is definitely striking: The relation between Sangha and laity was characterized at both levels by a ritualized network of segregation and exchange, and by the notion of a division of labor and complementarity between the two – best conveyed in the potent image of the two wheels of dharma, both necessary to the "soteriological machinery of cosmos and society."[70] Nevertheless, the question arises of the extent of Buddhism's ultimate dependence on the existence of a normative Buddhist kingship.[71] The issue here is whether the interaction between Sangha and laity at the village level was not, in some sense, more crucial to the resilience of Sangha and *sasana* than was a true Buddhist kingship. It seems at any rate to have proven more stable than the relation between Sangha and king, and to have rested, ultimately, on the essential self-sufficiency of the village monastery and its local lay audience as a "dharma realm" – less momentous than the "dharma realm" of the capital, but ideologically autonomous and endlessly replicable as the basic Theravada civilizational unit.[72]

[70] Reynolds and Clifford, "Sangha, Society," p. 60. The idea receives ample treatment in G. Obeyesekere, F. Reynolds, and B. L. Smith (eds.), *The Two Wheels of Dhamma: Essays on the Theravada Tradition in India and Ceylon* (Chambersburg, Pa.: American Academy of Religion, 1972).

[71] The idea of the relatively contingent nature of kingship is articulated in the most extreme fashion by Charles Keyes in his review of Tambiah's *World Conqueror:* "The prediction of Buddhism's status as a world religion on the existence of a monarchy informed by the Dhamma creates a parameter which is not essential; lay Buddhist ethics are not dependent on the existence of a monarchy; a Buddhist monarch is an historical development, not a structural imperative." Keyes, "Structure and History."

I would side with Tambiah's argument that an archconception connecting Buddhism and polity, and Sangha and kingship, is traceable to the earliest stages of Buddhist history; once launched, this interconnection created a number of structural possibilities between which the Theravada social order seems to have oscillated. Within this framework, however, I view Buddhist kingship as being in many important ways "frailer" than the basic cell of village sangha and laity.

[72] See Reynolds and Clifford, "Sangha, Society," especially pp. 73–9. The capital as dharma realm hosts the highest-status adherents of both paths (*dharmmaraja, sangharaja*). However, surrounding satellites did not necessarily accept the capital as their symbolic center. As conveyed in Tambiah's model of the "pulsating galactic polity," traditional Southeast Asian kingdoms oscillated between moments of strength and centralization and times of weakness and decentraliza-

The question remains whether this basic unit itself would have been successfully maintained through the centuries without periodic affirmation of its viability at the macrosocial level. Moreover, it would be hard to understand the cell-like expansion of the Sangha without the expansion of Buddhist kingdoms, or the close collaboration of Sangha and king in establishing centers of learning in the capitals and disseminating the Buddhist message over extended geographical spaces. A suggestive example of this intimate connection between Buddhism and kingdom- or even empire-building, is the close collaboration between King Aniruddha and the monk Shin Arahan in the "founding myth" of Pagan.[73] In general, Buddhism might well have first diffused in mainland Southeast Asia in or near the major political centers, and only later radiated into more peripheral areas – although such an assessment might also be an artifact of the historical and archaeological evidence available.[74] There seems to have obtained, at any rate, a very basic compatibility between village-based Buddhism and the decentralized, cellular character of the administrative–political environment and of the rural village structure, itself a correlate of the center's relative weakness.

Social stratification and economic context

Another important factor in the historical resilience of the village "civilizational unit" and the virtuoso–layman interaction at its core may have been the characteristic weakness of "secondary" aristocratic elites, that, like kings, had little hereditary or "dynastic" continuity. Even in Thailand, where nobility was a matter of royal birth, rank depended above all on the mother's status among the king's wives, and diminished generation by generation until the family dropped back into the untitled commonalty in the fifth generation, unless later marriages had brought new titles or ranks.[75] In Burma, every appointment, down to the humblest village headmanship, was the gift of the king, and lapsed at the end of each reign.[76] In practice, local authority was often hereditary, and many a head-

tion. The primacy of the capital is also limited by the relative autonomy of the village dharma realm already referred to.

[73] See Ray, *Theravada Buddhism in Burma*, pp. 98 ff.

[74] See C. F. Keyes, "Theravada Buddhism and its Worldly Transformations in Thailand: Reflections on the work of S.J. Tambiah," *Contributions to Indian Sociology* 21, no. 1 (1987): 133 ff. Not only are the historical data limited, but they might naturally be expected to survive better in political centers where large resources would be invested in the Sangha as well as in monument building and record keeping.

[75] See P. J. Bennet, *Conference under the Tamarind Tree: Three Essays in Burmese History* (New Haven, Conn.: Yale University Press, 1971).

[76] On the relative independence of the village unit, the absence of a hereditary aristocracy, and the weak social stratification of Burmese traditional society, see Bechert, *Buddhismus, Staat und Gesellschaft*, vol. 2, especially pp. 11 ff.

manship remained in the same family for centuries. What is crucial, however, is that "there was no feudal class whose political and landholding privileges enjoyed legal sanction against royal interference."[77] The higher strata's status was mostly based on personal vassalship to the king (apt to change with the next ruler), and on local, clientelistic relations with their own vassals, from whom they were not very different in many respects. Moreover, the power of princely elites were plagued by the same inherent weakness as the power of kingship itself. This is a basic aspect of what Tambiah called the "galactic polity," characterized by "lesser political replicas revolving around the central entity and in perpetual motion of fission and incorporation."[78] Within this framework, aristocratic families sometimes amassed sufficient local power to stand in the way of a "strong" king's centralizing claims, as for example during the reign of Parakramabahu I in Polonnavura Sri Lanka. It is perhaps in medieval Sri Lanka indeed that one may find the closest equivalent to an embryonic stratum of nobility, recruited from a number of powerful and eminent clans mostly from the warrior (*kshatrya*) caste, and enjoying significant privileges and immunities.[79] Despite superficial similarities to the "vertical" relationships of Western feudalism, however, what is strikingly absent from this social structure is the horizontal, translocal, and even transnational class consciousness developed by the aristocracy in medieval Europe.

An important implication of the political and symbolical weakness of the aristocracy – which will be better brought into relief through later comparison with the Christian case – is the absence of networks of allegiance and authority beyond the local kinship and village unit that could have competed with the village Sangha for local resources and loyalty. Perhaps not unrelated, the nearly total absence of competing intellectual–cultural elites or educational institutions undoubtedly helped sustain the overall cultural ascendancy of the Sangha.

Last, the overall agricultural, peasant character of South Asian societies also played its part. Trade was confined to the sea coasts and largely geared, at least up to the eleventh century, to international trade.

For a comparison of Thai and Burmese premodern social structures, see Bennet, *Conference under the Tamarind Tree,* p. 61 ff. See also Lingat, "Law in Burma and Siam," p. 22 especially.

[77] See V. B. Lieberman, *Burmese Administrative Cycles: Anarchy and Conquest c. 1580–1760* (Princeton, N.J.: Princeton University Press, 1984), p. 10. Lieberman emphasizes the presence in Tongoo Burma, from the end of the sixteenth to the mid-seventeenth century, of a cyclical pattern stemming from the recurrent crystallization of private power centers that have insufficient sanction in the formal hierarchy. See also G. E. Harvey, *Outline of Burmese History* (Bombay: Orient Longmans, 1954), pp. 187 ff. Harvey also emphasizes the role of intricate sumptuary laws in preventing the development of autonomous foci of status.

[78] Tambiah, "Galactic Polity."

[79] See Gunawardana, "Hydraulic Society in Medieval Ceylon," pp. 24 ff.

None of the Theravada kingdoms, but rather Java, Cambodia, and Sumatra, were the dominant commercial forces in the area. The withdrawal of the mainland states of Burma and Thailand from the international trade system in the eleventh and twelfth centuries corresponded to a relative expansion of their own more regional commercial networks, and the Burmese empire in particular did become a focal point of regional commerce at the time.[80] Much of the impulse to the trading activity, however, seems to have been due to the Chinese penetration of the internal commercial networks during this era. Even the expansion of trade in the fourteenth century and the increasing integration of Southeast Asia into the emerging world trade network do not seem to have led to any radical changes in social structure – such as the rise of a merchant class with distinctive social and political aspirations – but rather further intensified, at least for a while, the land-based, wet-rice economy. Whatever the general instability of the region and the existence of discernible changes at the economic level, no wave of extensive socioeconomic change (like the one said to have assisted the emergence of Buddhism and its divorce from Brahmanism), shook the material and political underpinnings of the classical virtuoso–layman relational structure during this long era of "traditional" Theravada Buddhism.[81]

Thus certain basic features of the Theravada sociopolitical environment seem to have played a role in sustaining the basic virtuoso–society relational structure, or at least providing it with a favorable context and facilitating its cultural centrality and resilience. Recurrent periods of political disorder, and major changes and variations in the sociopolitical environment – such as the shift from the "dry" to the "wet" zone in Sri Lanka around the thirteenth century,[82] or the contrast between the more benevolent and flexible structure of the Thai kingdom of Sukhodaya and the more rigid and centralized Khmer-influenced structure of Ayutthaya[83] – obviously affected the relationship between Sangha and political center in a variety of ways. At the same time, however, such macropolitical trends seem to have had little effect on the basic form and definition of the virtuoso–layman relation at the local level, and to have had no repercussions on the doctrinal articulation of this most essential dimension of Theravada tradition.

[80] See K. R. Hall, *Maritime Trade and State Development in Early Southeast Asia,* (Honolulu: University of Hawaii Press, 1985), chs. 1, 2, 7, 8 especially.

[81] Rural culture was also important in providing a primordial imagery (e.g., house, vegetation, river imagery) supporting the "psychological reality" of high Buddhism's intellectual concepts, even when counterintuitive, both relating perhaps to common underlying, unconscious cognitive structures pervasive in Indian culture at large. Collins, *Selfless Persons,* especially pp. 165–77, 218–25.

[82] See K. Indrapala (ed.), *The Collapse of the Rajarata Civilization in Ceylon and the Drift to the Southwest* (Peradinya: University of Ceylon, 1971).

[83] Kasetsiri, *Rise of Ayadhuya.*

5 Virtuoso radicalism: the triumph of a sociological complex

It is evident that the *bhikkhu,* originally enjoined to forsake all ordinary social bonds, eventually became enmeshed in but another network of social relations both within the Sangha and without, in his interaction with lay society. Hermits and wandering mendicants, representing the more asocial pole of the monastic ideal, became a quantitatively negligible phenomenon but did not entirely disappear. The tension between more and less socialized forms of renunciation persisted and even became from very early on (if not always in a uniform fashion) a significant factor in the various splits and divisions undergone by the Sangha in all Theravada countries.

Out of the divergent emphases on "practice" versus "study" already voiced in the first Buddhist councils developed the distinction between two major types of monastic vocations: *ganthadura,* the vocation of books, that is, of studying and teaching (by implication, teaching the laity); and *vipassanadhura,* the vocation of meditation (implying less of a connection to the laity). Another distinction that not necessarily fully coincided with the former was that between *arannavasi,* or *vanavasi* – forest dwellers – and *gamavasi* – dwellers in monasteries in towns and villages. Forest dwellers were not necessarily hermits,[1] but they did live a more secluded life than *gamavasi,* either individually or in groups, devoting most of their time to meditation and keeping their contact with lay life to a minimum.

These categories could designate differences between individual monks as well as between monasteries or entire branches of the Sangha with regard to their emphasis on lay-oriented activities versus meditation. But forest dwellers and town dwellers also came to be recognized as distinct, major branches of the Sangha. In twelfth-century Sri Lanka, under King Parakramabahu I, the division of the Sangha into village and forest monks was made to supersede the older division into three *nikayas* (Mahaviharasin, Abhayagirivasin, and Jetavanavasin). In nineteenth-century Thailand, too, *vipassanadhura* monks formed one of the three formal divisions of the Mahanikaya sect.[2] Forest dwellers, however, al-

---

[1] "Forest," moreover, would often be taken in a symbolic sense, meaning simply residing at the outer fringe of the settlement. Within the Syam Nikaya in modern Sri Lanka, the Malvatta and Asgirya branches are said to represent respectively the *gamavasi* and *arannavasi* traditions. In fact, Asgiryi monks live in villages and towns no less than Malvatta monks.

[2] See Bechert, *Buddhismus, Staat und Gesellschaft,* vol. 2, p. 185.

ways remained a minority, representing a living criticism, explicit or not, of the dominant majority of monks who opted for greater involvement in lay society.

Virtuoso radicalism and monastic sectarianism

Radical renouncers engaged in the single-minded pursuit of nirvana through meditation, either in total isolation or in forest hermitages, might thus be understood as a marginal group of deviant extremists or even "sectarians," opposing a religious establishment who favored a vocation of teaching and interaction with the lay world.[3] Such assessment, however, needs to be qualified by a better understanding of the nature of sectarianism in the Theravada Buddhist Sangha.

Splits in the Sangha, even when accompanied by arguments about *Vinaya,* were often triggered by entirely ad hoc reasons, such as personal conflicts, regional considerations, or disputes over property and lay patronage. As Kemper notes (albeit addressing himself mainly to the flurry of Sangha divisions in nineteenth-century Sri Lanka – not fully equivalent to processes of segmentation in the earlier, traditional era):[4] "Reform alone never seems to give rise to new *nikayas.* Often differences in monastic practice and argument about *Vinaya* serve to communicate the fact that segmentation has taken place. Sometimes, 'reform' is altogether irrelevant."[5] Moreover, it has been often observed that splits within the Sangha concerned matters of discipline rather than of doctrine. As a result, the seriousness of divisions within the Sangha has been somewhat underestimated, perhaps by implied contrast with Christianity, where sects and other divisions are deemed to usually arise from doctrinal divergences. The absence of a central authority functioning as keeper of dogma and orthodoxy has probably encouraged this line of interpretation.[6]

---

[3] Suggestive of the potential of deviance that might be attached to the forest option is the historiographic issue concerning the identity of the so-called wayward monks purged out of the Sangha in Burma in the eleventh century and sometimes identified with forest-dwelling monks. See E. M. Mendelson, *Sangha and State in Burma: A Study of Monastic Sectarianism* (Ithaca, N.Y.: Cornell University Press, 1975), pp. 36 and 46–52, for discussion of this issue and of other connections between the forest tradition and sectarianism in Burma.

[4] More generally, indeed, the richest material and analyses on the subject of the Sangha's divisions and sectarianism pertain to the later, "modern" period, in which problems of confrontation with alien rulers and disestablishment of the Sangha played a part in triggering a broad spectrum of dissension.

[5] S. Kemper, "Reform and Segmentation in Monastic Fraternities in Low Country Sri Lanka," *Journal of Asian Studies* 15 (1980): 40.

[6] See Bareau's stress on the absence of this factor already in the very early history of Buddhist sectarianism, in *Les sectes du petit véhicule*, p. 42.

Whatever the nature of the issue involved, though, the intensity of the controversies and of the ensuing hostilities leaves no doubt as to their importance. If branches of the Sangha often differed on what seem to be minor disciplinary matters – the manner of wearing a robe, drinking or not after noon meals, blessing or not after receiving a gift, and so forth – they also differed on matters of more evident importance, such as the handling of money and property, the importance given to meditation, and, in general, the degree of strictness in observing the *Vinaya* rules.[7] In Burma, for example, the distinction between forest dwellers and village dwellers seems to have originated in a thirteenth-century dispute concerning the rules for looking after the fields associated with the monasteries, a dispute upon which three monks are said to have left for the forest.[8]

Distinctions such as those between forest-dwellers and town-dwellers or between *ganthadura* and *vipassanadhura,* to my mind, can hardly be dismissed as merely disciplinary. For that matter, minor practices can be invested with important symbolic significance, and it is perhaps this symbolic meaning rather than the practices themselves that should be taken into account. Gautama Buddha himself is said to have emphasized practice rather than doctrine, and to have dissuaded his disciples from pondering over "metaphysical" issues. In a sense, if a way or method is the central tenet of a religious creed, controversies on matters of discipline have no less gravity than controversies on matters of dogma in a creed that stresses doctrine.

What seems to have conferred importance to what could appear to be mere differences in practice was the degree to which these could be taken to symbolize steadfastness to the original teachings of the Way as expressed in the *Vinaya* and to a distant past of pristine purity in the pursuit of salvation. The man who achieved enlightenment – the arhat – remained the ideal; someone who isolated himself for meditation and self-restraint, only temporarily joining the monastery, was understood to be closer to the ultimate goal. Whatever the actual realization of this ideal, it never totally disappeared as the ultimate yardstick for the evaluation of one's spiritual standing. Anti-institutional or rather a-institutional as it may have been, it also played an active part in the emergence of reformist monasteries, in the relation between these and other branches of the Sangha, and in the interaction between monks and laymen – although in no simple fashion. To say that something is the supreme ideal

---

[7] There is even disagreement concerning the extensive sectarian movement that beset Buddhism in the second century following Buddha's death. Some see doctrinal matters as bearing sole responsibility for it, others, rules of discipline. See Prebish, *Buddhist Monastic Discipline,* p. 27.

[8] See Mendelson, *Sangha and State in Burma,* p. 47.

does not necessarily mean that there is a consensus of feelings about it, nor that these feelings are monolithic. Some of the complexity involved is conveyed by the element of uncertainty introduced into the basic gift relationship with the emergence of individuals or branches of the Sangha dedicated to a better approximation of the pristine ideal.

The impact of virtuoso radicalism on the gift relationship

Not surprisingly, wealthy and established monasteries resented the appearance of reformist branches, not the least because laymen might prefer to give alms to those they considered truer to the ideal. The evidence, however, seems here to be somewhat contradictory. According to Malalgoda, for example, Silvat Samagama in eighteenth-century Sri Lanka diverted the flow of alms and indeed aroused the jealousy of other monasteries. Writing about an earlier period, though, Malalgoda also mentions that forest monks, although enjoying awe and respect for exemplifying the ultimate Buddhist ideals, did not attract gifts from kings and other laymen – a fact he attributes to their "renouncing of all social ties and their consequent lack of social significance."[9] In contrast, Geiger recounts that *tapassin* – a general term for radical ascetics – and in particular the major group of them, *pamsukulins,* were highly revered and presented with gifts in medieval Sri Lanka.[10] As for more modern times, Obeyesekere remarks that some laymen prefer to give alms to Amarapura monks, believed to lead a more ascetic life, and that hermit monks are so prestigious that, despite their isolation, their fame spreads and laymen pursue them with gifts to the most secluded spots.[11] This phenomenon seems to obtain in Burma as well, where magnificent monasteries stand abandoned, erected for some withdrawn holy man who has no intention of inhabiting them. Studies focusing upon contemporary Thailand, in contrast, have found that the most highly regarded monk is not the recluse dedicated to self-improvement, and reported varying degrees of resentment against monks who withdraw from communal life.[12] This in turn would seem to be partially contradicted by Tambiah's (more recent) report on the renewed "charisma" of forest

---

[9] Malalgoda, *Buddhism in Sinhalese Society,* pp. 19, 60.

[10] Geiger, *Culture of Ceylon,* p. 202.

[11] Obeyesekere, "Theodicy, Sin and Salvation," p. 38.

[12] Jane Bunnag, *Buddhist Monk, Buddhist Layman: A Study of Urban Monastic Organization in Central Thailand* (Cambridge University Press, 1973), p. 55; Mulder, *Merit, Monks and Motivation,* p. 41. This, incidentally, is consistent with Pfanner and Ingersoll's finding that Thai monks were more parish-oriented (vs. monastic-oriented) and more involved in village activities than Burmese monks. See D. Pfanner and J. Ingersoll, "Theravada Buddhism and Village Economic Behavior: A Burmese and Thai Comparison," *Journal of Asian Studies* 21 (1962): 341–61.

saints in Thailand, although the forest monks he deals with are also deeply involved in teaching both monks and laity – periodically coming out from seclusion and remoteness for that purpose.[13]

Attitudes toward the more zealous observers of the Way seem thus to vary greatly; whatever systematic pattern might underlie such variance, if any, cannot be assessed for want of a wider range of historical information. There is enough evidence, however, that religious virtuosi in Theravada Buddhist countries can be both revered for their ultra-orthodoxy and shunned for their deviance from what came to be accepted as the more orthodox path of renunciation, represented by monks remaining in closer touch with lay society. The ambivalence toward these radical virtuosi can probably be taken to reflect the reluctance of Buddhist laymen, and monks as well, to be reminded of the gap between them and Buddhism's supreme ideals. As such, it is a token of both their distance from the ideal and their awareness of it. Nonetheless, these radical virtuosi also represent a threat to the modus vivendi worked out between monks and laymen and between the Buddhist ideals and more worldly orientations. The institutionalized, highly socialized model of renunciation, after all, provides laymen with a relatively easy accumulation of merit and participation in the renouncer's pursuit of salvation, without interfering with their worldly activity. In deviating from it, radical virtuosi appear to disavow not only institutionalized renunciation, but also the division of labor that has become essential to the legitimacy and workings of the Theravada social order. More immediately, they also introduce an element of uncertainty in the pattern of exchange between monks and laymen, a break in the gift relationship that forms such an essential axis of what Werblowsky has suggestively called the "magnetic field of Sangha and laity."[14]

The ambivalence toward more radical, withdrawn virtuosi was never transformed, however, into outright and sustained condemnation, and radical virtuosi never came to embody a full-fledged heterodoxy. One can only speculate whether, given a stronger centralization and power of control, the Sangha might have forced them into such a position – as it occasionally did in conjunction with the king in the case of Mahayanist or Jainist tendencies. Furthermore, although radical virtuosi played a part in the emergence of reformist monasteries and sectarian branches of the Sangha, their influence never really overflowed beyond the Sangha into wider society: They never brought any change either in the basic pattern of interaction between Sangha and society or in worldly

---

[13] Tambiah, *Buddhist Saints of the Forest*. Tambiah, however, focuses on the eager interest in relics and amulets connected with these new forest saints, and does not explicitly relate to any effect this might have had on lay *dana*.

[14] Werblowsky, *Beyond Tradition and Modernity*, p. 92.

spheres of activity.[15] This could be seen as simply consistent with their tenacious adherence to the ideal of renunciation; yet a number of other factors seem to have played a part in blunting the potential of radical virtuosity as a source of actual dissent and/or religious change. Although an element of uncertainty was indeed introduced into the virtuoso–layman relationship, as suggested, what is crucial for our own purposes is that the basic segregative/interactive arrangement itself was never really challenged. In some cases, in fact, the more withdrawn virtuosi can even be said to have been instrumental in reviving rather than challenging it.

The conservative features of virtuoso radicalism

First, ascetic practices beyond those demanded in the *Vinaya* always retained an ambiguous doctrinal status.[16] Not only did the Buddha oppose systematic mortification, but connotations of schism and heresy were soon attached to the idea of greater ascetic rigor in the canonical precedent of Devadatta, who threatened to split the Sangha by advocating that additional ascetic practices (*duthanga*) and more reclusive living be made obligatory – which the Buddha refused to do.[17] *Duthanga* practices thus ever remained optional. It is not even clear that the way to *arhatship* necessarily passes through such practices, although they do appear in such eminently "orthodox" and influential texts as *Milinda's Questions* and Buddhagosa's *Visuddhimagga,* as an integral part of the mediator's progress.[18] Moreover, the stringency of *duthanga* practices was qualified by degrees of rigor (traditionally three), and by the fact that they were practiced only one or a few at a time.[19]

Second, the distinction between the way of mainstream village monks and the more radical, ascetic, reclusive, meditative way of forest monks did not necessarily crystallize into groupings of monks that are exclu-

---

[15] I have developed this point in I. F. Silber, "Dissent through Holiness: The Case of the Radical Renouncer in Theravada Buddhist Countries," *Numen* 18 (1981): 163–93.

[16] The ambiguous status of optional *duthanga* practices is also stressed in Carrithers, *Forest Monks of Sri Lanka,* p. 64, who thinks that *duthangas* were well established by the fourth or early third century BC, but that their significance and justification was by no means settled until the beginning of the Christian era. The doctrinal status of ascetic practices and, more generally, the institutional position of ascetic-leaning *bhikkhus,* has also been amply discussed in Tambiah, *Buddhist Saints of the Forest,* pp. 18–19.

[17] *Cullavagga* VII, 3:15, *Vinaya Texts,* part 3, p. 253.

[18] See *Milinda's Questions,* translated by I. B. Horner (London: Luzac, 1964), vol. 2, pp. 201–77; *Visuddhimagga,* translated by Bhikkhu Nanamoli (Berkeley: Samshala Publications, 1976), ch. 2.

[19] See Tambiah, *Buddhist Saints of the Forest,* pp. 33–5.

sively one or the other.[20] Dichotomies such as forest monks versus village monks, and learning versus practice, often overlapped in actuality and did not produce exclusive groupings of monks so much as two kinds of emphases and orientations. Many sects had both branches; indeed any monastic community could have *bhikkhus* who favored one orientation or the other. Moreover, monasteries or branches formed in reaction to the practices of the village mainstream monkhood were usually unable to sustain their ascetic aspirations and soon manifested internal cleavages reproducing the original dichotomies.[21]

Third, forest monkhood was far from anarchic and unstructured. This is most evident in Sri Lanka, where village monks and forest dwellers became equally recognized, official divisions of the Sangha, endowed with the same organizational structure and equally centralized control upon the ordination process. In some cases, as clearly illustrated by the nineteenth-century Burmese Shwegyin sect,[22] forest monkhood actually displayed a tendency to self-structuring and organization superior to that of village monks. In general, most forest monks remained within recognized lines of ordination shared with more lenient branches, of which they were not necessarily adamant critics even if they themselves opted for what they deemed the purer, better way. Those who remained outside any such recognized lineage of ordination may be seen, by implication, as more critical of the more established Sangha. However, it is also worth noting that there is no evidence, in the history of Theravada religious radicalism, for the potentially much more rebellious rejection of the very principle of the *upasampada,* the lineage of ordination as cardinal to monastic purity.[23]

Although it stands out as a type of protest unknown in the traditional era, even the rising of the Amarapura fraternity – challenging the Kandyan monopoly on ordination in eighteenth-century Sri Lanka – is far from entailing a radical deviation from established patterns. The refusal of chief monks in Kandy to grant higher ordination to those monks not of Goyigama caste – a refusal endorsed by the king if clearly contrary to the *Vinaya* – set off a bitter conflict, further amplified through polarization in terms of caste hierarchy and regional origins (low-caste monks from the coastal regions opposing the inland Kandy

[20] See Gombrich, *Theravada Buddhism*, p. 157; Mendelson, *Sangha and State in Burma*, p. 46.

[21] Mendelson, *Sangha and State in Burma*, pp. 53, 165.

[22] For a detailed account of the Shwegyin sect, see Ferguson, "Quest for Legitimation."

[23] Even recent attempts to undermine the differentiation between monks and laymen and give the laity much greater access to meditative practices are not the same as saying that a monk can ordain himself or does not need ordination at all.

Goyigama establishment). The Amarapura protest is unique in the history of monasticism in Sri Lanka in that it did not depend on the king of Kandy to make its reformist activity a success, and stood against a royal decree – the first time the right of secular authorities to regulate the affairs of the order had even been questioned. Yet as Malalgoda notes, it did not involve principled opposition to secular interference, but rather embodied, more simply, "a fraternity of the traditionally disinherited who challenged the right of the establishment, both religious and political, to keep them permanently excluded."[24] Furthermore, although it arose mainly in protest against caste exclusivism, and was indeed more heterogeneous in caste composition, the Amarapura soon underwent a process of segmentation in which caste distinctions reemerged to play an important role.

Fourth, forest monks became closely involved with the political establishment. As Bechert notes, it was usually in the king's interest to side with the stricter sections of the Sangha, precisely because they were more strongly committed to keeping at a distance from political and economic activities.[25] Kings were also interested in maintaining forest monks as a useful instrument in eventual campaigns of purification. On the other hand, kingly promotion of centralization and opposition to segmentation could hamper a fuller development of centrifugal tendencies among forest monkhood. A salient example of this complex relationship is King Parakramabahu's (1153–86) appeal to Mahakassapa, the leading elder of a withdrawn but large forest monastery, to assist him in reforming and unifying the Sangha. As Carrithers points out, this was the first time in Sri Lanka's history that the king's power actually reached within the Sangha to impose centralization and new regulations (some of them implicitly diverging from the *Vinaya*), enforced by "the double stamp of royal authority and forest-dwelling strictness."[26]

It is no less significant that the merging of these two distinct "reforming" impulses, despite the deviations from *Vinaya* regulations, is not explicitly acknowledged as such in the *katikavatas,* or new codices for the Sangha. This is in line with a characteristic tendency of Sinhalese texts, in Carrithers's words, "to present themselves as of a piece with the Vinaya texts," and to introduce "a deep polysemy into the key concep-

---

24 Malalgoda, *Buddhism in Sinhalese Society,* p. 102.
25 Bechert,"EinigeFragen der Religionssoziologie und Struktur des sudasiatischen Buddhismus."
26 Carrithers, *Forest Monks,* pp. 172–3. One may note that Mahakassapa is believed to have embodied all possible and conflicting aspirations for a monk (p. 174). This is perhaps the closest analogy to Saint Bernard in the Christian setting. The latter, however, is usually presented as a contradictory, paradoxical figure, whereas no stress is placed on any sort of inner contradictions in Mahakassapa's image.

tions of the Sangha and of purity," making it "possible to espouse quite different visions of reform in practically the same words."[27] In the process of close association with kingly reform, in other words, forest monkhood's reforming discourse lost some of its edge, some of its more autonomous and distinctive potential for criticism and dissent.

We should, however, avoid a simplistic association between reforming tendencies and strong kingship, perceiving monkhood as centralized, hierarchical, and reformed under strong kings, and decentralized, unorganized, and decadent under weak kings:[28] A trend to decentralization of the Sangha could also correspond, as happened in Burma, for example, to the urge to form small, self-governed monastic communities away from and in reaction against strong government intervention.[29]

Another important aspect of the role of forest monks in the Theravada social order is their role in colonizing and civilizing the forest frontiers and attracting settlements, thus enlarging the kingdom and strengthening it on the periphery.[30] However, as stressed especially by Tambiah, forest monks played an even more crucial role at the center, when there was need (in times of dissension, wars, epidemics, droughts, rebellions, and so forth) "to recharge and fortify monarchical legitimacy and creative powers by tapping the purity and charisma of the untarnished forest ascetics. Their very distance from everyday mundane affairs, their disinterest in ephemeral gains, and their alleged capacity to act in detachment in the spirit of cosmic love (*metta*), guaranteed their ability to replenish and revitalize the realm, whenever the center could not hold."[31] That this was a recurrent pattern is all the more impressive in light of the fact that there is certainly no doctrinal encouragement for the Sangha to play that type of role, and in light of the fact that the "forest" option, traditionally, precisely implies insisting upon distance from lay society. In other words, radical virtuosi played a crucial part in revitalizing, reestablishing, or even disseminating further the classical pattern, rather than changing or expanding its definition, seeking structurally different arrangements, or even simply reaffirming the renouncers' social and spriritual autonomy.

Perhaps the most important factor blunting any real potential for dissent or innovation on the part of the more "radical" and withdrawn forest monks, I submit, was that they did not necessarily try to escape, but only to minimize their dependence on and interaction with the laity.

[27] Ibid., p. 74.
[28] See Kemper, "Reform and Segmentation," 28.
[29] See Mendelson, *Sangha and State in Burma.*
[30] See Tambiah, *Buddhist Saints of the Forest,* p. 77. This role has also been noted, for example, in thirteenth-century Burma. See Mendelson, *Sangha and State in Burma,* p. 47.
[31] Tambiah, *Buddhist Saints of the Forest.*

A significant factor here is the fact that wealth was never understood as corrupting as such, but on the contrary, was seen as the legitimate instrument of lay merit making and a valid recognition of monks' superior spiritual status.[32] Whatever corruption of the monkhood might take place, as forcefully stressed by Kemper in the specific case of Sri Lanka, it was not perceived as resulting from wealth in itself, but from failing discipline in the use of wealth, dangerously blurring the distinction between monks and laymen.[33] At no point did a Christianlike ideal of radical monastic poverty emerge, which might have inspired a radical criticism and potential transformation of the traditional pattern of interaction between monks and laymen.

Even more essentially, forest monks are not known to have ever voiced any principled opposition to the basic cleavage between virtuosi and laymen, or to have envisioned any significant change to the usual pattern of interaction between monks and laymen. This may perhaps help explain why the more radical virtuosi left no distinctive spiritual or ethical impact on the laity. It is striking, as Obeyesekere notes, that divisions in the Sangha, even where they were endemic, "were of greater importance to the monastic world than to the laity: unlike Christian sects and denominations, the several Buddhist fraternities had very little influence on lay religiosity, and hardly affected the cultural unity of Buddhism."[34] Nor did the laity itself ever really contest the legitimacy of the Sangha in its more "domesticated," lay-oriented forms, even when acknowledging, and at times actually displaying, preference for the more withdrawn, purer forms.

Divergent forms of religious radicalism

We must still consider the occasional emergence of a type of holy men who might seem to diverge from the dominant pattern already described. Such holy men are not necessarily ordained *bhikkhus,*[35] but are related to the forest tradition to the extent that they generally display some form of intensified virtuoso asceticism and go through a phase of eremitic withdrawal. They also display, however, a more expansive,

---

[32] For a rich examination of the Theravada attitude to wealth, see R. F. Sizemore and D. K. Swearer, (eds.) *Ethics, Wealth and Salvation.*

[33] See Kemper, "Wealth and Reformation in Sinhalese Buddhist Monasticism."

[34] Obeyesekere, "Religion and Polity," 629.

[35] *Weikzas,* for example, who are the active leaders of Burmese millenarian groups (*gaings*), are not monks as a rule, even if these groups may include some *bhikkhu* members. See J. P. Ferguson and E. M. Mendelson, "Masters of the Buddhist Occult: The Burmese *Weikzas,*" *Contemporary Asian Studies* 16 (1981): 62–80; E. M. Mendelson, "A Messianic Buddhist Association in Upper Burma," *Bulletin of the School of Oriental and African Studies* 14 (1961): 560–80.

outreaching type of charisma somehow at variance with what has been seen until now. One may distinguish here, on the basis of a cluster of recent works,[36] three distinct (but sometimes combined) types of holy men: those forming the foci of active magical cults catering to the immediate, personal needs of their followers; those becoming meditation masters, attracting a network of disciples and often spreading the methods and benefits of meditation among the laity; and those related to various types of millenarian formations.

All evidence for this type of holy men is taken from the last two centuries only, however, and thus technically lies beyond the boundaries of the present study. Their emergence seems to have been triggered in some places by conditions – such as economic crises, or local and ethnic protests against the central religious and political establishment – that may have obtained as well in the traditional era, but have formed the typical background of revivalist reactions to the advent of modern colonial rule in many other settings as well. To that extent, and despite the undeniable continuity with past ascetic and popular Buddhistic traditions displayed by this type of charismatic religious figures, one should be cautious in presuming the existence of fully analogous equivalents in traditional Theravada Buddhism.

To some extent, one may find in this type of holy men, and in the militant millenarian movements even more especially, the seeds of a centrifugal religious radicalism that, when combined with popular appeal, might verge on heterodox and political protest – a form of "counterculture or counterstructure to domesticated organized Buddhism."[37] On the whole, however, these trends tend to represent a basically peripheral phenomenon with rather weak staying power. Moreover, even the utopian visions they carried with them were not radically different from those moving the central, traditional vision of an ideal Buddhist polity, focusing as they usually did on the image of an ideal ruler caring for the karmic and/ or nibbanic aspirations of his subjects.

Most crucial for our own purposes, millennial Buddhism, again, leaves the traditional virtuoso–layman structure basically untouched. In its militant phase, it might tend to fuse renouncer and ruler (since the ruler-to-be first appears or is announced as an ascetic virtuoso of extraordinary powers), which in the more common state of things are neatly separated. Nevertheless, as Tambiah stresses, and as is amply developed in Chapter 3, this convergence at the apex of the principles of world

---

[36] Carrithers, *Forest Monks of Sri Lanka;* C. Keyes, "Millenialism, Theravada Buddhism and Thai Society," *Journal of Asian Studies* 36 (1976): 283–303; K. Malalgoda, "Millenialism in Relation to Buddhism," *Comparative Studies in Society and History* 12 (1970): 424–41; Tambiah, *Buddhist Saints of the Forest;* Ferguson and Mendelson, "Masters of the Buddhist Occult."

[37] Tambiah, *Buddhist Saints of the Forest,* p. 319.

renunciation and world ruling is already a characteristic of the interpenetrating canonical perceptions of Buddha and kingship, at least at the
level of images and metaphors.[38] Moreover, such fusion of the otherworldly and worldly principles never spread to lower levels of the social
and spiritual ladder,[39] to the average layman and monk, whose duties
and definitions were left untouched.

In sum, the element of protest existing in early Buddhism (reacting in
particular against Brahmanic ritualism and divine dependence) did not
have significant historical ramifications in the form of protest movements or revolutionary orientations. Neither did the significant antistructural connotations attached in Buddhism, as in all Indian religions, to the notion of the forest – the symbol of chaos against the
known order of settled society[40] – become a lever for actual dissent and/
or change. This relative absence of antistructural trends of dissent may
be viewed by some as a sign of stagnation, of an inability to transcend
established forms of social order. I prefer, however, to interpret it as the
result of an exceptionally successful "harnessing" of chaos to settled
order, of monastery to village and forest to capital, through what formed
a most resilient, ubiquitous, and flexible mechanism, the virtuoso–
layman relational structure.

[38] Ibid., p. 320.
[39] Swearer's study of the "layman extraordinaire" in northern Thailand offers
     fascinating corroboration of this careful disconnection between the lay and
     monkish roles as they coexist in individuals with outstanding credentials in both
     roles: Although forming a type of lay religious leadership, their function does
     not go beyond providing proper mediation in the various traditional forms of
     interaction between monkhood and laity. See D. K. Swearer, "The Role of the
     Layman Extraordinaire in Northern Thai Buddhism," *Journal of the Siam Soci-
     ety* 64 (1976): 151–68.
[40] See Thapar, "Householder and the Renouncer," p. 190. In Thapar's view, "inter-
     woven with the notion of exile and of going out was that of creating or starting a
     new order."

Part III
Virtuosi and society in medieval Catholicism

6 Ideological groundings: plurality and conditional exchange

When we examine the ideological premises of virtuosity and of the virtuoso–society relation in Western Christianity, the overriding fact, in contrast to Theravada Buddhism, is how ambiguous the doctrinal status of monasticism originally was. Undeniably, the Gospels include both a powerful world-rejecting strand and very strong "virtuoso orientations," that is, orientations encouraging the emergence of religious rigorism and perfectionism. However, neither monasticism itself nor a definite, specific pattern of interaction with the laity enjoyed unequivocal doctrinal anchoring. Much of the ambiguity in the theological status of monasticism may be traced to a Christian mode of managing the tension between otherworldly and worldly orientations very different from that characteristic of Theravada Buddhism. As we shall see, in fact, Christianity may even be said to pose serious obstacles to the type of virtuoso–society relation found in Theravada Buddhism.

Notwithstanding the doctrinal ambiguities and obstacles, monastic life did come to represent the foremost ideal and the surest way to salvation for many Christians. The relationship between virtuosi and the rest of the Church gradually received ideological articulation. Underpinning this ideological incorporation of monasticism, however, was a conception of the Christian collective, and of religious authority, that has no equivalent in canonical Buddhism and can even be said to go against its grain.

Doctrinal open-enedness

Christian monasticism made its first appearance in Egypt and Palestine toward the end of the third century, and is thought to have emerged partly as a continuation of the spirit of martyrdom fostered by Roman persecution and partly in protest of the Church's increasing involvement with the world and relaxation of spiritual standards, both drastically accelerated following Constantine's establishment of Christianity in 313.[1] The emergence of monasticism, however, cannot be understood

[1] See H. B. Workman, *The Evolution of the Monastic Ideal* (Boston: Beacon, 1962), pp. 6–11 for a stress (by a Methodist historian) on the element of protest at the origin of monasticism. This is in contrast with the stress on continuity with the early Church in, for example, C. H. Lawrence, *Medieval Monasticism: Forms of Religious Life in Western Europe in the Middle Ages* (London: Longman Group, 1984).

119

independently of preceding developments through which a total sexual renunciation (in itself not necessarily enacted in a monastic framework) gradually became a widely acclaimed feature of the early Christian world.[2] Given that monasticism was originally a lay movement, at any rate, it is remarkable that monastic life rapidly became the ideal for some of the most influential intellectual figures in late antique and early medieval Christianity.[3] For its advocates, monasticism constituted the best means of attaining eternal salvation and gave rise, as such, to a whole chain of interwoven and evocative themes. As the earthly framework for the perpetual praise of God, it represented the anticipation of the heavenly life to come, or *vita angelica*. It was also believed to provide the possibility of a second baptism, of constant penance and purification from sin in a lifelong martyrdom. For Augustine, monasticism was the fullest possible realization of the City of God in the here and now. However, the dominant motif perhaps was the striving for *imitatio Christi* – the emulation of or even union with Christ's suffering and martyrdom in the hope of thereby approximating his relationship with God.[4]

Jesus himself offered the prototypical example by his own absolute chastity and poverty. The apostles, in the description of the first community of Jerusalem, provided an important model of brotherhood in shared poverty. Moreover, the Christian Scriptures repeatedly propound the search for perfection through the practice of ascetic virtues such as chastity, poverty, meekness, and renunciation of family ties:

Be ye therefore perfect, even as your father which is in heaven is perfect. (Matt. 5:48)

If thou will be perfect, go and sell what thou hast, and give to the poor, and thou shalt have treasure in heaven: and come and follow me. (Matt. 19:21)

All men cannot receive this saying, save they to whom it is given . . . and there be eunuchs which have made themselves eunuchs for the kingdom of heaven's sake. He that is able to receive it, let him receive it. (Matt. 19:11–12)

If anyone comes to me and does not hate his father and mother, and wife and children, and brethren and sisters, yes, and his own life also, he cannot be my disciple. (Luke 14:26)

[2] For a superb and now indispensable exploration of this process, see P. Brown, *The Body and Society: Men, Women and Sexual Renunciation in Early Christianity* (New York: Columbia University Press, 1988).

[3] On the early intellectual and institutional support of monasticism, see G. Ladner, *The Idea of Reform: Its Import on Christian Thought and Action in the Age of the Fathers* (New York: Harper & Row, 1967).

[4] For the early development and interconnectedness of these various themes, see M. Viller, "Martyre et perfection," *Revue d'Ascèse et de Mystique,* 6 (1925): 3–25, and idem, "Le martyre et l'ascèse," ibid., 105–42; Ladner, *Idea of Reform,* pp. 319–73. On Augustine's conception of monasticism in particular, see ibid., pp. 350 ff.

These and other classical loci of the ascetic tradition attest to the undeniable existence of a strongly perfectionist and world-rejecting strand in the Gospels.[5] Yet what quickly came to be perceived as the dominant axis in Christian teaching does not revolve around small and insulated communities of virtuoso ascetics,[6] but rather around a universal Church and ethic, that is, norms of faith, love, and charity incumbent upon all within the framework of a hierarchy dispensing the sacraments. The explicit endorsement of marriage, as legitimate and even indissoluble, clearly places limits on the isolated mortification of celibate collectivities.[7] The issues of chastity, virginity, and marriage were often at the crux of the controversies over perfection and the distinction between "two sorts of Christian," "two sorts of law," and so on. A distinction between the perfect and the ordinary Christian, and between precepts (for all) and counsels of perfection (for a minority) already appears in the patristic literature,[8] but it never led to the articulation of a full-fledged dual standard as it did in Buddhism. Christianity's strongly inclusive, universal Church-like leanings could only clash with, and prevent the full blossoming of, the perfectionist, elitist tendencies also in its midst. In time, mainstream Christianity came in fact to favor a rather "antiperfectible" stance – denying the possibility of total sinlessness in life and man's capacity to perfect himself without the help of divine grace – a stance most forcefully expressed in the reaction to the Pelagian

---

5 See here the classical controversy around Schweitzer's thesis of Jesus' teachings as "interim ethos." See M. Werner, *The Formation of the Christian Dogma* (Boston: Beacon, 1957).

6 On the early opposition to monks, see L. Gougaud, "Les critiques formulées contre les premiers moines d'Occident," *Revue Mabillon* 24 (1943): 145–63; H. R. Bitterman, "The Beginning of the Struggle between the Regular and Secular Clergy," in J. L. Cole and E. N. Anderson (eds.), *Medieval and Historiographical Studies in Honor of James Westfale Thompson* (Chicago: University of Chicago Press, 1938), pp. 19–26; P. Rousseau, *Ascetics, Authority and the Church in the Age of Jerome* (Oxford: Oxford University Press, 1978), pp. 9–11.

7 Paul became the crucial source on this issue: 1 Cor. 7:25–8: "Now Concerning virgins, I have no commandment of the Lord: but I give counsel, as having obtained mercy of the Lord, to be faithful. I think therefore that this is good for the present necessity: that it is good for man so to be. . . . But if thou take a wife, thou hast not sinned."

8 See D. Heyd, *Supererogation: Its Status in Ethical Theory* (Cambridge University Press, 1982), pp. 19 ff. The first explicit allusion to that distinction appears in the second half of the fourth century in Saint Ambrose's discussion of chastity; see Ambrose, *Concerning Widows* (Washington, D.C.: Catholic University of America Press, 1953), pp. 341–52; see also, soon after, Augustine, in connection with the story of the rich man (*Letters,* 157; *Holy Virginity,* 14). Ambrose further identifies the precepts with law and the counsels with grace in R. J. Deferrari (ed.), *Treatises on Marriage and Other Subjects* (New York: Fathers of the Church, 1955). The higher standard is for those who are under grace and the lower for those under law.

heresy.[9] Ironically, this position reflects lesser faith in the perfectibility of man here and now than found in the more "otherworldly" original Buddhism.[10] The issue was never fully resolved, however, and confrontation between so-called Pelagian and Augustinian views on perfectibility and on the related issue of predestination has had momentous importance throughout the history of Christianity.[11] Monasticism cannot, moreover, be systematically aligned with either side of the controversy, since one could not hold a Pelagian or Augustinian view of monasticism itself. Augustine himself, taken to represent the antiperfectible stance, was a fervent supporter of monasticism, and did believe that the *summum bonum,* communion with God, could be enjoyed within this life.

Another factor diminishing the centrality of the distinction between perfect and ordinary Christians was the overshadowing priority of the distinction between clergy and laity, imposing itself from the beginning of the third century on,[12] where the criterion was not the search for perfection but the administration of the sacraments. Many saw the priest as the epitome of Christian life, superior to the monk, who safely kept his distance from the world's entanglements and temptations.[13] In addition, the definitions of both the way to perfection and of the Church itself remained ambiguous, offering a wide range of possible interpretations and historical developments. Monasticism represented only one of the possible paths to perfection, and was torn between different definitions of the monastic ideal itself (much more so than Theravada monasticism). Early Christian doctrine did not spell out any guidelines for the interaction between virtuosi and laity, thus leaving the otherworldly, ascetic strand in a situation of doctrinal and practical open-endedness.[14]

[9] See Passmore, *Perfectibility of Man,* especially pp. 94–148; Ladner, *Idea of Reform,* especially pp. 319–40; R. Newton Flew, *The Idea of Perfection in Christian Theology* (New York: Humanities Press, 1968); also, Heyd, *Supererogation,* ch. 2 especially.

[10] See this volume, Part II, pp. 41–2.

[11] For the history of this tension up to its modern expressions, see especially Passmore, *Perfectibility of Man.* It should be noted that the notion of perfection did not necessarily carry the absolute tinge normally associated with the word in common usage. Ambrose, for example, would distinguish between two forms of perfection, ordinary vs. highest; the one in accordance with human powers, the other corresponding to the perfection of the world to come.

[12] See A. Faivre, "Clercs/laïcs: histoire d'une frontière," *Revue des Sciences Religieuses* 57 (1983): 195–220.

[13] This argument is already used by John Chrysostom, but he also believes that except for marriage, the Christian who lived in the world had the same obligation as the monk: detachment in the world. See Ladner, *Idea of Reform,* p. 126.

[14] On this uncertainty and open-endedness of the ascetic tradition in its earliest stage, see Ladner, *Idea of Reform,* pp. 320–1; Rousseau, *Ascetics, Authority, and the Church,* chs. 2,3, and 4.

The interpenetration of otherworldly and worldly orientations

At the root of this complexity and open-endedness lies Christianity's characteristic intertwining of other- or outworldliness with worldlier orientations: otherworldly not only in the general sense of supramundane or transcendent, but also in the more specific sense of a strong world-negating, world-devaluing tendency; and worldly in the countervailing tendency to invest the world, man, and man's institutions in the world with religious value. This intertwining is already present in the doctrine of Christ himself as truly and fully both man and God – a paradox intrinsic to the Christian "mystery."[15] However, it is also at work in such basic concepts as the Kingdom of God, the City of God, and of course the Church as the universal communion of the faithful and the body of Christ itself.[16] The very verses on which the foundations of the Church were laid are striking in this respect: "Thou art Peter and upon this rock I will build my church . . . and I will give unto thee the keys of the kingdom of heaven: and whatever thou shalt bind on earth shall be bound in heaven; and whatsoever thou shalt loose on earth shall be loosed in heaven." (Matt 16:18–19)

The history of Christianity is in fact often related as a gradual "unpacking" of this otherworldly/worldly Christian "bundle," with the progressive increase of worldly orientations and concomitant weakening of otherworldliness.[17] The original strength of the otherworldly strand, however, is open to debate. Louis Dumont accords it both ideological and historical primacy.[18] Ideologically, the more worldly orientations are seen as subordinated to, and encompassed by, the otherworldly ones in a hierarchy determined by their relative relevance to salvation. This original ideological structure is not very different, in his mind,

[15] For a succinct review of these trends, see E. Peters, *Heresy and Authority in Medieval Europe* (Philadelphia: University of Pennsylvania Press, 1978), introduction.

[16] See, for example, Y. Congar, "Concepts et images de l'église" in J. Congar, *L'ecclésiologie du haut Moyen-Age* (Paris: Cerf, 1958). For an emphasis on the worldly implications of variant conceptions of the Church, the kingdom, and Christ in early Christian history, see J. F. Gager, *Kingdom or Community: The Social World of Early Christianity* (Englewood Cliffs, N.J.: Prentice-Hall, 1975) and E. Pagels, *The Gnostic Gospels* (New York: Random House, 1979).

[17] See for example, R. N. Bellah, "Religious Evolution," *American Sociological Review* 29 (1964): 358–74. Such a conception also tends to assume, however, the myth of a golden age of otherworldly religiosity. See M. Hill's overview in *A Sociology of Religion* (London: Heinemann, 1973), pp. 228–51.

[18] L. Dumont, "A Modified View of our Origins: The Christian Origins of Modern Individualism," *Religion* 12 (1982): 1–27, followed by Bellah, Burridge, and Robertson, "Responses to Louis Dumont"; and Eisenstadt, "Transcendental Visions."

from that obtaining in Indian religions. The world is not condemned (although the temptation to do so, distinctive of the gnostic heresies, would recur in the history of Christianity), and there is definite latitude in worldly matters. Historically, Dumont sees the latter strengthening of worldly orientations essentially as the result of external events that, from Constantine on, influenced Christianity's gradual deviation from its original ideological structure.

Somehow contradicting his own argument, however, Dumont also stresses the transition between the out-worldly and the inner-worldly, "the incarnation of value," as lying at the very essence of Christianity. Indeed, it is rather this uneasy mediation of otherworldliness and worldliness – as well as of the corresponding antitheses of flesh/spirit, law/grace, Church/world, that inform Christian thought from the start[19] – that will receive emphasis here, contra Dumont, as an essential rather than contingent feature of Christianity, of critical importance for the history of Christian virtuosity. The Christian interpenetration of worldliness and otherworldliness is radically different from their neatly segregated and hierarchized coexistence in canonical Buddhism. It is also further deepened by the eschatological-chiliastic strand in Christianity, which invested the here and now of the primitive Church with millenarian expectation; the world and history were given soteriological meaning and a future direction,[20] in sharp contrast to the dominant Buddhist conception of the passage of time as only another aspect of samsara and of the general decay of things.[21]

[19] I refer here to Caspary's analysis of the dyadic structure characteristic of the classical Pauline pairs – flesh/spirit, law/grace, church/world, letter/spirit, etc. – where the two poles are "not merely complementary" but truly opposed. Confirming the importance, for the understanding of Christian thought, of the strain to mediate between them, Caspary notes that this dyadic structure coexists with a triadic structure, stemming from the messianic conception of Christ, in which regard "the tension inherited from Jewish apocalyptic thought between this world or the present age (ha-olam ha-zeh) and the next world or Messianic Age (ha-olam ha-bah), though still essential, was no longer quite enough." See G. E. Caspary, *Politics and Exegesis: Origen and the Two Swords* (Berkeley and Los Angeles: University of California Press, 1979), especially p. 118.

[20] There is, however, much debate concerning the nature, extent, and survival of this eschatological dimension in Christian theology. See Werner, *Formation of the Christian Dogma*. For some recent discussions of early Christianity as a millenarian or eschatological movement, see Gager, *Kingdom or Community;* S. R. Isenberg, "Millenarism in Greco-Roman Palestine," *Religion* 4 (1974): 26–46.

[21] Limited historical recording and the sporadic development of millenarian expectations and movements in Theravada Buddhism do not contradict the overriding pessimistic conception of time and the fact that salvation (as opposed to merit) can be attained only through the utter escape from worldly involvements and from the here and now. See Chai-Shin Yu, *Early Buddhism and Christianity: A Comparative Study of the Founders' Authority, the Community and the Discipline* (Delhi: Motilal Banarsidass, 1981), which contrasts early Buddhism and Christianity as "gnostic" vs. "eschatological."

If the ideological hierarchy noted by Dumont is indeed present in early and medieval Christianity, it is basically an unstable and fragile arrangement, constantly in need of reassertion to counter the basic ambiguities of the Christian message. Troeltsch's classic interpretation of this inner plurality or multivocality of Christianity distinguished a variety of tendencies – ascetic, secular, and theocratic – manifest as early as the Gospels; at times contradictory, these tendencies continued to exist side by side, eventually becoming bound in a "cosmos of mutual recognition and mutual help."[22] Within this framework, moreover, the ascetic tendency itself did not necessarily develop in only one specific direction, but could become oriented to a great variety of ends – the open-endedness referred to earlier: "Neither in theory nor in practice has asceticism evolved in a logical sense; it has simply grown out of the most divergent and contradictory ideas, and while these ideas have been to some extent fused with each other, the system contains within itself very varied possibilities."[23]

The intertwining of and unavoidable tension between the various inner tendencies of Christianity is acutely reflected in the search for perfection itself, ridden from the outset with basic dilemmas in determining the relative emphasis and precise meaning to be given to such key motifs of the ascetic life as contemplation, mortification, poverty, learning, good works, pastoral functions, individual prayer, liturgical functions, and manual labor. Underlying these dilemmas was the perennial tension between the lesser and greater otherworldly tendencies just mentioned, often couched in terms of the tension between a *vita contemplativa* and a *vita activa* that, ideally, should somehow be combined: "No man ought to be so completely inactive as not to think of his neighbor's advantage, nor so active as to neglect the contemplation of God."[24]

Much would depend on the terms of combination, however, and on the precise definition of the *vita activa*. A related but distinct question involved the preeminence of an inward- versus outward-oriented form of life in the search for perfection: In particular, was it enough to exercise the altruistic Christian virtues within the monastic community itself – Basil, for example, even considered that the monastic community was so self-sufficient that it needed neither secular clergy nor laity[25] – or should one turn to the outside, secular world? The same issue would arise from attempts to assess the relative value of eremitism

---

[22] E. Troeltsch, *The Social Teachings of the Christian Church* (New York: Harper, 1960), especially pp. 238–54.

[23] Ibid., p. 244.

[24] Augustine, *The City of God against the Pagans*, Book 19, ch. 19. Edited with translation by W. C. Greene (Cambridge, Mass.: Harvard University Press, 1960), p. 203.

[25] See Flew, *Idea of Perfection in Christian Theology*, p. 177.

and cenobitism: For many, the fact that the former did not allow for the enactment of the other-oriented Christian virtues made it automatically inferior to cenobitic monasticism.[26]

Monastic rules – such as those left by Basil, Pachomius, Columbanus, Caesarius, and Augustine, and the Master's Rule from which the most influential, that of Saint Benedict (480–550), is believed to be in great part derived – soon came to regularize the renunciatory life. Benedict's Rule would increasingly provide monasticism – mainly from the eighth century, when it reached a broad scope of diffusion with the backing of the Carolingian kings – with a quasi-dominant normative framework.[27] The rule itself, however, was not always unambiguous, and received varying interpretations, often in the name of a return to a "purer" enactment of its original injunctions. The issue of poverty in particular, with its various possible interpretations, received new meaning and prominence from the eleventh to the thirteenth centuries with the strong surge of eremitic and apostolic movements throughout that period, and the mendicant orders in the thirteenth century, all undermining the supremacy of the traditional Benedictine model. The Benedictine Rule, clearly, was not able to prevent the emergence of other trends, within and without the monastic world, each emphasizing different elements from the range of ideological and institutional options facing the ascetic life.

Division of labor and explicit exchange

In time, Christian theologians, too, developed conceptions approximating a double standard, articulating the relationship between virtuosi and others in terms of a division of labor that assigned specific functions to virtuosi within the collective of the Church. For example, monks were very early perceived as "crying on the sins of the world," "expiating the sins of others," and "praying for the world,"[28] all implying a notion of intercession and indirect penance, or, in Troeltsch's terms, "vicarious

---

[26] The traditional cleavage on this issue is between Cassian, for whom the solitary life is ultimately superior to the common life, and Basil, followed by Chrysostom and Jerome, for whom the communal, cenobitic ideal is superior to the solitary, individual one. For Benedict, eremitic life is the superior, end stage – destined for the very few only – to whom cenobitism is only the preparatory school. Aquinas, too, conceived the solitary ideal as ultimately superior.

[27] Cassian's *De Institutis Coenobium* was also very influential in the early shaping of the monastic idea, even if he did not write a rule; see J. Cassien, *Les institutions cénobitiques* (Paris: Cerf, 1965). The Rule of Saint Augustine, dating in its oldest form from the eighth century, was adopted and modified in the eleventh century by the new order of regular canons.

[28] Viller, "Le martyre et l'ascèse," p. 129; Lawrence, *Medieval Monasticism*, pp. 61–2; G. Tellenbach, *Church, State and Society at the Time of the Investiture Contest* (Oxford: B. Blackwell 1940), pp. 46–7.

oblation," which appears as the direct extension of notions originally applied to the relation between Christ and the world:

> The idea of vicarious repentance and achievement is really a living category of religious thought; the vicarious offering of Christ both as a punishment and as a source of merit is only a special instance of a general conception. . . . Thus the duty of those who live "in the world" towards the whole is that of preserving and procreating the race – a task in which ascetics cannot share, while they for their part have the duty of showing forth the ideal in an intensified form, and of rendering service through intercession, penitence and the acquisition of merit. This is the reason for the enormous gifts and endowments to monasteries; men wanted to make certain of their own part in the oblation offered by monasticism.[29]

This notion was expanded by scholastic theology into a full-blown model of the "circulation of grace" between virtuosi – not only monks but also saints, often but not always of monastic background[30] – and the rest of the faithful. The two key principles were the transferability of merit from one person to another and from the living to the dead, and the mediation of salvation through the Church – a tenet altogether alien to canonical Buddhism. In short, the holier, more virtuous members of the Church accumulate a treasure of supererogatory merits; it is the task of the Church to manage this treasure and redistribute it to the less virtuous so as to help them to salvation.

This theory, it must be noted, had the advantage of acknowledging the special standing, and even superiority, of virtuosi, while at the same time sustaining the key position of the secular clergy in the regulation and supervision of lay access to the means of grace. It was certainly more compatible with the clergy's interests to activate this "circulation of grace" than to let monks and saints increasingly concentrate in their hands a role of intercession potentially threatening the ecclesiastical monopoly on the mediation of salvation.

Essential to the development of this model was the idea already present in Augustine that the prayers of the living could improve a dead person's status in the next world, a notion that culminated in the Cluniac order's institution of All Souls Day to help the dead.[31] Moreover, one did not have necessarily to expiate one's sins oneself: It was a common practice, fully endorsed by the Church, for those who wished and could afford to, either to substitute the amount of money deemed equivalent to the inflicted penance, or to find someone who, for a payment, would fulfill the penance in one's stead.[32] Reliance on the intercessory value of

---

[29] Troeltsch, *Social Teachings*, p. 242.

[30] See Vauchez, *La sainteté en Occident.*

[31] In later formulations of the purgatory (an idea shown by Jacques Le Goff not to be fully explicit until the twelfth century) the dead could also intercede for the living.

[32] For the full analysis of these trends, see J. Le Goff, *La naissance du purgatoire* (Paris: Gallimard, 1981).

the monastic order was thus deeply related to broader notions and practices of transmutation and absolution of penance, which it long supported and complemented. On the other hand, increased or easier access to modes of penance and absolution mediated by the secular clergy could also compete with and eventually lessen the role of the monastic order in the overall process of salvation.

The increasing "commercialization" of religious supererogation is a later phenomenon, starting with the Crusades and culminating in the sale of indulgences by the Church, so vehemently opposed by Luther.[33] However, this only brings into relief a characteristic of the relation between virtuosi and society already present in earlier stages; namely, that whatever the terms of the exchange established between them – mainly intercessory prayers for the remission of sins as against endowments and donations – these terms received fully explicit and legitimate ideological articulation. Although the notion of lay acquisition of merit, linked as it was with gift giving to the virtuoso, is strongly reminiscent of the Theravada *dana* relationship, it is important to stress that the latter does not involve such explicit exchange. Theoretically at least, no return is expected from the *bhikkhu* who merely provides the laity with a field of merit, that is, with the occasion to acquire merit through selfless giving; at the limit, to recall, the best gift is the one given without thought to its karmic benefits – something that holds even in the more reciprocal versions of the *dana* theory when monks reciprocate by the countergift of teaching the doctrine, or *dharmadana*.

A number of doctrinal features facilitate the idiom of explicit, voluntary exchange in the Christian setting relative to the Buddhist one. Although transferability of merit and related practices were already accepted features of Theravada Buddhism at a very early stage, they somehow remained of dubious canonical validity. At any rate, they certainly seem to contradict the canonical Theravada emphasis on self-reliance – however problematic the notion of "self" in this context – in the striving for salvation. In contrast, similar notions seem to have been present in Christianity from the very beginning, and to have had full-blown theological and scholastic support. Moreover, explicit exchange was made possible by the notion of a division of labor between the sides involved, itself taking place within the context of holistic, unitary, and organistic notions of the Christian collective;[34] the equivalent of these

[33] On the transferability of merit from one person to the other, see for example G. Tellenbach, *Church, State and Society at the Time of the Investiture Contest* (Oxford: B. Blackwell, 1940) pp. 47, 78.

[34] Gager emphasizes, as already characteristic of early Christianity, the radical sense of community – open but asking for absolute and exclusive loyalty, and concerned with every aspect of the believer's life – which he sees as one of the most important factors in its success in institution building. See *Kingdom and Community:*

are much weaker, if not totally absent, in canonical Theravada Buddhism. This prevented the interaction between virtuosi and other Christians from becoming one of hierarchical interdependence – the Theravada model – and encouraged instead the notion of a more "egalitarian" explicit exchange within the framework of a differentiated but cohesive collective.

The horizontal and vertical principles

This "horizontal" emphasis on solidarity forms one of the major principles at work in the Christian ideological matrix. But the Church was always conceived in two dimensions: Horizontally it was the communion of people in Christ, a corporate organism sometimes almost coalescing with the notion of social harmony and order; vertically, it was the means for such communion, and, more specifically, "an institution formed from above and hierarchically structured, not only a simple association or corporation but an ideal superior and antecedent to its individual members."[35] It is important to stress that the hierarchy implied is thus not, or not only, one of spiritual or soteriological worth, but also one of institutional control and power of superiors over inferiors. This vertical "hierarchy of command,"[36] which is perhaps directly derived from the heteronomous character of the Christian faith propounding an individualized relationship to a personal God and His authoritative revelation from outside and above, is totally absent in Theravada Buddhism.

Much of the ideological incorporation and actual "functionalization" (in the sense developed in Chapter 2) of monkhood and virtuosi within Christian society can be accounted for in terms of the joint operation of these horizontal and vertical ideological principles. Although monasticism catered primarily to the individual religious aspirations of its members, it was also defined with respect to these two parameters. It perceived itself and was perceived horizontally as fulfilling specific and important functions in the life of the Christian whole.[37] Nevertheless, it also positioned itself vertically within the ecclesiastical hierarchy of control, which it never ultimately contested (one of the essential differences, incidentally, between monasticism and sects). Even the component of exchange in the relation between monks and nonmonks, to which both sides came voluntarily, freely, and to a certain extent, as

---

[35] Y. Congar, *Jalons pour une théologie du laïcat* (Paris: Cerf, 1951), p. 53.

[36] The formation of this "chain of command" in the early Christian community is analyzed in Chai-Shin Yu, *Early Buddhism and Christianity,* especially pp. 183 ff.

[37] On the development of this self-perception of the early ascetic community within the larger Christian whole, see Rousseau, *Ascetics, Authority and the Church,* pp. 56–67.

equals, was stamped by the legitimacy given it by the ecclesiastical hierarchy, which gradually came to regulate and use it on its own terms.

The monastic replication of the horizontal and vertical principles

No less important, the horizontal and vertical principles were replicated in the microcosm of the monastic world itself. This is most evident, horizontally, in the ideological valuation of the monastic "family," of communal brotherhood and internal solidarity within the individual monastery as the ideal community and self-contained whole – a theme much less salient in Theravada Buddhism;[38] and vertically, in the vow of obedience and the commitment to stability, that is, to lifelong affiliation with one's monastery of profession, as well as in the quasi-monarchic, absolutist definition of the abbot's authority.[39]

Vertically again, it is important to emphasize that Christian renouncers may not have been expected, any more than their Theravada counterparts, to be directly involved in the supervision and management of the social order. Nevertheless, the mutual reinforcement of the vertical parameter within the monastic world and the Church at large may have made Christian monasticism much more ideologically attuned to the sources and exercise of institutional power and to the exercise of religious power in the world.

This monastic replication of the horizontal and vertical principles, the equivalents of which are, it should be stressed again, much weaker in traditional Theravada Buddhist monasticism, should be interpreted as a double-edged phenomenon: It might support the corresponding mother principles operative in the Church and Christian society at large; but it might just as well invest Christian monasticism with an esprit de corps and institutional autonomy making it into a powerful and potentially independent rather than a smoothly integrated sector, operating with, against, or simply independently of the established secular and religious authorities. Indeed, much of the historical development of Christian monasticism can be understood as an oscillation between these two poles.

As a result, the doctrinal articulation of a neat division of labor and exchange between virtuosi and nonvirtuosi, under the benevolent regula-

---

[38] This contrast is richly analyzed in Collins, "Monasticism."

[39] The origin and development of obedience into the cardinal monastic virtue is analyzed by D. Knowles, "The Evolution of the Doctrine of Obedience," in idem, *From Pachomius to Ignatius: A Study in the Constitutional History of the Religious Orders* (Oxford: Clarendon, 1966), pp. 69–94; see also P. Salmon, *L'abbé dans la tradition monastique: contribution à l'histoire du charactère perpétuel des supérieurs religieux en Occident* (Paris: Sirey, 1962).

tion of the Church, gives only a partial picture of the actual historical situation, which was loaded, as will be explained later, with tension and increasing competition among the three parts involved: monks, secular clergy, and laity. As a matter of fact, the doctrinal model just outlined can be seen as the extreme example of a long-standing but not fully successful effort by medieval society and the Church in particular to define the social and spiritual status of monkhood. A clear expression of the ambiguous status of monks is that although medieval society, with its well-known concern with the hierarchical organization of the world, formulated elaborate schemes of social hierarchy, the place of monks in that hierarchy was extremely variable – sometimes at the very apex, above bishops and kings, at times grouped with the secular clergy, at other times kept distinct, and sometimes much lower or not even mentioned at all.[40] For example, Dionysius, the Pseudo-Areopagite (ca. 500) in his *Ecclesiastic Hierarchy* sets monks, albeit "perfect," below the "sacerdotal orders" (priests, ministers, mediators of the sacraments), and just above ordinary Christians within the large category of the (lay) "initiated."[41] In contrast, Abbo of Fleury, in the late tenth century, placed monks in the very first rank of both the social hierarchy and the scale of spiritual perfection. Although in earlier stages monks were most usually understood as a third order, next to the clergy and laity, later they were often merged with the clergy in a bipartite model of the Christian order, focusing rather on the distinction between clergy and laity. This bipartite ordering was itself to be displaced around the beginning of the eleventh century by a new tripartite model once again grouping monks with clergy within the category of prayers (*oratores*), but distinguishing them from fighters (*bellatores*), and tillers (*laborantes*).[42] Early expressions of this new tripartite model attributed to bishops Burchard of Worms and Gerard of Cambrai, in fact, appear more preoccupied with emphasizing the differentiation and interdependence than the relative hierarchical ordering between the various orders.[43] Different social sectors could favor different models, according to their own posi-

[40] See Tellenbach, *Church, State and Society,* pp. 50 ff. Tellenbach also notes that for Hugh of Fleury in the early twelfth century, bishops and priests were the very foundations of the Church, whereas monks and lower clergy were only its servants. Hugh of Flavigny, in contrast, placed holy hermits and perfect monks right after the apostles and before good bishops and priests in order of precedence at the Last Judgment.

[41] See *Hierarchie Ecclesiastique,* Books 5–6. See *Oeuvres complètes du Pseudo-Denys l'Areopagite,* translated with an introduction by M. de Gandillac (Paris: Aubier-Montaigne, 1943), pp. 293–312.

[42] See G. Duby, *The Three Orders: Feudal Society Imagined,* translated by A. Goldhammer (Chicago: University of Chicago Press, 1980).

[43] See G. Constable, "The Diversity of Religious Life and the Acceptance of Social Pluralism in the Twelfth Century," in B. McGinn and J. Meyendorff (eds.), *Christian Spirituality,* p. 33.

tion and interests. Uncertainty and fluctuation could be found at times even in the same author: For Aquinas the great mid-thirteenth-century systematizer, a man who acts under a vow merits far more from God than one who is not under any such obligation; all could attain to perfection, without vows and orders, but the religious state is clearly the shortcut to perfection; further, he deemed the contemplative life as superior to the active life,[44] and the solitary ideal as ultimately superior to the cenobitic one.[45] Nevertheless, laying out a complex system of criteria of excellence, he also saw orders devoted to preaching and teaching as the "most excellent," and when forming a hierarchy of the state of perfection, he placed bishops first, religious orders second, and parish priests and archdeacons third.[46]

Whatever these oscillations in the social position and status of monasticism (and perhaps because of them), monastic virtuosity – as in the Theravada model – implied segregation between virtuosi and society. This segregation was two-faceted, distinguishing monks not only from the laity but also from the clergy. Segregation was also a prerequisite of the Christian scheme of explicit exchange and division of labor: Monks must be pure and secluded from society (however seclusion is defined) for their intercessory role to be effective.

In the early phase of monasticism's ideological incorporation within the Church, one also encounters another form of "segregation" not found in the Theravada setting, namely, the need for monasticism to distinguish and dissociate itself from heretical and charismatic groups at odds with the emerging ecclesiastical hierarchy. On the whole, monasticism is usually understood to have sided with, rather than against, the evolving orthodoxy in coping with the heterodox challenge. The confrontation with the Arian docetist heresies was to be especially important both in the shaping of Christian orthodoxy and in the identification of monasticism with the orthodox camp. In Gager's opinion, however, there may well be here an orthodox reconstruction by late monasticism of a case that may not have been so clear-cut.[47] This may have helped to

---

[44] *Summa Theologica,* Part II, 2, Question 182, art. 1, in Thomas Aquinas, *Summa Theologica,* translated by Fathers of the English Dominican Province (Westminster, Md.: Christian Classics, 1981), vol. 4, p. 1937.

[45] *Summa Theologica,* Part II, 2, Question 188, art. 8; ibid., vol. 4, p. 1997.

[46] *Summa Theologica,* Part II, 2, Question 184, arts. 7 and 8; ibid., vol. 4, pp. 1950–3. Aquinas distinguishes here between state, order, and office, and then between intrinsic goodness and difficulty as criteria of excellence. Like Dionysius (see this chapter, fn. 41), he saw bishops in the position of perfecters, above monks as perfected.

[47] See J. F. Gager, "Body-Symbols and Social Reality: Resurrection, Incarnation and Asceticism in Early Christianity," *Religion* 12 (1982): 359. On charges of heresy (Manicheism and Priscillianism especially) against monasticism, see Bitterman, "The Beginning of the Struggle between the Regular and the Secular Clergy."

establish monasticism's own credentials despite certain dangerous affinities between the ascetic ideal and some of the nascent heterodoxies, especially those with dualist leanings. At any rate, one factor in the incorporation of monasticism into the Christian collective was the monastic acceptance of and alliance with ecclesiastical authority. Congruent with the vertical principle already discussed, this acceptance could not but contrast with heretical and charismatic assertions of freedom from ecclesiastical mediation and authority, or even claims at constituting the only true Church.

This has brought us very far from the meticulous and detailed doctrinal regulation of the virtuoso–layman relation in canonical Buddhism, dominated, as explained, by a "segregative–connective" arrangement: instituting a clear-cut distinction and double standard between virtuoso and layman, but also avoiding any real disconnection between the two and maintaining them in a sort of necessary, hierarchical interdependence. The Christian model – also "segregative," but "transactional" as well – is built on much shakier and less-defined doctrinal foundations, and remains a secondary and contingent rather than a central feature of Christian life. It is contingent on the priesthood–laity cleavage, which forms the very cornerstone of the Christian Church; on a more multivocal and open-ended conception of the ideal of religious perfection itself; and on an explicit, "free," and thus dissolvable relation of exchange rather than on hierarchical interdependence. The doctrinal grounds for a historically resilient virtuoso–layman relationship seem thus to be less solid than in Theravada Buddhism, and there seems to be little to prevent disconnection between them.

Ideological plurality and the principle of hierarchization

Despite the many ambiguities and uncertainties, however, Christian doctrine did entail a strong "virtuoso impulse," encouraging the emergence of ascetic rigorism and the quest for spiritual perfection. In fact, one may see this virtuoso impulse as enhanced rather than hampered by a differentiation in Christian spirituality between the striving for perfection and the striving for salvation, conceived as two intimately related but not overlapping motifs. Such a differentiation is in fact already announced in the story of the rich man (Matt. 19:16–24), alluded to earlier. The rich man asks, "What good shall I do that I may have life everlasting?" to which Jesus answers, "If thou will enter into life, keep the commandments," and only then adds, "If thou will be perfect, go and sell what thou hast, and give to the poor, and thou shalt have treasure in heaven: and come and follow me."

Historically speaking, the striving for perfection, though never unrelated to the soteriological motif, acquired a dynamic of its own. Despite the incorporation of monkhood into the Church, ultimately a distinction remained between the priesthood, corresponding to an office, and monkhood, defined as a mode of life: A monk might be either lay or clerical, and monkhood was never erected into an office or function. Even at times when monks and clerics seemed to be fusing in the fundamental bipartite division of Christians into clergy and laity, "the essential distinction between office and mode of life and relatedly, between matters of the cult and matters of perfection would remain."[48] Comcomitantly, no matter how uncertain and fluctuating monasticism's spiritual status and social prestige, "matters of perfection" always retained the potential to determine the ultimate hierarchization of human beings, thus catapulting monks and even hermits to the very apex of the hierarchical order.

Although hierarchization was certainly a pervasive feature of medieval society, it could evolve along a number of competing and potentially conflicting axes. Tellenbach thus was able to discern three different principles of hierarchization – the ascetic, theocratic-ecclesiastical, and monarchical; individuals and groups might hold to one or more of these principles simultaneously (the first and last of these principles forming a more compatible combination than the others) or perhaps shift from one to the other.[49] Georges Duby has analyzed the development of alternative systems of classification in medieval society, and in particular the development from the beginning of the eleventh century, as already mentioned, of a tripartite system of social classification – men of prayer, of combat, and of labor – a process he has traced to a number of major changes affecting the balance of power among bishops, lay princes, and kings at the time.[50] Walter Ullman distinguished between two major medieval theories of government, an ascending one – chronologically earlier – locating original power in the people or in the community, and a descending one – according to which all power descends from God. The latter would drive the former underground and dominate the scene from the earlier middle ages until the late thirteenth century (the period focused upon in the present study), to be in turn gradually displaced in the succeeding centuries. Integral to these developments, in Ullman's view, is the fusion of Roman and Frankish conceptions of kingship and government, rather than "Christian" orientations proper.[51]

[48] Congar, L'ecclesiologie du haut Moyen-Age.
[49] See Tellenbach, Church, State and Society.
[50] Duby, Three Orders; idem, The Chivalrous Society (Berkeley and Los Angeles: University of California Press, 1977), pp. 88–93. See also Le Goff, La civilisation de l'Occident médiéval (Paris: Flammarion, 1982), pp. 234–43.
[51] W. Ullmann, Medieval Political Thought (Harmondsworth, Middlesex: Penguin Books, 1975).

To understand this ideological plurality of medieval society, it is indeed necessary to place Christianity within the wider context of a medieval civilization incorporating a range of pre- and non-Christian cultural orientations.[52] In contrast to the rather smooth coexistence of "high" Buddhism with non-Buddhist symbolic orientations in Theravada countries, medieval Western culture seems to have been characterized by a much greater and steadily increasing level of ideological tension and competition among the various cultural orientations and traditions evolving in its midst.[53] This was obviously intensified by the existence of an ecclesiastical institution that considered itself to be the mediator and gatekeeper of religious orthodoxy. Moreover, the incorporation of a worldly strand within the Christian renunciatory salvational orientation itself forced the latter to compete over arenas of worldly activity with other cultural tendencies – "pagan" magico-ritual orientations and "secular" Roman Imperial, Germanic-tribal, or Hellenistic-urban orientations. In addition, worldly orientations tended to acquire autonomous soteriological value, enabling them to compete with renunciatory asceticism as avenues of perfection and salvation. This had crucial implications for the status of ascetic virtuoso orientations within the cultural system as a whole: Whereas in Theravada societies the virtuoso renunciatory strand was rather tolerant of "lower" orientations, yet also safely insulated at the apex of the hierarchy of symbolic orientations, in the context of medieval Christianity it was increasingly challenged and ultimately defeated by competing ideological orientations, both religious and secular.

Much of monasticism's subsequent historical development is foreshadowed in this analysis of Christian ideological matrix. To some extent, we can argue that here again, as in Theravada Buddhism, there was a congruity between doctrinal premises and institutional developments. But it was a congruity based, to a great extent, on open-endedness and plurality, making for a wider range of options than in Theravada. The virtuoso search for perfection maintained a powerful momentum of its own, but oscillated among the multiple options offered by the dilemmas of the ascetic life; although some of these were present in Theravada Buddhism as well, they reached greater extremes and encompassed a much greater range of possible variations in medieval Christianity.

---

[52] Reaching for this pre-Christian stratum and exploring its functioning in medieval culture, see G. Gurevitch, *Les catégories de la mentalité médiévale* (Paris: Presses Universitaires de France, 1985).

[53] This is most clearly exemplified by the complex confrontation between "pagan" magico-ritual orientations and Christian ecclesiastical "high" culture, which has given rise to too extensive a scholarly literature to be referred to here. See especially E. Peters, *The Magician, the Witch and the Law* (Philadelphia: University of Pennsylvania Press, 1978); Van Engen, J. "The Christian Middle Ages as an Historiographic Problem," *American Historical Review* 91 (1986): 519–52.

Christian virtuosity initially stabilized in the monastic, Benedictine form and developed a network of interaction with society and laity that was in many ways similar to the Theravada virtuoso relational structure. From early times, Christian monasticism displayed a strength of organizational structure, overall institutional autonomy, and political power that were not easily contained by mechanisms of segregation and exchange and that made for a more forceful interaction – perhaps even competition – with other groups and sectors. The result was a somewhat paradoxical combination of inherent instability and open-endedness, on the one hand, and institutional strength on the other – an inverse image of the Theravada combination of "looseness" or even weakness on many institutional parameters with an impressive degree of overall historical stability.

Later, starting with the early stages of the Gregorian reform, around the mid-eleventh century, the monastic sector attained an unparalleled degree of political and religious influence over society at large. However, as shown in the next chapter, it also underwent a process of internal differentiation and polarization that not only overflowed the classical, monastic forms of its institutionalization and dissolved their preeminence, but also undermined the elements of segregation and exchange between virtuoso and layman and thus, ultimately, the very existence of a distinct virtuoso sector.

7 Virtuosity institutionalized: monasticism in social context

Christian asceticism is thought to have started with the practice of various forms of supererogatory self-denial within the framework of ordinary family life. It is only gradually that ascetic ideals became intimately associated with the idea of total sexual abstinence and permanent separation from social life.[1] A pattern of withdrawal to the desert or the mountains, however, is recorded as early as the third century in Egypt and Syria, reaching the West (at first Italy and Gaul) only around the fourth century. Significantly for our present purposes, this desert tradition already stamped Christian monasticism with one of its most fundamental ambiguities. Whether as the domain of wild animals and demons, or at the extreme opposite, as the paradisiac place of encounter with God, the desert represented the anti-city and anti-civilization. However, under the impact of monasticism it was also quickly transformed, as conveyed in what has become a locus classicus of monastic literature – the *Life* of Saint Anthony – into a "city" of sorts.[2] The desert came to constitute, in fact, "a 'counter-world,' a place where an alternative 'city' could grow."[3]

Even at this stage, in what appears to have been a very fluid milieu where eremitic, semieremitic, and fully cenobitic forms of life coexisted,[4] ascetic life could assume a highly structured, quasi-military character, as in the densely populated monasteries founded in the Egyptian Thebaid by Pachomius in the first half of the fourth century. Pachomius gave the cenobitic tradition what was probably its earliest rule, characterized by the emphasis upon manual labor and total obedience to the superior. The Pachomian monastery, with church, refectory, hospital, guest house, and groups of monks organized according to occupation, was already an impressively self-sustained and differentiated structure, epitomizing the "desert city" paradox.[5]

---

[1] For the detailed analysis of this development as a complex and not self-evident process, see Brown, *The Body and Society*.

[2] See D. Chitty, *The Desert a City* (Oxford: B. Blackwell, 1961); also J. Le Goff, "Le désert-forêt dans l'Occident médieval." In idem, *L'imaginaire médiéval*, pp. 59–75.

[3] Brown, *Body and Society*, p. 217.

[4] Chitty, *Desert a City*. This element of lability of the various emerging forms of religious life in the very early stages, where individuals and even groups evolved from one form of life into another, is emphasized in Rousseau, *Ascetics, Authority and the Church*.

[5] H. Bacht, "L'importance de l'idéal monastique de Saint Pachôme pour l'histoire du monachisme chrétien," *Revue d'Ascétique et de Mystique* 26 (1950): 308–26;

Organizational structures

Throughout its history, Christian monasticism has displayed a strong tendency to self-structuring and organization, at first in self-sufficient and autonomous monasteries – the original Benedictine model – but later also in centralized networks of monasteries striving to unify observance and discipline. Of crucial importance in the creation of such powerful structures were the vows of obedience to the abbot, the existence of irrevocable vows, and the commitment to stability – elements totally absent in the Buddhist Sangha.[6] (It is noteworthy, in this respect, that no counsel of obedience is explicitly formulated in the New Testament, in contrast with the vows of chastity and poverty, which do have clearer doctrinal grounding). Be that as it may, it is ironic that these premises, enshrined in the Rule of Saint Benedict, came to sustain a powerful organizational development that was in fact a perversion of Benedict's original model, where the emphasis had been on the autonomy of the individual monastery and the absolute authority of the abbot within a self-contained monastic unit.

Until the seventh and even eighth centuries, however, Western monasticism as it first appeared in Gaul and Italy retained a certain looseness: There were a number of rules (only some of which were preserved), often quite fluid and complemented by local customs; many monasteries actually functioned with no written rules at all.[7] Benedict of Aniane's reform, culminating with the Synod of Aachen (815) during the reign of Charlemagne's son, Louis the Pious, played a role in tightening and unifying the organization of monasticism by imposing the Benedictine Rule throughout the Carolingian empire.[8]

With the expansion of Cluniac monasticism in the tenth century (itself intended as a return to a purer enactment of Benedict of Aniane's reform), monasteries lost their classical Benedictine independence and became subject to the abbot of the motherhouse of Cluny, to whom each

for a recent, somewhat modified picture of Pachomius's militarylike institutional rigor, see P. Rousseau, *Pachomius: The Making of a Community in Fourth-Century Egypt* (Berkeley and Los Angeles: University of California Press, 1985).

[6] On the early emergence of the principle of obedience in the ascetic community, see Rousseau, *Ascetics, Authority and the Church,* especially pp. 49–55. Obedience was seen to be implied, by later theologians, in Christ's injunction to "follow him."

[7] C. Courtois, "L'évolution du monachisme en Gaule," in *Il monachesimo nell' alto mediaevo e la formazione de la civilizatione occidentale* (Spoleto: Presso la Sede del Centro, 1957), especially pp. 59–65.

[8] See P. Schmitz, "L'influence de Saint Benoit d'Aniane dans l'histoire de l'Ordre de Saint Benoît," in *Il monachesimo nell' alto mediaevo;* C. Butler, *Benedictine Monachism* (Cambridge University Press, 1961), pp. 236–7; Knowles, *From Pachomius to Ignatius,* p. 8.

individual monk of any house made profession. This elaboration of a unified and hierarchical system would seem to form a strangely nonfeudal or antifeudal development, posing a sharp contrast to contemporary trends of territorial and political fragmentation.[9] The organizational potency and administrative rationality of the Cluniac "empire" should not be overestimated, however: It had little organizational or governmental apparatus and was based to a great extent on the reproduction of the feudal principles at work in society at large:[10]

A majority of the houses of the Cluniac body were integrated by a charter specifying their obligations of obedience, limitations of autonomy, and a small annual census or tax. Externally therefore, the relationship was one of vertical dependence, not of horizontal equality, and the model was not a commune or federation but the feudal bond which was being elaborately developed in contemporary Europe and particularly in France. Cluny thus made use of the two most powerful ideas in early medieval society, that of the religious obedience of a monk to his abbot, and that of the fidelity and mutual obligations of vassal and lord.[11]

The Cistercian order partially reinstated the autonomy of the cenobitic unit: Each had its own abbot; daughter houses were subject to the control but not authority of the motherhouse; and all the houses were governed by decisions made in common at general chapters, in what seems to have formed a more "democratic" structure. Both the Cluniac and the Cistercian model, however, involved a characteristic attempt at some form of supralocal and centralized structure. It must be stressed, moreover, that Christian monasticism produced some important constitutional innovations in the articulation of such structures, which cannot be seen as just the internalization of principles of social organization prevalent in society at large. In particular, it retained crucial "egalitarian" features, mainly within monasteries but also in some of its overarching institutions, and thus remained a parallel and even antithetic form of organization vis-à-vis the ecclesiastical and secular hierarchies.

The overriding difference with the Sangha, however, is not only the nature, degree, and scope of organizational structuring and centralization, but the fact that these structures were developed and sustained

[9] For the emphasis on Cluny's organizational principles as contrary to those of the feudal structure at large, see J. F. Lemarignier, "Political and Monastic Structures in France at the End of the Tenth and Beginning of the Eleventh Century," in F. L. Cheyette, *Lordship and Community in Medieval Europe* (New York: Holt, Rinehart, & Winston, 1968), p. 117; J. F. Lemarignier, *La France médiévale: institutions et société* (Paris: Armand Colin, 1970), pp. 199–200.

[10] Knowles, *From Pachomius to Ignatius,* p. 12. There is, more generally, much debate around the extent to which Cluny constituted a feudal or antifeudal structure. This debate does not so much focus on the internal organizational principles of the Cluniac network, but rather on Cluny's relations with local feudal lords – a topic to be treated later in this chapter (see fn. 46).

[11] Ibid., p. 12.

from within the monastic sector rather than by the political establishment. Kings and other laymen could and often did aim at influencing the choice of abbots; but the organizational structures themselves were never originated by them or based on their indispensable control and support.

The tendency to centralization and uniformity did not culminate within Benedictine monasticism, but in the new mendicant orders of the thirteenth century. It was only with the Dominicans that "the complete supranational religious order, at once fully centralized and fully articulated, achieved adult status."[12] In contrast with the Cluniac reproduction of the feudal principles at work in society at large, this new kind of centralization also furthered the "democracy" already initiated in the Cistercian constitution: It replaced the Benedictine authoritarian conception of the abbot elected for life with priors and a master-general accountable to elected general chapters. At the same time, though, these new structures were also put under the pope's direct control. What was involved here, therefore, was not a "democratic" opposition to authority and hierarchy as such, but rather the use of a "skillful combination of egalitarian opportunities, elected merit, and authoritative direction" to serve the order's main purposes, studying and preaching.[13] In pursuing these aims, many traditional features of monastic life – particularly monastic stability and enclosure – were discarded: As the necessary corollary of the new emphasis on preaching, the individual monk was made fully mobile, at the disposal of the order's head to be dispatched wherever need be. For Saint Francis, who heralded it, this new mobility may have been, if not a sign of individualistic freedom, at least another expression of utter poverty and renunciation and of his own attempt to free the religious vocation from its overgrowth of legalistic strictures. But even Francis, who had originally recoiled from imposing any elaborate rule and preferred his religious group to be bound only by ties of mutual charity and a common vocation, eventually did evolve a rule – albeit after much delay, and under papal pressure. Moreover, by combining the individual friar's state of utter disposal and the absence of effective constitutional checks upon the head of the order, Francis's rule opened the way, in fact, to absolutist and ultimately despotic use of religious authority.[14]

Another expression of strong organizational structuring and of the combined operation of the vertical and horizontal principles discussed in the previous chapter is the monastery's tendency to encompass people and functions normally external to them or on their margins – a variant

---

[12] Ibid., p. 53.
[13] Ibid., p. 57.
[14] Ibid., p. 48.

of the desert city paradox alluded to earlier. Benedict's ideal monastery was, economically and spiritually, a rather self-contained unit that could fulfill many functions either by drawing on its own members or by hiring external manpower when need be. Many of the large monasteries came, in fact, to display elaborate internal organization and differentiation replicating all the crucial functions of a self-governing unit, as exemplified in the celebrated plan of Saint Gall, the ideal plan of a monastery drawn at Reichenau around 820.[15] However, they also came to incorporate, within the walls of the monastery and under the abbot's control, sectors of the population that were not properly monastic. Long before the emergence of the lay brothers (as in Vallombrosa in the eleventh century and the Cistercian order in the twelfth) and of the third orders (thirteenth century), laymen would occasionally "give" themselves with their possessions to the monastery and commit themselves to some specific task for the monastery, which from then on was responsible for their daily care.[16] This capacity to incorporate nonmonastic members reached its epitome in the extreme and uncharacteristic example of Saint Riquier, a prominent monastery in Gaul that was destroyed in the 881 Norman invasion and later equaled in size only by Cluny and Clairvaux. Saint Riquier was a fortified city, a bourg, in which the monastery owned all the houses and where both the lay population (some seven thousand inhabitants obligated to pay taxes and perform military and other services for the monastery) and some three hundred monks were organized for practical and religious-ritual purposes under the strict regime of a lay-abbot.[17] This extreme example of totalistic and expansive monastic organization had no known historical offshoot. The more usual pattern of extramonastic expansion of the monastic community involved the establishment of monastic confraternities that monks from other monasteries, secular clergy, or laymen could join to be assured of prayers for their own souls or for those of their relatives.[18] Even this looser formula,

---

[15] See W. Horn and E. Born, *The Plan of St. Gall: A Study of the Architecture and Economy of, and Life in, a Paradigmatic Carolingian Monastery* (Berkeley and Los Angeles: University of California Press, 1979).

[16] Lawrence, *Medieval Monasticism,* p. 111. This was done according to various formulas regulating the specific disposal of property, which sometimes remained partially in the layman's possession. See J. Avril, *Le gouvernement des évêques et la vie religieuse dans le diocèse d'Angers, 1148–1240* (Lille: Cerf, 1984), pp. 812–3.

[17] J. Hubert, "Saint-Riquier et le monachisme bénédictin en Gaule à l'époque carolingienne," in *Il monachesimo nell'alto mediaevo,* pp. 293–309.

[18] Dealing more especially with the Cluniac commemorative *fraternitas,* but also amply discussing the development of such monastic confraternities in general, see J. Wollasch, "Les obituaires, témoins de la vie clunisienne," *Cahiers de Civilisation Médiévale* 22, no. 2 (1979): 139–171. Also on Cluny, see H. E. J. Cowdrey, "Unions and Confraternity with Cluny," *Journal of Ecclesiastical History* 16 (1956): 152–62.

however, entails a formalized incorporation of the laity within some extended framework of monastic solidarity, often cutting across local and national boundaries, and of a sort that did not emerge in the Theravada setting.

As a clear result of this general capacity for self-structuring, Christian monasticism was never as systematically dependent upon external political forces to enforce its inner purity as the Sangha was (which of course does not imply that purity was always successfully maintained). Kings or nobles occasionally took it upon themselves to intervene in these matters. This was notably the case in the Carolingian era, with the imperial support given to the spread of Benedictine monasticism at the expense of previous monastic traditions through both Boniface's missionary efforts and Benedict of Aniane's reform. Underlying the support to Benedict's Rule was perhaps less a concern for ascetic rigor than a legalistic and institutional interest in monastic unity and standardized discipline, facilitated by the Rule of Saint Benedict's acceptance of episcopal supervision. Be that as it may, even Charlemagne's and his son Louis the Pious's active support of monastic reform never attained the exemplary power of the Ashokan *sasana* reform as a model for a recurrent, traditional pattern of monastic reform through external, secular intervention. On a more localized level, many nobles, from the tenth century on, developed a strong personal interest in the purity of the monasteries of which they were the founders or patrons.[19] It was by then accepted to consider the monastery as the private property of whomever founded it on his lands; in contradiction to Saint Benedict's emphasis on free and autonomous election of the abbot, the founder's proprietary right also involved the right of choosing the abbot – a major way of controlling monastic discipline and purity. On the whole, however, this kind of lay involvement with monastic reform remained confined to the use of the monastery as a sort of private status symbol asserting the nobles' new strength and legitimacy vis-à-vis an enfeebled monarchy, and did not entail any principled conception of lay guardianship of monastic purity.

Organizational strength can thus be taken as a clear criterion of institutional vigor and autonomy. Nevertheless, it also placed monasticism at the better disposal of the ecclesiastical hierarchy and papacy – a trend already evident with Cluny and culminating with the (admittedly not classically monastic) mendicant orders – and could be used to better incorporate the virtuoso ascetic life into the wider social scene (as in the case of Carolingian monasticism). Indeed, as already suggested, monasticism's overall institutional strength should be assessed on the basis not

[19] See P. D. Johnson, *Prayer, Patronage and Power: The Abbey of La Trinité, Vendôme, 1032–1187* (New York: New York University Press, 1981), pp. 41–3; Avril, *Le gouvernement des évêques*, pp. 811–12.

only of its organizational structures alone, but also of the position of these structures in society at large.

Monastic economy

Christian monks could work, farm, and manage their collective property as they wished. Consequently, they were never as dependent on the laity for material support, least of all for food, as were their Buddhist counterparts. In time, monasteries displayed such craft and entrepreneurship in the cultivation and management of their property that they "gradually came to represent the largest single concentration of wealth in many parts of Western Europe."[20]

The accumulation of wealth, however, should not be seen as directly stemming from an ascetic, productive mystique of work. The monastic attitude toward work, primarily conceived as manual labor, retained a marked ambiguity. There is evidence of early itinerant Christian monks strikingly similar, in their total reliance on lay offerings, to the ideal early Buddhist wandering monks.[21] Nevertheless, early monks and hermits did work, as a rule, for their subsistence. The Pachomian regime certainly involved a great deal of manual labor as both the best expedient against the dangers of *accedia* – boredom – and a necessary means of self-support. On the whole, however, early monks probably despised all work and trade, which were perceived by them, as by all their contemporaries, as signs of a lowly, peasant condition. What came to prevail, though, was the more positive attitude to work, exemplified in Benedict's Rule, as an essential ingredient of ascetic life and a sign of humility, if never the object of glorification as such and never an end in itself.[22] Manual labor receded in importance with Benedict of Aniane's reforms, yielding to a new emphasis on the liturgy as the "work of God," a

---

[20] On the economic aspects of Christian monasticism, see J. A. Raftis, "Western Monasticism and Economic Organization," *Comparative Studies in Society and History* 8, no. 4 (1961): 452–67; R. Génestal, *Role des monastères comme établissements de crédit, étudié en Normandie du XIe à la fin du XIIIe siècle* (Paris: Rousseau, 1901); G. Duby, "Le monachisme et l'économie rurale," in *Hommes et structures du Moyen-Age*, pp. 381–93; idem, "Economie domaniale et économie monétaire: le budget de l'abbaye de Cluny entre 1080 et 1155," *Annales E.S.C.* 7 (1952): 155–71, also in *Hommes et structures du Moyen-Age* (Paris: Mouton, 1973), pp. 61–83; P. Schmitz, *Histoire de l'Ordre de Saint-Benoît* (Maredsous: Les Editions de Maredsous, 1942), pp. 11–50.

[21] See A. Guillaumont, "Le travail manuel dans le monachisme ancien: contestation et valorisation," in *Aux origines du monachisme chrétien: pour une phénoménologie du monachisme* (Begrolles en Mauges: Abbaye de Bellefontaine, 1979), ch. 7.

[22] See F. Prinz, "Monchtum und Arbeitsethos," in *Arkese und Kultur, Vor- und Frühbenediktinisches Mönchtum an der Wiege Europas* (Munich: Beck, 1980); A. J. Gurevitch, *Les catégories de la culture médiévale*, especially pp. 266–7.

tendency that climaxed in the tenth century with Cluny's permanent *opus Dei*. Manual labor made a temporary comeback in the early phases of the Cistercian order and some eremitic orders; as is well known, however, the Cistercians soon introduced lay brothers to work the land and to take care of economic and managerial tasks, thus freeing the monks for spiritual endeavors.

The sheer scope, dynamism, and highly rationalized nature of monastic economy relative to the rest of contemporary society are undeniable. Monasteries not only held a huge proportion of all cultivated lands,[23] but also led the way in the application of new technologies (the water mill, the mechanical clock, intensive methods of cultivation, bookkeeping) and often operated as the equivalent of banking institutions and even insurance companies. In a situation where usury was outlawed, if not nonexistent, monasteries provided alternative, legitimate forms of credit.[24] Leasing, mortgaging, and pawning property to monks were convenient ways to obtain money, often used by Crusaders in particular in the eleventh and twelfth centuries. In addition, monasteries encouraged the operation of local fairs around their precincts and promoted translocal trade, triggered urban development, in their vicinities and supported a host of arts and crafts related to monastic practices and ceremonial needs.

At the same time, however, we must be careful not to project upon traditional monasticism as a whole a picture of economic expansion and "rationalization" generated mainly on the basis of the economic successes of the Cistercian order in its early stages – itself now undergoing a certain amount of reassessment.[25] Many monasteries suffered impoverishment through mismanagement. Moreover, there was never any absolute injunction that monks be entirely self-supporting; that monks engaged in agricultural labor and general economic activity should not divert our attention from the even more significant fact that much of the monastic economy was nurtured as much by the input of lay endowments (to be discussed in greater detail), ecclesiastical tithes, and by a number of trading and other crucial privileges, as by economic entrepreneurship proper.

As a result of their extensive wealth and their direct involvement in the

---

[23] No precise numbers exist concerning monastic wealth and different types of wealth in the High Middle Ages. Herlihy assesses ecclesiastical landed property in general rather than monastic property in particular to have reached about a third of all cultivated land around the eleventh century. See "The Ecclesiastical Economy of Medieval Europe," *Journal of Ecclesiastical History* 4 (1986): pp. 227–31.

[24] Génestal, *Role des monastères*.

[25] I have dealt with these issues in greater detail in "Monasticism and the 'Protestant Ethic.'"

economic sphere, monasteries frequently became entangled in legal and economic struggles, and incurred a great deal of resentment in the process.[26] Among others, the payment of tithes – by monks or to monks – was a recurrent subject of dispute between monks and secular clergy. The issue was not purely economic, since it involved long-standing controversies over the legal status of monks within the Church.[27] Although in the early Middle Ages monks were as a rule forbidden to receive and required to pay tithes, by the twelfth century, most monks received tithes, and many were exempt from paying them. The short-lived attempt of the Cistercians to refuse tithes was also an attempt to reject the worldly strife that accompanied them: Monastic wealth brought with it the many rights and duties of feudal lordship, thus unavoidably involving monks in a whole network of entanglements with both vassals and other lords.

The rapid failure of those religious orders that tried to disengage from the corrupting influences of economic entanglements with the world – the early Cistercians and Franciscans in particular – may attest to the strength of the forces pulling away from monastic poverty and toward wealth and involvement. We should note, however, that although deeply involved in a network of economic exchange with the outside world, monasteries were on the whole powerful and autonomous partners in the process of exchange, and displayed a type of entrepreneurship (and a degree of rationalization) in economic matters uncharacteristic of the Theravada Sangha.[28] These undoubtedly strengthened their general institutional autonomy and bargaining power in their interaction with both laity and Church.

The gift relationship

Here too a gift relationship emerged, albeit ad hoc and without any doctrinal basis at first, and only gradually receiving ideological articulation.[29] Unlike the donations to the Theravada Sangha, endowments to

[26] On lay resentment and even physical violence against monks, see U. Berlière, "Monastères et sujets au Moyen-Age," *Revue Bénedictine* 43 (1931): B22–41; 44 (1932): 44–70.

[27] See G. Constable, *Monastic Tithes from their Origins to the Twelfth Century* (Cambridge University Press, 1964). Such developments provide important clues as to changes in the position of monks within the Church, and their increasing incorporation within the clergy.

[28] Sri Lanka's monastic "landlordism," however, would seem the closest to Western monasticism in this respect.

[29] Donations to monasteries have recently become an important focus of historical study. See B. Rosenwein, *To Be the Neighbor of St. Peter: The Social Meaning of Cluny's Property, 909–1049* (Ithaca, N.Y.: Cornell University Press, 1989); C. B. Bouchard, *Sword, Miter and Cloister: Nobility and the Church in Burgundy, 980–1198* (Ithaca, N.Y.: Cornell University Press, 1988); J. Wardrop, *Fountains Abbey and its Benefactors, 1132–300* (Kalamazoo, Mich.: Cistercian, 1987); S.

Christian monks never represented a routine practice involving the offering of their daily bread, and hence never represented as primordial and necessary a relation of interdependence. Although gifts of property by noble donors are mentioned in the Rule of Saint Benedict (ch. 59), it is only incidentally, as it were, as something that noble families might want to do when offering one of their sons to the monastic life. Otherwise, and except for forbidding all private possession and all acceptance of gifts by individual monks, the rule does not concern itself with the issue of donations to the monastery, and nothing in this basic text of monastic discipline would predict the scope and significance that donations to monasteries were to acquire in later centuries. The gift relationship did develop, however, on a very large scale and involved, among else, vast tracts of land. As Raftis notes, it is difficult to determine how the grant of land in particular originally became a characteristic form of donation.[30] It may well have been, as Southern seems to think, simply the most fruitful use that wealthy lords could make of huge and sparsely populated wastes that they had in any case no means of exploiting.[31] It may have also provided a convenient way to get rid of lands burdened with taxes and feudal obligations. Be that as it may, lay donations of land and various sources of income (churches, annuities, pasture and forest rights, tolls, etc.) played an enormous role in monasteries' accumulation of wealth at least until the end of the twelfth century. At that point, donations of land sharply decreased, to be replaced in part by endowments in money.

It must be noted that, even in the best of times, monasteries were often expected to reciprocate their benefactors' generosity not only in spiritual but sometimes in a very practical and material manner. Merovingian and Carolingian kings, for example, were generous benefactors and may even be said to have played a decisive role in launching Western monasticism on its road to the huge concentration of wealth; but they also felt free to allocate monastic properties to vassals or use them for their own purposes, especially in wartime. Monasteries might also be asked to loan

D. White, *Custom, Kinship and Gifts to Saints: The Laudatio Parentum in Western France, 1050–1150* (Chapel Hill, N.C.: University of North Carolina Press, 1988); E. Mason, "The Donors of Westminster Abbey Charters, ca. 1066–1240," *Medieval Prosopography* 8 (1987): 23–39; idem, "Timeo Barones et Donas Ferentes," in D. Baker (ed.), *Religious Motivation: Biographical and Sociological Problems for the Church Historian* (Oxford: B. Blackwell, 1978), pp. 61–75; C. M. Miller, "Donors, their Gifts and Religious Innovation in Medieval Verona," *Speculum* 66 (1991): 27–42.

[30] Raftis, "Western Monasticism and Economic Organization."

[31] Southern, *Western Society and the Church*, p. 229; this was also argued in the case of the Cistercians by B. Hill, *English Cistercian Monasteries and Their Patrons in the Twelfth Century* (Urbana: University of Illinois Press, 1968), p. 50 ff.

money to the king or provide him with military contingents when need be, recruited from the population on their territory. Even lesser founders and patrons of monasteries sometimes considered these as their personal property, whose economic resources they could tap as they wished. The duty of hospitality in particular, not only to a noble or royal benefactor but also to his whole entourage, could be a heavy economic drain.

Donations, moreover, could not only be given with very tangible and material returns in mind, but also become fully and explicitly "transactional." An endowment could be made, for example, against the explicit commitment of the monastery to provide the donor with food, clothing, or even lodging for the rest of his life. In time, indeed, there seems to have developed a whole spectrum of donations ranging from the relatively disinterested *pro anima* gift – in the sense of involving otherworldly spiritual interests only, and carrying no expectation for any reciprocity from the monks but for the promise of intercessory prayers for the donor's or his relatives' souls – to transactions involving gifts and counter-gifts with various degrees of reciprocity coming sometimes close, in their practical results, to buying and selling.[32]

Here too, and perhaps even more so than in the Theravada setting, gift giving obviously became tied to particular and localized interests. Donations to monasteries could become a way of preventing property from passing into the hands of more powerful lords, or of somehow consolidating family property – especially in cases where the abbot himself was a relative. Endowing a monastery where one had a child or other kin was also a way of contributing to the relative's well-being and living standard. Moreover, donations, were most often given with nothing but the donor's individual salvation in mind, and that of his closest relatives. However, here too donations to monasteries could occasionally acquire more generalizing, collective overtones. Witness the wording in Cluny's foundation charter (910):

I give moreover, all these things . . . first for the love of God; then for the soul of my lord king Odo, of my father and my mother; for myself and my wife – for the salvation, namely, of our souls and bodies; and not least, for that of Ava who left me these things in her will; for the souls also of our brothers and sisters and nephews, and of all our relatives of both sexes; for our faithful ones who adhere to our service; for the advancement, also, and integrity of the catholic religion.

[32] All these, however, were most often perceived as pious donations *pro anima*, indicating the absence of clear distinctions in types of reciprocity for those involved. See M. Castaing-Sicard, "Donations toulousaines du Xe au XIIe siecle," *Annales du Midi* 70 (1958): 288–54. See, however, for evidence of a clear distinction, in the donor's mind, between donations *pro anima* and other transactions with the monkhood, Bouchard, *Sword, Miter and Cloister*. Further emphasizing, perhaps, the "otherworldly" orientation of monastic endowments is the fact that a fair share of them were enacted just before the donor's death.

Finally, since all of us Christians are held together by one bond of love and faith, let this donation be for all – for the orthodox, namely, of past, present or future times.[33]

In the case of royal monasteries in particular, that is, monasteries founded and endowed by kings, and serving as places of kingly burial as well as repositories of kingly regalia, donations acquired a broader, "public" significance by contributing to the glamour of a monastic worship closely associated with the interests of kingship or even empire.[34] A similar process obtained, on a lower scale, around lesser monasteries that acquired saintly relics attracting lay donations and becoming public emblems of collective pride. Donations, moreover, could also acquire a broader collective or redistributive orientation due to the monasteries' involvement in charitable relief, theoretically resulting in the redistribution of a tenth of their overall income to the poor,[35] and specifically mentioned in many a foundation charter as a principal function of the monastery.[36] Although monastic charity was often of a purely ritualistic nature, limiting itself to the taking in charge of a symbolic number of "poor" attached to the monastery's family of dependents, it could also at times reach significant proportions and even become, as in the case of Cluny, a heavy economic burden. More generally, however, charity to the poor did not necessarily have to be mediated through the monks. Neither the interpretation of monks as the most truly "poor" because committed to voluntary poverty in the ascetic life, nor monasteries' active involvement in charity to the poor, would ever obliterate the fact that giving to monasteries was never the only form of religious donation available to either common layman or king in the Christian Middle Ages. Relatedly, while generous gift giving was one of the traits early associated with the idea of kingship,[37] it never became as crucial a component of kingly legitimacy as in the case of Buddhist kingship, and it did not necessarily focus on giving to monasteries (or even the Church at large) in particular.

As it is well known, monastic wealth became a major source of corruption and relaxation of ascetic standards. Paradoxically, laymen tended to

[33] E. F. Henderson, *Select Documents of the Middle Ages*, (London: G. Bell, 1892), pp. 329–33.

[34] See the analysis of the Abbey of Saint Denis in particular in Duby, *Age of the Cathedrals*, ch. 5.

[35] See W. Witters, "Pauvres et pauvreté dans les coutumes monastiques du Moyen-Age," in M. Mollat (ed.), *Etudes sur l'histoire de la pauvreté* (Paris: Publications de la Sorbonne, 1974), pp. 177–217.

[36] M. Mollat, *The Poor in the Middle Ages* (New Haven, Conn: Yale University Press, 1986), pp. 177–217; D. Knowles, *The Monastic Order in England, 943–1216* (Cambridge University Press, 1950), p. 479.

[37] On the impact and evolution of pre-Christian noble and Viking notions of generosity, see Gurevitch, *Catégories de la culture médiévale*, pp. 219–241, 251–63.

bestow donations and protection on monasteries or orders that they perceived as purer and holier, in a process usually leading to further monastic slackening and need for reform. Admittedly, there were ambiguities in the original injuction of poverty: Did it mean "poverty in spirit" or actual material poverty; and did it address only individual or also collective poverty? Wealth, moreover, made it possible to better fulfill the duty of Christian charity. This may explain in part, beyond the assumption of an ever-lurking and all-too-human greediness, why monks were so easily and systematically swept into the acceptance of donations that ultimately contradicted the original renunciatory ideals of monasticism and, unlike in Buddhism, were not backed by any specific doctrinal injunction. But as stressed by Georges Duby,[38] a determinant factor might be found in the extant images of consumption to which both monks and laymen were captive. When it came to the praise of God – up to the eleventh century at least – nothing less than splendid ceremony would do; monastic wealth, rather than being refused or redistributed, went to feed the sumptuous glorification of God, of which Cluny offered the prototype. For the Cluniacs indeed, as confirmed in Cowdrey's skillful interpretation, material splendor and the importunity with which gifts were solicited were neither mere preoccupation with corporate material wealth for its own sake nor just a reward for their faithful monastic observance, but an integral part of the monks' work of intercession for the living and the dead: "Every part of Cluny's buildings, every embellishment of its worship, and every parcel of the endowments which sustained it, spoke of the glories of heaven and commended to St. Peter and St. Paul the souls of the benefactors for whose salvation the monastic round was performed."[39]

With the Cistercian reaction and search for a more inward and sober worship, the fruits of systematic labor – mostly by the lay brothers – came to be rechanneled into the management of land and property. This, in turn, as the standard account goes, contributed to the further expansion of wealth and to the rapid corruption of the early Cistercian ideals.[40] Strikingly, at any rate, even the Cistercians did not disentangle themselves from the acceptance of donations that they only partially redefined – refusing only property burdened with feudal obligations (and otherwise taking advantage of all the usual indemnities and privileges).

---

[38] G. Duby, *Saint Bernard et l'art cistercien* (Paris: Flammarion, 1979).

[39] H. E. J. Cowdrey, *The Cluniacs and the Gregorian Reform* (Oxford: Clarendon, 1970), p. 131.

[40] See L. J. Lekai, *The Cistercians: Ideals and Reality* (Kent, Ohio: Kent State University Press, 1977). There is now increasing evidence, however, that what were thought to be later signs of "corruption" were already in evidence in even the first "wave" of Cistercian expansion, thus questioning the very nature of the Cistercian endeavor from its very beginning.

However, modes of consumption among the laity, and related concepts of worship, were themselves affected by changes in the socioeconomic environment, with crucial implications for the flow of donations. With growing urbanization and commercial activity in the twelfth century, Duby argues, the interest of princes shifted from endowing splendid monasteries to promoting a clerical technocracy to help run their worldly business. More generally, it has been often noted that the far-reaching economic and ideological changes of the twelfth century marked the beginning of the decline in lay donations and consequently in monastic wealth. It is remarkable, however, that despite the emergence of such trends as early as the first half of the eleventh century, Benedictine monasticism apparently withstood, and better than is often thought (at least up to the mid-twelfth century), what many have seen as a major "crisis" of the monastic institution. Only toward the end of the twelfth century can one really speak of a decline in donations.[41] The sharp contemporaneous decline in the practice of child oblation, that is, committing children to the monastic life – may also have been an important factor in the crisis. Before it rather abruptly fell out of favor, this previously common practice, as already mentioned often induced wealthy aristocratic families to endow the monastery to which their child was devoted, and even to ensure that aristocratic standards of living were maintained.[42]

Be that as it may, the relation of exchange between monks and laymen – which, as we have said, was purely voluntary and also, doctrinally at least, of a relatively secondary and "dissolvable" kind – was then undoubtedly undermined. As long as it did obtain, however (roughly from the sixth to the twelfth centuries, and even beyond, if in a much attenuated form), it displayed some similarities to the Theravada gift relationship. On the diverging side, however, the explicit reciprocity that characterized it (in contrast to the Theravada *dana* relation) received further accentuation, as monasteries increasingly provided not only spiritual intangibles but also a variety of concrete economic and social services in holding their part of the exchange.

Between autonomy and incorporation

Another indication of the greater autonomy of Christian monkhood (stated negatively) is that, in contrast with what happened in Burma and Thailand, monastic life was never incorporated as a normal, temporary stage in the average life cycle, or in other words, never became a sort of rite of passage. There was some link to the life cycle among the highest

[41] J. Van Engen, "The 'Crisis of Cenobitism' Reconsidered: Benedictine Monasticism in the Years 1050–1150," *Speculum* 61, no. 2 (1986): 266–304.
[42] Southern, *Western Society and the Church*, pp. 228–9.

strata, both secular and clerical, where young men would be sent to a prestigious monastery for a few years of schooling, or one might retire to a monastery in old age.[43] This remained, however, a totally unsystematic and voluntary pattern limited to the social elites, rather than a norm applicable to all. Nobles and princes, moreover, were usually satisfied with the *vestitudo ad succurendum,* ensuring that they died and were buried dressed in a monk's cowl in the hope of enhancing their chances of salvation.[44]

Christian monasticism also displayed, in contrast with the Sangha, an increasing and self-conscious tendency to acquire independence from local units and authorities – both ecclesiastical and secular. This tendency, already noted with regard to the development of broad supralocal and supranational structures, is only the more noteworthy in the light of contrary beginnings. Monastic communities were made formally subservient to the ecclesiastical hierarchy as early as the Council of Chalcedon (451), whose resolutions were repeatedly invoked by bishops in their attempts to maintain their diocesan right of control over the monasteries. The Rule of Saint Benedict (ch. 64) enjoined the monastic community (then still essentially lay) to refer to the external authority of the local bishop when need be, for instance in cases in which difficulties arose over the election of the abbot. Early medieval monasteries not only accepted, but even relied on the hierarchical authority and sanction of the secular Church. The Church was made the protector (at least in theory) of the monasteries' spiritual interests – a role not unlike that of the king vis-à-vis the Sangha – helping the abbot maintain internal discipline, and even supervising the abbot himself.

Such power of supervision and interference could easily be abused, however. The history of the relation between monasteries and bishops is one of pervasive tension and recurrent conflict, involving not only matters of moral and spiritual rights but also, more often than not, the control of temporal wealth.[45] Monasteries strove to become exempt from obedience to local bishops, with varying success: Exemption could be total or partial, and was more common in certain areas than others. It appears to have been especially weak in Germany, where it nearly totally disappeared in the eleventh century. Lay patrons, or nobles and other vassals to whom kings would give monasteries and/or monastic offices (including the position of abbot), could also be the source of

[43] See for example Johnson, *Prayer, Patronage and Power,* pp. 41–3; Avril, *Le gouvernement des évêques,* pp. 811–12.

[44] L. Gougaud, *Dévotions et pratiques ascétiques du Moyen-Age* (Paris: Pax, 1925), pp. 129–42.

[45] On the relation between bishops and the regular clergy, see for example, Dom P. Schmitz, *Histoire de l'Ordre de Saint Benôit,* ch. 3; Avril, *Gouvernement des évêques,* pp. 813–20.

serious interference, disposing of monastic property and interfering with monastic life as they saw fit.

Cluny's recommending itself to the sole authority and protection of the Holy See – a still rather distant and ineffective force at that stage – and thereby removing itself entirely from the control of both secular lord and bishop, is the best-known if far from unique example of Christian monasticism's struggle for autonomy, of no equivalent in the Theravada context. Although Cluny's insistence on exemption from episcopal authority and local lay interference seems to be clearly antifeudal in orientation, there is now much evidence that Cluny, in fact, was not necessarily always at odds with local authorities, and was even willing to entertain positive and mutually supportive relations with many local lords and bishops.[46] Be that as it may, one has to recall that Cluniac independence from local lay and ecclesiastical authority was ultimately warranted by another, external, and in fact superior authority, that of Rome, to which Cluny admitted allegiance. It might well not have been able to develop and maintain its unique autonomy without the active support of the Papacy.[47] Cluniac autonomy, in fact, did undergo a temporary setback when Pope Benedict IX (1033–45) withdrew papal support, leaving Cluny vulnerable to the attacks of the bishop of Macon.[48] On the other hand, Cluny was far from totally subject to the Papacy, even at the time of its close alliance with the Gregorian papacy, and repeatedly displayed marks of independent policy. This applies even in such crucial matters as papal theocratic claims against the empire, which Cluny did not fully sustain,[49] or the opposition to lay investiture of bishoprics, in which Cluny came out more moderate than Rome – perhaps due to the development of a tight network of interactions with the aristocracy, a class that the Gregorian project was envisioned to weaken.[50]

Beyond the (in many way unique) case of Cluny, the Gregorian Reform may be seen as having had the same effect on monasteries as on all other ecclesiastical offices and property, namely, ensuring their greater freedom from lay interference. Nevertheless, it also contributed, ultimately, to strengthening both papal and episcopal authority over monks. The historical process is thus one of oscillation between phases of lesser

---

[46] See H. Diener, "Das Verhaltnis Clunys zu den Bischofen vor allem in der Zeit seines Abtes Hugo (1049–1109)," in G. Tellenbach (ed.), *Neue Forschungen uber Cluny und die Cluniacenser* (Freiburg: Verlag Herder, 1959), pp. 219–338; H. E. Mager, "Studien uber das Verhaltnis der Cluniacenser zum Eigenkirchenwese," in Tellenbach (ed.), *Neue Forschungen*, pp. 167–214.

[47] For the development and gradual enhancement of Cluny's autonomy through a unique pattern of relationship with the Papacy, see Cowdrey, *Cluniacs and the Gregorian Reform*.

[48] Ibid., pp. 44 ff.

[49] Ibid., pp. 157 ff.

[50] See especially Mager, "Studien uber das Verhaltnis."

and greater autonomy, if always within the framework of ecclesiastical discipline.

Indeed, the difference with the Sangha does not lie simply in Christian monasticism's greater potential for institutional autonomy, but rather in its greater tendency to oscillate between autonomy and incorporation. In many respects, we can see Christian monasticism in the first stage, from the sixth to the eleventh century (and during the Carolingian era in particular), as sharing with the Sangha a common baseline of social incorporation and deautonomization, despite the many differences of detail.

First, western monasteries, like those of the Sangha, came to provide society at large with extensive services. The major type of service was the saying of masses for the donor or deceased members of his family: Believing in the solidarity of the dead and the living, laymen were eager to enter into the *societas et fraternitas* of monastic communities for the purpose of commemorating the dead through the mediation of monks' prayers.[51] Giving a sense of the amplitude of that drive, Reichenau's *Liber memorialis,* or book of commemorative fraternity, starting from Carolingian times up to the eleventh century, contained no fewer than forty thousand names.[52] This commemorative function was developed in a particularly systematic and extensive fashion by Cluny, which also endeavored to multiply its intercessory effect by having the same anniversary and commemorative masses performed throughout all Cluniac communities at the same time. Computerized examination of all known obituaries from Cluniac monasteries, in the strictest sense of that term,[53] has now produced a list of some forty-eight thousand names of the dead.[54] Death and the afterlife, in fact, were perhaps the most important point of confluence between monks – the "dead to the world" – and society. This was also reflected in laymen's desire, beginning in the second half of the sixth century, to be buried in or near a monastery, resulting in the growth of huge cemeteries around the latter's precincts. As for the great of this world, they often managed to be buried within the walls of the monastery itself. With the increasing medieval preoccupation with death, the funerary role of monks expanded, yielding an

---

[51] See K. Schmid and J. Wollasch, "Die Gemeinschaft der Lebenden und Berstorbenen in Zeugnissen des Mittelalters," *Fruhmittelalterliche Studien* 1 (1967): 365–405.

[52] Wollasch, "Les obituaires," p. 143.

[53] Strictly Cluniac houses are those legally subject to Cluny, whose monks were all individually professed to the abbot Cluny. Cluny's influence, however, reached much beyond strictly Cluniac houses.

[54] See J. Wollasch, W. D. Heim, H. Mehne, F. Neiske and D. Poeck, (eds.), *Synopse der cluniacensichen Necrologien* (Munich: Wilhelm Fink, 1982). This is a huge collective work of computerized compilation and analysis of Cluniac necrologies.

increasing number of obituaries in the course of the eleventh and twelfth centuries especially, when funerary services came to play a growing part in the liturgy, and monasteries were besieged by a periphery of graves.

More collectively oriented were monks' prayers for the material and spiritual welfare of Christian kingdoms and their rulers. Monks were seen as a militant elite protecting Christian society through their heroic struggle against malevolent supernatural powers. The theme of *miles Christi,* present already in the desert tradition, where it denoted the solitary combat of the individual ascetic with evil spirits, received an additional twist, and came to be applied to the collective relation between monks and Christian society as a whole. The military imagery entailed is well conveyed in King Edgar's foundation charter for New Minster, Winchester (966):

> The abbot is armed with spiritual weapons and supported by a troop of monks anointed with the dew of heavenly graces. They fight together in the strength of Christ with the sword of the spirit against the aery wiles of the devils. They defend the king and clergy of the realm from the onslaughts of their invisible enemies.[55]

Furthermore, monasteries performed a range of variegated functions, although not always to the same extent: They served not only as necropolises but also as medieval equivalents of banks, hotels, old-age homes, and even asylums; they absorbed unmarried women of great families;[56] cared for unwanted children, as long as child oblation (allowed in Benedict's Rule) was in vogue; and provided clerical help to princes. No less important, monasteries were – at least until the emergence of the cathedral schools and the universities – the main educational and intellectual institution of Christendom.[57] In this latter function, however, they catered primarily to their own needs, to the education of oblates and novices, or the education of the nobility; only rarely – unlike the

---

[55] Quoted by Southern, *Western Society and the Church,* p. 225.

[56] This is far from being the only significance of the absorption of women into the monastic sector, a topic that demands fuller analysis on its own. Convents often functioned under the spiritual supervision of a monastery to which they were annexed, the few and later cases (such as the Brigittines or Fontevrault) where both men and women could come under the authority of an abbess remaining exceptions. At any rate, both convents and female recluses were no less accepted a phenomenon than their male counterparts, and the place of women in all forms of religious virtuosity (and heresy) increased from the eleventh century on and beyond the period under study in the present work. Christian monasticism's ability, in contrast with the Buddhist Sangha, to encompass both sexes, should perhaps be taken as another sign of autonomy (from extant categories of gender and kinship in this case).

[57] See J. Leclercq, *L'amour des lettres et le désir de Dieu: initiation aux auteurs monastiques du Moyen-Age* (Paris: Cerf, 1957). Idem, "Il y a-t-il une culture monastique?" in *Il Monachesimo.* I do not claim to consider the (to my mind, fascinating) issue of the intellectual contribution of monasticism and the development of a specifically monastic "culture," but stress only some of the most salient institutional aspects.

Sangha – did they maintain schools serving larger sections of the laity. Monasteries also served as the depositories and guardians of saintly relics, a function that, perhaps more than any other, was of significance to all strata of medieval society, but on which they did not have the monopoly.[58] (The possession of relics can hardly be seen as a distinguishing hallmark of monasteries at a time when every church altar and many aristocratic houses could boast some relics of sorts. Relics, moreover, were highly mobile and transportable goods, easily subject to trade, theft, and forgery, by monasteries or anybody else.)[59]

There is even some similarity with the Sangha in the loss of autonomy vis-à-vis secular rulers. Besides being subordinated to episcopal control, Christian monasticism, like its Theravada Buddhist counterpart, was very much affected by the policies and fortunes of kings and emperors. Not unlike the Sangha at some stages, monasticism brought its missionary impulse to the service of the colonizing and "civilizing" aims of both empire and papacy. The missionary impetus, absent in the earlier phases of monasticism, became first and most salient among Irish monks, and received further encouragement from Pope Gregory the Great (590–604), who actively promoted the expansion, among Anglo-Saxon populations, of Benedictine monasteries intended to serve as so many centers of Christian life and instruments of Christianization.[60] A similar "civilizing" tendency asserted itself, albeit later, on the Continent as well, first with the dissemination of Irish-Frankish monasteries into the countryside under Merovingian kings in the seventh century, and the evangelization of Germanic populations by Benedictine monks in the eight century. Although popes and bishops were at first the main initiators and supporters of these trends, there is no doubt that kings remained far from indifferent to their political implications. The active role of Merovingian kings in promoting monasticism may have been in part due to sincere religious motives, but one cannot fail to note that it was also conveniently compatible with political expansion.[61] The part played by the Carolingian regime in monastic reform and uniformization has already been mentioned. Through its agency, "support of the Benedictine Rule became a feature of

---

[58] See for example Duby, *Age of the Cathedrals*, pp. 59–61.

[59] See P. Geary, *Furta Sacra: Thefts of Relics in the Central Middle Ages* (Princeton, N.J.: Princeton University Press, 1978). The highly mobile and transportable nature of relics in Western Christendom (but not Germany, where their holiness was more tightly bound to geographical location) has been emphasized, with regard to the later centuries of the Middles Ages in particular, in L. Rothkrug, "German Holiness and Western Sanctity in Medieval and Modern History," *Historical Reflections/Reflexions Historiques* 15 (1988): 161–248.

[60] See M. Pacaut, *Les ordres monastiques et religieux au Moyen-Age* (Paris: F. Nathan, 1970), ch. 4.

[61] See Geary, *Before France and Germany: The Creation and Transformation of the Merovingian World* (New York: Oxford University Press, 1988), pp. 177–8.

central government."[62] The spread and imposition of Benedictine monasticism at the expense of older Irish-Frankish and Gallo-Roman forms actually became a measure of the growing Carolingian control in the Frankish world.[63] Moreover, the monasticism favored by Charlemagne was not contemplative and withdrawn, but expected to be "useful" and contribute its share to the Carolingian renaissance.[64] This entailed, among other things, a great expansion in monasteries' scholarly and educational activities, both within the monastery proper and in "external" schools where monks would come to teach, at the expense of the more traditional emphasis on work and prayer – again emphasizing the role of monasteries as centers of culture and civilization.

All this, obviously, was a far cry from the original flight into the desert by individuals in search of their own religious salvation. What the trends just described denote is a social involvement and "functionalization" (in the sense explained in Chapter 2) of the monastic institution different in many aspects from the Sangha's, but certainly no weaker, and in some respects even more systematic and thorough.

Monasticism and royalty

One might see a further similarity with the Theravada Buddhist case in that here too a pattern of interaction that obtained on a microsocial level with individual laymen was "stretched" with little modification to the macrosocietal level, to the interaction with kings as rulers of society. Nevertheless, the relative importance and meaning of the relationship at this level was very different from the one it achieved in Southeast Asia. First, as already announced by the doctrinal–ideological differences in this regard, the relationship fundamentally remained one of explicit exchange, involving both material and symbolic resources on both sides. In fact, it was so explicit and reciprocal that it tended to assume the character of an economic transaction corresponding to a functional division of labor, hence vulnerable to changes in the balance and "fair" reciprocity of the exchange. Second, Christian monarchs never became as dependent on their relationship to the monastic sector as did Buddhist kings. To begin with, the existence of a secular clergy provided an alternative source of religious absolution and legitimization. Most impor-

---

[62] Southern, *Western Society and the Church,* p. 218.
[63] See Geary, *Before France and Germany,* pp. 215–17.
[64] See Pacaut, *Les ordres,* pp. 46 ff. Benedict of Aniane's reform meant to reemphasize withdrawal from the world (and its concomitant prayer) in the definition of the monastic vocation through a more uniform enforcement of the Benedictine Rule. This itself was made possible and promoted by the support of a ruler, Louis the Pious, who was more sympathetic to the contemplative aims of monasticism than his father, Charlemagne.

tantly, however, their own sacral legitimacy (stemming partly from pre-Christian Germanic traditions) was in some important respects stronger and more autonomous than that of the Buddhist kings. Kingship in Christendom was strengthened and stabilized by the principle of royal dynasties and blood lineage, in contrast with the weakness of ascriptive principles in Theravada, where kings had to prove their karmic merit and personal charisma. Further weakening the king's dependence on legitimization by religious authorities was the notion of the king's direct election by God, which the Church only comes to confirm. This the Church had no problem doing, willing as it was to recognize that "all power is of God," as long as its own ultimate superiority was acknowledged. In fact, however, this was not always the case. Kings also perceived themselves in roles that could only clash with the Church's conception of its own supremacy. If they did not view themselves as priests (the king-priest, or *rex sacerdos,* rooted in the tradition of Melchisedek, had no powerful offshoot in Western Christianity), they did consider themselves at least as supreme among the *oratores.* A last dimension in the symbolics of sacral kingship were the supernatural powers of the "*rois thaumaturges,*" so brilliantly expounded by Marc Bloch.[65] This, however, was a later phenomenon, that appeared only in the twelfth century, and was perhaps symptomatic of the resurgence of royal power after a temporary decline in the tenth.

Especially telling, from this point of view, is the special relationship that developed between monarchy and certain royal monasteries, such as Fleury or Saint Denis, where kings had themselves buried and kept the symbols of their royal power, and upon which they lavished their benefactions and personal interest. First launched under the reign of the Merovingian king Dagobert I (629–38),[66] the special connection between Saint Denis and royal power culminated under the direction of the abbot Suger (1122–51), who was propelled to the summit of political influence through his long personal friendship with Louis VI, and remained a principal counselor to Louis VII, in whose absence he actually governed the realm of France for two years (1147–9). The point, however, is that these select monasteries became strongholds of royal cults and ideology, developing the praise of the monarch to an extent unknown even in the capital monasteries of the Theravada Buddhist setting.[67] Indeed, this special relationship between the monarchy and the monastic sector – or more precisely, specific, prestigious monasteries – must be placed within the

[65] M. Bloch, *Les rois thaumaturges* (Paris: Albin, 1961).

[66] Dagobert was the first to endow Saint-Denis with enormous amounts of land and wealth – and expect from it the perpetual offering of prayers for the king, his family and his kingdom. See Geary, *Before France and Germany,* p. 167.

[67] See Duby, *Age of the Cathedrals,* especially pp. 97 ff.

context of the perpetual struggle between religious and secular authorities in medieval Europe. The tendency of kings to turn to monasteries might be interpreted as a way in which they preserved a "window on the sacred" and an important basis of legitimacy – a pattern replicated by the lesser nobility. This relationship also had the advantage of not being as burdened by comprehensive political implications as relationships with the secular ecclesiastical hierarchy. Admittedly, this special tie between kings and monasteries was more than counterbalanced by the tendency of important parts of the monastic sector to develop allegiance to Rome rather than to local church authorities and national kings.[68] Nevertheless, it still may be taken as the epitome of Christian monasticism's potential for social involvement and incorporation, despite its no-less-real and impressive institutional autonomy.

Monasticism and social elites

A crucial characteristic of Christian monasticism's social incorporation, alluded to earlier, was the development of an especially tight and manifold (if never exclusive) connection to the nobility and to social elites in general.[69] This presents an important contrast with the Sangha, where the major factor of "domestication" was the grass-roots embedment within a local and weakly stratified village laity, with no special linkage to higher strata. (Here again, Sri Lanka was the deviant case, coming closer to the Western situation, with a society that was caste-stratified – albeit much less rigidly than the Indian caste system – and where recruitment to the Sangha was very early limited to the highest caste.)

This connection between Christian monasticism and the social elites had many expressions: Nobles – oblates and other recruits – accounted for a large share of the monastic population and were predominant among its leadership;[70] some monasteries even became reserved for the

---

[68] There were, however, significant geographical and historical variations in these tendencies. The *Regularis Concordia* (c. 970), for example, shows English monasticism to have a distinctive, even intimate connection with British monarchy and national identity. See Knowles, *Monastic Order in England,* pp. 44–6.

[69] See F. Prinz, "Mönchtum und Frühmittelalterliche Adelgesellschaft im Spiegel der Hagiographie," in *Askese und Kultur,* pp. 75–86; J. Wollasch, "Parenté noble et monachisme réformateur: observation sur les 'conversions' à la vie monastique aux XIe et XIIe siecles," *Revue Historique* 535 (1980): 3–24.

[70] This was already the case in pre-Columbian Merovingian monasticism: "Abbots and bishops were members of a highly cultured elite, joined together by education and above all by the bonds of *amicitia*. Although members of the most significant aristocratic families tended to look to episcopal rather than abbatial office, no hard and fast line can be drawn between the bishops and abbots of this period with respect to their social origins or their cultural attainments." See I. Wood, "A Prelude to Columbanus: The Monastic Achievement in the Burgundian Territories," in H. B. Clarke and M. Brennan (eds.), *Columbanus and*

nobility though in theory monasteries were open to all classes; monasteries were founded and supported through noble patronage; and many of monasticism's social functions and services were particularly and sometimes even exclusively oriented toward the nobility. This was true even of the function of intercessory prayer, since it was customary for noble families to offer very young children to a monastery where they could then pray all their lives for the salvation of their relatives, who remained in the world.[71] Monastic "external" education chiefly involved children from elevated backgrounds, and at least before the great apostolic revival, women's monasteries catered mostly to women of noble backgrounds. It came to be taken for granted that monasticism would be able to provide its members of elevated social origins with the aristocratic standards of living they were accustomed to, despite the obvious contradiction with ascetic ideals of renunciation; this was one of the most significant factors in the eventual corruption of monastic ideals.[72]

Irish monasticism may have played a crucial role in the early establishment of this relation to the aristocratic elites. According to Prinz,[73] the Columbian missionary wave had the effect of detaching monasticism from its previous urban episcopal connection (itself contrary to its original antiurban character), leading it to the countryside, where it took on the form of aristocratic or royal monasteries with manorial organization.[74] Moreover, the spectacular success of Columbanus was mainly determined, in Prinz's view, by close personal connections with the Frankish aristocracy: Outstanding pupils at Luxeuil were influential aristocrats and officeholders at the Merovingian court who, precisely because of their old political connections, could do much for the material advancement of monasteries.[75]

It seems possible to extend this idea beyond the Merovingian era and apply it to the close relations of both Cluniacs and Cistercians with the

Merovingian Monasticism (Oxford: B.A.R., 1981), p. 5. Furthermore, noble ascetics did not necessarily disconnect themselves from their kinship ties: first, they did not stray too far from civilization, and often journeyed to the marginal land just within or slightly beyond the boundaries of the family estate. Wood also notes that saints who had begun by dissociating themselves entirely from their families came into closer contact with their relatives once sanctity was achieved; the break from secular ties of a family was thus followed by religious influence that worked through family connections (p. 8).

[71] Duby, *Age of Cathedrals,* p. 59.
[72] The role played by infant oblation in this trend has already been mentioned.
[73] F. Prinz, "Columbanus, the Frankish Nobility and the Territories East of the Rhine," in Clark and Brennan, *Columbanus and Merovingian Monasticism,* pp. 73–90.
[74] Prinz also perceives here the influence of the Irish monastic church, with its close interrelation of political and monastic structures: The office of abbot was handed down in the family of the original founder, who in his turn was frequently the head of the tribe or a member of the ruling circle.
[75] See also Geary, *Before France and Germany,* pp. 171–8 especially.

aristocratic classes.[76] In general, monasticism appears to be very much an "elite game." In this game, the nobility played a prominent part, and royal dynasties developed close associations with specific monasteries. It was not infrequent for kings (most notably Robert and Louis the Pious in France, or Edward the Confessor and Henry III in England) to display monastic inclinations. Kings often kept monks in their entourage and in some cases even abdicated the crown in order to adopt the monastic life.[77] In the case of Louis the Pious, for one, Benedictine notions of the abbot's authority and accountability to God for the soul of his brethren may have even shaped conceptions of imperial rule and responsibility.[78] Abbots, on the other hand, developed close connections with the highest secular and clerical elites. Many popes and bishops came from a monastic background; not infrequently they maintained the custom of periods of monastic or even eremitic retreat. Saint Bernard, abbot of Clairvaux, born to a knightly family, is the prime example, as he was not only the spiritual leader of the Cistercian order but also powerful enough to influence the fate of popes and even Christendom as a whole in his time.

This relationship with the social elites favored the easy access by Christian monasticism to political power through a network of connections to the very highest echelons of both the secular and ecclesiastical hierarchy. However, the connection between monasticism and nobility is also of a more intrinsic and not merely "political" nature. Underlying it was the widespread belief in a deep and necessary kinship between noble blood and virtue (also evident in the social background and definition of medieval sainthood),[79] that could have no equivalent in the Theravada Buddhist context. Moreover, the relationship was accompa-

---

[76] Cluny mainly spread at first in regions where kingship was weakest, and through connection to local powerful lords and princes.

[77] See C. Stancliffe, "Kings who Opted Out," in P. Wormald, D. Bullough, and R. Collins (eds.), *Ideal and Reality in Frankish and Anglo-Saxon Society* (Oxford: B. Blackwell, 1983), pp. 155–76. Stancliffe studied a wave, starting in England in the sixth and seventh centuries and peaking in the last quarter of the eighth century, of kings who voluntarily abdicated for the sake of religious life (either entering a monastery or going on an extended pilgrimage). This pattern seems, however, to be unique to England and to have little equivalent on the Continent in the same period. It corresponds, in Stancliffe's view, to a peak in the prestige of monasticism under the influence of Irish spirituality, not counterbalanced by a strong-enough conception of Christian kingship. On the Continent, by contrast, both clergy and kings, perhaps in a continuity of Greco-Roman orientations to the political arena, carried a more positive conception of kingship in general and of the potential contribution of Christian kingship in promoting Christianity. Joining the monastic life could also be, however, an honorable way of stepping down when a king's position, for whatever reason, became untenable.

[78] T. F. X. Noble, "The Monastic Idea as a Model for Empire: The Case of Louis the Pious," *Revue Bénédictine* 86 (1976): 235–50.

[79] A. Vauchez, "Beata stirps: sainteté et lignage en Occident," in G. Duby and J. Le Goff (eds.), *Famille et parenté dans l'Occident médiéval* (Rome: Ecole Française, 1977).

nied by mutual influence and even interpretation at the ideological level – aristocratic values, in their historical variants, affecting monastic spirituality, which itself played an important role in the evolution of these same values – in a complex, dialectical process that exceeds the scope of the present discussion.[80]

The association with social elites through networks of kinship, friendship, and political and ideological influence could work in two seemingly opposite directions: It functioned as perhaps the most important factor of monastic incorporation and deautonomization, but was no less important in sustaining a monastic impact on the external environment very different from that of the Sangha. A number of aspects of monks' interaction with wider society not found in the Theravada context highlight a pattern of forceful interpenetration, mutual impingement, or even competition between monasticism and other groups and social sectors; a more forceful, even if not necessarily direct, political involvement; and a far-reaching ascetic influence on society at large, loaded with innovative and even "transformative" implications.

Monasticism and the secular clergy

Rather than remaining confined to a clear-cut definition of its vocation, monasticism tended in time to encompass many religious and secular functions otherwise differentiated in Christian society at large. In particular, monasticism often penetrated domains of activity normally reserved for the secular clergy – for example, administering some of the sacraments and even providing entire parishes with full-fledged *cura animarum* indistinguishable from that provided by the secular clergy. This was partly a result of the multivocality of the monastic ideal itself oscillating between its more and less socially involved orientations – which prevented it from remaining as clearly segregated and confined to specific domains of activity as the Sangha – and partly because of the increasing role of liturgy in monastic life. In fact, only two features clearly distinguished monks from priests, at least institutionally: Priests were not devoted to the search for Christian perfection, their primary function being to administer sacraments and the *cura animarum;* though clearly distinct from laymen, priests were not committed to seclusion and to the type of segregation from society that goes along with it.

One might have thought that Church and monastery would eventually settle into clear-cut differentiated roles – monks totally devoting them-

---

[80] This process of mutual impingement is finely suggested, with regard to the relation between Irish monasticism and Frankish aristocracy in Geary, *Before France and Germany,* pp. 171 ff.; and with regard to Cistercian spirituality in Duby, St. Bernard et l'art cistercien, pp. 149 ff.

selves to a perfect imitation of Christ and the search for individual
salvation, whereas priests would handle the *vita activa,* the distribution
of sacraments, and the *cura animarum.* Yet the history of the relation
between monks and priests is one of constant interpenetration and even
competition in most of these areas. This combination of interpenetration
and competition was already present in the early, less-differentiated
stages. Starting as a lay perfectionist movement in flight from a Christianity it saw as increasingly corrupted by worldliness, monasticism was
ultimately at odds with the clergy of which it implied a basic criticism,
even if it never actually rejected its authority.[81] At the same time, the
Church found it hard not to welcome the tendency of monasticism to
expand into originally extramonastic spheres of activity in times when
the secular clergy was often corrupt and illiterate, and hence less efficient in serving the Christianizing and expansionist endeavors of both
Church and empire. By the ninth century, many monks (assessments
range from a quarter to a half) were also ordained priests. Following
Benedict of Aniane's reform, the liturgical function acquired increasing
centrality in monastic life, and even became a dominant feature in the
Cluniac order from the tenth century on. As for the clergy, it developed
a type of *vita mixta* in the order of regular canons – priests taking upon
themselves a common life and other elements typical of the monastic
life. Popes themselves frequently came from a monastic background.

The Gregorian reform, to be later discussed in greater detail, is
especially significant from the point of view of the relation between
regular and secular clergy. Commonly considered to stretch from the
Council of Rheims (1049) to the first Lateran Council (1123) but owing
its name to Pope Gregory VII (1073–85), who was one of its chief
exponents, the Gregorian project involved, among other things, the
attempt to reassert the cleavage between clergy and laity – a cleavage
that had been much weakened by the corrupting influence of simony
(the sale and purchase of church offices), lay investiture (lay preroga-
tives in the selection and ordination of clergymen), nicolaism (the marriage of priests), and generally low standards of priesthood. This reforming policy, moreover, has to be understood as part and parcel of
the Gregorians' intent to promote papal supremacy within the church
and even within Christendom at large.[82] A crucial aspect of Gregorian

[81] See Bitterman, "The Beginning of the Struggle between the Regular and the
Secular Clergy," pp. 19–26.
[82] The literature on the Gregorian era is voluminous and still growing. See among
the more contemporary works, Tellenbach, *Church, State and Society;* N. F.
Cantor, *Church, Kingship, and Lay Investiture in England, 1089–1135* (Princeton, N.J.: Princeton University Press, 1958); Cowdrey, *Cluniacs and the Gregorian Reform;* K. Morrison, "The Gregorian Reform," in McGinn et al. (eds.),
Christian Spirituality, pp. 177–93.

policy, at any rate, was the attempt to enforce celibacy as well as higher standards of morality, knowledge, and spirituality, or in other words, to "monachize" the clergy.[83] With these aims in mind, a succession of Gregorian popes also developed a close partnership – the precise nature of which has been much debated by historians – with important parts of the monastic sector and Cluny in particular.[84] In a later phase, however, the papacy attempted to reestablish a clearer distinction between monks and priests, and switched to favoring the more withdrawn monastic orders, whose vocation was more clearly distinct from that of the secular clergy.

The emergence of the mendicant orders in the thirteenth century further complicated the picture, since these explicitly took upon themselves the activity of preaching and hearing confession, until then the preserve of the secular clergy. These multiple trends of mutual interpenetration and competition were accompanied by much struggle and antagonism – monks proving to be no less polemical than the others – that especially intensified from the tenth to the thirteenth centuries with the increasing differentiation of the monastic sector, the emergence of various types of canons, and finally, the appearance of the friars and their own orders.[85] The laity itself may be said to have joined this area of competition over the same period, developing new forms of religious expression (at times heretical and often anticlerical), and giving rise to a whole range of groups and organizations (such as penitential groups, popular movements, lay fraternities, or lay orders) that, albeit often monastically inspired in spiritual orientation, increasingly operated outside and independently of the monastic and mendicant sectors.[86]

[83] See, for example, Morrison, "Gregorian Reform," p. 188 ff.

[84] The literature on the relation of Cluny and other reformed monastic branches to the various phases and aspects of the Gregorian project is extensive and rife with controversies. The earlier historical stance that tended to see the Gregorian reform as a direct outgrowth of Cluny's reform has now been long superseded by a much more complex analysis of the various forces at work in the Gregorian reform and of an only temporary convergence, or even superficial compatibility between monastic and papal aims. This is especially emphasized in H. J. White, "The Gregorian Ideal and Saint Bernard of Clairvaux," *Journal of the History of Ideas* 21 (1960): 321–48; also Tellenbach, *Church, State and Christian Society,* especially pp. 186 ff; Cowdrey, *Cluniacs and the Gregorian Reform;* idem, "Cluny and the First Crusade," *Revue Bénédictine* 23 (1973): 285–311.

[85] See especially M. D. Chenu, "Monks, Canons and Laymen in Search of the Apostolic Life in idem, *Nature, Man, Society: Essays on New Theological Perspectives in the Latin West* (Chicago: University of Chicago Press, 1968); E. W. McDonnel, "The Vita Apostolica: Diversity or Dissent?", *Church History* 24 (1955): 15–31; G. Constable, "The Diversity of Religious Life and Acceptance of Social Pluralism in the Twelfth Century," in McGinn et al. (eds.), *Christian Spirituality,* pp. 29–47.

[86] For the gradual development of a distinctive spirituality of the laity in the first millenium, see J. Fontaine, "The Practice of Christian Life: The Birth of the

Monasticism and political power

From a more specifically "political" perspective, that is, focusing on issues of control, power and authority, monasticism came to hold a great deal of power in a competitive social arena. Worldly political involvement was to be avoided by those who had opted for monastic seclusion from a world they despised. Monks never became as fully autonomous a political force as the secular hierarchy and the papacy, to which they always remained subordinate in one way or another. Their impact, like the Sangha's, most often operated indirectly and informally. There are, however, basic differences between the two: First, monasticism simply commanded greater coalitional power in the perennial clashes between kings and church, empire and papacy, nobles and kings, and nobles among themselves – all competing to draw monasteries into their respective spheres of influence to boost their own power and legitimacy; second, the manifold network of connection to the elites, already described, ensured rapid access to effective foci of institutional authority; third, the existence of the Church itself, of which monasticism was a part and that it never altogether rejected, provided monks with a religious institution in the world to which they could return and in which they could even assume leadership once clad with the prestige of their previous ascetic seclusion.

These various aspects of monks' political involvement reflect the vertical principle that made monasticism essentially consonant with, rather than antithetical to, authority and power (be it secular or religious), and thus much better equipped for struggles in the political sphere. This may already be discerned in the formative stages of the ascetic movement: The intense concern with issues of authority, the appeal of spiritual ascetic authority inside and outside the monastic milieu, and the oscillation between retreat to the desert and the return to positions of institutional power (giving rise to the somewhat paradoxical figure of the monk-bishop in fifth-century Gaul), were all in tune with later developments.[87] As Bowersock has emphasized, the ability to create a new and characteristic form of institutional authority at that stage may have given Christianity a definite edge over competing contemporary intellectual and soteriological movements. The adherents of the latter might opt out of ordinary life for some sort of with-

Laity," in McGinn et al. (eds.), *Christian Spirituality,* pp. 453–91. On the increasing religious activization of the laity as such from the tenth to the thirteenth centuries, see Chenu, "Monks, Canons and Laymen; J. R. Strayer, "The Laicization of French and English Society in the Thirteenth Century," in S. Thrupp (ed.), *Change in Medieval Society* (New York: Appleton, Century & Crofts, 1964), pp. 103–16.

[87] Rousseau, *Ascetics, Authority and the Church.*

drawn and even eremitic life – a common mark of the philosophic life among various schools at the time – and even become close friends or advisors of secular rulers. But they did not combine ascetic withdrawal and institutional authority, a revolutionary and effective combination to be found time and again in later stages of Christian history.[88] Significantly, however, political involvement was never the domain of entire monasteries or orders, but only of abbots – responsible for the monastery's interaction with the external world, and clearly differentiated from other members of the community in this function – frequently traveling and entertaining guests from the outside world (within the monastery, but on distinct premises) and disposing of a budget kept distinct from the monastic budget proper. Furthermore, political influence usually affirmed itself not as a routine, taken-for-granted property of the monastic institution as such or of abbots in general, but only through monastic leaders of outstanding personality – such as Wala of Corbie, Suger of Saint Denis, or Bernard of Clairvaux – and not without reservations and dilemmas for both the abbots themselves and their communities.[89]

Religious and cultural impact

On the whole, monastic political behavior remained within the established rules of the game and showed little innovative or radical potential before the eleventh century. However, monasticism also exerted a significant religious and cultural, rather than specifically political, impact upon society at large, one increasingly loaded, at least up to the thirteenth century, with dynamic and innovative potential for Christian society. Throughout the period under study, there was a significant and increasing diffusion of monastic standards of spirituality into other sectors of Christian society, both lay and clerical. This was especially evident in the increasingly elaborate patterns of penitence, originally adopted from the monastic world;[90] the gradual enforcement of priestly celibacy;[91] the emergence in the tenth century of ideals of lay sanctity fed by monastic

[88] G. Bowersock, "Architects of Competing Transcendental Visions in Late Antiquity," in S. N. Eisenstadt (ed.), *The Origins and Diversity of the Axial Age Civilizations* (Albany, N.Y.: SUNY Press, 1986); Drijvers, "Askese und Monchtum," pp. 444–65.

[89] See H. Mayr-Haring, "Two Abbots in Politics: Wala of Corbie and Bernard of Clairvaux," *Transactions of the Royal Historical Society* 5, no. 40 (1990): 217–37.

[90] C. Vogel, *La discipline pénitentielle en Gaule des origines à la fin du VIIe siecle* (Paris: Letouzoy et Aré 1952); N. T. Tentler, *Sin and Confession on the Eve of the Reformation* (Princeton, N.J.: Princeton University Press, 1977).

[91] H. C. Lea, *History of Sacerdotal Celibacy in the Christian Church* (London: Watts, 1932).

models and criteria – as in Odo's biography of Count Gerald of Aurillac (d. 909);[92] the incorporation of lay brothers into the monastic community, followed later by the formation of lay third orders; and the strong ascetic tendencies of lay religious movements, some of which were subsequently condemned as heretical (the Cathars, Arnoldians, Patarins, and Waldensians).[93] Knighthood itself is often analyzed nowadays as entailing, at some stage of its development, a strong element of "monastization of the warrior,"[94] in what is clearly a case of ideological cross-fertilization, since knightly values also penetrated the monastic world, leading to a merger of the two ideals in the Order of the Templars, initially supported by Saint Bernard of Clairvaux.[95] As already mentioned, a number of kings were clearly influenced by monastic values (Robert, Louis the Pious, Edward the Confessor, and Henry III) or had abbots among their closest friends and counselors (Alcuin with Charlemagne; Benedict of Aniane with Louis the Pious; and Lanfranc with William the Conqueror being the most famous examples).

Only with the movement of the Peace of God, which began in 989, can one discern a shift toward a more directly active role for monks in the "ascetic shaping" of their social environment. At stake in this movement was the attempt to reinstate a degree of peace and safety in areas where the decline of the monarchy left widespread disorder and warfare, and to provide protection not only for church property but also for the poor from the violence of lords, knights, and *milites* of all sorts.[96] Monks

[92] See J. C. Poulin, *L'idéal de sainteté dans l'Aquitaine carolingienne d'après les sources hagiographiques 750–950* (Québec: Presses de l'Université Laval, 1971).

[93] H. Gründmann, *Religiöse Bewegungen im Mittelalter* (Darmstadt: Wissenschaftliche Buchgesellschaft, 1961); T. Manteuffel, *Naissance d'une hérésie: les adeptes de la pauvreté volontaire au Moyen-Age* (Paris: Mouton, 1970); M. D. Lambert, *Medieval Heresy: Popular Movements from Bogomil to Hus* (London: Arnold, 1977). The Cathars are especially interesting from this point of view, since they also propounded the distinction and double standard between an ascetic elite and average believers (*perfecti* and *credentes*) taken over from the Manichean tradition.

[94] See, for example, G. Duby, "The Origins of Knighthood," in idem, *The Chivalrous Society* (Berkeley and Los Angeles: University of California Press, 1977), pp. 158–67.

[95] Cistercian monasticism itself is infused with religiously transposed knightly values. See Bernard of Clairvaux, "In Praise of the New Knighthood," pp. 125–68 in idem, *Treatises III* (Kalamazoo, Mich.: Cistercian, 1977), and the introduction by R. J. Z. Werblowsky; also Duby, *Saint Bernard: l'art cistercien,* pp. 77–82, 150 ff. A variant of this thesis of the transmutation of knightly orientations has even been applied to Benedictine monasticism in general. See B. H. Rosenwein and L. K. Little, "Social Meaning in Monastic and Mendicant Spiritualities," *Past and Present* 63 (1974): especially 15.

[96] See J. P. Poly and E. Bournazel, *La mutation féodale, Xe–XIIe siècle* (Paris: Presses Universitaires de France, 1980), pp. 251 ff.; H. E. J. Cowdrey, "The Peace of God and the Truce of God in the Eleventh Century," *Past and Present* 46 (1970): 42–67; G. Duby, "Laity and the Peace of God," in idem, *Chivalrous Society,* pp. 123–33.

played a prominent role in the great assemblies convened with the aim of committing the *bellatores* to peace, first through a general, overly ambitious attempt to contain violence by the threat of excommunication, later by the more partial (but more effective) banning of violence on specific days of the week. Cluny in particular threw all its authority behind the movement; Odo of Cluny's *Life* of Gerard d'Aurillac, already mentioned, undoubtedly played an important part in the emergence of a new ideal of Christian knighthood, promoting the (very impractical) image of a lay lord imbued with monastic ideals of abstinence and dedicated to nonviolence and the protection of Church and poor.[97] The authors of the peace initiative, however, also included the bishops, some of whom were in fact indignant at monks' emerging from their monasteries to interfere in worldly matters and assume functions of social control reserved for kings and bishops.

Not unrelated to the widespread millenarian belief in the imminence of the Second Coming around the end of the tenth century, the monastic ideal reached what was probably the climax of its prestige and influence in the eleventh, when the Church increasingly advocated higher (and thus closer to monastic) standards of poverty and chastity not only for the clergy but for all Christians.[98] This trend culminated during the Gregorian period, which at least in its early stages, as already noted, provided the monastic-ascetic ideal with broad institutional and political backing.[99] Some have been tempted to see this period as a revolutionary turning point in the history of Western civilization, as important as the Reformation itself.[100] In this vein, one is even reminded, indeed, of Luther's later attempt to "turn the world into a huge monastery."[101] The analogy, however, should not be exaggerated: Modern historians are now careful to distinguish between various phases of the Gregorian era and to emphasize that the intentions of abbots and popes, even at times of close collaboration, did not necessarily coincide.[102] Even in the case of Cluny, whose autonomy from local feudal interference and total subservience to the papacy were understood by a succession of Gregorian popes as the model of true ecclesiastic "*libertas,*" it may be more precise to talk of a broad compatibility rather than tight identification of monastic and papal objec-

---

[97] See Duby, *Chivalrous Society,* pp. 166–7.
[98] The thesis of a connection between eschatological fervor and the diffusion of monastic ideals into Christian society at large is especially propounded by Georges Duby. See for example, *Age of Cathedrals,* pp. 57–8.
[99] See this chapter, fn. 82.
[100] See, for example, N. F. Cantor, "The Crisis of Western Monasticism, 1050–1130," *American Historical Review* 67 (1960): 55; useful as an introduction to alternative interpretations, see S. Williams (ed.), *The Gregorian Epoch: Reformation, Revolution, Reaction?* (Boston: Heath, 1964)
[101] See Weber, *Protestant Ethic and the Spirit of Capitalism,* pp. 153–4.
[102] See this chapter, fn. 84.

tives. Although also concerned with impressing higher standards of religious life on both clergy and laity, Cluniac abbots were on the whole less virulently in conflict with their feudal environment, and ultimately gave priority to monastic goals proper rather than aim at a radical restructuring of Christian society as a whole.[103] As for the papacy itself, its overriding, ultimate aim was, rather, imposing Roman spiritual and temporal primacy (papal "monarchialism" or "theocracy")[104] and consolidating the sacerdotal hierarchy, than promoting ascetic ideals proper. In fact, the Gregorian reform may even be understood, using Tellenbach's nomenclature, as an attempt to try to substitute the sacerdotal–sacramental for the monastic–ascetic hierarchy of values.[105] Be that as it may, this era offers a forceful example of the tremendous impact of monasticism upon the entire structure of Christian society at a crucial stage of the confrontation between religious and secular authorities: The alliance between monasticism and papacy reached its peak here in the attempt to impose a maximal overlap between Church and society, through the subordination and desacralization of secular authorities, the systematic attack on lay interference in ecclesiastic matters, and the general raising of Christian standards of behavior for all. This alliance and the systematic attempt, in at least some phases of the Gregorian era, to spread the ascetic impulse beyond the walls of the monastery itself represent a phenomenon unknown in the history of Theravada monasticism. It is also important to note that the Gregorian reform, in its first stage at least, drew much of its inspiration and leadership not only from Cluny, but also from the new wave of eremitic and semieremitic reform movements within the monastic world itself. It is remarkable indeed that a leading eremitic figure such as Peter Damian could become a part of these far-reaching political processes, being induced to join the reform effort and propelled for this purpose to the very apex of the ecclesiastical hierarchy.[106]

It should be obvious that the political and cultural impact of monasticism just analyzed could not but help blur the boundaries between the

---

[103] For a detailed analysis of the relation between Cluny and the Gregorians, see Cowdrey, *Cluniacs and the Gregorian Reform.* Comparing their respective objectives, especially see pp. 121–56.

[104] See Lemarignier, *La France médiévale,* p. 211. Lemarignier himself prefers the label "papal theocracy." Using rather "papal monarchialism," see, e.g., White, "Gregorian Ideal," p. 324.

[105] See White, "Gregorian Ideal," pp. 324 ff.

[106] See J. Leclercq, *Pierre Damien, ermite et homme d'église* (Rome: Storia e Letteratura, 1960); B. Hamilton, "Saint Pierre Damien et les mouvements monastiques de son temps," in *Monastic Reform, Catharism and the Crusades* (London: Variorum, 1979), pp. 177–202; Little, L. K., "The Personal Development of Peter Damiani," in W. C. Jordan, B. M. Nob, and T. F. Ruiz, *Order and Innovation in the Middle Ages: Essays in Honor of J. R. Strayer* (Princeton, N.J.: Princeton University Press, 1976), pp. 317–42. Damien, it must be noted, was not hostile to Cluny.

monastic and other social sectors and contradict the ideological–
theological model of a neat division of labor and segregation between
virtuosi and nonvirtuosi described earlier. It must be stressed, however,
that whatever "active" influence monasticism had upon its social surroundings was usually facilitated, supported, and channeled through
the ecclesiastical authorities, in relation to whom the monastic leadership generally retained the conservative "vertical" stance already mentioned. It is only with the advent of Saint Bernard of Clairvaux, signaling the waning of the Gregorian impetus, that one may speak of a
more autonomous and "charismatic" anti-institutional impetus in the
interaction between monasticism and society at large.

What Bernard of Clairvaux represents is not so much the fluid translation of monastic, ascetic prestige into institutional power through
access to the highest levels of the ecclesiastical hierarchy, as the combination of ascetic prestige and political power within one stormy individual, independently of and eventually against the ecclesiastical hierarchy. Bernard did not hesitate to interfere in the choice of a pope at the
time of the double election of Anacletus II and Innocent II and the
consequent schism of 1130 – heavily sponsoring the candidate of his
choice irrespective of curial considerations of procedural regularity.
This interference entailed "the assumption that a disputed papal election might be adjudicated by an abbot, no matter how great his sanctity, in itself evidence of the waning prestige of Gregorianism . . . a
tacit admission that both official and charismatic power now resided
elsewhere than in Rome."[107] What Bernard brought to this involvement was not only his specific personal influence, however, but an
alternative, charismatic ideology of religious leadership.[108] For Bernard, in White's words,

> the hierocracy constructed by the Gregorians must yield in all matters of univer-
> sal importance to the general will of the community of believers led and taught
> by the monk. Ultimate authority resides not in sacerdotal hierarchy, but in
> spiritual hierarchy. . . . For the first time since the election of Leo IX a pope was
> created, not in Rome, but in the provinces, by the representatives of the popular
> morality and in conformity to the charismatic idea of religious leadership.[109]

Later, Bernard even attempted to translate monastic ascetic values into
a viable principle of hierarchical leadership. In this view, not unlike that of
Peter Damian, "the true leader becomes a spiritual teacher not trained in
dialectic, law, arms, diplomacy, but humility, charity, contemplation,"
and the pope is transformed "from a figurehead of the sacerdotal hierar-

---

[107] White, "Gregorian Ideal," p. 337.
[108] See also Mayr-Harting, "Two Abbots in Politics," pp. 231–7.
[109] White, "Gregorian Ideal," p. 339. Knowles cautions, however, against over-
inflating Saint Bernard's role.

chy into the true leader of the community of saints."[110] Such a conception could not but clash with (and was in fact partly a reaction to) the recent development of canon law and the enhanced emphasis on legalism, both inside and outside the ecclesiastical institution.

The following decades saw a return of monasticism to the more classical confines of its withdrawn vocation. The papacy itself came to favor those orders most committed to withdrawal and contemplation. By starting to grant plenary indulgences from 1300 on (a custom first launched by Boniface VIII), the papacy also contributed to undermining the need for monks' intercession in the remission of sins and salvational process. More generally, the increasing secularization of the state and secular power as such (greatly desacralized by the Gregorian era itself), now increasingly independent from the Church and from religious legitimacy in general, implied an overall decline of monastic political influence. These trends could not but further weaken monasticism's resources in its relations of exchange with society at large, already undermined by the convergence, in the twelfth century, of broad economic, social, and cultural changes unfavorable to the classic pattern of interaction between virtuosi and society.

An important aspect of this period of massive social and cultural change is the emergence of new urban and commercial strata as a result of the increasingly market- and money-oriented economy, and of accelerated urbanization – itself implying the emergence of new types of wealth as well as of poverty. But no less crucial was the advent of new types of nonmonastic, secular cultural elites and institutions (first cathedral schools and then universities) that undermined the monks' long-standing monopoly as carriers and transmitters of the West's intellectual-cultural traditions.

Another major feature of this era is the tremendous differentiation within the virtuoso sector itself, challenging and overflowing the classical monastic forms of virtuosity, as is explained in greater detail in the next chapter. It is often argued that traditional Benedictine monasticism was well-adapted to the Carolingian system and to agrarian and feudal structures, whereas mendicant spirituality corresponded to the development of new urban needs. The relationship between religious and social-structural differentiation has become a historiographical commonplace:

For several centuries, until nearly the end of the eleventh century, the tendency had been to develop an ever-greater degree of identity of purpose and organization, and to delight in the unity of an achieved ideal. Then, within little more than a hundred years, all the main varieties of medieval religious organization came into existence. We shall certainly not be wrong in associating the stability of religious ideals before about 1100 with the relatively static society of the early

[110] Ibid., p. 344.

Middle Ages, and the rapid diversification of religious organization after this date with the expansion and growing complexity of western society.[111]

In contrast to the overall stability of the virtuoso–society relational structure in the Theravada Buddhism setting, the overriding characteristic of the relationship of Christian monasticism to its macrosocietal context would seem to be one of plasticity and progressive internal differentiation, favored by and responding to changes in the wider environment. This partially explains the greater similarity between the two cases in the earlier stage. In the first stage, monasticism interacted with a more static and less differentiated environment. The similarity with traditional Theravada Buddhism is also enhanced by the fact that Church and state constituted relatively weaker macrosocietal frameworks at that stage, undergoing increasing fragmentation in the era of feudalism; in addition, monasticism had then to interact and compete with fewer alternative elites, and even represented, like the Sangha, the only effective cultural–ideological elite.

Nevertheless, it is important to stress that the relationship with the environment is not simply one of direct reflection. The element of *antithesis* – what we called in the Introduction "alternative structure" – remained and accompanied these drastic transformations. Rosenwein and Little, examining what they see as the close relations between Cluniac and mendicant spirituality and the dominant orientations of their respective historical sociocultural environment, emphasize the element not only of extension and reflection, but also that of antithetic, dialectical transposition: Cluniac patience and prayer, in this view, were part of a complex of responses to feudal warfare, whereas mendicant poverty and preaching were one of a number of related responses to urban money making.[112]

[111] Southern, *Western Society and the Church,* p. 215.
[112] See Rosenwein and Little, "Social Meaning," p. 31: "The religious life of the friars, like that of the monks before them, involved the Christianizing of an activity that had been seen as wholly exploitative and therefore morally unacceptable. In both instances this activity was the occupation of the dominant class of a sector of society. In urban society, dominated by merchants and professionals, money making had been condemned, while in feudal society, dominated by knights, lay violence had been unacceptable.

"The spiritualities that responded to these conditions did so, on one level, by repudiating the unacceptable activities; the friars rejected money; the monks abandoned the battle field. But on a second level, the response . . . developed spiritualities that in themselves suggested a way to separate out the useful aspects from the exploitative ones. The monks fought spiritual battles without shedding blood, thus exercising violence as truly Christian knights. The friars negotiated the Gospel without using money, thus exercising commerce as truly Christian merchants." A similar element of "antithetic reflection" in the relation between virtuosity and its environment is emphasized by Duby, *Age of the Cathedrals,* p. 118.

This tendency of religious virtuosity to link up dialectically with whatever strata or institutions are dominant is rooted in the fact that these dominant groups and institutions were not only foci of economic or organizational power, but themselves also possessed a high degree of ideological–symbolic autonomy. As suggested before, although hierarchization was certainly a pervasive organizational device in medieval society, it could evolve along a number of competing and potentially conflicting principles or axes. The greater ideological strength and autonomy of monarchy and aristocracy in particular have been stressed. In general, one of the overriding characteristics of Christian monasticism's macrosocietal environment, especially when contrasted with the Theravada case, is the existence of a plurality of foci of authority, both secular and religious, often competing over and interfering in each other's domains of influence, with only occasional periods of clear-cut division of labor and complementarity. Furthermore, their interaction and confrontation could take place not only at the level of king and national Church, but also on the broader macrosocietal scope of empire and Papacy, as in the Carolingian and Gregorian eras, or on a smaller local scale, between kings or princes and local bishops.

Three implications for monasticism need to be stressed here. First, monasticism was constantly caught up in a shifting network of alliances, seeking protection and providing support in a rather opportunistic fashion, according to the interests of the moment – which can be considered as much a sign of social incorporation as the maintenance of a certain degree of "outsiderhood" and autonomy. Second, the symbolic status and prestige of monasticism fluctuated with the principles of social hierarchization favored by a specific balance of power, and never attained the stability and exclusive preeminence of the Buddhist renouncer vis-à-vis kings and laymen. Third, and easily overlooked, the various foci of political power and institutional authority already mentioned provided monasticism with relatively forceful exemplars of institutional formalization, legalistic and centralizing tendencies, and massive administrative structure that had no equivalent in the Theravada setting. Most essentially, perhaps, this greater ideological plurality of the Christian setting favored a transactional mode of interaction between virtuosi and the environment, and ultimately defeated the existence of a distinct virtuoso sector within an increasingly differentiated and competitive economic and ideological marketplace.

8 Virtuoso radicalism: a self-defeating triumph

It is clear from the previous chapter that Christian monasticism was a more "dynamic" and autonomous institution than the Theravada Sangha, forcefully interacting with other social sectors and playing an important part in an arena of shifting social forces and coalitions. Up to the eleventh century, this part was mostly conservative. Abbots usually bowed to and even supported the external authority of kings and popes, while fending for their own material and ideal interests in a world they basically accepted as it was. The strong influence of monasticism in the Gregorian attempt to restructure Christian society was a sign of monasticism's vitality and prestige. Ultimately, however, this influence should be understood as the result of a close collaboration with the ecclesiastical hierarchy – an effective alloy of monastic prestige and ecclesiastical institutional power. On the whole, therefore, Christian monasticism cannot be said to have been much more anti- or counterstructural than its Theravada equivalent, despite its criticism of the world – and of the Church in the world especially – so important at its emergence, and maintained in a more subdued fashion throughout its subsequent stages. Seguy's conception of Christian monasticism as a form of "implicit protest" (see this volume, Chapter 2) may be applied without much reservation throughout the period under study, although this aspect may seem at times to be completely superseded by the elaborate network of mutual support and exchange between monasteries and society.

Reform and internal differentiation

The virtuoso sector, as already suggested, was not altogether homogeneous; it went through a process of increasing internal differentiation. It is precisely in this process of differentiation that one may still discern the periodic resurgence of the basically asocial, antisocial, or countersocial premises of the monastic form of life. The overriding difference from the Sangha is that Christian monasticism very early became characterized by a much greater degree of differentiation and polarization, eventually leading to the emergence of forms of virtuosity overflowing the boundaries of classical monasticism. In a first, less-differentiated stage, which ran roughly up to the end of the tenth century, Benedict's Rule was the normative standard, even if modified in many areas by the surviving influence of various layers of local monastic tradition. However, from

173

the eleventh century on, one can discern a number of trends that significantly modified the mostly "conservative" picture of the monasticism–society relationship already described – such as, in particular, the emergence of changing forms of virtuoso radicalism and the immense acceleration in differentiation of the virtuoso sector in the eleventh and twelfth centuries.

From its emergence up to and including tenth-century Cluny, Christian monasticism was gradually incorporated into an elaborate network of competition and exchange with other social sectors. This was not necessarily perceived as contradicting the monastic ideal, which even in its dominant, Benedictine version could be interpreted with a certain range of freedom. Increased entanglement in worldly affairs and interests, coupled as it was with other forms of slackening of monastic discipline, however, did lead the more rigorist minded to periodic attempts at reform, usually couched in the terms of a return to the pristine purity of the Benedictine Rule. One may see this as a repetition of the process through which monasticism itself emerged, at least in part – as a reaction to and a product of the growing institutionalization and routinization of the mother church.

At first, reform did not necessarily mean the introduction of new divisions into the monastic world: Benedict of Aniane's reform brought Western and especially Gallic monasticism to an unprecedented level of uniformity and standardization, while introducing a number of innovations – such as a new emphasis on the liturgy, as well as an increased centralization and its enforcement by an act of state – clearly at variance with the original Benedictine spirit. Eventually, however, the reforming impulse also led to the emergence of a range of new forms of monastic life and to sharp variations within the monastic sector: Beginning with Cluny (itself intended as a return to a stricter observance of Saint Benedict of Aniane's reform); expanding with the emergence of the Cistercians and of a range of eremitical, canonial, and then military orders; further continuing with the formation of women's orders in the twelfth and thirteenth centuries; and culminating with the appearance of the mendicant orders from the early thirteenth century on. Here I shall concentrate on the historical development of the eremitic strand – the closest equivalent of the Theravada Buddhist forest monks – that strikingly exemplifies the typical features of the relation between virtuosi and society in medieval Christianity.[1]

---

[1] On the historical development of the eremitic strand, see especially the invaluable collection of articles in *L'eremitismo in Occidente nei secoli XI–XII* (Milan: Universite cattolica del Sacre Cuore, 1965); "Érémitisme et hérésie au Moyen-Age," in *Hérésies et sociétes dans l'Europe pré-industrielle* (Paris: Mouton, 1968), pp. 139–145; H. Leyser, *Hermits and the New Monasticism: A Study of*

Eremitism "old" and "new"

To begin with, the medieval Christian equivalent of the Sangha's differentiation into forest and village monks seems to have given rise to a greater institutional differentiation and polarization, not only between eremitic and cenobitic monasticism but also between forms of withdrawal – either eremitic or cenobitic – more fully disconnected from their social surroundings than their Theravada correspondents, and forms of involvement with the laity – whether monastic, eremitic (paradoxical as it may seem) or, later, mendicant – that made the "worldoriented" pole of Christian virtuosity more worldly than even the worldliest Buddhist village monks.

The eremitic and cenobitic traditions appear to have coexisted from the very beginning: Contemporary with Anthony (c. 251–356), who is said to have spent twenty years in isolation before coming out to lead others to the solitary life, was Pachomius, who founded the first known cenobitic community in 315 and wrote what is probably the earliest rule. The two forms of life were far from being necessarily antagonistic, although disagreement as to their respective preeminence and worth obtained at times. Not only did eremitic, semieremitic, and fully cenobitic forms of life coexist; they were tried in succession by individual ascetics and easily transformed from one into the other in what appears to have been a very fluid ascetic milieu.[2] This fluidity could even be extended to the secular Church, which, as noted, could rechannel the special holiness of desert ascetics back into the ecclesiastical leadership. Thus there was no sharp opposition between ascetics and the established ecclesiastical hierarchy; it would be mistaken to see the desert ascetics of early monasticism as the carriers of anti-institutional charisma.[3] This was not contradicted by later history: The Rule of Saint Benedict acknowledged eremitism as the final stage, for which cenobitic monasticism was deemed to be a preparatory school. Cluny itself, often considered the powerful prototype of cenobitic, established monasticism, provided

Religious Communities in Western Europe, 1000–1150 (London: Macmillan Press, 1984); J. Heuclin, *Aux origines monastiques de la Gaule du nord: ermites et reclus du Ve aux XIe siècles.* (Lille: Presses Universitaires de Lille, 1988); L. Gougaud, "La vie érémitique au Moyen-Age," *Revue d'Ascétique et de Mystique* 1 (1920): 209–40, 313–28; C. Kingsley, *The Hermits* (London: Macmillan Press, 1869); R. Doyere, "Érémitisme," in *Dictionnaire de spiritualité ascétique et mystique* vol. 4 (Paris: G. Beauchesne, 1960).

[2] Rousseau, *Ascetics, Authority and the Church.*

[3] In Drijvers's words, "The ascetic represented in a paradigmatic, exemplary way what was actually a requirement of everybody . . . 'das ausseralltagliche' was from its beginning, an institution with an exemplary function, for the ecclesiastical authories as well as for the bulk of the believers." See Drijvers, "Askese und Mönchtum."

room within its domains for solitary ascetics. Hermits often maintained ties with their monastery and abbot, and remained willingly dependent on monks for the sacraments. It was not uncommon, moreover, for bishops or abbots to go off to temporary eremitic retreats while in office, or to become hermits upon retirement.

Among the laity, the hermit aroused admiration for his spiritual worth, and, not unlike the holy men of late antiquity in Peter Brown's analysis, attracted the interest of those seeking the disinterested advice of outside "bearers of objectivity."[4] A similar function seems to have been fulfilled by the recluse, a solitary ascetic whose cell was typically located right next to the parish church, that is, at the very center of the local community.[5] Kings themselves were not indifferent to hermits of special holiness, bestowing forests and monasteries upon them, seeking their blessing before going to war, or even forcing them to take up residence at court.

The distinction between a rather conservative first stage and a more dynamic and potentially revolutionary second stage, beginning around the eleventh century, is here again of major significance, as will be emphasized later in this section. Nevertheless, even in the first long, conservative stage, when the coexistence between the eremitic and cenobitic strands and between eremitism and the world (including the church) was relatively peaceful and uneventful, one may already note a number of important differences with the Theravada eremitic forest tradition that bring into relief Christian eremitism's more anarchic and subversive character.

First, whereas the Buddhist hermit virtuoso, no less than other monks, referred himself to the *Vinaya* and other classical Buddhist scriptures that clearly defined the prototypical stages of spiritual progress and perfection, Christian hermits were on the whole left on their own "in the wilderness," to pursue an individual quest that led Christian eremitism to greater ideological and practical variety than its Buddhist counterpart. This eremitic individualism, with its potential for spiritual anarchy and deviance, could arouse monastic, clerical, or lay suspicion and even opposition. Only at a rather late stage did eremitic rules make a rather weak appearance (in contrast with Theravada Buddhism, where there was never any specialized eremitic rule differentiated from the *Vinaya*). Even in the case of the highly regulated institution of anchoritism in England, rules for anchorites are merely sets of suggestions and advice, in contrast to monastic rules formulated as demands.[6]

---

[4] See this volume, Chapter 2.
[5] See, for example, H. Mayr-Harting, "Functions of a Twelfth-Century Recluse," *History* 60 (1975): 344–5.
[6] A. K. Warren, *Anchorites and their Patrons in Medieval England* (Berkeley and Los Angeles: University of California Press, 1985), p. 101.

Second, even if one ignores for the moment the methodological problem, relevant to both settings, posed by those hermits who withdrew from all contact with society and left no historical record, the possibility of full detachment from society seems much less plausible in the Theravada tradition. Even if theoretically implied by the Buddhist ideal of radical world renunciation, it seems to be hampered by the various doctrinal injunctions that prevent the renouncer from providing for his own food and shelter, and the highly detailed (if never compulsory) pattern of interaction with the laity.[7] Furthermore, whereas the prime element in the definition of Buddhist hermitages is a greater disconnection from the laity, as symbolized by the opposition between village and forest – a forest that, as noted, need not be very distant – Christian hermits could also be defined by withdrawal from any community, be it monastic or lay, and by their striving for total, individual isolation, *solum cum solo*. From the perspective of the second phase of the development of eremitism and of the virtuoso sector in general, starting after the tenth century, we may be tempted to see this easier and more total disconnection of the virtuoso ascetic from all social unit as a case of *reculer pour mieux sauter*. The extraordinary revival of the eremitic movement in the eleventh and twelfth centuries, when, in Peter Damian's phrase, "it seemed as if the whole world would be turned into a hermitage," represents in fact a new form of eremitism: rekindling, to be sure, the traditional controversies between eremitism and cenobitism, but also adopting a more agressive stance, more critical of both monks and clergy, and, even more important, more insistent on reforming the laity and society at large (thus explaining its temporary convergence with the aims of the Gregorian reform).[8]

A major characteristic of the new eremitic movements, starting with the founding of Calmaldoli by Romuald of Ravenna at the beginning of the eleventh century in Italy, is the discontent with the corporate wealth and worldly involvement of traditional monasticism as epitomized by Cluny and Gorze, and the yearning for a return to greater solitude, poverty, and simplicity. Nevertheless, in contradistinction to traditional eremitism, and in what represented a confluence of the eremitic and apostolic traditions, the new hermits did not seek solitude for one or two individuals, but formed collective groups in remote, uninhabited locations. Furthermore, some of these new "hermits" engaged, somewhat paradoxically from the point of view of more traditional categories, in preaching to the laity, trying to communicate their discontent with the

---

[7] These very basic strictures upon the individuality of the Buddhist renouncer have been emphasized in Tambiah, "Renouncer."

[8] See Chenu, "Monks, Canons and Laymen"; Cantor, "Crisis of Western Monasticism;" Leclercq, "The Monastic Crisis of the Eleventh and Twelfth Century," in N. Hunt (ed.), *Cluniac Monasticism in the Central Middle Ages* (Hamden, Conn.: Archon, 1971), pp. 217–37; Leyser, *Hermits and the New Monasticism.*

contemporary state of Christianity at large and their impulse for religious reform.

The response elicited by this new type of hermit was not always uniform. As a rule, the hermits appealed to the masses who thronged to their preaching; and although receiving the support of local bishops, they generally clashed with traditional monks and the secular priests in whose domain (and with whose livelihood) they were seen to interfere. Given the intensity of their criticism, and the fact that they were deviating from normal patterns of monastic obedience, it is surprising that they remained, with few exceptions, within the pale of orthodoxy. This may be seen, at least in part, as the result of the initial alliance with the Gregorian reform, where someone like Peter Damian, deeply involved in the eremitic movement, played a pioneering role. However, it is also important to note that these new hermits were seeking not a free, formless life, but rather a better and more stringent rule. They did not necessarily intend to be innovative. On the contrary, the new groups and movements all referred themselves to one or more of three major traditions: the apostolic life of the primitive Church in Jerusalem, as described in the Gospels; the desert fathers; and the Benedictine Rule itself, in its pristine purity. The progressive abandonment of their original, rather inchoate forms of life – often to join a recognized order, albeit cleaving to a more rigorous enactment of its rule – should not be seen as a classical case of routinization of charisma, of the weakening and compromise of ideals, but on the contrary as a conscious, sustained concern with the search for rules, as the expression even of a legalistic bent, to be placed in the context of the new, contemporary concern with legal forms and order.[9]

The ultimate acceptance of ecclesiastical authority, the dependence on the support of bishops, and the concern with legal structure all exemplify the reproduction, within the eremitic sector, of the vertical principle identified earlier. It is remarkable that this vertical principle functioned as a powerful force of incorporation and structuration even among those strands of the virtuoso sector that might have been thought most a- or anti-institutional, and thus most immune to its impact.

Some of these new groupings, such as the Camaldoli and Carthusians, did give rise to eremitic or semieremitic forms of monastic organization too novel to fit into any traditional cenobitic pattern. An important innovation, most productively put to use by the Cistercians, was the use of lay brothers, freeing a contemplative elite from the burden of economic and

---

[9] Leyser, *Hermits and the New Monasticism,* p. 3. This was not true of all eremitic trends of the period. The Grandmontese refused to acknowledge the necessity of an order, denying that they were either monks, canons, or hermits, and claiming the Gospel for their only rule (ibid., p. 88).

administrative duties and acting as a buffer between the hermitage or convent and the secular world. Indeed, it has been pointed out that the overall conservative and even fundamentalist orientation to pristine monastic traditions coexisted in some cases with a not altogether unconscious positive attitude to religious novelty, to the conscious creation of new forms of religious life – an element with no equivalent, it seems, in any form of virtuoso radicalism in traditional Theravada Buddhism.[10]

In general, the eremitic revival of the eleventh and twelfth centuries and its various eremitic, semieremitic, and apostolic offshoots involved, in varying degrees, not so much an attempt at reviving the solitary forms of eremitic life as an attempt at recovering a true enactment of religious "poverty" by disentangling the monastic collective from the corrupting influence of corporate wealth and the elaborate network of exchange with the laity.[11] The radical, albeit still monastic (rather than eremitic) solution to that problem, was first of all to establish themselves on a remote, uninhabited territory and withdraw from the *cura animarum,* as well as to reemphasize the place of manual labor and autonomous economic production in the monastic regime, to refuse many traditional sources of monastic income (tithes, manorial rents, serfs, churches, etc.), and, not least, to refuse childoblates. (There is now increasing evidence, however, that this view of the Cistercians' pristine impetus may have been somewhat exaggerated: Far from always settling in deserted, wild locations, they also set up residence in places that were already settled and even cultivated, and from which they actually expulsed the previous population, as well as retaining many of the traditional "feudal" features and entanglements).[12] At the same time, they introduced both lay brothers and hired labor so as to allow enough time for prayer, meditation, and study. The illiterate lay brothers were not recruited, however, on purely instrumental, economic grounds. An important element in the remarkable spread of the Cistercian order was the formal incorporation of laymen into the monastic community (a potential feature of Christian monasticism we have already noted); this

[10] See G. Constable, "Renewal and Reform in Religious Life: Concepts and Realities," in R. Benson and G. Constable (eds.), *Renaissance and Renewal in the Twelfth Century* (Oxford University Press, 1982), pp. 37–67.

[11] McDonnel, "Vita Apostolica"; A. Vauchez, "La pauvreté volontaire au Moyen-Age," *Annales* 25 (1970): 1566–73; Manteuffel, *Naissance d'une hérésie;* L. K. Little, *Religious Poverty and the Profit Economy in Medieval Europe* (Ithaca, N.Y.: Cornell University Press, 1978); M. D. Lambert, *Franciscan Poverty: The Doctrine of the Absolute Poverty of Christ and the Apostles in the Franciscan Order, 1210–1323* (London: S. P. C. K., 1961).

[12] See C. H. Berman, *Medieval Agriculture, the Southern French Countryside, and the Early Cistercians: A Study of Forty-three Monasteries,* (Philadelphia: American Philosophical Society, 1986); G. Despy, "Les richesses de la terre: Citeaux et Prémontré devant l'économie de profit aux XIIe et XIIe siècles," *Problèmes d'Histoire du Christianisme* (1974), 58–80; Lekai, *Cistercians.*

provided laymen with a form of spiritual justification, sanctification of labor, and asceticism that, although not making them equal to the choirmonks, were at least a partial response to the wave of lay religious fervor that spread through eleventh- and twelfth-century Europe. The well-known paradox of the Cistercian order is that, through skillful management of great estates and aggressive commercial entrepreneurship, it quickly became extremely wealthy. At the root of that wealth, however, was not only their own labor but a generous flow of endowments, at least in the early decades of the order. The basic gift relationship was therefore maintained, a striking fact considering that at the same time so many other elements of interaction with the laity had been rejected.

It is important to note that many of the eremitic and semieremitic formations were often a fluid and transitory phenomenon. Individuals and even entire groups could pass back and forth from one form of life to another – especially between the eremitical and canonical options,[13] often ending up returning with little modification, as mentioned, to the Benedictine fold. It has even been suggested that the new eremitic formations corresponded to a social and economic structure itself in a state of transition, when cities were already sufficiently developed to cause religious flight but not enough to motivate what would come later, namely the apostolic, mendicant duty to urban populations.[14] At any rate, it was only with the new combination of corporate poverty and preaching to the masses in the mendicant orders of the early thirteenth century, and most notably the early Franciscans, that reliance upon endowments, together with so many other classical features of the religious life – such as monastic enclosure and stability – was seriously (if temporarily) challenged.

The new forms of religious life did not, however, completely supersede the more traditional ones, either monastic or eremitic. In fact, the hermit saint remained a recurrent figure in medieval French literature.[15] His role in the Arthurian romance, especially, has been analyzed as a benevolent utility figure, performing a variety of minor services for

[13] See L. Millis, "Ermites et chanoines réguliers au XII siècle," *Cahiers de Civilization Médiévale* 22 (1979): 39–80. The Augustianian order of canons was the outcome of attempts to replace the Capitula of Aix (816) by a much more rigorous concept of the canonical life, one that emphasized the *vita apostolica*, the need for poverty. The ideals of these and of the hermits were therefore closely allied; many of the first communities of regular canons were formed either by hermits or as a result of their teaching; some allowed for private property, whereas others opposed it.

[14] L. Genicot, "L'erémitisme du XIe siècle dans son contexte économique et social," in *L'eremitismo in Occidente*, pp. 45–71.

[15] A. J. Kennedy, "The Hermit's Role in French Arthurian Romance (c. 1170–1530), *Romania* 91 (1974): 54–81; E. Franceschini, "La figura dell'eremita nella letteratura latina medioevale," in *L'eremitismo in Occidente*, pp. 561–9; Kingsley, *Hermits*, pp. 219–23.

knight-errantry, but also, more important, as a didactic figure, a vigorous exponent of Christian chivalry (particularly in the Grail texts composed around 1180–1230), or a severe critic of contemporary Christianity. It is interesting that Christian hermits, in the literary imagination of the period, were not necessarily defined by disconnection from the laity, but on the contrary by a special proximity to knights and kings and, in general, to the common people.[16] In Jacques Le Goff's analysis, the hermit emerges as the closest of all religious figures to popular folklore and sensibility, located in a "forest" embodying distance from high, learned culture (rather than from society as a whole).

The affinities between eremitic and popular spirituality have been finely examined, together with the heretic, heterodox potential that these might have implied; the stress has usually been, however, on the fact that hermits, as a rule, remained within the confines of orthodoxy.[17] Nevertheless, some of the wide range of groupings and trends loosely lumped together under the flexible title of the eremitic–apostolic revival did come into confrontation with the ecclesiastical authority and were ultimately condemned as heretical (these include the Cathars, Arnoldians, Patarins, Humiliati, Waldensians, and the direct offshoots of a specifically mendicant, Franciscan spirituality, the Fraticelli and Apostolic Brethren.[18] The impact of Joachim of Fiore upon the Fraticelli in particular may be seen as a case of the potentially subversive confluence of ascetic and millenarian orientations. His vision of the historical development of the Church and even mankind in three stages, the last of them characterized by the dominance of the ascetic virtuosi, is the culmination of the unmistakably increasing claim of Christian virtuosi to shape not only their own fate and salvation, but that of Christian society as a whole. It has been pointed out, however, that the dividing line between orthodoxy and heresy in this remarkable efflorescence of reli-

[16] Le Goff notes among other characteristics of the hermit – such as the hermit as "wild man," as the counterpart and conversant of kings in the forest as a sacred place, and as close to the outlaws in the same forest that is also the locus of the wild and untamed – his special closeness to people, who come to him to confess, ask for advice, or seek blessing or healing. See "Le désert-forêt dans l'Occident médiéval," in *L'imaginaire médiéval* (Paris: Gallimard, 1985), pp. 59–75.

[17] See E. Delaruelle, "Les ermites et la spiritualité populaire," in *L'eremitismo in Occidente*, pp. 212–41; J. Becquet, "L'érémitisme clérical et laïc dans l'ouest de la France," in ibid, pp. 182–204; "Érémitisme et hérésie au Moyen-Age," in *Hérésies et sociétés dans l'Europe pré-industrielle*, pp. 139–45. Although hermits could easily arouse suspicions of heresy, Becquet is of the opinion that historically they did not display any special predisposition to heresy. Nevertheless, the problem of documentation remains, as noted in Chapter 2, as well as that of the definition, doctrinal vs. institutional, of heresy.

[18] See Lambert, *Medieval Heresy*, pp. 182–208; idem, *Franciscan Poverty;* G. Leff, *Heresy in the Later Middle Ages: The Relation of Heterodoxy to Dissent, c. 1250–1450* (New York: Manchester University Press, 1967), pp. 167–238.

gious movements seems to lie not so much in differences of religious beliefs and doctrines, but rather in the willingness to come to terms with ecclesiastic authority, that is, to acknowledge the vertical principle in the regulation of religious virtuosity within the Church.[19] One may surmise that acknowledgment of this vertical regulation was made even more vital in light of the obvious threat not only to the ecclesiastical, but to the social order in general, that was entailed by the radical attack against both individual and corporate wealth.

We shall not go further into the historical development of the mendicant orders nor of virtuoso radicalism in general. Of primary interest here is the impact that the remarkable internal differentiation of the virtuoso sector had upon the more traditional patterns of segregation, competition, and exchange between virtuosi and society. Clearly, monasticism lost its monopoly and was overtaken by new forms of monastically inspired virtuosity, critical of Benedictine wealth and laxity, and aspiring to stricter forms of ascetic abnegation. The latter, however, would go one of two ways in redefining the relation to the laity: One possibility was to withdraw even further from the laity; the other – in what forms a brand of virtuoso radicalism with no equivalent in the traditional Theravada Buddhist setting – was to intensify interaction with the laity and cater to its religious needs in the world to an extent and manner as yet unprecedented. Both options undoubtedly deviated from the previous balance of segregation and exchange between monks and laymen.

In any case, both virtuosi and laymen now found themselves facing a rich and bewildering spectrum of virtuosity, enhancing the elements of choice, competition, and explicit exchange present in the earlier stage.[20]

---

[19] This is strongly argued in Manteuffel, *Naissance d'une hérésie,* who stresses the relativity of heresy to the degree of centralization of the Church. It is no accident, in his view, that the most violent persecution of adepts of poverty coincided with the efforts of the Avignon Papacy to make of the Church an "administrative monarchy." Waldensians were condemned, in this view, because they believed that poverty gave them the right to preach without any need to receive clerical legitimacy. In Vauchez's view, many trends may be approved as long as they remained a clerical phenomenon, and may be condemned only when reaching the laity, thus threatening the very basis of social order. See Vauchez, "La pauvreté volontaire au Moyen Age."

[20] On the tension and competition among the various options and sectors, see Chenu, "Monks, Canons and Laymen"; C. Dereine, "Odon de Tournai et la crise du cénobitisme au XIe siècle," *Revue du Moyen-Age Latin* 4 (1948): 137–154; D. G. Morin, "Rainaud l'Ermite et Ives de Chartres: un épisode de la crise du cénobitisme au XIe–XIIe siècle," *Revue Bénédictine* 15 (1928): 99–115; J. Leclercq, "Le poème de Payen Bolotin contre les faux ermites," *Revue Bénédictine* 73 (1958): 52–84; Milis, "Ermites et chanoines réguliers"; McDonnel, "Vita Apostolica"; G. Constable and B. Smith, *Libellus de Diversis Ordinibus et Professionibus qui sunt in Ecclesia* (Oxford: Clarendon, 1972). This twelfth-century document nicely conveys the attempt by a contemporary to make sense of and tolerate the enormous new variety of religious callings. The Fourth

This could only underline the basically precarious (because increasingly contingent and conditional) nature of whatever bonds were formed between virtuosi and society. Finally, the increasing access of the laity itself to forms of religious virtuosity of its own – in a wide range of orders and confraternities – would further contribute to undermining the segregation and distinction between virtuosi and nonvirtuosi, and thus the very possibility of a differentiated virtuoso institution.

> Lateran Council in 1215 tried indeed to restrain the emergence of new forms of religious life by requiring that any new group join one of the already acknowledged orders. See also Constable, "Diversity of Religious Life," pp. 29–47.

Part IV
Virtuosity, charisma, and social order

9 Virtuosity and the virtuoso–society complex

The institutionalization of religious virtuosity in traditional Theravada Buddhism and medieval Catholicism displays some fundamental similarities. Most obviously, virtuosity gave rise, in both settings, to monastic "alternative structures" (in the sense defined in Chapter 2) that shared a number of features and dilemmas. I have tried to show, however, that these inherently precarious structures also relied on different, even contrasting, patterns of institutionalization. A major aim of the comparision was to contradict the frequent assertions of a contrast between otherworldly Buddhist "weakness" and "looseness" vis-à-vis Western Christian "power" and "dynamism" in matters of institutional building and worldly involvement. Buddhism developed in *and around* the monastic institution a social structure of impressive historical strength and effectiveness that could be properly identified and assessed, it was argued, only by distinguishing between a number of criteria of institutionalization.

In terms of formal organization, autonomy (organizational, economic, and social), and political power, Theravada Buddhist monasticism was shown to be much weaker an institution than its Christian equivalent. In terms of the position of monasticism within the social structure at large, however, Buddhist monasticism appears to have been more solidly institutionalized, retaining, with impressive stability and with only minor variations, a specific social position and pattern of relationship with wider society. In contrast, the position of monasticism in medieval Europe changed with time, was a constant focus of controversy, and was seriously undermined toward the end of the period under study.

Up to that point, however, the greater organizational capacity of Christian monasticism, on the one hand, and its more ambiguous and unstable social position, on the other, may be understood as two complementary aspects of Christian monasticism taken as a more powerful "alternative structure" within society at large: an alternative structure, that is, displaying both a stronger autonomy from and a more forceful interaction and even competition with other groups and social sectors.

In contrast, the institutional strength of monasticism in traditional Theravada Buddhism – where it also formed an alternative structure in the sense of presenting a form of life antithetical and alternative to average social life – was to be found not so much in its own organizational-

187

institutional structures and direct political power (both relatively elusive), but rather in its forming the nexus of a virtuoso–layman relation that came to form an essential axis of social organization in Theravada Buddhist societies. In other words, institution building may be viewed not only in terms of organizational-corporate status, but also, as suggested in the Introduction, in terms of sets of relationships or relational structures.

The Theravada virtuoso–layman relational structure was also shown to have had a partial and temporary equivalent in medieval Catholicism: Christian monasticism was also sustained for a long period (roughly from the sixth to the twelfth centuries) by a pattern of interaction and exchange with nonvirtuosi that resembled the Theravada pattern. At the end of that period, however, it was drastically shattered (if not completely eradicated), together with the overall social position and cultural significance of monasticism itself. Emphasizing this temporary convergence has a double significance from a comparative sociological perspective. One is historical and substantive, in that the convergence has usually been overlooked in comparative interpretations more intent on uncovering those unique features of the medieval West that may explain the advent of capitalism and modernity. The other is theoretical, in that the virtuoso–layman relation entails a distinctive cluster of sociological processes – that is, a sociological "complex" – that has not received its due attention and typological elaboration. Although fundamentally related to charisma in the very largest sense of this term, I submit that this virtuoso–society complex is also clearly distinguishable from the cluster of sociological processes associated either with the compelling appeal of "pure," "concentrated," personal charisma, or with the notion of routinized, "institutional" charisma.

Virtuosity and charisma

First, it is necessary to define the core features of religious virtuosity itself, independently of its ties to any specific religious and historical context. An important contribution toward such a definition is Michael Hill's analysis of the religious order, which he defines, among other things, as "a collection of religious virtuosi with an uncompromising interpretation of the Gospel ethic which is sanctioned by the church but is not put forward as necessary for all." Hill's analysis confines itself to the area of Christianity and does not claim cross-cultural validity. Furthermore, it is intended to also encompass nonmonastic religious orders, and does not address itself to the issue of monasticism proper. Of primary interest to us, however, is his conception of virtuosity itself, and the fact that he defines it, ideal-typically, mainly through distinguishing it from charisma, a Weberian concept that has enjoyed much greater impact in the sociological study of religion and under which religious virtuosity has often been too readily subsumed.[1]

Weber himself, in fact, occasionally used the term "charisma" in connection with religious virtuosi.[2] On such occasions, however, he used it in the usual sense of an exceptional religious gift and an essentially personal attribute, rather than in the sense of his own (later) analytical elaboration of charisma as part of a typology of forms of authority.[3] Charisma in the latter sense seems in fact to refer to a range of phenomena that only partially overlap, and in some important ways even stand in contrast to those associated with religious virtuosity.

Whereas Weber emphasized the contrast between virtuoso religion and mass religion and did not try to clarify its analytical relation to charisma, Hill sees virtuoso religion – correctly, in my opinion – as distinguishable from both mass religion and the religion of charismatic figures. Virtuosi and charismatics may be related empirically, but there is, to his mind, a basic difference between the two types: One represents the rigorous restatement of an existing religious tradition, the other, a shattering of tradition and the articulation of a new basis of normative obligation.

Hill argues that virtuosity has characteristically relied on a traditional type of legitimation – such as a pristine model of religious purity or the original rule of the order – even if this did not necessarily prevent it from eventually functioning as a lever for change under certain circumstances. He does not deny, however, that members of religious orders and monastic communities have often exhibited charismatic characteristics, or that the origins of Christian monasticism entailed a strong charismatic component. But it is claims to traditional legitimacy, he asserts, that have played the dominant role in the accommodation between virtuoso religion and church religion. Furthermore, he is struck by the high degree of formal organization of Christian virtuosi in comparison to those in other religions – a fact he attributes to their "characteristic capacity to embody tradition."

The weakness of this argument notwithstanding – both the lesser capacity of virtuosity in other religions to "embody tradition" and the causal relationship between such a capacity and formal organization being far from evident – it should be recalled that Hill's primary concern is with the religious order, that is, with formally organized virtuosity, and not with virtuosity in its various possible manifestations, includ-

[1] Hill, *Religious Order*.
[2] See for example his use of the word "charisma" in the definition of religious virtuosity at the beginning of Chapter 2.
[3] Weber, *Economy and Society*, pp. 241–51, 1111–56.

ing the less institutionalized and less tradition-affirming ones. Another problem with this distinction – virtuosity as entailing the rigorous restatement of tradition versus charisma that shatters tradition – is that (as Hill himself has pointed out in another work)[4] a charismatic breakthrough can very well entail the rigorous restatement of tradition. Finally, he contrasts virtuosity with dynamic, subversive charisma only, ignoring its relation to other forms of charisma, and in particular to what Weber called "official" or institutional charisma – defined as one of the possible results of the routinization of charisma, whereby charisma comes to reside in the position or office rather than in the person. This last notion, and its later elaboration in the work (each in his own way) of Shils and Eisenstadt,[5] has been much criticized as widening the notion of charisma to the point of trivializing it. Nevertheless, it may have to be taken into account, precisely because of certain features of monastic virtuosity that, as will be clarified later in this section, appear to locate it somewhere between charisma in its genuine, "dynamic" pole and its more institutionalized pole, and to thus indicate the need for more refined categories of analysis. Redefining virtuosity and its relation to charisma in both the "genuine" and "institutional" sense will be a crucial step in establishing the distinctive cluster of sociological phenomena associated with the institutionalization of virtuosity in the two specific historical settings under study. Virtuoso and charismatic figures appear to share some important features: They both display a privileged and single-minded connection to the realm of ultimate goals and values, however conceived. Both entail, in different ways but with similar intensity, something outside, beyond, and even antithetical to the socially "normal" and "ordinary." Yet it would be mistaken to subsume religious virtuosi under the general category of charismatic religious figures and see them as just another instance of the perennial "charisma versus institution" antithesis.

It may be useful at this point to define virtuosity by a number of core features independent of particular ideological contents and institutional expressions, making it possible to use the concept across cultural contexts and historical periods. First, religious virtuosity is a matter of individual choice, a voluntary option implying an intense personal commitment, in contrast with the more or less compulsory and/or routine norms and expectations of common religious behavior. Second, it entails a search for perfection, an extreme urge to go beyond everyday life and average

---

[4] Hill, *Sociology of Religion*, pp. 153–7.

[5] For the full elaboration and amplification of charisma as a crucial component of institutional life and social order in general, see E. Shils, "Charisma, Order and Status," *American Sociological Review* 30 (1965): 199–213; S. N. Eisenstadt, "Introduction," in idem (ed.), *Max Weber*, pp. ix–lvi.

norms of achievement as defined in each cultural setting. It is this general attitude of straining toward perfection that should be seen as the primary feature, independent of its precise orientation (worldly or otherworldly, activistic or contemplative, ascetic or mystical, etc.). Third, this search for perfection is sustained in a disciplined, systematic fashion, entailing a singleminded adherence to fixed principles of behavior, a defined rule or method. Fourth, it implies a normative double standard: Its rigor is considered neither possible nor necessary for all, from either a virtuoso or nonvirtuoso point of view.[6] Fifth, it is based on achievement. Virtuosity is in principle an option open to all, even if actually valid for a "heroic" minority only. There is thus an element of elitism – one based, however, on achievement and nonascriptive criteria.

Looking at this list of features, it is clear that some of them might fully apply to "pure," personal charisma as well. Virtuoso and charismatic types, indeed, may well be empirically related, and even occasionally coincide. In fact, there may be a fluidity or actual liability between the two: Virtuosi may develop into charismatic figures, and the latter may in turn give rise to new forms of virtuosity. Virtuosi, however, do not as a rule turn into charismatic figures; and as long as they do not, they constitute a sociological type with distinctive, if indeed "quieter" (but not necessarily less socially significant) features. "Pure," personal charisma is credited, in Weber's well-known discussion of charismatic authority, with an essentially dynamic and subversive, anti-institutional potential. Religious virtuosi, in contrast, are not typically anti-institutional – Hill even emphasized their "conservative" character – even if they clearly represent something that is not altogether institutionalized and may even stand in tension with established authorities.

The last three features in the list are especially useful in bringing out interesting ideal-typical differences between virtuosity and charisma and giving us a better understanding of the distinctive features of monasticism as a "virtuoso institution" and of the "virtuoso-society" sociological complex with which it came to be associated in Theravada Buddhism and medieval Catholicism.

The first major difference lies in virtuosity's disciplined, methodic character, contrasting with one of the basic features of Weber's pure, genuine charisma, namely its resistance to any form of rational planning and discipline. This "practical religious rationalism," to use Schluchter's

---

[6] One may note the relevance of philosophical discussions of "supererogatory" actions, i.e., actions that possess moral value and that an agent may feel called upon to perform, but that cannot be demanded, and whose omission cannot be called wrongdoing. See, for example, J. O. Urmson, "Saints and Heroes," in J. Feinberg (ed.), *Moral Concepts* (Oxford: Oxford University Press, 1969); Heyd, *Supererogation*.

term,[7] predisposes virtuosity to formalization and organization. It does not, however, automatically identify virtuosity with institutional or routinized charisma, which is not necessarily characterized by rationality in general (in whatever sense of the term) or by this specific mode of rationality in particular. At any rate, it lends virtuosity a sustained character that contrasts with the volatile character of genuine charisma, which typically cannot be sustained for long and is bound either to disappear, or undergo routinization, transforming itself in the process into something radically opposed to its original nature.

The next distinction concerns the type of elitism involved. In a sense, charisma too transcends primordial and ascriptive attributes and is thus "open" to all, at the same time as it clearly pertains to the very few only. Nevertheless, it tends to be conceived as a spontaneous, extraordinary personal gift, one which may have to unfold, reveal, and sustain itself, but, unlike virtuosity, cannot be learned, and is not, nor should be revealed as, achieved, acquired, or developed.

Furthermore, there is a crucial difference in the type of relationship established with a following or "audience." The relational nature of charisma has often been emphasized: Only those individuals – and by extension, those ideals, values, or institutions – are charismatic that are recognized as such by other people. Charisma depends on its attribution, confirmation, and maintenance by an audience. Similarly, virtuosity presupposes the existence of nonvirtuosi and can be fully comprehended only when a nonvirtuoso vantage point is reckoned with. Nevertheless, significant differences between the two might be found precisely along this "relational" dimension.

A major difference is that virtuosity entails a normative double standard, whereas charisma need not. The virtuoso's rigor is considered neither possible nor necessary for all; it does not automatically determine the religious status and worth of nonvirtuosi – even, however paradoxical it may seem, where the virtuoso's superiority is clearly recognized. In a sense, charisma – as an exceptional, personal gift reserved to the extraordinary few – implies an even more radical, quasi-ontological demarcation between the charismatic individual and others. This demarcation is too sharp to be accounted for by a "merely" normative, ethical double standard. Charisma originates a more demanding, total kind of relation – which made Weber include it, significantly, within his general typology of forms of authority. As such, it is said to call for total devotion and commitment, and for a relation of deep personal identification from the followers of the charismatic figure. Virtuosity, in contrast, seems to call for dissociation and differentiation between virtuosi and

---

[7] Schluchter, "Paradox of Rationalization," p. 15.

nonvirtuosi, and implies a less direct and comprehensive commitment on the audience's part. Although virtuosity does presuppose a non-virtuoso point of reference, it is less dependent on external recognition than charisma, which is by definition dependent on an intense emotional bond between the charismatic figure and his followers.

Finally, virtuosi's tendencies to dissociation can take the form of radical (individual or collective) withdrawal from normal patterns of social relationships. This contrasts with the outreaching, communicative social tendencies of dynamic charisma, whatever the size of the audience it aims at. It is important to note, however, that dissociation and withdrawal can become the basis of and a stage in the accumulation of charismatic potential, as suggested earlier, whether the latter is taken in its more "institutional" and dispersed, or "dynamic" and concentrated, sense.

All these differences do not necessarily obviate the "rigorous restatement of tradition" that Hill considered a determining characteristic of virtuosity; but we should distinguish, when assessing the precise relation of virtuosi to tradition, between the virtuosi's perspective and that of society. Although virtuosi do tend to perceive themselves as representing or rigorously restoring the pristine purity of an impaired or corrupted tradition (a tendency also found, as already mentioned, in charismatic breakthroughs – sometimes mixed with a conscious attempt at religious innovation), their relation to tradition as perceived by society at large, and by the religious establishment in particular, ought to be seen as an empirical variable to be gauged in each specific case.

The same argument applies to virtuosi's potential for "charismatization" vis-à-vis or within the outside world, whether referring to charisma in its more dynamic or in its institutional forms. Virtuosi may come to represent, in certain cases, a form of countertradition or protest. Indeed, it is precisely their direct, single-minded commitment to the realm of ultimate concerns and values – in other words, to the charismatic dimension of human action in Shils's sense – and the consequent attempt to reestablish a pure, rigorous enactment of a religious tradition they perceive as endangered or transformed by the forces of routinization and institutionalization, that make them apt to develop countertradition and dissent.[8]

The crucial characteristic, however, is virtuosi's distinctive capacity to maintain themselves, in the process, in an ambiguous stance within soci-

---

[8] For a most suggestive study in this regard, see the analysis of religious "precisionist" movements in M. Fulbrook, *Piety and Politics: Religion and the Rise of Absolutism in England, Württemberg and Prussia* (Cambridge University Press, 1983); and B. Mazlich, *The Revolutionary Ascetic: Evolution of a Political Type* (New York: Basic, 1976).

ety at large, bringing with them the formation of virtuoso "alternative structures" in the sense defined earlier (see Chapter 2). Presenting a reversed image of society at large in many respects, even while remaining within its ideological and institutional boundaries, these "alternative structures" may be seen as one way in which "the element of potential dissent [is introduced] as an inherent and continuous component of the social order."[9] As such, religious virtuosity underlines the need for a more differentiated and comparative analysis of the manifold forms of expression and incorporation of the charismatic motive in social life in general.[10] What virtuoso alternative structures exemplify, in other words, is a form of charisma that differs (for the reasons already outlined) from "pure," genuine charisma in Weber's stronger formulations of the term, entails a definitive component of institutionalized charisma, and yet also maintains an element of potential dissent or antistructure (or even counter structure) that is differently expressed and actualized in each case, and that was only partly captured by Shils's analysis of either segregated (see this volume, Chapter 2) or diffuse institutional charisma.[11]

The virtuoso complex

Virtuosity, as defined by the core features already discussed, was able to give rise to a distinctive cluster of social processes – a complex – no less significant (if less dramatic) than those associated with the better-known and often overused "charisma versus institution" complex derived from Weber's original formulation.

The first element in this complex is the formation of virtuoso alternative structures, in the sense defined in Chapter 2. There is a vast difference indeed between virtuosity as a purely individual, occasional, and localized phenomenon, and those few historical instances in which virtuosity became institutionally sustained and reinforced to the point of engendering a specialized virtuoso institution – monasticism. The characteristics of monasticism as a distinctive type of social formation have already been analyzed. It may be noted at this point that its strong propensities for rationalization and its "total institution" aspects are

---

9 See S. N. Eisenstadt, "Comparative Liminality and Dynamics of Civilization," *Religion* 15 (1985): 324–5.

10 For the recent exploration of a very different mode of incorporation of charisma into broader societal contexts (specifically, through the transformation of millenarian charismatic orientations in seventeenth-century England and New England), see A. B. Seligman, "Charisma and the Transformation of Grace in the Early Modern Era," *Social Research* 58, no. 3 (1991): 591–622.

11 Although Shils emphasized segregation, among other things, as coping with the generally disruptive nature of intense and concentrated charisma, he did not dwell on the disruptive, subversive potential specifically entailed in monasticism's central ideological and institutional features.

obviously antagonistic to the basic features of genuine charisma. On the other hand, it also retained a strong component of systematic antithesis to ordinary social life, as well as an element of personal, optional striving and achievement, that are not usually connected with the idea of official or institutional charisma.

Another important element of the virtuoso–society complex is the enforcement of some form of segregation between virtuosi and society – a dimension rightly if only partly captured in Shils's notion of "segregated charisma." Although obviously facilitated by the existence of the monastic institution (of which it is in turn an essential condition), segregation does not necessarily take on the same character in all settings and periods: What is perceived as a threat to proper segregation in one cultural setting may not be seen as such in another. Segregation, at any rate, may be viewed as the culmination of the element of dissociation and differentiation between virtuosi and their audience intrinsic to the very notion of virtuosity and contrasting, as mentioned, with the intense emotional bond associated with charisma. As such, it should be understood as a two-sided process, encouraged by the virtuosi themselves, but also sustained (or undermined) by the nonvirtuoso environment.

Segregation, however, is also counterbalanced by the development of an intricate network of material and symbolic exchange between the virtuoso sector and society – another important feature of the virtuoso complex. This is epitomized in the gift relationship (laymen giving, virtuosi receiving) that is, in a form of exchange couched in the idiom of voluntariness and nonreciprocity, and signaling the presence of some form of solidary relationship betweeen the parties. The extent to which some form of reciprocity (material or symbolic) is nevertheless implicitly expected may vary. What actually occurs is the donation of mostly material goods by laymen to virtuosi, who in return are expected to provide some form of intangible, symbolic resources (merit, soteriological intercession, religious edification, or even – as more salient in the Theravada context – magico-ritual protection), as well as a variety of more tangible secular (educational, economic, therapeutic, and social) services. Paradoxically, the validity of this exchange is also dependent on the virtuosi's maintaining a degree of closure to reciprocity and negotiability, situating them without, or above, the range of ordinary social interactions and transactions. It is not incidental, in this regard, that monks came to provide ritual services, in both cases, in one sphere mostly: that of death and relation to the dead, confirming once again their ambiguous position as "outsiders" on the margins of ordinary social life and interaction.

Underlying this special form of exchange are distinctive ideological structures intrinsic to the virtuoso–society complex: First, the interaction between virtuosi and nonvirtuosi articulates and revolves about commonly acknowledged (if not equally enacted) ultimate, noninstrumental values; second, it entails the articulation of notions of a religious double standard, distinguishing between a virtuoso norm and an average norm but also locating them on a shared soteriological continuum, allowing for a gradient in religious performance and commitment to the search for perfection; third, it tends to be accompanied by notions of a symbolic "division of labor" between the two, nonvirtuosi delegating to the virtuoso sector the direct enactment of religious ideals that they are unable or unwilling to take upon themselves (a process aptly conveyed by Troeltsch's notion of "vicarious oblation"), and virtuosi acknowledging the necessary part of nonvirtuosi in the fulfillment of basic worldly tasks and duties (e.g., material survival and procreation).

It is crucial to note that the various components of the virtuoso–society complex would not be able to develop to the same extent and in the same fashion if not for the very first component upon which they depend, that is, the institutionalization of virtuosity in the form of monastic alternative structures. This institutional dimension once recognized, however, it is also characteristic that the virtuoso–layman relationship was never fully institutionalized: However well-established, institutionalized, and ideologically articulated the relationship became, it also remained totally optional and voluntary on both sides, and is supported by only informal sanctions. Furthermore, the relationship itself – again on both sides – is rich in ambivalences and dilemmas. The perennial quandaries besetting monasticism have already been analyzed. On the laity's side, one may mention two major kinds of dilemmas. The first refers to the tendency to make the virtuoso increasingly accessible and functional – perhaps to the point of endangering whatever special spiritual valence he may have – rather than enforcing his segregation and risking total disconnection between virtuosi and laymen, and thus total "defunctionalization" of the virtuoso sector from society's point of view. The second dilemma, more psychological, entails the tension between acknowledging, admiring, and sustaining the virtuoso's spiritual superiority, versus feeling threatened by and eventually rejecting or denying it. In the final chapter, we also address a complex range of more implicit symbolic dilemmas and ambiguities (as distinguished from the more explicit and widely acknowledged ideological structures already mentioned), important for a fuller understanding of the gift relationship in particular, and of the virtuosi's distinctive form of "ideological power."

For the moment, though, it is enough to recognize that the virtuoso–society complex, as a result of its basically voluntary character and of the many sociological ambivalences besetting it,[12] is a precarious sociological phenomenon. This precariousness is further enhanced by the ever-present possibility of corruption on either side. Economic, political, or cultural changes may unsettle it. Gift giving on the laity's side may deteriorate into a potlatchlike, competitive form of conspicious consumption and destruction of wealth.[13] The gift relationship may be transformed into an ordinary transaction, thus losing its crucial symbolic dimensions of nonreciprocity and nonnegotiability. Last but not least, virtuoso radicalism may emerge, within or without monasticism, bringing an element of instability into, or even basically undermining, the established network of relationships.

It is striking that, under certain conditions, and despite its seemingly fragile and precarious character, the virtuoso–society complex did not remain a merely localized, particularistic, and peripheral phenomenon, but could also apply at the central, macrosocietal level. In some sense, rulers had an obvious interest in supporting a politically withdrawn virtuoso sector, perhaps easier to interact with than a more politically involved religious establishment. Be that as it may, the basic virtuoso–society complex, through its very capacity to disperse at the local, peripheral level and stretch to the central level, and to bridge sectors of the population displaying differential degrees of commitment to central religious values, could come to form an overarching, macrosocietal structure, invested with diffuse but momentous political and even civilizational significance.

Crucial to the development and maintenance of macrosocietal, civilizational entities is the formation of overarching psychosocial structures, encompassing social heterogeneity and differentiation within a common cultural framework. Religious virtuosi were able to become the nexus of a wider sociological complex, of a cluster of social relationships and processes sustaining such an overarching, generalized structure. This type of structure, which is distinct from and independent of more obvious political ones, may sustain or even replace them when the latter disintegrate or fail. The virtuoso–society complex cannot be expected to develop in all societies, and might appear, when it does, in

---

[12] These could be shown to comprise *all* the various types of sociological ambivalence distinguished by R. K. Merton in *Sociological Ambivalence and Other Essays* (New York: Free Press, 1976).

[13] Such a process is fully documented, for example, in Gernet, *Aspects économiques du bouddhisme*. For another, interesting variation, in which donations develop as a sort of tribute to a nonascetic aristocracy of holy men themselves indulging in conspicuous consumption, see D. Cruise O'Brien, "Don divin, don terrestre: l'économie de la confrérie mouride," *Archives Européennes de Sociologie* 15 (1974): 82–101.

significant variants of the ideal-typical configuration defined above. In the next chapter, I seek to define the broader social and cultural conditions favorable to its historical crystallization and persistence, as well as to explain the major variations it displayed in the two settings selected for comparison.

10 The virtuoso complex compared

Only rarely do all the features essential to the virtuoso syndrome co-
alesce with enough strength to form a lasting and influential structure. In
this chapter, I try to sum up the ideological and institutional conditions
that have facilitated this unusual process of coalescence and institutionalization in the two settings examined here. Following the multidimensional approach defined earlier (see Chapter 2), the stress will be on the
combined impact, in each setting, of religious-ideological premises, patterns of monastic institutionalization within and in relation to a specific
macrosocietal context, and patterns of virtuoso radicalism.

The ideological premises

Religious virtuosity in the sense developed in the previous chapter can be
expected to develop only on the basis of cultural orientations that encourage belief in the perfectability of man and allow for the possibility of
voluntary and individual choice in committing oneself to the search for
perfection. Moreover, it would seem especially apt to thrive and develop
into a wider virtuoso–society complex when some of the commonly acknowledged, central cultural premises are fundamentally incompatible
with the worldly concerns of ordinary life, thus demanding a level of
commitment that cannot typically be expected from all. Although all
ideals may be somewhat incompatible with day-to-day life, the incompati-
bility is undoubtedly made especially acute in the case of out- or otherworldly salvational orientations. The virtuoso complex will not develop,
however, where otherworldly ideologies remain confined to small schools
or ephemeral groups, but only in those very few and rare cases where
otherworldly religious premises are combined with a universalist thrust
and thereby come to be part of the cultural system of macrosocietal
civilizational entities. In those cases, the complementary mechanisms of
segregation and exchange associated with the virtuoso–society complex
may be seen as mitigating the rift between those committing themselves to
the enactment of unworldly premises and those unable or unwilling to do
so – a specific instance of the more general problem of the internal heterogeneity of macrosocietal entities already mentioned.

The problems and paradoxes entailed in upholding otherworldly cultural premises on a macrosocietal scope were more especially acute,
however (and hence more conducive to the development of the virtuoso–

199

society complex), in the case of Theravada Buddhism, often taken to be the otherworldly religion par excellence. Indeed, traditional Theravada Buddhism offers a fuller and historically more resilient expression of the ideal-typical virtuoso–society complex already delineated. However, most crucial from this point of view were not so much differences in degree of worldliness or otherworldliness, but rather in the pattern of relation between otherworldly and worldlier orientations that developed in the two cultural systems. Theravada Buddhism's dominant tendency – understood now as the outcome of a sustained historical process of ideological selection and retention – was to enshrine otherworldliness at the peak of a relatively stable and unidimensional hierarchy of symbolic orientations. This process of hierarchization had the effect of insulating the supreme otherworldly ideals from impingement by or intertwining with more worldly, lower orientations. Christianity, on the contrary, displayed stronger and increasing worldly orientations, and a strong interpenetration between otherworldly and worldly tendencies. Here too, significantly, hierarchization emerged as an important principle of cultural organization regulating the relation between alternative symbolic orientations. Nevertheless, although otherworldly ideals appear to have indeed governed the process of symbolic hierarchization for a while, they were never as safely insulated from a whole range of worldlier cultural orientations that themselves would in time develop into alternative, competing principles of symbolic hierarchization.

These differences are reflected in the monastic institution itself. In Christianity, the intertwining of otherworldliness and worldlier orientations seems to have made, logically enough, for a monasticism displaying a greater capacity for institution building in the here and now. Conversely, Theravada virtuosi, committed to more exclusively otherworldly ideals, have given rise to a loose form of institution, in line with the general indifference to and "weakness" in institution building commonly attributed to otherworldly religions.

Resorting to a simple otherworldly/worldly dichotomy, however, is not sufficient to account for what has been diagnosed here as a very strong and enduring pattern of institutionalization of virtuosity in the Buddhist context. This peculiar pattern of institutionalization is not to be seen as the result of either otherworldly or worldly orientations proper, but rather of what I called the worldly "facets" of Theravada Buddhism's essentially otherworldly soteriological message. What this nuanced if admittedly unwieldy formulation is meant to record is, if not a positive soteriological valuation of activity in this world, at least a sustained awareness of and interest in the worldly context in which the search for salvation necessarily begins and unfolds. The most important expression of this stance, in my view, was the doctrinal elaboration of a very articulate and highly specified model of interaction between virtuosi and laymen, which played a decisive role in the incorporation of virtuosi within the wider social collective and in the "anchoring" of otherworldly ideals in the social here and now.

This model unequivocally buttressed the virtuoso's spiritual superiority, but also propounded a religious double standard investing the laity and worldly activity with a significant range of freedom and autonomy. Although insisting upon a clear-cut segregation of virtuosi and laity, it also kept them strongly interconnected and mutually dependent – a pattern in which the gift relationship played a central role. Unlike the Christian case, the doctrinal model did not elaborate explicit notions of reciprocal exchange and division of labor; nor did it propound any principles of religious authority or power in this world, either among virtuosi themselves or in their interaction with the laity, relying instead on the purely voluntary and formally unregulated participation of the two sides involved.

Religious ideology, monastic structures, and macrosocietal context in Theravada Buddhism

Theravada Buddhism's staunch renunciatory ideals were undoubtedly attenuated during its widespread diffusion and establishment in Southeast Asia. In the process, the Sangha became deeply embedded into its social environment as well as characterized by a low level of institutional autonomy. This so-called domestication of the Sangha also entailed the tendency for the Sangha to provide the laity with a variety of secular or magico-ritual services in tension with a stricter, more otherworldly definition of their virtuoso vocation. I have tried to show, however, that the basic segregative/interactive character of the relationship between virtuosi and laymen delineated at the doctrinal–ideological level, was in fact enforced and its scope of application even drastically expanded: First, it was effectively reproduced over large geographical areas in cellular, decentralized fashion, at the grass-roots village level; second, it came to apply at the polity's level as well, in the relationship between Sangha and king. In the process, the virtuoso–layman relation came to constitute a central axis of macrosocietal organization, cutting across regional differences, bridging center and periphery, and ending up forming the backbone of the interrelation of Buddhism and polity for Theravada countries.

Most striking for our own purposes, the strengthening and broadening of Theravada Buddhism's worldlier facets – sustained as it was, at least in part, by ideological developments of equivocal doctrinal status – never undermined the basic requisite for the virtuoso–society complex, namely, the very distinction between virtuosi and laymen, with the double standard that this entailed. Neither did it challenge the classical hierarchy of ultimate values. In fact, the resilience of the virtuoso–society complex on the one hand, and of the hierarchy of symbolic orientations as dominated by the renunciatory, otherworldly ideology on the other, formed deeply interrelated and mutually sustaining historical phenomena.

The resulting congruence between the doctrinal–ideological model and its actual historical embodiment was further reinforced by some dominant institutional characteristics of the macrosocietal context. Of special importance in this regard was the decentralized, cellular character of the administrative–political environment, at both the organizational and symbolic level. Such a framework, most obviously, could not provide the Sangha with powerful models of centralized authority or organization. More important, neither kingship and center, nor secondary aristocratic elites, nor even any alternative religious specialists or intellectual elites appear to have mustered sufficient strength and autonomy to compete with the village Sangha for local resources and loyalty. Buddhist polities, however unstable and fluctuating, undoubtedly contributed a framework that was crucial to the historical resilience and expansion of the Sangha and themselves acquired, in time, a considerable ideological momentum. In the long run, however, the typical Buddhist polity seems to have built upon but never fully superseded the village monastery and its local lay audience as an ideologically self-sufficient civilizational unit. Last, but not least, socioeconomic conditions remained relatively constant; stated negatively, no pervasive socioeconomic changes emerged that might have shaken the material and ideological underpinnings of the classical Sangha–society relationship.

It would be difficult, and probably mistaken, to try and determine the causal relations between the virtuoso–society complex and these major characteristics of the macrosocietal context. A posteriori, at any rate, the "fit" or compatibility between them is rather impressive, and the Theravada sociopolitical environment seems to have provided a favorable context for the basic virtuoso–society structure of relations, facilitating its cultural centrality and historical resilence. On the other hand, the virtuoso–society complex itself, so solidly entrenched, could impose constraints upon and mold the course of developments in society at large. Whatever the ultimate basis of this syndrome and the nature of the forces that brought it into being and kept it going for centuries, it also acquired a structuring power of its own. As such, it seems very close to Anthony Giddens's notion of a "structural set": "a distinct clustering of transformation and mediation relations implied in the designation of structural principles, i.e., principles of organization of societal totalities."[1] I try in the next and concluding chapter to penetrate a bit deeper into the nature of the implied relations of mediation. My point for the moment is that the virtuoso complex is to be understood as a key formation in the historical settings discussed, shaped by but also shaping in turn significant economic, political, and cultural aspects of social behavior at large, facilitating certain developments and hampering others. Indeed, it is this development of the virtuoso–layman relation into a major axis of social organization capable of operating at both local and macrosocietal level that sustained the long-term endurance of monasticism as an essential component of the social structure at large in traditional Theravada Buddhist societies. In other words, we have here the rather paradoxical case of a monasticism maintaining the major "alternative," antistructural features essential to the monastic institution as explained in our previous chapter, but also coming to interweave and interlock with wider social frameworks in such a way as to constitute a dominant, even determinant feature of the social structure at large.

Virtuoso radicalism in the Theravada configuration

Even virtuoso radicalism, which might have been thought to pose (and to some extent did pose) a challenge to the established pattern of institutionalization and "domestication" of virtuosity, was not only contained within the bounds of this established pattern, but even acted at times in such a way as to reinforce and revitalize the whole configuration. On the one hand, radical renouncers striving for more extreme forms of withdrawal from the world undoubtedly challenged the established modus vivendi between Sangha and society; as has been noted, they also introduced a significant element of uncertainty into the gift relationship so essential to this modus vivendi. On the other hand, the ideology of outworldliness itself implied the existence of the always-legitimate option of retreating further from the social order and thereby recharging the virtuoso's charismatic potency, itself essential to the cultural viability of the virtuoso–society complex. The more radical renouncers, moreover, were far from constituting an altogether anarchic element; they did not necessarily strive for a clear-cut differentiation from the established, village Sangha. More important, they tended to become enmeshed with the political center and the latter's campaigns of purification. As a result, they may be

[1] A. Giddens, *The Constitution of Society: Outline of the Theory of Structuration* (Cambridge: Polity Press and B. Blackwell, 1984), pp. 185 ff. I allow myself to borrow the concept of structural set without necessarily endorsing Giddens's broader theory of structuration – a usage Giddens himself expected and encouraged. There have been in fact very few attempts to apply Giddens's highly theoretical concepts, even fewer regarding the analysis of premodern phenomena.

said to have contributed to revitalizing, reestablishing, or even disseminating the classical pattern of interaction between virtuosi and society rather than seeking structurally different arrangements. Most crucially, Theravada virtuoso radicalism never seems to have aimed, at least during the long period under study, at a total escape from the basic pattern of interaction with the laity, but only at minimizing it, voicing no principled opposition to the basic cleavage between virtuosi and laymen, and achieving no distinctive impact upon the laity.

It may be possible to further explain the historical resilience of the Theravada virtuoso–society complex by its very flexibility: As has been noted, it allowed for a largely tolerant stance vis-à-vis world and laity as well as heterogeneous "lower" cultural orientations – a feature enhanced by the absence of any mediating ecclesiastical institution or keeper of dogmatic orthodoxy. Moreover, it could be basically indifferent to and untouched by the vagaries and failures of the social order, which the virtuoso otherworldly ideology did not claim to model to begin with. Third, the ability of the virtuoso–society complex to function at both local and macrosocietal level, together with its typical village-based cellularity, endowed it with the lizard-like capacity, when impaired at one point or level, to survive or reform itself at another level. All this should not be taken to imply in any ways that the basic structure of the relations between virtuosi and society never broke down. The crucial point, rather, is that even if it did (as happened recurrently and most dramatically following wars and invasions), it re-emerged later with little modification, and that no alternative arrangement ever achieved a comparable social status.

Religious ideology, monastic structures, and macrosocietal context in medieval Catholicism

Within medieval Christianity, by contrast, developments at the ideological and institutional level interacted in such a way as to encourage the emergence of a variant of the virtuoso–society complex, but at the same time also prevent it from ever acquiring the cultural centrality and solid social anchorings it was able to achieve in the Theravada setting.

To begin with, the virtuoso–society complex had to rely on far less solid doctrinal and ideological groundings, *despite* the presence, from the outset, of strong virtuoso inclinations clearly encouraging the emergence of ascetic rigorism and perfectionism. Most crucial perhaps, these original virtuoso orientations were not endowed with a specific model of relation to the world, and retained a characteristic ideological open-endedness. Moreover, the multivocality of the Christian message itself, with its deep intertwining of otherworldliness and worldliness, further contributed to the oscillation of the virtuoso impulse among various conflicting conceptions of the search for perfection.

The doctrinal model of relations between virtuosi and other Christians that developed in time displayed some critical differences from its Theravada equivalent. First, although also entailing, like the Theravada model, an element of segregation, it was more distinctly "transactional," based upon reciprocal and explicit exchange between virtuosi and others. Second, the traffic in symbolic and material resources was sustained by notions of a division of labor between the parties. Third, this division of labor was understood to take place within the bounds of what have been designated here as the Church's vertical and horizontal parameters: It was regulated, in the final instance, by the ecclesiastical hierarchy, as well as founded upon holistic and organistic conceptions of the Christian collective. Such a model might seem to form, at first sight, an ideological edifice no weaker and perhaps even stronger than that obtaining in the Buddhist context. The crucial point, however, is that Christian monasticism developed a degree of organizational structure, overall institutional autonomy, political power, and cultural impact upon society at large too extensive and forceful to be effectively contained by mechanisms of segregation, division of labor, and exchange.

For a time though (roughly up to the eleventh century), Christian monasticism did maintain a network of interaction and exchange with society at large that superficially resembled the Theravada pattern, whatever the crucial differences in ideological underpinnings. Not unlike and in certain respects even more than the Sangha, it too became deeply "functionalized" (in the sense of being made useful for society at large and providing the laity with a broad range of religious and social services). Christian monks were on the whole less engaged in providing the laity with magical or magico-ritual services – probably reflecting the lesser tolerance of "high" Christianity in general with magical orientations seen as competing with its own scheme of (magico)-sacramental devices. Nevertheless, they too did intervene as specialists invested with some form of distinctive ritual capacity in one important sphere at least, that of relation to death and the dead. Moreover, Christian monasticism as well became at times heavily dependent upon lay patronage in general and the political center in particular. However, it also displayed a characteristic tendency to penetrate nonmonastic spheres of activity and a capacity to transform ascetic prestige into power in the world, which, together with the steady and increasing diffusion of virtuoso orientations into society at large, formed a sharp contrast with the Theravada situation. What thus obtained was a monastic institution that came to constitute much more of an "alternative" structure than in the Buddhist situation, standing in a relation of greater opposition and competition to other institutional sectors – in part because also more similar to them in institutional structures and dynamics.

These characteristics of Christian monasticism may be attributed, at least in part, to the worldly strand ingrained within the ascetic tradition itself, as well as to the replication, within the monastic institution, of what I have designated as the horizontal and vertical principles of organization operative in the Church at large – all making for a greater potential in corporate strength and social involvement. They were also much facilitated by the special (if never exclusive) connection to the upper strata and aristocratic elites, enabling easy access to the centers of secular or ecclesiastical political power – in contrast to the dominant (if not exclusive either) Theravada pattern of grassroots embedment at the local village level. At any rate, these institutional characteristics of monasticism obviously enhanced its overall institutional and transactional power for a while. But they also helped blur the boundaries between the virtuoso sector and society at large in the long run, and as a result, defeated the possibility of a clear-cut segregation and division of labor between them. Paradoxically, thus, the very strength of Christian virtuosity's penetration of and impact upon society at large may be said to have contributed to the undermining of a separate virtuoso "alternative structure," and of the virtuoso–society complex of which that structure is a necessary element.

Moreover, the very fact that the relation between virtuosi and the others tended to be couched in a transactional, at times even quasi-commercial idiom, enhanced the element of precariousness intrinsic to the virtuoso–society complex in general. Being based on conditional, reciprocal exchange, it was automatically undermined by changes that affected the laity's interest in entering or maintaining the relationship – a fact that may explain its rapid erosion from the twelfth century on. The element of option on the laity's side had been present from the very beginning: Laymen could always content themselves with the soteriological intercession provided by the secular clergy, or even decide to do without any intercession or mediation at all – a recurring theme of medieval lay religious protest. However, it is mainly from the twelfth century on, in the wake of major institutional and ideological changes in society at large, that laymen started to withdraw from the relation of exchange with religious virtuosi, channeling whatever material surplus they had at their disposal in new directions. Whereas the segregative aspect of the relation between virtuosi and society became increasingly blurred, its transactional and thus essentially contingent aspect was, on the contrary, enhanced.

Although a number of features of the Christian ideological matrix contributed to these trends and developments, it is necessary to also consider the impact of various characteristics of the macrosocietal context without which these trends might not have evolved. From this point of view, the distiguishing characteristic of medieval Christian society, relative to the Theravada Buddhist case, is the coexistence of multiple foci of authority, ecclesiastic and secular, competing and interfering in each other's domains of influence at the various levels of social organization (from the local to the national and the supranational), with only occasional periods of clear-cut division of labor and complementarity. In this, my analysis converges with other works in comparative historical sociology that have all emphasized, despite otherwise great differences in approach, the plurality of centers of power and/or authority as a distinguishing characteristic of the medieval West. These foci of political power and institutional authority, to begin with, provided monasticism with forceful exemplars of institutional formalization, legalistic and centralizing tendencies, and massive administrative structures, having no equivalent in the Theravada setting. Moreover, monasticism was caught up, as a result, in a shifting network of alliances between the various clerical and secular political forces; its symbolic status and prestige tended to fluctuate with the principles of social hierarchization favored by a specific balance of power.

The crucial point is that, although hierarchization was a pervasive device of organization in medieval society, it could evolve along a number of competing and potentially conflicting axes. Concomitantly, the various political forces were able, in alternation, to attain a high degree of ideological–symbolic autonomy. The greater ideological strength and autonomy of kingship and aristocracy, in particular, have been stressed, contrasting as they do with the relative weakness of their Buddhist equivalents and with their consequent relative ideological dependence upon the Sangha. Although the view that matters of perfection may determine the ultimate hierarchical position of human beings – placing monks and even hermits at the very apex of the hierarchical order – never vanished and was at times dominant, it was always in competition with other, equally influential models of hierarchization. This was a major factor hampering the consolidation of the virtuoso–society interaction into a major axis of social organization in the Theravada fashion.

Moreover, the overall ideological and institutional plurality of the Christian setting further enhanced the competitive, transactional, and thus ultimately contingent aspect of the relationship between virtuosi and their social environment. In sum, this relationship would never be able to reach the status of a central "structural set" in the sense already defined – although it may have seemed to approach that status from the seventh to the tenth century. The status it achieved was rather that, ultimately less central and less solidly entrenched, of what may be called a principle of "structural alternation": a principle, that is, whose impact appears to lie in constituting one of a plurality of forcefully competing, interpenetrating, and historically alternating structural principles in the same societal entity.

It is important to stress that the greater (if always partial) similarity to the traditional Theravada Buddhist pattern that obtained in the earlier phase of medieval Christianity, running roughly from the sixth to the eleventh centuries, was also favored by a greater similarity in macrosocietal configuration at that stage. Not only did a mostly agrarian, subsistence-level economic structure with little economic surplus and fluidity of exchange prevail, but the Church was not yet so strong and centralized, no competing intellectual elites or institutions had yet come into being, and macrosocietal political frameworks themselves displayed much fluctuation in political power and centralization. Macrosocietal political frameworks, which had almost vanished with the dismantling of the Roman Empire, may be said to have regained strength under Charlemagne; but they were much weakened again by the end of the ninth century, when the Carolingian Empire was successfully challenged by other kingdoms. The consequent feudal decentralization or even atomization persisted until the reemergence of political centers in the course of the twelfth and thirteenth centuries, in conflict with a Church itself considerably stronger and centralized.

On the other hand, the overall strengthening of both state and church apparatus coincided with the gradual decline in the scope and centrality of the virtuoso complex in the medieval West. This would seem to indicate that the virtuoso complex is apt to become an overarching generalized structure in agrarian societies where macrosocietal, state structures may be present, but rather weak or inefficient, and where the degree of cultural–ideological pluralization and elite differentiation is relatively limited. Again, the great turning point was the twelfth century, when the acceleration of a market economy, the burgeoning of national kingship and state, the overall strengthening of the secular clergy itself and of the Church's bureaucratic apparatus, and the emergence of new types of cultural–ideological elites and institutions greatly undermined virtuosi's power of survival as a separate sector within an increasingly differentiated and competitive ideological marketplace.

It should be emphasized, however, that the contingent, transactional nature of the interaction between virtuosi and society in general was enhanced not only by the increasing pluralization and "marketlike" character of the ideological and institutional macrosocietal context, but also by the very existence, at least up to the Great Schism, of a global and holistic conception of Christendom – perhaps providing the taken-for-granted, "precontractual" arena in which transactional market processes could better develop: "Competition and contractual relationships fare best within an area of agreement and consensus."[2] Neither "state" nor "church" in their Theravada equivalents appear to have operated in such a global precontractual fashion.

The foregoing interpretation of the main institutional structures of the medieval West and of the place in it (and demise) of monasticism is rather consistent, by and large, with other extant macrosociological interpretations of that period of Western history. Where I would deviate, however, is in the interpretation of the church, in some of these works, as the equivalent of a powerful bureaucracy and state – or statelike – structure.[3] This difference may simply stem from the fact that I address myself to the earlier rather than later parts of the Middle Ages, where such a characterization is hardly applicable. Indeed, as already suggested, it is perhaps the relative weakness until the twelfth century of both secular and ecclesiastic "state" structures that allowed monastic structures and the attendant virtuoso complex to acquire such an important role, thus facilitating some important similarities with Theravada Southeast Asia.

Virtuoso radicalism in the Christian configuration

A number of developments in the virtuoso sector itself converged with the trends just described to further shake the foundations of the virtuoso–society complex as they obtained in the earlier stage. First, the virtuoso sector itself underwent increasing internal differentiation and polarization, much more so than in the Theravada case. Not only was the polarization between withdrawn and socially involved forms of virtuosity more pronounced, it also combined with a whole range of other ideological variations in an expanding spectrum of virtuoso options. This ideological plurality of the virtuoso sector led not only to institutional divisions within the monastic sector, but also to the emergence of new forms of virtuoso radicalism, overflowing the boundaries of monasticism itself (and even in some cases, of orthodoxy in general). The implications for the basic segregative/transactional mode of interaction between virtuosi and other social groups were momentous. In particular, both those forms of virtuoso radicalism striving at greater and even total withdrawal from the laity, and those striving, on the contrary, to intensify interaction with the laity, represented a deviation from the previous balance of segregation and exchange between monks and laymen. Even the eremitic strand reproduced the basic ideological and institutional

---

[2] Hall, "Religion and the Rise of Capitalism." A similar argument has been advanced in Mann, *Sources of Social Power*, chs. 10, 12 especially.

[3] See especially Collins, *Weberian Sociological Theory*.

features of the virtuoso "establishment" at large: the intertwining and tension between otherworldliness and worldliness, the impact of the vertical and horizontal principles, and the translatability of ascetic, outworldly prestige into power in the world – all ultimately inimical, as noted, to the maintenance of a pattern of clear-cut segregation between virtuosi and society. Moreover, the laity's increasing access to forms of religious virtuosity of its own further blurred the boundaries between the virtuoso and nonvirtuoso sectors and challenged the very plausibility of a differentiated virtuoso institution – a process that culminated with the Reformation. But perhaps most crucial, the existence of a broad spectrum of virtuosity further enhanced the elements of choice, competition, and transactional exchange that had already made the interaction between virtuosi and society characteristically precarious and contingent in the earlier medieval setting.

Summing up, we have thus reached a multidimensional analysis of the virtuoso complex, showing its precise development to be shaped by a constellation of ideological and institutional forces or variables. Although I believe that these variables were the most significant ones in shaping the historical trajectory of religious virtuosity in each civilization, I do not claim that the same variables should be invariably and automatically used in comparative macrosociological analysis more generally (of religious or any other type of phenomena). Neither should the interaction between them always be expected to be conceptualized in the same way – as one of overall mutual reinforcement. Religious–ideological orientations, to be sure, are given place of pride in my argument; but they are never considered independently of a whole range of other variables with which they powerfully interact. In the concluding chapter, I try to address the precise significance of religious–ideological orientations in the interaction between virtuoso elites and society, and thereby better define the sources and nature of virtuosity as a distinctive form of ideological power.

Conclusion
Religious virtuosity as ideological power: some implications for the comparative study of civilizations

Like any style or method of work, comparative macrosociology has distinctive strengths but also limitations. Following the development of a constellation of variables over many centuries and across civilizations makes it perhaps possible to highlight ideal-typical formations and broad structures, but does not claim to engage in the kind of rich and detailed analysis of more limited material – something akin to Geertz's programmatic call for "thick description" – better able to render the rich texture and "fine grain" of social life. Although this is true of any aspect of social life in general, I find the problem especially acute and challenging, for my own purposes, concerning the study of cultural orientations in particular. Stating the dilemma from the Weberian angle, the problem is how to conciliate the Weberian quintessential emphasis on the interpretation of meaning and the equally Weberian emphasis on the importance of multifactorial comparative sociological analysis.

The aim of the two preceding chapters was, first, to define the essential features of the virtuoso–society complex, and second, to identify the ideological and institutional forces shaping the expression of this complex in the two civilizations in which it achieved its fullest deployment. Having thus gone through rather "normal" motions of a comparative macroscopic analysis, I intend now to probe a bit further into the ideological appeal and symbolic meaning of virtuoso elites. More generally, I submit, the difficult issue of meaning cannot be simply brushed aside if one is aiming at a fuller understanding of the place of religious ideology and structures in the dynamics of macrosocietal, civilizational entities.

Recent macrocomparative treatments of these topics, in contrast, have tended to address religion not in terms of ideological contents and symbolic meaning, but rather in terms of the economic and institutional facets or solidarity functions of religious organizations.[1] Significantly,

[1] See the Introduction, fn. 4. See also Gellner, *Plough, Sword and Book,* especially pp. 93–103. (Gellner, however, does otherwise give weight to ideological contents in other parts of this same work and objects to any principled theoretical stance on this matter.) The main functions referred to, typically, have to do either with some form of social control (such as socialization, the diffusion and regulation of literacy, the legitimization of power, or general enforcement of order) or with the contribution to some form of normative pacification and social solidarity. Despite the self-conscious refusal to submit religious substan-

however, such perspective has not necessarily denied, and in some cases has even contributed, to emphasizing the distinctive importance of religion in the comparative understanding of civilizational dynamics. Of special interest for our present purposes is the approach of Michael Mann: similarly bracketing out issues of ideological content or meaning, yet granting religion a large share of autonomy and the capacity to constitute a highly distinctive and influential source of ideological power. Although otherwise sharply opposed to what he defines as the more "conventional" style of comparative macrosociology to which the present book probably belongs, Mann's general emphasis on "networks of power" as the prime ingredients of his comparative world-historical approach is in fact rather compatible with my present emphasis on the virtuoso complex as a specific type of relational macrostructure.[2] More important, I find the notion of ideological power especially suggestive and relevant to what I have addressed, in the Introduction, as the capacity of virtuoso elites to achieve institutional strength and collective relevance – Nietzsche's contradictory "triumph." Yet the basis of religious ideological power, in Mann's perspective, is said to lie not so much in religious contents and beliefs, however genuinely adhered to, but rather in its capacity "to convert into a distinctive form of social organisation, pursuing a diversity of ends, 'secular' and 'material' (e.g. the legitimation of particular forms of authority) as well as those conventionally considered as religious or ideal (e.g. the search of meaning)."[3]

Understanding the social position of virtuoso elites in the medieval West and traditional Southeast Asia, however, may give us a unique opportunity to counteract these recent expressions of a "neomaterialist" interpretation of the role of religion in premodern macrosocietal entities. Monasticism and virtuoso elites, after all, are eminently and primarily ideological, or at least ideologically oriented phenomena; so is, at least in part, society's response and attitude to them. It is not my intent, however, to argue for a purely idealist interpretation of virtuosi and their relationship with society at large. Rather, it seems to me important to give their due to both ideological as well as institutional dynamics, and even more specifically, to the intricate intertwining and interpenetration of the two in the understanding of religious virtuosity as a specific form of ideological power.

tive contents, like any other variable, to systematic theoretical and comparative scrutiny, one does encounter in these works occasional and inconsistent references to the importance of religious doctrines and orientations, albeit again without admitting them any systematic theoretical status.

[2] Although Michael Mann advances this conception in strident opposition to what he sees as flawed, conventional macrosociology, it could be shown that the gap is far from unbridgeable and somewhat an artifact of Mann's perception of "conventional" macrosociology.

[3] Mann, *Source of Social Power*, p. 22.

The point is, indeed, that religious virtuosi in the two civilizational settings selected for comparison have given rise to an inextricable cluster of "symbolic-cum-organizational" processes in their historical interaction with society at large. On the one hand, virtuoso religion undoubtedly spawned a specific form of organization – monasticism. Furthermore, this organization often entailed the provision of a variety of "secular" services (educational, economic, and social) that account, at least in part, for its powerful position in these two settings. It is of course true that in both cases monasticism "provided not just soteriological subtleties, but concrete social services,"[4] all amply discussed in previous chapters of this volume. However, it is also true that soteriological subtleties were far from irrelevant for the sides involved, and were a necessary condition for whatever social services were provided. It is not the organized provision of social services, but rather the effective combination of the two aspects – soteriological and organizational – that underlies the social significance of the monastic elites in these two settings. The ability of monks to provide most of these services ultimately rested, for the laity, on their special prestige as carriers of specific cultural values and their theoretically withdrawn, "disinterested" asceticism. Overemphasis on social services could threaten monks' spiritual vocation, and consequently their soteriological functions for the laity (be it active intercession, as in the Christian case, or the more passive provision of a field of merit, as in the Buddhist case) – their major and prime service to society at large. In other words, there is a basic tension between the functional and ideological aspects of monasticism that, among other things, engendered much of the recurrent corruption-and-reform cycle in the history of monasticism in both settings.

Recognizing this tension is essential to the analysis of the ideological power of the virtuoso sector. To some extent, monasticism did give rise to a sort of "diffused power, spreading in a . . . spontaneous, unconscious, and decentered way throughout a population," of the kind associated by Mann with ideological power in its more "autonomous" configuration.[5] The appeal or influence displayed by virtuoso elites, however, cannot be fully captured by the notion of an ideological power relying either on its functional, "practical" bases or on a straightforward process of ideological diffusion and persuasion. What is involved, as repeatedly stressed in the previous chapters, is a more ambiguous and contradictory phenomenon, relying on a complex process of segregation and exchange in the mediation between virtuosi and society at large.

It may be useful at this point to turn again to Mauss's pioneering work on gift giving – a tradition of inquiry seldom made to encounter the

---

[4] Hall, *Powers and Liberties*, p. 74
[5] Mann, *Sources of Social Power*, p. 8.

comparative sociological one.[6] (Having already noted the need for a mutual fructification of the Weberian and Durkheimian approach to the study of religion, it is perhaps not incidental that it is to one of Durkheim's closest collaborators that we are now turning for additional insights.) To judge from the massive stream of donations received by monks, they obviously struck a chord among a laity willing to dispossess of a significant part of their material resources for the monks' material support. Far from being totally "disinterested" gifts, however, lay donations can be shown to make sense within the framework of certain ideological beliefs and to entail highly valued soteriological remuneration, such as an increased store of merit (for Buddhist laymen), or a better chance at salvation in the world to come (for Christians). It may also be tempting to interpret these donations as a tacit payment for the various social services already alluded to. Lying at the essence of gift giving, however, as recognized by Mauss, is precisely a distinct and delicate combination of "interestedness" and "disinterestedness," denying reciprocity yet constituting an important mechanism of solidarity in the long term.

Lay donations, in short, are not just a payment for monastic secular or religious services. Neither are they, however, equivalent to a straightforward commitment to the virtuoso ideals. A more adequate interpretation of donations, rather, is that they contribute to mediating between two otherwise polarized and even antagonistic sectors, between a religious elite exemplifying certain ideals, and lay believers willing to acknowledge the same ideals but unable or unwilling to commit themselves to their fullest enactment. The gift, in this case at least, is perhaps "total" (in Mauss's sense of being simultaneously economic, religious, political, etc.), but it is also, ideologically, a highly pliant and multivocal phenomenon.

It is useful, in this regard, to draw attention to the contradictory character of a gift relationship that undoubtedly testifies to the importance of otherworldly ideals, but also obviously gives tremendous importance to the proper circulation of material things in and of this world. After all, if worldly goods were not important, why should it be so important to get rid of them in the proper fashion and to the proper person? The significance of the virtuoso, from such a perspective, may be not so much, or not only his commitment to otherworldly ideals, but also his highly codified, "professional-like" way of life. At a time in

---

[6] See, however, for a suggestive example of encounter between Weberian and Maussian themes of inquiry, Tambiah, *Buddhist Saints of the Forest;* J. Parry, "The Gift, the Indian Gift, and the 'Indian' Gift," *Man* n.s. 21 (1986), 453–73. See also the monumental application of a historical sociological perspective to the study of "evergetic" giving in Greco-Roman antiquity in P. Veyne, *Le pain et le cirque: sociologie historique d'un pluralisme politique* (Paris: Seuil, 1976).

which neither market nor banking institutions in the modern sense were available, monasteries came to constitute the most reliable channels for the conservation, fructification, and display of wealth.[7] Paradoxically, it is precisely through what Peter Brown has aptly called his prolonged "rituals of dissociation" from the world and its ordinary web of social mutualities, and his resulting "professionalization" and "objectivity"[8] that the ascetic virtuoso may well offer the donor one of the most trustworthy, because most controlled and rationalized, ways of consuming his possessions and goods in this world. The trustworthiness is here further enhanced by the corporate continuity and (at least theoretically) inalienability of monastic wealth, by the fact that the receivers and receptacles of donations were monastic institutions ensuring a degree of continuity beyond the life span of individual virtuosi and of the donors themselves.

Although undoubtedly testifying to the appeal of otherworldly ideals,[9] the gift should thus also be seen as standing at the very nexus of otherworldliness and worldliness. Circulating things in this world, but also becoming quasi-thing-like itself in the process, the gift represents a sort of buffer zone in which the uneasy process of segregation and interaction between monk and layman, and between otherworldly and worldly, is thus regularly reenacted. It expresses the contradictory impulse to reaffirm the legitimacy of the average man's activity and wealth in the world while supporting a small elite withdrawn from the world, and to acknowledge the soteriological import of otherworldliness but also to negate or partly neutralize its impact.

The critical point is not only that the gift mediates between virtuosi and laymen, but also that it does so by coming "in place" of some other form of interaction for which it may be a substitute. What the religious gift of the kind discussed here would seem to connote and come in place of is not so much the possibility of conflict between donor and receiver – especially emphasized, for example, in Sahlins's reading of Mauss.[10] Rather, it is the oscillation between two possibilities no less threatening in nature: The first one is a polarization so deep and dichotomic that it may lead to total indifference or disconnection, that is, to the absence or dissolution of any sort of ties between renouncer and layman; the second one, at the opposite extreme, is a more involving, total form of commit-

---

[7] A similar function of donations to religious institutions in general is suggested by Ernst Gellner, who sees them mainly as a way of protecting surplus wealth from confiscation by eventual predators. See Gellner, *Plough, Sword and Book*, p. 103.

[8] Brown, "Social Functions of the Holy Man."

[9] For a stress on the importance of otherworldly orientations for religious (especially charitable) giving, see Parry, "Gift." See however, a more nuanced analysis of the relation between Christianity in particular and charity (vs. other forms of giving), in Veyne, *Le pain et le cirque*, pp. 44–65.

[10] See M. Sahlins, *Stone Age Economics* (Chicago: Aldine, 1972), pp. 169 ff.

ment, in the face of which the gift is a form of surrogate and compromise. It is, after all, undoubtedly easier to give a gift to a monastery than to surrender oneself to the monastic life. In this regard, therefore, the gift may be understood as a form of mediation between total disconnection and total commitment, and constitutes as much a way of establishing or reestablishing long-term solidarity as of testing or retesting options and boundaries.

It would be mistaken, however, to think that we have now exposed the one exhaustive and fundamental "meaning" of donations to the monks. As a matter of fact, the precise set and mix of motivations – conscious and unconscious, explicit and implicit – probably varied not only between the two settings examined, but even in each specific act of giftgiving.[11] A similar observation led Ernst Gellner to simply conclude that "when men perform acts which are part of their cultural repertoire, the ascribed motives come as part of a package deal, and need not be taken too seriously in any one individual case. . . . What does matter are the situational constraints which operate overall."[12] This, however, leaves unexplained what allowed these acts of donations to become such an ingrained part of the cultural repertoire – a question I believe can be answered only within the context of a more general understanding of the virtuoso–society complex and of the combination of ideological and institutional conditions affecting its deployment. But what Gellner's "situational" approach also overlooks is the distinctive operation of the gift as a mechanism of ideological mediation, relying, precisely, upon its pliable and multivocal character, its capacity to become the focal point or common locus of many possible types and layers of meaning, however differentially actualized in each discrete act of donation.[13]

If virtuoso elites did tend to generate a pattern of ideological power, therefore, it was one ridden – as all power perhaps – with basic tensions, ongoing instability and a fundamental ambivalence. Their ideological power is, to a very large extent, the power of ideology; but the power of ideology is itself, in this case, of a very specific and complex kind. In terms of our original comparison of virtuosity with charisma, here confirmed once again, the ideological power entailed does not call

---

[11] This is also why it may be not be helpful to lump together all forms of donations to religious institutions under one interpretation. Donations to priestly elites may well constitute a different pattern of giving than donations to virtuoso elites in the sense developed here.

[12] See Gellner, *Plow, Sword and Book,* p. 103.

[13] The high variability and plasticity of gifts' symbolic meaning across contexts and situations has been strongly emphasized in R. Firth, "Symbolism in Giving and Getting," in idem, *Symbols, Public and Private* (Ithaca, N.Y.: Cornell University Press, 1973), pp. 368–402. I am adding here the possible element of symbolic pliancy and multivocalness even in one single act, type, and context of gift-giving.

for total identification and commitment but rather an ongoing balancing of identification and differentiation, internalization and externalization, closeness and distance.

Recognizing the intrinsic ambiguities and complexities of this major form of ideological power in the two great traditions examined implies acknowledging the capacity for tolerating and even actively nurturing ideological ambiguity as an essential rather than peripheral dimension in the analysis of both past and contemporary cultures.[14] Conversely, if a number of recent studies have tended to understate the role of ideological beliefs and contents in their analysis of the place of religious structures in macrosocietal formations, it is perhaps, at least in part, because they have assumed (like more traditional analyses of central value-systems before them) an overly monolithic and "cognitive rational" model of what ideological beliefs and orientations can be about.[15] Emphasizing both the presence of an inextricable cluster of ideological-cum-organizational dimensions and the ambiguous, dynamic nature of the ideological dimension itself in the interaction between virtuosi and society has certainly brought us, at any rate, a long way from any simple version, Durkheimian or otherwise, of virtuosi's "exemplary" ideological impact or symbolic "function."

A major aim of this study is to reassert the importance of relational structures in macrosocietal analysis – a style of interpretation usually giving priority to more obvious and "visible" organizational-institutional structures. This, however, should not lead us to reify such relational structures, nor to overrate their strength. The prominent position of religious elites and their general, macrosocietal significance as the acknowledged carriers of major religious ideals, were shown to be based, ultimately, on a voluntary and in many ways ambiguous and precarious process of interaction and exchange between these elites and their lay audiences. This, in turn, should instill in us a solid sociological respect for those (very few) cases in which these seemingly fluid and unsteady symbolic-ideological structures were successfully upheld over extensive stretches of time and space. Such exceptional endurance and scope can hardly be fitted into a static and passive conception of cultural continuity and tradition. Rather, it was shown to depend on the development of a

---

[14] For an important theoretical discussion of this general issue, see D. N. Levine, *The Flight from Ambiguity: Essays in Social and Cultural Theory* (Chicago: University of Chicago Press, 1985), especially ch. 3.

[15] For a brief critique of conventional forms of value analysis, see J. C. Alexander and P. Smith, "The Discourse of American Civil Society: A New Proposal for Cultural Studies," *Theory and Society* 22, no. 2 (1993): 151–5 especially. From a very different angle, see A. Swidler, "Culture in Action." See also the critique of Western-biased notions of religious beliefs in Deborah E. Tooker, "Identity Systems of Highland Burma: Belief, *Akha zan* and a Critique of Interiorized Notions of Ethno-religious Identity," *Man* 27, no. 4 (1992): 799–820.

complex cluster of institutional and ideological processes allowing not only virtuosi, but also vast masses of average believers, to negotiate their relationship to otherworldly ideals hardly applicable to all.

To that extent, this analysis of the virtuoso complex certainly confirms the need to approach cultural values and value systems as "themselves the outcome of processes of defining what is valuable."[16] This process of defining the valuable, moreover, involves not only "the association of groups, conflict among groups, domination of some groups by others, and the settlement of conflicts among rival societal groups,"[17] but also, as I tried to demonstrate in a more detailed analysis of the gift relationship in particular, complex processes of symbolic mediation through a network of material and symbolic exchange. In this perspective, in fact, I hope not only to have contributed to the ongoing theoretical and empirical exploration of the mutual interrelations between micro- and macroprocesses, but also to have provided the example of a form of "traditional" process or mechanism capable of playing a privileged role in the mutual encounter and interconnection of micro and macro aspects of social life – and perhaps as a result, in the production and reproduction of certain sets of values and practices over vast expanses of social space and time.

Coming back to Weber, there is by now general agreement that he tended to underestimate the worldly, social potential of Buddhism, whether dated to the latter's origins or the result of a gradual accommodation with the world, and whether conceived as a "betrayal" of its original ideals or as a "genuine," straightforward development basically in line with its initial premises.[18] It is not incidental, in this regard, that his classical nomenclature of religious orientations is much more easily and readily applicable to Christianity, from which it obviously sprang, than to Buddhism, where I had to devise the (admittedly awkward) notion of "worldly facets of otherworldliness" in order to account for orientations that are not otherworldly, and yet neither affirmatively worldly in Weber's sense. What I hope to have demonstrated here, at any rate, is that Weber definitely underestimated the special kind of ideological and institutional capacity that Theravada Buddhism did evince in the process of upholding and diffusing its otherworldly premises across vast expanses of time, population, and territorial space.

It may still be basically true that an "essential peculiarity of Buddhism [is] the complete elimination of any form of inner-worldly motivation to

---

[16] See Munch and Smelser, "Relating the Micro and Macro," in Alexander et al. (eds.), *Micro–Macro Link*, p. 372.

[17] Ibid.

[18] See the Introduction, fn. 18.

conduct of a rational purpose in nature."[19] In line with Weber's own opposition to overdeterminism, however, it may be recalled that the history of religions is replete with unexpected twists of fate, unintended consequences of religious messages, or transformations of religious contents. The core of rationalization entailed in the systematic and disciplined search for salvation in Buddhism as in all "religious rationalization"[20] might well have expanded, intentionally or not, into other spheres of life. If it did not, or did so much less than in the Western setting, the explanation is perhaps to be found not, or not only, in its religious–ideological premises, but in a certain pattern of interaction between virtuosi and society at large – called here a virtuoso–society complex – that developed into a major and enduring axis of social organization, and as a result, also imposed very real constraints and limits on further ideological and institutional trends. These constraints and limits should not be assessed, however, in a purely negative way, as a sign of weakness or lack of institutional vigor. On the contrary, what deserves to be stressed much more than it has been until now, is the impressive diffusion and resilience of Theravada Buddhist outworldliness in the context of Southeast Asia, a resilience that cannot be understood as mere survival, but rather as the result of powerful supporting mechanisms. Not only are these mechanisms no weaker than those obtaining in Western civilization, but they may be seen, as perhaps stronger and more effective from the point of view of their capacity to secure lasting collective identification with outworldly ideals.

The resulting institutional capacity, as has been shown, has to be assessed according to different criteria of social significance and vitality than the more usual – because Western in origin – criteria of rationality, formal structuration, political power, or innovative potential. As for the admittedly greater efficiency and institutional capacity of Christian monasticism along those latter lines, they should be understood as deriving not, or not only, from an intrinsic tendency to rationality and/or worldly religious–cultural orientation, but also, and crucially so, from the interaction with a very different type of macrosocial context.[21] The importance of contextual structures was dramatically confirmed in the Western setting when a cluster of sweeping socioeconomic changes played a crucial part in deflecting the virtuoso impulse away from the monastic institution,

---

[19] Weber, *Religion of India*, p. 222.
[20] See S. Kalberg, *"The Rationalization of Action in Max Weber's Sociology of Religion,"* *Sociological Theory* 8, no. 1 (1990): 57–84.
[21] This is, of course, fully in line with Weber's analysis of the historical development of Western rationality in general (and capitalism in particular) in terms of a multidimensional combination of cultural orientations and institutional factors – as mostly evident in his *General Economic History,* last chapter especially.

"dispersing" it as it were into the lay sector, and thus eventually defeating the very principle of a neatly differentiated virtuoso sector.

From that point on, resistance to the separate existence of virtuoso elites has become an ingrained feature of the Western tradition. Undergoing momentous transformations throughout the later Middle Ages, the Reformation and the post-Reformation eras (and displaying to this day a rather surprising and paradoxical tenacity)[22] the virtuoso impulse in its more traditional ascetic–religious sense eventually lost much of its previous appeal and significance. Resistance to virtuosity could only be enhanced by the diffusion of modern democratic ideologies, theoretically hostile to the very principle of a hierarchical distinction between elites from the rest of society, and to the very idea of a normative double standard. Yet virtuosity itself, despite its connotations of elitism and double standard, did not altogether disappear from Western culture and the Western social landscape. In fact, it may be suggestive to extend the notion of virtuosity beyond the domain of traditional religions and into modern, secularized settings. As Guenther Roth once proposed, for example, it is possible to see certain kinds of secular revolutionaries or religious fundamentalists as modern examples of "ideological virtuosi" – marginal minorities characterized by an ethic of maximal commitment and single-minded conviction, with a largely indirect, exemplary influence on society at large.[23] In a more philosophical vein, one may also want to pursue the virtuoso motif in the theme – running from Nietzsche to Foucault's later writings – of the individual's disciplined self-transcendence and solitary labor in shaping himself into a "work of art."[24] Paradoxically enough, from such an angle, there may be some underlying similarity between religious forms of ascetic withdrawal and present forms of resistance to dominant cultural trends and social structures.

As repeatedly stressed in this book, however, the existence of individual virtuosi or even groups of virtuosi in a specific social setting does not necessarily mean the emergence of a broader virtuoso–society complex, that is, of a constellation of ideological and institutional structures regulating the relation between virtuosi and society. In newer and secular

---

[22] I am thinking here not only of the survival of a broad range of Catholic religious orders, but also of the paradoxical emergence of monastic forms of life among contemporary Protestants. Traditional types of virtuosi also keep emerging, with even greater tenacity, from within the classical Asian traditions of religious asceticism.

[23] Roth and Schluchter, *Max Weber's Vision of History,* pp. 144–162. Roth, however, follows Weber's rather loose definition of virtuosity and lack of conceptual distinction from charisma.

[24] See the comparison of this theme in Nietzsche's work with Weber's conception of individual fulfillment in D. Owen, "Autonomy and 'Inner Distance': A Trace of Nietzsche in Weber," *History of the Human Sciences* 4 (1991): 79–92.

forms, and beyond the domain of modern political ideology, virtuosity survives now perhaps most clearly, if obviously with modifications, in the professions,[25] the arts and sciences, and in sports.[26] It is in these spheres that the individual search for perfection has remained a potent motif, together with elements of ascetic discipline as well as combined notions of distance from and exchange with a lay public audience. Modern forms of sponsoring and patronage in these various fields may even bear some similarity to the gift relationship that was an integral part of the more traditional virtuoso complex.[27] It remains to be seen, however, whether contemporary civilization will nurture enough of a sustained interest in the search for perfection on the one hand, and the mediation of ideological ambiguities on the other, to endow these possible fragments of newer virtuoso structures with a cultural resonance comparable to that achieved in the context of medieval Christendom and Southeast Asian Buddhism.

[25] See M. Sarfatti Larson, *The Rise of Professionalism: A Sociological Analysis* (Berkeley and Los Angeles: University of California Press, 1977).

[26] The theme of solitude and withdrawal has recently been shown to have served as a powerful metaphor in the early cultural construction of, and discourse about, the scientific endeavor. See S. Shapin, "Mind in its Own Place: Science and Solitude in Seventeenth-Century England," *Science in Context* 4 (1991): 191–18. Intriguingly related, see the analysis of the phenomenon of *prouesse* (prowess) – defined as "a conspicuous act by which an individual signals his success in reaching, within particular circumstances, the highest possible level of value achievement attainable by man" – in modern French culture, in Jesse R. Pitts, "Continuity and Change in Bourgeois France," in S. Hoffman (ed), *In Search of France* (Cambridge, Mass: Harvard University Press, 1964), reprinted in part in J. C. Alexander and S. Seidman, *Culture and Society: Contemporary Debates* (Cambridge University Press, 1990).

[27] "Philanthropic" sponsoring and patronage have only most recently started to attract their due attention in comparative historical sociology. See especially R. Wuthnow, *Meaning and Moral Order: Explorations in Cultural Analysis* (Berkeley and Los Angeles: University of California Press, 1987), pp. 279–88, and idem, *Communities of Discourse: Ideology and Social Structure in the Reformation, the Enlightenment, and European Socialism* (Cambridge, Mass.: Harvard University Press, 1989).

Bibliography

General

Abu-Lughod, J. *Before European Hegemony: The World System, A.D. 1250–1350.* New York: Oxford University Press, 1989.

Alatas, H. S. "The Protestant Ethic and Southeast Asia." *Archives de Sociologie des Religions* 15 (1963): 21–34.

Alexander, J. C. (ed.). *Durkheimian Sociology: Cultural Studies.* Cambridge University Press, 1988.

Alexander, J. C., and P. Smith. "The Discourse of American Civil Society: A New Proposal for Cultural Studies." *Theory and Society* 22, no. 2 (1993): 151–207.

Alexander, J. C., B. Giesen, B. Münch, and N. Smelser (eds.). *The Micro–Macro Link.* Berkeley and Los Angeles: University of California Press, 1987.

Baechler, J. *The Origins of Capitalism.* Oxford: B. Blackwell, 1975.

"Aux origines de la modernité: castes et féodalités: Europe, Inde, Japon." *Archives Européennes de Sociologie* 27 (1986): 31–57.

Bellah, R. N. "Religious Evolution." *American Sociological Review* 29 (1964): 354–74.

Religion and Progress in Modern Asia. New York: Free Press, 1965.

Bellah, R. N., K. Burridge, and R. Robertson. "Responses to Louis Dumont." *Religion* 12 (1982): 83–8.

Bergman, W. "Das frühe Mönchtum als soziale Bewegung." *Kölner Zeitschrift für Soziologie und Sozialpsychologie* 37 (1985): 30–59.

Bourdieu, P. "Une interprétation de la sociologie religieuse de Max Weber." *Archives Européennes de Sociologie* 12 (1971): 3–25.

Calhoun, C. "Beyond the Problem of Meaning: Robert Wuthnow's Historical Sociology of Culture." *Theory and Society* 21, no. 3 (1992): 419–44.

Chirot, D. "The Rise of the West." *American Sociological Review* 56 (1985): 181–95.

Collins, R. *Weberian Sociology.* Cambridge University Press, 1986.

"Maturation of the State-Centered Theory of Revolution and Ideology." *Sociological Theory* 11 (1993): 117–128.

Collins, S. "Monasticism, Utopias and Comparative Social Theory." *Religion* 18 (1988): 101–35.

Creel, A. B., and V. Narayanan (eds.). *Monastic Life in the Christian and Hindu Traditions: A Comparative Study.* Lewiston, N.Y.: Mellen, 1990.

Cruise O'Brien, D. "Don divin, don terrestre: l'économie de la confrérie mouride." *Archives Européennes de Sociologie* 15 (1974): 82–101.

Czarnowski, S. *Le culte des héros et ses conditions sociales: St. Patrick, héros national de l'Irlande.* Preface by H. Hubert. Paris: Alcan, 1919.

Dumont, L. *Religion, Politics and History in India: Collected Papers in Indian Sociology.* The Hague: Mouton, 1970.

Homo Hierarchicus. Chicago: University of Chicago Press, 1970.

From Mandeville to Marx: The Genesis and Triumph of Economic Ideology. Chicago: University of Chicago Press, 1977.

"A Modified View of our Origins: The Christian Origins of Modern Individualism." *Religion* 12 (1982): 1–27.

Durkheim, E. *The Elementary Forms of Religious Life.* Glencoe, Ill: Free Press, 1965.

Eisenstadt, S. N. *The Political System of Empires.* New York: Free Press, 1963.

"The Axial Age: The Emergence of Trancendental Visions and the Rise of Clerics." *Archives Européennes de Sociologie* 23 (1982): 294–314.

"Transcendental Visions – Other-Worldliness and its Transformations: Some More Comments on Louis Dumont." *Religion* 13 (1983): 1–19.

"Die Paradoxie von Zivilisationen mit ausserwertlichen Orientierungen: Uberlungen zu Max Webers Studie über Hinduismus und Buddhismus." In W. Schluchter (ed.), *Max Webers Studie über Hinduismus und Buddhismus,* pp. 333–62. Frankfort: Suhrkampf, 1984.

"Comparative Liminality and Dynamics of Civilization." *Religion* 15 (1985): 315–338.

"Macrosociology and Sociological Theory: Some New Directions." *Contemporary Sociology* 16 (1987): 602–9.

European Civilization in Comparative Perspective. Oslo: Norwegian University Press, 1987.

"The Expansion of Religions: Some Comparative Observations on Different Modes." *Comparative Social Research,* 13 (1991): 45–70.

Eisenstadt, S. N. (ed.). *Max Weber on Charisma and Institution Building.* Chicago: University of Chicago Press, 1963.

Eisenstadt, S. N., and S. R. Graubard (eds.). *Intellectuals and Traditions.* New York: Humanities Press, 1973.

Eisenstadt, S. N., and H. J. Helle, "General Introduction to Perspectives on Sociological Theory." In S. N. Eisenstadt and H. J. Helle (eds.), *Macrosociological Theory: Perspectives on Sociological Theory,* vol. 1. London: Sage, 1985.

"The Expansion of Religions: Some Comparative Observations on Different Modes." *Comparative Social Research,* 13 (1991): 45–70.

Firth, R. *Symbols, Public and Private.* Ithaca, N.Y.: Cornell University Press, 1973.

Fulbrook, M. *Piety and Politics: Religion and the Rise of Absolutism in England, Württemberg and Prussia.* Cambridge University Press, 1983.

Garret, W. R. "Maligned Mysticism: The Maledicted Career of Troeltsch's Third Type." *Sociological Analysis* 36, no. 3 (1975): 205–23.

Gellner, E. *Saints of the Atlas.* Chicago: University of Chicago Press, 1969.

Plough, Sword and Book: The Structure of Human History. London: Paladin, 1991.

Gerth, H. H., and C. Wright Mills (eds.). *From Max Weber: Essays in Sociology.* New York: Oxford University Press, 1975.

Giddens, A. *The Constitution of Society: Outline of the Theory of Structuration.* Cambridge, Eng.: Polity Press and B. Blackwell, 1984.

Goddijn, H. P. M. "The Sociology of Religious Orders and Congregations." *Social Compass* 7 (1960): 431–47.

Goffman, E. *Asylums.* Chicago: Aldine, 1961.

Goldstone, J. A. "Ideology, Cultural Frameworks, and the Process of Revolution." *Theory and Society* 20 (1991): 405–54.

Greenfeld, L. *Nationalism: Five Roads to Modernity.* Cambridge, Mass.: Harvard University Press, 1992.

Hall, J. *Powers and Liberties: The Causes and Consequences of the Rise of the West.* Berkeley and Los Angeles: University of California Press, 1985.

"Religion and the Rise of Capitalism." *Archives Européennes de Sociologie* 26 (1985): 193–223.

Hawley, J. S. (ed.). *Saints and Virtues.* Berkeley and Los Angeles: University of California Press, 1987.

Hill, M. "Typologie sociologique de l'ordre religieux." *Social Compass* 17 (1971): 45–64.

The Religious Order: A Study of Virtuoso Religion and Its Legitimation in the Nineteenth-Century Church of England. London: Heinemann, 1973.

Sociology of Religion. London: Heinemann, 1973.

Hillery, G. A. Jr. "The Convent: Community, Prison or Task Force?" *Journal for the Scientific Study of Religion* 8 (1969): 140–51.

Hillery, G. A. Jr., and P. C. Morrow. "The Monastery as a Commune." *International Review of Modern Sociology* 6 (1976): 139–54.

Kalberg, S. "Max Weber's Types of Rationality: Cornerstones for the Analysis of Rationalization Processes in History." *American Journal of Sociology* 85, no. 5 (1980): 1145–80.

"The Origin and Expansion of *Kultur/Pessimismus:* The Relationship between Public and Private Spheres in Early Twentieth Century Germany." *Sociological Theory* 5, no. 2 (1987): 57–84.

Max Weber's Comparative-Historical Sociology. Oxford: Polity Press, 1994.

Kane, A. "Cultural Analysis in Historical Sociology: The Analytic and Concrete forms of the Autonomy of Culture." *Sociological Theory* 53 (1990): 53–70.

Kapferer, B. (ed.). *Transaction and Meaning.* Philadelphia: ISHI, 1976.

Levine, D. N. *The Flight from Ambiguity: Essays in Social and Cultural Theory.* Chicago: University of Chicago Press, 1985.

Mann, M. *The Sources of Social Power,* vol. 1. Cambridge University Press, 1986.

Martin, D. *Pacifism: An Historical and Sociological Study.* New York: Schocken, 1965.

Mauss, M. *The Gift.* New York: Norton, 1976.

Mazlich, B. *The Revolutionary Ascetic: Evolution of a Political Type.* New York: Basic, 1976.

Mecklin, J. *The Passing of the Saint: A Study of a Cultural Type.* Chicago: University of Chicago Press, 1941.

Merton, R. K. *Sociological Ambivalence and Other Essays.* New York: Free Press, 1976.

Moulin, L. "Pour une sociologie des ordres religieux." *Social Compass* 10 (1963): 145–70.

Nietzsche, F. *On the Genealogy of Morals.* Translated and edited by W. Kaufmann. New York: Vintage, 1969.

Owen, D. "Autonomy and 'Inner Distance': A Trace of Nietzsche in Weber." *History of the Human Sciences* 4 (1991): 79–92.

Paine, R. "Two Modes of Exchange and Mediation." In B. Kapferer (ed.), *Transaction and Meaning,* pp. 63–86. Philadelphia: ISHI, 1976.

Parry, J. "The Gift, the Indian Gift, and the 'Indian' Gift." *Man,* n.s. 21 (1986): 453–73.

Peacock, J. L. "Mystics and Merchants in Fourteenth-Century Germany: A

Speculative Reconstruction of their Psychological Bond and its Implications for Social Change." *Journal for the Scientific Study of Religion* 8 (1969): 47–59.

Pitts, J. R. "Continuity and Change in Bourgeois France." In S. Hoffman (ed.), *In Search of France*. Cambridge, Mass: Harvard University Press, 1964.

Plé, M. (ed.). *La séparation du monde*. Paris: Cerf, 1901.

Reynolds, F. "Contrasting Modes of Action: A Comparative Study of Buddhist and Christian Ethics." *History of Religion* 20 (1980): 128–46.

Ritzer, G. "Micro–Macro Linkage in Sociological Theory: Applying a Meta-theoretical Tool." In G. Ritzer (ed.), *Frontiers of Social Theory: The New Syntheses*. New York: Columbia University Press, 1990.

Robertson, R. "On the Analysis of Mysticism: Pre-Weberian, Weberian and Post-Weberian Perspectives." *Sociological Analysis* 36, no. 3 (1975): 241–66.

Roth, G., and W. Schluchter, *Max Weber's Vision of History: Ethics and Methods*. Berkeley and Los Angeles: University of California Press, 1979.

Sahlins, M. *Stone Age Economics*. Chicago: Aldine, 1972.

Sarfatti Larson, M. *The Rise of Professionalism: A Sociological Analysis*. Berkeley and Los Angeles: University of California Press, 1977.

Schluchter, W. "The Paradox of Rationalization: On the Relation of Ethics and World." In G. Roth and W. Schluchter, *Max Weber's Vision of History: Ethics and Methods,* pp. 11–64. Berkeley and Los Angeles: University of California Press, 1979.

"Weltflüchtiges Erlösungsstreben und organische Sozialethik. Uberlegungen zu Max Webers Analysen der indischen Kulturreeligionen." In W. Schluchter (ed.), *Max Webers Studie über Hinduismus und Buddhismus: Interpretation un Kritik,* pp. 11–71. Frankfurt: Suhrkampf, 1984.

Schluchter, W. (ed.). *Max Webers Studie über Hinduismus und Buddhismus: Interpretation und Kritik*. Frankfurt: Suhrkampf, 1984,
   Max Webers Sicht des okzidentalen Christentums. Frankfurt: Suhrkampf, 1988.

Schreuder, O. "Les ordres religieux: litérature." *Social Compass* 18 (1971): 160–4.

Schwartz, B. J. "The Age of Transcendence." *Daedalus* 104, no. 2 (1975): 1–7.

Seguy, J. "Une sociologie des sociétés imaginées: monachisme et utopie." *Annales E.S.C.* 26 (1971): 328–54.
   "Pour une sociologie de l'ordre religieux." *Archives de Sciences Sociales des Religions* 57 (1984): 55–68.

Seligman, A. B. "Charisma and the Transformation of Grace in the Early Modern Era." *Social Research* 58, no. 3 (1991): 591–622.

Servais, E., and F. Hambye. "Structure et méthode: Problème et méthode en sociologie des organisations claustrales." *Social Compass* 18 (1971): 27–44.

Shapin, S. "Mind and its Own Place: Science and Solitude in Seventeenth-Century England." *Science in Context* 1 (1991): 191–218.

Shils, E. *Center and Periphery: Essays in Macrosociology*. Chicago: University of Chicago Press, 1975.

Silber, I. F. " 'Opting Out' in Theravada Buddhism and Medieval Christianity: A Comparative Study of Monasticism as Alternative Structure." *Religion* 15 (1985): 251–77.
   "Monasticism and the Protestant Ethic: Asceticism, Ideology and Wealth in the Medieval West." *British Journal of Sociology* 44, no. 1 (1993): 103–23.

Skocpol, T. (ed.). *Vision and Method in Historical Sociology.* Cambridge University Press, 1984.

Smith, D. *The Rise of Historical Sociology.* Philadelphia: Temple University Press, 1991.

Swidler, A. "The Concept of Rationality in the Work of Max Weber." *Sociological Enquiry* 43 (1973): 35–42.

"Culture in Action: Symbols and Strategies." *American Sociological Review* 5 (1986): 273–86.

Troeltsch, E. *The Social Teachings of the Christian Church.* New York: Allen & Unwin, 1931.

Turner, B. *Religion and Social Theory: A Materialist Perspective.* London: Heinemann, 1983.

Turner, V. *Dramas, Fields and Metaphors: Symbolic Action in Human Society.* Ithaca, N.Y.: Cornell University Press, 1974.

Veyne, P. *Le pain et le cirque: sociologie historique d'un pluralisme politique.* Paris: Seuil, 1976.

Wach, J. *Sociology of Religion.* Chicago: University of Chicago Press, 1971.

Weber, M. *The Protestant Ethic and the Spirit of Capitalism.* New York: Scribner, 1958.

General Economic History. New York: Collier, 1961.

The Sociology of Religion. Boston: Beacon, 1964.

Economy and Society: An Outline of Interpretative Sociology. New York: Bedminster, 1968.

Weber, M. *The Religion of India.* Glencoe, Ill.: Free Press, 1958.

Werblowsky, R. J. Z. *Beyond Tradition and Modernity: Changing Religions in a Changing World.* London: Athlone, 1976.

Wiley, R. "The Micro–Macro Problem in Social Theory." *Sociological Theory* 6 (1988): 254–61.

Wuthnow, R. *Meaning and Moral Order: Explorations in Cultural Analysis.* Berkeley and Los Angeles: University of California Press, 1987.

Communities of Discourse: Ideology and Social Structure in the Reformation, the Enlightenment and European Socialism. Cambridge, Mass.: Harvard University Press, 1989.

Zaret, D. "Religion, Science and Printing in the Public Spheres in Seventeenth-Century England." In C. Calhoun (ed.), *Habermas and the Public Sphere,* pp. 212–36. Cambridge, Mass.: MIT Press, 1992.

Zerubavel, Y. "The Benedictine Ethic and the Modern Spirit of Scheduling: On Schedules and Social Organization." *Sociological Inquiry* 50 (1980): 157–69.

Theravada Buddhism

Akin, R. *The Organization of Thai Society in the Early Bangkok Period (1782–1873).* Ithaca, N.Y.: Cornell University, Southeast Asia Program, 1969.

Ames, M. "Magical-Animism and Buddhism: A Structural Analysis of the Sinhalese System." *Journal of Asian Studies* 23 (1964): 21–52.

"Ritual Prestations and the Structure of the Sinhalese Pantheon." In M. Nash et al., *Anthropological Studies in Theravada Buddhism,* pp. 27–50. New Haven, Conn.: Yale University Press, 1966.

Ariyapala, M. B. *Society in Medieval Ceylon: The State of Society in Ceylon as Depicted in the Saddharmaratynaye and Other Literature of the Thirteenth Century.* Colombo: K. V. G. de Silva, 1970.

Aung, S. Z., and Rhys Davids (eds.). *Points of Controversy or Subjects of Discourse.* Translation of the *Katha-vathu* from the *Abhidamma-Pitaka.* London: Luzac, 1969.

Aung-Thwin, M. "Kingship, the Sangha, and Society in Pagan." In K. R. Hall and J. K. Whitmore (eds.), *Explorations in Early Southeast Asian History: The Origins of Southeast Asian Statecraft.* Ann Arbor: Center for South and Southeast Asian Studies, University of Michigan, 1976.

"The Role of *Sasana* Reform in Burmese History: Economic Dimensions of a Religious Purification." *Journal of Asian Studies* 38 (1979): 671–88.

"A Reply to Lieberman." *Journal of Asian Studies* 39 (1980): 87–90.

"Jambudipa: Classical Burma's Camelot." *Contributions to Asian Studies* 16 (1981): 38–61.

"Prophecies, Omens and Dialogue: Tools of the Trade in Burmese Historiography." In D. K. Wyatt and A. Woodside (eds.), *Moral Order and the Question of Change: Essays on Southeast Asian Thought.* New Haven, Conn.: Yale University Press, 1983.

"Divinity, Spirit and Human: Conceptions of Classical Burmese Kingship." In L. Gesick (ed.), *Center, Symbols and Hierarchies: Essays on the Classical States of Southeast Asia.* New Haven, Conn.: Yale University Press, 1983.

"Hierarchy and Order in Pre-Colonial Burma." *Journal of Southeast Asian Studies* 15, no. 2 (1984): 224–32.

Pagan: The Origins of Modern Burma. Honolulu: University of Hawaii Press, 1985.

Bareau, A. *Les premiers conciles bouddhiques.* Paris: Presses Universitaires de France, 1955.

Les sectes du petit véhicule. Saigon: Ecole française d'Extrême-Orient, 1955.

"The Superhuman Personality of the Buddha and its Symbolism in the *Mahaparinirvanasutra* of the *Dharmaguptaka.*" In J. M. Kitagawa and C. H. Long (eds.), *Myth and Symbols.* Chicago: University of Chicago Press, 1971.

Bechert, H. "Ways of *Sansana* Reform in Theravada Buddhism." In V. Nanaloka (ed.), *Rhys Davids Memorial Volume,* pp. 145–57. Colombo: University of Ceylon, 1965.

Buddhismus, Staat und Gesellschaft in den Landern des Theravada Buddhismus. Frankfurt: Alfred Metzner Verlag, 1966.

"Einige Fragen der Religionssoziologie und Struktur des Sudasiasischen Buddhismus." *Internationales Jahrbuch für Religionssoziologie* 4 (1968): 251–95.

"Contradictions in Sinhalese Buddhism." *Contributions to Asian Studies* 4 (1973): 7–17.

"Sangha, State, Society, 'Nation': Persistence of Traditions." *Daedalus* 102, no. 1 (1973): 85–96.

"The Beginnings of Buddhist Historiography: Mahavamsa and Political Thinking." In B. L. Smith (ed.), *Religion and Legitimation of Power in Sri Lanka,* pp. 1–12. Chambersburg, Pa.: Anima, 1978.

"The Structure of the Sangha in Burma: A Comparative View." In A. K. Narain (ed.), *Studies in History of Buddhism,* pp. 33–42. Delhi: B.R. Publishing, 1980.

"Theravada Buddhist Sangha: Some General Observations on Historical and Political Factors in its Development." *Journal of Asian Studies* 29 (1970): 761–78.

"The Sangha as a Factor in the Social Life of Sri Lanka and Burma." In

P.E.P. Deraniyagala Commemoration Volume. Colombo: University of Ceylon, 1980.

Bellah, R. N. "Reflections on the Protestant Ethic Analogy in Asia." *Journal of Social Issues* 19 (1963): 52–60.

Bennet, P. J. *Conference Under the Tamarind Tree: Three Essays in Burmese History.* New Haven, Conn.: Yale University Press, 1971.

Bond, G. D. "The Development and Elaboration of the *Arahant* Ideal in the Theravada Buddhist Tradition." *Journal of the American Academy of Religion* 52 (1985): 227–42.

Brand, A. "Merit, Hierarchy, and Royal Gift-Giving in Traditional Thai Society." *Bijdragen tot de Taal-, Land- en Volkenkunde* 131 (1975): 111–37.

Bunnag, J. *Buddhist Monk, Buddhist Layman: A Study of Urban Monastic Organization in Central Thailand.* Cambridge University Press, 1973.

Burghart, R. "Renunciation in the Religious Traditions of South Asia." *Man* 18, no. 4 (1983): 635–53.

Butt, J. "Thai Kingship and Religious Reform (18th–19th Centuries)." In B. L. Smith (ed.), *Religion and Legitimation in Thailand, Laos and Burma,* pp. 34–51. Chambersburg, Pa.: Anima, 1978.

Cady, J. F. *A History of Modern Burma.* Ithaca, N.Y.: Cornell University Press, 1958.

Carrithers, M. "The Social Organization of the Sinhalese Sangha in an Historical Perspective." In G. Krishna (ed.), *Contributions to South Asian Studies,* vol. 1, pp. 121–36. Delhi: Oxford University Press, 1979.

"The Modern Ascetics of Lanka and the Pattern of Change in Buddhism." *Man* 14 (1979): 294–310.

The Forest-Monks of Sri Lanka: An Anthropological and Historical Study. Delhi: Oxford University Press, 1983.

Clifford, R. T. "The *Dhammadipa* Tradition of Sri Lanka: Three Models within the Sinhalese Chronicles." In B. L. Smith (ed.), *Religion and the Legitimation of Power in Sri Lanka,* pp. 36–47. Chambersburg, Pa.: Anima, 1978.

Coedes, G. *The Indianized States of Southeast Asia.* Honolulu: W. Vella, 1968.

Cohen, E. "Sociocultural Change in Thailand: A Reconceptualization." In E. Cohen, M. Lissak, and U. Almagor (eds.), *Comparative Social Dynamics: Essays in Honor of S. N. Eisenstadt,* pp. 82–94. Boulder, Colo.: Westview, 1985.

Collins, S. *Selfless Persons: Imagery and Thought in Theravada Buddhism.* Cambridge University Press, 1982.

"On the Very Idea of the Pali Canon." *Journal of the Pali Text Society* 15 (1990): 89–126.

Conze, E. *Buddhism: Its Essence and Development.* New York: Harper & Row, 1959.

"Dharma as a Spiritual, Social, and Cosmic Force." In P. Kuntz (ed.), *The Concept of Order.* Seattle: University of Washington Press, 1967.

Corpus Inscriptionum Indicarum. Ootacumund: Government Epigraphist for India, 1963.

Dasavatthuppakarana. Edited and translated by J. Ver Eecke. Saigon: Ecole française d'Extreme-Orient, 1976.

Day, T. P. *Great Tradition and Little Tradition in Theravada Buddhist Studies.* Lewiston, N.Y.: Mellen, 1988.

De Gokuldas. *Democracy in the Early Buddhist Sangha.* Calcutta: Calcutta University, 1955.

Dhammapada: The Path of Perfection. Translated from the Pali with an introduction by J. Mascaro. Harmondsworth: Penguin Books, 1973.

Dialogues of the Buddha (Digha Nikaya). Edited and translated by T. W. Rhys Davids and C. A. F. Rhys Davids. London: Luzac, 1897, 1921.

Dumont, L. "The Conception of Kingship in Ancient India." *Contributions to Indian Sociology* 6 (1962): 48–77.

Dunnington, J. M. *Arahantship*. Kandy: Buddhist Publication Society, 1974.

Dutt, S. *Early Buddhist Monachism: 600 B.C.–100 B.C.* London: Kegan Paul, Trench & Trubner, 1924.

    Buddhist Monks and Monasteries of India. London: Allen & Unwin, 1962.

Epigraphica Birmanica. Rangoon: Archeological Survey of Burma, 1920.

Epigraphica Zeylanica. London: Archeological Survey of Ceylon, 1912.

Evers, H. D. "Kinship and Property Rights in a Buddhist Monastery in Central Ceylon." *American Anthropologist* 69 (1967): 703–10.

    "The Buddhist Sangha in Ceylon and Thailand." *Sociologus* n.s. 28 (1968): 20–35.

    "Monastic Landlordism in Ceylon: A Traditional System in a Modern Setting." *Journal of Asian Studies* 28, no. 4 (1969): 685–92.

Evers, H. D. (ed.). *Loosely Structured Social Systems: Thailand in Comparative Perspective*. New Haven, Conn.: Yale University Press, 1969.

Ferguson, J. P. "The Symbolic Dimensions of the Burmese Sangha." Ph.D. diss., Cornell University, 1975.

    "The Quest for Legitimacy by Burmese Monks and Kings: The Case of the Shwegyin Sect." In B. L. Smith (ed.), *Religion and Legitimation of Power in Thailand, Laos and Burma*. Chambersburg, Pa: Anima, 1978.

Ferguson, J. P., and E. M. Mendelson. "Masters of the Buddhist Occult: The Burmese Weikzas." *Contemporary Asian Studies* 16 (1981): 62–80.

Frauwallner, E. *The Earliest Vinaya and the Beginnings of Buddhist Literature*. Rome: ISMEO, 1956.

Geertz, C. *Negara: The Theater State in Nineteenth-Century Bali*. Princeton, N.J.: Princeton University Press, 1980.

Geiger, W. *Culture of Ceylon in Medieval Times*. Edited by H. Bechert. Wiesbaden: Harrassowitz, 1960.

Gernet, J. *Les aspects économiques du bouddhisme dans la société chinoise du Ve au Xe siècles*. Saigon: Ecole française d'Extrême-Orient, 1956.

Gesick, L. (ed.). *Centers, Symbols, and Hierarchies: Essays on the Classical States of Southeast Asia*. New Haven, Conn.: Yale University Press, 1983.

Ghoshal, U. N. *A History of Indian Political Ideas*. Bombay: Oxford University Press, 1959.

Gokhale, B. G. "Early Buddhist Kingship." *Journal of Asian Studies* 26 (1960): 15–22.

    "Early Buddhist View of the State." *Journal of the American Oriental Society* 89 (1969): 731–38.

Gombrich, R. F. "Merit Transference in Sinhalese Buddhism." *History of Religions* 11 (1971): 203–19.

    Precept and Practice: Traditional Buddhism in the Rural Highlands of Ceylon. Oxford: Clarendon, 1971.

Greenwald, A. "The Relic on the Spear: Historiography and the Saga of Dutthagamani." In B. L. Smith (ed.), *Religion and Legitimation of Power in Sri Lanka*, pp. 13–35. Chambersburg, Pa: Anima, 1978.

Griswold, A. B. "On Kingship and Society at Sukhodaya." In G. W. Skinner and A. T. Kirsch (eds.), *Change and Persistence in Thai Society*, pp. 29–92. Ithaca, N.Y.: Cornell University Press, 1975.

Gunawardana, R. A. L. H. "Buddhist Nikayas in Medieval Ceylon." *Ceylon Journal of Historical and Social Studies* 9 (1966): 55–66.

"Irrigation and Hydraulic Society in Medieval Ceylon." *Past and Present* 53 (1971): 3–27.

Robe and Plough: Monasticism and Economic Interest In Early Medieval Sri Lanka. Association for Asian Studies, Monograph 35. Tucson: University of Arizona Press, 1979.

Hall, K. R. *Maritime Trade and State Development in Early Southeast Asia.* Honolulu: University of Hawaii Press, 1985.

Halverson, J. "Religious and Psychosocial Development in Sinhalese Behavior." *Journal of Asian Studies* 37 (1978): 221–32.

Hanks, L. M. "Merit and Power in the Thai Social Order." *American Anthropologist* 54 (1962): 1247–61.

Harvey, G. E. *Outline of Burmese History.* Bombay: Orient Longmans, 1954.

Heesterman, J. C. "Brahmin, Ritual and Renouncer." *Wiener Zeitschrift für die Kunde Süd- und Ostasiens* 8 (1964): 1–31.

The Inner Conflict of Tradition: Essays in Indian Ritual, Kingship, and Society. Chicago: University of Chicago Press, 1985.

Heine-Geldern, R. von. "State and Kingship in Southeast Asia." *Far Eastern Quarterly* 5 (1942): 1–15.

Conceptions of State and Kingship in Southeast Asia. Ithaca, N.Y.: Cornell University Press, 1957.

Heinze, R. I. *The Role of the Sangha in Modern Thailand.* Taipei: Chinese Association for Folklore, 1977.

Holt, J. C. "Sinhalese Sectarianism: Robe, Ploughs and Revivals." *History of Religion* 20 (1981): 368–74.

Buddha in the Crown: Avalokitesvara in the Buddhist Traditions of Sri Lanka. New York: Oxford University Press, 1991.

Horner, I. B. *The Early Buddhist Theory of Man Perfected.* London: William & Norgate, 1936.

Htin Aung, M. *A History of Burma.* New York: Columbia University Press, 1967.

Indrapala, K. (ed.). *The Collapse of the Rajarata Civilization in Ceylon and the Drift to the Southwest.* Peradinya: University of Ceylon, 1971.

Jackson, P. *Buddhadasa: A Buddhist Thinker for the Modern World.* Bangkok: Siam Society, 1988.

Kasetsiri, C. *The Rise of Ayudhya: A History of Siam in the Fourteenth and Fifteenth Centuries.* Kuala Lumpur: Oxford University Press, 1976.

Kaufman, H. K. *Bangkhuad: A Community Study in Thailand.* Locust Valley, N.Y.: Augustin, 1960.

Kemper, S. "Buddhism without Bhikkhus: The Sri Lanka Vinaya Vardena Society." In B. L. Smith (ed.), *Religion and Legitimation of Power in Sri Lanka,* pp. 212–35. Chambersburg, Pa.: Anima, 1978.

"Reform and Segmentation in Monastic Fraternities in Low Country Sri Lanka." *Journal of Asian Studies* 15 (1980): 27–42.

"The Buddhist Monkhood, the Law, and the State in Colonial Sri Lanka." *Comparative Studies in Society and History* 26, no. 3 (1984): 401–27.

"Radical Asceticism and the Sinhalese Case." *Man* 15 (1984): 195–6.

Keyes, C. F. "Buddhism and National Integration in Thailand." *Journal of Asian Studies* 30 (1971): 551–68.

"Millenialism, Theravada Buddhism and Thai Society." *Journal of Asian Studies* 36 (1976): 283–303.

The Golden Peninsula: Culture and Adaptation in Mainland Southeast Asia.
New York: Macmillan, 1977.

"Structure and History in the Study of the Relationship between Theravada
Buddhism and Political Order." *Numen* 25 (1978): 156–70.

"Merit-Transference in the Karmic Theory of Popular Buddhism." In C. F.
Keyes and E. Valentine Daniel (eds.), *Karma: An Anthropological En-
quiry,* pp. 261–86. Berkeley and Los Angeles: University of California
Press, 1983.

"Theravada Buddhism and its Worldly Transformations in Thailand: Reflections on the Work of S. J. Tambiah." *Contributions to Indian Sociology* 21
(1987): 123–47.

King, W. L. *In the Hope of Nibbana: An Essay on Theravada Buddhist Ethics.*
Casalle, Ill.: Open Court, 1964.

A Thousand Lives Away: Buddhism in Contemporary Burma. Cambridge,
Mass.: Harvard University Press, 1965.

Knox, R. *An Historical Relation of the Island of Ceylon in East Indies.* Colombo:
K. V. G. de Silva, 1956.

Lamotte, E. *Histoire du Bouddhisme indien.* Louvain: Bibliothèque du Museon,
1958.

Leach, E. (ed.) *Dialectic in Practical Religion.* Cambridge University Press,
1968.

Lieberman, V. B. *Burmese Administration Cycles: Anarchy and Conquest, c.
1580–1760.* Princeton, N.J.: Princeton University Press, 1984.

"The Political Significance of Religious Wealth in Burmese History: Some
Further Thoughts." *Journal of Asian Studies* 39 (1980): 753–69.

Lingat, R. "Vinaya et droit laïque: études sur les conflits de la loi religieuse et de
la loi laïque dans l'Indochine hindanayiste." *Bulletin de l'Ecole Française
d'Extrême-Orient* 37 (1937): 415–77.

"Evolution of the Conception of Law in Burma and Siam." *Journal of the
Siam Society* 38 (1950): 9–31.

"La double crise de l'église bouddhique au Siam (1767–1851)." *Cahiers
d'Historie Mondiale* 4 (1958): 402–10.

Luce, G. H. *Old Burma, Early Pagan.* Ascona, Switzerland: Artibus Asiae,
1970.

Madan, T. N. (ed.). *Way of Life: King, Householder, Renouncer: Essays in
Honour of Louis Dumont.* New Delhi: Vikas, 1982.

Mahavamsa or The Great Chronicle of Ceylon. Translated by W. Geiger. London: Oxford University Press, 1912.

Malalgoda, K. "Millenialism in Relation to Buddhism." *Comparative Studies in
Society and History* 12 (1970): 424–41.

Buddhism in Sinhalese Society, 1750–1900. Berkeley and Los Angeles: University of California Press, 1976.

Masefield, P. *Divine Revelation in Early Buddhism.* Colombo: Sri Lanka
Institute of Traditional Studies, in conjunction with Allen & Unwin,
1988.

Masson, J. *La religion populaire dans le canon bouddhique.* Louvain: Museon,
1942.

McClung, L. G. *The Vessantara Jataka: Paradigm for a Buddhist Utopian Ideal.*
Princeton, N.J.: Princeton University Press, 1985.

McDermott, R. "Is There Group Karma in Theravada Buddhism?" *Numen* 23,
no. 1 (1985): 67–80.

Mendelson, E. M. "A Messianic Buddhist Association in Upper Burma." *Bulletin of the School of Oriental and African Studies* 14 (1961): 560–80.

"Buddhism and the Burmese Establishment." *Archives de Sociologie des Religions* 17 (1964): 85–95.

Sangha and State in Burma: A Study of Monastic Sectarianism. Ithaca, N.Y.: Cornell University Press, 1975.

Milinda's Questions. Translated by I. B. Horner. London: Luzac, 1964.

Moerman, M. "Ban Ping's Temple: The Center of a Loosely Structured Society." In M. Nash et al., *Anthropological Studies in Theravada Buddhism.* New Haven, Conn.: Yale University Press, 1966.

Mulder, M. *Merit, Monks and Motivation: An Investigation of the Motivational Qualities of Buddhism in Thailand.* De Kalb, Ill.: Northern University Press, 1968.

Narain, A. K. (ed.). *Studies in the History of Buddhism.* Delhi: B.R. Publishing, 1980.

Nash, M., G. Obeyesekere, H. M. Ames, J. Ingersoll, D. E. Pfanner, J. C. Nash, M. Moerman, M. Ebihars, and N. Yalman. *Anthropological Studies in Theravada Buddhism.* New Haven, Conn.: Yale University Press, 1966.

Obeyesekere, G. "Theodicy, Sin and Salvation in a Sociology of Buddhism." In E. R. Leach (ed.), *Dialectic in Practical Religion,* pp. 7–40. Cambridge University Press, 1968.

"Gajabahu and the Gajabahu Synchronism: An Inquiry into the Relationship between Myth and History." In B. L. Smith (ed.), *Religion and Legitimation of Power in Sri Lanka,* pp. 155–76. Chambersburg, Pa.: Anima, 1978.

"Religion and Polity in Theravada Buddhism: Continuity and Change in a Great Tradition." *Comparative Studies in Society and History* 21, no. 4 (1979): 626–39.

"Exemplarische Prophetie oder etish geleitete Askese? Uberlegungen zur fruhbuddhistischen Reform." In W. Schluchter (ed.), *Max Webers Studie uber Hinduismus und Buddhismus: Interpretation und Kritik.* Frankfurt: Suhrkamp, 1984.

Obeyesekere, G., F. Reynolds, and B. L. Smith (eds.), *The Two Wheels of Dhamma: Essays on the Theravada Tradition in India and Ceylon.* Chambersburg, Pa.: American Academy of Religion, 1972.

O'Flaherty, W. D., and J. D. M. Derret (eds.). *The Concept of Duty in South Asia.* New Delhi: Vikas, for the School of Oriental and African Studies, 1969.

Oldenburg, H. *Buddha: His Life, His Doctrine, His Order.* London: Williams & Norgate, 1880.

Pardue, P. A. *Buddhism: A Historical Introduction.* New York: Macmillan, 1976.

Pfanner, D., and J. Ingersoll. "Theravada Buddhism and Village Economic Behavior: A Burmese and Thai Comparison." *Journal of Asian Studies* 21 (1962): 341–61.

Prebish, C. S. "A Review of Scholarship on the Buddhist Councils." *Journal of Asian Studies* 33, no. 2 (1974), 239–54.

Buddhist Monastic Discipline: The Sanskrit Pratimoksa Sutras of the Mahasamghikas and Mulasarvastivadins. University Park: Pennsylvania University Press, 1975.

Przyluski, J. *The Legend of Emperor Ashoka in Indian and Chinese Texts.* Translated by D. K. Biwas. Calcutta: K. L. Mukhopadyay, 1967.

Rahula, W. *History of Buddhism in Ceylon.* Colombo: Gunasena, 1956.

Ratnapala, N. *The Katikavatas, Laws of the Buddhist Order of Ceylon from the Twelfth to the Eighteenth Century.* Munich: J. Kitzinger, Munchener Studien zur Sprachwissenschaft, 1971.

Ray, N. *Theravada Buddhism in Burma.* Calcutta University Press, 1946.

Reynolds, C. "The Buddhist Monkhood in Nineteenth-Century Thailand." Ph.D. diss., Cornell University, 1973.

Reynolds, F. E. "The Two Wheels of Dhamma: A Study of Early Buddhism." In G. Obeyesekere, F. Reynolds, and B. L. Smith (eds.), *The Two Wheels of Dhamma: Essays on the Theravada Tradition in India and Ceylon.* Chambersburg, Pa.: American Academy of Religion, 1972.

"Buddhism as Universal Religion and as Civic Religion: Some Observations on a Tour of Buddhist Centers in Central Thailand." *Journal of the Siam Society* 63, no. 1 (1975): 28–43.

"Four Modes of Theravada Action." *Journal of Religious Ethics* 7 (1979): 12–27.

"Contrasting Modes of Action: A Comparative Study of Buddhist and Christian Ethics." *History of Religion* 20 (1980): 128–46.

Reynolds, F. E., and R. T. Clifford. "Sangha, Society and the Struggle for National Integration." In F. E. Reynolds and T. Ludwig (eds.), *Transitions and Transformations in the History of Religions: Essays in Honor of Joseph M. Kitagawa.* Supplement to *Numen* 39. Leiden: Brill, 1980.

Ryan, B. *Caste in Modern Ceylon: The Sinhalese System in Transition.* New Brunswick, N.J.: Rutgers University Press, 1953.

Sadler, A. W. "Pagoda and Monastery: Reflections on the Social Morphology of Burmese Buddhism." *Journal of Asian and African Studies* 5 (1975): 282–91.

Sarkisyanz, E. *Buddhist Backgrounds of the Burmese Revolution.* The Hague: Nijhoff, 1965.

Schlucter, W. (ed.). *Max Webers Studie uber Hinduismus und Buddhismus: Interpretation und Kritik.* Frankfurt: Suhrkamp, 1984.

Schopen, G. "Two Problems in the History of Indian Buddhism: The Layman/Monk Distinction and the Doctrines of the Transference of Merit. *Studien zur Indologie und Iranistik* 10 (1985): 9–47.

Seneviratne, H. L. *Rituals of the Kandyan State.* Cambridge University Press, 1978.

Shulman, D. "Kingship and Prestation in South Indian Myth and Epic." *Asian and African Studies* 19 (1985): 93–117.

Silber, I. F. "Dissent through Holiness: The Case of the Radical Renouncer in Theravada Buddhist Countries." *Numen* 18 (1981): 163–93.

Singer, M. "Max Weber, *The Religion of India:* The Sociology of Hinduism and Buddhism." *American Anthropologist* 43 (1961): 143–51.

Sizemore, R. F., and D. K. Swearer (eds.). *Ethics, Wealth and Salvation: A Study in Buddhist Social Ethics.* Columbia: University of South Carolina Press, 1990.

Smith, B. L. "Polonnaruva as a Ceremonial Complex: Sinhalese Cultural Identity and the Dilemmas of Pluralism." In A. K. Narain (ed.), *Studies in the History of Buddhism,* pp. 295–320. Delhi: B. R. Publishing, 1980.

Smith, B. L. (ed.), *The Two Wheels of Dhamma* Chambersburg, Pa.: American Academy of Religion, 1972.

Religion and Legitimation of Power in Sri Lanka. Chambersburg, Pa.: Anima, 1978.

(ed.). *Religion and Legitimation of Power in Thailand, Laos and Burma.* Chambersburg, Pa.: Anima, 1978.

Smith, D. E. *Religion and Politics in Burma.* Princeton, N.J.: Princeton University Press, 1965.

Spiro, M. *Buddhism and Society: A Great Tradition and its Burmese Vicissitudes.* London: Allen & Unwin, 1971.

Strenski, I. "On Generalized Exchange and the Domestication of the Sangha." *Man* n.s. 18 (1983): 403–78.

Swearer, D. "The Role of the Layman Extraordinaire in Northern Thai Buddhism." *Journal of the Siam Society* 64 (1976): 151–68.

Tambiah, S. J. "The Ideology of Merit and the Social Correlates of Buddhism in a Thai Village." In E. R. Leach (ed.), *Dialectic in Practical Religion.* Cambridge University Press, 1968.

Buddhism and the Spirit Cults in North-East Thailand. Cambridge University Press, 1970.

World Conqueror and World Renouncer: A Study of Buddhism and Polity in Thailand Against Historical Background. Cambridge University Press, 1973.

"Buddhism and This-Worldly Activity," *Modern Asian Studies* 7 (1973): 1–20.

"The Persistence and Transformation of Tradition in Southeast Asia, with Special Reference to Thailand." *Daedalus* 102, no. 1 (1973): 55–85.

"The Renouncer, his Individuality and his Community." In T. N. Madan (ed.), *Way of Life: King, Householder, Renouncer: Essays in Honour of Louis Dumont.* New Delhi: Vikas, 1982.

The Buddhist Saints of the Forest and the Cult of Amulets. Cambridge University Press, 1984.

Culture, Thought and Action: An Anthropological Perspective. Cambridge, Mass.: Harvard University Press, 1985.

"The Galactic Polity in Southeast Asia." In idem, *Culture, Thought and Action: An Anthropological Perspective,* pp. 252–86. Cambridge, Mass.: Harvard University Press, 1985.

Terwiel, B. J. *Monks and Magic: An Analysis of Religious Ceremonies in Central Thailand.* London: Curzon, 1975; revised ed., 1979.

"A Model for the Study of Thai Buddhism." *Journal of Asian Studies* 35 (1976): 391–403.

Than Tun. "Religion in Burma. A. D. 1000–1300." *Journal of the Burma Research Society* 42 (1959): 47–69.

Ancient Indian Social History: Some Interpretations. New Delhi: Orient Longman, 1978.

Thapar, R. "The Householder and the Renouncer in the Brahmanical and Buddhist Traditions." In T. N. Madan (ed.), *Way of Life: King, Householder, Renouncer: Essays in Honour of Louis Dumont,* pp. 273–98. New Delhi: Vikas, 1982.

Three Worlds According to King Ruang. Translated by F. Reynolds and M. Reynolds. Stanford, Calif.: Stanford University Press, 1978.

Tooker, D. "Identity Systems of Highland Burma: Belief, *Akha zan* and a Critique of Interiorized Notions of Ethno-Religious Identity." *Man* n.s. 27, no. 4 (1992): 799–820.

Vallee Poussin, L. *The Way to Nirvana: Six Lectures on Ancient Buddhism as a Discipline of Salvation.* Cambridge, Eng.: Hibbert Lectures, 1917.

Vinaya Text. Translated by T. W. Rhys Davids and H. Oldenburg. Delhi: Oxford University Press, 1966.

Visuddhimagga (*Path of Purification*). Translated by Bhikkhu Nanamoli. Berkeley: Samshala, 1976.

Wales, H. G. Q. *Siamese State Ceremonies: Their History and Function.* London: Quaritsch, 1931.

Watson Andaya, B. "Statecraft in the Reign of Lu Tai of Sukhodaya (ca. 1347–1374)." In B. L. Smith (ed.), *Religion and Legitimation of Power in Thailand, Laos and Burma,* pp. 2–19. Chambersburg, Pa.: Anima, 1978.

Werblowsky, R. J. Z. *Beyond Tradition and Modernity.* London: Athlone, 1976.
  "Modernism and Modernization in Buddhism." In *The Search for Absolute Values in a Changing World,* Proceedings of the Sixth International Conference on the Unity of the Sciences, San Francisco, 1977.

Wijayaratna, M. *Buddhist Monastic Life According to the Texts of the Theravada Tradition.* Translated by C. Grangier and S. Collins. Cambridge University Press, 1990.

Wyatt, D. K. "The Buddhist Monkhood as an Avenue of Social Mobility in Traditional Thai Society." *Social Science Review* 10 (1966): 49–52.
  The Politics of Reform in Thailand: Education in the Reign of Chulalongkorn. New Haven, Conn.: Yale University Press, 1969.

Yalman, N. "The Ascetic Buddhist Monks of Ceylon." *Ethnology* 1 (1962): 315–28.

Medieval Catholicism

Anson, P. F. *The Call of the Desert: The Solitary Life in the Christian Church.* London: S.P.C.K., 1964

Augustine. *Letters.* Translated by W. Parsons. Washington, D.C.: The Catholic University of America Press, 1953.
  Holy Virginity. In R. J. Deferrari (ed.), *Treatises on Marriage and Other Subjects.* New York: Fathers of the Church, 1955.
  The City of God Against the Pagans. Edited and translated by W. C. Greene. Cambridge, Mass.: Harvard University Press, 1960.

Avril, J. *Le gouvernement des évêques et la vie religieuse dans le diocèse d'Angers, 1148–1240.* Lille: Cerf, 1984.

Becquet, J. "L'érémitisme clérical et laïc dans l'ouest de la France." In *L'eremitisimo in Occidente nei secoli XI–XII.* Milan: Universita cattolica del Sacro Cuore, 1965.
  "Erémitisme et hérésie au Moyen Age." In *Hérésies et sociétés dans l'Europe pré-industrielle, pp. 139–45.* Paris: Mouton, 1968.
  "Chanoines réguliers et érémitisme clérical." *Revue d'Historie de la Spiritualité* 27 (1972): 361–70.

Benson, R., and G. Constable (eds.). *Renaissance and Renewal in the Twelfth Century.* Oxford: Clarendon, 1982.

Bergman, W. "Das frühe Mönchtum als soziale Bewegung." *Kölner Zeitschrift für Soziologie und Sozialpsychologie* 37 (1985): 30–59.

Berliére, U. "L'exercice du ministère paroissal par les moines du XIIe au XVII siècles." *Revue Bénédictine* 39 (1927): 340–64.
  "Monastères et sujets au Moyen Age." *Revue Bénédictine* 43 (1931): 322–41; and 44 (1932): 47–70.

Berman, C. H. *Medieval Agriculture, the Southern French Countryside and the Early Cistercians: A Study of Forty-Three Monasteries.* Philadelphia: American Philosophical Society, 1986.

Bitterman, H. R. "The Beginning of the Struggle between the Regular and Secular Clergy." In J. L. Cate and E. N. Anderson (eds.), *Medieval and Historiographical Studies in Honor of James Westfale Thompson*. Chicago: University of Chicago Press, 1938.

Blazovitch, A. *Soziologie des Monchtums und der Benediktinerregel*. Wien: Verlag Herder, 1954.

Bligny, B. *L'Eglise et les ordres religieux dans le royaume de Bourgogne aux XIe et XIIe siècles*. Paris: Presses Universitaires de France, 1960.

Bloch, M. *Les rois thaumaturges*. Paris: Albin, 1961.

Bolton, B. "Paupertas Christi: Old Wealth and New Poverty in the Twelfth Century." In D. Baker (ed.), *Renaissance and Renewal in Christian History*. Oxford: B. Blackwell, 1977.

Bouchard, C. B. *Sword, Miter and Cloister: Nobility and the Church in Burgundy, 980–1198*. Ithaca, N.Y.: Cornell University Press, 1988.

Bowersock, G. "Architects of Competing Transcendental Visions in Late Antiquity." In S. N. Eisenstadt (ed.), *The Origins and Diversity of Axial Age Civilizations*, pp. 280–90. Albany, N.Y.: SUNY Press, 1986.

Brooke R., and C. Brooke. *Popular Religion in the Middle Ages*. London: Thames & Hudson, 1984.

Brown, P. "The Rise and Function of the Holy Man in Late Antiquity." *Journal of Roman Studies* 61 (1971): 80–101.

The Cult of the Saints: Its Rise and Function in Latin Christianity. Chicago: University of Chicago Press, 1981.

Society and the Holy in Late Antiquity. London: Faber & Faber, 1982.

"Late Antiquity." In P. Veyne (ed.), *A History of Private Life,* translated by A. Goldhammer, pp. 237–312. Cambridge, Mass.: Harvard University Press, 1987.

The Body and Society: Men, Women and Sexual Renunciation in Early Christianity. New York: Columbia University Press, 1988.

Bultot, R. "Mépris du monde au XIe siècle." *Annales* 22, no. 1 (1967): 219–28.

Butler, C. *Benedictine Monachism*. Cambridge University Press, 1961.

Bynum, C. W. *Jesus as Mother: Studies in the Spirituality of the High Middle Ages*. Berkeley and Los Angeles: University of California Press, 1982.

Cantor, N. "The Crisis of Western Monasticism, 1050–1130." *American Historical Review,* 67 (1960): 47–67.

Caspary, G. E. *Politics and Exegesis: Origen and the Two Swords*. Berkeley and Los Angeles: University of California Press, 1979.

Cassien, J. *Les institutions cénobitiques*. Paris: Cerf, 1965.

Castaing-Sicard, M. "Donations toulousaines du Xe au XIIe siècle." *Annales du Midi* 70 (1958): 288–54.

Chenu, M. D. "Monks, Canons and Laymen in Search of the Apostolic Life." In idem, *Nature, Man, Society: Essays on New Theological Perspectives in the Latin West*. Chicago: University of Chicago Press, 1968.

Chitty, D. *The Desert a City*. Oxford: B. Blackwell, 1961.

Colvin, H. M. *The White Canons in England*. Oxford: Clarendon, 1951.

Congar, J. *Jalons pour une théologie du laïcat*. Paris: Cerf, 1951.

L'ecclésiologie du haut Moyen-Age. Paris: Cerf, 1958.

"Modèle monastique et modèle sacerdotal en Occident de Grégoire V (1073–1185) à Innocent III (1198). In *Etudes de civilisation médiévale (IX–XIIe): Mélanges offerts à Edmond-Marie Labande*. Poitiers: C.E.S.M., 1973.

Constable, G. *Monastic Tithes from their Origins to the Twelfth Century.* Cambridge University Press, 1964.

"*Famili* et *Conversi* at Cluny." *Revue Bénédictine* 83 (1973): 326–56.

Religious Life and Thought: Eleventh and Twelfth Centuries. London: Variorum, 1979.

"The Diversity of Religious Life and Acceptance of Social Pluralism in the Twelfth Century." In B. McGinn, J. Meyendorff, and J. Leclercq (eds.), *Christian Spirituality,* pp. 29–47. London: Routledge & Kegan Paul, 1986.

Constable, G., and B. Smith. *Libellus de Diversis Ordinibus et Professionibus qui sunt in Ecclesia.* Oxford: Clarendon, 1972.

Coulton, G. B. *Scottish Abbeys and Social Life.* Cambridge University Press, 1933.

Courtois, C. "L'évolution du monachisme en Gaule." In *Il Monachesimo nell alto medioevo* (Settimane di studio del Centro Italiano di studi sull'alto medioevo), pp. 47–72. Spoleto: Presso la Sede del Centro, 1957.

Cowdrey, H. E. J. "Unions and Confraternity with Cluny." *Journal of Ecclesiastical History* 16 (1965): 152–62.

"The Peace of God and the Truce of God in the Eleventh Century." *Past and Present* 46 (1970): 42–67.

The Cluniacs and the Gregorian Reform. Oxford: Clarendon, 1970.

Daly L. J. *Benedictine Monachism: Its Formation and Development Through the Twelfth Century.* New York: Sheed and Ward, 1965.

Darwin, F. D. *The English Mediaeval Recluse.* London: Society for Promoting Christian Knowledge, 1944.

Delaruelle, E. "Les ermites et la spiritualité populaire." In *L'eremitismo in Occidente nei secoli XI–XII,* pp. 212–247. Milan: Universita cattolica del Sacro Cuore, 1965.

Dereine, C. "Vie commune, règle de Saint Augustin et chanoines réguliers au XIe siècle." *Revue d'Histoire Écclésiastique* 41 (1946): 365–406.

"Odon de Tournai et la crise du cénobitisme au XIe siècle." *Revue du Moyen Age Latin* 4 (1948): 137–54.

Doyere, R. "Erémitisme." *Dictionnaire de spiritualité ascetique et mystique,* vol. 4. Paris: G. Beauchesne, 1960.

Drijvers, H. J. D. "Askese und Mönchtum im frühen Christentum." In W. Schluchter (ed.), *Max Webers Sicht des antiken Christentums.* Frankfurt: Suhrkampf, 1985.

Duby, G. *Hommes et structures du Moyen-Age.* Paris: Mouton, 1973.

The Chivalrous Society. Translated by C. Postan. Berkeley and Los Angeles: University of California Press, 1977.

Saint Bernard et l'art cistercien. Paris: Flammarion, 1979.

The Three Orders: Feudal Society Imagined. Translated by A. Goldhammer. Chicago: University of Chicago Press, 1980.

The Age of the Cathedrals: Art and Society, 980–1420. Translated by E. Levieux and B. Thompson. Chicago: University of Chicago Press, 1981.

Duckett, E. S. *Monasticism.* Ann Arbor: University of Michigan Press, 1961.

Dumont, L. "A Modified View of our Origins: The Christian Origins of Modern Individualism." *Religion* 12 (1982): 1–27.

Fechter, J. "Cluny, Adel und Volk (910–1154). Ph.D. diss., Tubingen, 1966.

Finoli, A. M. "La Figura dell'Eremita nella Letteratura Antico-Francese." In *L'eremitismo in Occidente nei secoli XI–XII,* pp. 581–91. Milan: Universita cattolica del Sacre Cuore, 1965.

Flew, R. N. *The Idea of Perfection in Christian Theology.* New York: Humanities Press, 1968.

Gager, J. F. *Kingdom of Community: The Social World of Early Christianity.* Englewood Cliffs, N.J.: PrenticeHall, 1975.

"Body-Symbols and Social Reality: Resurrection, Incarnation and Asceticism in Early Christianity." *Religion* 12 (1982): 345–63.

Geary, P. *Furta Sacra: Thefts of Relics in the Central Middle Ages.* Princeton, N.J.: Princeton University Press 1978.

Before France and Germany: The Creation and Transformation of the Merovingian World. New York: Oxford University Press, 1988.

Génestal, R. *Role des monastères comme établissements de crédit, étudié en Normandie du XIe à la fin du XIIIe siècle.* Paris: A. Rousseau, 1901.

Génicot, L. "L'érémitisme du XIe siècle dans son contexte économique et social." In *L'eremitismo in Occidente nei secoli XI–XII.* Milan: Universita cattolica del Sacre Cuore, 1965.

Goodich, M. "The Politics of Canonization in the Thirteenth Century: Lay and Mendicant Saints." *Church History* 44 (1975): 294–307.

Gougaud, L. "La vie érémitique au Moyen-Age." *Revue d'Ascétique et de Mystique* 1 (1920): 209–40, 313–28.

Dévotions et pratiques ascétiques du Moyen-Age. Paris: Pax, 1925.

Grundmann, H. *Religiöse Bewegungen im Mittelalter.* Darmstadt: Wissenschaftliche Buchgesellschaft, 1961.

Guillaumont, A. *Aux origines du monachisme chrétien: pour une phénoménologie du monachisme.* Begrolles en Mauges: Abbaye de Bellefontaine, 1979.

Gurevitch, A. J. *Les catégories de la culture médiévale.* Paris: Gallimard, 1983.

"Medieval Culture and Mentality according to the New French Historiography." *Archives Européennes de Sociologie* 24 (1983): 167–95.

"Popular and Scholarly Medieval Cultural Traditions: Notes in the Margin of Jacques Le Goff's Book." *Journal of Medieval History* 9 (1983): 71–90.

Hamilton, B. "Saint Pierre Damien et les mouvements monastiques de son temps." In idem, *Monastic Reform, Catharism and the Crusades,* pp. 177–202. London: Variorum, 1979.

Henderson, E. F. *Select Documents of the Middle Ages.* London: G. Bell & Sons, 1892.

Herlihy, R. "The Ecclesiastical Economy of Medieval Europe." *Journal of Eccelesiastical History* 4 (1986): pp. 227–31.

Heuclin, J. *Aux origines monastiques de la Gaule du nord: ermites et reclus du Ve aux XIe siècles.* Lille: Presses Universitaires de Lille, 1988.

Hill, B. *English Cistercian Monasteries and Their Patrons in the Twelfth Century.* Urbana: University of Illinois Press, 1968.

Horn, W., and E. Born. *The Plan of St. Gall: A Study of the Architecture and Economy of, and Life in, a Paradigmatic Carolingian Monastery.* Berkeley and Los Angeles: University of California Press, 1979.

Hubert, J. "Saint-Riquier et le monachisme bénédictin en Gaule à l'époque carolingienne." In *Il Monachesimo nell'alto medioevo e la formazione della civilizatione occidentale* (Settimane di studio del Centro Italiano di studi sull'alto medioevo), pp. 293–309. Spoleto: Presso la Sede del Centro, 1957.

Hunt, N. (ed.). *Cluniac Monasticism in the Central Middle Ages.* Hamden, Conn.: Archon, 1971.

Isenberg, S. R. "Millenarism in Greco-Roman Palestine." *Religion* 4 (1974): 24–46.

Johnson, P. D. *Prayer, Patronage and Power: The Abbey of la Trinité, Vendôme, 1032–1187.* New York: New York University Press, 1981.

Kennedy, A. J. "The Hermit's Role in French Arthurian Romance (c. 1170–1530)." *Romania* 91 (1974): 54–81.

Kingsley, C. *The Hermits.* London: Macmillan, 1913.

Knowles, D. *The Monastic Order in England, 943–1216.* Cambridge University Press, 1950.

"Cistercians and Cluniacs: The Controversy between St. Bernard and Peter the Venerable." In idem, *The Historian and Character and Other Essays,* pp. 50–75. Cambridge University Press, 1963.

From Pachomius to Ignatius: A Study in the Constitutional History of the Religious Orders. Oxford: Clarendon, 1966.

Kolakowski, L. *Chrétiens sans église.* Paris: Gallimard, 1969.

Ladner, G. *The Idea of Reform: Its Impact on Christian Thought and Action in the Age of the Fathers.* New York: Harper & Row, 1967.

Lambert, M. D. *Franciscan Poverty: The Doctrine of the Absolute Poverty of Christ and the Apostles in the Franciscan Order, 1210–1323.* London: S.P.C.K., 1961.

Medieval Heresy: Popular Movements from Bogomil to Hus. London: E. Arnold, 1977.

La vita commune del clero della origini alla Reforma Grigoriania. Rome: Storia e Letterature, 1968.

La vita commune del clero nei secoli XI e XII. Milan: Universita cattolica del Sacro Cuore, 1962.

Lawrence, C. H. *Medieval Monasticism: Forms of Religious Life in Western Europe in the Middle Ages.* London: Longman Group, 1984.

Lea, H. C. *History of Sacerdotal Celibacy in the Christian Church.* London: Watts, 1932.

Leclerq, J., *L'amour des lettres et le désir de Dieu: initiation aux auteurs monastiques du Moyen-Age.* Paris: Cerf, 1957.

"Il y a-t-il une culture monastique?" In *Il monachesimo nell'alto medioevo et la formazione della civilizatione occidentale* (Settimana di studio del centro italiano di studi sull'alto medioevo), pp. 339–356. Spoleto: Presso la Sede del Centro, 1957.

"Le poème de Payen Bolotin contre les faux ermites." *Revue Bénédictine* 73 (1958): 52–84.

Pierre Damien, ermite et homme d'Eglise. Romse: Storia e Letteratura, 1960.

"L'érémitisme en Occident jusqu'a l'An Mil." In *L'eremitismo in Occidente nei secoli XI–XII,* pp. 28–38. Milan: Universita cattolica del Sacro Cuore, 1965.

"The Monastic Crisis of the Eleventh and Twelfth Century." In N. Hunt (ed.), *Cluniac Monasticism in the Central Middle Ages,* pp. 217–37. Hamden, Conn.: Archon, 1971.

Leff, G. *Heresy in the Later Middle Ages: The Relation of Heterodoxy to Dissent, c. 1250–1450.* New York: Manchester University Press, 1967.

Le Goff, J. *La civilisation de l'Occident médiéval.* Paris: Flammarion, 1964.

Time, Work and Culture in the Middle Ages. Chicago: University of Chicago Press, 1980.

La naissance du purgatoire. Paris: Gallimard, 1981.

L'imaginaire médiéval. Paris: Gallimard, 1985.

Lekai, L. J. *The Cistercians: Ideals and Reality*. Kent, Ohio: Kent State University Press, 1977.

Lemarignier, J. F. "Aspects politiques des fondations de collégiales dans le royaume de France au XIe siècle." In *La Vita Commune del clero nei secoli XI–XIIe*. Milan: Universita cattolica del Sacro Cuore, 1962.

"Political and Monastic Structures in France at the End of the Tenth and Beginning of the Eleventh Century." In F. L. Cheyette, *Lordship and Community in Medieval Europe*. New York: Holt, Rinehart, & Winston, 1968.

La France médiévale: institutions et société. Paris: Armand Colin, 1970.

Leyser, H. *Hermits and the New Monasticism: A Study of Religious Communities in Western Europe, 1000–1150*. London: Macmillan, 1984.

Little, L. K. "The Personal Development of Peter Damiani." In W. C. Jordan, B. M. Nob, and T. F. Ruiz (eds), *Order and Innovation in the Middle Ages: Essays in Honor of J. R. Strayer*, pp. 317–342. Princeton, N.J.: Princeton University Press, 1976.

Religious Poverty and the Profit Economy in Medieval Europe. Ithaca, N.Y.: Cornell University Press, 1978.

McCann, J. (ed. and trans.) *The Rule of Saint Benedict*. London: Burns Oates, 1952.

McDonnel, E. W. "The Vita Apostolica: Diversity or Dissent?" *Church History* 24 (1955): 15–31.

McGinn, B., J. Meyendorff, and J. Leclercq (eds.). *Christian Spirituality: Origins to the Twelfth Century*. London: Routledge & Kegan Paul, 1986.

Manteuffel, T. *Naissance d'une hérésie: les adeptes de la pauvreté volontaire au Moyen-Age*. Paris: Mouton, 1970.

Mason, E. "Timeo Barones et Donas Ferentes." In D. Baker (ed.), *Religious Motivation: Biographical and Sociological Problems for the Church Historian*, pp. 61–75. (Oxford: B. Blackwell, 1978).

"The Donors of Westminister Abbey Charters, ca. 1066–1240." *Medieval Prosopography* 8 (1987): 23–39.

Mayr-Harding H. "Functions of a Twelfth-Century Recluse." *History* 60 (1975): 337–52.

Milis, L. "Ermites et chanoines réguliers au XIIe siècle." *Cahiers de Civilisation Médiévale* 22 (1979): 39–80.

Miller, C. M. "Donors, their Gifts, and Religious Innovation in Medieval Verona." *Speculum* 66 (1991): 27–42.

Mollat, M. (ed.). *Etudes sur l'histoire de la pauvreté*. Paris: Publications de la Sorbonne, 1974.

The Poor in the Middle Ages. New Haven, Conn.: Yale University Press, 1986.

Morin, D. G. "Rainaud l'ermite et Ives de Chartres: un épisode de la crise du cénobitisme aux XIe–XIIe siècles." *Revue Bénédictine* 15 (1928): 99–115.

Morris, C. *The Discovery of the Individual, 1050–1200*. New York: Harper, 1972.

Murray, A. *Reason and Society in the Middle Ages*. Oxford: Clarendon, 1978.

Nagel, P. *Die Motivierung des Askese in der Alten Kirche und der Ursprung des Mönchtums*. Berlin: Akademie Verlag, 1966.

Noble, T. F. X. "The Monastic Ideal as a Model for Empire: The Case of Louis the Pious." *Revue Bénédictine* 86 (1976): 235–50.

Oliger, P. *Les évêques réguliers: recherches sur leur condition juridique depuis les origines du monachisme jusqu'a la fin du Moyen-Age* Paris: Louvain, 1958.

Pacaut, M. *Les ordres monastiques et religieux au Moyen-Age.* Paris: F. Nathan, 1970.

Passmore, J. *The Perfectibility of Man.* London: Duckworth, 1970.

Peters, E. *Heresy and Authority in Medieval Europe.* Philadelphia: University of Pennsylvania Press, 1978.

Poly, J. P., and E. Bournazel. *La mutation féodale, Xe–XIIe siècles.* Paris: Presses Universitaires de France, 1980.

Poulin, J. C. *L'idéal de sainteté dans l'Aquitaine carolingienne d'après les sources hagiographiques, W. C. Jordan, B. M. Nob and T. F. Ruiz, 750–950.* Québec: Presses de l'Université Laval, 1973.

Prinz, F. "Aristocracy and Christianity in Merovingian Gaul. In K. Bosl (ed.), *Gesellschaft-Kultur-Literatur: Beitrage Luitpold Wallach gewidmet.* Stuttgart: A. Hiersemann, 1975.

——— "Mönchtum und Arbeitsethos." In F. Prinz, *Askese und Kultur, Vor- und Frühbenediktinisches Mönchtum an der Wiege Europas.* Munich: C.H. Beck, 1980.

——— "Mönchtum und Frühmittelalterliche Adelgesellschaft im Spiegel der Hagiographie." In F. Prinz, *Askese und Kultur, Vor- un Frübenediktinisches Mönchtum an der Wiege Europas,* pp. 75–86. Munich: C.H.Beck, 1980.

——— "Columbanus, the Frankish Nobility and the Territories East of the Rhine." In H. B. Clarke and M. Brennan (eds.)., *Columbanus and Merovingian Monasticism.* Oxford: B.A.R., 1981.

Pseudo-Denys, l'Aréopagite. *Oeuvres Completes.* Translated with introduction by M. de Gandillac. Paris: Aubier-Montaigne, 1943.

Raftis, J. A. "Western Monasticism and Economic Organization." *Comparative Studies in Society and History* 8, no. 4 (1961): 452–67.

Reeves, M. "The Originality and Influence of Joachim of Fiore." *Traditio* 36 (1980): 269–316.

Riche, P. "Columbanus, his Followers and the Merovingian Church." In H. B. Clarke and M. Brennan (eds.), *Columbanus and Merovingian Monasticism.* Oxford: B.A.R., 1981.

Rosenthal, J.T. "Edward the Confessor and Robert the Pious: Eleventh Century Kingship and Biography." *Mediaeval Studies* 33 (1971): 7–20.

Rosenwein, B. H. *Rhinoceros Bound: Cluny in the Tenth Century.* Philadelphia: University of Pennsylvania Press, 1982.

——— *To Be the Neighbor of St. Peter: The Social Meaning of Cluny's Property, 909–1049.* Ithaca, N.Y.: Cornell University Press, 1989.

Rosenwein, B. H., and L. K. Little. "Social Meaning in the Monastic and Mendicant Spiritualities." *Past and Present* 63 (1974): 4–32.

Rothkrug, L. "German Holiness and Western Sanctity in Medieval and Modern History." *Historican Reflections/Reflexions Historiques* 15 (1988): 161–248.

Rousseau, P. *Ascetics, Authority and the Church in the Age of Jerome.* Oxford: Oxford University Press, 1978.

——— *Pachomius: The Making of a Community in Fourth-Century Egypt.* Berkeley and Los Angeles: University of California Press, 1985.

Ruether, R., and E. C. McLaughlin (eds.), *Women of Spirit.* New York: Simon & Schuster, 1979.

Salmon, P. *L'abbé dans la tradition monastique: contribution à l'histoire du caractére perpétuel des supérieurs religieux en Occident.* Paris: Sirey, 1962.

Schmidt, K., and J. Wollasch. "Die Gemeinschaft der Lebenden und Bestorbenen in Zeugnissen des Mittelalters." *Frühmittelalterliche Studien* 1 (1967): 365–405.

Schmitz, P. *Histoire de l'Ordre de Saint-Benoît.* Maredsous: Les Editions de Maredsous, 1942.

Schmitz, P. "L'influence de Saint Benoît d'Aniane dans l'histoire de l'Ordre de Saint Benoit." In *Il monachesimo nell'alto mediaevo e la formazione della civilizatione occidentale* (Settimane di studio del Centro Italiano di studi sull'alto medioevo), pp. 401–15. Spoleto: Presso la Sede del Centro, 1957.

Sommerfeldt, J. R. (ed.). *Cistercian Ideals and Reality.* Kalamazoo, Mich.: Cistercian, 1978.

Southern, R. W. *The Making of the Middle Ages.* New Haven, Conn.: Yale University Press, 1953.

Western Society and the Church in the Middle Ages. Harmondsworth: Pelican Books, 1970.

Stancliffe, C. "Kings Who Opted Out." In P. Wormald, D. Bullough, and R. Collins (eds.), *Ideal and Reality in Frankish and Anglo-Saxon Society,* pp. 155–76. Oxford: B.Blackwell, 1983.

Strayer, J. R. "The Laicization of French and English Society in the Thirteenth Century." In S. Thrupp (ed)., *Change in Medieval Society,* pp. 103–16. New York: Appleton, Century & Crofts, 1964.

Tellenbach, G. *Church, State and Society at the Time of the Investiture Contest.* Oxford: B. Blackwell, 1940.

Tellenbach, G. (ed.). *Neue Forschungen über Cluny und die Cluniacenser.* Freiburg: Verlag Herder, 1959.

Tentler, N. T. *Sin and Confession on the Eve of the Reformation.* Princeton, N.J.: Princeton University Press, 1977.

Thomas Aquinas, *Summa Theologica.* Translated by Fathers of the English Dominican Province. Westminister, Md.: Christian Classics, 1981.

Troeltsch, E. *The Social Teachings of the Christian Churches.* New York: Harper, 1960.

Ullman, W. *Medieval Political Thought.* Harmondsworth: Penguin Books, 1979.

Van Engen, J. "The 'Crisis of Cenobitism' Reconsidered: Benedictine Monasticism in the Years 1050–1150." *Speculum* 61 (1986): 266–304.

"The Christian Middle Ages as a Historiographical Problem." *American Historical Review* 91 (1986): 519–52.

Vauchez, A. "La pauvreté volontaire au Moyen-Age." *Annales* 25 (1970): 1566–73.

"Beata stirps: sainteté et lignage en Occident." In G. Duby and J. Le Goff (eds.), *Famille et parenté dans l'Occident mediéval.* Rome: Ecole française, 1977.

La sainteté en Occident aux derniers siècles du Moyen-Age. Rome: Ecole française, 1981.

Violante, C. "Il monachesimo clunaciense di fronte al mondo politico de ecclesiastico secoli 10–11." *Studi Sulla Christianita Medioevale,* pp. 34–9. Milan: Vita e Pensiero, 1972.

Vogel, C. *La discipline pénitentiellle en Gaule des origines à la fin du VIIe siècle.* Paris: Letouzay et Ané, 1952.

Ward, J. C. "Fashions in Monastic Endowment: the Foundations of the Clara Family, 1066–1324." *Journal of Ecclesiastical History* 32 (1981): 427–53.

Wardrop, J. *Fountains Abbey and its Benefactors, 1132–1300.* Kalamazoo, Mich.: Cistercian, 1987.

Warren, A. *Anchorites and their Patrons in Medieval England.* Berkeley and Los Angeles: University of California Press, 1985.

Wemple, S. *Women in Frankish Society: Marriage and the Cloister, 500–900.* Philadelphia: University of Pennsylvania Press, 1983.

Werner, E. *Pauperes Christi: Studien zu Sozialreligösen Bewegungen in Zeitalter des Reformpapstums.* Leipzig: Koehler & Amelang, 1956.

White, H. J. "The Gregorian Ideal and Saint Bernard of Clairvaux." *Journal of the History of Ideas* 21 (1960): 321–48.

White, S. D. *Custom, Kinship and Gifts to Saints: The* Laudatio Parentum *in Western France, 1050–1150.* Chapel Hill: University of North Carolina Press, 1988.

Williams, W. "A Dialogue between a Cluniac and a Cistercian." *Journal of Theological Studies* 31 (1930): 164–75.

Wilmart, A. "Une riposte de l'ancien monachisme au manifeste de St. Bernard." *Revue Bénédictine* 46 (1934): 296–344.

Witters, W. "Pauvres et pauvreté dans les coutumes monastiques du Moyen-Age." In M. Mollat (ed.), *Etudes sur l'histoire de la pauvreté,* pp. 177–217. Paris: Publications de la Sorbonne, 1974.

Wollasch, J. "Les obituaires, témoins de la vie clunisienne." *Cahiers de Civilisation Médiévale* 22, no. 2 (1979): 139–71.

"Parenté noble et monachisme réformateur: observations sur les 'conversions' à la vie monastique aux XIe et XIIe siècles." *Revue Historique* 535 (1980): 3–24.

Wollasch, J., W. D. Heim, J. Mehne, F. Neiske, and D. Poeck (eds.). Synopse der cluniacensichen Necrologien. Munich: Wilheim Fink, 1982.

Wood, I. "A Prelude to Columbanus: The Monastic Achievement in the Burgundian Territories." In H. B. Clarke and M. Brennan (eds.), *Columbanus and Merovingian Monasticism.* Oxford: B.A.R., 1981.

Zerubavel, E. "The Benedictine Ethic and the Modern Spirit of Scheduling: On Schedules and Social Organization." *Sociological Inquiry* 50 (1980): 157–69.

Index

activist–ascetic virtuoso religion, 26, 27, 32; Church's ambivalence toward, 28

Alcuin, as abbot counselor to Charlemagne, 166

alternative structure, monasticism as, 38–41, 43, 51, 187, 194; in medieval Christianity, 187, 205–6; in Theravada Buddhism, 187–8

Amapura, 111

ambiguity: of aspects of Benedictine rule, 126; in attitude of Buddhist canon to magical beliefs and practices, 70; in definition of monastic vocation, 65; in definitions of the way to perfection and of the Church, 122; of doctrinal status of ascetic practices, 110; of doctrinal status of Christian monasticism, 119; ideological, 216; of ideological premises' interaction with institutional structures, 50; in monastic attitude to work, 138; in nature of the ideological dimension, 217; in notion of dharma, 60; of social position of Christian monasticism, 187, 193–4

ambiguous orientation to the social order and kingship, 60, 63

ambiguous stance of canonical texts toward magico-animistic practices, 76

ambiguous status of monks, 131

ambivalence: toward virtuoso radicalism, 109; toward virtuoso religion, 28, 44; in virtuoso–laymen relation, 196, 197, 216

anatta, 63

anchoritic monasticism, 44, 176

Aniruddha, 102

Anthony, 175

Anuradhapura, 94

antistructure, in monasticism, 40–1, 53

Apostolic Brethren, in eremitic–apostolic revival, 181

apostolic movement, in medieval Europe, 17

Aquinas, on medieval Catholic religious hierarchy, 132

arannavasi, 105

arhat, 69, 72, 107–8

arhatship, 110

aristocracy (*see also* elites; nobility), Christian monastery recruitment from, 158–9, 172

Arnoldians: in eremitic–apostolic revival, 181; as lay religious movement, 166

Arthurian legend, hermit–saint figure in, 180–1

arya sangha, 72–3

ascetic virtuosi, 1, 2, 9, 18, 36, 71, 137 (*see also* eremitism; hermits); convertible aspect of, 45; Durkheim functionalist approach to, 43; role of, 7, 13; safety-valve model for, 44

Ashoka, 61, 62; role in spread of Buddhism, 15, 57n, 58n, 74, 142

Augustine, 120, 122, 126

Aung-Thwin, M., 86

autonomy: of Christian monasteries, 52, 138, 150–6, 173; of religious institutions, 50; of Theravada Buddhism monasteries, 155, 173

Axial Age religions, 4–5

Ayutthaya, 104

Basil, 125, 126

Bechert, Heinz, on definition of traditional Theravada Buddhism, 14, 112

begging, by Theravada Buddhist monks, 66–7

Bellah, Robert, 4n, 6

Benedictine form of Christian virtuosity, 17, 136

Benedictine monasteries, 166n, 170; eremitism in, 166n, 170; expansion of, 142, 155; organizational structure of, 138, 140, 141; wealth of, 182

Benedictine Rule, for monastic life, 126, 138, 142, 143, 146, 151, 154, 155–6, 160, 173, 174, 175–6, 182

Benedict of Aniane: as abbot counselor to Louis the Pious, 166; monastic reform of, 138, 142, 143–4, 162, 174

Berger, Peter, 6

bhikkhus, 80, 86, 90, 91, 92, 95, 98, 105, 114, 128

Bimbisara, 68

Bloch, M., 157

bodhisattva, 61–2, 65, 66, 72, 100

Bourdieu, Pierre: on Weber, 35n

Bowersock, G., 164

Brahmanism: renunciation and, 8, 9n, 46

Brown, Peter, 31, 45–6, 47, 176

Springs of Scientific Creativity
Essays on Founders of Modern Science

The McKnight Foundation has provided
support toward the publication of this book.
The University of Minnesota Press
gratefully acknowledges this assistance.

Springs of Scientific Creativity

Essays on Founders of Modern Science

Rutherford Aris
H. Ted Davis
Roger H. Stuewer
Editors

University of Minnesota Press
Minneapolis

Copyright © 1983 by the University of Minnesota.
All rights reserved.
Published by the University of Minnesota Press,
2037 University Avenue Southeast, Minneapolis, MN 55414
Printed in the United States of America.

Library of Congress Cataloging in Publication Data

Main entry under title:

Springs of scientific creativity.

    Includes index.
    1. Physics—History. 2. Physicists. 3. Scientists.
4. Creative ability in science. I. Aris, Rutherford.
II. Davis, H. Ted (Howard Ted) III. Stuewer, Roger H.
QC7.S77 1983   509'.2'2   82-23715
ISBN 0-8166-1087-8

The University of Minnesota
is an equal-opportunity
educator and employer.

Preface

It would have been more than a little fascinating to have been at the high table of Trinity the night that Hardy tackled Housman about the opening paragraphs of his Leslie Stephen lecture, "The Name and Nature of Poetry."[1] Though as precise and exacting a scholar as Housman, Hardy reacted violently to Housman's putting the literary critic above the literary creator. Housman had referred to his 1911 Inaugural where he had said that though poets and others, "if rare in comparison with blackberries are yet commoner than the appearance of Halley's comet; literary critics are less common."[2] Admitting that he had improved in some respects but deteriorated in others, he went on to say: "I have not so much improved as to be a literary critic, nor so much deteriorated as to fancy that I have become one."[3] Hardy, the pure mathematician par excellence, thought the life of the finest of critics to be unworthy of comparison with that of the poet or scholar, and Housman seems to have conceded that his remarks were "perhaps not entirely" to be taken seriously. In his Inaugural however Housman had defined a literary critic as one "who has things to say about literature which are both true and new,"[4] and what were Hardy's mathematical discoveries but things about mathematics which were both true and new?

Yet Hardy's instincts were entirely right, for the scientist and mathematician prize originality above all, and Hardy uses this very instance in his 'Apology' as an apology for writing *about* mathematics at all. It is scarcely surprising that of all kinds of scientists it is the mathematicians who have most often been concerned with the roots and conditions of creativity and that we have personal insights from no less a master than Poincaré.[5] Frequently their testimony has been to the sudden moment of insight coming at a point when the preliminary cogitation and the working of the subconscious have prepared the mind for the intuitive flash of recognition. Poincaré had just put his foot on the step of the bus in Coutances when he realised that the transformations of non-Euclidean geometry were just those he needed in the theory of Fuschians. He did not need to interrupt his conversation, still less to verify the equation in detail; his insight was complete at that point.

There have been many analyses of creativity from all points of view.[7,8] Arthur Koestler[9] has built on the analogy with humor where two habitually incompatible aspects of life meet in the explosive moment; while Hanson[10] saw a model of creative insight in the way an observed pattern can suddenly change its significance. Bronowski[11] has stressed the discovery of new unity in diversity and pointed out that the construction of a scientific theory gives as much play to the imagination as the writing of a novel or poem and that it is only to the man who makes the theory that 'it may seem as inevitable as the ending of Othello did to Shakespeare'. In a recent study Sasso[12] has looked at what he calls 'constructive action' as the bridge between imitation and creation. One could go on and on, but the only conclusion that seems to emerge is that there cannot be any prescribed method of creativity however much may be learned of the conditions that promote it. Popper,[13] from his greater knowledge of the practice of science, saw that the verificationism of the Vienna circle was sterile and introduced the canon of falsifiability as a guide in the construction of scientific theories. 'What we read in him most deeply', Bronowski[14] wrote, 'was a passion for science, not as a system but as an activity — a method to foster the growth of knowledge.' On the other hand Feyerabend[15] saw method itself as a barrier to creativity and scientific progress.

Amid such a wealth, not to say welter, of insights, the question may well be raised whether creativity is patient of an essential characterization or whether, like a craft, it lives in its instances. The working scientist is usually ready enough to leave it unexamined and often regards philosophy as a debilitating befuddlement and shuns the vagueness and generality of much that has been said and written about creativity. Yet its fascination remains, and one way of satisfying our curiosity is to get to know more of the intellectual lives of those who, on any count, must be regarded as creative thinkers.

The idea behind the series of lectures that gave birth to this volume was a suggestion of Ted Davis, that a refreshing way to approach this question would be through a biographical look at a selection of scientists and mathematicians. We recognized from the start that there was no hope of being comprehensive and that any selection would be open to the criticisms of "Why not A?" or "Should you really have B when you don't have C?". We accepted this hazard hoping that our main principle of organization would compensate the reader disappointed of his or her favorite subject. In organizing such lectures there is only one way to go and that is to ask that person of lively mind whom you judge to be best qualified in each area to contribute a paper, indicate the general thrust and intention of the series, and then give them all their head. Any attempt to prescribe too narrowly the purview of each talk is self-defeating as well as inconsistent with the confidence that a scholar deserves. In the choice of speakers, now authors, we leaned heavily on Roger Stuewer's knowledge of people in the field and benefitted from the help of Alan Shapiro. We were not only gratified, but also encouraged, to find such a ready response to the suggestion and are most grateful to the authors of the ensuing chapters for their willingness not only to give the lectures in the first place but also to write them up for publication. We are particularly grateful to the deans of the Graduate School and the Institute of Technology, for supplementing the financial support that our departments needed to mount this enterprise.

Our hope is that the reader will find these essays as stimulating in their written form as the lectures were in the spoken word and that they will lead to further insight into the creative springs of the scientific enterprise. For the rest, they may speak for themselves.

Notes

1. G. H. Hardy, *A Mathematician's Apology* (Cambridge: Cambridge University Press, 1940).

2. A. E. Housman, *The Confines of Criticism* (The Cambridge Inaugural, 1911) (Cambridge: Cambridge University Press, 1969).

3. A. E. Housman, *The Name and Nature of Poetry* (Cambridge: Cambridge University Press, 1933). Reprinted in *A. E. Housman: Selected Prose*, ed. J. Carter (Cambridge: Cambridge University Press, 1961).

4. Hardy cannot be blamed for overlooking this, as Housman did not go on to quote his definition of the critic. The inaugural of 1911 had never been published, as Housman had been unable to verify a quotation from Shelley that he used to point out the vacuity of unscientific criticism. Cf. Carter's preface to Housman, *The Confines of Criticism,* and the articles of Carter and Sparrow in the *Times Literary Supplements* of 6.ix.1963 and 21.xi.1968.

5. H. Poincaré, "La raisonnement mathématique," in *Science et Méthode* (Paris: E. Flammarion, 1908). Cf. J. Hadamard, *The Psychology of Invention in the Mathematical Field* (Princeton: Princeton University Press, 1949).

6. G. Wallas. *The Art of Thought* (London: Cape, 1926).

7. A. Rothenburg and B. Greenberg, *The Index of Scientific Writings on Creativity: Creative Men and Women* (Hamden, CT: Shoe String Press, 1974).

8. B. Ghiselin, *The Creative Process* (Los Angeles: California University Press, 1952).

9. A. Koestler, *The Act of Creation* (New York: Macmillan, 1964).

10. N. R. Hanson, *Patterns of Discovery* (Cambridge: Cambridge University Press, 1961).

11. J. Bronowski, *A Sense of the Future* (Cambridge, MA: M.I.T. Press, 1977). Reprints "The Creative Process" from *Scientific American,* September 1958.

12. J. Sasso, "The Stages of the Creative Process," *Proceedings of the American Philosophical Society* 124 (1980), pp. 119-132.

13. K. Popper, *The Logic of Scientific Discovery* (London: Hutchinson, 1959).

14. J. Bronowski, "Humanism and the Growth of Knowledge," in *A Sense of the Future,* p. 83.

15. P. K. Feyerabend, *Against Method* (London: Verso, 1975).

Contents

Springs of Scientific Creativity
Essays on Founders of Modern Science

Chapter *1*

Galileo and Early Experimentation

Thomas B. Settle

In the last two decades scholars have provided much new evidence of Galileo's use of experiment. Argument continues about particulars, but it can now at least be safely assumed that he did design and use experiments in the course of his many researches.[1] Some basic questions, however, are still unanswered: how early did he begin the practice, how mature or developed was his experimental sense when he first began, and did he begin out of nothing, from scratch, or rather did he build on and possibly transform an already existing tradition?

That he did not uniquely invent the art of experiment ought to be clear from the fact that his father before him, Vincenzo Galilei, a musician and musical theorist, already was an effective experimenter in musical accoustics in the decade of the 1580s when the young Galileo was in his late teens and early twenties.[2] In this period Vincenzo undertook to resolve a musical dispute, and this led him to investigate the proportionalities of the lengths, tensions, and "weights" of the strings of musical instruments and their resulting tones. Eventually he rejected all arguments based on a priori judgements about the primacy of ratios of small natural numbers and,

I should like to thank Dr. Donald R. Miklich (2235 Julian Street, Denver CO 80211) who conceived and directed the experiment described in this paper. He did the work when he was with the National Asthma Center of Denver, an institution which has since ceased to exist. Together we thank the Research Society of Sigma Xi for the Grant-in-Aid which covered Dr. Miklich's expenses. I should also like to thank Ronald Breland and Len Lowy of McCaffrey & McCall, Inc. for their invaluable help in having the photographs processed.

experimenting with a monocord, devised rules for the ratios on the basis of empirical evidence. Under Vincenzo's tutelage Galileo himself became an accomplished lutanist, and he went on to extend his father's experimental work and to revise and improve his theories. Unfortunately for us, Galileo reported these results much later in the *Discorsi* (1638),[3] so it is difficult to have a good idea of the sequence of his own ideas or experiments or of what thread or threads led him on.

We are in a better position, however, with regard to Galileo's work on natural motion. Here many datable texts exist, from his ca. 1590 manuscript *De motu*,[4] through the correspondence, notes, and publications of the early 1600s,[5] to the *Dialogo*[6] and the *Discorsi* of the 1630s. These documents are now beginning to yield a picture of Galileo the investigator, the seeker, a picture with some movement through time replacing the flat, motionless portraits which emphasized Galileo's final positive accomplishments. In this new picture we can see Galileo starting with certain assumptions and practices, changing his mind, using experiment to criticize and revise theory, using theory to criticize and revise experiment, making up his mind, wavering, leading himself into dead ends, and so on: just as we ought to expect from a person with his penetrating, persistent, and sometimes obstinate intelligence, working actively over a span of fifty-five-odd years. But the questions remain; where and how did he begin?

Galileo's First Trials

The earliest direct evidence of Galileo's interest in natural motion is in the *De motu*[7] or *De motu antiquiora,* composed primarily during his first tenure as a teacher of mathematics at the University of Pisa in the years 1589 to 1592. In this tract, Galileo proposed a theory of natural motion according to which a body in free fall is presumed to move with a characteristic uniform speed. In this case the uniform speed is not one that results from the resistance of a medium; it is the uniform speed that a body would exhibit most perfectly, in fact, in a vacuum. And the degree of this uniform speed for a given body is determined by and directly proportional to its specific gravity. That is, if a ball of gold and a ball of silver were dropped simultaneously from a high place, one ought to see the ball of gold hit the ground while the silver ball is still half way down from the point of release, gold having about twice the specific gravity of silver. And it would seem that Galileo devised an experiment on the matter, in this case an unsuccessful experiment; he writes:

Plate 1. Galileo. Portrait by Justus Susterman, Uffizi Gallery, Florence.

These then are the general rules governing the ratio of the speeds of [natural] motion of bodies made of the same or different material, in the same medium or in different media, and moving upward or downward. But note that a great difficulty arises at this point, because those ratios will not be observable by one who makes the experiment. For if one takes two different bodies, which have properties such that the first should fall twice as fast as the second, and if one lets them fall from a tower, the first will not reach the ground appreciably faster or twice as fast.[8]

We do not have to suppose that Galileo used gold and silver balls; any two similarly diverse bodies would suffice. Nevertheless, in the trial two such bodies seem to drop pretty much side by side, *contrary to hypothesis,* and it is in this sense that Galileo could view the experiment a failure in 1590. At this juncture, then, he had accepted a fairly precise rule about the nature of free fall; he had already wished to see that rule exhibited materially, so he had performed trials; and he found and reported that nature seemed not to conform to his primary theory. His response seems to have been two-fold. He developed subsidiary hypotheses which would allow him to keep his primary assumption while explaining away the divergent phenomena, and he continued to explore by experiment in the hope of actually finding the primary rule directly confirmed in nature. These two interacting lines of investigation led him, by the end of a decade or so, to drop the uniform motion rule and to decide that the essential phenomenon in free fall was instead a uniform acceleration according to the specific relationship we know as Galileo's Law: $S \propto T^2$, the distances from release being directly proportional to the squares of the time intervals from release. The details of this transformation, in so far as we can reconstruct them, have been treated elsewhere.[9] What is important to note is that already in the first work on motion Galileo expects theory and practice to agree and that, instead of dismissing the phenomena as evidence of a recalcitrant and inherently imprecise nature, he reports the results and accepts them as a challenge to his ingenuity. It would seem that even at this early date he was experimenting at a fairly mature level. But we can probe even further.

Galileo and Girolamo Borro

In a continuation of the *De motu* passage cited above, Galileo describes his observation even more precisely:

Indeed, if an observation is made, the lighter body will, at the beginning of the motion, move ahead of the heavier and will be swifter.[10]

And in another version he writes:

For we find in experience that if two spheres of equal size, one of which is double the other in weight, are dropped from a tower, the heavier one does not reach the ground twice as quickly. Indeed, at the beginning of the motion the lighter one will move ahead of the heavier, and for some distance will move more swiftly than it.[11]

It is clear from the second passage that when Galileo mentions light and heavy bodies he means also less dense and more dense ones. It is also clear that he wants us to accept that he has seen such light bodies move ahead of the heavier ones, at least at the beginning of their fall. And he takes his observation so seriously that later on in this tract he devotes an entire chapter to accounting for it, a chapter entitled, "In which the cause is given why, at the beginning of their natural motion, bodies that are less heavy move more swiftly than heavier ones."[12] In it he evokes an assumption subsidiary to his primary rule, with which he explains both why two bodies will be seen to fall more or less side by side and why light bodies may even precede heavy ones for a while.

The details of the subsidiary hypothesis do not concern us here; it was Galileo's chief means of defending or saving his primary rule, and he eventually gave it up. But there is an obvious problem. We know, or we think we know, that light bodies do not fall ahead of heavy ones. A natural response might be either that Galileo was a very poor experimenter or that he was trying to mislead us.[13] In either case we should conclude that we ought to view with extreme skepticism not only this but any other claim of Galileo to have done any critical observational or experimental research. Certainly it casts a shadow on his associated claim of having seen bodies fall more or less together.

Yet he does write convincingly that he actually saw the light body precede the heavy one at first. He even cites a predecessor at Pisa who claimed to have seen the same thing. The predecessor was Girolamo Borro, an Aristotelian philosopher who was teaching at Pisa when Galileo was a student there[14] and who published in Florence in 1575 a book entitled *De motu gravium et levium*.[15] In the passage indicated by Galileo we find Borro probing a certain problem concerning the weight of the air and a related problem of whether a heavier or lighter "mixed" body will fall faster in the air. Unable to resolve the latter question by reason, he and a small group decided to put the matter to test:

since, among us, discussions always grow and no end to them could be found, we took refuge in experience, the teacher of all things. . . .[16]

In this case he took a piece of wood and a piece of lead such that they were of equal weight and dropped them simultaneously from a high place.

we threw (*proiiciemus*) these two pieces of equal weight from a rather high window of our house at the same time and with the same force (*pari impulsu*). The lead descended more slowly, namely [it descended] above the wood, which had fallen to the ground first; however many times we were all there waiting for the results of this occurrence, we saw the latter [i.e., the wood] fall downward [before the lead]. Not only once but many times we tried it with the same results. . . .[17]

Now this test is somewhat different from Galileo's. In the first place the bodies were of equal weight but not of equal size. Since Borro evidently was not interested in looking at the differences in fall according to differences in absolute weight, we can infer that implicitly, if perhaps vaguely, he had in mind to test the differences according to density or specific gravity. Later on Galileo would be much more precise in his language, possibly a result of *his* greater exposure to Archimedean, hydrostatic considerations. In the second place, Borro seems to have "projected" the two pieces from his window, instead of just dropping them vertically. It is hard to know how to understand the *proiiciemus*. Perhaps he rested the two weights on the window ledge and "pushed" them horizontally out into space. Or possibly he held them in his hands and threw them horizontally just enough to ensure that they would clear the facade of his house as they fell. I say "horizontally" (that is, with no vertical component) because he would have had to take some care not to "favor" the fall of either of the weights. With the group of colleagues and students present, some undoubtedly antagonistic to his ideas, he would want to be seen to be "fair." But whatever the details, Borro was sure of the result: the wood fell ahead of the lead, many times. These results, if not precisely equivalent to those of Galileo, at least argue in the same direction. But how are we to interpret them? The world simply does not act in the way indicated. Were both men simply inventing phenomena and theories to fit the inventions?

Benedetto Varchi, Giovanni Francesco Beato, and Luca Ghini

Before resolving that issue it will be instructive to leave Galileo and Borro and examine additional sixteenth-century texts for evidence of other Italians who seem to have performed dropping experiments. One early tract was written by Benedetto Varchi, the Florentine historian and early and continuing member of Grand Duke Cosimo de' Medici's Accademia Fiorentina. In 1544 he wrote an essay on alchemy in which he took up the question of whether base metals could be transmuted into gold. He reviewed all the arguments, classical and medieval, pro and con, and remained skeptical on the possibility, though not dogmatically so.[18] On the other hand he was quite certain that the healthy, modern society in which he lived required the other alchemical arts such as the refining and processing of metals, dye and drug making, the ceramic arts and many others, and he cited gunpowder as evidence that at least some alchemy works spectacularly. In a section discussing the opinions of Albert the Great he allowed himself a digression on experiment in general:

Albert, who even if he was not a saint, deserved, nonetheless, at his time and for his learning the title the Great, in the third book of his *Minerals* in chapter nine, put the question of whether the metals could be changed from one species into another, as the alchemists claim. He concluded *yes,* following Avicenna who in his book on alchemy stated that it was not the *arte* which made the metals but nature and nature aided by *arte,* as we mentioned above. And without doubt the authority of Albert the Great ought to be considered not small for his being not only a philosopher, but a very great experimenter (*sperimentatore grandissimo*), that is, according to my poor judgement, a true and perfect philosopher. . . . And who would doubt that if philosophy could rouse itself from its laziness and from the shade and get out in the dust under the sun, as M. Tullio said of rhetoric, that it would not be much more esteemed and much more fruitful than it is. But this is beside the point and I have said it more in order to rescue Albert from those who, when they ought to have praised him highly, in fact blamed him severely for having wished to experiment on so many things. These many things pleased me greatly even if those impossible miracles and those unnatural things recounted by him or about him did not. And even if the custom of modern philosophers is always to believe and never to test (*non provar mai*) that which they find written in good authors, especially Aristotle, that does not mean that it would not be both safer (*più sicuro*) and more delightful to do otherwise and sometimes descend to experience (*sperienza*) in some cases, as for example in the motion of heavy bodies, in which both Aristotle and all other philosophers without ever doubting the fact, have believed and affirmed that according to how much a body is more heavy, by so much more [speed] will it descend, the test (*prova*) of which shows it not to be true. And if I were not afraid of getting too far from my subject, I would discourse at length in order to prove this opinion, which I have found some others to hold, for example, particularly, the Reverend Father and no less learned philosopher than good theologian Fra Francesco Beato, metaphysician at Pisa, and Messer Luca Ghini, most worthy physician and botanist (*Medico e Semplicista*) and also expert in the theoretical and practical knowledge of all the minerals, as it seemed to me when I heard it from him publicly at the University of Bologna.[19]

Varchi evidently had strong feelings about some contemporary philosophers and about experience or experiment. Unfortunately he does not describe the particulars of the *prova* of dropping unequal weights; nor does he indicate whether he is reporting his own experiences or those of either Fra Beato[20] or Luca Ghini;[21] nor, finally, does he give any of the details of the objections of Beato and Ghini. He is only clear in his rejection of what he takes to be Aristotle's theory. Nevertheless, we can guess that all three had performed or had seen performed the *prova,* at least in some informal way, in the previous decade. Until Varchi himself returned to Florence in the winter of 1542-1543, he had lived many years as an exile in several north Italian cities, among them Padua and Bologna. While in Padua he studied with Fra Beato before the latter came to Tuscany in the early 1540s,[22] and in Bologna he attended Luca Ghini's lectures in botany and minerology. So it is possible that these two universities had already seen experiment used in the very limited sense of providing a visual argument against a widely taught theory. And the later presence of Beato and Ghini at Pisa suggests that by mid-century there might have been established there a tradition of challenging Aristotle by making such dropping experiments, a tradition that both Borro and Galileo would have been following in their own times.

Giuseppe Moletti

If the tests of nature and Aristotelian theory were limited in both scope and execution in the 1530s and 1540s, they were considerably more developed a generation later. Borro's questioning and experimental technique were already much more detailed, and in the north Giuseppe Moletti was pursuing his own investigations.[23] In his later years Moletti was a mathematician at the University of Padua; he occupied the same chair that Galileo would hold when the latter came to Padua in 1592. And he counted among his friends in Padua the same erudite scholar, collector and patron who would later befriend Galileo, Gianvincenzo Pinelli. His interest in the problem of natural motion is demonstrated in a manuscript tract now in the Pinelli collection of Biblioteca Ambrosiana of Milan, a tract dated 1 October, 1576, and entitled *On Artillery*.[24] It is written in the form of a dialogue between "P" and "A," a prince and the author;[25] in this case the prince is the learned member of the pair and the author plays the openminded student. Here the prince continues a discussion already in progress:

P. Now a heavy body moving naturally can move with a greater or lesser velocity with respect to the medium. Thus, for a more subtle medium it moves with a greater velocity and for a denser (*più crasso*) medium a lesser velocity. All this you can well understand with reference to those things that fall first in water and then in air. If you take a body of water one hundred *passi* [about 174 meters][26] deep, and let a weight drop in it, and observe the time it takes to touch bottom, and make note of the time; and if again you pick an equal height of a hundred *passi* and let drop from it a body of the same weight, substance and figure as the other, and take count of the time it takes to reach the bottom, you will find this time to be much less than the other.

A. Why did you want the body to be the same substance, weight and figure as the other?

P. To avoid any reason (*cagione*) for ambiguity.

A. And what doubt could there be concerning these things?

P. Very great indeed, because Aristotle has given reason (*cagione*) for doubting, saying that in the same medium the velocity of things that move in natural motion, being of the same nature and figure, is as their powers (*potenze*). That is, if from the top of a tower we release two balls, one of lead of twenty pounds and the other equally of lead but of one pound, the motion of the larger will be twenty times greater in velocity than that of the smaller.

A. This appears reasonable enough to me; actually if I were asked about it I would concede it as a principle.

P. My dear sir, you would err; they both arrive at the same time and I have made the test (*prova*) of it not once but many times. And there is more: a ball of wood more or less the same size as the lead one, and released from the same height, descends and reaches the ground or soil in the same moment of time.

A. If Your Highness had not told me that you have made the test (*prova*) I would not believe it. — Well, how can one save Aristotle?

P. Many have tried to save him in various ways but in fact he is not to be saved. Actually to tell you the truth, I once believed that I had found a way to save him, but upon thinking better on it, it was not so.[27]

In comparison with Benedetto Varchi's vague mention of a *prova*, Moletti offers a set of very sharp images. One knows precisely what he is talking about and one can argue with him on the details. His initial case must be a thought experiment, at least as it is written; not even the Mediterranean offers a place where one can see clearly to a depth of 174 meters, nor are there towers of that height. Of course he may have tried this *prova* at more modest heights. But he delineates the problem he is posing very precisely, and he specifically recommends the making and recording of the exact intervals of time involved.

In the second case, however, he procedes to refute Aristotle in not one but two specific instances. The first concerns the fall of two bodies of the same substance but of different weight moving in the same medium. The second has to do with balls of the same volume but of different substance and thereby different weight, again in the same medium. In both sets of circumstances the balls reached the ground at the same instant. Clearly he has dissected, analysed, the variants of the problem of fall to a much greater critical depth than had Varchi, and he has devised much more probing tests. But note: he claims that he has performed these experiments many times, and yet he claims that the falling objects hit the ground simultaneously.

Now there is no particular reason to doubt that he made the trials. What we can doubt is that the objects hit the ground together. Anyone who has tried the experiment, releasing hand-held balls together and watching them drop, knows that it does not work that way.[28] They land close after one another, to be sure, especially in comparison with what the Aristotelian theory predicted; but not simultaneously. Quite probably what he did in reporting his results was, as we say, to round them out. If so, however, he has done this uncritically; or certainly he has not presented any justification for such rounding out.

By contrast, both Borro and Galileo saw balls fall *not* quite side by side, though each in his own fashion. What we seem to find in both of them is a willingness to attend quite closely to the raw data of sense experience and to take those data quite seriously. Both must have at one time or another been tempted to round out their data in the same way that Moletti had. And ultimately Galileo saw even more than Borro had; he not only saw the light object initially move ahead of the heavy, he also saw the heavy overtake the light.

Much later on, after refining his investigative techniques and gaining a broader mastery of the phenomena of natural motion, Galileo would assert that in principle bodies should fall side by side and that, in so far as they did not, that fact was to be ascribed to the accidents of the experiment, i.e., experimental artifact. At that later stage, in the *Discorsi*, Galileo's claim that bodies fall side by side had a different status from Moletti's superficially similar one; that is, instead of uncritically rejecting discrepancies, Galileo then had reasonably sound experimental and theoretical criteria for doing so.[29] By that point his mastery of the arts of experimental natural philosophy had reached quite an advanced level. But could Borro and Galileo actually have seen light bodies precede heavy ones in the first part of their fall? It turns out that the phenomenon is real; it has now been confirmed by two separate and distinct sets of experiments, the first of which will be described briefly below.

The Experiment

The experiment in question was designed by Dr. Donald R. Miklich in consultation with myself; and it was executed by Dr. Miklich.[30] We assumed at the outset that Galileo may indeed have worked in such a way as to see light bodies fall ahead of heavy ones, and we hoped to discover a set of plausible circumstances in which that would occur. After discussing the possibilities, we decided that a good place to start would be with the premise that in these early trials Galileo would have held the two balls, one in each hand, palms down, and then would have tried to release them simultaneously.[31] We also supposed that such a technique on Galileo's part might offer an explanation for the phenomenon: that the increased muscular or nervous fatigue (or combination of both) induced in the arm required to hold the heavier of the two balls would delay the release time of that ball by enough for the effect to occur, even though the "dropper" was subjectively certain that he had released the balls together. In the experimental work to date the latter physiological cause of the phenomenon has not been explored or isolated in detail, but the "Galileo effect," we believe, has been demonstrated.

For the experiment Dr. Miklich acquired two sets of spheres. The larger set was about 4 inches in diameter and consisted of an iron ball (about 10 pounds) and a wooden ball (about 1 pound). The smaller set was likewise a pair of equal diameter, iron and wooden balls. The two sizes were required to check the possibility that object size might make a difference in the result. Miklich also recruited 51 student-subject "droppers." Each of the subjects was to drop 4 times for the record, twice with the large set and twice with the small set. For each set, the subject was to drop once with the heavy ball held by the dominant hand and once with the light ball so held. There are 24 permutations of the sequence in which these 4 drops can be performed. These 24 permutations were listed and their order randomized for a master control sheet. Each subject in turn followed the successive drop sequences indicated on the master sheet. Only after a complete cycle of the 24 permutations was the cycle started over again.

The subject droppers were not told that they were taking part in the investigation of a historical problem. They were told that this was a study in engineering psychology designed to find out if people could perform simultaneous hand and finger movements while handling objects of different weight. It was explained that no one actually knew if it was possible to release heavy and light objects simultaneously, and that it was not an "error" if in a given instance one of the balls seemed to go ahead of the other even though both were apparently released together. They were asked to inform the experimentor if they knew, in a given instance, that they had accidentally let one of the balls drop first; in that case the drop would be repeated immediately. In fact, this never happened.

The drops themselves were arranged in such a way that each pair of spheres fell in front of a vertical stand on which were painted parallel horizontal lines. This background was illuminated, and each drop was recorded on Regular 8mm film at the rate of 24 frames per second. The results were scored both by watching the films played at full speed and by reviewing the films, frame by frame, in a film editor; the two scorings were comparable. It turned out that in the vast majority of drops one ball (whether heavy or light) obviously led the other. In only two instances of the roughly 200 drops (4 x 51) were the balls so close together that the lead one could not be determined. But the significant finding was that in only 12 percent of the drops did the heavy ball either precede or fall alongside the light one. In 88 percent of the trials the light ball clearly preceded the heavy one, and the results were essentially the same for both the large and the small sets of balls.

The photographs in the figure show a sequence typical of the trials in which the lighter of two balls precedes the heavier.[32] They are enlargements from successive frames of the 8mm record of one of the runs. The first two frames show the subject holding a pair of the smaller spheres at the starting level; the dark sphere is the iron one and the lighter the wood. The next frame shows the subject's fingers beginning to open. The fingers on the light ball are slightly more open than the fingers on the heavy, even though the subject "feels" that she has released both simultaneously. Both balls have begun to move, and the light one is already slightly ahead. In the fourth frame the light one is even more ahead, and the hand that held the iron ball already shows more vertical rebound than the other.[33] The remaining frames show the balls falling past the field of view, the wooden one always unmistakably ahead. This, then, is the "Galileo phenomenon," or at least it would seem to be a reasonable reproduction of it, lacking as we do any more complete description of the trials that Galileo performed at the early stage of the research he discussed in the 1590 *De motu*. Light objects do precede heavy objects when dropped together from a palms-down hand hold.

Back to Galileo

If we can accept these results and accept that it was reasonable for Galileo to take corresponding results seriously for a while, then we can conclude that not only was he experimenting right at the beginning of the early *De motu* research, but also that he was already experimenting quite effectively. He would go on to polish his practice and to change his ideas with regard to natural fall and to experiment itself, but he was already well started. Moreover, it seems that with regard to the problem of understanding natural motion he did

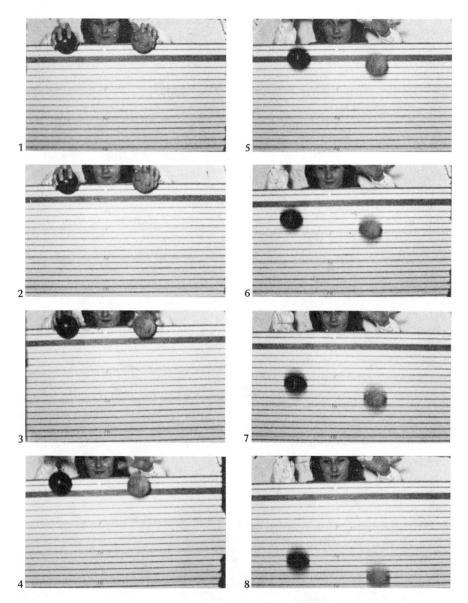

Figure 1. This sequence of eight frames comes from the 8mm film record of a typical "drop." The camera speed was 24 frames per second. The frames before no. 1 show no motion in either hand. The black ball is iron and the lighter ball is wood. Frames 1 & 2 continue to show no motion on the part of the balls, although a close inspection of the original of 2 (and, to a certain extent, of the print shown here) reveals a slight blurring of the index and middle fingers of the subject's left hand, perhaps indicating the very beginning of the opening of that hand. In frame 3 the subject's left hand is clearly wider open than her right hand. Both hands have now released their balls; the subject believes the balls to have been released simultaneously; and the lighter ball is already clearly ahead. In the remaining frames, the light ball continues to outpace the heavier, as the hand that held the heavier ball obviously rebounds the most.

inherit a nascent tradition of empirical testing, and in his own work he vastly refined experiment as a tool of critical inquiry and as an agent in the reformation of accepted knowledge.

One might object that the trials reported by Varchi, Borro, and Moletti and the erroneous observation of the Galileo phenomenon hardly constitute "experiment" in any but the most crude and uninteresting sense. But this would miss the historical and perhaps the methodological point. No craft or art or practice (experimental science included) comes into existence fully developed. Nor is it guaranteed that any craft, art, or practice has a final, definitive set of techniques and methods. Our ancestors did not make fine bone china the first time they put clay into a campfire, yet over the years we developed and are still developing a multitude of ceramic arts. The first hunters to pluck their strung bows were not professional lutanists, yet we developed lutes and many other stringed instruments along with the musicians to play them, such as Vincenzo and Galileo Galilei. Likewise, experiment had to begin somewhere (probably in many places and at many times, depending on the topic of interest), and effective experiment had to be learned, improved, diversified, and expanded in scope and technique, all over time, over generations. Nor would it serve any but the most arbitrary purposes to locate some moment in our story before which the empirical activity was not experiment in the "true" sense and after which it was. In the example offered there was going on, in more or less continuous reinforcement, a refinement of the quality and precision of the observations made, the quality and precision of the theoretical questions asked, and the quality and precision of the experimental means employed. What is interesting historically is the movement, the progression.

What we have seen is evidence that by the 1540s a few, even if not yet a great many, natural philosophers had already tested empirically what they took to be Aristotle's assumptions about natural motion and found them wanting. Unfortunately, their investigations bore no immediate fruit. Natural philosophers apparently lacked the capacity or inspiration to keep questioning the phenomena in such a way as to lead to the formulation of alternative positions, and their empirical tactics were relatively undeveloped. Perhaps their chief focus still lay, as in the thought of Moletti's interlocutor, in attempts to save the basic Aristotelian position theoretically. If this is the case, then it appears that by the 1560s some natural philosophers were beginning to move out of those bounds. Instead of just noting that Aristotle was wrong in a particular instance, they were questioning the phenomena more closely. For them Aristotle's theoretical assumptions no longer had pride of place. For Girolamo Borro and Giuseppe Moletti one or another experimentally derived version of physical reality occupied the forefront: for Borro the fact that light bodies precede heavy ones in their fall; for Moletti the fact that all bodies, regardless of weight or density, fall exactly side by side. In addition, both dissected and described the phenomena in greater analytical depth than had Varchi and his friends, and both provided more operational and procedural detail.

Then in the 1580s Galileo could profit from all these predecessors. We know that he read Borro, and it is possible that he also attended his lectures. And we know that Galileo had sufficient Florentine connections almost to guarantee that he had access to the information that Varchi provided. Finally, towards the end of the 1580s, he had enough in the way of indirect contact with Moletti to make it reasonably certain that he would have known of the latter's arguments even if he had not yet seen the text quoted above.[34] With all this as a base, Galileo quickly learned to ask more precise empirical questions and to attend more perceptively to nature's answers. Most importantly he was using the empirical information to force the revision of his own theoretical understanding. It would seem that even at this early point in Galileo's career he had already developed a considerable talent for empirical research. From what we know, both this talent and the persistence with which he perfected it served him well and were, in fact, at the core of his productive scientific life.

Notes

1. For an introduction to the topic and further references see S. Drake, *Galileo at Work: His Scientific Biography* (Chicago: University of Chicago Press, 1978); R. H. Naylor, "Galileo's Theory of Projectile Motion," *Isis* 71 (1980), pp. 550-570. See also J. MacLachlan, "A Test of an 'Imaginary' Experiment of Galileo's," *Isis* 64 (1973), pp. 374-379; P. D. Sherman, "Galileo and the Inclined Plane Controversy," *The Physics Teacher* 12 (1974), pp. 343-348; T. B. Settle, "Galileo's Use of Experiment as a Tool of Investigation," in E. McMullin, ed., *Galileo: Man of Science* (New York: Basic, 1967, pp. 315-337; T. B. Settle, "An Experiment in the History of Science," *Science* 133 (1961), pp. 19-23. For a balanced discussion written before some of the more recent publications see: M. A. Hoskin, "Galileo as an Experimenter," in *Saggi su Galileo Galilei*, Vol. 1 (unpublished but off-print issued: Florence, Barbèra, 1967), 12 pp.

2. C. V. Palisca, "Scientific Empiricism in Musical Thought," in H. H. Rhys, ed., *Seventeenth Century Science and the Arts* (Princeton: Princeton University Press, 1960), pp. 91-137; C. V. Palisca, *Girolamo Mei (1519-1594), Letters on Ancient and Modern Music to Vincenzo Galilei and Giovanni Bardi* (Musicological Studies and Documents No. 3, American

Institute of Musicology, 1960); C. V. Palisca, "Vincenzo Galilei's Counterpoint Treatise: A Code for the *Seconda Pratica*," *Journal of the American Musicological Society* 9 (1956), pp. 81-96; S. Drake, "Renaissance Music and Experimental Science," *Journal of the History of Ideas* 31 (1970), pp. 483-500, revised as "Vincenzo Galilei and Galileo" in S. Drake, *Galileo Studies* (Ann Arbor: University of Michigan Press, 1970), pp. 43-62. See also D. P. Walker, *Studies in Musical Science in the Late Renaissance* (Studies of the Warburg Institute, Vol. 37, Leiden, E. J. Brill, 1978), pp. 14-33.

3. In English as the *Two New Sciences* (var. eds.); Antonio Favaro, ed., *Le Opere di Galileo Galilei*, 20 Vols. (Florence: Barbèra, 1890-1909), Vol. 8.

4. *Le Opere di Galileo Galilei*, Vol. 1.

5. In addition to the works cited in note 1, see W. L. Wisan, "The New Science of Motion: A Study of Galileo's *De motu locali*," *Archive for History of Exact Sciences* 13 (1974), pp. 103-306.

6. In English as the *Dialogue Concerning (on) the Two Chief (Great) Systems* (var. eds.); *Le Opere di Galileo Galilei*, Vol. 7.

7. Translated and edited by I. E. Drabkin, in I. E. Drabkin and S. Drake, *Galileo Galilei on Motion and on Mechanics* (Madison: University of Wisconsin Press, 1960). For the *De motu* see E. A. Moody, "Galileo and Avempace: the Dynamics of the Leaning Tower Experiment," *Journal of the History of Ideas* 12 (1951), pp. 163-193, 375-422; T. B. Settle, "Galileo's Use of Experiment"; R. Fredette, *Les De Motu 'plus anciens' de Galileo Galilei*, 2 Vols. (Ph.D. Thesis, Institute d'Etudes Médiévales, Université de Montréal, 1969); R. Fredette, "Galileo's *De motu antiquiora*," *Physis* 14 (1972), pp. 321-348.

8. Drabkin and Drake, *Galileo Galilei*, pp. 37-38.

9. T. B. Settle, "Galileo's Use of Experiment"; cited above; T. B. Settle, "on Normal and Extraordinary Science," *Vistas in Astronomy* 17 (1975), 105-111; R. Fredette, "Galileo's *De motu antiquiora*."

10. Drabkin and Drake, *Galileo Galilei*, p. 38.

11. Ibid., pp. 31n-32n.

12. Ibid., pp. 106-110.

13. C. B. Schmitt, "Experience and Experiment: A Comparison of Zabarella's View with Galileo's in *De Motu*," *Studies in the Renaissance* 16 (1969), pp. 80-138, esp. pp. 117-123. See also the comments of G. de Santillana, ed., *Dialogue on the Great World Systems* (Chicago: University of Chicago Press, 1953), pp. 27n-28n, 212n.

14. Galileo was a student at Pisa from 1581 to 1585. Borro taught at Pisa in the years 1553-1559, 1575-1582, and 1583-1586.

15. Hieronymus Borrius Arretinus, *De Motu Gravium & Levium* (Florence, Marescotti, 1575). On Borro (1512-1592) see: C. B. Schmitt, "The Faculty of Arts at Pisa at the Time of Galileo," *Physis* 14 (1972), 243-272; C. B. Schmitt, "Girolamo Borro's *Multae sunt Nostrarum Ignorationum Causae* (Ms. Vat. Ross. 1009)," in E. P. Mahoney, ed., *Philosophy and Humanism* (Leiden: E. J. Brill, 1976), pp. 462-476; C. B. Schmitt, "Borro, Girolamo," *Dictionary of Scientific Biography* 15 (1978), pp. 44-46; G. Stabile, "Borri (Borro, Borrius), Girolamo," *Dizionario Biografico degli Italiani* 13 (1971), pp. 13-17.

16. Borro, *De Motu*, p. 215. I am using the translation of C. B. Schmitt, "The Faculty of Arts at Pisa," p. 269.

17. Borro, *De Motu*, p. 215; C. B. Schmitt, "The Faculty of Arts at Pisa," p. 270.

18. Biblioteca Nazionale Centrale di Firenze: Ms. Magl. XVI. 126 & Ms. Conv. Soppr. B. 8. 1856 (cc. 1-46r); Domenico Moreni, ed., *Questione sull' Alchimia di Benedetto Varchi* (Florence: Magheri, 1827). On Varchi see: U. Pirotti, *Benedetto Varchi e la Cultura del suo Tempo* (Florence: Olschki, 1971).

19. Moreni, ed., *Questione sull' Alchimia de Benedetto Varchi*, pp. 32-34. Part of this

passage is published in Raffaello Caverni, *Storia del Metodo Sperimentale in Italia,* 6 Vols. (Florence: 1891-1900; reprinted: Bologna, Forni, 1970), Vol. 4, p. 270.

20. Giovanni Francesco Beato or Beati. Luigi Ferrari, *Onomasticon: Repertorio Bibliografico degli Scrittori Italiani dal 1501 ad 1850,* (Milan: Hoepli, 1947), p. 85, gives his dates as 1475-1547. See also G. M. Mazzuchelli, *Gli Scrittori d'Italia,* Vol. 2, Part 2 (Brescia: Bossini, 1760), pp. 569-570; E. Narducci, *Giunte all'Opera 'Gli Scrittori d'Italia' del Conte Giammaria Mazzuchelli* (Rome: Salviucci, 1884), 65; J. Quétif and J. Echard, *Scriptores Ordinis Praedicatorum,* Vol. 2 (New York: B. Franklin, 1959), p. 123.

21. For Ghini (1490-1556) see G. B. De Toni, "Luca Ghini," in A. Mieli, ed., *Gli Scienziati Italiani,* Vol. 1, Part 1 (Rome: Nardecchia, 1921), pp. 1-4; A. G. Keller, "Luca Ghini," *Dictionary of Scientific Biography,* 5 (1972), pp. 383-384; C. B. Schmitt, "The University of Pisa in the Renaissance," *History of Education* 3 (1974), pp. 3-17.

22. Fra Beato seems to have been in Padua as late as December 1543; see Narducci, *Giunte all'Opera.*

23. For Moletti (1531-1588) see A. Favaro, "Giuseppe Moletti," in A. Mieli, ed., *Gli Scienziati Italiani* Vol. 1, Part 1 (Rome, 1921), pp. 36-39; A. Favaro, "Amici e Corrispondenti di Galileo Galilei. XL. Giuseppe Moletti," *Atti del R. Istituto Veneto de Scienze, Lettere ed Arti,* Tome 77, Part 2 (1918), pp. 47-118.

24. Biblioteca Ambrosiana de Milano: Ms. S. 100 Sup. The exerpt that interests us is transcribed in Biblioteca Nazionale Centrale di Firenze: Ms. Gal. 329. And an excerpt of the latter is published in R. Caverni, cited above, Vol. 4, pp. 271-274.

25. Moletti came to Padua in 1577 from service at the Court of Mantua where he was tutor to Prince Vincenzo Gonzaga.

26. H. Doursther, *Dictionnaire Universel des Poids et Mesures Anciens et Modernes* (1840; reprint Amsterdam: Meridian, 1965), p. 379; the Venetian *passo* was about 1.74 meters.

27. R. Caverni, *Storia del Metodo Sperimentale,* Vol. 4, pp. 271-272.

28. For recent attempts to investigate Galileo's "Leaning Tower Experiments" see C. G. Adler and B. L. Coulter, "Aristotle: Villain or Victim?," *Physics Teacher* 13 (Jan., 1975), pp. 35-37; C. G. Adler and B. L. Coulter, "Quasi-History Revisited," *Physics Education* 14 (1979), pp. 398-399; B. L. Coulter and C. G. Adler, "Can a Body Pass a Body Falling through the Air?," *American Journal of Physics* 47 (Oct., 1979), pp. 841-846; G. Feinberg, "Fall of Bodies Near the Earth," *American Journal of Physics* 33 (June, 1965), pp. 501-502. See also B. M. Casper, "Galileo and the Fall of Aristotle: A Case of Historical Injustice?," *American Journal of Physics* 45 (Apr., 1977), pp. 325-330, for a further discussion of various aspects of the problem.

29. Galileo discusses these and other issues in the "First Day" of the *Discorsi.*

30. A full description and discussion of this experiment will appear elsewhere. A second experiment, with a different basic design, was performed recently by a group at the Polytechnic Institute of New York. It confirmed the results indicated below, and it too will be described separately.

31. Had Galileo used some sort of trap or mechanical release he might not have elicited the effect, but see the C. G. Adler and B. L. Coulter papers cited above. Other hand-hold positions seemed to offer difficulties in achieving simultaneous release.

32. This sequence is actually from the preliminary trials, before the recording of the data summarized above. It was chosen to illustrate an experimental run because of its photographic quality; the phenomena correspond to those in the recorded runs in every way.

33. The greater rebound comes from the effort of holding the heavier ball.

34. A full account of the complex network of engineers, artists, mathematicians, scholars, and others who knew each other and passed information around both by the written

word and in conversation remains to be written, but one can have some idea of the *ambiente* from many of the works cited above. In addition see L. Spezzaferro, "La Cultura del Cardinale Del Monte e il Primo Tempo del Caravaggio," *Storia dell'Arte* 9/10 (1971), pp. 57-92. Cardinal Francesco Maria del Monte was the brother of Guidubaldo del Monte (who figures importantly in this paper), friend and patron of Galileo, well placed in Paduan circles, and active on many technical and scientific fronts in Italy in this pre-Galilean period.

Chapter 2

Newton's Development of the *Principia*

Richard S. Westfall

By nature I am incurably empirical. Faced with the assignment to contribute to a book on the springs of scientific creativity, I turned spontaneously to a specific example. I offer no excuse, however, for I am convinced that the entire history of science affords no other example of a creative leap forward equal to that made by Newton in the period of two and a half years that culminated in the publication of the *Principia*. If we can find the springs of scientific creativity anywhere, surely we can find them here. If we cannot find them here, it is probably pointless to look further.

My topic is hardly new. I shall not need to tell you that I did not discover the *Principia*. It has been the object of extensive study ever since its initial publication, and its monumental significance is universally recognized. Nevertheless I do have a different story to tell. I shall be concerned, not with the structure and argument of the book, but with its history, how it reached the form in which it appeared. It is a compelling story of a creative genius at work, constantly expanding his conception of the work on which he was engaged. Aside from the early thoughts that Newton entertained about universal gravitation, the book went through three distinct phases, for which manuscript evidence survives, during the period I am concerned with here—in effect, three different works animated by three different concepts. I want to insist that what I have to say rests on a manuscript record. In no sense am I engaged in rational reconstruction. Historians must always interpret their evidence, of course, but the story I want to tell stands on a foundation of solid manuscript evidence, which I shall try to indicate as I proceed. It is also a story that is not confined to abstract intellectual development. Rather it concerns a living man engaged in the most intense endeavor, and without attention to the human dimension the narrative would be radically incomplete.

Newton's creative work during these months is intelligible only against the background of the problem with which he concerned himself. Let me go back as far as Kepler and his version of the heliocentric system. As Kepler perceived his situation, Tycho Brahe's destruction of the crystalline spheres was a fundamental reality. Kepler himself embodied their destruction in his ellipses. The crystalline spheres were more than abstract intellectual constructs. They had provided the physical structure of the universe, and with their destruction Kepler was left with the apparent fact that planets, in the immensity of space, without visible support or assistance, follow the same paths in eternal repetition. How is it possible that they do so? This question provided the thread of Ariadne that guided Kepler through the maze of planetary astronomy. He couched the answer he devised to it in terms of Aristotelian mechanics at the very time when the Aristotelian science of mechanics was being outmoded. Later answers to the same question employed the new mechanics. Central to the new mechanics was the principle of inertia, enunciated early in the seventeenth century by the combined efforts of Galileo and Descartes. Despite their insight, the establishment of the principle of inertia involved a more complicated history than is usually understood. As it appears to me, its final establishment was one aspect of Newton's endeavor in the period that I am examining in this paper, and flowed directly from his solution to the problem Kepler left.

Meanwhile another aspect of the new science of mechanics, its understanding of circular motion, was more obviously involved in that problem. For Kepler, if a planet moves at all it moves in a closed orbit. With the new mechanics, rectilinear motion became primary while circular motion became a resultant of rectilinear motions and tendencies. Problems with the conceptualization of circular motion nevertheless remained. There was something in circular motion inherently similar to rest. A spinning top can turn forever on its own axis without disturbing bodies around it any more than the same top at rest. Similarly a body moving in a circular orbit always maintains the same relation to the center about which it turns. From such perceptions emerged the idea of circular motion as an implicit equilibrium. A body constrained to move in a circle, seventeenth-century students of mechanics said, tends to recede from the center. Christiaan Huygens coined the phrase "centrifugal force," literally force fleeing the center, to express this tendency. It was understood by Huygens and by everyone else that if a body does in fact move in a circle, the centrifugal force must be opposed. Hence a body in circular motion was looked upon as a body in equilibrium exactly like one lying on a table where its tendency to fall toward the center of the earth is held in equilibrium by the table. Huygens proceeded beyond coining a name and gave a quantitative measure to the force, and the publication of his work in 1673 opened the way to a new assault on the cosmic problem posed by Kepler. Newton was one who defined the problem in the new terms. He was by no means the only one to define it so.

One of the best known Newtonian stories—the one about the fall of an apple, which led him to begin speculating on how far the force of gravity extends—belongs to a period approximately twenty years before the composition of the *Principia.* In his old age, Newton told the story to at least four different people, and the incident may indeed have occurred. To it historians have joined an autobiographical passage, describing the same early period of discovery, which asserted that when he began to think of gravity extending to the moon he compared the force holding the moon in its orbit with the force of gravity at the surface of the earth and found them to "answer pretty nearly."[1] From these combined sources have emerged the myth of Newton's twenty-year delay in publishing the *Principia* and theories to explain the delay. Although the story falls well before the period with which I am primarily concerned, I shall briefly start my consideration of Newton at this point. He had taken his Bachelor's degree less than a year before. While an undergraduate, he had discovered the literature of the new natural philosophy, the writings of Descartes, Galileo, and others, and within this literature the new science of mechanics. For a time, he had turned his attention to it. Within the mechanical philosophy of nature, impact was the only recognized means by which one body might influence another. Descartes had defined the centrality of impact but had bungled his own attempt to state its laws. While he was still an undergraduate, Newton attacked the problem and pursued it to the conclusion that the common center of gravity of an isolated system of two bodies in motion will remain in an inertial state whether or not the two bodies meet in impact.[2] He proceeded to circular motion, and applying his understanding of impact to a body moving inside a circular wall against which it bounces, he succeeded

Plate 1. Newton in 1689. Portrait by Sir Godfrey Kneller. Courtesy of Lord Portsmouth and the Trustees of the Portsmouth Estates.

SIR ISAAC NEWTON
Painted by
Sir Godfrey Kneller.
1702

Plate 2. Newton in 1702. Portrait by Sir Godfrey Kneller. Courtesy of the Trustees of the National Portrait Gallery.

in deriving the same quantitative law of centrifugal force (a name he did not, of course, use), which Huygens would publish eight or nine years later in the *Horologium*.[3]

Two other papers from this period applied the quantitative measure of centrifugal force to questions related to the cosmic problem. One of the papers took up an issue raised in Galileo's *Dialogue*: would the centrifugal effects of the earth's rotation throw bodies off its surface? Newton's calculation showed that gravity as measured by a pendulum is about three hundred times greater than the centrifugal force at the equator.[4] As far as Newton was concerned, Galileo's argument with opponents of a moving earth had long been settled; nevertheless, his calculation showed that their objection contained no substance. In the second paper, Newton substituted the ratio of Kepler's third law into his formula for centrifugal force and found that the centrifugal forces of the planets vary inversely as the squares of their distances from the sun. He went on in the same paper to compare the moon's centrifugal force with gravity at the surface of the earth. Since he set the moon's distance at sixty terrestrial radii, an inverse square relation would have yielded a ratio of 3600; he obtained instead a ratio of a bit over 4000. As we now know, and as he later discovered, he was using an incorrect figure for the size of the earth.[5] I am convinced that the paper in question is what Newton had in mind when he wrote more than fifty years later that he found the two to answer pretty nearly. At any rate, I shall examine it under that assumption. The first thing one notices is that the paper did not contain the idea of universal gravitation. Quite the contrary, it spoke of the tendencies of bodies in orbit to recede from the center. Nevertheless, it appears to me that Newton must have had some inchoate idea at the back of his mind. It is a strange comparison to have carried out, finding the ratio between the tendency of one body to recede from a center and that of another to approach it. As I say, it appears to me that he must have had some idea in his mind to make such a comparison, for he did remember the paper years later and at that time considered it to have marked an important step in his own development. But the idea, whatever it was, was only partially formed. It required time to mature, and fortunately Newton had the time.

After his early explorations of mechanics, Newton did not, as far as we know, touch the subject for more than a decade. Late in 1679, he unexpectedly received a letter from Robert Hooke which started a brief correspondence about the path of a falling body on the surface of the earth. Since Newton, who introduced the topic, treated the path as a segment of the longer curve the body would follow if the earth itself offered no resistance and motion continued beneath its surface, they effectively converted the problem of fall into the problem of orbital motion. In his first letter, Newton blundered and treated the path as a spiral that ended at the center of the earth. Hooke corrected him with explicit reference to his own theory of orbital motion, to wit, that orbital motion is compounded from a tangential motion and an attraction toward the center. Flustered by the correction, something he never enjoyed, Newton blundered a second time; he drew the shape of an orbit under the assumption that gravity is constant, only to receive from Hooke a second reply that he considered gravity to vary inversely as the square of the distance.[6] That letter formed the basis of Hooke's later charge of plagiarism. Remembering his early paper in which he had derived the inverse-square relation from Kepler's third law, and recognizing in Hooke's letter the lack of a solid foundation for the assertion, Newton always refused to consider that Hooke had any claim whatever.

Concentrating on the inverse square law, both of them neglected the other aspect of the correspondence, which appears more important to me, Hooke's conception of orbital motion. As far as we know, Hooke was the first one to reformulate the conception of circular motion in order to state it as we now do—i.e., to consider it, not as an equilibrium, but as a disequilibrium in which an unbalanced force continually deflects a body from its rectilinear path and holds it in a closed orbit. No one, including Newton, had conceived orbital motion in such terms before. The correspondence of 1679-1680 proved to be a permanent lesson for him; he later embodied it in his term "centripetal force," force seeking the center, which he coined in conscious correction of Huygens's earlier phrase. Meanwhile, according to his own assertion, the correspondence with Hooke led Newton early in 1680 to demonstrate that motion in an ellipse entails an inverse square force toward one focus. As Proposition XI, the demonstration later served as one of the foundation stones of the *Principia.*

We must not, however, mistakenly equate the demonstration of 1680 with the concept of universal gravitation. We know that roughly a year later Newton exchanged several letters with John Flamsteed, the Astronomer Royal, about the great comet of 1680-1681.[7] As far as Newton was concerned, one should rather say great comets. In November 1680 one had appeared in the eastern sky just before dawn and had moved toward the sun until it disappeared. About two weeks later another comet which moved away from the sun appeared in the western sky after sunset. Flamsteed insisted that the two were a single comet which reversed its direction nearly 180° in the vicinity of the sun. Unfortunately he dressed his theory up in a fantastic physics that had the comet turn short of the sun; Newton was bound to reject such an arrangement. What is most interesting, however, is the fact that he also refused to see Flamsteed's proposal as an instance of the orbital mechanics he had worked out only a year earlier; hence he did not at that time believe that the two appearances belonged to a single comet. It was generally accepted that comets were bodies foreign to the solar system; as such they might not be subject to attractions between the sun and the planets. It appears to me that Newton applied such reasoning. Whatever his reasoning, the correspondence with Flamsteed shows that in 1681 he had not yet adopted the idea of universal gravitation.

All of the above serves as background for the fateful period of thirty months that began with a visit from Edmond Halley in August 1684. Halley had previously engaged in a conversation with Christopher Wren and Robert Hooke about the shape of the orbit that a body in an inverse-square force field would follow. One should not neglect to notice the significance of that conversation; as I suggested earlier, the problem central to the *Principia* was defining itself in a number of minds. The conversation in London had not reached any conclusion, however, and Halley now put the same question to Newton. The orbit would be an ellipse, Newton replied immediately. How did he know? He had calculated it. Could Halley see the calculation? Recalling his blunders in 1679-1680 when he replied too hastily to Hooke, Newton pretended that he could not find the paper, but he did accede to Halley's request that he work out the demonstration anew and send it to him.[8] As a result, about three months later, Halley received a nine-page treatise that is universally known by a name it did not carry, *De motu.* The treatise embodied the first of the three stages through which the *Principia* progressed during the period that I am considering.

Already upon its dispatch to Halley, the process from which the ultimate work appeared—the process of steady expansion as Newton perceived ever deeper levels of meaning in his original conceptions—was at work. One cannot fully appreciate that process without considering aspects of Newton's personal history. During the fifteen years prior to Halley's visit, Newton had not concerned himself much with the topics on which his enduring reputation stands. He had, it is true, worked some at mathematics, though only spasmodically, with decreasing frequency, and mostly as a result of external stimuli. He had devoted himself to optics only to the extent of preparing earlier work for presentation to the Royal Society in two different papers and in the correspondence they provoked. Except for the correspondence with Hooke, he had not concerned himself with mechanics at all. Meanwhile two other topics far removed from these, alchemy and theology, had dominated his attention. Something about the question Halley raised grasped his interest, however. It did more than grasp. It seized him and refused to let him go.

From Newton's Cambridge years there survived a number of stories about the strange fellow who lived beside the great gate of Trinity College. We know that some of them came from the period of the *Principia's* composition; it is likely that many of the others did. He would set out for dinner in the hall, take a wrong turn, find himself out on the street, and, forgetting where he had intended to go, return to his chamber. When he did make it to the hall, he would show up dishevelled and dressed in the wrong gown, and then he was apt to sit lost in thought while the meal on his plate sat untouched. When other fellows of the college walked in the gardens, they would discover strange geometric diagrams drawn in the gravel, diagrams all the stranger to an unambitious group who preferred to avoid even simple sums. Be it said in their favor, however, that they were as awed by their strange peer as they were amused, and they carefully walked around the diagrams so as to leave them undisturbed. The thirty months following Halley's visit are a virtual blank in Newton's life. Almost no correspondence from the period survives, and what little does exist, with one exception, devotes itself to the work in progress.

Early in February 1685, Charles II died; the city fathers of Cambridge proclaimed James II King of England at a number of places throughout the city, one of them immediately ouside Newton's chamber. The crisis implied by James's succession took two years to reach Cambridge, almost precisely the time that Newton required to complete his book. In the spring of 1687, an abstracted don, who had consistently held himself aloof from the university, but who was newly released from his long period of steady concentration, emerged as a leader of the university's resistance to James's effort to Catholicize it. As a result, Newton eventually found himself translated to London and an office in the Royal Mint. In fact the *Principia*, the completion of which was the preliminary to these events, changed his life even more. For twenty years Newton had been littering his chamber with unfinished treatises—on mathematics, mechanics, optics, alchemy, theology. It is difficult to assess the work in alchemy, but in all the other fields at least he had taken immense strides. Yet he had so far completed almost nothing. This time the problem refused to release him and carried him through to its completion, changing a life of tentative endeavor into one of magnificent achievement.

De motu, the first stage of the work, was a treatise on orbital dynamics based on the principle of a central attraction. From the principle it succeeded in extracting dynamic demonstrations of all of Kepler's three laws.[9] The very essence of the process that I am describing, the steady unfolding of new meaning as Newton peered more deeply into the principles with which he began, meant that *De motu* could not be a final product.

Even as he sent it off to Halley in London, Newton was already at work revising it. Two major developments emerged as he worked over *De motu.* The first of these was the perfection of Newton's basic dynamics. One cannot over-emphasize the crudity of the dynamic foundation on which the brilliant results of *De motu* rested. The treatise employed two basic concepts, inherent force and impressed force, and the content of the dynamics it proposed lay in the interaction of the two forces. "I call that by which a body endeavors to persevere in its motion in a right line the force of a body or the force inherent in a body," Newton stated. That is, the first stage of the *Principia,* the book that stated the principle of inertia as the first law of motion, employed as one of its fundamental elements a conception of motion directly contrary to the principle of inertia, a conception which held that uniform rectilinear motion is the product of a force internal to the body in motion. Impressed force, the other element in his dynamics at this time, was an external action that changes a body's state of motion. Orbital motion resulted from the interaction of the two forces; the parallelogram of forces was *De motu's* central dynamic device to relate the two. The problem with the dynamics of the treatise lay in the fact that via the parallelogram he was trying to compound different entities, a force that maintains uniform motion (measured by mv) and a force that alters uniform motion (measured by ma). Indeed the difficulties of the treatise were increased by the fact that it employed two different concepts of the second force. To derive the area law, Newton used the concept of a series of impulses. As he stated it, the force "acts with a single but great impulse" at equal intervals of time. Such forces are measured by Δmv. Other theorems employed continuous forces that continually divert a moving body from its rectilinear path, forces that are, of course, measured by *ma*.

It is beyond the range of this paper to treat in detail all of the changes that Newton introduced into his dynamics as he revised *De motu.* I have in any case written about them at excessive length elsewhere.[10] The essence of the change appears to me to have been associated with the principle of inertia. As he refined his dynamics, Newton confronted the riddle of circular motion. He was working with the concept that the inherent force internal to a body is the product of the external forces that have acted upon it. As long as he confined himself to rectilinear motion, this concept raised no problems. With circular motion, however, the problems became insoluble. In our terms, in circular motion the continuous action of a uniform force performs no work. In Newton's terms, in circular motion the continuous action of a uniform external force, which is necessary to divert a body from its rectilinear path, produces no increase in its linear speed, the measure of the body's internal force. Newton eventually resolved the problem by embracing the principle of inertia. He now recognized that circular motion is a uniformly accelerated motion, dynamically equivalent to the motion that had hitherto appeared to be its antithesis, uniformly accelerated motion in a straight line. Since the time of Galileo and Descartes, only Christiaan Huygens had understood inertia without ambiguity and embraced it fully; others had employed concepts similar to Newton's inherent force, which in many contexts, though not in circular motion, was surprisingly similar to the principle of inertia. It appears correct to insist that only with this development in Newton's dynamics, which occurred in the early months of 1685 and determined the form of the laws of motion in the *Principia,* was inertia established as the prevailing concept of motion.

With the principle of inertia in hand, the rest of his mature dynamics fell quickly into place. Newton did not eliminate inherent force from his dynamics. It is still to be found as Definition III of the published *Principia,* and he still conceived of dynamics as the interaction of inherent force with impressed force, an interaction finally embodied in his third law of motion. Inherent force had undergone a change, however. Whereas in *De motu* it maintained a body's uniform motion, it now operated as a resistance to change that established a constant proportion between an impressed force and the change in motion it produces.[11] We have forgotten the existence of this strange force and no longer realize that it remains buried in our concept of mass. Hence we avoid the paradox it contains, the paradox of a force latent in matter which manifests itself solely when external forces attempt to alter a body's state of rest. Newton embodied the paradox in another phrase we have also forgotten, *vis inertiae,* which we might translate freely as the activity of inactivity.

The second major development that belonged to the period of *De motu* concerned the nature of the attraction it employed. The attractive force of *De motu* was not yet universal gravitation. To be sure, Newton was flirting with the idea. Initially he called the attraction "gravity," though he then went back through the treatise changing that word everywhere to the neutral term "centripetal attraction." Already in December he was writing to John Flamsteed for information about Jupiter and Saturn in conjunction and about comets, inquiries that seem to look toward universal gravitation. On the other hand, neither the first nor the second draft of *De motu* contained a correlation of the moon's orbit with the measured acceleration of gravity, the cornerstone of the final argument for universal gravitation.

Moreover, other elements in papers associated with *De motu* confirm what the absence of the correlation implies. The quantity of a body, he stated in a paper of definitions that followed the third draft of the tract, is calculated "from the bulk of the corporeal matter which is usually proportional to its weight." The statement is incompatible with Newton's final concept of universal gravitation. Indeed Newton went on at the time to underline this fact by suggesting a device by which to compare the quantity of matter in two bodies of equal weight. Hang them on pendulums of equal length; their quantities of matter will be inversely proportional to the number of oscillations they make in equal time. Newton crossed the passage out and beside it entered the following note: "When experiments were carefully made with gold, silver, lead, glass, sand, common salt, water, wood, and wheat, however, they resulted always in the same number of oscillations."[12] Then he realized that an analogous experiment was being carried out constantly in the heavens. If the planets obey Kepler's third law, the sun must attract them in exact proportion to their quantities of matter. Moreover, since Jupiter's satellites also obey Kepler's third law, Jupiter must attract them in the same proportion, and since they maintain concentric orbits around Jupiter, the sun must attract both them and Jupiter in proportion to their quantities of matter.

Now at last Newton was ready to explore the full implications of an idea which had been vaguely present in his mind for twenty years. There is no indication that anyone in Trinity College realized something exceptional was transpiring beside the great gate, but in the early months of 1685 the concept of universal gravitation silently unfolded before Newton's gaze. Apparently it occurred very near the time when Samuel Newton, Alderman of Cambridge, was proclaiming James Stuart King of England outside Isaac Newton's chamber.

Clearly an idea as grandiose as universal gravitation demanded more than a nine-page tract to expound it. During the following eight or nine months, Newton expanded *De motu* into a treatise in two books, in all approximately ten times as long, to which he affixed the title *De motu corporum*. It is sometimes referred to as the *Lectiones de motu* since Newton later deposited the manuscript in the university library as the text of his lectures for the years 1684, 1685, and 1687.[13] The statutes of the Lucasian chair demanded the deposit of texts for ten lectures delivered each year. At this time Cambridge was going through a catastrophic decline, one aspect of which was the conversion of professorships to sinecures. Newton proved to be as susceptible as other professors to the mores of the times. After 1687 he never lectured again, as far as surviving evidence indicates; he continued to draw the income from the chair for five years after he had departed from Cambridge. In the late eighties he simply took the manuscript of the second stage of the *Principia,* after it had been supplanted, wrote dates in the margins at suitable intervals, and deposited it as the text of lectures. He did not even bother to put the papers in order, and at one point the series of dates advances unconcerned through two successive drafts of the same material. Not all of this second stage of the *Principia* survives, but enough does that we can comprehend its nature.

Whereas *De motu* was a treatise on orbital dynamics, *De motu corporum* was a demonstration of the concept of universal gravitation. It subsumed the orbital dynamics, of course, and to it added several new elements. One of these was the demonstration that a homogeneous sphere attracts every body outside it with a force directly proportional to the mass of the sphere and inversely proportional to the square of the distance from the center of the sphere. The demonstration revealed an incredible parallel, itself embodying the principle of universal gravitation, which Newton did not fail to notice: a composite homogeneous sphere made up of particles that attract with forces that vary inversely as the square of the distance attracts by the same law as do its particles.[14] Only with this demonstration did the correlation between the moon and the measured acceleration of gravity become valid, and the application of the word "gravity" (or "gravitas") to the centripetal accelerations demonstrated to exist in the heavens rested directly on the correlation.

The internal logic of the new treatise also required that Newton address himself to the mutuality of attractions. The basic propositions of orbital dynamics derived Kepler's three laws from the assumption of an unmoved central attraction. If universal gravitation was a reality, this assumption had to be false. Newton approached the issue first through the two body problem, in effect the sun and one planet. He demonstrated that the mutual attraction between the two does not upset strict conformance to Kepler's laws. Throughout this section of the work, Kepler's laws functioned as the empirical standard to which theory had to conform. Newton went on to develop formulas for the periods and principal axes of ellipses in the case of mutual attraction in comparison to those that hold when equal forces attract toward an unmoved center.[15] Manifestly, however, the two-body problem did not dispose of the objection. Empirical reality consists not of a sun circled by one planet but (to speak of the solar system alone) a sun circled by six planets, three of which were then known to have satellites circling them. If the theory of universal gravitation was in fact true, all of these bodies had to attract each other. Would not their mutual attractions upset the observed facts of Kepler's three laws?

A full solution of the many-body problem proved to be beyond Newton's reach. As we now know, it is impossible. Nevertheless, he did succeed in developing an analysis of the three-body problem which served as the foundation of a convincing answer to the question posed. This analysis he expounded in Proposition XXXV (later renumbered XXXVI, by which I shall refer to it, and corresponding to Proposition LXVI of the published work). Let S be a large central body circled by two planets, P and Q. (See Figure 1.) The goal of the analysis is to determine what disturbance the outer planet Q causes in the orbit of the inner planet P. Let the attraction be expressed by the line LQ. KQ, the mean distance of the planet P from Q, furnishes the metric of the analysis. When P is at distance KQ, the attraction of Q equals KQ. Since the force varies inversely as the square of the distance, the attraction will be greater than KQ when the planet is closer (as it is in the diagram) and less when it is farther removed. Newton proceeded by analyzing LQ into two components, LM parallel to PS, and MQ parallel to SQ. Since LM is radial, it does not upset the description of areas in proportion to time. When it is

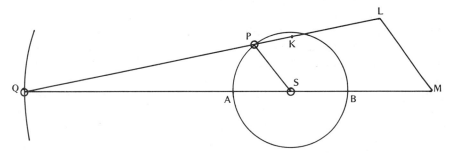

Figure 1: Newton's original diagram for the three body problem.

added to the attraction that S exerts on P, however, that force is no longer exactly proportional to the inverse square of the distance. Hence the presence of component LM must destroy the perfect ellipticity of P's orbit.

Since the component MQ is neither radial nor inversely proportional to the square of the distance, it must upset both the first and the second laws of Kepler. The effect of MQ is largely offset, however, by the fact that Q also attracts S. Only the part MS, by which MQ differs from SQ, operates to perturb the orbit. Under what conditions, Newton asked, would the perturbations introduced by the presence of Q be minimal? When distances are large and angles small, he replied, so that MS is minimal in relation to the attraction of S on P (which is of course not measured by the line SP in this diagram). But especially, he added, it is the mutuality of attraction whereby the force MQ is effectively reduced to MS, the very universality that introduced the problem in the first place, that keeps perturbations at a minimum. Thus Newton concluded Proposition XXXVI with a single corollary which embodied the principal conclusion of his analysis. If several planets revolve about a great central body, "the motion of the innermost revolving body P is least disturbed by the attractions of the others, when the great body is attracted and agitated by the others equally in proportion to weights and distances and they by each other."[16] That is, in a world such as ours is, Kepler's laws cannot hold exactly, but they can be closely approximated, so closely indeed that in most cases the perturbations lie below the threshold of observation as it stood in Newton's day.

No stage of the *Principia* was composed in such a way that every line in it contributed to a single logical plan. *De motu* set out initially to be a treatise on orbital mechanics, but before he completed it Newton saw a way to treat motion through a resisting medium and consequently added two propositions on that topic which did not have a close connection with the rest of the tract. Apparently he expanded that aspect of the work considerably in *De motu corporum.* This part of the second stage does not survive, but in Book II there is a reference to a Proposition LXXII, which can be identified from the content with Proposition XXII of Book II in the published version. Proposition XXII is the next to the last one in Section V, Book II, which treats the pressure in the atmosphere that is caused by the earth's attraction of the air. The preceding four sections in published Book II all concern themselves with motion through resisting media; they have no real connection with the argument for universal gravitation although they constitute a considerable step forward for the science of mechanics. It is reasonable to assume that at this point Newton had composed what later constituted the first five sections of Book II. If we do make that assumption, we can then account with assurance for all but four of the preceding fifty propositions in Book I of *De motu corporum.*

With the discarded manuscript for Book I, Newton also deposited an incomplete copy of Book II as the text of lectures, in this case for 1687. After his death, a complete manuscript was found among his papers and published under the title *De mundi systemate.* An English translation of it appears at the end of the Cajori edition of the *Principia,* the one in common use throughout the English-speaking world. From various pieces of evidence that I shall not try to state here, it appears to have been composed in the autumn of 1685. It consisted of a prose essay on the subject later given it as a title, the system of the world, an essay which established first the necessity of attractive forces, then the necessity of inverse square attractive forces, and finally the necessity of a single inverse square attractive force which arises, he said, "from the universal nature of matter."[17] The book went on briefly to suggest further possibilities that this conclusion raised. One short paragraph, devoid of quantitative details, suggested that this force might explain the inequalities of the moon's motion; a second paragraph, equally free of quantitative details, further suggested that it might predict new, as yet unobserved, inequalities. Two other paragraphs, which also lacked any details, added that it might explain the tides and the precession of the equinoxes. The book then closed with a long essay on comets which failed to reduce any observed comet to a conic orbit.

In fact Book II of *De motu corporum* never existed in the form I have just described. Even before he completed it, Newton began to transform it. He cancelled the paragraph on the tides before he had had time to compose the following ones, and for it he substituted a greatly expanded treatment substantially identical to that in the published *Principia.* In the manuscript we can see the analysis take shape before our eyes. Most of the manuscript is in the hand of Humphrey Newton, Isaac Newton's amanuensis, but several times, in difficult passages, Newton himself took the pen to complete sentences or paragraphs. In the expanded discussion he referred to the twenty-two corollaries of Proposition XXXVI. The surviving version of Proposition XXXVI has a single corollary (which I quoted above). The twenty-one new ones, which we know from Proposition LXVI of the published *Principia,* constitute the very heart of the transformation of the work into its third and final form.

The new corollaries reversed the intent of the proposition almost exactly. In version three of *De motu,* when he had referred briefly to the perturbations in orbits arising from the mutual attraction of all the bodies in the solar system, Newton had offered the opinion that reducing them to exact calculation "exceeds, unless I am mistaken, the force of the entire human intellect."[18] He now began to see that perhaps it did not exceed the entire human intellect after all. With the new corollaries, he could use a proposition, developed originally to argue that most perturbations are extremely small, to subject certain perturbations to exact calculation. He changed the diagram. The great central body became T (for *Terra*) and the outer planet S (for *Sol*), thus creating the anomaly of a geocentric diagram in the work that supplied the dynamic foundation for the heliocentric system. (Figure 2.) Perhaps he could have altered the letter of the inner planet to L (for *Luna*), but he left it as P, probably because it

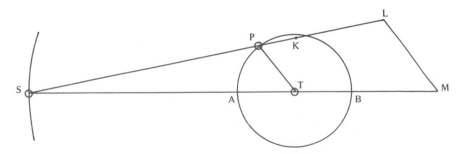

Figure 2: The diagram for the three body problem as it appears in the *Principia.*

functioned in his analysis as several things, not only as the moon, but also as a ring of water or of solid matter around the earth. The new corollaries that applied to the moon became the basis of a lunar theory that did indeed explain the observed inequalities of the lunar motion and propose new ones. Those that considered a ring of water furnished the explanation of the tides, and those concerned with a ring of solid matter reduced the precession of the equinoxes to exact calculation. That is, the new corollaries looked forward to a final work radically different from the one he had written.

Other changes in Book I looked in the same direction. He composed what became Section IX, in which he employed the perturbing attraction of the sun to explain the progressive motion of the lunar apsides. An interesting note connected with the last demonstration reveals the extent to which Newton understood what a new departure he was undertaking. The demonstration was both a triumph and a failure. It was a triumph in proposing the cause of a phenomenon long known but never explained. Alas, the calculated motion of the line of apsides came to only one half the observed amount. Newton could not bring himself to admit his failure and published the calculation without comment. Manifestly he regarded the lunar theory as incomplete. It was one of the last things he added before publication; no doubt he expected to remove the discrepancy with further work. Lunar theory was indeed the major topic on which he worked in the period between the first and second editions, but the line of apsides still resisted his efforts. Only in the third edition did he finally add a brief comment that the observed motion is about twice as great as the one he had calculated.

The changes that I have been describing probably belonged to the winter of 1685-1686. They included other additions to Book I beyond those I have mentioned. As a result the book was becoming excessively long. Newton decided to divide it in two, so that the entire work would contain three books, and in April 1686 he dispatched the manuscript of Book I (in the final numbering scheme) to the Royal Society. From Halley, who not only had a personal connection with the work because of his original visit to Cambridge but also was Secretary of the Royal Society, he received a reply in two paragraphs. The first contained praise as lavish as any man might ever need to hear. The second reported Hooke's claim on the concepts central to the book. It is typical of Newton that he concentrated exclusively on the second paragraph. For three weeks he simultaneously nourished his anger and fed upon it, and then, appropriately for the man who had just defined the mathematics of orbital motion, he went into orbit himself:

Now is not this very fine? Mathematicians that find out, settle & do all the business must content themselves with being nothing but dry calculators & drudges & another that does nothing but pretend & grasp at all things must carry away all the invention as well of those that were to follow him as of those that went before. . . . And why should I record a man for an Invention who founds his claim upon an error therein & on that score gives me trouble? He imagins he obliged me by telling me his Theory, but I thought my self disobliged by being upon his own mistake corrected magisterially & taught a Theory wᶜʰ every body knew & I had a truer notion of then himself. Should a man who thinks himself knowing, & loves to shew it in correcting & instructing others, come to you when you are busy, & nothwithstanding your excuse, press discourses upon you & through his own mistakes correct you & multiply discourses & then make this use of it, to boast that he taught you all he spake & oblige you to acknowledge it & cry out injury & injustice if you do not, I beleive you would think him a man of a strange unsociable temper. . . . Philosophy [he lamented, with a cry of anguish] is such an impertinently litigious Lady that a man had as good be engaged in Law suits as have to do with her.[19]

He concluded his complaint by threatening to suppress Book III.

Since Halley talked him out of the threat immediately, I cannot believe that Newton ever meant it seriously. As I read the situation, all that Hooke expected from him was some sort of acknowledgment in the preface. As it happened, one of the last changes that Newton had introduced into the concluding book had been a laudatory mention of Hooke in its introductory passages. Newton now returned to his manuscript and cancelled the reference. Acknowledge Hooke? Not likely. He went through the manuscript cancelling other references to Hooke as well, although he later had to reinsert his name into the discussion of comets where he used some of Hooke's observations of the comet of 1680-1681 that he could not replace from other sources. To the introduction to Book III he also added a passage that indicated that he had originally composed the book in a popular form; "but afterwards, considering that such as had not sufficiently entered into the principles could not easily discern the strength of the consequences, nor lay aside the prejudices to which they had been many years accustomed, therefore, to prevent the disputes which might be raised upon such accounts, I chose to reduce the substance of this Book into the form of Propositions (in the mathematical way), which should be read by those only who had first made themselves masters of the principles established in the preceding Books."[20] Years later he told his friend William Derham that he had deliberately made the *Principia* difficult in order to avoid "being baited by little Smatterers in Mathematicks."[21]

In both cases it appears obvious that Newton had Hooke in mind. But Newton's account will not do. It is true that he recast the form of the final book into the mathematical language of propositions, lemmas, and the like. If one compares the original form of the book with the corresponding parts of the published form, however, he is bound to conclude that the change was purely cosmetic. The first eighteen propositions of Book III plus the general discussion of comets, the parts involved, still remained a prose essay on the system of the world. The abstruse mathematics in Book III appeared in the new additions, and as I have just argued, the alterations that prepared the way for these additions were already under way before Newton's outburst.

He introduced analogous changes in the new Book II. The parts of it composed earlier had consisted mostly of the abstract mathematical description of motion through any resistance. As I have indicated, these passages had no close relation to the central arguments of the *Principia.* He now added four new sections devoted to the physics of the material world. Two of them examined the origin of resistance in material media and the resistance that such media must offer to projectiles. One derived the velocity of sound in the air from first principles of dynamics, and the last considered the dynamics of vortices. The velocity of sound, though it was one of the master strokes of the *Principia,* was another sideshow to the central theme. The other three new sections all made use of mathematical physics to destroy the validity of the Cartesian system. On the one hand Newton demonstrated—at least to his own satisfaction—that the heavens must be void, or so close to void as to be indistinguishable from it. On the other hand he demonstrated that a vortex can neither yield Kepler's laws nor sustain itself without some source that constantly supplies new motion.

In its final stage, the *Principia* proposed much more than the law of universal gravitation. It still embodied that law, of course, just as it still embodied the orbital dynamics of *De motu.* It had expanded, however, into a general mathematical science of dynamics to which he now gave the title, not *De motu corporum,* but *Philosophiae naturalis principia mathematica.* As its most central feature it presented a new ideal of science. It was not Newton who proposed that science is essentially the mathematical description of phenomena. Kepler, Galileo, and Huygens, to name only Newton's most distinguished predecessors in this respect, had already firmly established this characteristic of modern science. With them, however, mathematical description had been confined to ideal entities and systems, and they had avoided or ignored the complications of physical reality. When Galileo brought up the question of friction, for example, he asserted that "no firm science" is possible in regard to such factors "which are variable in infinitely many ways. Hence to deal with such matters scientifically, it is necessary to abstract from them. We must find and demonstrate conclusions abstracted from the impediments, in order to make use of them in practice under those limitations that experience will teach."[22] With the final stage of the *Principia,* Newton transcended confinement to ideal situations. He extended the meaning of "science" beyond the ideal case and made it apply as well to the exact extent to which the physical world fails to conform to the ideal. This was a new program for science, one without any serious precedent. It appears to me to be the ultimate foundation of the *Principia's* enduring influence. The concept of universal gravitation was a monumental generalization; on a public unschooled in science it could and did exert a dramatic impact. For the scientific community, the new ideal of science was more important. It rapidly came to define their activity during the eighteenth century; it continues to do so today.

What then can one conclude about the springs of scientific creativity from this concrete example? In his old age, Newton was asked how he had discovered the law of universal gravitation. "By thinking on it continually," was his succinct reply.[23] On another occasion he described his procedure, not with sole reference to the law of universal gravitation, in similar terms: "I keep the subject constantly before me, and wait 'till the first dawnings open slowly, by little and little, into a full and clear light."[24] The two statements do seem to me to offer accurate descriptions of the process I have tried to describe. Central to it was incredibly intensive concentration sustained some thirty months. As he probed the orbital dynamics with which he began, Newton uncovered ever deeper levels of meaning, first the law of universal gravitation, then a new ideal of science itself. One thinks inevitably of Wordsworth's lines inspired by the statue in the Trinity College chapel:

> The marble index of a mind for ever
> Voyaging through strange seas of Thought, alone.

I would not care to offer his example as a universal pattern. Human nature appears essentially diverse and multifarious to me. With other men I would expect other stories, and while I did begin with the assertion that the case I have described has no equal, I do not in any sense intend to deny the phrase "scientific creativity" to other examples. I note with approval that the organizers of this volume gave it the title, not "The Spring of Scientific Creativity" but the "Springs." In Newton's case, as in others, no one would wish to leave out the role of sheer genius. Nevertheless it appears to me that what made his genius productive was a rare capacity for sustained concentration which allowed him, in the brief period of two and a half years, to move science forward through the greatest single stride it has ever experienced.

Notes

1. Cambridge University Library, *Add. MS. 3968.41*, f.85.

2. John Herivel, *The Background to Newton's 'Principia,'* (Oxford: Clarendon Press, 1965), pp. 133-79. Herivel prints the text of Newton's investigation, which is what I am citing.

3. Ibid., pp. 129-31.

4. Ibid., pp. 183-8.

5. Ibid., pp. 193-5.

6. *The Correspondence of Isaac Newton,* ed. H. W. Turnbull, J. F. Scott, A. R. Hall, and L. Tilling, 7 vols. (London: Cambridge Univ. Press, 1959-1977), 2, pp. 297-313.

7. Ibid., 2, pp. 340-367.

8. The best account of the visit is found in a memorandum about Newton by Abraham DeMoivre, which is in the Joseph Halle Schaffner Collection, University of Chicago Library.

9. Herivel, *Background,* pp. 257-74.

10. R. S. Westfall, *Force in Newton's Physics* (London: MacDonald and Co., 1971), pp. 424-56.

11. *Principia,* trans. Andrew Motte and Florian Cajori, (Berkeley: Univ. of Calif. Press, (1934), p. 2.

12. Herivel, *Background,* pp. 306 and 316-317. Herivel has misplaced the correction as though it belonged with another manuscript.

13. Cambridge University Library, *Dd. 4.18* and *Dd. 9.46.*

14. *The Mathematical Papers of Isaac Newton,* ed. D. T. Whiteside, 8 vols. (Cambridge: Cambridge University Press, 1967-1981), 6, pp. 180-2.

15. This part of the MS does not survive, but internal references make its existence clear. It corresponded to Propositions LVII-LXIII of the published *Principia* (pp. 164-169).

16. Cambridge University Library, *Add. MS. 3965.3,* ff. 7-10. The folios are part of a fascicle of eight folios that belonged to *De motu corporum* but was somehow separated from the rest.

17. *Principia,* p. 571.

18. Herivel, *Background,* p. 297.

19. *Correspondence,* 2, pp. 437-439.

20. *Principia,* p. 397.

21. King's College, Cambridge, *Keynes MS 133,* p. 10.

22. Galileo, *Two New Sciences,* trans. Stillman Drake, (Madison: Univ. of Wisconsin Press, 1974), p. 225.

23. This anecdote appeared in French (*en y pensant sans cesse*) as a note to Voltaire's *Eléméns de la philosophie de Newton* in the so-called Kehl edition of his *Oeuvres* (1785-1789). There is some reason to think that the note rested on Voltaire's authority and that the story derived from his stay in England.

24. *Biographia Britannica,* 7, p. 3241.

Chapter 3

The Origins and Consequences of Certain of J. P. Joule's Scientific Ideas

Donald S. L. Cardwell

It is easy to assume that inevitability is the hallmark of the historical progress of science; that, in other words, each scientific advance contains the germs of, and points towards, the next advance. It is also easy to believe that every scientific revolution poses a stark choice between right and wrong, between the new theory and the old one. But the inevitability of scientific progress is refuted by the well-known fact that few, if any, scientists have successfully predicted the future course of science, in general or in particular. And the choice available at any time of crisis or revolution is seldom a simple one. I hope that the following paper will confirm these elementary truths and, more importantly, throw new light on the origins of James Prescott Joule's scientific ideas and on their immediate consequences.

The scientific study of heat was developed by chemists and medical men in the eighteenth century. Explicitly or implicitly their work rested on the axiom of the conservation of heat, which asserted that in such familiar operations as the communication of heat, change of state, and the performance of work by heat, no heat is lost or converted into anything else. The material, or "caloric," theory of heat is consistent with this axiom. Towards the end of the century the "physicists" began to make their bid to take over heat. (The unpleasant word "physicist" with its repeated sibilants was coined by Whewell in 1840.) This was a notable step towards the establishment

I am grateful to the Syndics of the Cambridge University Library and the Librarian of the University of Glasgow for permission to quote from the Joule-Thomson letters they hold.

of the discipline as we know it today.[1] The movement was largely French in inspiration. In the English-speaking world the chemists and medical men still predominated, while the engineers, the heirs of James Watt, tacitly abandoned this part of their scientific inheritance. For them the revolutionary new steam engines were essentially vapor pressure engines, driven by steam pressure in the same way that all hydraulic engines were driven by water pressure. In short, the steam engineer had much more in common with the hydraulic engineer than he had with the chemist or doctor.[2]

I mention the engineers and the steam engine because the period I am concerned with was one that witnessed intense industrialization. In the van of the industrial revolution were the twin English towns of Manchester and Salford. Rapid industrial growth meant equally rapid population increase. In 1801 the combined population of the two towns was about 90,000; by 1831 it had grown to 230,000, and by 1851 it stood at 367,000.[3] This enormous expansion was accompanied by severe social stress. In August 1819 the "Peterloo Massacre" took place, when the yeomanry—roughly equivalent to the National Guard—killed eleven people and injured many more while dispersing a large crowd of demonstrators. But all this passed by my subject, for James Prescott Joule was only nine months old at the time, and in any case his father, an affluent brewer, had no concern with such matters. His brewery and its profits would naturally expand with the towns. And this was of some significance, for brewers were among the leaders in scientific and technological innovation.[4] Nor, as we shall see, was the affluence unimportant.

James, the second surviving child, had an elder and a younger brother and two younger sisters, one of whom died in childhood. He was too delicate for school, so he had private tutors instead. When he was fourteen he and his elder brother, Benjamin, were sent to learn mathematics and science under John Dalton, the doyen of Manchester science. The Joule boys studied for three years under Dalton, at the Manchester Literary and Philosophical Society,[5] after which they assisted their father in the brewery. I doubt if the work was onerous, for young Joule was able to carry out his early scientific work there before his father built him a laboratory at home.

This looks like a rather indulged childhood and adolescence. But considering Joule's social status I doubt if it was untypical. As the family increased in wealth and security, so the sons gave up the dissenting church of their fathers—Dr. Roby's Independent Chapel—and joined the Church of England, the established church;[6] a transition that was fairly common among those rising in the world.[7] By

George Patten. A R A pinx. 1863.   Imp Wittmann Paris.   H Manesse sc

Plate 1. James Prescott Joule, 1818-1889. The original portrait, from which this engraving was taken, was destroyed when the Manchester Literary and Philosophical Society's House was burned down during an air raid in December 1940.

the time he was thirty-six Joule had given up work at the brewery, which in any case the family were soon to sell. The brothers became gentlemen of leisure. Benjamin had estates in Ireland and spent his time training church choirs, playing the organ, and composing hymns and chants. John, the youngest, retired to the vacation Isle of Man, where he died comparatively young. James's career was outwardly similar to those of many other nineteenth-century British scientists who, having made or inherited a comfortable sum of money, went on to devote themselves to science. Such was the common career pattern of, for example, W. H. Perkin, David Edward Hughes, Henry Wilde, and James Nasmyth.[8] You made your hundred thousand pounds or more, invested it in sound public utilities, railroad stock, or government securities to yield, say, three percent, and retired to a comfortable life of science in the secure knowledge that things were getting better and cheaper all the time.

It was a different lifestyle from the one most of us are familiar with. And so, too, was the intellectual milieu. There was no university in Manchester at that time. But there was the Literary and Philosophical Society, a strictly voluntary institution that owed its origins to the physicians and surgeons of the nearby infirmary and to various clergymen, lawyers, businessmen, and gentlemen of leisure, all of whom were interested in science. In the 1830s and 1840s the Society was the intellectual hub of Manchester, which, it is important to remember, was a developing, challenging, and exciting town as well as a place with acute social problems. At the Society Joule would be in the company of such engineers as Eaton Hodgkinson, William Fairbairn, and Richard Roberts. He would meet Lyon Playfair, the ambitious young chemist who later became a minister in one of Gladstone's administrations; Edward Binney, attorney and geologist, who made a huge fortune out of the early oil industry; and, of course, the venerable John Dalton.

What sort of man was Joule? We are told that he was shy and retiring; and even his best friends admitted that he was an unimpressive public speaker. He gave only half a dozen public lectures in the whole course of his career, and these were to local societies of strictly amateur status. Unlike Dalton, he never spoke at the Royal Institution in London and he never delivered a named lecture to the Royal Society, although he was a Copley medallist. I doubt if he was too easily led, but he was certainly ready to put his experimental gifts in the service of others, particularly those with commanding personalities such as William Thomson and Lyon Playfair. He suffered from a spinal weakness that caused him to be slightly hunchbacked.

To the Editor of the Annals of Electricity, &c.

Manchester, September 17, 1838.

Dear Sir,

I have often during thunder storms noticed that the flashes of lightning do not always appear momentary, but frequently as if there were two distinct flashes, one succeeding the other at an interval of about $\frac{1}{4}''$ of time.

And indeed, this fact cannot have escaped the observation of any attentive person, who has seen the lightning of a distant storm at night; then, the flame of light is in general seen to shine brightly at first, then partly to die away, and at last to end with about the same lustre with which it began; the whole scene taking up in some cases a length of time so palpable as one second. In this case, the lightning has lost so much of its dazzling brilliancy, that the evidence of our senses may safely be trusted.

For my own part I feel quite unable to furnish any hypothesis at all calculated to account for the above phenomenon; I present it therefore to you and your many scientific readers for explanation.

I am, dear sir,
Your obedient servant,
J. P. J.

Plate 2. Joule's letter to Sturgeon's *Annals of Electricity* and detail from the index of Volume III.

He married a woman five years older than himself, Amelia Grimes, who was thirty-three when they married in 1847.[9] He seems to have been deeply attached to his mother, who died in 1836, and to his younger sister Alice, who died in 1834, aged 14. In due course Joule showed himself to be a most affectionate father of his two children.

Joule's scientific credentials and qualifications are of considerable interest. In his personal library, in our possession in Manchester, there is a complete set of William Sturgeon's *Annals of Electricity* (1836-1843) annotated by him in ink. In 1838 the *Annals* printed a short letter in which it was asserted that individual lightning flashes are usually multiple; that is, more than one discrete flash follows the same channel with quiescent periods in between. The writer added that the interval between the flashes was of the order of one-quarter of a second.[10] Now this is correct; many, if not most, lightning flashes are multiple, the periods of quiescence being between 100 and 250 milliseconds.[11] The letter was signed "P" and the address given as Manchester. In Joule's volume the initial "J" is written in, before and after the letter "P." The writer was Joule himself. Evidently we can learn something about a man by studying his library. And we see too that Joule had excellent powers of observation, for photographic studies of lightning were not feasible at that time. Another of his early and little known experiments was to examine the effects of electricity on human beings. His subject was a servant girl who reported her sensations as the voltage was stepped up—he used a large battery—to the moment when she became unconscious, whereat he felt it advisable to stop the experiment.[12] Unfortunately the young lady's opinions were not recorded.

Joule was no narrow specialist. His *Collected Scientific Papers* and his private correspondence show that throughout his active life he had a truly inquiring mind, curious about any unusual phenomenon or effect that came his way and deeply appreciative of the natural beauties of land, sea, and sky. So we find him studying such diverse matters as the formation of hail and its association with thunderstorms, the total eclipse of the sun of 1858, a novel way of measuring the velocity of sound, the green flash to be seen just as the sun sets over the sea. Is it reasonable to suppose that a persistent curiosity about nature is one of the indicators of the scientific spirit; one of the ways in which we can distinguish the born scientist from the incurious layman? I must, however, admit that, apart from some early and rather sadistic experiments to decide whether spiders can survive in sulfuric acid (they cannot), Joule did not show much interest in the world of living things. His activities were confined to physics, geophysics, mechanical engineering, electrical technology, and some forays into chemistry.

As we know, in these particular fields Joule strove for, and achieved, remarkable standards of accuracy of measurement. It is also familiar knowledge that some of his early critics refused to accept his work on the mechanical equivalent of heat on the ground that it depended on temperature readings accurate to within one hundredth of a degree. But this reflects more on the critics' standards of accuracy than on Joule's and, in any case, confuses the validity of the concept of a mechanical equivalent of heat with the accuracy of its determination. Helmholtz and others might, initially, carp at the latter, but Joule's data were sufficiently unambiguous to establish the former. However, it was not just a question of measurements made to the nth decimal place; he sought also to eliminate all possible sources of error and ambiguity. In his first paper on the mechanical equivalent of heat, in 1843, he even allowed for the heat lost by sparks at the commutator of his small electric generator. In his last determination, in 1878, he reduced his weights to their values in vacuo and his final calculation to its value at sea level from the altitude at which the experiments were made, 120 feet. Necessary though consistent accuracy was for his work, it did not determine the immediate course of his researches; there was no critical measurement, or series of measurements, that changed his views or suddenly clarified everything, as was the case with the Rutherford-Marsden scattering experiment of 1909; the eclipse measurements of 1919. Rather his experiments were carried out to test intuitively formed hypotheses and the course of his researches determined by their own logic and the singleness of mind with which he carried them through. Accordingly I now turn to the first experiments he made, in the late 1830s and early 1840s.

Joule's introduction to what I may call his mainstream science was a result of the exaggerated hopes raised by the first electric motors, or "electro-magnetic engines" as they were called. No one then knew the ultimate capacity of the electric battery, and there were seemingly good grounds for hoping that the voltaic cell driving a well designed electric motor could provide virtually limitless power. (The word "power" is used here in its contemporary and very general sense.) In a masterly paper M. H. Jacobi described the theoretical advantages of the rotative electric motor. He mentioned the limiting effect of what was later to be called back EMF but expressed the hope that this could be overcome, if not turned to positive advantage.[13] A perfected motor without back EMF and in the absence of friction and air resistance could, in theory reach an infinite velocity. The accelerative force between two electromagnets is unaffected by relative motion and as the armature is rotating there is no point at which motion and acceleration have to stop, as in the case of a reciprocating steam engine. The scientific and technical public at once foresaw the prospects, if not of perpetual motion at least of something approximating to it. The clumsy, dirty, noisy steam engine was to be replaced by the compact, clean, quiet and above all supremely economical "electro-magnetic engine", or motor. What I have called an electric euphoria swept Europe, including Russia, and the United States.[14] Joule, at an impressionable age, was caught up in the prevailing enthusiasm. The hopes, however, were to be disappointed, largely because of Joule's own researches.

Joule possessed great experimental skills, but he was also lucky in his basic training and his intellectual inheritance. He would know of the kinetic theories of heat put forward by Davy and Rumford and the dynamical theory of gases proposed by John Herapath.[15] He would have learned from John Dalton and, at one remove, from the engineer Peter Ewart[16] the importance of the concept of work in mechanics; a concept particularly acceptable in an engineering community. For in Britain the measure of work had been developed in the context of a native engineering tradition that went back to the eighteenth century and in particular to John Smeaton. In other words, Joule's training would have ensured that he was substantially immune to the insular prejudices of British mathematicians and natural philosophers who had exalted the Newtonian measure of force at the expense of the Continental notion of vis viva with its necessary correlate, potential or latent vis viva. He would also have readily accepted that the efficiency of an engine is measured in terms of its "duty"; that is, the work it would do for the combustion of a given amount of coal in its furnace. This measure would be doubly familiar to him, for the Joule brewery was big enough to have a steam engine. What, then, could be more natural than for Joule to assess the performance of his electric motors by their "duty": the work they would do for the "combustion" of a given weight of metal in the driving battery? Finally, he must have shared in the common conviction that the three related agencies of light, heat, and electricity shall, as Joule's mentor Dalton put it, "be shown to arise from the same principle;" and "in the meantime is it not most consistent to conclude that these agents are of the same nature? And if any one of the three, *heat, light* and *electricity* be deemed a fluid then the other two must also be deemed *fluids*. If any one of these three be deemed *powers* or *properties* then all three must be deemed *powers* or *properties* of matter.''[17] Dalton was not the first, and he was certainly not the last, to hope and expect that the related agencies of heat, light, electricity, and magnetism would be shown to be different manifestations of a common underlying substance or agency. (This speculation was not necessarily inconsistent with, or destructive of, the axiom of the conservation of heat.) In fact the expectation was fairly common at that time. As we know, Dalton voted for the fluid theory, but by Joule's time the tide of opinion was moving in the other direction. The undulatory theory of light was increasingly accepted and with it the undulatory nature of radiant heat. But the cautious man of science would probably prefer to keep his options open by professing agnosticism as to the nature of heat, while at the same time accepting, even if only implicitly, the axiom of its conservation.[18]

In the course of his interesting study of the origins of the axiom of the conservation of energy, Yehuda Elkana claims that Naturphilosophie played a significant part in guiding the speculations of J. R. Mayer and von Helmholtz. With its emphasis on the unity of nature and on the common links between phenomena, Naturphilosophie helped pave the way for the axiom of the conservation of energy. This original suggestion may be valid in the context of German scientific thought in the early nineteenth century but, applied universally, it would devalue the widespread conviction among British men of science — a conviction that owed nothing to Naturphilosophie — that heat, light, electricity and magnetism were all different manifestations of a common fundamental cause.[19] It is also unfair, by default, to Joule, with whose works Elkana appears to be unfamiliar.[20] But let me return to the mundane studies of electromagnets, motors, and experimental physics.

Joule's quantitative experiments proved conclusively that, weight for weight of "fuel" consumed, even the best electric motor could not compete with the Cornish steam engine, at that time the most efficient in the world. And as the battery fuel, zinc, was much more expensive than coal, he felt compelled to write: "I confess I almost despair of the success of electromagnetic attractions as an economical source of power."[21] A few years later the electric euphoria was over, and electric motors, from which so much had been expected, were little more than philosophical toys. In the meantime, however, Joule had turned his attention to the study of the heat generated by an electric current. The motive for this, apart from scientific curiosity, would be straightforward. Practical engineers had recognized for many years that the appearance of heat and the optimum performance of work are not compatible in any machine; hence the need for lubrication. Perhaps, therefore, the appearance of heat in an electric circuit was an analogous indication of a loss of power? Joule soon discovered that the heat generated in a circuit was proportional to the square of the current and to the resistance.[22] And he went on to show that a given weight of fuel burned in a battery generates the same amount of heat in the circuit, including the battery itself, as it would if ignited and burned in an atmosphere of oxygen. This led him to the pregnant generalization, "Electricity may be regarded as a grand agent for carrying, arranging and converting chemical heat."[23] We should note the significance of the word "converting" in this context.

At this point I must mention another book in Joule's library that may have influenced him in these researches. This was his volume of the second edition of Adair Crawford's *Animal Heat* (London, 1788). Joule refers to Crawford on two occasions—in 1841 and in 1843—and we know that Dalton had a high opinion of Crawford's work.[24] Now according to Crawford's theory of animal heat the physico-chemical processes of the heart-lung system convert the air we breathe into "fixed air," or carbon dioxide, which has a markedly lower specific heat capacity than atmospheric air. The excess heat left behind by the exhaled "fixed air" would be carried off by the arterial blood, pumped out of the heart into the body. The returning, venous blood, had, Crawford showed, an appropriately lower specific heat capacity than the arterial blood; the difference was, he argued, accounted for by the heat of the body. This theory, based on some excellent experimental work, represented a most ingenious attempt to explain the origins of bodily heat. Its correctness is of less importance than the possibility that it *may* have provided Joule with a model or a fruitful analogy for the process of electrical heating and the operation of the battery. The heart-lung system is analogous to the battery, the blood to the current, and the body to an electrical resistance or load. In both cases we have the quantitative study of the generation and distribution of heat in a closed circuit or system.

Whatever the role of Crawford's work in the development of Joule's ideas, the position he had now reached was, we may say, critical. On the one hand he had demonstrated the equivalence between chemical action, electricity, and heat. He had shown that the heat generated in an electric circuit was equivalent to the chemical action in the battery and, further, that if a motor was included in the circuit, *less* heat was generated as *more* work was done. It was at this point the key question arose. Electricity may be generated mechanically, by means of a "magneto-electric engine"; but in this case where does the associated heat come from? It cannot, as is the case with a battery operated circuit, come from chemical action, for there is none. Does the "magneto-electric engine" act as a heat-pump, transferring heat from armature and magnet to the outside circuit? In this case there should be a measurable degree of cooling within the engine itself. In an extremely careful series of experiments Joule found that there was no such cooling; at every point in the engine and in the circuit heat was generated in accordance with the $i^2 r$ law. The conclusion was inescapable: the heat represented the mechanical work done to drive the engine; it could come from no other source, for the only changes had been the performance of work and the production of heat.

In 1843 Joule described these experiments and gave his conclusions in a paper on the calorific effects of magneto-electricity and the mechanical equivalent of heat that he read to a meeting of the British Association, held in Cork, in Ireland. At the end of the paper he announced a value for the mechanical equivalent of heat derived from measurements of the heat generated electrically by a magneto-electric engine driven by falling weights.[25] He added, in an appendix, a value obtained by forcing water through narrow glass tubes bound together to form a kind of porous piston that he drove up and down inside a cylindrical vessel full of water.[26] The last series of experiments gave a remarkably accurate result. Joule was asked to read his paper to Section B (Chemistry) as Section A (Mathematics and Physics) was full.[27] And indeed, during these years the Chemistry Section of the British Association could show only about half the number of papers read to the Mathematics and Physics Section, for these were years of great activity in physics. I imagine that Section B had to be filled out somehow in those lean years for chemistry. Joule was not the only one to be shanghaied: W. G. Armstrong, the engineer, read his paper on the electricity of high-pressure steam with a description of his hydroelectric machine to Section B.

All this tends to refute the argument recently put forward by J. Forrester that, during these early years, Joule was predominantly interested in chemistry.[28] This view ignores Joule's evident concern with electric motors and the design of electro-magnets.[29] It also raises the awkward question why, if the suggestion is true, did his interest change from "physics" to "chemistry"? Forrester's view is also unfortunate in that it implies that our present, rather rigid, classifications are applicable to the scientific world of the 1840s. In fact the frontiers between disciplines were, in those days, far less clearly marked than they subsequently became. Subjects such as electricity, magnetism, and heat, which were later to be incorporated in "physics," were still, as we have seen, considered branches of "chemistry." It is true that Joule's work did have important implications for chemistry (see below), and some of his researches can fairly be described as chemical, but this does not make him a chemist.[30] Had one asked Joule how he regarded himself, he would surely have replied—after saying he was a gentleman—that he was an experimental philosopher and a man of science. In fact, he went wherever his scientific intuition and his researches directed him without bothering about disciplines and their classifications.

Such freedom was essential, for his next task was to show that, by whatever means mechanical work was converted into heat, whatever substances or agencies were involved, the exchange rate was always the same; that it was a constant of nature. He measured the heat generated by fluid friction between different liquids and solids and by dry friction between metals. He related the adiabatic heating of gases to the work done, and he deduced a value for the mechanical equivalent of heat from the converse effect, the heat lost when work is done by an expanding gas. In all cases the value obtained was, within the limits of experimental error, the same.

It would, however, be wrong to assume that Joule made a simple choice between the "wrong" theory of heat and the "correct" theory; between the caloric theory or the conservation of heat axiom in the positivistic form adopted by Fourier and his disciples and the modern dynamical theory. On the contrary, there was a two-stage transfer from the one to the other. Joule's first theory was that atoms are surrounded by atmospheres of an electrical fluid, and that it was the speed, or rather the energy, of rotation of these atmospheres that constituted heat.[31] W. J. M. Rankine put forward another transitional model for the dynamical theory of heat. In Rankine's model all thermal phenomena are ascribed to the rotational energy of vortices in the atmosphere (substance unspecified) surrounding all atoms.[32]

In spite of the evident carefulness of Joule's experiments, and the rigor of his arguments, he failed to make much impression on his scientific peers. He was, as I have already suggested, neither a Huxley nor a Tyndall. It is only fair to add that the positivistic or operational interpretation of the theory of heat still had strong supporters. But then, on a famous occasion, at the Oxford meeting of the B.A. in 1847, William Thomson, at that time only twenty-three years old, dragged the whole issue into the forefront of scientific debate, at least as far as Britain was concerned.

The numerous accounts of that famous meeting confirm that Thomson was deeply impressed by Joule's work and ideas but could not accept his conclusions. From his early teens Thomson had had a precocious understanding; he was an ardent admirer of Fourier's *Analytical Theory*.[33] He had spent a postgraduate year in Paris, working in Regnault's laboratory, so it is easy to see why he would have tended to favor the older, positivist view of the theory of heat. In a letter to his brother James, written just after his meeting with Joule, he conceded that the latter had important things to say but argued that there must be a serious flaw somewhere in his work.[34] But—and this has not been published up to now—Thomson soon revised his opinion, drastically.

The Oxford meeting of the British Association was held unusually early that year, in June, and after it was all over young Thomson set off on a long tour that took him first to Paris and then on to Geneva and the Alps. Immediately after he got back to Glasgow in the fall he set about repeating Joule's experiments for himself. At Oxford Joule had described how he had established the dynamical nature of heat and measured its mechanical equivalent by experiments on liquid friction. He had constructed two suitable calorimeters, fitted with baffles and revolving paddle wheels, and filled one with water, the other with mercury. As measurable work was done in driving the paddle wheels against the friction of the liquids, the temperature rose. This was the experiment that Thomson set about repeating. He described it in a letter, dated December 5, 1847, which he wrote to J. D. Forbes, Professor of Natural Philosophy at St. Andrews University:

Perhaps before then (Friday 7) I may have succeeded in boiling water by friction. This is not very probable, however, as the machine I have made being not strong enough. In the first experiment made with it the temperature rose from 45°, 46° to 57° at about the rate of 1° every five minutes during a continued turning of the instrument (a very flat disc with narrow vanes turning in a thin tin box about 8 inches in diameter of which the bottom and lid were furnished with thin fixed vanes. The bearings of the paddle were entirely within the box which was full of water). In a second experiment we began with water at 98° & the temperature rose to about 99½° when part of the machine gave way before the experiment could be considered quite decisive. My assistant was preparing to make an experiment today with water at 80°, 90° & to go on grinding (along with another for relief) for about 4 hours, but I have not heard yet whether it went on.[35]

Joule and Thomson had begun a friendly correspondence just after the Oxford meeting, but the correspondence had lapsed for about a year, to be resumed on October 6, 1848 when Joule, disappointed at not having met Thomson, at the Swansea meeting of the British Association, wrote some comments on Thomson's paper "On an Absolute Thermometric Scale".[36] He went on to give a brief justification of some of his previous ideas, followed by an account of an experiment he said he intended to make. A small compressed air engine was to be wholly enclosed in a tight metal box submerged in water in a calorimeter. The engine was to be coupled up either to raise a weight external to the calorimeter or to drive paddles in the water. In the first case Joule expected that the temperature of the water would fall; in the second case that it would be unchanged. There is no evidence that this experiment was ever made. More interesting however is his account of the thought-experiment with which he ended his letter. Plate 3 reproduces the sketch he included. "e" is a tiny steam engine enclosed in an evacuated metal box, abcd. The boiler is heated by a small gas flame supplied by the pipe t; t' carries off the products of combustion. The engine may be used to raise the external weight W; or it may be stopped and the steam blown off through a safety valve into the box abcd. Now according to the axiom of the conservation of heat, the temperature of the surrounding water must be raised by exactly the same amount in both cases, although in the first instance work is done, and in the second it is not. Joule remarks:

It appears to me that a theory of the steam engine which does not admit of the conversion of heat into power leads to an absurd conclusion. For instance suppose that a quantity of fuel A will raise 1,000 lb of water $1°$ – then according to a theory which does not admit the convertibility of heat into power the same quantity A of fuel working a steam engine will produce a certain mechanical effect, and besides that will be found to have raised 1,000 lb of water $1°$. But the mechanical effect of the engine might have been employed in agitating water and thereby raising 100 lb of water $1°$ which added to the other makes 1,100 lb of water heated $1°$ in the case of the engine. But in the other case, namely without the engine, the same amount of fuel only heats 1,000 lb of water. The conclusion from this would be that a steam engine is a *manufacturer* of heat, which seems to me contrary to all analogy and reason.[37]

Thomson wrote a long reply, dated October 27, 1848.[38] Unfortunately parts of the letter are illegible, but enough can be deciphered to indicate its importance. For one thing Thomson gives Joule details of his experiments on fluid friction. The vanes are described as being

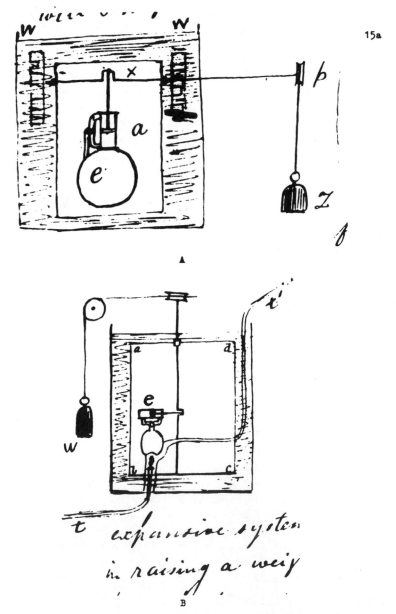

15a

Plate 3. Joule's proposed compressed air engine (A) and steam engine (B). From the sketches in his letter to Thomson of October 6, 1848 (C.U.L.).

1/10th of an inch broad and the drum, of tinplate, 1 inch deep. He has even adapted the apparatus for drive by machinery in a cotton mill. (This was an interesting anticipation of his later experiments in collaboration with Joule when they used the steam engine at the brewery (Joule-Thomson effect).) He predicted, "I shall not be surprised if, by keeping the paddle going at 10 turns per second and preventing as much as possible the loss of heat by radiation we shall be able to boil the water by friction alone."

Thomson goes on to admit the force of Joule's arguments against Carnot and Clapeyron, which Joule had set out in his paper on the rarefaction and condensation of air: "Believing that the power to destroy belongs to the Creator alone I entirely coincide with Roget and Faraday in the opinion that any theory which, when carried out, demands the annihilation of force, is necessarily erroneous."[39]

And Thomson ended by proposing another thought-experiment to demonstrate the difficulty Joule had so clearly exposed. The essence of this was a simple apparent paradox: heat may flow from a hot body to a cold body by conduction, or it may flow through a perfect engine in which case work is done. The question then is, "what has become of the work that might have been gained in arriving at the same result after having gone through the process first described? I see no way as yet of explaining this difficulty; but there must be an answer."

These words were soon to be echoed in the memorable paper he read on January 2, 1849, "An Account of Carnot's Theory of the Motive Power of Heat with Numerical Results deduced from Regnault's Experiments on Steam": "When 'thermal agency' is thus spent in conducting heat through a solid what becomes of the mechanical effect which it might produce? Nothing can be lost in the operations of nature—no energy can be destroyed. . . . A perfect theory of heat imperatively demands an answer to this question, yet no answer can be given in the present state of science."[40]

This perceptive and eloquent passage aroused the admiration of Thomson's biographer, Silvanus P. Thompson.[41] We now see that it did not originate with Thomson's own reflections on the problem but was provoked directly by Joule's letters and by his relentless exposé of what one might call the apparent paradox of power.

The position Thomson adopted in his first paper of 1849 seems, at first sight, to be rather ambiguous. He mentions Mr. Joule's experiments and expresses guarded approval. He then goes on to say that "in the present state of science, however, no operation is known by which heat can be absorbed into a body without either elevating its temperature or becoming latent and producing some alteration in its physical condition; and the fundamental axiom adopted by Carnot may be considered as still the most probable basis for an investigation of the motive power of heat."[42]

In his earlier paper, "On an Absolute Thermometric Scale", of June 1848, he had used almost exactly the same words except at the end where he had asserted, more boldly, "the conversion of heat (or *caloric*) into mechanical effect is probably impossible, certainly undiscovered."[43]

If Thomson's public attitude seems to be one of caution, the subsequent development of his paper on Carnot's theory, based on the axiom of the conservation of heat, may lead us to suppose that he had mentioned Joule's work and ideas solely as an act of academic propriety, in the spirit in which one mentions theories that one cannot accept. But his letters to Forbes and to Joule before 1849 make it clear that through his own experiments, as well as through Joule's papers and letters, he had come to accept that mechanical "effect" (energy) *can* be converted into heat. I think we do well to remember that, in all historical studies what people do *not* say, or do, can be as revealing as the words they use or the actions they carry out. Thomson did not puzzle over the results of his Joule-type experiments, nor did he try to reconcile them with the axiom of the conservation of heat. On the other hand it is clear that his experiments on the lowering of the melting point of ice under pressure confirmed his faith in Carnot and persuaded him that mechanical effect can be obtained only through the passage, or fall, of heat from a high to a low temperature. The image and the analogy of the water fall driving the water wheel is, we may say, a convincing and persistent one.

Thomson's position, therefore, seems to have been less ambiguous than has been assumed. He agreed with Joule that heat could be generated by the destruction, or rather the transformation, of mechanical effect. And he agreed with Carnot that mechanical effect could be generated only by the passage of heat from hot to cold.[44] It is only through the wisdom, or perhaps in the distorting mirror, of hindsight that such a position will seem untenable. In contemporary physics asymmetry had been a key feature of Faraday's discovery of electromagnetic induction: a steady electric current is accompanied by a magnetic field, but a magnetic field does not result in a steady current. And, as was soon to be established, while mechanical effect can, without restriction, be transformed into heat, the converse effect is strictly limited by the second law of thermodynamics. The axiom that cause equals effect is a tricky one to apply in physics.

Thomson was not the only one to adopt, for a time, an intermediate position between the axiom of the conservation of heat and the complete energy doctrine. G. A. Hirn, for one, in the early stages of his long and vitally important series of experiments on the conversion of heat into mechanical effect through the operation of the Woolf-type compound high-pressure engines, thought that it was only in the adiabatic, or expansive, stage that heat was actually transformed into work. If the engine was worked nonexpansively, no heat, he thought, was converted into work.[45] Consequently his early measurements of the mechanical equivalent of heat through the converse method (heat into work) yielded wildly discordant results.

This brings me back to the point I made at the beginning. During this period of the development of thermodynamics there was never, as far as Thomson was concerned, a clear choice between two mutually exclusive theories, those of Carnot and of Joule. Indeed, it would surely be an oversimplification to suppose that at any given time human ingenuity is so limited that the range of choice is restricted to two. Generally all sorts of theories are available, all kinds of compromises are possible. For Thomson the real dilemma was that posed by what I have called the apparent paradox of power.

As for Joule, it is surely a pity that so much emphasis has been put on these purely thermomechanical investigations. His mechanization of the laws of electricity and of electrochemistry was immensely important, as Thomson was well aware.[46] The scientific study of electricity was, in the middle years of the nineteenth century, the branch of physical science that was undergoing the most rapid change. It commanded the attention of such figures as Faraday, Arago, Lenz, Weber, Neumann, Helmholtz, and Maxwell as well as of Thomson himself. In short, unless and until the energy doctrine could be extended to include electricity, the axiom of the conservation of energy could never be established in its generality. It was Joule who did this. He was, beyond doubt, the first to bridge the gaps between heat, chemistry, mechanics, and electricity and magnetism.

As we have seen, Joule's initial researches were guided by a technological ambition that was never realized. It is appropriate, therefore, to examine one or two, at least, of the technological consequences of some of the researches he so successfully completed. Although the concepts of energy and thermodynamics were closely related to the development of steam and internal combustion engines, it is doubtful that Joule's researches were, with the exception of his work on the surface condenser,[47] of direct importance in these quarters. It was in the field of electro-technology that he had the greatest impact. His membership of the B.A. Committee on Electrical Units was significant.[48] That Committee rendered a notable service to world science and technology by establishing standardized and rational electrical units. The initiative had come in the first place from the telegraph engineers; but—and the point should be stressed—the great electrical supply industries on which all developed economies now depend sell energy in units of measurement made possible by Joule's work. Before any commodity can be sold there must be a measure by which to sell it; Joule provided the measure for the sale of electricity. And more, the i^2r heating law indicated that the highest possible voltage should be used for the maximum economy in transmission. Before his death, in 1889, high voltage transmission had begun, in the United States and in Europe.[49]

Many detailed innovations can be credited to Joule, but they are outside the scope of this paper. One point, of present-day interest, may be made, however. In 1865 W. S. Jevons published his book *The Coal Question,* which, as far as my reading goes, was the first diagnosis of the incipient energy crisis. No such book could have been written before the establishment of the energy doctrine in the 1850s. Surely it was no accident that this one was written by a man who, with Joule, was a member of the Manchester Literary and Philosophical Society.

In view of the nature and range of Joule's scientific work, it is natural to inquire a little further into his intellectual background. Joule's scientific circle consisted of his friends in the Manchester Society together with Scoresby in Bradford, Thomson in Glasgow, and Stokes and Hopkins in Cambridge.[50] London seems to have had little to offer him. And this fact offers us a new perspective on the social structure of science in mid-nineteenth-century Britain. The London "establishment," dominated by the Royal Society and the Royal Institution, was powerful, vociferous, and relatively numerous; but it was by no means always the center of science, or the leader in scientifiic thought. At the risk of repetition I must emphasize that Joule was fortunate in both his Manchester background and residence and in his scientific friends. Had he had a conventional "scientific" training[51] and lived thereafter in London, moving in the circle of Faraday, Wheatstone, John Herschel, Daniell, Lardner, Sabine, etc., I, for one, doubt if he would—or could—have made the scientific advances he did. The traditions and ideas of a practical engineering community, the company of the Literary and Philosophical Society members, and the down-to-earth common sense of John Dalton were, I submit, essential factors in the development of his powerful scientific character.

And that, in the present state of knowledge, is all that can be said under this heading. His letters—I have transcribed about 450 of them —are entirely innocent of references to philosophical issues, whether relevant to science or not. Hume, Kant, Hegel, and their successors are never mentioned, nor are their works to be found in his library. Although it is reasonable to suppose that Joule's sincerely held religious faith helped to convince him of the rationality and order of nature, significant references to the Almighty are rare in his papers— one of the few is quoted above, p. 59—and in his correspondence. God is invoked in his letters only in times of acute personal distress. And it should not be overlooked that all discussion of religious matters was, and is, strictly forbidden at meetings of the Literary and Philosophical Society. It follows that those who are interested in assessing the religious motivations of nineteenth-century scientists will find little of interest in the career of James Prescott Joule. In political matters he was always deeply conservative. He detested radical politicians and carried his conservatism to the extent of opposing all movements for change in his beloved Society.[52]

A conspicuous feature of Joule's scientific personality was, as I pointed out at the beginning of this essay, his enduring and wide interest in nature. No phenomenon slightly out of the ordinary failed to attract his interest, whether it was the sea flooding in over the sands at night and bringing with it phosphorescence like liquid silver, the great 20-foot waves off the Atlantic coast of Ireland and the skills of the Irish boatmen with their superbly designed craft, the wheeling flight of seagulls, the sunsets after the eruption of Krakatoa. . . . Sometimes his never dormant scientific impulse led him into curious situations:

It has been blowing a hard gale of wind all day with occasional gusts and lulls. As there was at the same time an overcast sky I thought it would be a good opportunity to try the effect on a thermometer. I first used one of my older ones with a 5/8 inch diameter bulb. I placed this on a stand on a ledge of the house. By elevating it six inches it became fully exposed to the wind but when lowered the wind did not blow so strongly on the bulb. In the former situation the temperature was 1/3 of a degree Fahr *lower* than in the latter, the difference in temperature indicating 5 divisions of the scale. . . .

I was proceeding further but towards noon the wind got so violent that I was fearful of breaking the thermometer or even of being blown off myself, so I waited till the afternoon when at 2 o.c. the wind had considerably abated.[53]

We may wonder what the neighbors thought.

Another conspicuous feature of his scientific personality was the immense skill and precision that marked his experiments from the very beginning. How did he acquire these gifts, characteristic of the thorough professional? Unfortunately we know little of his early tutors; they are shadowy figures. And Dalton was never renowned for experimental accuracy. For the rest we may suppose that experience at the brewery would have familiarized him with temperature measurements and the working of the steam engine. But in the final analysis I must conclude that these particular gifts were bestowed by Providence and not by his fellow men.

How can we sum up Joule? He was essentially a private man; he himself said as much.[54] But he was also a most unusual man, even by the standards of nineteenth-century science. For he combined in his person two attributes that are commonly thought of as opposed, although complementary in the scheme of science. Nineteenth-century thermodynamics was the creation of theoreticians and speculative thinkers like Carnot, Helmholtz, Gibbs and Maxwell on the one hand, and of experimentalists such as Victor Regnault who provided the accurate, reliable data on the other. But Joule was unique, for he covered both fields. A bold and original thinker, as the few letters quoted above indicate, and a masterly experimenter, he provided much of the firm base on which the new science could be built. To do this he had to dispose of the difficulties and objections, some minor, some major, and all potentially fatal to the new doctrines that the speculative thinker is liable to overlook in his enthusiasm and the historian to ignore in his desire to tell as coherent a story as possible. Joule was, in a few words, a scientist's scientist; the quintessential physicist. Of the independence of his thought there can be no question. He owed nothing to J. R. Mayer,[55] the man who was set up, by others, as his great rival. But there is little profit and much danger in trying to decide which one of these two was the more important. When we consider the disputes of long ago we should remember that, as the saying goes, the past is a foreign country; they do things differently there.

Notes

1. D. S. L. Cardwell, "Theories of Heat and the Rise of Physics," *History of Science* 15 (1977), pp. 138-145.

2. D. S. L. Cardwell, "Science and the Steam Engine Reconsidered" (Thirteenth Dickinson Memorial Lecture), *Transactions of the Newcomen Society* 49 (1977-1978), pp. 111-120.

3. B. R. Mitchell and Phyllis Deane, *Abstracts of British Historical Statistics* (Cambridge: Cambridge University Press, 1976), pp. 24-26. Details of the populations of Manchester, Salford, and nearby towns and villages are given in the directories that, beginning with the one published by Elizabeth Raffald in 1772, appeared at irregular but frequent intervals. Other directories, covering the period of this paper, were published by Holmes, Bancks, and Pigot and Dean. The hardships and pollution caused by the industrial revolution in Manchester are among the most familiar facts in social and economic history, thanks in large measure to Friedrich Engels's *Condition of the Working Classes in England in 1844.* It is only fair to point out that previous observers had commented on the effects of industrialization in terms no less severe than those used by Engels. For a modern criticism, see Steven Marcus, "Reading the Illegible," *The Victorian City: Images and Reality,* vol. 1 (London: Routledge and Kegan Paul, 1973), pp. 257-276. It is equally fair, and most revealing, to point out that none of these observers saw anything in Manchester beyond tremendous material production, hardship, pollution, and the amassing of wealth.

4. Peter Mathias, *The Brewing Industry in England, 1700-1830* (Cambridge: Cambridge University Press, 1959), pp. 64, 81. Professor Mathias remarks that "few brewers thought seriously about (a steam) engine until their annual production was well over 20,000 barrels." As the Joule brewery had a steam engine theirs must have been one of the larger ones in the rapidly expanding conurbation.

5. F. Greenway, *John Dalton and the Atom* (London: Heinemann, 1966), p. 1; Elizabeth C. Patterson, *John Dalton and the Atomic Theory* (New York: Doubleday & Co., 1970), pp. 75, 251.

6. I am grateful to Professor J. R. Prescott for pointing this out to me. In addition to the sources mentioned by Professor Prescott in his forthcoming short paper, reference can also be made to J. T. Slugg, *Reminiscences of Manchester Fifty Years Ago* (Manchester: J. E. Cornish, 1881), pp. 131-133.

7. It was noted, for example, by Tocqueville in his *Journeys to England and Ireland,* trans. George Lawrence and K. P. Mayer (London: Faber and Faber, 1958), p. 79. Tocqueville quoted a correspondent who wrote: "One notices that when a family becomes rich, when it reaches an income of five or six thousand pounds it leaves the *dissenters* to join the Established Church."

8. William Henry Perkin (1838-1907) was a young student when, in 1856, he discovered the first aniline dyestuff, "mauveine." He promptly set up as a manufacturer of the new dye, built up a substantial business, and retired at the advanced age of 36 to devote himself to scientific research. See *Dictionary of Scientific Biography,* vol. 10 (New York: Scribners, 1974), pp. 515-517. David Edward Hughes (1831-1900) invented the system of printing telegraphy used in continental Europe, made a large fortune, and returned to England to devote himself to a life of science. See J. O. Marsh and R. G. Roberts, "David Edward Hughes: Inventor, Engineer and Scientist", *Proceedings of the Institution of Electrical Engineers* 126 (Sept. 1979), pp. 929-935. Henry Wilde (1833-1919), the son of a working mechanic, made a fortune as an inventor and consulting engineer. At the age of fifty-one he retired from business and, in the words of W. W. Haldane Gee, "decided to devote his

time to scientific research." See *Memoirs and Proceedings of the Manchester Literary and Philosophical Society* 63 (1918-1919) No. V, pp. 1-16. Wilde's most notable contribution was the substitution of electro-magnets for permanent magnets in "magneto-electric engines," a vital step in the invention of the dynamo. Wilde's successful innovation was followed up by Siemens and Wheatstone. James Nasmyth (1808-1890), engineer, artist, and industrialist, invented the steam-hammer and made many improvements to machine-tools. In his later years he turned to astronomy and, when he was 66, published a book on the subject. See *James Nasmyth — Engineer, an Autobiography,* ed. Samuel Smiles (London: John Murray, 1883), p. 323 et seq.

9. A recently discovered letter in the few surviving archives of the Literary and Philosophical Society confirms that, after the death of his wife, Joule fell in love with his cousin, Frances Charlotte, the daughter of his former tutor and uncle by marriage, William Tappenden. Nothing came of it, however, and the young woman later married someone else. She lived to an advanced age, dying in 1923. See the letter from L. B. Tappenden to J. R. Ashworth, dated December 6, 1931. I am indebted to Mr. A. G. Pate for discovering the letter and telling me about it.

10. Letter signed "P" and dated Sept. 13, 1838, *Annals of Electricity, Magnetism and Chemistry and Guardian of Experimental Science* (sic!), 3 (1838-1839), p. 508 and index; 7 (1841), 226. See also M. Faraday, "On Some Supposed Forms of Lightning," *Philosophical Magazine* 19 (1841), p. 104. Faraday argued that the apparent effect was due to the edges of clouds being sharply outlined by distant and different flashes.

11. K. Berger, "The Earth Flash" in R. H. Golde, ed., *Lightning, Volume 1: The Physics of Lightning* (London: The Academic Press, 1977), pp. 119-190. The phenomenon can easily be demonstrated by exposing an ordinary camera, pointing it in the direction of a thunderstorm on a dark night, and swinging it from side to side. Whether or not Joule could actually resolve the flashes through direct visual observation is less important than the scientific attitude and intuition the claim reveals.

12. From an early notebook (1841) in the possession of my Department (UMIST, Manchester M60 1QD, England), Joule published two other short items on thunderstorms: *Collected Scientific Papers of James Prescott Joule,* vol. 1 (London: The Physical Society, 1887; Dawson Reprint, 1963), pp. 329, 500 (referred to hereafter as *C.S.P.*). There are scattered references to his observations on lightning and thunderstorms in his correspondence with William Thomson.

13. M. H. Jacobi, "On the Application of Electro-magnetism to the Moving of Machines," *Annals of Electricity* 1 (1836-1837), pp. 408-415, 419-444. Jacobi ended his paper by remarking: "I think I may assert that the superiority of this new mover is placed beyond a doubt, as regards the absence of all danger, the simplicity of application, and the expense attending it." As late as 1856 John Tyndall, while accepting the principle of the conversation of energy, still believed that it might be possible to turn the back EMF to useful account. See the discussion following Robert Hunt's paper, "Electromagnetism as a Motive Power," *Minutes of Proceedings of the Institution of Civil Engineers,* 16 (1856-57), p. 386. The implications of the energy doctrine were by no means fully evident even to informed scientists who accepted it.

14. D. S. L. Cardwell, "Science and Technology: The Work of James Prescott Joule," *Technology and Culture* 17 (Oct. 1976), pp. 674-687, a paper presented to a conference held at the Burndy Library in 1973.

15. Eric Mendoza, "A Critical Examination of Herapath's Dynamical Theory of Gases," *British Journal for the History of Science* 8 (July 1975), pp. 155-165.

16. Peter Ewart wrote a long defense of the work concept in mechanics, which was published as "On the Measure of Moving Force," *Manchester Memoirs,* Vol. II, 2nd Series

(1813, pp. 105-258. Dalton dedicated the second volume of his *New System of Chemical Philosophy* (Manchester: S. Russell, 1827; Dawson reprint, London 1953) to John Sharpe and Peter Ewart jointly. See D. S. L. Cardwell, "Reflections on Some Problems in the History of Science," *Manchester Memoirs* 106 (1963-64), pp. 108-123; and *From Watt to Clausius* (London: Heinemann, 1970), pp. 162-164.

17. Quoted by A. R. Hall, "Precursors of Dalton," in D. S. L. Cardwell, ed., *John Dalton and the Progress of Science* (Manchester: Manchester University Press, 1968), pp. 40-56. Professor Hall points out that "this idea was later given more specific form as the 'correlation of physical forces.'" J. J. Berzelius also called attention to the obvious connections between "caloric," light, and electricity. See his "Explanatory Statement. . .," *Nicholson's Journal* 34 (Feb. 1813), p. 142. It was not necessary to be a genius to infer the existence of a fundamental substance or agency. See Joseph Lucock, "On Specific Heats," *Philosophical Magazine* 53 (1819), p. 44. Lucock invented the name "fluidium" for the common elemental substance.

18. This was the attitude taken by J. B. J. Fourier and his disciples. See J. B. J. Fourier, *Analytical Theory of Heat*, trans. A. Freeman (New York: Dover Books, 1955). As a positivist Fourier was not interested in discussing the nature of heat. Nevertheless his analysis assumes conservation. He explicitly denied any connection between heat and the science of mechanics: "This part of natural philosophy cannot be connected with dynamical theories. . . ." (P. 23)

19. This belief can be traced back to the period of the scientific revolution and more particularly to Newton's program set out in *The Opticks*. Although Newtonian exegesis allowed for a good deal of flexibility, the ideal of bringing all natural phenomena within a comprehensive mechanical theory was never forgotten. It was well expressed by John Robison: "The Laws which regulate the formation of elastic vapors, of the general phenomena which it exhibits, give us that link which connects chemistry with mechanical philosophy. Here we see chemical affinities and mechanical forces set in opposition to each other and the one made the indication, characteristic and measure of the other. We do not have the least doubt that they make one science, the Science of Universal Mechanics." Article "Steam", 3rd ed. *Encyclopaedia Britannica*, (London, 1797).

20. Yehuda Elkana, *The Discovery of the Conservation of Energy* (London: Hutchinson, 1974). On page 127 Elkana repeats Helmholtz's error in crediting the i^2r law of electric heating to Lenz who "discovered" it over two years after Joule had announced it in *Proceedings of the Royal Society* (December 17, 1840) and in *Philosophical Magazine* 19 (1841), p. 260. On page 184 he repeats Thomson's assertion that Joule seemingly did not know of Carnot until Thomson told him. But in one of the best known passages in one of Joule's best known papers we find the following: "This view [that a steam engine works solely by the flow of caloric] has been adopted by Mr. E. Clapeyron in a very able theoretical paper, of which there is a translation in the 3rd part of Taylor's Scientific Memoirs. This philosopher agrees with Mr. Carnot. . .," *Philosophical Magazine* 26 (1845), p. 369; *C.S.P.*, pp. 172-189. This paper was published two years before Joule and Thomson met or corresponded.

21. In 1841. *C.S.P.*, p. 48.

22. In 1840. *C.S.P.*, pp. 59-60 and in 1841, *C.S.P.*, p. 60 et seq.

23. In 1843. *C.S.P.*, p. 120.

24. *C.S.P.*, pp. 78, 158. In John Dalton, *New Systems of Chemical Philosophy*, vol. 1 (Manchester, 1808) there are frequent and respectful references to Crawford's works, particularly after the section headed "On the Specific Heat of Bodies," p. 74 et seq.

25. The paper was published as "On the Calorific Effects of Magneto-Electricity and the Mechanical Value of Heat," *Philosophical Magazine* 23 (1843), pp. 263, 347, 435; *C.S.P.*,

pp. 123-159. The *Report of the British Association* (1843), *The Athenaeum*, and the *Literary Gazette* made only the briefest references to the paper.

26. More details of this experiment than are given in the above paper are contained in a letter Joule wrote to Thomson on July 21, 1863, now in Glasgow University Library.

27. J. R. Ashworth, "List of Apparatus now in Manchester which Belonged to Dr. J. P. Joule, F.R.S.; with Remarks on his MSS, Letters and Autobiography," *Manchester Memoirs* 75 (1930), pp. 105-117. The short autobiography was written towards the end of 1866 in response to a request from P. G. Tait, Professor of Natural Philosophy at Edinburgh. Joule says, in the autobiography, that his supporters at Cork were the Earl of Rosse, the astronomer who later became President of the Royal Society; Dr. Apjohn, a Dublin chemist who was interested in the physics of gases and geology as well as chemistry; and Eaton Hodgkinson, the distinguished engineer and fellow member of the Manchester Literary and Philosophical Society. A year later Hodgkinson was to write an obituary notice of Peter Ewart in *Manchester Memoirs*, dealing in particular with Ewart's contribution to the development of the concept of work in Britain.

28. J. Forrester, "Chemistry and the Conservation of Energy: the Work of James Prescott Joule," *Studies in the History and Philosophy of Science* 6 (1975), pp. 274-313. The importance of Joule's debt to Faraday for such fruitful advances as the doctrine of electrochemical equivalents is indisputable. See Osborne Reynolds, "Memoir of James Prescott Joule", *Manchester Memoirs*, 6 (1892), pp. 39-43, 56, 189-191. In all other respects—personal and intellectual—the two men had remarkably little contact with each other. Their temperaments were entirely different.

29. The first eight letters and papers in *C.S.P.* are concerned with matters that would now be regarded as indisputable in the areas of physics or electrical engineering; they are followed by a short note on the voltaic battery (chemistry) and three more communications on electromagnets (physics).

30. Joule collaborated with the chemist Lyon Playfair in researches on the atomic volumes of substances in solution. But Joule makes it clear (*C.S.P.*, vol. 2, p. 11, footnote) that the theory was all due to Playfair; he merely did the lab. work. In any case the experiments have been authoritatively described as "laborious, but ultimately fruitless" (*Dictionary of Scientific Biography*, vol. 11 (1975), pp. 36-37). A case for Joule as a chemist cannot, therefore, be built on the strength of the papers he published in collaboration with Playfair.

31. H. J. Steffens, *James Prescott Joule and the Concept of Energy* (New York: Neale Watson, 1979), p. 19 et seq.

32. Keith Hutchison, *W. J. M. Rankine and the Rise of Thermodynamics* (Oxford: D.Phil. Thesis, 1976).

33. Silvanus P. Thompson, *Life of William Thomson, Baron Kelvin of Largs*, vol. 1 (London: Macmillan and Co., 1910), pp. 13-17.

34. Letter dated July 12, 1847. In Cambridge University Library, Add MSS 7342 T429. See *Catalogue of the Kelvin and Stokes Collections*, compiled by David B. Wilson (Cambridge University Library, 1976) (Hereafter cited as *C.U.L., K. & S.C.*). Also quoted in Thompson, *Life of William Thomson*, p. 266.

35. *C.U.L., K. & S.C.*, F190.

36. William Thomson, "On an Absolute Thermometric Scale," *Mathematical and Physical Papers* (hereafter cited as *M.P.P.*), vol. 1 (Cambridge: At the University Press, 1882), pp. 100-106. Significantly, Joule's paper was accorded a full page in the report from the (still crowded) Section A meeting at Swansea.

37. *C.U.L., K. & S.C.*, J61.

38. *C.U.L., K. & S.C.*, J62.

39. *C.S.P.*, 172-189.

40. *M.P.P.*, vol. 1, 113-55.

41. Thompson, *Life of William Thomson*, p. 271.

42. Thomson, *M.P.P.*, p. 117.

43. Thomson, "On an Absolute Thermometric Scale," p. 102. In his letter of October 6, 1848, Joule remarked that in his experiments on the compression and rarefaction of air, "I thought I had proved the convertibility of heat into power; for I found that on letting compressed air escape into the atmosphere a degree of cold was produced *equivalent* to the mechanical effect estimated by the column of atmosphere displaced. The cold could not be explained by an increase in the capacity of the rarefied air because no cold was produced on the *whole* when air was let to escape into a vacuum". No doubt this clear statement from an experimentalist he had learned to respect made Thomson adopt a less dogmatic line on the conversion of heat into mechanical energy. The notion that the specific heat capacity of a gas increased as it expanded was an important element in the caloric theory and was held (wrongly) to have been confirmed by the otherwise excellent experiments of Delaroche and Bérard.

44. Sadi Carnot, *Réflexions sur la puissance motrice du feu* (Paris, 1824), p. 9.

45. Alfred Kastler, "L'Oeuvre Scientifique de Gustave-Adolphe Hirn, 1815-1890," *Révue Générale des Sciences* 65 (1958), pp. 277-97. Historians have for too long underestimated the difficulties that confronted Hirn in these experiments, and the brilliant and devoted skill with which he overcame them. A detailed study of the life and work of Hirn is overdue.

46. William Thomson, "On the Mechanical Theory of Electrolysis," *Philosophical Magazine*, 2 (1851), pp. 429-442 and *M.P.P.*, pp. 472-489. Thomson begins by remarking that "Certain principles discovered by Mr. Joule and published for the first time in his various papers in this Magazine, must ultimately become an important part of the foundation of a mechanical theory of chemistry."

47. J. P. Joule, "On the Surface Condensation of Steam," *Philosophical Transactions of the Royal Society* 151 (1861), p. 133, and *C.S.P.*, p. 502. The development of the surface condenser for marine steam engines was of the utmost economic, social, and finally political importance. The subsequent revolution in ocean transport has irreversibly changed the conditions of life for all nations.

48. This Committee sat from 1861 to 1867. It defined the fundamental units of electrical measurement in terms of force and work using the CGS system. Joule joined the Committee in 1863. The other members included Wheatstone, C. W. Siemens, Maxwell, Thomson, and Balfour Stewart.

49. The Niagara Falls scheme had been proposed over a hundred years ago. Some credit for its completion belongs to Thomson for in his presidential lecture to the Physics Section of the British Association in 1881 he discussed the economics of high-voltage transmission. Thomson later became Chairman of the Niagara Falls Commission. See Thompson, *Life of William Thomson*, vol. 2, p. 895.

50. For William Scoresby, see T. and C. Stamp, *William Scoresby, Arctic Scientist* (Whitby, Eng: Whitby Press, 1975).

51. It is not easy to define, in a few words, what would have constituted a conventional "scientific training" in Britain in the 1830s and 1840s. As Joule contemplated going to Cambridge to take the Mathematical Tripos after his wife died in 1854 we may certainly include mathematics degrees at Cambridge, Dublin, or Oxford, a medical training at one of the Scottish universities, and apprenticeship to a pharmacist, physician, surgeon, or engineer. The German universities had only just begun to attract American, British, and other foreign students.

52. Sir Arthur Schuster, *Biographical Fragments* (London: Macmillan & Co., 1932), pp. 201-206.

53. Letter dated March 14, 1857, *C.U.L., K. & S.C.*.

54. Ashworth, "List of Apparatus."

55. Joule's letter to Thomson of December 9, 1848, makes it clear that he has only just learned of Mayer's work. (*C.U.L., K. & S.C.*, J64) Steffens's conjecture (*James Prescott Joule*, pp. 61-76) that Joule may have learned of Mayer's work just after he published his first paper on the mechanical equivalent of heat in 1843 cannot be sustained. See E. Mendoza and D. S. L. Cardwell, "A Note on a Suggestion Concerning the Work of J. P. Joule," *British Journal for the History of Science* 14 (1981), pp. 177-180.

Chapter 4

Maxwell's Scientific Creativity
C. W. F. Everitt

James Clerk Maxwell (1831-1879) is properly regarded along with Isaac Newton and Albert Einstein as one of the three supreme creative geniuses of modern theoretical physics. Others have contributed magnificently to the development of physical theory (one thinks of Lagrange and Laplace) or to changing the world view underlying it (one thinks of Bohr and Heisenberg), but these three men, Newton, Maxwell, and Einstein, are hewn on a grander scale, and both in personal stature and pervasiveness of influence they demand the attention of all who wish to understand scientific creativity.

Maxwell's two largest achievements are his creation of the electromagnetic theory of light and his introduction and systematic development of statistical methods in physics through his work on the kinetic theory of gases. The electromagnetic theory of light unified the fields of electricity, magnetism, and optics under a system of equations, Maxwell's equations, which not only surpassed all previous accounts of the phenomena in explanatory power, but also changed the course of physics by articulating a new kind of theory: field theory. The idea of interpreting the forces between magnets and currents in terms of stresses in the intervening space rather than direct action at a distance originated with Faraday rather than Maxwell, but Maxwell by mathematizing it and introducing the new concepts of the displacement current, the energy density in the

Some of the research on which this chapter is based was undertaken with support from a Fellowship in 1976-1977 from the John Simon Guggenheim Memorial Foundation.

field, and the Maxwell stress tensor made it uniquely his own. Besides providing a startlingly original theory of light, which succeeded technically where earlier theories had failed, Maxwell's work implied the existence of radio waves twenty-five years before they were detected experimentally by Hertz. And Maxwell went further. His vast *Treatise on Electricity and Magnetism,* published in two volumes in 1873, opened so many new lines of research that it became the chief source of progress in physics over the next forty years. In 1950 Robert Andrews Millikan, author of the famous oil-drop experiment to measure the charge on the electron, looking back over his own long career as a physicist which began when the influence of the *Treatise* was at its height, joined Maxwell's *Treatise* with Newton's *Principia* as the two most far-reaching books in the history of physics—"the one creating our modern mechanical world, the other our modern electrical world."[1]

In the development of electromagnetic theory Maxwell (to adapt Newton's phrase) stood on the shoulders of two giants: Michael Faraday and William Thomson (Lord Kelvin). In the development of statistical mechanics he was the giant on whose shoulders two other men, Ludwig Boltzmann and Willard Gibbs, stood. The story of Maxwell's introduction of the velocity distribution function into kinetic theory in 1859 is an enlightening one for the student of scientific creativity. It originated in the coming together of three apparently unconnected fields of research: Maxwell's study between 1855 and 1859 of the rings of Saturn, which proved that Saturn's rings had to be made up of large numbers of independent but possibly colliding bodies; his chance reading early in 1859 of a paper on gas theory by Rudolf Clausius, in which Clausius introduced the idea that gas molecules, though traveling at high velocities, are continually colliding with each other and starting off in new directions; and another chance reading ten years earlier of an essay-review by John Herschel of Adolphe Quetelet's *Theory of Probability as Applied to the Moral and Social Sciences.* Herschel had given a new popular derivation of the law of least squares applied to random distributions of point in a space of two dimensions. Maxwell had been thinking about the collisions between the bodies making up Saturn's rings but saw no way of doing useful calculations on them. Clausius's paper made him realize that although it was hopeless to try to follow the paths of vast numbers of individual colliding bodies, one might learn something from their statistical behavior, just as social scientists learn something from statistical investigations of human phenomena. What was needed was a formula giving the most probable distribution of velocities among a large number of gas molecules. Maxwell applied Herschel's idea to derive such a formula. He analyzed properties of gases never before investigated, the so-called transport phenomena—viscosity, diffusion, and thermal conduction. He discovered the "equipartition theorem," which in its original form stated that the average translational energy and average rotational energy of large numbers of colliding molecules, whether of the same or different species, are equal. He then discovered the first breakdown in classical mechanics, since calculations from the equipartition theorem turned out to be inconsistent with the measured ratios of the specific heats of gases: a puzzle that remained unsolved until the rise of quantum theory 40 years later. Another surprising result was that over a wide range of pressures the viscosity of a gas should be independent of its pressure. When Maxwell and his wife verified this prediction experimentally between 1863 and 1865, the kinetic theory of gases became widely accepted.

Maxwell's later work in gas theory and statistical mechanics took three principal directions, one of which led to Boltzmann, one along with Boltzmann's work to Gibbs, and the third into a new area to which neither Boltzmann nor Gibbs contributed but which came into its own much later, the science of rarefied gas dynamics. The route to Boltzmann came with Maxwell's second published paper on kinetic theory (1867). This paper greatly improved the analysis of transport phenomena, taking into account the long-range forces between gas molecules, and gave a new derivation of the velocity distribution law. Boltzmann, from 1868 on, set about generalizing Maxwell's work. Following up one result of Maxwell's, he showed how to incorporate the action of external forces such as gravitation into the theory. He also extended the equipartition theorem, investigated the approach of a velocity distribution to equilibrium, and rewrote Maxwell's transfer equations in the form usually known today as the Boltzmann equation. Some of Boltzmann's results were more than a little disturbing. The arguments they were based on were so general that they would seem to apply to the molecules of liquids and solids as well as gases, yet it was hard to conceive how they could. In Maxwell's words, "Boltzmann has proved too much."[2] It was in following out this issue that Maxwell in 1878, a year before his death, produced the paper that in Joseph Larmor's words "marks the emergence of Statistical Dynamics into the rank of a special exact science."[3] In it, among other things, Maxwell developed the concept of "ensemble averaging" that was to become central in Gibbs's work. The question of whether statistical mechanics applied to solids and liquids as well as gases remained, like the growing number of discrepancies between the equipartition theorem and observation, a mystery until the rise of quantum theory. It then became clear that the methods of Boltzmann, Maxwell, and Gibbs work even for solids if classical statistics is replaced with the appropriate quantum statistics.

To have been the central figure in the two greatest theoretical achievements of one's age would be enough for most scientists. Maxwell did more. His other discoveries, though smaller by comparison, would have secured the reputations of half a dozen lesser men. He founded the science of quantitative colorimetry and projected in 1860 the first color photograph. He made important contributions to the theory of photoelasticity. His essay on Saturn's rings, published in 1859, was described by G. B. Airy, the English Astronomer Royal, as "the most remarkable contribution to mechanical astronomy that has appeared for many years."[4] He invented the method of reciprocal diagrams for analyzing stresses in bridge structures. He wrote in 1868 the first important paper on control theory. His work on thermodynamics led to the Maxwell relations between thermodynamic quantities, as well as to the famous "very small BUT lively being"[5] the Maxwell demon. He made notable contributions to geometrical optics, including the first practical developments of what later became known through the work of Henrich Bruns as the "eikonal method." He invented the standard notation of dimensional analysis. He influenced the course of mathematical technique through his discussion of the classification of vector quantities and his coining of the terms *gradient, convergence* (divergence), and *curl* for the different actions of Hamilton's vector operator ∇ on vector and scalar quantities. He invented the polar representation of spherical harmonic functions.

Such a range of activity in a man who died at 48 suggests a most unusual personality, and Maxwell, though at a distance he sometimes appeared as a "quiet and rather silent man,"[6] impressed those who came closer as someone entirely out of the ordinary. When Henry Augustus Rowland, the newly appointed Professor of Physics at Johns Hopkins University, visited Britain in 1875, he saw most of the physics laboratories in the country and stayed as Maxwell's guest at his home in the southwest of Scotland as well as at Cambridge. On the whole the professors did not impress him: "They are men like the rest of us." But there was one exception: "After seeing Maxwell I felt somewhat discouraged for here I met with a mind whose superiority was almost oppressive."[7]

II

Granting the unusual qualities that must be present in a Maxwell, it is yet necessary to recognize that genius does not flower in a vacuum. The romantic view always tends to link creativity with rebellion, and even a man with so many estimable qualities as Einstein may not be above the charming egotism that emphasizes how little rather than how much he owes to his environment. But if Maxwell had been born in Afghanistan, or even two hundred years earlier in the Scottish Borders, he might, as the expert horseman he was, have become a great brigand; he would not have become a great physicist. Even the classic cases of genius seemingly materializing out of thin air, like the Indian mathematician Ramanujan, prove otherwise on closer examination. To G. H. Hardy from the fastnesses of Trinity College, Cambridge, Ramanujan may have seemed a child of Nature, but in reality his interest in mathematics had been stimulated by good teachers, by the opportunity he had at the age of sixteen to borrow an English text, Carr's *Synopsis of Pure Mathematics,* by a fellowship to the Government College at Kumbakonen, Madras, and by warm encouragement from Ramaswami Aiyar, founder of the Indian Mathematical Society. Maxwell, who well knew how much he owed to his environment, stood in two great scientific traditions: the Scottish tradition centering in Edinburgh, where he spent his formative years from ten to nineteen between 1841 and 1850; and the tradition of applied mathematics at Cambridge, where he was an undergraduate from 1850 to 1854, a Fellow of Trinity College from 1854 to 1856, an examiner in the Mathematical Tripos for the four years, 1866, 1867, 1869, and 1870, and Professor of Experimental Physics from 1871 until his death in 1879. Before looking into the personal aspects of Maxwell's genius we must learn its background, in both the broad influence of Edinburgh culture on his family and the particular impact of the Scottish and English educational systems on Maxwell himself.

Among all the varied themes in Scottish history none deserves more admiring attention than the cultural flowering of Edinburgh during the century that followed the Union with England in 1707. Having lost their Parliament, the Scots struck out in a new direction, and Edinburgh swiftly advanced from being the capital of a small and poor country on the periphery of things to become one of the great European intellectual centers, a city to whose fame over a golden age lasting nearly 150 years, David Hume and Adam Smith,

James Hutton and Joseph Black, Robert Burns and Sir Walter Scott, to name but six of the more obvious figures, each in his own way contributed. The seeds of change had been planted in the seventeenth century when sectarian strife or simple need had forced large numbers of Scotsmen to seek an education in Leiden or Paris or Rome, but by the middle of the eighteenth century the tide had turned. Edinburgh Medical School, established by the Monros, two of whom, father and son, had studied under Hermann Boerhaave at Leiden, was equal to any in Europe. For English Dissenters, excluded from Oxford and Cambridge by the religious tests, Edinburgh University was the obvious place to go, and once there they would meet professors of wider interests and greater distinction than any to be found in the two English universities. Even so notable a European as Benjamin Constant found the two years he spent in Edinburgh the happiest and most intellectually stimulating of his life. Nor was the eminence of Edinburgh limited to things of the intellect. Art flourished with Raeburn, Allan Ramsay the younger, and a worthy group of lesser painters; architecture with the Adams brothers and William Craig, the man who laid out the designs for Edinburgh New Town, built between 1770 and 1820, one of the few cities in Britain with a coherent and graceful plan; while in the countryside around Edinburgh new farming methods brought a cheerful prosperity largely free of the squalors that accompanied the money-making of the Industrial Revolution elsewhere in Britain.

Behind the famous figures who came and went across the Edinburgh stage between 1720 and 1850 was a group of talented persons, small in absolute numbers but substantial enough to form a distinctive culture. Among the families making up this group one of the strongest was the Clerks of Penicuik, whose 7000-acre estate at Penicuik (pronounced Penny-cook) about twelve miles south of Edinburgh was and remains one of the most beautiful landed properties in Scotland. The family had begun its rise early in the seventeenth century under William Clerk, a merchant of Montrose. His son, John Clerk, went to Paris in 1634, acquired there a large fortune in commerce, and after returning to Scotland in 1646, bought the barony of Penicuik. He died in 1674. His eldest son John served in the Scottish Parliament and was created a baronet of Nova Scotia in 1679, which makes the Clerk baronetcy the oldest now surviving in Scotland. He was a man of great personal courage and unbending Presbyterian principles. He married Elizabeth Henderson, granddaughter of William Drummond of Hawthornden, the poet, a singularly accomplished lady, especially in music, to whose influence the later artistic proclivities of the family may probably be traced. They had two sons, John and William, of markedly different character. John, the elder, who succeeded to the baronetcy in 1720, had the gifts and temperament of the successful man of affairs: talent, learning, industry, lack of humor, and a calculating sense of the loci of power. William was a charming, feckless, ne'er-do-well, always at odds with his father.

Towards the end of his life (he died in 1755) the second Sir John Clerk wrote an autobiographical memoir, which was eventually published by the Scottish Record Society in 1892. To anyone who is not put off by the sight of an elderly gentleman offering, in a private document addressed to his family, patent half-truths with an air of bluff honesty, the memoir makes absorbing reading, both as a tale in itself and for the insight it gives into the rise of Edinburgh culture and of the Clerk family in it. In 1695 at the age of nineteen young Clerk had gone to Leiden, where he studied medicine under Boerhaave and drawing under William Mieris. The next two years he spent in Florence and Rome, studying painting and music. He wrote an opera, which was performed in Rome. He returned to Scotland in 1698, took up the law, and by 1705 had become sufficiently well known to be chosen as one of the Commissioners of the Union with England. Talent and industry made him, young as he was, the principal Scottish financial negotiator. His memoir contains a lively account of the journey from London to Edinburgh in which he accompanied the mule train carrying the English gold that was the price of settlement. He became a judge and eventually a Baron of the Exchequer (one of the Scottish law lords), married, and settled down to a long safe career during which he adroitly navigated through the rocks and shoals of disputes between Hanoverians and Jacobites on which so many others made shipwreck during the rebellions of 1715 and 1745. He remained a skillful musician and became a patron of the arts, as well as a famous—to his sons a tedious—antiquary. One story that he does not himself tell is that his fifth son, John, a talented sculptor, made a number of ancient Roman heads, which were buried at appropriate sites near Penicuik and duly discovered, to the delight and amazement of Clerk and his antiquarian friends.

While John Clerk was building a successful life, brother William was making a mess of his. The Clerk papers contain two drafts of a pitiless document compiled by his father, the first baronet, in 1709, cataloging in lurid detail all the young man's errors, debts, changes of plan, and low amours over the previous decade. He entered Glasgow University but was sent down for an entanglement with a servant girl. He spent a year at Leiden but made nothing of it, though he shared his brother's talent for drawing. He returned to Edinburgh and promptly landed in another amatory pickle. He tried his hand at the law and failed. His restless spirit and inability to settle anywhere earned him the nickname "Wandering Willie." Just as it seemed that he would come to the inevitable bad end, he fell in love with Agnes Maxwell, heiress of the Maxwells of Middlebie in Dumfriesshire, married, and for the few remaining years of his life continued a model husband and father. It was through this marriage that the name Maxwell became linked with that of the Clerks, and hence more than 100 years later that Maxwell the physicist inherited the double name Clerk Maxwell.

William and Agnes both died young, leaving one seven-year-old daughter, Dorothea, heiress to the Middlebie estate. Her uncle, the Baron of Exchequer, became her guardian. In 1732 she married his second son George, she being then seventeen and he twenty-one. Clerk in his memoirs states in one place that he had no part in bringing about the marriage, and in another, a few pages away, that it was done in accordance with her mother's dying wish ten years earlier. Be that as it may, the marriage had the advantage of keeping the Middlebie property snugly in the family. By some ingenious manipulations, more easily carried through by an eminent jurist than a layman, the entail on the Middlebie estate was broken by special Act of Parliament, and the property was put up for sale to liquidate the Maxwell debts, bought in by Clerk himself at a price far below market value, and thus secured free and clear in his son George's name. At the same time it was arranged that Middlebie should not be held together with Penicuik. The separation of properties went into abeyance when Sir James Clerk, the third baronet, died without issue in 1782 and George Clerk Maxwell succeeded him; but it was revived after the fifth baronet died in 1798, when the estates again descended to two brothers, sons of the fifth baronet's younger brother James. The elder, Sir George Clerk, succeeded to Penicuik and in due course became a prominent Conservative politician. The younger, John Clerk, lived in Edinburgh under that name until 1826, when at the age of thirty-six he married a lady by the name of Frances Cay, took the name Maxwell, and set about cultivating the 2000 acres near Dalbeattie in the southwest of Scotland that were all that was now left of the enormous Middlebie property after a succession of imprudent business speculations by Sir George Clerk Maxwell. John Clerk Maxwell and his wife had two children, a daughter Elizabeth born in

1828 who died at the age of two, and James, the physicist, son and heir, born in Edinburgh on 13 June 1831.

Strong individuality, practical good sense, artistic talent, and a tradition of the law characterized the Clerk family over several generations, and the closeness of Penicuik to Edinburgh gave them ample opportunity to shine. Penicuik House, rebuilt by the third baronet in 1767, was one of the showplaces of Scotland, with sixty rooms and a grand dining hall whose ceiling was magnificently decorated by Alexander Runciman with paintings illustrating scenes from Macpherson's fraudulent Gaelic poem *Ossian*. The persistence of the artistic gift in a family so practical in outlook is a striking fact, one that must be born in mind in analyzing Maxwell's genius. Each generation threw up clever artists, among whom not the least able was Maxwell's cousin Jemima—daughter of John Clerk Maxwell's sister, Mrs. Wedderburn—whose brilliant water-color paintings of Maxwell's childhood are a perpetual delight to Maxwell scholars.

Many of the men who constituted Edinburgh society in the late eighteenth and early nineteenth century had been trained as lawyers, but they dabbled in literary, scientific, or antiquarian pursuits. Young men, even with inherited wealth, were expected to take up a profession. Walter Scott was one, Maxwell's father another, and Maxwell himself in one of these brief remarks that cast a flood of light on the difference in outlook between one historical period and another says in one place, "I should naturally have become an advocate by profession, with scientific proclivities, but the existence of exclusively scientific men, and in particular of [Professor J. D. Forbes] convinced my father and myself that a profession was not necessary to a useful life."[8] Maxwell may not have appreciated that his decision was one of the signs that physics was just then beginning to emerge as a profession. It was no accident that the words *physicist* and *scientist,* coined by William Whewell in 1840, only came into general use in the 1870s.

Even in the eighteenth century several of the Clerks had scientific interests, mostly of a practical kind. Sir George Clerk Maxwell, the fourth baronet, and his brother John Clerk of Eldin were both friends of James Hutton, the geologist. Clerk of Eldin—the same who had teased his father by burying fake Roman sculptures at Penicuik—accompanied Hutton on that famous expedition to Glen Tilt in 1785, where Hutton verified a crucial point in his theory of the earth by observing the exposed contact between granite and country rock in the river bed, becoming so excited thereby that the guides who were with them were convinced that he had found gold.[9] Clerk's drawings of the geological sites on his expeditions with Hutton are classics.[10] His son John Clerk, Lord Eldin, became a famous lawyer and judge, noted for his caustic repartees, besides being a great antiquary and collector in his own right. Another son, William, to whom Maxwell's father was close, was an intimate friend of Sir Walter Scott's, often referred to in Lockhart's *Life of Scott.*

Although Maxwell's father was trained for the law and used his legal knowledge to good effect in local affairs after he had moved to the country, he never practiced extensively. His great interests were architecture and scientific matters. He was elected a Fellow of the Royal Society of Edinburgh in 1822, along with his friend John Cay, the son of another of Scott's close friends and brother of his future wife, with whom he spent many hours planning technical devices of various kinds. John Clerk Maxwell's one published scientific paper appeared in the *Edinburgh Medical and Philosophical Journal* a few months before Maxwell's birth, "Outlines for a Plan combining Machinery with the Manual Printing Press." The details are not important; yet the paper is important to students of Mr. Maxwell's son. There in the neatly thought out, carefully drawn contrivance for an automatic feed printing press are the qualities that reappeared later in Maxwell's experimental work on color vision, electromagnetism, and the viscosity of gases. Every experiment Maxwell did involved a specific device, thought out from beginning to end, manufactured to precise designs by an instrument maker; as different as could be imagined from the string-and-sealing-wax improvisations characteristic of Faraday, Stokes, J. J. Thomson, and a century of English physicists from 1840 on.

The Scottish genius seems to embody two contrasting daemons that may be called for want of better terms the classical and the romantic, or perhaps the spirit of order and the spirit of invention. Among men disclosing the two strains, two of the best known are Hume and Scott, yet when their works are examined in detail the contrast between the great rationalist and the great romantic chiefly reveals the elusive character of a division whose origins seem definable only by negations. The difference is not between religion and irreligion; no institution in Scotland embodies the spirit of order and reason more completely than the Kirk. Nor is it the contrast between Highlands and Lowlands, though Lowland writers like Scott, Robert Louis Stevenson, and John Buchan have found in tales of Highland life an outlet for their romantic imaginings. Least of all do they correspond to the division between doers and thinkers: Livingstone the explorer was a man of order, Carlyle the prophet-philosopher a man of chaotic invention. Yet elusive as the actions of the daemons may be, they often provide insight into the workings of Scotland and Scotsmen, and nowhere do they appear more dramatically than in the contrasting histories of the two families whose names are joined in that of Maxwell the physicist: the Clerks and the Maxwells.

The story of the Clerks is of a steady upward climb. Talented, hard-headed, industrious, self-sufficient, they moved from strength to strength, skillfully consolidating their gains, capable of every action except the grand romantic gesture. Canny is the Scots word that perfectly fits their character. A sharper contrast than with the Maxwells would be hard to imagine. One of the great Border families going back to the twelfth century, probably of Anglo-Norman descent, theirs was a history of violent ups and downs. Hereditary keepers from the fourteenth century of Caerlaverock Castle near Dumfries, where the river Nith enters the Solway Firth some twelve miles east of Maxwell's home at Glenlair, they continued for three centuries in steady feuding with their neighbors the Douglases and the Johnstones. The Maxwell peerage dates from 1428. James IV of Scotland enters the line through his illegitimate daughter Lady Katherine Stewart, who married James Douglas, Third Earl of Morton, and whose daughter Beatrice married the Fifth Lord Maxwell. Their descendant Lord Maxwell the Eighth was, through his illegitimate son John, the ancestor of the Maxwells of Middlebie, and so of James Clerk Maxwell

Toward the end of the sixteenth century the ancient feud between the Maxwells and Johnstones erupted in blood. A series of lurid events culminated in 1593 in a pitched battle at Dryffe Sands between Lord Maxwell the Seventh at the head of 2000 men and a smaller army of the Johnstones with their allies. The Maxwells were routed, and Lord Maxwell, who had fallen, was brutally put to death after having his hand slashed off as he extended it for quarter. Lord Maxwell the Eighth publicly swore vengeance and, after escaping in 1608 from preventive detention in Edinburgh, approached Sir James Johnstone for a secret meeting to discuss terms. Thereupon he shot his enemy from his horse with "two poysonit bullets"[11] and castrated him as he lay dying. Lord Maxwell fled to France; venturing four years later to return to Scotland, he was caught and charged with treason as well as murder, and beheaded in 1613. His brother, who succeeded him in the absence of legitimate descendants, was not recognized as Ninth Lord Maxwell nor restored to his lands until 1619. Probably Middlebie went to Lord Maxwell's natural son at the same time. The feud with the Johnstones became famous in Scottish popular history through the ballad "Lord Maxwell's Goodnight," printed from an old manuscript by Walter Scott in his *Minstrelsy of the Scottish Border* (1799), which celebrates in language of haunting beauty the grandeur of revenge. The feud did not end with Lord Maxwell's execution. In 1639 John Maxwell of Middlebie, Maxwell's ancestor, was taken by might in his house by a party of Johnstones and murdered.

The Maxwells from the sixteenth to the eighteenth century were traditionally adherents of the Stuarts, and like most who touched that fatal flawed beauty gave away their own interests in exchange for moments of high glory and fickle princely charm. Lord Maxwell the Sixth served as proxy for James V of Scotland in his marriage with Mary of Guise; while it was at Terregles, near Kirkcudbright, home of that Lord's younger brother Sir John Maxwell, afterward Fourth Lord Herries, that Mary Queen of Scots spent two of her last three nights on Scottish soil and took her ill-omened decision to seek refuge in England rather than France. Among the possessions that descended to Maxwell the physicist was a clock, said to have belonged to the Queen, presented by her to Lord Maxwell as she left. The family fortunes continued to fluctuate. Lord Maxwell the 10th, the 1st Earl of Nithsdale and a staunch supporter of Charles I, had much of his property seized by the Army of the Estates during the rupture between the King and Covenanters in 1640, when Caerlaverock Castle was bombarded and taken. Other members of the family duly found themselves ruined with the Stuarts during the 1715 rebellion, though the Maxwells of Middlebie survived, probably because the inheritance lay in the female line. Clerk of Penicuik made no such mistake. After the death of Queen Anne he quietly withdrew to the country for some months and then emerged as a vigorous supporter of the Hanoverian cause, active in helping stamp out the 1715 and 1745 rebellions.

Maxwell, the most modest and least snobbish of men, who, as Lewis Campbell observes, alarmed his high-born relatives when he was young by traveling third-class on trains because he liked a hard seat, and by "speaking to gentle and simple in exactly the same tone,"[12] was the last man to value anyone for another's merit. Yet he felt the strength of the past, and a remark of his to Campbell that no man knows how much in him is due to his progenitors, seems true in his own case. The student of Maxwell's scientific papers cannot but be impressed by the nice mixture of Clerk-like canniness and Maxwell-like cavalier recklessness by which his work is characterized,

as witnessed, for example, in the contrast between the daring imagi-
nativeness of the molecular vortex model of the aether, from which
in 1861 Maxwell gained his first inkling of the electromagnetic
theory of light, and the sober phenomenology of the paper that
followed it in 1863, in which he deduced the relationship between
electromagnetic quantities and the velocity of light from purely
dimensional arguments, independent of theories of the aether.

So far I have said almost nothing about Maxwell's mother or the
Cay family from which she sprang. But Frances Cay is too striking
and powerful a woman to be described at the end of a section; we
must come back to her later.

III

In attempting to penetrate the mind of a nineteenth century Scots-
man, especially one who had contact with England, one essential is
to form some appreciation of the profound gulfs that separated the
educational systems of the two countries from each other and from
systems now existing. The differences went far deeper than details
of curricula, organization, and church influence, important as such
matters were in the debates of the period: they represented, rather,
fundamental divergencies of educational theory.

Nowadays even those who deplore excessive specialization in
education seldom deny that someone who wishes to become an
engineer should at some stage of his university career choose a course
of study broadly related to engineering, that a future physicist
should study physics, a historian history, and a clergyman some
group of subjects including theology, church history, and psychology. In the early nineteenth century it was not so. Formal study was
seen in a different light. Its purpose was not to fit a man for a career
but to enlarge his mind. In England—at least in that part of the
English educational system that was embodied in Oxford, Cambridge, and the "public" schools—the guiding principle was the notion of an intellectual discipline. To achieve mental strength, so the
theory ran, one should be subjected to a rigorous training in one
particular field over a period of several years. When that was done all
else would follow. The Greek scholar could quickly assimilate whatever information might be needed in his life's work as an engineer or
builder of Empire; the Latinist could go on to become an architect
or Member of Parliament; the mathematician could pursue his career
as a lawyer or a bishop. As for the educational merit of different
disciplines, that was a matter of frequent, bitter debate: in practice

the possibilities reduced to two: at Oxford, classics, or more accurately, classics combined with logic; at Cambridge, mathematics, or mathematics combined with classics. Such and none other were the two rival collections of gymnastic apparatus on which a young Englishman with the right social background or unusual good luck, and a willingness to subscribe to the thirty-nine articles of the Church of England, could expect to undertake his intellectual muscle-building.

In Scotland also the preference was for mental over vocational training, but in a different framework. The Scottish system has been termed by G. E. Davie "democratic intellectualism." The universities were democratic in the sense that they were emphatically not the abodes of privilege that the English ones were. The plowboy, who swung his sack of oats over his shoulder and trudged seventy miles to the city for an education, was a reality, recognized and allowed for in the long summer vacations and the thrifty expedients of class tickets and *viva voce* examinations. It was no accident that Scotland, with less than half the population, had five ancient universities to England's two. As for Scottish intellectualism, its essence lay in teaching at a fairly elementary level a wide range of subjects organized around the philosophy class, the theory being that the broad views and logical habits of thought so developed would give the student a sound footing for his later specialized interest. To sum up in a sentence, the English aimed to make particular studies the foundation of a general education; the Scots aimed to make a general education the foundation for particular technical studies. Anyone, therefore, like Maxwell, who passed through both systems had to execute a sharp, possibly bewildering, *volte-face,* the consequences of which would critically depend on his intellectual, and still more his emotional, maturity at the time of transition. And here was another difference between the two systems. In England the normal university entrance age, then as now, was eighteen. In Scotland the range was much wider: the majority of the class entered at the age of sixteen and remained at college four years, but there was always a proportion of poor undergraduates in their twenties and early thirties, earnest young men, anxious for opportunity, who imparted to the classes a seriousness of purpose little known to the privileged youth of England.

In Maxwell's time both systems were under attack. In England, Oxford and Cambridge were easy targets for the outcries of reformers against privilege and exclusiveness. To the complaints of religious nonconformists, who though they could attend the two

Plate 1. Maxwell about 1866 (age 35).

Plate 2. Maxwell in 1855 (age 24).

Plate 3. "Puck with an Owl" — James Clerk Maxwell, age 2, by William Dyce.

The authenticating letter from Maxwell's cousin Albert Cay to his sister Elizabeth Dunn reads:

23 March 1915

My dear Lizzie

I think you may like to have this photograph of a drawing by Uncle William Dyce of James Clerk Maxwell as "Puck". It does not come out very well but the drawing is wonderfully like the picture of James with Aunt Fanny [Maxwell's mother] that we have in the Dining room here (also by Uncle William) — the roguish eyes are excellent.

With much love from us both to you both

Your affectionate brother
Albert Cay

Plate 4. Tubbing on the Duck Pond at Glenlair by Jemima Wedderburn (1840, age 9). Figures from left clockwise: Jemima Wedderburn, Bobby, Maxwell's tutor, Johnny, Mrs. Wedderburn, John Clerk Maxwell, Toby, 3 ducks among the onlookers.

ancient universities after 1829, could not graduate from them without foreswearing their consciences, were added the objections of utilitarians who claimed that everything taught there was useless and out of date. Why was so much wealth concentrated in anachronistic survivals, while up-to-date institutions like University College, London, struggled and starved? Such questions were loudly argued when Maxwell was a student at Cambridge in the early 1850s, and his return there in 1871 to become Professor of Experimental Physics was one part of the University's response to changing times.

The crisis in Scottish education has been analyzed by Dr. Davie. As in England the utilitarian voices were heard calling for radical reform, but another factor that preoccupied the minds of Scotsmen, then as now, was the impact of England and English educational ideals. Whatever the theoretical merits or demerits of the Scottish system might be, it was a painful fact that Scotsmen leaving the university at twenty often found themselves at a disadvantage in competition with the better Oxford or Cambridge graduates. The institution of Civil Service examinations in the 1840s, which went some way towards eliminating abuses so far as the English were concerned, only made matters worse for the Scots, since the examinations were designed for products of English universities and public schools. While the Scots tended too much to attribute their woes to the sinister plottings of the London government, forgetting that the English, with the sectarian debates between Church of England and Dissenters, had troubles enough of their own, they did face special difficulties. The early entrance age to the universities made it difficult to raise university standards without first reforming the schools, yet no one was agreed on how to reform the schools.

Into these problems at the age of ten, all unknown to himself, Maxwell was projected. His early years had been spent running wild on the Glenlair estate remote from any school. His education was in his mother's hands. She taught him to read and write, encouraged (as did his father) his curiosity in all things, and took pride in his wonderful memory. At seven he could recite long passages from Milton; he knew by heart all 176 verses of Psalm 119. Then in 1839, when Maxwell was eight, she died. It was a stunning blow and one whose repercussions went beyond those that affect any small boy whose mother dies, since it also utterly disrupted Maxwell's education. For two years a tutor was tried, with ill results. The tutor and Maxwell held different opinions about the utility of Latin grammar as an educational instrument, and Maxwell even at that age was not one to yield an opinion. He balked, the tutor bashed, and Mr. Maxwell was so absorbed in his own schemes that two years went by before the sharp eyes of Miss Jane Cay, Mrs. Maxwell's sister, on a visit to Glenlair, spotted what was going on and the tutor was dismissed. Mr. Maxwell decided to send his son to school in Edinburgh, but since he himself remained generally in the country, Maxwell for the next eight years spent an uneasy existence shuttled back and forth between his father at Glenlair and one or another of his two Edinburgh aunts, Mrs. Wedderburn and Miss Cay.

Edinburgh Academy, to which Maxwell went, had been founded in 1824 by a group of prominent Edinburgh men, including Sir Walter Scott and Lord Cockburn, the lawyer and memorialist, as a counterweight to the old Edinburgh High School. The headmaster, or Rector, to use his correct title, was a Welshman, the Reverend John Williams, imported via Balliol College with the express purpose of imparting to Edinburgh youth a classical education with all the most up-to-date Oxford refinements. He was an efficient teacher, known to the boys as "Punch" and popular with them because—in Maxwell's words to his father—"We have lots of jokes, and he speaks

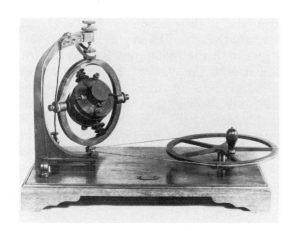

Plate 5. Apparatus used by Maxwell in 1861 in an attempt to observe a gyromagnetic effect (subsequently detected in 1908 by S. J. Barnett).

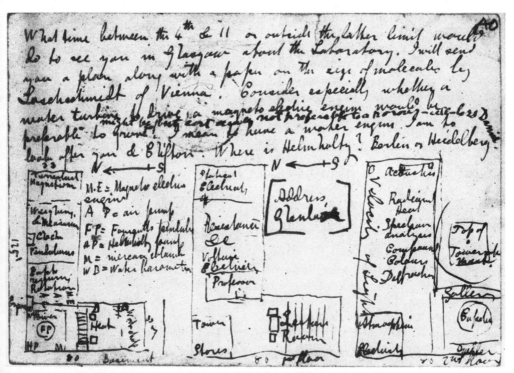

Plate 6. Postcard from Maxwell to Thomson written a few weeks after his appointment to the Cavendish Professorship at Cambridge in 1871 showing the plan of the Cavendish Laboratory in a form nearly identical to the architect's final designs.

a great deal, and we do not have so much monotonous parsing."[13] He rapidly made the Academy the leading school in Scotland and became prominent in the party that was out to anglicize the universities. His aim was, indeed, to smash the metaphysical structure of Scottish education and replace it with the classics. Times and values change in strange ways. If it seems odd now that a clergyman propounding classical education should be cast as a leader of the advanced reform party, that is only one of the oddities the student of education in nineteenth-century Scotland must grapple with. Even in the Academy, however, Williams did not always get his way. Most of the staff were Scotsmen with their own opinions about the activities of the Oxford interloper, not least among them the mathematics master James Gloag, "a teacher of strenuous character and quaint originality" for whom mathematics was, in the old Scottish tradition, a "mental and moral discipline." More than one tale has survived of Gloag's gritty confrontations with the Rector and his "classical pets."[14]

To arrive at school several weeks after the beginning of term, dressed in eccentric clothes designed and made by one's father, speaking Scots in a Gallowegian accent that no right-minded Edinburgh boy has heard, are not the actions of a young man versed in the ways of the world. Maxwell came home from school the first day with his clothes torn to ribbons, an air of brave amusement on his face, and murder in his heart. For the next two years his school life was a misery. He was harrassed in the Academy yard and did badly in class because of his awkwardness and hesitancy of speech. That in due course he came to enjoy Edinburgh Academy and ended by writing a song in its honor with the refrain

> Dear old Academy,
> Queer old Academy,
> A merry lot we were, I wot,
> When at the old Academy.[15]

is a tribute to the excellence of the senior masters, especially Gloag and the Rector, and still more to the vital friendships he formed with two boys, Lewis Campbell and Peter Guthrie Tait. Maxwell's friendship with Tait, which began when both boys were about fifteen, was based chiefly on their common interest in physics and mathematics. With Campbell, who was to become Maxwell's biographer as well as a distinguished Greek scholar and author in his own right, his relationship went deeper. Modestly Campbell recalls the occasion two years after Maxwell entered the Academy when he (Campbell) came to Maxwell's rescue in a fight, with "the warm rush of chivalrous emotion, and the look of affectionate recognition in Maxwell's eyes. However imperturbable he was one could see he was not thick-skinned."[16]

In a fascinating response to a questionnaire sent out by Francis Galton in 1876 while gathering materials for his book *English Men of Science,* Maxwell wrote that his education "included French, German, logic, natural philosophy, chemistry, besides mathematics. I lived in a house where I saw many people whose interests were of various kinds, and I went to a day-school where I mixed with the boys only when they were fresh and active. Thus I had two outer worlds to balance against each other. On the whole, I had, I think, the greatest degree of freedom possible to a boy."[17] Campbell's brilliant portrayal of Maxwell's boyhood confirms this and adds more on Maxwell's other interests: his early excellence at English literature and Scripture knowledge; his verse translations of the Latin classics; his cooperation with cousin Jemima, by then in her early twenties, in knitting, pottery-making, and woodcutting; his weird letters to his father, full of puns and acrostics; his experiments with his uncle John Cay on electrotyping; his trips to study the geology of Salisbury crags and the engineering works of the Granton railway; the dancing lessons where he mastered the most intricate steps; his first attendance when twelve at a Shakespearean play, *As You Like It,* with Mrs. Charles Kean as Rosalind; and his casual report, with deliberately perverse spelling, in a letter to his father, written when he was thirteen: "I have made a Tetra hedron, a dodeca hedron, and 2 other hedrons I don't know the wright names for."[18]

One friend of the family was D. R. Hay, a decorative artist interested in the principles of design. In 1845 Hay had been seeking a geometrical method of drawing oval curves similar to the string property of an ellipse. By attaching a pencil to a continuous string passed around three pins rather than two, he made a curve of roughly oval form combining segments of three ellipses. Maxwell's interest was aroused. At fourteen he discovered that if one keeps two foci but folds the string back on itself m times towards one focus and n times towards the other, like the block and tackle of a crane, a true oval is formed, which as afterwards appeared, is identical with the ovals first studied in 1683 by Descartes in connection with the refraction of light. Maxwell's father excitedly showed the idea to J. D. Forbes, the Professor of Natural Philosophy at Edinburgh University, who made the link to Descartes, verified that this method of describing Cartesian ovals was new, presented an account of it at the meeting of the Royal Society of Edinburgh on April 6, 1846, and wrote up in Maxwell's name a summary for the Society's *Proceedings*. Thus Maxwell made his entrance into the Edinburgh scientific world, and met one of the men who was to exercise a decisive influence on his career.

I have remarked elsewhere[19] that it is a mistake to see Maxwell as an infant mathematical prodigy like Pascal or Gauss. Clever he undoubtedly was, but the idea about ovals was one that might with luck have occurred to any very clever schoolboy familiar with the string property of the ellipse, who had seen cranes and lifting tackle at work. It was not the kind of profound mathematical insight that Pascal had at a comparable age, nor would it have been published if John Clerk Maxwell had not happened to know the right people. Range rather than concentration is the true mark of Maxwell's childhood genius, and many of the early signs point to a flowering in literature rather than science. Nevertheless for Maxwell the discovery was an event of high importance. His father, who had already taken him to one or two meetings of the Royal Society of Edinburgh, now started attending the meetings regularly with him. In April 1847 his uncle John Cay took him and Lewis Campbell to visit the private scientific laboratory of William Nicol, inventor of the Nicol's polarizing prism, a meeting Maxwell afterwards described as a turning point in his life. When Nicol a few months later sent him a pair of prisms, Maxwell began his first serious research in physics by studying the phenomenon of induced double refraction in strained glass, which had been discovered in 1826 by another famous Scottish experimenter, Sir David Brewster. Meanwhile mathematics was not neglected. Maxwell followed up his first work on ovals by an impressively thorough manuscript on the geometrical and optical properties of ovals and related curves of higher order. Gloag's teaching continued and the friendship with Tait ripened. Tait records how in 1847 he and Maxwell got into the habit of exchanging mathematical manuscripts and discussing "with schoolboy enthusiasm, numerous curious problems, among which I remember particularly the various plane sections of a ring or tore, and the form of a cylindrical mirror which should show one his image unperverted."[20] The groundwork had been laid.

Maxwell was enrolled at the University of Edinburgh in November 1847. At sixteen he was one of the few boys from the Academy's entering class of 1841 who had stayed the whole course. For all his obvious talent, no one had attempted to push him ahead. His record is worth comparing with those of his friends Campbell and Tait. Tait was in the class below Campbell and Maxwell. In the 1846 competition for the Edinburgh Academical Club Prize, which was open to all boys from the three senior classes, Campbell was first, Tait was third, and Maxwell sixth, the first three in mathematics being Tait, Campbell, and Maxwell, in that order. In the following year, Campbell having left, Maxwell was second and Tait third in the overall competition, and the two were first and second respectively in mathematics. Maxwell continued to excel in English, being top of his class in that and high in Latin; but it was Tait, not Maxwell, who was confidently (and rightly) hailed at school as a future Senior Wrangler in the Cambridge Mathematical Tripos.

The leisurely pace continued. Whereas Tait, who entered Edinburgh University at the same time as Maxwell, rushed immediately into the second-year classes in mathematics and natural philosophy, ignoring everything else, and then went up to Cambridge after one year, Maxwell spent three unhurried years on an almost wholly traditional Scottish university education with classes in logic and metaphysics, moral philosophy, mathematics, natural philosophy, and chemistry. All that was missing from the traditional mix were Latin and Greek, and in these subjects the English-style classical education Maxwell had received at Edinburgh Academy put him far ahead of anything he would have learned at the University.

Campbell attributed Maxwell's long stay at Edinburgh to his father's inveterate habit of procrastination, heightened by the lurid fears of Mr. Maxwell's Presbyterian friends about the corrupt moral and religious influences of the English universities. He deplored it on the grounds that an earlier experience of college life, in contrast to the non-resident existence of a Scottish university, might have rubbed off some of Maxwell's social awkwardnesses. Debate on such matters is difficult, but much can be said on the other side. In the intellectual life there are advantages to a period of some relaxation around the age of eighteen or nineteen. If the zest for learning has been established, it is then that fresh ideas may be germinated. At Edinburgh Maxwell was free to come and go as he pleased without the fierce competitive drive of the Cambridge Tripos examinations. Besides attending classes he had time to devour the university library. To this period belong some of his most fruitful plantings. What would have happened if he had gone straight to Cambridge is hard to guess. It is enough that Maxwell's course exposed him more than any of his contemporaries to the dichotomy between the Scottish and English educational systems and made him enter Cambridge one year older and far more mature intellectually than most English undergraduates. To say more requires a look at the two Edinburgh professors who most influenced him: Forbes and Sir William Hamilton, the metaphysician.

Two men more sharply contrasted than Forbes and Hamilton would be hard to find. Forbes, who was thirty-seven when Maxwell first met him, was an experimental physicist, who without quite being in the front rank had to his credit a good corpus of research. He is remembered for the invention of the seismometer; the discovery (sometimes wrongly attributed to Melloni) that radiant heat, like light, can be polarized; the discovery of the temperature dependence of the electrical resistivity of metals; and a pioneer investigation of the motions of glaciers, made during his vacations in the Swiss Alps, he being one of the earliest British Alpinists. He was a fine lecturer with an eloquent style, which he polished to precision by taking elocution lessons from Mrs. Siddons, the actress. During Maxwell's years at Edinburgh, Forbes gave him the run of his laboratory, enlisted his aid in the experiments on color vision that started Maxwell in that field, imparted to him some of his own impressive grasp of the history of physics, and provided for Maxwell's other researches a nice mixture of encouragement and sharp-tongued criticism.

Hamilton, the Professor of Logic and Metaphysics, was a much older man (he was fifty-nine when Maxwell entered the university). He had come to his chair later than Forbes after a varied career during which he had studied medicine and practiced law, as well as pursuing philosophy at Glasgow and Oxford Universities, and in Germany. A man of vast erudition and dominating personality, he had an extraordinary gift for stimulating young minds. Unlike Forbes, who had become enamored of the Cambridge educational system with its written examinations, Hamilton kept his classes in the traditional Scottish pattern, with two hours a week out of five being discussion periods guided by the great man himself. His home was open in the evenings for students to drop in, and his magnificent library of ten thousand volumes, many extremely rare, was at their command. He had married late, and his young family added to the liveliness of the atmosphere. Nothing could have been more captivating than this unusual combination of generosity and erudition. The influence of so many Scotsmen in revitalizing British philosophy during the latter half of the nineteenth century may be traced antecedently to Hamilton. By the time Maxwell knew him, Hamilton's health had begun to fail, and he needed a teaching assistant. The following passage from a letter of Maxwell's to Lewis Campbell in November 1847 describes his mode of conducting classes and a typical morning at Edinburgh University.

I look over notes and such like till 9:35, then I go to Coll., and I always go one way and cross streets at the same places; then at 10 comes Kelland [the Professor of Mathematics]. He is telling us about arithmetic and how the common rules are the best. At 11 there is Forbes, who has finished the introduction and properties of bodies and is beginning mechanics in earnest. Then at 12 if it is fine, I perambulate the Meadows; if not, I go to the Library and do references. At 1, I go to Logic. Sir W. reads the first ½ of his lecture, and commits the rest to his man, but reserves to himself the right of making remarks . . . we sit in seats lettered according to name and Sir W. takes and puts his hand into a jam pig [jar] full of metal letters (very classical) and pulls one out and examines the bench of the letter. The Logic lectures are far the most solid and take most notes.[21]

Forbes and Hamilton were bitter enemies. They differed on politics (Hamilton was a Whig, Forbes a Tory), on religion (Forbes was an Episcopalian, Hamilton a Presbyterian), and above all on universities policies. Whether it was the choice of a new colleague or the plan for a new pension fund, one thing was sure: whatever side Forbes came down on, Hamilton would come down on the other. In one place only did they ever meet constructively, and that was in the mind of the seventeen-year-old Maxwell. Here their combined influence was magnificently beneficial. Forbes helped develop in Maxwell a practical down-to-earth interest in experimental technique rare in a theoretical physicist; Hamilton gave him the ranging philosophic vision that is so evident in the many interesting philosophical asides that occur throughout his papers.

One point of angry contention between Forbes and Hamilton had been the appointment in 1839 of a Cambridge mathematician, Philip Kelland, to succeed William Wallace in the chair of mathematics at Edinburgh. Forbes, through his early involvement in the founding of the British Association in 1830, had become deeply impressed by William Whewell, Charles Babbage, John Herschel, and other Cambridge men, while on the other hand he had found Wallace's teaching, concentrated on geometry—with the traditional Scottish emphasis on philosophical foundations—woefully inadequate as a preparation for his own physics classes. Kelland, an Englishman who had acquired a great reputation as a Cambridge college tutor, was his candidate. Naturally such a choice offended local patriotism. It also aroused the horror of Hamilton, who was just then engaged in an acrimonious dispute with Whewell about the educational value of mathematics. Whewell, who was really arguing for Cambridge against Oxford, claimed that mathematics had a special value in sharpening the logical facilities. Hamilton retorted that logical thought is best promoted by a training in logic, and that in any case the Cambridge system fostered manipulative skills at the expense of a true understanding of the foundations of mathematics. Forbes's opponents produced an admirable rival candidate in D. F. Gregory, another Cambridge man, but one who had also been to Edinburgh University, being the latest descendent of the brilliant Gregory family that had made such a mark on Scottish intellectual history during the previous two centuries; but after a number of maneuverings more notable for ingenuity than the narrower forms of rectitude, Forbes won his point and Kelland was elected. It was Kelland who taught Maxwell calculus, and who in February 1849 read before the Royal Society of Edinburgh Maxwell's second published paper "On the Theory of Rolling Curves," since "it was not thought proper for a boy in a round jacket to mount the rostrum there."[22]

A favorite theme of Hamilton's metaphysical teaching was the relativity of human knowledge. By this Hamilton meant primarily that all human knowledge is of relations among objects rather than of objects in themselves. One does not know a table directly; one infers its properties from its interaction with light and other phenomena in the external world. This was an idea that entered deeply into Maxwell's scientific consciousness. Like all radical philosophical doctrines it can only be carried through by making certain distinctions. Taken to an extreme it could be interpreted as signifying that objects in themselves have no existence. In Hamilton's theory of perception an important distinction was that between knowledge and belief. One may believe in the existence of objects in some absolute sense; one perceives them, however, only in a relative sense. The same kind of distinction appears in Maxwell's theory of light. Although Maxwell assumed the existence of an aether, in his final version of the theory there is no attempt to determine the aether's properties; instead the existence of electromagnetic waves is deduced solely from electrical equations. A relationship is established between two classes of phenomena, light and electricity, without the need for a mechanical theory of either.

The philosophical asides in Maxwell's scientific papers, as well as his occasional essays on larger questions written at different times throughout his life, show how seriously he took the philosophic quest. He read widely. Letters from his student days at Edinburgh and Cambridge refer to Descartes, Hume, Berkeley, Hobbes, Leibnitz, Spinoza, and Kant, as well as more modern philosophers. For several years, however, he tended to return to Hamilton: one of his letters to

Campbell written during his last year at Edinburgh contains the curiously self-satirical remark that he is studying "Kant's Kritik of Pure Reason in German, read with a determination to make it agree with Sir. W. Hamilton."[23] Hamilton watched Maxwell with a genial eye. In part, his interest had a personal background because Hamilton, together with John Lockhart, the biographer of Scott, had in his younger days been an intimate friend of Maxwell's uncle John Cay. But it went deeper. One of the documents reproduced by Maxwell's biographers is an essay on "The Properties of Matter" written for Hamilton by Maxwell when he was seventeen, and afterwards discovered in Hamilton's private drawer by T. S. Baynes, Hamilton's assistant and the future editor of the famous 9th edition of the *Encyclopaedia Britannica.* Hamilton recognized Maxwell's quality.

And so did Forbes. Few things are more arresting about the young Maxwell than that he could simultaneously and successfully choose as his mentors two such bitter foes as Forbes and Hamilton. Forbes's comment on Maxwell for his class certificate at the end of his second undergraduate year was: "His proficiency gave evidence of an original and penetrating mind."[24] But Forbes was no easy guide. Shortly before leaving Edinburgh for Cambridge, Maxwell completed the manuscript of his third scientific paper (his first on physics)—"On the Equilibrium of Elastic Solids," a combination of theoretical and experimental work in which Maxwell put forward the strain theory of photoelasticity to account for induced double refraction in strained objects. It was an impressive effort for a young man not yet nineteen, and Maxwell was obviously proud of it. On 4 May 1850, he received from Forbes the following letter:

My dear Sir—Professor Kelland, to whom your paper was referred by the Council [of the Edinburgh] R[oyal] S[ociety], reports favourably upon it, but complains of the great obscurity of the several parts, owing to the *abrupt transitions* and want of distinction between what is *assumed* and what is *proved* in various passages, which he has marked with a pencil, and which I trust that you will use your utmost effort to make plain and intelligible. It is perfectly evident that it must be useless to publish a paper for the use of scientific readers generally, the steps of which cannot, in many places, be followed by so expert an algebraist as Prof. Kelland;—if, indeed, they be steps at all and not assumptions of theorems from other writers who are not quoted. You will please to pay particular attention to clear up these passages, and return the MS by post to Professor Kelland, West Cottage, Wardie, Edinburgh, so that he may receive it by Saturday the 11th, as I shall then have left town—Believe me, yours sincerely, James D. Forbes.[25]

It is impossible not to like Forbes. He had a tiger on his hands, but he was not going to allow the tiger to get away with anything less than the very best work. Maxwell must have felt furious when he read these stinging words about "great obscurity" which it would be "useless to publish," along with the insinuation that some of the results appeared to have been surreptitiously taken from other writers without acknowledgement. But the effect was salutary. When one compares the rambling obscurity of so much scientific writing with Maxwell's papers at their best: beautifully written, full of ideas, generous to other workers, still fresh and suggestive after a hundred years: one can only wish there were more professors like Forbes about—and more Maxwells to benefit from their criticisms.

Maxwell entered Cambridge in October 1850. It was another world: English, privileged, collegiate. Church-dominated: a university that with 3500 undergraduates was nearly three times the size of Edinburgh University, where the intellectual life was ruled by competition for a high place in the Tripos examinations, but where students of a more jocund temperament preferred the lure of Newmarket race course or nightly escapades followed by a late return over the college walls. Maxwell's first term was spent at Peterhouse, or St. Peter's College as it was then called, which was where William Thomson and Tait had been undergraduates. He then migrated to Trinity, chiefly, it seems, because the chances of winning a college fellowship later on were better there. Peterhouse, being small, had few fellowships, and one of the other entering undergraduates was E. J. Routh, a promising mathematician who three years later beat Maxwell to the position of Senior Wrangler in the Tripos examination.

The Mathematical Tripos was the glory of Victorian Cambridge. Everyone attending the university had to take the examination, even those who later would aim for distinction in the Classical Tripos. The doings of the leading candidates stirred an excitement that in modern universities is reserved for the performance of football heroes. The examination occupied seven (later eight) full days. The student was called upon to face this trial in a very inadequately heated Senate House during the January of his fourth academic year. To allow for the varied abilities of the candidates, the examination was divided into two parts. Those not ambitious for high honors were content to be placed in the "Poll"[26] by answering the first three days of papers, where the questions mainly concerned standard bookwork, including knowledge of Euclid's *Elements* and Newton's *Principia.* To the serious mathematician the challenge came during the last four days, but even he dared not treat the earlier papers lightly, for the custom of allowing any number of questions to be answered put a tremendous premium on speed. The questions in the last four days emphasized analytical ingenuity: the art of solving them turned on spotting the right trick. Their content in Maxwell's time included a great deal of dynamics and practical mathematics: differential equations, summation of series, three-dimensional geometry, and so on. To complete the performance a few of the best candidates would take the Smith's Prize examinations, which contained questions of still higher difficulty. In addition to monetary rewards from the will of Dr. Smith, the early eighteenth-century mathematician, these offered the outstanding man who had failed to do himself justice in the Tripos examination the chance to redeem his reputation. William Thomson, though Second Wrangler, was first Smith's prizeman; Maxwell, similarly placed, was bracketed equal first with Routh.

Hamilton's critique of the Mathematical Tripos seems at first glance eminently sane. Few people now would claim with Whewell that massive doses of algebra, geometry, and calculus are the best prescription for strengthening the powers of general reasoning. But before we follow a distinguished twentieth-century writer, himself a Cambridge man, and dismiss the old Tripos as an example of the "remarkable woodenness of the English in deciding what examinations should be like,"[27] we should pause and reflect. An education that could cultivate such varied talents as Tennyson, Darwin, Babbage, Herschel, Whewell, the historian Macaulay, the theologian and social reformer F. D. Maurice, the novelist Charles Kingsley, Bishops Westcott, Lightfoot, and Colenso, the critic Leslie Stephen, the philosopher and educator Henry Sidgwick—not to mention physicists as able as Stokes, William Thomson, Maxwell, Rayleigh, and J. J. Thomson, and pure mathematicians of the stature of Cayley, De Morgan, Sylvester, Clifford, Burnside, and Forsyth, all of whom received their training at Cambridge when the old Tripos system was at its height—demands respectful attention.

Much the most penetrating account ever given of Victorian Cambridge is to be found in a little known book, *Five Years in an English University,* written in 1852 by Charles Astor Bristed, a New Yorker who had spent three years at Yale before entering Trinity College in 1840. Bristed's first reaction to Cambridge—a reaction Maxwell was to share—was one of disappointment, even disgust. Drunkenness, wenching, schoolboy pranks in the lecture rooms, were the order of the day: "These youths of eighteen or nineteen . . . seemed years behind American students considerably their juniors except that some of them—and only some of them—executed beautiful Latin verses with great facility."[28] But soon Bristed noticed a strange thing. During the two or three years after graduation, large numbers of Cambridge men would blossom in the most surprising way. Without guidance, without apparent effort, they would form a range of new interests, mastering them with a rapidity and critical intelligence that was breathtaking. "The great change and improvement effected by a few years of collegiate life," remarks Bristed, "was to me one of the first problems connected with the English universities. Home experience had not led me to expect such a start between the ages of twenty-two and twenty-five."[29] Bristed saw the change most among the bachelor-scholars: men like Maxwell who remained at Cambridge after taking their degrees, reading for a college fellowship. But many who left immediately flowered similarly. William Thomson was one; another was Charles Darwin, who, after a college career seemingly distinguished only for a slightly larger than average accumulation of debts to Cambridge tradesmen, was appointed naturalist to the ship H.M.S. Beagle on a casual recommendation from the Professor of Botany, the Reverend J. S. Henslow, with whom he was in the habit of discussing his collection of beetles, to return after a five-year voyage spent out of touch with other scientists to write one of the great classics of observational biology, and with the seeds of evolutionary theory already planted in his mind. Biographers who are too much moved to pity by the hideous groans that rend the air above the examination battlefield, or who study a career like Darwin's in isolation, are naturally shocked by the harshness and inefficiency of the old Cambridge system. In fact, Darwin's story, though exceptional in scope, is by no means untypical of early nineteenth-century Cambridge.

In October 1851, one year after going up to Cambridge, Maxwell was admitted into the class of the great private tutor, William Hopkins. Among the many curious features of the educational scene in Victorian Cambridge, private tuition was the most distinctive and anomalous. It had no official place in the university scheme. The tutor assembled, usually in his own home, a hand-picked team of students, ranging in number from three or four, if classicists, to more than a dozen if mathematicians, and trained them in all things for the rapid and accurate answering of the barrage of written questions they would face in the examinations. The system had weaknesses, but for anyone with academic ambitions the private tutor served as important a function as the river coach to the boating man. He gave the Cambridge mathematician a critical knowledge of the textbooks and a facility with problems that was unmatched anywhere in the world. And against that widely criticized deficiency of modern universities, professors' neglect of teaching duties for research, or—if truth were told—for academic infighting, the system had the most effective of all safeguards: idealism was harnessed to cupidity: the tutors were paid by the students, not the university—for results.

And Hopkins produced results. During the period of his ascendancy, between 1830 and 1858, he trained altogether 200 Wranglers, including seventeen Seniors and forty-four Seconds, most of whom went on to distinguished careers. Cayley, Stokes, William Thomson, Tait, Routh, and Maxwell were all Hopkins's men. Hopkins was more than a tutor. His interests embraced almost every field of science, and extended to music, painting, literature, and politics. His original work on the inertia and internal structure of the earth, together with his influence on William Thomson, and through Thomson on George Darwin and a line of distinguished Cambridge figures, gives him a claim to be regarded as the founder of theoretical geophysics. About his claim to be the greatest teacher Cambridge has ever produced, no one who has studied his impact can have a doubt. It is peculiarly shameful that modern Cambridge, while dignifying nonentities, has complacently allowed Hopkins's name to fade from its memory. The only surviving portrait of him is stored out of sight in a basement at Peterhouse.

Hopkins soon saw what he had on his hands. In a conversation with another of his students, W. N. Lawson, he described Maxwell as "unquestionably the most extraordinary man he has met with in the whole range of his experience; he says it appears impossible for Maxwell to think incorrectly on physical subjects; that in his analysis, however, he is far more deficient; he looks upon him as a great genius with all its eccentricities, and predicts that one day he will shine as a light in physical science."[30] Maxwell for his part liked "Old Hop" and did not object to the Tripos grind. In June 1853 he wrote to his aunt Jane Cay: "If any one asks how I am getting on in mathematics, say that I am busy arranging everything so as to be able to express all distinctly, so that examiners may be satisfied now and pupils edified hereafter. It is pleasant work and very strengthening, but not nearly finished."[31]

Two other Cambridge men who had an impact on Maxwell were George Gabriel Stokes, the Lucasian Professor of Mathematics, then still a relatively young man, and William Whewell, the Master of Trinity College and Professor of Moral Philosophy. Stokes's fame as a physicist, both mathematical and experimental, survives through his work on hydrodynamics, elasticity, and optics. His critical papers on optics provided a background for the optical side of Maxwell's electromagnetic theory nicely complementary to Thomson's contributions on the electrical side. Equally important was his mere presence at Cambridge. Half the secret of doing good work is to believe that good work is within one's grasp. To meet and talk with one of the leading mathematical physicists of Europe, to see his strengths and limitations—and Stokes had obvious limitations—is itself a liberal education. After Maxwell returned to Cambridge in 1871, the two men and their wives[32] became close friends; Stokes was one of the executors of Maxwell's will.

Of Whewell many things have been said by many people: none neater than Sydney Smith's "science was his forte and omniscience his foible," to which may be adjoined the words of a prizefighter, who, seeing Whewell's magnificent physique, exclaimed, "What a man was lost when they made you a parson!"[33] The closest thing in English university life to the self-made man, born in 1794 the son of a master-carpenter, Whewell entered Cambridge in 1812 on a scholarship and graduated Second Wrangler in 1816. His early works on dynamics played a notable part in the reform of Cambridge mathematics then taking place, but he was soon ranging in other fields, including the philosophy of Kant. Concerning Whewell's omniscience; his books on architecture, mathematics, and mineralogy; his encyclopedia articles on electricity, political economy, and Chinese musical instruments, little need be said: for Maxwell his importance lay in his two massive works on the *History and Philosophy of the Inductive Sciences* and his interest in scientific terminology.

Although Whewell and Sir William Hamilton were enemies on educational subjects, their philosophical positions had something in common. Each had been influenced by Kant, and each in his own way had become convinced that the notion of bare scientific fact was a delusion. The merit in Whewell's two works lay in their being the first real attempt in English to describe the scientific process in terms other than Baconian inductivism. According to Whewell, big scientific advances come about not through the accumulation of facts but through the formulation of clear general ideas. He distinguished different stages in the progress of each science: the Epoch of Induction, the Epoch of Verification, and the Epoch of Application, each with its own special characteristics. He combined this sequential view of scientific progress with a hierarchical view of the universe. Nature has been ordered by the Creator in a series of tiers, each more or less complete in itself, each built on the one below. The key to successful discovery lies in finding the set of ideas appropriate to the tier one is occupied with: once that is done, the new knowledge becomes a permanent part of the scientific heritage, independent of future investigation at a deeper level, and even to some extent independent of experiment.

In detail, Whewell's interpretations, like all attempts to expound universal ideas, contained much that was debatable, but compared with the writings of his contemporary rivals, Comte, Mill, and Herbert Spencer, his had one inestimable advantage: they were based on a knowledge of scientific research from the inside. The shaping force behind Whewell's doctrine of *appropriate ideas* was his recognition from personal experience of the different intellectual patterns of different sciences. The same experience was reflected in his life-long preoccupation with scientific terminology and definition. Both interests reappear constantly in Maxwell. Thus in working on his first paper on electricity in June 1855 Maxwell wrote to his Cambridge friend R. B. Litchfield: "It is hard work grinding out 'appropriate ideas' as Whewell calls them. However I think they are coming out at last, and by dint of knocking them against all the facts and ½-digested theories afloat, I hope to bring them into shape, after which I hope to understand something more about inductive philosophy then I do at present."[34]

An important feature of Cambridge education was the informal exchanges in the long "constitutionalizing" walks taken every day by pairs of students or students and dons. According to Bristed the average constitutional of his day took two hours and covered eight miles. The good effect on the Cambridge physique was obvious, as was the opportunity for the interchange of ideas. Nothing in the young Darwin's record is more telling than his becoming known as "the man who walks with Henslow."[35] Maxwell's friendships were mostly among the brilliant circle of liberal classical scholars who graced the courts of Trinity College. Through their influence he was elected in 1853 to the "Apostles Club," the famous quasisecret intellectual society founded in 1824 by a certain "immortal Tomlinson," among whose early members had been figures as diverse as Tennyson, Richard Monckton Milnes (Lord Houghton), and one man beyond all whose fierce integrity permeated the society for many years: F. D. Maurice. The Apostles were primarily classicists rather than mathematicians. Maxwell was one of the rare exceptions, although years later two other Cambridge mathematicians of note, A. N. Whitehead and Bertrand Russell, also entered the charmed circle.

The dramatic influence of the Apostles' meetings is widely attested.

Maxwell's friend F. J. A. Hort, the Biblical scholar, described them as the "strongest and also on the whole the most salutary"[36] influence he had known. Henry Sidgwick regarded his accession as the turning point of his life. The meetings were held on Saturday evenings in one of the Apostles' rooms. After a light meal of tea, toast, and anchovies, a member would read an essay on any subject of his choosing, after which there would be a relentless critical discussion ending in the small hours of Sunday morning with each person present entering his signed opinion in the Society's record book. Maxwell's biographers print portions of a dozen of his essays. They deal with subjects ranging from "Idiotic Imps," an essay on magic and the dark sciences, to a study of beauty and symmetry in art and their relation to beauty in nature. Most important was the essay on "Analogy," read in April 1856, two months after Maxwell had completed his first paper on electricity. To the role of analogy in Maxwell's scientific thinking we must return later.

At this point it is useful to reflect once more on the quarrel between Whewell and Hamilton about training in logic versus training in mathematics. Both men were half wrong and half right, because what in the last analysis underlay their dispute was not the choice of an educational medium but the ambience of a university. As for Whewell's defense of mathematics, even those who admire the old Cambridge Tripos may well consider his position to have been misconceived, even unfair to himself. For Whewell's personal enthusiasm for logic and philosophy was quite unrepresentative of Cambridge. Bristed had a far clearer insight when he claimed intellectual self-discipline as the true virtue of Cambridge. And therein lay its advantage over the Scottish training, where the glib student, through his familiarity with broad philosophical principles, could sometimes get away with airy generalities that a Cambridge man, particularly if he were an Apostle, would have pounced on.

If a criticism of Cambridge is needed, it is the one Bristed made when he remarked in a searching phrase that it tended to yield "consumers rather than producers of knowledge."[37] The critical powers were sometimes so brilliantly developed that they strangled the creative impulse. In Maxwell the critical attitude was balanced by the speculative and experimental views he had imbibed from Forbes and Hamilton in Edinburgh. The same inevitable Cambridge tendency to particularize dominated the Tripos examinations. The successful candidate had at his fingertips an impressive array of mathematical techniques, but not necessarily any large insight into the foundations of mathematics. Since many educators and mathematicians today scorn such training, it is well to emphasize the advantage that accrues to a working scientist, whether in theory or experiment, from sheer familiarity with technique. Life is too short to be always starting from general principles. One of the most impressive characteristics of the best nineteenth-century Cambridge applied mathematicians, of whom Rayleigh may be taken as the archetype, was their ready confidence in tackling new problems. They had already seen so many.

For Maxwell, Cambridge was a time of consolidation. For three years he wrote no more scientific papers. Outwardly he changed little. "During the time I knew him," wrote Hort, "I can recall no perceptible sign of change other than quiet growth, and suspect that he attained too early and too stable a maturity to receive a new direction from any kind of intercourse with his university contemporaries."[38] His strong personality and strong Gallowegian accent impressed all who met him, as did his willingness to talk on any matter that came up. On January 1, 1854, a few days before the Tripos examinations, his friend Lawson wrote in his diary about a tea where Maxwell was "as usual, showing himself acquainted with every subject upon which the conversation turned. I never met a man like him. I do believe there is not a single subject on which he cannot talk, and talk well too, displaying always the most curious and out of the way information."[39]

"Of all decades in [English] history," wrote G. M. Young in his *Portrait of an Age,* "a wise man would choose the 1850s to be young in." Maxwell, having made that choice, had enjoyed for more than six years a process of university education as effective and varied as any to be found in Europe. He entered his career as a tide of optimism was sweeping Britain. Suddenly it became clear that things had been bad, that they were getting better, and that well-intended effort would make them get better faster. The Great Exhibition of 1851 proved that British achievements and British genius astonished the world. At home prosperity was rising; the conditions of the poor improving; Royalty, strangest transformation of all, had in the persons of Prince Albert and his Queen become worthy of respect. Abroad, Livingstone in Africa, Burton at Mecca, the railway-builders everywhere, exemplified foreign adventure in its idealistic, romantic, and mercantile phases. Even the evils of the Crimean War and the Indian Mutiny served as spurs to reform. Maxwell's life, both as a physicist and as a Christian gentleman teaching evening classes for working men, mirrors the optimism of that happy decade. But education and opportunity, however spendid, do not in themselves explain creative genius. There must be some deeper driving force at work. To understand that we must examine another of Maxwell's choices: his choice of parents.

IV

In every child's relation to its parents there is an outer circle and an inner circle. The outer circle is the circle of interests, attitudes, and opinions that parent and child share within the context of a larger society. The inner circle is the world of emotion: love, hope, fear, jealousy, conflict, joy, anger, doubt, trust.

The sustained influence of John Clerk Maxwell in forming his son's interest in things practical and scientific is plain to see. It ran from the early years at Glenlair, through the period in Edinburgh when he took Maxwell to the Royal Society of Edinburgh meetings, right until the occasion in 1853 when Maxwell, working full stretch for the Cambridge Tripos examination, proposed to take a short break during the Easter vacation to stay with his friend Johnson Gedge at Birmingham, only to receive from his father, who had himself visited Birmingham as a young man, the following letter:

Ask Gedge to get you instructions to Brummagem [Birmingham] workshops. View, if you can, armourers, gunmaking and gunproving—swordmaking and proving—*Papier-mâché* and japanning—silver-plating by cementation and rolling —ditto, electrotype—Elkington's works—Brazier's works, by founding and by striking up in dies—turning—spinning teapot bodies in white metal, etc.— making buttons of sorts, steel pens, needles, pins, and any sorts of small articles which are curiously done by subdivision of labour and by ingenious tools— glass of sorts is among the works of the place, and all kinds of foundry work— engine-making—tools and instruments—optical and [philosophical], both coarse and fine. If you have had enough of the town lots of Birmingham, you could vary the recreation by viewing Kenilworth, Warwick, Leamington, Stratford-on-Avon, or such like.[40]

Any spare moments could presumably be spent playing croquet with Gedge's sisters.

The Clerk family for generations was patriarchal. It is the men who stand out as forceful and original personalities. Very different is the story of the Cays. An English family stemming from a long line of Newcastle merchants, they had been seated at North Charlton, not far south of the Scottish border since 1695, but maintained close ties with Edinburgh after John Cay (1727-1782) took refuge at Holyrood during the course of a "grievous law plea"[41] with the

Earl of Northumberland. Three things characterize their history, first, a strong religious nonconformity; second, the interest of later members of the family in law and antiquarianism; third, a genealogy characterized by a succession of powerful and singularly independent-minded women.

One such was Barbara Carr, wife of Robert Cay (1634-1682), a "prominent nonconformist" in Newcastle. In 1684 after Robert's death, Barbara "adventured her malt-loft to be a place of assembly for preaching and praying"[42] at a time when the Conventicle and Five Mile Acts placed severe restrictions on nonconformist worship. Her first son Jabez (1666-1703), the most interesting of the male Cays, graduated in medicine from Padua University (not an unusual place for nonconformists excluded from the English universities). Besides practicing medicine in Newcastle, he became a close friend of Ralph Thoresby, the Yorkshire antiquary, and made noteworthy experiments on fire-damp in coal mines. It was he who purchased North Charlton. He married a woman of distinction, but died without issue, leaving the property to his brother John (1668-1731), who in 1691 had married Grace Woolf, daughter and co-heiress of Henry Woolf, a wealthy Yorkshire Quaker. Grace's mother, also Grace, was described by one of her admirers as a "good gentlewoman of great experience."[43] Good she may have been, and experienced she must have been, but gentle is a word that can be used of her only to define social standing, not character. Deeply religious, she was a powerful supporter of Ambrose Barnes, the ardent Puritan alderman of Newcastle, to whom she wrote a letter considered important enough to be preserved by Barnes's memorialist, breathing all the uncompromising fervor of the matriarch "to whom it comes natural to be a fierce partisan of those who think like her, but can spare no pity or understanding for weaker mortals of frailer persuasions."[44]

Robert Cay (1694-1754), son of John Cay and Grace Woolf the younger, was another prominent Newcastle nonconformist with antiquarian interests. He at the age of 32 married Elizabeth, daughter of Reynold Hall of Carcleugh, who appears from evidence in a letter to Cay from the minister of Morpeth meeting house to have been another powerful woman. Then came the most astonishing marriage of all. John Cay (1727-1782), the Cay who started the family connection with Edinburgh by taking sanctuary at Holyrood during his lawsuit with the Earl of Northumberland, in 1756 married a Roman Catholic, Frances, daughter of Ralph Hodshon of Lintz, Switzerland. How John Cay and Frances Hodshon met is a mystery. Presumably her family had fled to Lintz because of their Roman Catholicism. But for a man of that age with five generations of ironclad nonconformity behind him to up and marry a Catholic was amazing, and it was equally amazing for her to marry him. Nor did either yield their faith. Their son, Robert Hodshon Cay (1758-1810), Maxwell's grandfather, friend of Sir Walter Scott and Judge of the Admiralty Court in Scotland, married in 1789 Elizabeth, daughter of John Liddell of North Shields, Yorkshire, a lady of extraordinary artistic talent. Over the next eighteen years they had seven children who lived, besides two who died in infancy. Maxwell's uncle John was the eldest, and his mother Frances, named after the Roman Catholic grandmother and born 25 March 1792, was the second. By this time the family had become Scottish Episcopalian. Frances Cay was thirty-four when she married John Clerk Maxwell, a Presbyterian, more than old enough to have a mind of her own. In those days a marriage between an Episcopalian and a Presbyterian, though not so startling as one between nonconformist and Roman Catholic, was not the casual event it might seem today. Concerning her character and faith in the context of Cay family history, two sentences are enough to place it: the capsule description Maxwell gave in answer to Francis Galton's questionnaire referred to earlier. She was, wrote Maxwell, "guided by religious thought and very independent of the exhortations of acquaintances, clerical or lay. Religion was a forbidden subject in her father's family as his mother was a Roman Catholic and all discussion was avoided religiously."[45] Like mother, like son! To Maxwell's statement that Frances Cay was "very independent of the exhortations of acquaintances" may be linked the statement of Lewis Campbell: "Few men, if any, would venture to argue or remonstrate with Maxwell when he had decided on a course of action in the council-chamber of his own breast."[46]

When a man of thirty-six, not previously married, joins himself to a "very independent" woman of thirty-four, even one whom he has known for several years, he may be in for surprises. When seven generations of matriarchy join seven generations of patriarchy, and together produce their first surviving child when the mother is thirty-nine and the father forty-one, the surprise is likely to be considerable. John Clerk Maxwell's practical knowledge and experience of the world would have been enough to dominate most women, but not Frances Cay. Lewis Campbell caught the secret of the marriage when he compared the two: John Clerk Maxwell, a large, slow, unwieldy man, thinking everything through to the last ingenious detail and then apt to be put out when plans went wrong; his wife just as practical, "but her practicality was different from his. She was of a strong and resolute nature,—as prompt as he was cautious and considerate,—more peremptory but less easily perturbed . . . with blunt determination she [an upper-class Edinburgh woman] entered heart and soul into that rustic life."[47] Once after a blasting accident, when her husband and everyone else were dithering about, she took charge and personally tended the injured men during the long wait until the doctor's carriage rattled to the scene.

When Maxwell was two years and ten months old in April 1834, his mother wrote a description of him in a letter to her sister, Jane Cay:

He is a very happy man, and has improved much since the weather got moderate; he has great work with doors, locks, keys, etc., and "show me how it doos" is never out of his mouth. He also investigates the hidden course of streams and bell-wires, the way the water gets from the pond through the wall and a pend or small bridge and down a drain into Water Orr, then past the smiddy, and down to the sea, where Maggy's ships sail. As to the bells, they will not rust; he stands sentry in the kitchen and Mag runs thro' the house ringing them all by turns, or he rings, and sends Bessy to see and shout to let him know, and he drags papa all over to show him holes where the wires go through. We went to the shop and ordered hats and bonnets, and as he was freckling with the sun, I got him a black and white straw till the other was ready, and as an apology to Meg said it would do to toss about; he heard me and acts accordingly. His great delight is to help Sandy Frazer with the water-barrel. . . . You would get letters and violets by a woman that was going back to her place; the latter would perhaps be rotten, but they were gathered by James for Aunt Jane.[48]

To have a strong father and a stronger mother for whom one is the center of attention, to find men who will allow one to help with the water-barrel, to be surrounded by adoring women who are prepared to run to and fro at one's bidding, is a heady existence for a boy of three. How Maxwell would have fared if his mother had not died when he was eight is an intriguing speculation; but she did die. The shock was immense. Writing in 1868 to the astronomer William Huggins, whose mother had just died, Maxwell remarked, "though my own mother was only eight years with me, and my father became my companion in all things, I felt her loss for many years, and can in some degree appreciate your happiness in having so long and so complete fellowship with your mother."[49]

How complex the relationship between parent and child is! In one view John Clerk Maxwell was an ideal father: stable, kindly, full of constructive interests. Lewis Campbell describes him as he appeared on visits to Edinburgh Academy: "His broad, benevolent face and paternal air, as of a gentler Dandie Dinmont, beaming with kindness for the companions of his son, is vividly remembered by those who were our schoolfellows in 1844-5."[50] In another view Mr. Maxwell's record is shocking. To let his son's affairs go astray for four years in the critical age between eight and twelve, right after his mother's death, first through the mischosen tutor and then through the inept handling of Maxwell's introduction to Edinburgh Academy, is inexcusable. Allowance can be made for Mr. Maxwell's own sense of loss, but not for his blindness to such obvious injuries as being (in Lewis Campbell's words) "smitten on the head with a ruler and having one's ears pulled till they bled."[51] But what was Maxwell's own part in all this? Why did he not complain? Campbell remarks of the first experience that "the young Spartan himself made no sign that his relations with his tutor were otherwise than smooth,"[52] and of the scene in which his clothes were ripped to shreds on the first day at Edinburgh Academy, that on his return home Maxwell maintained the appearance of being "excessively amused by his experiences, and showing not the smallest sign of irritation."[53]

Such an elaborate hiding of normal emotion must have a meaning. First, parenthetically in the tutor's defense, Maxwell could, when he chose, be utterly infuriating. Campbell has a tale of how "one evening at Glenlair, just as the maid-servant was coming in with the tea-tray, Jamsie blew out the light in the narrow passage and lay down across the doorway."[54] But joined to the natural inheritance of the spoiled brat, there was in Maxwell, certainly at age eight and therefore presumably much earlier, a quality that continued to manifest itself throughout his later life: a compelling need to endure pain, and seemingly also to hide, if possible, that pain from his father and (later) his friends.

Much in Maxwell's later life confirms this statement. His strongly expressed preference as a young man for a hard seat on the railway train is a trivial example. More significant is his grievous failure in the last two years of his life to consult a doctor about the severe abdominal pains which were the signs of the incipient cancer from which he died. The baffling issue of Maxwell's marriage lies outside the scope of this paper, but one vignette of Campbell's is interesting: "Once at Cambridge when his wife was lying ill in her room, and a terrier, who had already shown 'a wild trick of his ancestors' was watching beside the bed, Maxwell happened to go in for the purpose of moving her. The dog sprang at him and fastened on his nose. In order not to disturb Mrs. Maxwell, he went out quietly, holding his arm beneath the creature, which was still hanging to his face."[55] Admirable in thoughtfulness, but surely an abnormal restraint of the usual human reaction to sudden pain. One of Maxwell's later essays at Cambridge is an attempt under the general title "On Modified Aspects of Pain" to answer the question, "Why is it that in all times and countries the endurance of pain has been looked upon with great respect and has been considered necessary, salutary, honourable or meritorious?"[56] Many of the points Maxwell makes are admirable good sense, but psychoanalytically the question has to be what led Maxwell to concentrate so much thought on such as issue.

Psychohistory is a dangerous subject. It is too easy to play God. There are reasons for guessing that Maxwell's need for pain was tied to his relationship with his mother: when told at the age of eight that she was in heaven, he exclaimed, "oh, I am so glad, now she will have no more pain."[57] There are reasons also for connecting that need with Maxwell's strong reaction against his own narcissism, as expressed in the poem "Reflection From Various Surfaces,"[58] which he wrote while a student at Cambridge. But in the absence of evidence that only Maxwell could have uncovered, and he only after hard psychoanalytic work, all such speculations remain speculations. The question for us is rather, what effect, if any, the drive for pain in Maxwell would have in turning him into a scientist, and in what way it might have determined the particular kind of scientist he actually became.

A quality that Maxwell shared with Newton and Einstein was an extraordinary tenacity. His powers of physical endurance are widely attested; they were matched in things intellectual by what Tait described as an "altogether unusual amount of patient determination."[59] Tenacity without creative imagination has small value, but given the imaginative power, it does drive great work to completion. In Maxwell the tenacity that made him spend six years of concentrated effort in writing his *Treatise on Electricity and Magnetism* is the rational expression of the quality that between the age of eight and ten enabled him to endure silently, for whatever perverse reason, his tutor's barbarous teaching methods.

Can we go further and see what it is in Maxwell's masochistic urge that turned him into a great natural philosopher rather than a mere skillful calculator? In Maxwell's Introductory Lecture on Experimental Physics at Cambridge in 1871 there is a passage in which he remarks that, whereas working on mathematics may be fatiguing to the mind and doing routine experiments "may perhaps tire our eyes and weary our backs but [does not] greatly fatigue our minds."

It is not until we attempt to bring the theoretical part of our training into contact with the practical that we begin to experience the full effect of what Faraday calls "mental inertia" not only the difficulty of recognizing, among the concrete objects before us, the abstract relation which we have learned from books, but the *distracting pain* [my italics] of wrenching the mind away from the symbols to the objects, and from the objects back to the symbols. This, however, is the price we have to pay for new ideas."[60]

Surely it is an act of genius to harness a psychic drive so inherently destructive as masochism to this kind of creative purpose.

The turning point in Maxwell's becoming a physicist was the memorable afternoon in April 1847 when Maxwell's uncle John Cay took him and Lewis Campbell to visit William Nicol's private laboratory. Years later, shortly before his death, Maxwell had occasion to review a book on physics for school children by Frederick Guthrie of University College, London. It was an unsatisfactory work full of dreary definitions: Maxwell treated it harshly—in fact with a harshness so extreme as to arouse psychoanalytic suspicion. Almost the only good word he had for it was in praise of some of Guthrie's experimental demonstrations. He suggested that Guthrie would have done better if instead of writing the book he had invited a group of schoolboys to his laboratory. He then went on to say in obvious reference to his own visit to Nicol: "If a child has any latent capacity for the study of nature, a visit to a real man of science in his laboratory may be a turning point in his life. He may not understand a word of what the man of science says to explain his operations; but he sees the operations themselves, and the pains and patience which are bestowed on them; and when they fail he sees how the man of science instead of getting angry, searches for the cause of failure among the conditions of the operations."[61]

Why did this visit make such an impression on the fifteen-year-old Maxwell? Lewis Campbell says this about Maxwell's father: "His temper was all but perfect; yet, as 'the best laid schemes of mice and men gang aft agley' the minute care with which he formed his plans sometimes exposed him to occasions which showed that his usual calm self-possession was not invulnerable. At such times he would appear, not angry, only discomposed or 'vexed' and, after donning his considering cap for a little while, would soon resume his benign equanimity."[62] How these moments of being "discomposed or 'vexed' " went in the presence of a wife who was "more peremptory but less easily perturbed" is a nice question. In any case, the contrast between Nicol's calm handling of a faulty apparatus and John Clerk Maxwell's distress at a failed plan struck Maxwell at a very deep level. If in one view by becoming a physicist he was following a line his father had drawn for him, in another he was rebelling with all the fury of adolescent rebellion, a rebellion all the more powerful because of the eminently rational disguise in which it came. Perhaps (but this is purest conjecture) the harshness of Maxwell's remarks about Guthrie should be interpreted as a displacement of the harsh feelings about his father, which Maxwell had redirected but not resolved.

In the response to Galton already quoted more than once, Maxwell offers a self-analysis. He attributed to himself "great continuity and steadiness; gratitude and resentment weak; στοργη [family affection] pretty strong; not gregarious; thoughts occupied more with things than persons; social affections limited in range; given to theological ideas and not reticent about them."[63] Most of this is so apt that one's first reaction on seeing "gratitude . . . weak" is bewilderment. The lifelong friendship with Campbell, starting with that "look of affectionate recognition in Maxwell's eyes"; the deep emotion expressed in Maxwell's remark to Campbell after Forbes' death, "I loved James Forbes"[64]; the night-long journey taken by Maxwell in 1876 to be with his aunt Jane at her death—all speak otherwise, and Campbell is manifestly right in saying that "Maxwell's gratitude to all for whom he had received any help or stimulus was imperishable."[65] So why the denial? Surely Maxwell harbored resentments so powerful and so dangerously directed that it was necessary to hide them from himself, even at the cost of denying gratitude. No deep psychoanalytic knowledge is needed to guess towards whom the resentments were directed.

Resentment can be a driving force in a scientist, not always for ill. On the few occasions when Maxwell's work was subject to attack, one sees an instantaneous bristling followed by a calmer but far more deadly response in which Maxwell gathers his intellectual forces to deliver a massive counterblow, not at the person, but at the scientific issues. An example (not the only one) was the time after Clausius in 1862 had pointed out, in a rather patronizing tone, several errors in Maxwell's earliest paper on kinetic theory. Maxwell's first reaction was simple anger. His next was to follow Clausius in attempting to patch up the original mean free path theory. Finally in 1867 came the great paper on transport theory, which grandly reorganized the whole subject and made everything Clausius had done obsolete.

In the period of Maxwell's early life about which most is known, from the age of ten on, he was continually being pulled in different directions. There was the tension between home and school, which gave him "two outer worlds to balance against each other"; but there were deeper tensions, not least a tug of war over the control of his life between his two Edinburgh aunts, Isabella Wedderburn (John Clerk Maxwell's sister) and Jane Cay (Mrs. Maxwell's sister). Ostensibly the tug was about religion, Mrs. Wedderburn being (like her brother) a Presbyterian and Jane Cay (like her sister) an Episcopalian. Religion was indeed an issue, but there were personal issues as well. Lewis Campbell's description of Jane Cay as "one of the warmest-hearted creatures in the world; somewhat wayward in her likes and dislikes, perhaps somewhat warm-tempered also, but boundless in affectionate kindness to those whom she loved"[66] does not portray a woman who, having discovered how badly John Clerk Maxwell had mismanaged his son's education, would stand back and let Mr. Maxwell's sister guide Maxwell's development unimpeded. She strongly disapproved of Mrs. Wedderburn's son George, "a young man about Edinburgh, and a humourist of a different order"[67] from Maxwell. She disliked the laissez-faire governance of her sister-in-law, and from 1845 on had Maxwell over to her house frequently, seeking "to bring him out amongst her friends, to soften his singularities, and to make him more like other youths of his age."[68]

The 1840s were a time of religious strife in Scotland. The great Disruption of 1843 split the Church of Scotland apart, and in the consequent turmoil (to quote Maxwell's words to Hort), "quite young people were carried away . . . and when the natural reaction came, they ceased to think about religious matters at all, and became unable to receive fresh impressions."[69] The General Assembly at which all this happened took place at St. Andrews Church, the church Maxwell attended with his father and Aunt Isabella. Aunt Jane, sensing the danger, poked and prodded at Mr. Maxwell to let Maxwell go to Episcopal as well as Presbyterian services and come under the influence of E. B. Ramsay, the Episcopal Dean of Edinburgh. To this Mr. Maxwell eventually agreed, "knowing him to be a good and sensible man."[70]

When a sensitive, intelligent, strong-willed boy finds himself and his education the focus of dispute amongst his elders, and sees other elders in violent disagreement over great issues, two things are bound to happen. He will experience emotional conflict, and he will be forced to think for himself. In many young idealists the religious wrangles might have destroyed belief, but for Maxwell the example of the "good and sensible" Dean Ramsay and the memory of a mother who, while "guided by religious thought," was "very independent of the exhortations of acquaintances, clerical or lay," were strong countervailing forces. Thus there was formed in him early an intense need to hold together conflicting ideas, a need that tied to and reinforced earlier conflicting emotions towards his parents.

It is my conviction that the strong unifying drive in Maxwell's scientific work is a response to the emotional turmoil he passed through in the five or more years following his mother's death. To connect previously unrelated ideas is not the same as resolving conflicting emotions, but a man privileged to achieve what Maxwell did will have emotional rewards. The elation with which he could write to his cousin Charles Cay on 5 January 1865 concerning his greatest feat of unification "I have also a paper afloat, with an electromagnetic theory of light, which, till I am convinced to the contrary, I hold to be great guns,"[71] is at once charming and infectious.

One comes to the baffling question of creativity and neurosis. Intense emotional conflict is normally debilitating, and yet in a man strong enough to withstand the conflict there may be a release of creative energy not found in ordinary mortals. Of Maxwell's strength there is no doubt. Few boys could have survived the battering he took between the ages of eight and thirteen. But the issue is deeper than a simple moral tale of strength in adversity. Maxwell, as we have seen, sought pain. That he had reasons for doing this is not the point. It is hard to imagine any emotional pattern inherently less creative than masochism. And if Maxwell sought pain he also sought conflict. It was no accident that at Edinburgh University he chose two mentors so much at loggerheads as Forbes and Hamilton. Here it is easier to provide an intelligent rationalization for his actions. At a certain stage of growth the reflective Maxwell would see that there is truth on both sides of every deeply felt argument, and with his unifying drive would wish to embrace the whole truth. Such an explanation, while valid, misses the psychoanalytic point, which is to arrive at some understanding of the unifying drive.

An important characteristic of Maxwell is the number and diversity of father-figures he found for himself in his young manhood. Forbes and Hamilton were the most powerful, but there were others. We have already seen the impact on Maxwell of his visit to William Nicol, a visit guided by another man in semiparental role, Maxwell's uncle John Cay. The influences of D. R. Hay, the artist, and Dean Ramsay, the good and sensible clergyman, though smaller, are not to be overlooked, nor at Edinburgh Academy the influences of James Gloag the mathematics master and "Punch" the Rector. Beyond these there was one other man in Edinburgh to whom Maxwell was especially drawn, George Wilson the Professor of Technology. Wilson was a chemist, a student of Thomas Graham's. He achieved wide public recognition as the founder of the Scottish Museum of Technology, but is now better remembered as the author of an admirable biography of Henry Cavendish, and as the man who carried out the first statistical survey of color blindness in Britain. The latter work was published in 1855 in a small volume containing in an appendix a letter from Maxwell to Wilson giving the first account of Maxwell's own researches on color vision. A man of deep Christian faith, Wilson impressed everyone who met him with his sensitivity of feeling and fineness of character. He had had the misfortune to have his leg amputated in 1843 three years before the introduction of anesthetics, a topic on which he wrote a moving public letter to James Young Simpson, the surgeon who introduced the use of chloroform, at a time when Simpson was under attack for giving anesthetics to women in childbirth. If ever a man knew pain it was Wilson. Campbell's throwaway remark that Wilson's "likeness hung beside that of Forbes in [Maxwell's] rooms at Trinity [College, Cambridge]"[72] tells much.

Whether or not Maxwell ever resolved his ambivalence towards his own father, he had excellent taste in father-figures. All the Edinburgh men we have referred to were estimable characters of unusual intelligence. At Cambridge his needs were different, but in Whewell, Hopkins, and Stokes he found first-class guides, and if he could view Hopkins with some casualness as "Old Hop" that was a sign that he had grown up. His handling of his own father in the same period shows equal self-assurance. Perhaps it was the memory of John Clerk Maxwell's year or more of procrastination about the decision to enter Cambridge that made Maxwell, when at Forbes's suggestion he applied for the chair of Natural Philosophy at Marischal College, Aberdeen, simply present his father with a fait accompli, in notable contrast to the close working together of William Thomson with his father when the young Thomson applied for the corresponding chair at Glasgow.

With this background we may reflect on the intellectual relationship between Maxwell and the man whom he called "the father of that enlarged science of electro-magnetism which takes in at one view all the phenomena which former inquirers had studied separately"[73] : Michael Faraday. The history of physics has few instances of a physicist of high stature becoming so involved in another man's work as Maxwell was in Faraday's. There are, of course, many examples of satellites circling the great orb: Newton's followers, Rutherford's young men, and the Copenhagen circle around Niels Bohr. But among these the men of distinction, like Kapitza and Blackett in Rutherford's group, were men whose creative work was largely independent of the master's. Maxwell's was a fresh creation arising directly out of a study of Faraday's researches. It was as if Dirac had started off by reading all of Rutherford's papers or Einstein all the papers of Lenard.

Maxwell again displayed admirable judgement in his choice of intellectual father-figure. In choosing Faraday and electricity Maxwell chose the greatest living scientist and the most important field of research then existing. Good judgment in the choice of research topic is essential to creativity, and Maxwell in the preface to his *Treatise* observed that the importance of electricity extended beyond the boundaries of the subject itself: "Its external relations, on the one hand, to dynamics, on the other to heat, light, chemical action, and the constitution of bodies, seem to indicate the special importance of electrical science as an aid to the interpretation of nature."[74] As taken up from Faraday electricity became in Maxwell's hands the key to understanding light. As passed to his successors it became the key to understanding the atom.

Of equal interest is Maxwell's observation, also in the preface to the *Treatise,* that he approached the dispute between Faraday and the mathematicians with the conviction gained from William Thomson that "the discrepancy did not arise from either party being wrong."[75] The idea that in physics there may occur genuine reconciliation of conflicting ideas, and that scientific truth may lie on both sides of the argument, appeals deeply to anyone who, like Maxwell, has seen his elders locked in deadly combat. As it turned out, Maxwell, though he saw both sides, came down on one—Faraday's—as corresponding "more faithfully with our actual knowledge, both in what it affirms and what it leaves undecided."[76]

Maxwell paid a price for making physics his way of escape from childhood turmoil. He had, and knew that he had, a blind spot about certain aspects of human behavior. In one passage, after commending the study of the history of ideas as "of all subjects that in which we, as thinking men, take the deepest interest," he went on to say with self-deprecating irony that "when the action of the mind passes out of the intellectual stage, in which truth and error are the alternatives, into the more violently emotional states of anger and passion, malice and envy, fury and madness; the student of science, though he is obliged to recognize the powerful influence which these wild forces have exercised on mankind, is perhaps in some measure disqualified from pursuing the study of this part of human nature."[77] Lewis Campbell spoke more directly: "Nor was Maxwell's power over others always equal to the keenness of his perceptions. For while his penetration often reached the secrets of the heart, his generosity sometimes overlooked the most obvious characteristics—especially in the shape of mean or vulgar motives."[78]

Generosity? Or was it fear, a fear of facing his own hidden resentments and hidden violence? Strangely, but perhaps not so strangely, there is a common thread in Maxwell's lack of perception about ordinary human behavior and the lack of worldly wisdom his father showed in exposing the young Maxwell to needless harrassment from the boys at Edinburgh Academy.

Having seen Maxwell's quest for a father-figure worked out along the path that led from William Nicol to Michael Faraday, one is tempted to ask how Maxwell fared in the other half of the great human equation: his relations with womankind. The plain answer is, not well. A serious investigation would take us into material which, though important, lies outside the scope of a discussion of scientific creativity. Certainly Maxwell was profoundly attracted by and attractive to women. Enough to say that at the age of twenty-seven he found himself confronted with a choice between two women, one his cousin Elizabeth Cay, a girl of eighteen of fine intelligence and stunning beauty, the other the woman he actually married, Katherine Mary Dewar, daughter of the Principal of Marischal College, Aberdeen, a woman of lesser gifts and seven years older than himself, who in later life was dogged by ill health and mental breakdowns. There may have been family pressure against a union with Elizabeth Cay on prudential grounds, though cousin marriages were far more common in Victorian times than they are now, but the choice was Maxwell's and there is evidence that in later life he perceived how momentous it had been.

Wonderful intelligence, yes; a wonderful education, yes; but more than these, a character at once complex and concentrated: that is the secret of Maxwell's creativity. A tenacity hardened in a five-year fight for psychic survival, powerful emotions of resentment and gratitude, an adolescent rebellion tamed and harnessed through the clear scientific intelligence of Nicol and the luminous scientific intelligence of Faraday, a unifying drive that constantly sought out and resolved conflicting principles, a willingness to endure distracting intellectual pain as "the price we have to pay for new ideas," and finally a daring scientific imagination, whose workings, easier to describe than explain, are the topic of the next section.

V

In an earlier comparison[79] of the three men who created modern electromagnetic theory I described Faraday as an accumulative thinker, William Thomson as an inspirational thinker, and Maxwell as an architectural thinker. Faraday worked by gradually collecting large arrays of facts, altering his ideas a little at a time, writing up progress each day in his carefully cross-referenced diary. Thomson would take up a subject, work at it furiously for a few weeks, throw forth a string of novel—in Maxwell's epithet, "science-forming"[80] — ideas, and then drop everything and pass on. Maxwell differed from both. Not for him the slow steady development of Faraday's ideas or the brilliant lightning flashes of Thomson's. Instead each of his major papers offers in sixty or seventy pages a new coherent view of some large subject, concise, complete in itself, yet opening the way to further discovery. The unity of Faraday's work consists in its slow progression from idea to idea and experiment to experiment; the unity of Maxwell's is an immediate unity of vision.

The question of form is central to an understanding of Maxwell's creativity. To grasp it better, another comparison is useful, between Maxwell and the two men who followed him in the development of statistical mechanics: Boltzmann and Gibbs. Here the differences are in style rather than substantive mode. Gibbs and Boltzmann both resembled Maxwell in presenting scientific panoramas, but their brushwork was different. Boltzmann was an example of a man, not born great, who achieved greatness through sheer stumbling perseverance. Long-winded, cluttered with unnecessary detail, stodgy, pedantic, his papers deter all but the bravest readers and often fail to solve the problems they set out to. Yet they contain deep discoveries. A fascinating theme in the development of kinetic theory during the 1870s is the complementary development of Maxwell and Boltzmann: Maxwell adroitly moving into new regions where he could side-step analytic difficulties; Boltzmann battering at the difficulties head on and finding that the methods extended much further than he or Maxwell had originally supposed. Much of Boltzmann's outlook is embodied in his remark that considerations of elegance belong to tailors and shoemakers rather than mathematicians, yet it was he who gave the finest appreciation of Maxwell's style in describing the paper that laid the foundation for his own life's work:

A mathematician will recognize Cauchy, Gauss, Jacobi, Helmholtz after reading a few pages, just as musicians recognize, from the first few bars, Mozart, Beethoven or Schubert. A supreme external elegance belongs to the French, though it is occasionally combined with some weakness in the construction of the conclusions; the greatest dramatic vigour belongs to the English [sic], and above all to Maxwell. Who does not know his dynamical theory of gases? First the variations of the velicities are deployed in majestic array; next enter from one side the equations of state, from the other the equations of central motion; higher and higher surges the chaotic flood of formulae, until suddenly the four words resound: "Put n = 5" and the malignant demon V [the relative velocity of two molecules] vanishes, just as a wild overpowering figure in the bass may suddenly be reduced to silence. As if by a magic wand an apparently hopeless confusion is reduced to order. There is no time to explain why one or the other substitution is made; let him who does not feel it in his bones put away the book. Maxwell is no composer of program music who has to preface his score by a written explanation. Obediently his formulae deliver result after result, until we reach the final surprise effect. The problem of the thermal equilibrium of a heavy gas is solved and the curtain falls.[81]

Gibbs had much in common with Maxwell. Like Maxwell he would choose some large topic—thermodynamics, vector analysis, or statistical mechanics—give it prolonged study, and then write a paper or book drawing all together in a grand synthesis. Among British physicists of the 1880s Gibbs was often referred to as the Maxwell of America. But Maxwell's genius was at once more varied and more careless than Gibbs's. Everything Gibbs wrote seems to have unassailable perfection: no equation is wrongly derived, no statement can be challenged, no section is inconsistent with any other section. And finished with a subject he saw no need to go over the ground again. Maxwell, on the other hand, was continually changing his outlook. His five leading papers on electromagnetic theory written between 1855 and 1868 each presented a complete view of the subject, and each viewed it from a different angle. It is this variety that makes Maxwell's writings, in Jeans's words, a kind of enchanted fairyland: one never knows what to expect next. Other great scientists, such as Gibbs, Ampère, and Fourier have equalled him in synoptic power; Maxwell had a unique ability for developing a subject up to a certain point, presenting it in a systematic manner and then detaching himself from it all and starting anew. He was a system builder but never a slave to his own systems.

The aspect of Maxwell's creative style that has attracted most attention is his use of mechanical models and physical analogies. At the risk of sounding perverse I would argue that the method of analogy, though interesting, is neither the first nor the second most important factor in Maxwell's creativity, and, insofar as it is important, is so as part of a wider process. Of more moment are first Maxwell's architectonic mind and second his sense of mathematical beauty and order. In the response to Galton already quoted so often, Maxwell remarked, "I always regarded mathematics as the method of obtaining the *best* shapes and dimensions of things, and this meant not only the most useful and economical, but chiefly the most harmonious and the most beautiful."[82] The child who fashioned models of the five regular solids with his own hands was the father of the man who formulated Maxwell's equations.

Maxwell's starting point in mathematics was Euclidean geometry. Euclid is now so out of fashion that few people know the excitement of his intellectual rigor, but a discipline that could stir three young minds as powerful as those of Maxwell, Bertrand Russell, and Einstein deserves respect. With Maxwell the love of geometry stayed. "I remember one day," wrote W. N. Lawson, "our lecturer [at Cambridge] had filled the blackboard three times with the investigation of some hard problem in the Geometry of Three Dimensions, and was not at the end of it, when Maxwell came up with a question whether it would not come out geometrically, and showed how with a figure, and in a few lines, there was the solution at once."[83] After the paper on ovals, three of his next four papers were on geometrical topics. Of these, one, "On the Transformation of Surfaces by Bending," (1854) notably extended Gauss's work on surface geometry by relating the curvature of a surface to the angular defect of a polygon inscribed in it. Geometry continued as a minor but pleasing theme in Maxwell's later research through his work on geometrical optics (1857, 1868, 1874), reciprocal diagrams in engineering structures (1864, 1870, 1876), Gibbs's thermodynamic surface (1875), and the intriguing paper of 1870, "On Hills and Dales." The love of geometry also helped interest Maxwell in Faraday's ideas about lines of force. As with physical models, however, its influence should not be exaggerated. Kelland's teaching at Edinburgh and Hopkins's at Cambridge gave Maxwell command of a wide range of analytic technique. Careless about analytic detail he may have been; narrow he was not.

The successive decades of Maxwell's career saw certain general developments of method. Typical of his mathematical grasp in the 1850s was the essay "On the Stability of the Motion of Saturn's Rings," an example of applied mathematics in the Cambridge tradition unusual only in its literary grace and massive assurance of style. The great papers of the 1860s continue at roughly the same analytic level with epoch-making advances in physical and philosophic insight. The books and articles of the 1870s display growing mastery of mathematical abstraction in the use of matrices, vectors, and quaternions, Hamiltonian dynamics, special functions, considerations of symmetry and topology. A difficult but rewarding task is to explore the contrasting ways in which these different phases of Maxwell's mature researches reflect his interactions with contemporaries and his influence on the next scientific generation. Thomson's was the strongest influence on Maxwell's early work in electromagnetism, but the man who influenced him most during his late thirties and early forties was—Tait. Tait's prickly personality has made him as unpopular among historians as he was among many of his contemporaries. Maxwell saw deeper. When the Thomson-Tait *Treatise on Natural Philosophy* came out in 1867, nearly all written by Tait, Maxwell at once perceived how much mathematical physics his friend had learned since they had been at school together. He was not ashamed to pick Tait's brains.

Most scientific reputations are built partly on luck. Someone who has mastered an experimental technique or mathematical method suddenly finds himself in circumstances that spring a great discovery. But careers so widely productive as Newton's, Maxwell's, or Einstein's are not accidental. Such men achieve what they do by finding creative principles to guide them through regions where others see only confusion. These principles of discovery are distinct from the discoveries themselves. Einstein's insights into the definitions of space and time, matter and energy involve questions of physics and philosophy; but in speculative origin they came, in part at least, from his wonderful ingenuity in inventing "thought experiments" to lay bare the essentials of a problem. With Maxwell much rests in a process which he called the "cross-fertilization of the sciences."[84] The idea behind that phrase needs to be distinguished from the more familiar one, propounded by advocates of "interdisciplinary studies," that new discoveries often occur in the boundaries between two fields of research. There is truth in that view: it underlies much of Faraday's phenomenal productiveness: but it is not what Maxwell meant. He was concerned with the unexpected, even accidental impact of one science on another. A case in point was Thomson's discovery in 1841 that the equations governing the distribution of electric charge on the surface of a conductor are formally equivalent to the equations governing the flow of heat through a solid body.

The phenomena were as remote as could be, but once Thomson had recognized their mathematical relation he could apply Fourier's methods from the theory of heat to solve previously intractable problems in electrostatics.

Thomson's discovery formed the starting-point (not the whole point) of Maxwell's first paper on electricity. Similar "cross-fertilizations" occur throughout his work. We have seen the influence of Herschel's article on social statistics on Maxwell's first paper on gas theory. The concept of "relaxation time," which was also to be crucial for gas theory, followed a study of viscosity in solids, which Maxwell learned of through Forbes's investigations of the motions of glaciers. Maxwell's analysis of the stability of governors, the first important paper on control theory, was partly based on methods he had encountered in analyzing the stability of Saturn's rings. The title of a note from the 1870s, "On the Application of Kirchhoff's Rules for Electric Circuits to the Solution of a Geometrical Problem," tells its own tale, while one of the subtlest cross-fertilizations occurred in Maxwell's last big paper, completed just before his death, in which he applied methods of spherical harmonic analysis from his *Treatise on Electricity and Magnetism* to calculate stresses in rarefied gases due to inequalities of temperature.

"I suppose," wrote Maxwell, "that when the bees crowd around the flowers it is for the sake of the honey they do so, never thinking that it is the dust which they are carrying from flower to flower which is to render possible a more splendid array of flowers, and a busier crowd of bees, in the years to come."[84] But Maxwell did think about what he was doing. Thomson's analogy between electrostatics and heat conduction impressed him deeply. Besides carrying analytic techniques from one field into the other, Thomson had shown that Faraday's ideas and experiments were after all consistent with traditional electrostatics, hence convincing Maxwell that the apparent discrepancy between "Faraday's way of conceiving the phenomena and that of the mathematicians . . . did not arise from either party being wrong." To understand Thomson's discovery, consider a point source of heat P embedded in a homogeneous solid. Since the surface area of a sphere is $4\pi r^2$, the heat flux ϕ through a small surface area dS at a distance r from P is proportional to $1/r^2$, in analogy with Coulomb's inverse square law of electric action; so (in Maxwell's words) "we have only to substitute *source of heat* for *centre of attraction, flow of heat* for *accelerating effect of attraction* at any point and *temperature* for *potential* and the solution of a problem in attraction is transformed into that of a problem in heat."[85]

One of the strangest discoveries in physics was Oersted's observation in 1821 that a magnet suspended above a wire carrying an electric current tends to set at right angles to the wire. A magnet below the wire also sets at right angles but pointing in the opposite direction. In Faraday's language the lines of magnetic force generated by the electric current form closed circles around the wire. In 1847 Thomson formulated a new mathematico-physical analogy to illustrate this relation. Think of a straight wire embedded along the axis of a solid cylinder of some elastic material. If one pulls on the wire while keeping the outer surface of the cylinder constrained, the material will distort through shear, and each element of solid will become twisted about an axis at right angles to the wire. Circles can thus be drawn around the wire indicating lines of equal twist. These correspond to the lines of magnetic force, and the amount of twist at a distance from the wire falls off as $1/r$, just as in electromagnetism the intensity of the magnetic force falls off inversely with distance from the wire carrying the current.

Thomson in the 1840s explicitly disclaimed any physical significance for the analogies he had discovered and seemed pointedly reluctant to search for deeper meaning. Maxwell inevitably thought further. He was the more willing to do so because of his dissatisfaction with Ampère's and Weber's attempts to reduce electromagnetism to the actions of complicated force laws between electric charges or elements of electric current: hypotheses that involved unphysical ideas and called for elaborate reinterpretations of the simple laws discovered by Oersted and Faraday. "The present state of electrical science," wrote Maxwell in 1855, "seems peculiarly unfavourable to speculation." Neither a purely mathematical nor a purely physical treatment was satisfactory. On one side "the student must make himself familiar with a considerable body of most intricate mathematics, the mere retention of which in the memory materially interferes with further progress." On the other hand to adopt prematurely a physical hypothesis like Weber's would make one "see the phenomena only through a medium, and [be] liable to that blindness to facts and rashness in assumption which a partial explanation encourages."[86] Analogies like Thomson's, rightly understood, supply a mean between these extremes.

The essence of analogy is a partial resemblance between two things. If the resemblance were complete, one would speak not of analogy but identity. Maxwell made this point many times, most forcefully in a rediscussion in the *Elementary Treatise on Electricity* (1876) of Thomson's analogy between electricity and the flow of heat: "We must not conclude from the partial similarity of some of the relations of the phenomena of heat and electricity that there is any real physical similarity between the causes of these phenomena. The similarity is a similarity between relations, not a similarity between things related."[87] Elsewhere, after describing this and the further analogy with the flow of an incompressible fluid, Maxwell wrote, "A fluid is certainly a substance, heat is as certainly not a substance, so that though we may find assistance from analogies of this kind in forming clear ideas of formal relations of electrical quantities, we must be careful not to let one or the other analogy suggest to us that electricity is either a substance like water, or a state of agitation like heat."[88]

The key is Maxwell's desire to form "clear ideas of formal relations of electrical quantities." The attention that has been focused on Maxwell's introductory discussion about physical analogy in the paper of 1855, "On Faraday's Lines of Force," makes it easy to forget that what makes the paper exciting is not the analogy in Part I between lines of force and streamlines, but the formal system of equations developed in Part II to represent electromagnetic phenomena. Maxwell generously entitled this section "On Faraday's Electrotonic State," though the results it contains are only loosely tied to the rather shadowy speculations put forth by Faraday under that name. He acknowledged influence from Thomson's analogy of the strained elastic solid, but confessed that the theory "has not yet presented itself to my mind in such a way that [the] nature and properties [of the electro-tonic state] may be clearly explained without reference to mere symbols, and therefore I propose . . . to use symbols freely, and to take for granted the ordinary mathematical operations."[89]

For electro-tonic state, read vector potential. But Maxwell is not just deriving some new abstract function. He does what Thomson seems never to have had the courage for—goes to the heart of the electromagnetic problem. Here he owed much to an important analytical theorem first given in a letter from Thomson to Stokes dated 2 July 1850[90] and first published by Stokes *as an examination question* in the Smith's Prize examination Maxwell had sat for in 1854.[91] This theorem, which, following Maxwell, we now call Stokes's theorem, states that the integral of a continuous function around a closed curve is equal to the integral of the curl of that function over the enclosed surface. Applying it to Ampère's observation that the actions of a small circulating current and a small magnet are identical, Maxwell worked out a set of equations summarizing all the relations between the four vectors E, I, B, and H, that describe electric and magnetic lines of force. These are the beginnings of what we now call Maxwell's equations. Maxwell used Cartesian coordinates and a special symbolism, but since he later invented the notation we now use, the results may legitimately be modernized. One was the circuital equation relating the magnetic force vector H to the current density I (without the displacement-current term)

$$\operatorname{curl} H = I. \tag{1}$$

Defining a new vector A (the electro-tonic function), Maxwell discovered an inverse circuital relation between A and the magnetic induction vector B

$$B = \operatorname{curl} A \tag{2}$$

where in a homogeneous isotropic magnetic medium of permeability μ, the quantities B and H are related by

$$B = \mu H. \tag{3}$$

In a vacuum μ is 1, and for most purposes B and H may be thought of as identical. If one wants analogies, the streamline analogy can be used to illustrate Equation (1) and Thomson's elastic solid analogy to illustrate Equation (2). For Equation (1) the lines of force may be thought of as a whirlpool circulating around the wire. The *curl* relation between the current and field lines may be visualized as the rotation of a paddlewheel at the center of the whirl. For Equation (2) the vector A corresponds to the displacement parallel to the wire in the elastic medium as the wire is pulled, and the vector B corresponds to the twist in the medium. There are thus two distinct ways of viewing the relation between the current and the lines of force, each depending on the operation *curl*. These are illustrated but not explained by our two analogies. Maxwell went on to show that the electromotive force develped in electromagnetic induction may be written $-\partial A/\partial t$, and that the total energy of an electromagnetic system is $\int I.A\ dV$. Thus the electro-tonic function provided equations to represent ordinary magnetic action, electromagnetic induction, and the forces between closed currents.

An important aspect of Maxwell's achievement was, as Norton Wise has emphasized,[92] to take seriously Faraday's picture of the relationship between electricity and magnetism as two mutually embracing curves. A circulating current creates interlocking loops of magnetic force. A magnet moving in a closed path through a loop of wire generates a circulating current. That is what underlies the symmetry of the two reciprocal circuital relations (1) and (2). But if one asks the secret of Maxwell's achievement, it is neither this nor the use of analogies, but rather having the courage to attack the constructive problem. Thomson had all the pieces in hand, but he never put them together. It is intriguing that Thomson, who in society appeared so self-confident, had for all his brilliance a streak of intellectual timidity, while Maxwell, who struck people on first meeting as shy and hesitant, met the scientific issues head on.

Courage was of the essence in Maxwell's extraordinary second paper on electrical theory, "On Physical Lines of Force" (1861-1862). So much has been written about the molecular-vortex model of the electromagnetic aether, with its intermeshed magnetic vortices and particles of electricity, that it hardly needs summary here. Two points only should be made. First, it is a sport among Maxwell's scientific papers. He wrote nothing like it before or after. Hence, fascinating as it is, it should not be taken as the key to Maxwell's creativity. Rather one should examine the corpus of Maxwell's work without it, and then, having grasped what one can of his genius, come back for a fresh look at "Physical Lines." Second, Maxwell wrote the paper as an experiment to see how far he could go in accounting by an aether model both for electromagnetic phenomena and the stresses Faraday had associated with lines of magnetic force. Both things were possible: then came the surprise. After completing the first two parts Maxwell tried the further idea of introducing elasticity into the model in order to account for electrostatic phenomena. Now an elastic medium transmits waves. The velocity of transverse waves calculated from the known ratio of electric to magnetic forces turned out to be equal to the velocity of light. One hundred and twenty years later the excitement still leaps from the page in Maxwell's italics. "We can scarcely avoid the inference that *light consists in the transverse undulations of the same medium which is the cause of electric and magnetic phenomena.*"[93]

In consolidating his work on electromagentic theory over the next twelve years, Maxwell's procedure was alternately to simplify and to generalize. In 1863 he wrote jointly with Fleeming Jenkin a paper, "On the Elementary Relations of Electrical Quantities," based on dimensional principles. The ratios of electric to magnetic units depend on a quantity having the dimensions of a velocity; five distinct methods exist for determining this velocity; data from an experiment by Kohlrausch and Weber (1856) make it close to the velocity of light. The connection between electrical quantities and the velocity of light stands independent of any visionary vortex machinery. In 1865 Maxwell produced his "great guns" paper, "A Dynamical Theory of the Electromagnetic Field." In it, besides much else, he formulated a Lagrangian theory of the field, wrote down Maxwell's equations in essentially complete form, and deduced from these equations alone that electromagnetic waves propagate through space with the velocity of light. His principal assumptions were as follows: (1) electric and magnetic energy, instead of being localized in material bodies, are disseminated through space, presumably in some kind of aethereal medium; (2) without knowing the mechanical properties of this aether, one can deduce expressions for the two kinds of energy from the equations of electromagnetism; (3) if the medium is subject to dynamical principles, phenomena occurring in it will be governed by the general equations of dynamics, i.e., Lagrange's equations; (4) the variables ordinarily used in Lagrange's equations, being mechanical, depend on differences between two kinds of energy, kinetic and potential; (5) in applying dynamics to electromagnetism one may substitute magnetic and electric energy for kinetic and potential energy to form a hybrid theory, dynamical in the sense that it is based on Lagrange's equations, electromagnetic in the sense that the quantities entering the equations are electric or magnetic; (6) according to the Faraday-Mossotti theory of dielectrics, when a potential difference is applied across a dielectric it becomes polarized, i.e., its molecules acquire a positive charge at one end and a negative charge at the other; (7) this means that electrical energy is stored in the dielectric, and further that when a potential difference is being set up across it, a transient electric current flows in it; (8) since the theory assumes that even apparently empty space stores up electrical energy, it is reasonable to expect space (or the aether), like a material dielectric, to become polarized by a potential difference; (9) hence in particular, even though the aether is a perfect insulator, a *changing* potential difference will produce in it a changing "current," *the displacement current*, with which is associated a changing magnetic field.

Equal physical and philosophic insight went to the making of the "Dynamical Theory." Philosophically the crux was Maxwell's recognition that it was neither necessary nor desirable to invent a mechanical model of the aether—undesirable because such models take one into speculative realms; unnecessary because the existence of electromagnetic waves propagating with the velocity of light follows from the electrical equations. Maxwell's theory established a relationship between light and electricity without the need for a mechanistic explanation of either. Not that Maxwell had abandoned the prospect of a dynamical explanation of electromagnetic phenomena, for the Lagrangian formulation makes the theory consistent with dynamical principles; rather, he had hit upon the "appropriate idea," the appropriate level of explanation, to suit the case. The influence on the one hand of Whewell, and on the other of Hamilton's doctrine of the relativity of knowledge, is clear. And if Maxwell's retreat from the vortex aether was an act of scientific caution, his step in introducing electromagnetic variables into the equations of dynamics was an act of marvelous philosophic courage. It anticipated by thirty years the debate of the 1890s between the "mechanical" and "electromagnetic" world-views: the question whether one should base electromagnetic theory on the laws of mechanics or mechanics on the laws of electromagnetism: a debate that ended in 1905 when Einstein fused the two views by modifying the laws of mechanics to account for the properties of bodies moving with velocities close to the velocity of light.

Maxwell's great physical insight was his notion of the displacement current. The displacement current was not a necessary consequence of experimental evidence available in Maxwell's day. He had stumbled upon the idea by accident in making the molecular-vortex aether elastic, since the elasticity meant that the electric particles disseminated through space in that theory were capable of transient motions. Having jettisoned the model, Maxwell needed other grounds for including the displacement current in his equations. The subtle way he pulled it off in developing assumptions (1), (2), (6), (7), (8), and (9) above showed the physicist— or was it the lawyer manqúe?— at work. From the known facts about light Maxwell argued that space (or the aether) must be capable of storing up energy; from the equations of electricity and magnetism he showed the forms electric and magnetic energy must have if disseminated throughout space; from a generalization of the Faraday-Mossotti theory of dielectrics he suggested that there will be a displacement current; and from the displacement current he was able to deduce the properties of the electromagnetic waves that account for light. Anyone with lingering doubts can always reflect that the relation between electromagnetism and the velocity of light rests on dimensional analysis.

Rather than pursue Maxwell's later work on electromagnetism, I turn to another example of cross-fertilization: his reformulation in 1866 of the theory of transport phenomena in gases. After Clausius had pointed out the errors in Maxwell's original theory of heat conduction in a gas, Maxwell spent some time in 1864 trying with fair success to patch up the theory by the mean free path method, only to discover experimentally that the viscosity of a gas, instead of being proportional to the square root of the absolute temperature T as expected from the simple theory is more nearly proportional to T. The implication had to be that molecular interactions depend on a long-range force rather than on simple collisions between billiard-ball-like objects. But if so, molecules no longer move in straight lines but in complicated orbits among each other. The mean free path method falls to pieces.

Some property descriptive of the heterogeneous structure of a gas was needed, however. Maxwell found it by considering a phenomenon that had first been discussed by Stokes in 1845 and then drawn to Maxwell's attention by Forbes in 1849 in connection with the motions of glaciers. Many substances like pitch or glass, which are ordinarily thought of as solids, flow viscously when left for long periods. The distinction between solids and liquids seems to be a matter of time. Considering how simple the issue is, it is odd that twenty years elapsed before someone—Maxwell—followed up Stokes's lead by writing down an equation to describe just how time enters these processes. With certain assumptions one can define a time τ, the "modulus of the time of relaxation" of stresses in a material such that for times shorter than τ the body behaves like an elastic solid, while for times longer than τ it behaves like a viscous liquid.

What has all this to do with gas theory? Here came one of Maxwell's most astounding insights. Consider a group of molecules moving about in a box with flexible walls. Their impacts on the walls exert a pressure that is just equal in the theory of elastic bodies to the coefficient of cubical elasticity. Suppose the pressure is reduced to make the free path much greater than the dimensions of the box. The molecules will fly from wall to wall. If the walls are rough, the molecules will rebound at random, so that in addition to the pressure there will be continued exchange of transverse momentum between the walls, making the box, even though it is flexible, resist shearing stresses. In other words a rarefied gas behaves like an elastic solid! Let this property of a rarefied gas be called *quasi-solidity.* Maxwell interpreted the viscosity of a gas at normal pressures as the relaxation of quasi-solidity by molecular encounters, and by replacing Clausius's idea of a characteristic distance with the characteristic time τ he was able to formulate a systematic procedure for relating the observed properties of a gas to the kinetic theory variables.

From the motions of glaciers to the conduction of heat in gases is a thrilling leap. The ingenuity that could parlay the relationship between liquids and solids into one between a gas at ordinary pressures and a rarefied gas is beyond praise. But there is more to Maxwell's paper of 1867 on gas theory than a startling analogy. Maxwell had to generalize Stokes' hydrodynamical equations, study the scattering of particles under a repulsive force, invent an elaborate but elegant notation to keep track of the variables, provide a new derivation of the velocity distribution law, and finally carry through that systematic reduction to experience so admired by Boltzmann in which his formulae "obediently . . . deliver result upon result." All were essential to his creative architecture.

Range is the grand characteristic of Maxwell's inventive genius. The man who wrote the first significant paper on control theory was the man who took the first color photograph. The same quality is seen in Maxwell's ability within a single paper to go from the most general to the most particular results. The "Dynamical Theory of the Electromagnetic Field" contains the electromagnetic theory of light and the Lagrangian formulation of the field equations. It also contains the first calculation of the correction to coefficients of induction arising from the "want of uniformity of the current in the different parts of the section of the wire at the commencement of the current"[94] — that is, the correction for the skin effect.

Most appealing of all in a man of conservative tastes was the forward-looking constructive character of Maxwell's thought. Ten years after his death Oliver Heaviside complained to Hertz about the "slavish way" in which most British writers on electricity followed Maxwell's *Treatise*: "I have struck out a path for myself and I am quite sure that if Maxwell had lived, he would, because he was a progressive man, have recognized the superior simplicity of my methods."[95] Heaviside was not aware, because Maxwell's papers had still not been published as a collection, that in 1868 Maxwell had actually written the equations in essentially that form. But he was right in describing Maxwell as a progressive man. One of Maxwell's last papers, a letter on the definition of "Potential," published in the *Electrician* in April 1879, twenty-five years after he began studying the subject, shows his sense of how much remained to be done, as well as the extent to which his mind-set had been influenced by his two philosophic mentors, Hamilton and Whewell.

There is no more satisfactory evidence of the progress of a science than when its cultivators, having settled all their differences about the connexions of the phenomena [Hamilton!], proceed to reconstruct the definitions [Whewell!]. Even in the most mature sciences, such as geometry and dynamics, the study of the definitions still leads original thinkers into new regions of investigation, and in a science like electricity, the growth of which has proceeded from so many centres, it is only to be expected that when the different departments have grown until they meet, their definitions will need some adjustment to make them consistent with each other.[96]

But we must still ask how Maxwell's creative ideas came to him.

VI

Men differ widely in their responses to problems. Some, faced with a new question, think out the answer step by step through conscious ratiocination. In others the mental processes go on behind the scenes. A great twentieth-century thinker, who had the second type of mind, has described its workings well. When such a man encounters a novel suggestion, "his mind goes blank; he will stare at the fire or walk about the room or otherwise keep conscious attention diverted from the problem. Then abruptly he will find that he has a question to ask or a counter-suggestion to make, after which the mental blank returns. At last, he is aware, once more abruptly, what is his judgement on the suggestion and subsequently, though sometimes very rapidly, he also becomes aware of the reasons which support or necessitate it."[97]

Maxwell seems to have had this second type of mind in extreme and peculiar form. The odd contrast between the clarity of his writing and the frequent obscurity of his speech was often remarked on. Some obscurity can be put down to the natural shyness of a man who has been mistreated as a child, but not all; indeed part of the difficulty between Maxwell and his tutor may well have been the result rather than the cause of his verbal obscurities. Two quotations, among several possible ones, illustrate the point. The first is from Arthur Schuster, giving an impression of Maxwell at the Cavendish Laboratory in the 1870s:

Maxwell often showed a certain absentmindness: a question put to him might remain unnoticed, or be answered by a remark which had no obvious connection with it. But it happened more than once that on the following day he would at once refer to the question in a manner which showed he had spent some time and thought on it. I never could quite make up my mind whether on these occasions the question had remained unconsciously dormant in his mind until something had brought it back to him, or whether he had consciously put it aside for future consideration, but it was quite usual for him to begin a conversation with the remark, 'You asked me a question the other day, and I have been thinking about it.' Such an opening usually led to an interesting and original treatment of the subject.[98]

The second quotation is from F. W. Farrar, the Dean of Canterbury Cathedral and popular writer, who had been a friend of Maxwell's at Cambridge and a fellow Apostle. Describing the Apostles' meetings he wrote that Maxwell's

interventions in the discussions, when each of us had to speak in turn, were often hardly intelligible to anyone who did not understand the characteristics of his mind, which were very marked in his conversation. If you said something to him, he would reply by a remark which seemed wide as the poles from what you had mentioned. This often had the effect of diverting the conversation from the subject in hand, because the remark appeared wholly irrelevant. When this was the case, he usually dropped the discussion altogether, and, indeed, many of those who casually met him regarded him as incomprehensible for this reason. But if you gave him his bent, he would soon show you that his observation, so far from being *nihil ad rem,* really bore very closely on the heart of the question at issue. To this he would gradually approach, until the relevance of his first remark which seemed so distant from the topic under consideration, became abundantly manifest.[99]

The idea that the mind "exerts energies, and is the subject of modifications, of neither of which it is conscious"[100] was familiar to Maxwell from Sir William Hamilton's teaching at Edinburgh. Hamilton strongly believed in the occurrence of "unconscious mental modifications," and his discussions of dreams and free association are among the liveliest parts of his lectures. The rise of Freudian psychology has made the role of the unconscious a popular, if ill-understood, cliché, but in the 1840s Hamilton's teaching struck with all the force of novelty. Maxwell became convinced of its truth by introspection, and especially convinced of the influence of "unconscious mental modifications" in his own creative processes. Once at Cambridge, when asked by a group of students how he solved problems, he said, "I dream about them." In a letter of 1857 to his undergraduate friend R. B. Litchfield he wrote: "I have not had a mathematical idea for about a fortnight, when I wrote them all away to Professor Thomson, and I have not got an answer yet with fresh ones. But I believe there is a department of mind conducted independent of consciousness, where things are fermented and decocted, so that when they are run off they come clear."[101]

With this view of Maxwell's mental processes it is instructive to return to the comparison with Faraday and Thomson and examine the expression of intellectual style in each man's private notebooks. Faraday seems to have been a thinker of the conscious type, reasoning along with few surprises. The seven volumes of his *Diary* offer a day to day record of his thoughts unparalleled in its completeness, almost as consecutive as his published papers. Thomson's "green books" have all his compulsiveness: grand schemes of research are continually being started, taken over twenty pages, and then dropped. He also seems to have written his notes with an eye to posterity, often setting down the exact day and hour at which the latest brilliant idea had struck him. Maxwell's notebooks are different again. He always carried a small one with him, but the entries are jotted at random. Unfinished calculations jostle against addresses of correspondents, lists of laboratory equipment, quotations from Italian and Spanish poets, even in one place an inventory of his wine cellar. Maxwell's phenomenal memory spared him Faraday's distressing need to write down everything he did, but the ultimate difference is in mode of work. His papers were the results of long periods of hidden thinking followed by three or four months' concentrated effort to distill the ideas that had been "fermented and decocted" in the preceding years. He had no need to commit ideas to paper till the moment of creation was on.

What is to be made of the more peculiar characteristic of Maxwell noted by Farrar and Schuster, that his responses in conversation were often "wide as the poles from what you had mentioned?" There is more to this than the "mental blank" or conscious diversion of attention of the nonratiocinative thinker. Psychoanalytically it is more an aggressive than an evasive act, but not destructive aggression because, as Farrar said, if you gave Maxwell his bent he would soon show you that his seemingly irrelevant observation "really bore very closely on the heart of the question at issue." Whether one can penetrate deeper into so strange a phenomenon remains a question; assuredly it lies close to the heart of Maxwell's creativity. Who, asking about the conduction of heat in gases, would look for a response on the motions of glaciers? Lewis Campbell, who knew his man, singled out for special attention a remark of Maxwell's: "no one who has once known can ever forget that instead of two views there are three, good, bad and grotesque,"[102] a remark that evokes the grotesque atmosphere pervading Maxwell's early letters to his father and some of his later letters to Tait. Somewhere in Maxwell was a strain of grotesque (in the twentieth century one might prefer to say surrealistic) fantasy — the necessary element of surprise — which fused with his classical sense of order and symmetry to produce great scientific work.

Much can be learned about a writer, especially one of Maxwell's literary distinction, by examining his choice of metaphors. Two classes of illustration used by Maxwell are particularly enlightening.

The first relates ideas to processes of growth. Thus in commending mathematical analogies he speaks of their advantages in "fertility of method."[103] Later of the molecular hypothesis, with its assumption of the existence of unnumbered individual things, all alike and unchangeable, he says it is an idea "which cannot enter the human mind and remain without fruit."[104] In an anonymous review he describes one of Thomson's electrical papers as "the germ of that course of speculation by which Maxwell has gradually developed the mathematical significance of Faraday's idea of the physical action of lines of force."[105] Similar notions of progress by growth occur in Maxwell's comments on teaching. To Tait he wrote "I am going to try, as I have already done, to sow 4nion [quaternion] seed at Cambridge. I hope and trust nothing I have yet done may produce tares";[106] to the audience at his "Introductory Lecture on Experimental Physics" he spoke of "the untried fertility of those fresh minds into which [the] riches [of creation] will continue to be poured."[107]

Such metaphors fill out the picture of Maxwell's hidden mental processes. They reflect also the influence on his mind of Biblical imagery, and the fact of his being a countryman. The incidental illustrations in his papers include many allusions to country life. A curious cancelled passage in the manuscript of his "Dynamical Theory of the Electromagnetic Field" compares the inductive coupling between two electric circuits to the action of two horses pulling alternately on the swingletree of a cart.[108] References to bees remind one that Maxwell had hives at Glenlair. The use of such homely metaphors occasions no surprise. More unexpected in this most peaceful of men, who would not touch a gun or fishing rod, is the second group of frequent metaphors, the military ones. To Lewis Campbell in 1857 he wrote about Saturn's rings, with a typical Maxwellian pun: "I have been battering away at Saturn, returning to the charge every now and then. I have effected several breaches in the solid ring, and now I am splash into the fluid one, amid a clash of symbols truly astounding."[109] Of some work for an experiment on gases he wrote to Charles Cay, "I set Prof. W. Thomson a prop[osition] which I had been working on for a long time. He sent me 18 pages of letter of suggestions about it, none of which would work; but on Jan 3 [1865], in the railway from Largs, he got the way to it, which is all right; so now we are jolly, having stormed the citadel, when we only hoped to sap it by approximations."[110] A passage in his "Introductory Lecture" that gives a further insight into his creative processes states that "there is no more powerful method for introducing knowledge into the mind than that of presenting it in as many different ways as we can. When the ideas, after entering through different gateways, effect a junction in the citadel of the mind, the position they occupy becomes impregnable."[111] Elsewhere in the same lecture he spoke of how Gauss and Weber set up the Magnetic Union to do worldwide experiments and "the scattered forces of science were converted into a regular army."[112] In another place he spoke of "keeping up operations on a broad front and an ever increasing scale,"[113] while a slightly different application, along with a passing nod at the fertility metaphor, occurs in a passage on molecular theory that may also shadow forth Maxwell's view of the work of Thomson and himself on electrical theory: "To conduct the operations of science in a perfectly legitimate manner by means of methodized experiment and strict demonstration requires a strategic skill which we must not look for, even among those whom science is most indebted to for original observations and fertile suggestions. It does not detract from the merit of the pioneers of science that their advances, being made on unknown ground, are often cut off for a time, from that system of communications with an established base of operations, which is the only security for any permanent extension of science."[114]

Maxwell's warlike metaphors have been noticed by Mr. J. G. Crowther, who refers them to Maxwell's ancestral relative John Clerk of Eldin, author of a celebrated treatise on naval strategy.[115] Most of the illustrations, however, refer to military rather than naval affairs, often to sieges. A more likely source is in the history of Galloway, with the constant fighting between the Maxwells and their neighbors, the sieges of Caerlaverock and Threave castles, and the more recent memories of the hated English dragoons from the 1745 rebellion, which Maxwell mentions in one letter as being still strong in Galloway when he was a boy. Another is the Crimean War. In one place Maxwell describes the condition of the rings of Saturn, made up of independent bodies as "something like the state of the air, supposing the siege of Sebastopol conducted from a forest of guns 100 miles one way and 30,000 the other, and the shot never to stop, but go spinning away round a circle, radius 170,000 miles."[116]

Whatever the hidden aggressions underlying such ferocious similes, issues of scientific strategy were essential to Maxwell. He seemed to know instinctively which problems to attack and which to leave alone. Often the reader feels himself tricked as Maxwell marches up, banners waving, guns bristling, against a seemingly impregnable scientific position, and then adroitly takes it by some unforeseen flank maneuver. Of this aspect of his research he was thoroughly conscious. Commenting on a point in the electromagnetic theory of light, Maxwell at one stage wrote, "my theory says nothing of what goes on at the boundary of the medium, because I felt it the essence of sound scientific strategy to avoid the difficulties of the problem."[117]

One further aspect of Maxwell's intellect is seen in the contrasting roles of philosophical speculation in his work and in that of a later Cambridge mathematician, A. N. Whitehead. Whitehead was intensely concerned with the bearing of science on the perennial problems of philosophy. The whole thrust of his *Process and Reality* is to apply the theories of evolution and relativity as extended philosophic metaphors. Now the merit of what Whitehead (and later Teilhard de Chardin) attempted is worthy of debate. Much depends on the perspective of the scientific theories being examined. But whatever the merits of the approach, it is not Maxwell's. Not that he was indifferent to the bearing of science on philosophy: far from it: his occasional writings discuss the influence of Leibniz and Newton on the course of philosophical speculation as well as the philosophical significance of statistical mechanics. But the tie he saw between the immanent scientific and transcendent philosophic questions was much broader. The more one reads Maxwell the clearer it becomes, not so much how scientific research affected his philosophical concern, but how philosophical convictions that he reached early in his career influenced and fructified his scientific ideas. His use of metaphor touches the same theme. He brought his interest in country life, military strategy, the applied arts, and other matters to illustrate and enlarge his scientific tales. And that is at least part of the reason for the elegant clarity of Maxwell's writing in contrast to the strange density of Whitehead's.

VII

Writing of Faraday in 1873 in the article accompanying the presentation portrait with which *Nature* began its series of "Scientific Worthies," Maxwell said:

Every great man of the first rank is unique. Each has his own office and his own place in the historic procession of the sages. The office did not exist even in the imagination, till he came to fill it, and none can succeed to his place when he has passed away. Others may gain distinction by adapting the exposition of sciences to the varying language of each generation of students, but their true function is not so much didactic as paedagogic—not to teach the phrases which enable us to persuade ourselves that we understand a science, but to bring the student into living contact with the two main sources of mental growth, the fathers of the sciences, for whose personal influence over the opening mind there is no substitute, and the material things to which their labours first gave a meaning.[118]

Nothing more aptly illustrates the truth of the dictum *l'homme, le temps, le milieu* than the comparison of Faraday and Maxwell. Each was a "great man of the first rank"; each seemed preternaturally fitted to the career he built, and yet deep as Faraday's influence on Maxwell was—an influence whose parental character is again caught in the phrase "the fathers of the sciences"—the office and place of each was as different as might be. Between the simple profundity of Faraday's mind and the profound complexities of Maxwell's were differences in social background, in temperament, in interest, in cast of mind, in education, as far-reaching as any to be found within the British Isles. And herein lies the best lesson of Maxwell's career. For the way to profit from great men—or women—whether at first hand or through their writings, is to perceive their special insights and personal qualities, and to pay them the highest compliment one human being can pay to another—to learn from them and not imitate them, as Faraday, the discoverer of electromagnetic induction learned from Davy, the discoverer of sodium; as Maxwell learned from Faraday and Thomson.

Notes

1. R. A. Millikan, *The Autobiography of Robert Andrews Millikan* (New York: Prentice-Hall, 1950), p. 205.

2. I am unable to track down this elusive reference, but compare A. Schuster, *The Progress of Physics 1875-1908* (Cambridge: At the University Press, 1911), p. 29: "I remember especially [Maxwell's] saying that Boltzmann's theorem, if true, ought to be applicable to liquids and solids as well as gases."

3. J. Larmor, *Mathematical and Physical Papers II* (Cambridge: At the University Press, 1929), Appendix III, p. 743.

4. G. B. Airy, *Monthly Notice of the Royal Astronomical Society* 19 (1859), p. 304.

5. C. G. Knott, *Life and Scientific Work of Peter Guthrie Tait* (Cambridge: Cambridge University Press, 1911), pp. 214-215.

6. Letter from Canon Richard Abbay to F. J. C. Hearnshaw in the latter's *The Centenary History of King's College, London 1828-1928* (London: G. G. Harrap & Co., 1929), p. 111. Compare C. Domb, "James Clerk Maxwell in London 1860-1865," *Notes and Records of the Royal Society of London*, 35, (1980A), pp. 101-103, where the Abbay letters are reprinted.

7. Letter from H. A. Rowland to Daniel Gilman, August 14, 1875. The Johns Hopkins University, Milton S. Eisenhower Library, Frieda C. Thies Manuscript Room, Daniel Coit Gilman Papers.

8. Victor L. Hilts, "A Guide to Francis Galton's English Men of Science," *Transactions of the American Philosophical Society* 65, (1975), Part 5, p. 59.

9. John Playfair, "Biographical Account of the late Dr. James Hutton, F.R.S. Edin," *Phil. Trans. Roy. Soc. Edin.* 5, (1805), pp. 39-99.

10. *Theory of the Earth: The Lost Drawings,* ed. G. Y. Craig, including explanatory text by D. B. Macintyre, C. D. Waterston, and A. Y. Craig (Edinburgh: Royal Society of Edinburgh, 1979).

11. Sir Walter Scott, *Minstrelsy of the Scottish Border,* (reprinted London: Murray, 1868), p. 236; quoting from an account in Spottiswoode 1677.

12. Lewis Campbell and William Garnett, *The Life of James Clerk Maxwell* (London: Macmillan and Co., 1882), pp. 105-106.

13. Ibid., p. 67.

14. C. G. Knott, *Peter Guthrie Tait,* p. 5; Magnus Magnusson, *The Clacken and the Slate* (London: Collins, 1974), pp. 102-103.

15. Campbell and Garnett, *James Clerk Maxwell,* 1st ed., p. 591.

16. Ibid., p. 55.

17. Hilts, "A Guide," p. 59.

18. Campbell and Garnett, *James Clerk Maxwell,* 1st ed., p. 60.

19. C. W. F. Everitt, *James Clerk Maxwell, Physicist and Natural Philosopher* (New York: Scribners, 1975), p. 48.

20. P. G. Tait, "James Clerk-Maxwell," *Proceedings of the Royal Society of Edinburgh* 10 (1880), p. 332.

21. Campbell and Garnett, *James Clerk Maxwell,* 1st ed., pp. 115-116.

22. Ibid., pp. 106-107.

23. Ibid., p. 135.

24. Ibid., p. 106n.

25. Ibid., pp. 137-138. "Abrupt transition" was a favorite remark of Forbes. See Maxwell's letter (Ibid., p. 124) poking fun at his superprecise pronunciation of it.

26. δι πολλοι, the crowd.

27. C. P. Snow, *Variety of Men* (New York: Scribners, 1967), p. 32.

28. Charles Astor Bristed, *Five Years in an English University* (New York: G. P. Putnam, 1852), vol. 1, p. 46.

29. Ibid., p. 50.

30. Campbell and Garnett, *James Clerk Maxwell,* 1st ed., p. 133n.

31. Ibid., pp. 186-187.

32. Mrs. Stokes seems to have been one of the few people who actually liked Mrs. Maxwell.

33. For Bristed's version see Bristed, *Five Years,* vol. 1, p. 119.

34. Campbell and Garnett, *James Clerk Maxwell,* 1st ed., p. 215.

35. Quoted in Alan Moorehead, *Darwin and the Beagle* (London: Hamish Hamilton, 1969), p. 26.

36. Campbell and Garnett, *James Clerk Maxwell,* 1st ed., p. 417.

37. Bristed, *Five Years,* vol. 2, p. 19.

38. Campbell and Garnett, *James Clerk Maxwell,* 1st ed., p. 417.

39. Ibid., p. 176.

40. Ibid., p. 185.

41. From a letter from Maxwell's uncle John to the Rev. John Hodgson, 10 April 1832, quoted in E. Bateson, ed., *A History of Northumberland* (Northumberland County History Committee, 1895), vol. 2, p. 297. For this and other researches on the Cays I am indebted to unpublished work by my brother, Professor A. M. Everitt.

42. Ibid., p. 298.

43. "Memoirs of the Life of Mr. Ambrose Barnes, Late Merchant and Sometime Alderman of Newcastle upon Tyne," published in *Proceedings of the Surtees Society* 50 (1867), p. 195.

44. A. M. Everitt, private communication.

45. Hilts, "A Guide," p. 59.

46. Campbell and Garnett, *James Clerk Maxwell,* 1st ed., p. 430.

47. Ibid., p. 12.

48. Ibid., pp. 27-28.

49. Lewis Campbell and William Garnett, *The Life of James Clerk Maxwell,* 2nd ed. (London: Macmillan and Co., 1884), p. 260.

50. Campbell and Garnett, *James Clerk Maxwell,* 1st ed., p. 72.

51. Ibid., p. 43.

52. Ibid., p. 44.

53. Ibid., p. 50.

54. Ibid., p. 41.

55. Ibid., p. 427.

56. Ibid., p. 447.

57. Ibid., p. 32.

58. Ibid., pp. 593-594.

59. Tait, "James Clerk-Maxwell," p. 33.

60. *The Scientific Papers of James Clerk Maxwell,* ed. W. D. Niven (Cambridge: At the University Press, 1890), vol. 2, p. 248.

61. *Nature* 19 (1879), p. 311. See p. 384 for Guthrie's angry response, which throws an interesting light on the status of the Cavendish Laboratory at the time.

62. Campbell and Garnett, *James Clerk Maxwell,* 1st ed., p. 10.

63. Victor L. Hilts, "A Guide," p. 59.

64. Campbell and Garnett, *James Clerk Maxwell,* 1st ed., p. 79.

65. Ibid., p. 79.

66. Ibid., p. 14.

67. Ibid., p. 71. Among the Clerk family paintings by Jemima Wedderburn preserved in the National Portrait Gallery London, there is one of George Wedderburn doing a female impersonation which gives a clue to the nature of his humor.

68. Ibid., p. 72.

69. Ibid., p. 420.

70. Ibid. Maxwell credits the move to his father, but Campbell, (Ibid., p. 55) makes it clear that the initiative was Miss Cay's.

71. Ibid., p. 342.

72. Ibid., p. 203.

73. Niven, ed., *Scientific Papers,* vol. 2, p. 358.

74. J. Clerk Maxwell, *Treatise on Electric and Magnetism,* 3rd ed. (Oxford: At the Clarendon Press, 1904), vol. 1, p. vi.

75. Ibid., p. viii.

76. Ibid., p. x.

77. Niven, ed., *Scientific Papers,* vol. 2, pp. 251-252.

78. Campbell and Garnett, *James Clerk Maxwell,* 1st ed., p. 430.

79. C. W. F. Everitt, "Maxwell's Scientific Papers," *Applied Optics* 4 (1967), p. 61.

80. Niven, ed., *Scientific Papers,* vol. 2, p. 301.

81. L. Boltzmann, *Gustav Robert Kirchhoff. Festrede zur Feier des 301 Grundungstages der Karl-Franzens-Universitat zu Graz* (Leipzig: J. A. Barth, 1888), pp. 29-30. See also S. G. Brush, *The Kind of Motion We Call Heat* (Amsterdam: North-Holland, 1976), vol. 2, p. 446. The translation is Arthur Schuster's *Biographical Fragments* (London: Macmillan and Co., 1932), p. 225.

82. Hilts, "A Guide," p. 59.

83. Campbell and Garnett, *James Clerk Maxwell*, 1st ed., p. 175.

84. Niven, ed., *Scientific Papers*, vol. 2, pp. 743-744.

85. Ibid., vol. 1, p. 157.

86. Ibid., vol. 1, pp. 155-156 for all the quotations in the paragraph.

87. James Clerk Maxwell, *Elementary Treatise on Electricity*, 2nd ed. (Oxford: At the Clarendon Press, 1888), p. 52.

88. Niven, ed., *Scientific Papers*, vol. 1, p. 79.

89. Ibid., vol. 1, pp. 187-188.

90. Cambridge University Library (Anderson Room), Stokes MSS, File Box 6.

91. G. G. Stokes, *Mathematical and Physical Papers* (Cambridge: At the University Press, 1905), vol. 5, p. 320, question 8.

92. M. N. Wise, "The Mutual Embrace of Electricity and Magnetism," *Science* 203 (1979), pp. 1310-1318.

93. Niven, ed., *Scientific Papers*, vol. 1, p. 500.

94. Ibid., vol. 2, p. 536.

95. Heaviside to Hertz, 14 February 1889; Institute of Electrical Engineers, London, Heaviside Papers. I am grateful to Professor Stuewer for drawing my attention to this letter.

96. *Electrician* 2 (1879), pp. 271-272 and letter of Robert E. Baynes to which Maxwell was replying on pp. 231-232.

97. William Temple, *Nature, Man and God* (London: Macmillan and Co., 1934), pp. viii-ix.

98. A. Schuster in *History of the Cavendish Laboratory* (London: Macmillan and Co., 1910), p. 31.

99. F. W. Farrar, *Men I Have Known* (Boston: T. Y. Crowell & Co., 1897), pp. 136-137.

100. Francis Bowen, *The Metaphysics of Sir William Hamilton Collected, Arranged and Abridged for the Use of College and Private Students* (Boston and Chicago: Sever and Francis, 1861), p. 235.

101. Campbell and Garnett, *James Clerk Maxwell*, 1st ed., p. 268.

102. Ibid., pp. 262-426.

103. Niven, ed., *Scientific Papers*, vol. 1, p. 156.

104. Ibid., vol. 2, p. 254.

105. Ibid., p. 304.

106. Cambridge University Library, Anderson Room, Maxwell papers, letter of 9 October 1872.

107. Niven, ed., *Scientific Papers*, vol. 2, p. 244.

108. Royal Society Archives, Maxwell Papers.

109. Campbell and Garnett, *James Clerk Maxwell*, 1st ed., p. 278.

110. Ibid., p. 341.

111. Niven, ed., *Scientific Papers*, vol. 2, p. 247.

112. Ibid., p. 245.

113. Ibid., p. 000.

114. Ibid., p. 420.

115. J. G. Crowther, *Men of Science* (New York: W. W. Norton & Co., 1936), p. 316. Maxwell's copy of Clerk's treatise is preserved at Edinburgh University Library.

116. Campbell and Garnett, *James Clerk Maxwell*, 1st ed., p. 278.

117. For similar caution with respect to surface phenomena in gases see S. G. Brush and C. W. F. Everitt, "Maxwell, Osborne Reynolds and the Radiometer," *Historical Studies in the Physical Sciences* 1, (1969), pp. 105-125.

118. Niven, ed., *Scientific Papers*, p. 358.

Chapter 5

The Scientific Style of Josiah Willard Gibbs

Martin J. Klein

The scientific writings of Josiah Willard Gibbs quickly acquired the well-deserved reputation for difficulty that they continue to enjoy in the scientific community. About fifteen years after their initial publication Wilhelm Ostwald translated Gibbs's papers on thermodynamics into German and collected them in one volume. In the preface to this book Ostwald warned his readers that they were embarking on a study that would "demand extraordinary attentiveness and devotion." He pointed out that Gibbs had chosen his mode of exposition, "abstract and often hard to understand," in order to achieve "the greatest possible generality in his investigation and the greatest possible precision in his expression."[1] As a result these papers were full of treasures that had yet to be unearthed. In the same year that Ostwald's translation appeared, Lord Rayleigh wrote to Gibbs urging him to expand his papers into a treatise on thermodynamics, so as to make his ideas more accessible. Rayleigh found Gibbs's original exposition "too condensed and too difficult for most, I might say all, readers."[2] (In assessing this remark one must remember that Rayleigh himself could be so terse as to be almost cryptic.) Even Einstein, who once referred to Gibbs's book on

Some of the material in this chapter has already been published in my paper "The Early Papers of J. Willard Gibbs: A Transformation of Thermodynamics," in *Human Implications of Scientific Advance. Proceedings of the XVth International Congress of the History of Science. Edinburgh 10-15 August 1977.*, ed. E. G. Forbes (Edinburgh: Edinburgh University Press, pp. 330-341. Some of the research reported here was done under a grant from the National Science Foundation.

statistical mechanics as "a masterpiece," qualified his praise by adding, "although it is hard to read and the main points have to be read between the lines."[3]

The abstract, general, and concise form in which Gibbs set forth his work made it difficult for scientists to master his methods and to survey his results. The same qualities in Gibbs's writing offer difficulties to the historian who approaches these papers as historical documents. His task is to enliven those records of scientific activity in the past, "to capture the processes in the course of which those records were produced and became what they are."[4] The historian wants to find out things like the questions Gibbs was answering when he formulated his theoretical systems, the choices available to Gibbs and his contemporaries in dealing with these questions, the various contexts within which he worked. The finished form of Gibbs's papers leaves very few clues for pursuing such historical studies. And yet their form is the completely appropriate expression of Gibbs's way of doing science, of his remarkable combination of the physicist's drive to understand the natural world with the mathematician's concern for logical structures.

These papers also show that "the most abstract and most algebraic scientific work can nevertheless reflect its author's temperament like a faithful mirror," as Pierre Duhem remarked in his essay on Gibbs.[5] It was Henry A. Bumstead, Gibbs's former student, who described his teacher as having been "of a retiring disposition,"[6] and Duhem seized on that phrase, recognizing that it characterized Gibbs's scientific style, and even what one might call his scientific personality.[7] That "retiring disposition" is so faithfully expressed in Gibbs's writings that it is often hard to realize just how much new insight lies behind even his way of posing the scientific issues he discussed, much less his way of resolving them.

In this paper I want to explore and illustrate some of those features of Gibbs's science that give it the individual character that is so distinctive. I shall concentrate on his first publications, the papers in which he introduced himself to the scientific public in 1873. These two works on geometrical methods in thermodynamics had but few readers at the time of their appearance, and their importance to the development of that subject has rarely been recognized by scientists or historians of science. Nevertheless they do exhibit the same characteristics as their author's longer and more famous writings; like them the first papers bear the unmistakable signs of the lion's claw.

When Josiah Willard Gibbs was appointed Professor of Mathematical Physics at Yale in 1871, he had already spent almost all of his thirty-two years in New Haven, Connecticut.[8] He would rarely leave it again except for summer holidays in the mountains. Gibbs's father, also Josiah Willard Gibbs, was the first Yale graduate in a family that had already sent four generations of its sons to Harvard College. The elder Gibbs was a distinguished philologist, Professor of Sacred Literature at Yale. He was known as "a genuine scholar," and despite the difference between their fields some of his intellectual traits resemble those of his son. "Mr. Gibbs loved system, and was never satisfied until he had cast his material into the proper form. His essays on special topics are marked by the nicest logical arrangement."[9] The younger Gibbs graduated from Yale College in 1858 having won a string of prizes and scholarships for excellence in Latin and especially mathematics. He continued his studies at Yale and was one of the first few scholars to be granted a Ph.D. by an American university. Yale had begun to award this degree in 1861, and Gibbs received his in 1863 in the field of engineering.

The dissertation Gibbs wrote bears the title, "On the Form of the Teeth of Wheels in Spur Gearing," not exactly what one might have expected from what we know about his later activities.[10] But as Gibbs pointed out in his first paragraph, "the subject reduces to one of plane geometry," and the thesis is really an exercise in that field. It was not published until 1947, at which time its editor wrote that in reading the thesis, one "feels that he is gradually reaching the summit of an intellectual structure that is firmly founded and well joined." The editor's subsequent comments on the style of this work could apply with only minor changes to much that Gibbs would write in later years. "If [the reader] has a natural friendliness for the niceties of geometrical reasoning, he will be rewarded with a sense of satisfaction akin to that felt upon completing, say, a book of Euclid; if he is not so endowed, he had perhaps better not trouble himself with the austerities of style and extreme economy (one might almost say parsimony) in the use of words that characterize the entire work."[11]

After he received his doctorate Gibbs was appointed a Tutor at Yale and spent the next three years teaching Latin and natural philosophy (physics) to undergraduates. During this period Gibbs continued to develop his engineering interests, and in 1866 he obtained a patent on his design of an improved brake for railway cars.[12] That same year he presented a paper to the Connecticut Academy of Arts and Sciences, of which he had been a member

Plate 1. J. W. Gibbs. Reproduced by permission of the AIP Niels Bohr Library.

since 1858, on "The Proper Magnitude of the Units of Length, and of other quantities used in Mechanics."[13] This unpublished paper includes a remarkably clear discussion of the dual roles played by the concept of mass in the structure of mechanics—inertial mass and gravitational mass—and of the confusion introduced by writers who would define mass as quantity of matter. "Yet it is evident," Gibbs wrote, "that when the matter of the bodies compared is different in kind, we cannot strictly speaking say that the quantity of matter of one is equal, greater, or less than that of the other. All that we have a right to say, except when the matter is the same in kind, is that the gravity is proportioned to the inertia. To say *that*, is to express a great law of nature,—a law by the way of that class which we learn by experience and not by a priori reasoning. It might have been otherwise, but its truth is abundantly attested by experience. But to say, that the intensities of these two properties are both proportioned to the quantity of matter, is to bring in an element of which we know *nothing*."[14]

In August 1866 Gibbs left New Haven for three years of study in Europe, his only extended absence from his native city. He spent a year each at the universities of Paris, Berlin, and Heidelberg, attending lectures on mathematics and physics and reading widely in both fields. While our information on his activities during this period is rather scanty, one thing is certain.[15] Gibbs did not work as a research student with any of the great scientists whose lectures he attended or whose papers he studied. Nor is there any indication in the notebooks he kept while in Europe that he had yet begun any research of his own or even decided what line he would try to follow in his work. Gibbs had apparently decided to use his time at the three scientific centers to broaden and deepen the somewhat limited education in mathematics and physics he had acquired at Yale, and to inform himself about the current concerns of those who were actively working in these areas. He would then be prepared to choose the subjects of his own researches after he returned to New Haven.

Gibbs's future was still uncertain when he came back in the summer of 1869. Of the next two years we know only that he taught French for at least one term at Yale's Sheffield Scientific School, and that he probably worked out his modification of Watt's governor for the steam engine at this time.[16] Gibbs was evidently able to manage financially on what he had inherited from his father, especially since he continued to live in the family home with his unmarried sister Anna and with his sister Julia and Julia's husband, Addison Van Name, Gibbs's college classmate who had become the

Librarian of Yale. This fortunate state of financial independence was certainly known within the academic community of New Haven when Gibbs was appointed on July 13, 1871 to a newly created position as Professor of Mathematical Physics. It explains to some extent the chilling phrase "without salary" that forms part of the official record of that appointment in the minutes of the Yale Corporation meeting of that date.[17] The new chair was not yet endowed, so there was no money available for paying its incumbent. In any case his teaching duties would be light, since the appointment was in the small graduate department; Gibbs actually taught only one or two students a year during his first decade or so in the new professorship. (Not until 1880, when Gibbs was on the point of accepting an attractive offer from the exciting, new, research-oriented Johns Hopkins University, did Yale pay him a regular salary.)

Gibbs's appointment to the chair of mathematical physics preceded his first published research by two years. Although this now seems like an inversion of the normal order of events, it was not so extraordinary at the time. Benjamin Silliman had been invited to become Yale's first professor of both chemistry and natural history while he was reading the law in New Haven, and before he had reached his twenty-second birthday.[18] Silliman knew essentially nothing of either science but was persuaded by Yale's President Timothy Dwight, who insisted that "the study will be full of interest and gratification, and the presentation which you will be able to make of it to the college classes and the public will afford much instruction and delight."[19] It was only after his appointment in 1802 that Silliman embarked on the systematic study of the sciences he was to profess. Half a century after Silliman's appointment another graduate of Yale was made professor of mathematics "at the early age of twenty-five," only five years after his graduation from the college. This was Hubert Anson Newton, who was then given a year's leave of absence to study modern mathematics in Paris.[20] Newton, only nine years older than Gibbs, was one of his teachers, and must have been one of those who strongly supported Gibbs's appointment to the faculty.

Evidently the thirty-two-year-old Gibbs, with his brilliant college record, his doctoral degree, his demonstrated abilities as an engineer, and his three years of postdoctoral study in Europe, had far more impressive qualifications for a professorship than most of his colleagues had had when they were appointed. Yale had every reason to express its confidence in Gibbs, who had, after all, been a member of this small academic community since his birth.

Gibbs began his first paper, "Graphical Methods in the Thermo-dynamics of Fluids,"[21] by remarking that although geometrical representations of thermodynamic concepts were in "general use" and had done "good service," they had not yet been developed with the "variety and generality of which they are capable." Such representations had been restricted to diagrams whose rectilinear coordinates denote volume and pressure, and he proposed to discuss a range of alternatives, "preferable . . . in many cases in respect of distinctness or of convenience." This beginning suggested that the paper would be primarily didactic, and was likely to be rather removed from the current concerns of scientists already actively involved in thermodynamic research. What followed seemed to bear out this suggestion, as Gibbs went on to list the quantities relevant to his discussion and to write down the relationships among them.

The quantities appropriate for describing the body in any given state were its volume v, pressure p, absolute temperature t, energy ϵ, and entropy η. In addition to these functions of the body's state, there were the work done W, and the heat received H, by the body in passing from one state to another. These quantities were related by the equations

$$d\epsilon = \tilde{d}H - \tilde{d}W, \tag{1}$$

$$\tilde{d}W = pdv, \tag{2}$$

$$\tilde{d}H = td\eta. \tag{3}$$

The first and third equations express the definitions of the state functions energy and entropy whose existence is required by the first and second laws of thermodynamics, respectively, while equation (2) is just the expression for the mechanical work done by an expanding fluid.[22] Gibbs then eliminated the work and heat to obtain the equation

$$d\epsilon = td\eta - pdv, \tag{4}$$

which he referred to as the differential form of "the fundamental thermodynamic equation of the fluid," the equation expressing the energy as a function of entropy and volume.

Gibbs used hardly any more words than I have just used in stating these matters, as though he too were simply reminding his readers of familiar, widely known truths, and were writing them down only to establish the notation of his paper. That is just what one might expect as the starting point of a first scientific paper, one that promised to be only a modest didactic exercise. Could there have been any doubt or disagreement that this was the proper starting point for any treatment of thermodynamics?

To answer this question one must look not at Gibbs's paper but rather at the general state of thermodynamics in 1873, when it was written. Almost a quarter of a century had gone by since Rudolf Clausius had set the subject on its proper, dual foundation, and William Thomson had endorsed and developed the idea that there are *two* basic laws of thermodynamics.[23] Clausius, especially, had explored the second law in a series of memoirs, searching for "the real nature of the theorem."[24] He was convinced that that "real nature" had been found with the help of his analysis of transformations, first for cyclic processes in 1854 and then for the general case in 1862.[25] It was not until 1865 that Clausius invented the word entropy as a suitable name for what he had been calling "the transformational content of the body."[26] The new word made it possible to state the second law in the brief but portentous form: "The entropy of the universe tends toward a maximum," but Clausius did not view entropy as the basic concept for understanding that law. He preferred to express the physical meaning of the second law in terms of the concept of disgregation, another word that he coined, a concept that never became part of the accepted structure of thermodynamics.[27] Clausius restricted his use of entropy to its convenient role as a summarizing concept; in the memoir of 1865 where it was introduced, he derived the experimentally useful consequences of the two laws without using the entropy function, or even the internal energy function.

Ten years later, when Clausius reworked his articles on thermodynamics into a treatise that would make a convenient textbook, he had not changed his mind about the status of both entropy and energy.[28] Although he showed how the two laws guarantee the existence of these two state functions, Clausius eliminated them from his working equations as soon as possible. In contrast to Gibbs, Clausius kept the original thermodynamic concepts, work and heat, at the center of his thinking, although he did devote a chapter to showing how the energy and entropy of a system could be determined from experimentally measurable quantities.

Since Clausius gave entropy such a secondary position in his writings, it is not surprising that his contemporaries paid little or no attention to the concept. Thomson had his own methods which bypassed the need for introducing the entropy function, as did Carl Neumann.[29] W. J. M. Rankine had independently introduced the same concept in 1854,[30] calling it the thermodynamic function, and using it in his book, *A Manual of the Steam Engine and Other Prime Movers* in 1859.[31] Although this must have been a popular text, since it was already in its sixth edition in 1873, Rankine's thermodynamic function was not used by many of his readers. As James Clerk Maxwell once put it, Rankine's exposition of fundamental concepts often "strained [the reader's] powers of deglutition"; and as for his statement of the second law, "its actual meaning is inscrutable."[32]

Clausius's word, entropy, did enter the thermodynamic literature in English, but only by an act of misappropriation. Peter Guthrie Tait liked Clausius's "excellent word," but preferred to use it in his *Sketch of Thermodynamics* in 1868 as the name of quite another concept. "It would only confuse the student," he wrote, "if we were to endeavor to invent another term for our purpose."[33] And so, acting like Lewis Carroll's Humpty Dumpty, Tait chose to make entropy mean available energy, a usage unfortunately followed by his friend Maxwell in the first edition of his *Theory of Heat* a few years later.[34]

If we now return to the opening pages of Gibbs's first paper, we see that his statements were by no means the conventional wisdom of scientists in 1873. Few, if any, of those working in thermodynamics would have chosen the approach that Gibbs set forth as though it were obvious. From the beginning he emphasized the properties of material systems rather than "the motive power of heat." As a result the state functions, energy and entropy, necessarily took precedence over those quantities that depend on the process carried out by the system—the work and heat it exchanges with its surroundings. No wonder then that Gibbs used the term fundamental equation for the relation of the system's energy to its entropy and volume, since "from it . . . may be derived all the thermodynamic properties of the fluid."[35] For Gibbs thermodynamics was the theory of the properties of matter at equilibrium, rather than the mechanical theory of heat that Clausius and Thomson had seen. But as it was expressed by a man "of a retiring disposition," this important change in viewpoint could easily be overlooked by his readers.

When Gibbs wrote of the "general use and good service" given by the geometrical representation of thermodynamic propositions, he was thinking of something more than mere illustrations. In the four decades since Clapeyron had introduced the indicator diagram (or pressure-volume diagram) into his exposition of Carnot's ideas, that diagram had been developed into a valuable technique.[36] Rankine had shown how this geometrical method could be used for "the solution of new questions especially those relating to the action of heat in all classes of engines," and for presenting "in a systematic form, those theoretical principles which are applicable to all methods of transforming heat to motive power by means of the changes of volume of an elastic substance."[37] To see how far Rankine could go in this fashion, one should examine his geometrical derivation of the equation for the difference between the heat capacities of a fluid at constant pressure and at constant volume. Rankine used these methods extensively in his *Manual of the Steam Engine,* as did the authors of other texts, such as Gustav Zeuner.[38]

Gibbs set out to free the geometrical approach from the limitations imposed by the particular choice of volume and pressure as basic variables. He wanted to find "a general graphical method which can exhibit at once all the thermodynamic properties of a fluid concerned in reversible processes, and serve alike for the demonstration of general theorems and the numerical solution of particular problems."[39] To this end he considered the general properties of any diagram in which the states of the fluid were mapped continuously on the points of a plane. The thermodynamic properties of the fluid would then be expressed in the geometrical properties of the several families of curves connecting states of equal volume, of equal temperature, of equal entropy, and so forth.

Since the equations relating work to pressure and volume, and heat to temperature and entropy (equations (2) and (3) above), are of exactly the same form, the temperature-entropy diagram must share many of the useful features of the pressure-volume diagram. As Gibbs pointed out, it has the additional advantage that the universal nature of Carnot's ideal cycle appears directly, since this cycle is always represented by a rectangle in the temperature-entropy diagram, regardless of the properties of the working substance. Gibbs saw that the real advantage of the temperature-entropy diagram is that it "makes the second law of thermodynamics so prominent, and gives it so clear and elementary an expression." He meant that although there is no formal difference between representing the work done in a process as the area under its curve in the pressure-volume diagram, and representing the heat exchanged in the process as the area under its curve in the temperature-entropy diagram, the former representation was only an expression of the definition of mechanical work. The latter, however, was "nothing more nor less than a geometrical expression of the second law of thermodynamics in its application to fluids, in a form exceedingly convenient for use, and from which the analytical expression of the same law can, if desired, be at once obtained."[40]

The potential value of a diagram so closely analogous to the pressure-volume diagram was seen by others at about the same time, but in more limited inquiries. In December 1872 the Royal Academy of Sciences at Brussels published a paper on the second law of thermodynamics by the civil engineer Th. Belpaire,[41] a paper described by one of the Academy's referees as "the first truly original work on this subject written in Belgium."[42] Belpaire's "new demonstration of the second law" was more original than it was cogent, unfortunately, but he did nevertheless introduce a diagram like Gibbs's and use it effectively. Several years later J. Macfarlane Gray, Chief Examiner of Marine Engineers for the Board of Trade in London, independently began to use such a diagram in his own analyses of engines.[43] When Gray presented the diagram and described its uses before the Institution of Naval Architects in 1880, he was told of Gibbs's work—one wonders by whom—which he proceeded to obtain and read. Gray reported that "Professor Gibbs's paper was a very high-class production," despite its "revelling in mathematics," and that he would limit his own claim to asserting that he had done "what others had only said could be done," namely, applied the diagram "for practical use by engineers."[44]

Gibbs did not consider the temperature-entropy diagram worth an extended discussion, and devoted only three of his thirty-two pages to it. The diagram "whose substantial advantages over any other method" made it most interesting and worth discussing in more detail, was that in which the coordinates of the point denoting the state were the volume and the entropy of the body.[45] The very nature of the fundamental thermodynamic equation, which expresses energy in terms of entropy and volume, would suggest the importance of an entropy-volume diagram. Such a diagram has a variable scale factor. In other words, the ratio of the work done in a small cyclic process to the area enclosed by the cycle representing that process in the diagram varies from one part of the volume-entropy plane to another. Both the pressure-volume and temperature-entropy diagrams have constant scale factors. Although a variable scale factor might offer difficulties, or at least some awkwardness, for engineering purposes, it was a definite advantage in studying the properties of matter at equilibrium.

Gibbs showed this advantage in his analysis of the states in which vapor, liquid, and solid coexist at a definite, unique set of values of the pressure and temperature. The scale factor, which is $(\partial p/\partial \eta)$ in this diagram, vanishes for such states. The region of coexistence of the three phases is represented by the interior of a triangle in the entropy-volume diagram, and, as Gibbs remarked, the information conveyed this way "can be but imperfectly represented" in any other diagram.

Some features of the thermodynamic diagrams, that is to say some aspects of the families of curves representing thermodynamic properties, are independent of the choice of coordinates. Gibbs carefully examined these invariant features, and especially the order of the curves of different kinds (such as the isobars, isotherms, and isentropics) as they cross at any point, and the geometrical nature of these intersections, which could involve contacts of higher order.

In closing his paper, Gibbs pointed out that what he had done was to start from the analytical expression of the laws of thermodynamics, taken as known, and "to show how the same relations may be expressed geometrically." The process could have been reversed. "It would, however, be easy, starting from the first and second laws of thermodynamics as usually enunciated, to arrive at the same results without the aid of analytical formulae, — to arrive, for example at the conception of energy, of entropy, of absolute temperature, in the construction of the diagram without the analytical definitions of these quantities, and to obtain the various properties of the diagram without the analytical expression of the thermodynamic properties which they involve." And Gibbs also emphasized the essential point, "that when the diagram is only used to demonstrate or illustrate general theorems, it is not necessary . . . to assume any particular method of forming the diagram; it is enough to suppose the different states of the body to be represented continuously by points upon a sheet."[46]

Gibbs's "natural friendliness for the niceties of geometrical reasoning," already demonstrated in his thesis, is very much in evidence in his work on thermodynamics. This surely was a major factor in the enthusiastic response his work evoked from Maxwell, who preferred to argue geometrically rather than analytically whenever possible, and who derived the four thermodynamic relations that bear his name by completely geometrical reasoning.[47]

Gibbs did not tell his readers what had drawn his attention to thermodynamics as the subject for his first professorial research. He had not attended lectures in this field during his years of study in Europe, and there was no stimulus for his work coming from his colleagues at Yale. What made this untried, but mature and independent thinker, as he at once showed himself to be, select this particular set of problems to begin with? It is true that in 1872 the pages of the *Philosophical Magazine,* probably the most widely read British journal of physics, carried a number of articles on thermodynamics. They were full of lively, pointed, and even angry words on the subject as Tait and Clausius debated the history, which to them meant the priorities, of the discovery of the second law.[48] Gibbs could hardly have avoided noticing this dispute, in which the names of Thomson and Maxwell were mentioned, and it might have prompted him to do some reading. But controversy repelled rather than attracted Gibbs, and he did not enter the debate in progress.

Another possible source for Gibbs's interest in thermodynamics is Maxwell's *Theory of Heat,* which appeared in London in 1871 and in a New York edition the following year.[49] The book was widely read, going through a number of editions within a few years. In 1873 J. D. van der Waals wrote of it as "the little book which is surely to be found in the hands of every physicist."[50] Although it appeared in a series described by its publisher as "text-books of science adapted for the use of artisans and of students in public and science schools,"[51] Maxwell did not keep his writing at an elementary level. Tait even thought that some of it was probably "more difficult to follow than any other of his writings,"[52] which was saying a great deal. In any event Maxwell did not hesitate to include discussions of whatever interested him in the latest developments of thermodynamics as his book went into its successive editions. One such development described in Maxwell's first edition was Thomas Andrews's recent discovery of the continuity of the two fluid states of matter, liquid and gas.[53] Whether Gibbs learned of Andrews's work from Maxwell's book or came across the paper Andrews presented to the Royal Society of London by reading the *Philosophical Transactions* for 1869, he certainly knew about Andrews's discovery of the critical point when he wrote his first paper. There is a footnote referring to Andrews at the place where Gibbs discusses the possible second order contact of the isobar and the isotherm corresponding to a particular state of the fluid: "An example of this is doubtless to be found at the critical point of a fluid."

Andrews's Royal Society paper reported the results of a decade of experimental work. It was the high point of his scientific career and Andrews was well aware of it, writing to his wife: "I really begin to think that Dame Nature has at last been kind to me, and rewarded me with a discovery of a higher order than I ever expected to make."[54] His careful measurements of the isotherms of carbon dioxide established the existence of a critical temperature: if the gas were compressed isothermally below this temperature it would eventually begin to liquefy and become a two-phase system with a visible surface of separation between gas and liquid. Further compression would lead to complete transformation of gas into liquid, the liquid then being almost incompressible. In sharp contrast to this behavior, an isothermal compression of the gas at a temperature above the critical one would never lead to two phases, although the density would eventually take on values appropriate to the liquid state. Above the critical temperature there was no distinction between liquid and gas. It was always possible to pass from a state clearly liquid to one that was equally clearly gas without ever going through the discontinuous two-phase region. These remarkable properties were by no means peculiar to carbon dioxide. They are "generally true of all bodies which can be obtained as gases and liquids," as Andrews confirmed by studies on some half dozen substances.[55] He did not theorize at all about the implications of his discovery, attempting neither a kinetic-molecular explanation nor a thermodynamic analysis.

Andrews's discovery—a new, surprising, and general feature of the behavior of matter, as yet quite unexplained—would have been just the sort of thing to attract Gibbs's attention as that promising new professor of mathematical physics sought for a suitable subject on which to work. As he advised one of his students many years later, "one good use to which anybody might put a superior training in pure mathematics was to the study of the problems set us by nature."[56]

By the time Gibbs wrote his second paper, which appeared only a few months after the first, his physical interests were much more apparent.[57] Although this paper, "A Method of Geometrical Representation of the Thermodynamic Properties of Substances by Means of Surfaces," might seem to be a mere extension of the geometrical methods from two dimensions to three, one does not have to read far to see that Gibbs is doing something quite different. The emphasis is no longer on methods as such but rather on the phenomena to be explained. His problem was to characterize the behavior of matter at equilibrium, to determine the nature of the equilibrium state of a body that can be solid, liquid, or gas, or some combination of these, according to the circumstances. Gibbs goes directly to a single, fundamental three-dimensional representation in which the three rectangular coordinates are the energy, entropy, and volume of the body, and the equilibrium states constitute a surface whose properties he proceeded to explore.

There was only one precedent for using a three-dimensional representation of equilibrium states, and that a very recent one. James Thomson, William's older brother and former collaborator in studies on heat, had introduced the thermodynamic surface in pressure-volume-temperature space to assist his thinking about Andrews's results.[58] Thomson was Andrews's colleague at Queen's College, Belfast, and had been thinking about Andrews's work and trying to interpret it since 1862, though he did not publish his ideas until 1871. Gibbs was aware of Thomson's publication and cited it at the start of his own paper. (It is possible, of course, that it was Thomson's work that had set Gibbs thinking about thermodynamics.) Thomson's "chief object" in his paper was to argue that Andrews had not gone far enough in his claim that the liquid and gas phases are continuously related. Below the critical temperature Andrews's isotherms included a straight line segment parallel to the axis of volume. This represented the states in which gas and liquid could co-exist at a fixed pressure, in proportions varying from all gas to all liquid. This pressure of the saturated vapor depends only on the temperature, for a given substance. At both ends of the two-phase region the slope of the isothermal curve changes abruptly, producing what Thomson called a "practical breach of continuity." He proposed to smooth this out by introducing a "theoretical continuity" that would require the isotherm to include "conditions of pressure, temperature, and volume in unstable equilibrium."[59] The isothermal curves that Thomson sketched freehand look much like the theoretical isotherms derived on quite different grounds by van der Waals in his dissertation two years later.

The crucial question about the isothermal curves that neither Thomson nor van der Waals could answer was: where must the horizontal line segment be drawn? In other words, what is the condition that determines the pressure at which gas and liquid can co-exist in equilibrium at a specified temperature? (This temperature must be below the critical temperature.) The problem of finding the condition for equilibrium between two phases had a relatively long history,[60] but not even Maxwell (who included a discussion of Thomson's work in his "elementary textbook") had been able to solve it.

What was missing from all these attempts was nothing less than the second law of thermodynamics. Gibbs, who started from the thermodynamic laws, settled the question in his usual brief and elegant manner. The fundamental equation – relating energy, entropy, and volume for a homogeneous phase – corresponds to what he called the primitive surface. It includes all equilibrium states, regardless of their stability. When the system consists of several homogeneous parts, its states form the derived surface. This is constructed by recognizing that "the volume, entropy, and energy of the whole body are equal to the sums of the volumes, entropies, and energies respectively of the parts, while the pressure and temperature of the whole are the same as those of each of the parts." In a two-phase system the point representing the compound state must then lie on the straight line joining the two pure (that is, single-phase) state points which are themselves on the primitive surface. The pressure and temperature are the same at all points on this line. But the direction of the tangent plane at any point of the primitive surface is determined by the pressure and temperature, since we have from equation (4),

$$p = - \left(\frac{\partial \epsilon}{\partial v} \right)_\eta \qquad , \qquad (5)$$

and also

$$t = \left(\frac{\partial \epsilon}{\partial \eta} \right)_v \qquad . \qquad (6)$$

Since the line joining the two points on the primitive surface that represent the two phases in equilibrium must lie in the tangent planes at both points, and since those planes are parallel, they must be the same plane. This condition, that there be a common tangent plane for the points representing two phases in equilibrium, is easily expressed analytically in the form

$$\epsilon_2 - \epsilon_1 = t(\eta_2 - \eta_1) - p(v_2 - v_1), \qquad (7)$$

where the subscripts 1 and 2 refer to the two phases and where p, t are the common values of pressure and temperature.

Gibbs referred to this second paper almost twenty years later in a letter to Wilhelm Ostwald. "It contains, I believe, the first solution of a problem of considerable importance, viz: the additional condition (besides equality of temperature and pressure) which is necessary in order that two states of a substance shall be in equilibrium in contact with each other. The matter seems simple enough now, yet it appears to have given considerable difficulty to physicists. . . . I suppose that Maxwell referred especially to this question when he said . . . that by means of this model, problems which had long resisted the efforts of himself and others could be solved at once."[61] Maxwell expressed his appreciation of Gibbs's thermodynamic surface by constructing a model of it for water and sending a cast of it to Gibbs. He also included a fourteen-page discussion of the Gibbs surface in the 1875 edition of his textbook, giving more details of its properties than Gibbs had. In that same year Maxwell developed an alternative form of the equilibrium condition—the Maxwell construction—which states that the horizontal, two-phase portion of the isotherm must cut off equal areas above and below in the van der Waals-Thomson loop. The proof involved a direct application of the second law carried out with what may be called genuinely Maxwellian ingenuity. Clausius independently arrived at Maxwell's result five years later by a slightly different argument.[62] He had apparently missed Maxwell's discussion of the Gibbs surface, and there is no sign that he ever read any of the reprints Gibbs regularly sent to him.

Gibbs arrived at a new, profound understanding of the critical point by analyzing the conditions for the stability of states of thermodynamic equilibrium. He showed that, for a system surrounded by a medium of constant pressure P and constant temperature T, the quantity $(\epsilon - T\eta + Pv)$ must be stationary in an equilibrium state, and must be a minimum if that equilibrium is to be stable. The possible instabilities are of two kinds. The first, "absolute instability," corresponds to states like those of a supercooled gas, stable against small variations but not against a radical split into two phases. The other, "essential instability," corresponds to states like those in the inner part of a van der Waals loop. The critical point is the common limit of both regions of instability; it is itself stable against both types of change. Gibbs's analysis of the critical point led to a series of explicit conditions that must be fulfilled, most of which had not been pointed out before.

Once again Gibbs's "retiring disposition" meant that the transformation of thermodynamics he had accomplished in these early papers was not properly appreciated. In 1902 Paul Saurel was quite justified in remarking: "It does not seem to be generally known that Gibbs, in his memoir on the energy surface, has given in outline a very elegant theory of the critical state of a one-component system and of the continuity of the liquid and gaseous states."[63] And in 1979, over a century after their publication, Arthur Wightman wrote: "For those who like their physics stated in simple general mathematical terms, the version of thermodynamics offered by

Gibbs's first two papers can scarcely be improved. Nevertheless, apart from its impact on Maxwell, it had very little influence on late nineteenth century textbooks. The notion of 'fundamental equation' and the simple expression it gives for the laws of thermodynamics . . . only became available with the publication of 'neo-Gibbsian' textbooks and monographs in the mid-twentieth century."[64]

When Gibbs accepted the Rumford Medal awarded to him by the American Academy of Arts and Sciences at Boston, he wrote: "One of the principal objects of theoretical research in any department of knowledge is to find the point of view from which the subject appears in its greatest simplicity."[65] His efforts to achieve that point of view were central to all his scientific activity, and he never presented his work to the public until he was satisfied with the logical structure he had constructed. But as a consequence, his readers are "deprived of the advantage of seeing his great structures in process of building . . . and of being in such ways encouraged to make for themselves attempts similar in character, however small their scale."[66]

Notes

1. J. W. Gibbs, *Thermodynamische Studien*, trans. W. Ostwald (Leipzig: W. Engelmann, 1892), p. v.

2. Lord Rayleigh to J. W. Gibbs, June 5, 1892.

3. A. Einstein to M. Besso, June 23, 1918, in A. Einstein, M. Besso, *Correspondance 1903-1955*, ed. P. Speziali (Paris: Hermann, 1972), p. 126.

4. E. Panofsky, *Meaning in the Visual Arts* (Garden City, N.Y.: Doubleday & Company, 1955), p. 24.

5. P. Duhem, *Josiah Willard Gibbs à propos de la publication de ses mémoires scientifiques* (Paris: A. Hermann, 1908), p. 6.

6. H. A. Bumstead, "Josiah Willard Gibbs," in *The Scientific Papers of J. Willard Gibbs*, eds. H. A. Bumstead and R. G. Van Name, 2 vols. (New York: Longmans, Green, and Co., 1906; reprinted 1961), I, p. xxiii. This collection will be noted as *Sci. Pap.* and page references to Gibbs's papers will refer to this edition.

7. Duhem, *Josiah Willard Gibbs,* p. 10.

8. Full information on Gibbs's life will be found in L. P. Wheeler, *Josiah Willard Gibbs. The History of a Great Mind* 2nd ed. (New Haven: Yale University Press, 1952).

9. See Wheeler, *Josiah Willard Gibbs,* p. 9. The quotations are descriptions of the elder Gibbs.

10. Gibbs's thesis is printed in *The Early Work of Willard Gibbs in Applied Mechanics*, eds. L. P. Wheeler, E. O. Waters, and S. W. Dudley (New York: H. Schuman, 1947), pp. 7-39.

11. E. O. Waters, "Commentary upon the Gibbs Monograph, *On the Form of the Teeth of Wheels in Spur Gearing,*" in Wheeler et al., eds., *The Early Work of Willard Gibbs,* p. 43.

12. S. W. Dudley, "An Improved Railway Car Brake and Notes on Other Mechanical Inventions," in Wheeler et al., eds., *The Early Work of Willard Gibbs,* pp. 51-61.

13. Printed in Wheeler, *Josiah Willard Gibbs,* Appendix II, pp. 207-218.

14. Ibid., p. 209.

15. See ibid., pp. 40-45 for a summary of Gibbs's European notebooks.

16. Ibid., pp. 54-55, 259. For Gibbs's governor see also L. P. Wheeler, "The Gibbs Governor for Steam Engines," in Wheeler et al., eds., *The Early Work of Willard Gibbs,* pp. 63-78.

17. Wheeler, *Josiah Willard Gibbs,* p. 57. For the later history of Gibbs's salary see pp. 59-60, 90-93.

18. L. G. Wilson, "Benjamin Silliman: A Biographical Sketch," in *Benjamin Silliman and His Circle: Studies on the Influence of Benjamin Silliman on Science in America,* ed. L. G. Wilson (New York: Science History Publications, 1979), pp. 1-10.

19. Quoted by J. C. Greene in ibid., p. 12.

20. J. W. Gibbs, "Hubert Anson Newton," *Sci. Pap.* II, p. 269.

21. J. W. Gibbs, "Graphical Methods in the Thermodynamics of Fluids," *Transactions of the Connecticut Academy* 2 (1873), pp. 309-342. Reprinted in *Sci. Pap.* I, pp. 1-32.

22. I have used Gibbs's notation except for adding the bar on d to denote an inexact differential as đ. This notation is due to C. Neumann, *Vorlesungen über die mechanische Theorie der Wärme* (Leipzig: B. G. Teubner, 1875). See p. ix.

23. See J. W. Gibbs, "Rudolf Julius Emanuel Clausius," *Sci. Pap.* II, pp. 261-267. Also see D. S. L. Cardwell, *From Watt to Clausius* (Ithaca, N.Y.: Cornell University Press, 1971).

24. R. Clausius, "Ueber eine veränderte Form des zweiten Hauptsatzes der mechanischen Wärmetheorie," *Ann. Phys.* 169 (1854), pp. 481-506.

25. R. Clausius, "Ueber die Anwendung des Satzes von der Aequivalenz der Verwandlungen auf die innere Arbeit," *Ann. Phys.* 192 (1862), pp. 73-112.

26. R. Clausius, "Ueber verschiedene für die Anwendung bequeme Formen der Hauptgleichungen der mechanischen Wärmetheorie," *Ann. Phys.* 201 (1865), pp. 353-400.

27. For an analysis of disgregation see M. J. Klein, "Gibbs on Clausius," *Historical Studies in the Physical Sciences* 1 (1969), pp. 127-149, and also K. Hutchison, "Der Ursprung der Entropiefunktion bei Rankine und Clausius," *Annals of Science* 30 (1973), pp. 341-364.

28. R. Clausius, *Die mechanische Wärmetheorie,* Vol. I (Braunschweig: F. Vieweg & Sohn, 1876).

29. See note 22.

30. W. J. M. Rankine, "On the Geometrical Representation of the Expansive Action of Heat, and the Theory of Thermodynamic Engines," *Philosophical Transactions of the Royal Society* 144 (1854), pp. 115-176. Reprinted in W. J. Macquorn Rankine, *Miscellaneous Scientific Papers,* ed. W. J. Millar (London: C. Griffin and Co., 1881), pp. 339-409. See also Hutchison, "Der Ursprung der Entropiefunktion."

31. W. J. M. Rankine, *A Manual of the Steam Engine and Other Prime Movers* (London: C. Griffin and Co., 1859). I have used the Sixth Edition, 1873.

32. J. C. Maxwell, "Tait's *Thermodynamics,*" *Nature* 17 (1878), p. 257. Reprinted in *The Scientific Papers of James Clerk Maxwell,* ed. W. D. Niven, 2 vols. (Cambridge: At the University Press, 1890; reprinted 2 vols. in 1 New York, 1965), II, pp. 663-664.

33. P. G. Tait, *Sketch of Thermodynamics* (Edinburgh: Edmundston and Douglas, 1868), p. 100.

34. J. C. Maxwell, *Theory of Heat* (London: Longmans, Green and Co., 1871), p. 186. Reading Gibbs's first paper persuaded Maxwell to correct the error he had "imbibed" from Tait. See my paper cited in note 27. Tait's misusage of "entropy" can also be found in G. Krebs, *Einleitung in die mechanische Wärmetheorie* (Leipzig: B. G. Teubner, 1874), pp. 216-218.

35. An approach similar to that used by Gibbs, deriving "all the properties of the body

that one considers in thermodynamics" from a single characteristic function, is to be found in two notes by François Massieu, "Sur les fonctions caractéristiques des divers fluides," *Comptes Rendus* 69 (1869), pp. 858-862, 1057-1061. Massieu does not carry the discussion very far in these notes, and there is no reason to think that Gibbs knew them in 1873. He does refer to them in 1875 in his work on heterogeneous equilibrium. See *Sci. Pap.* I, p. 86 fn.

36. É. Clapeyron, "Mémoire sur la puissance motrice de la chaleur," *Journal de l'École Polytechnique* 14 (1834), pp. 153-190. The earlier history of the indicator diagram is discussed in D. S. L. Cardwell, note 23, pp. 80-83, 220-221. Cardwell remarks that the diagram had been a closely guarded trade secret of the firm of Boulton and Watt, and that John Farey, the English engineer, learned about it only in 1826 in Russia, presumably from one of Boulton and Watt's engineers working there. Since Clapeyron was also in Russia during the late 1820s he may have acquired his knowledge of the indicator diagram in the same way.

37. W. J. M. Rankine, *Papers*, note 30, pp. 359-360.

38. G. Zeuner, *Grundzüge der mechanischen Wärmetheorie* (Leipzig: Arthur Felix, 2nd ed., 1866).

39. J. W. Gibbs, *Sci. Pap.* I, p. 1.

40. J. W. Gibbs, *Sci. Pap.* I, p. 11.

41. T. Belpaire, "Note sur le second principe de la thermodynamique," *Bulletins de l'Académie Royale des Sciences, des Lettres, et des Beaux-Arts de Belgique,* 34 (1872), pp. 509-526. It seems safe to conclude that Gibbs had not read this paper even though the *Bulletins* were received by the Connecticut Academy on an exchange basis: the pages of Belpaire's paper in the Connecticut Academy's volume of the *Bulletins* for 1872, now in the Yale University library, were still uncut in the early summer of 1977.

42. See the "Rapport" on Belpaire's paper by F. Folie, in the same journal, pp. 448-451.

43. J. M. Gray, "The Rationalization of Regnault's Experiments on Steam," *Proceedings of the Institution of Mechanical Engineers* (1889), pp. 399-450. Discussion of this paper, pp. 451-468. See in particular pp. 412-414.

44. Ibid., pp. 463-464.

45. J. W. Gibbs, *Sci. Pap.* I, pp. 20-28.

46. J. W. Gibbs, *Sci. Pap.* I, p. 32.

47. J. C. Maxwell, *Theory of Heat,* 5th ed. (London: Longmans, Green, and Co., 1877), pp. 165-171. For his geometrical preferences see, for example, L. Campbell and W. Garnett, *The Life of James Clerk Maxwell* (London: Macmillan and Co., 1882; reprinted in New York: Johnson Reprint Corporation, 1969), p. 175.

48. For a discussion and references see my paper in note 27. Also see C. G. Knott, *Life and Scientific Work of Peter Guthrie Tait* (Cambridge: At the University Press, 1911), pp. 208-226.

49. See note 34.

50. J. D. van der Waals, *Over de continuiteit van den gas-en vloeistoftoestand* (Leiden: A. W. Sijthoff, 1873), p. 81.

51. Advertisement of the publisher (Longmans, Green, and Co.) for the series, printed at the end of the text in some editions.

52. P. G. Tait, "Clerk-Maxwell's Scientific Work," *Nature* 21 (1880), pp. 317-321.

53. T. Andrews, "On the Continuity of the Gaseous and Liquid States of Matter," *Phil. Trans. Roy. Soc.* 159 (1869), pp. 575-590. Reprinted in *The Scientific Papers of Thomas Andrews* (London: Macmillan and Co., 1889), pp. 296-317. Further references are to this edition.

54. Andrews, *Scientific Papers,* p. xxxi.

55. Ibid., p. 315.

56. In June 1902 Gibbs advised his former student, Edwin B. Wilson, who was leaving for a year's study in Paris, to take some work in applied mathematics. "He ventured the opinion that one good use to which anybody might put a superior training in pure mathematics was to the study of the problems set us by nature." E. B. Wilson, "Reminiscences of Gibbs by a Student and Colleague," *Scientific Monthly* 32 (1931), pp. 210-227. Quotation from p. 221.

57. J. W. Gibbs, "A Method of Geometrical Representation of the Thermodynamic Properties of Substances by Means of Surfaces," *Transactions of the Connecticut Academy* 2 (1873), pp. 382-404. Reprinted in *Sci. Pap.* I, pp. 33-54.

58. James Thomson, "Considerations on the Abrupt Change at Boiling or Condensing in Reference to the Continuity of the Fluid State of Matter," *Proc. Roy. Soc.* 20 (1871), pp. 1-8. Reprinted in James Thomson, *Collected Papers in Physics and Engineering* (Cambridge: At the University Press, 1912), pp. 278-286. References will be to this reprinting. Related papers and unpublished notes by Thomson are to be found at pp. 276-277 and pp. 286-333. Although Gibbs does not refer to them, he may well have read Thomson's papers to the British Association for the Advancement of Science in 1871 and 1872 (pp. 286-291, 297-307) in which the triple point is first named and discussed.

59. See Thomson, *Collected Papers,* p. 279.

60. See van der Waals, *Over de continuiteit,* pp. 120-121.

61. J. W. Gibbs to W. Ostwald, March 27, 1891. Printed in *Aus dem wissenschaftlichen Briefwechsel Wilhelm Ostwalds,* ed. H.-G. Körber (Berlin: Akademie-Verlag, 1961) I, pp. 97-98.

62. R. Clausius, "On the Behavior of Carbonic Acid in Relation to Pressure, Volume, and Temperature," *Philosophical Magazine* 9 (1880), pp. 393-408. See particularly pp. 405-407.

63. P. Saurel, "On the Critical State of a One-Component System," *Journal of Physical Chemistry* 6 (1902), pp. 474-491.

64. A. S. Wightman, "Introduction: Convexity and the Notion of Equilibrium State in Thermodynamics and Statistical Mechanics," in R. B. Israel, *Convexity in the Theory of Lattice Gases* (Princeton: Princeton University Press, 1979), pp. ix-lxxxv. Quote from p. xiii.

65. Quoted in Wheeler, *Josiah Willard Gibbs,* pp. 88-89.

66. H. A. Bumstead in J. W. Gibbs, *Sci. Pap.* I, p. xxiv.

Chapter 6

Principal Scientific Contributions of John William Strutt, Third Baron Rayleigh

John N. Howard

Family Background

What makes Lord Rayleigh remarkably different from most other scientists is that he was born rich. Not fabulously rich, but comfortably rich. His father, John James Strutt (1796-1873), the second Baron Rayleigh, was a prosperous Essex farmer, who raised a large family of six sons and a daughter. In spite of J. J. Strutt's being an Oxford man himself, his eldest son, John William Strutt (1842-1919), showed such a mathematical bent that it was decided to send him to Trinity College, Cambridge. (He established such a reputation at Cambridge that some of his younger brothers also went there.) When John James Strutt died in 1873, John William Strutt became the third Baron Rayleigh and equipped part of the mansion at Terling as a private laboratory. The farms were at that time mostly in the hands of tenants, but Rayleigh was not particularly inclined toward managing the estate, and in 1876 he entrusted the management to his younger brother Edward Strutt (1854-1930), who had just come down from Cambridge. Edward was almost immediately faced with the agricultural depression of 1878-1879; wheat prices fell, harvests were bad, and most of the tenants left. He converted part of the estate to dairy farming, introduced new scientific principles of crop rotation, kept careful records of milk yield, and weeded out those milkers of low yield. By 1928 the estate had a herd of eight hundred and fifty cows and employed sixty milkers. In order to be independent of middle-men, a shop with the legend "Lord Rayleigh's Dairies" was established in Great Russell Street, London, in 1897, and this was followed by others in different parts of London. At the end of Rayleigh's life there were eight in all. Rayleigh's name became more familiar to the general public from these shops and from the milk carts seen throughout the London streets with his name on them than from his scientific activities. (The family sold their interest in the London retail stores in 1929, but the family dairies in Essex continue to be one of the largest milk producers in England.)

When John William Strutt died in 1919, his son Robert John Strutt (1875-1947) succeeded as fourth Baron Rayleigh. Robert's son, the present Lord Rayleigh, John Arthur Strutt (b. 1908) succeeded as fifth Baron in 1947.

Schooling and Cambridge

John William Strutt was born at Langford Grove, Maldon, Essex on November 12, 1842. His early education was frequently interrupted by ill health. At the age of ten he entered Eton, but he stayed less than a year. Later he went for a short time to Harrow. Ultimately he attended a school in Torquay, where he was prepared for the University. In October 1861 he went up to Trinity College, Cambridge, beginning his university career without expectation of a high place, but his confidence gradually increased as he proceeded in his studies. In the annual college examinations he always occupied a high place, although still a long way from the top, for these examinations included classical and other subjects; but among the pupils of Routh he was looked upon as the most likely to come out as a Senior Wrangler.

At that time Cambridge University in general, and Trinity College in particular, dominated the production of British mathematicians and natural scientists, and boasted such early graduates as Bacon, Newton, and Cavendish. A student attended college, heard lectures, and read courses, but the mark of his achievement and even his future career depended on his standing in the Natural Sciences or Mathematical Tripos examinations. The top man in Class I of the latter examination was called (until 1912) the Senior Wrangler, the next, Second Wrangler, then Third Wrangler, etc. The outcome of the Tripos and the ranking of the candidates was published in the newspapers, as well as in the bulletin of the University, and these placements were used as a basis for awarding fellowships and even awarding professorships. Lord Kelvin (who was Second Wrangler in 1845) described this system as "miserable." The coveted position of Senior Wrangler was not always awarded to the best mathematician of his year, but to the one who had been best groomed for the race by constant drill and coaching by his tutor. J. J. Thomson, who had been second to Joseph Larmor in 1880, likewise decried this system. The mathematician Hopkins was famed for having had seventeen Senior Wranglers among his pupils, but this record was surpassed by his successor E. J. Routh, who in thirty-three years had twenty-seven Senior Wranglers among his pupils. Routh himself had been Senior Wrangler the year in which Clerk Maxwell was second. Routh coached his pupils in a series of exceedingly clear lectures, given to an audience larger than those attending the lectures of the mathematical professors of the University. J. J. Thomson remarked also on Routh's extreme regularity: one who had attended his lectures could tell what he had been lecturing about on any particular day and hour over a twenty-five year period.

Among Strutt's recreations during college were tennis and photography. One of his early papers was "On the irregular flight of a tennis ball." His interest in wet-plate photography made him acutely aware of the absence of any provision in the University curriculum for experimental work. He attended the optics lectures of Stokes, and strongly hinted to his professor that he would like to assist in the demonstrations; but Stokes, a taciturn man, did not respond.

In January 1865 J. W. Strutt took his degree and was Senior Wrangler in the Tripos. Several of the questions concerned geometrical and physical optics. One of them even anticipated the much later Michelson-Morley experiment: "Fresnel supposes that, when bodies move in the medium, the relative velocity of the medium with respect to the body is in the same direction, but in proportion $1:\mu$. Show that the retardation of a plate of glass will be independent of the motion of the earth, if the square of the velocity of the earth to the velocity of light be neglected." One of the examiners said at the time that "Strutt's papers were so good that they could have been sent straight to press without revision."[1]

Strutt then capped his triumph by submitting the winning paper for the Smith's Prize, the other mark of achievement at Cambridge in natural science. Kelvin had been a First Smith's Prizeman, and Maxwell had bracketed with Routh for First. At the age of twenty-two Strutt was now recognized throughout Britain as a mathematical physicist of great ability and promise. The only reservation expressed was that, when he ultimately succeeded to the peerage, his social obligations would not leave him time for scientific activities.

The First Scientific Period and Terling

Schuster has given a brief account of the position of physics at the time John Strutt began work in 1865. Joule's experiments on the conservation of energy had only recently received general acceptance, and William Thomson (later Lord Kelvin), barely forty years old, had given his formulation of the second law of thermodynamics while Strutt was in school. About the time he (Strutt) entered the University, Maxwell applied the laws of probability to the kinetic theory of gases, and, while Strutt was getting ready for the Tripos, Maxwell's paper on "A dynamical theory of the electromagnetic field" was communicated to the Royal Society. Green and Stokes had put the undulatory theory of light on a sound basis; Foucault had shown experimentally that light was propagated more slowly through water than through air. Michael Faraday was still alive, although old and ailing. Bunsen and Kirchhoff had just introduced spectrum analysis, photography was still in its infancy, and the first observations had been made of the glows observed when electric discharges pass through vacuum tubes. In the laboratory, a vacuum was achieved only after hours of hand-operation of a Töpler pump; electricity came from hand-operated generators or batteries, and the Bunsen burner was but eight years old.

Four years passed between Strutt's degree in 1865 and his first paper of 1869. During this period, he was a fellow of Trinity College, attending additional lectures, such as those of Stokes, but mostly reading and studying the scientific literature. One of his professors told him he should learn German, and he selected Helmholtz's "Die Lehre von den Tonempfindungen" (which had appeared in 1862) as his text. Thus began his great interest in acoustics and in the physiology of hearing. This introduction also led him on to Helmholtz's work on color vision. Young and Maxwell had also written on color perception, a subject that became one of Strutt's first experimental investigations. But chiefly during this period he practiced and perfected mathematical techniques, and, in particular, the methods of Lagrange. In many physical problems in optics, acoustics, electricity, and hydrodynamics, in which we do not observe the motions of material particles directly, it is still possible to describe such concepts as energy and momentum in terms of generalized coordinates by using the Lagrange function. Such an approach is particularly useful in the analysis of vibrations, as in generalized coordinates the terms involving the fundamental and harmonic frequencies are much simpler in form, with fewer cross-terms, and are more amenable to manipulation. Rayleigh was certainly not the first to apply such techniques, but he seems to have been the most successful and versatile in recognizing related problems in dynamics, acoustics, optics, and electricity. When he had solved a problem in one field, he was able to solve immediately the analogous problem in each other field.

As Lindsay has put it, the intensive coaching of Routh ground the methods of mathematics so thoroughly into each of his students that these methods became a natural part of his thinking: "It was not *rigorous* mathematics in the pure sense, but it was *vigorous* mathematics."[2] Although Rayleigh's degree was actually in mathematics, he ordinarily approached a problem from a physical point of view and considered the mathematics an auxiliary technique. As Rayleigh himself described his approach (in the preface to "The Theory of Sound"):

In the mathematical investigations I have usually employed such methods as present themselves naturally to a physicist. The pure mathematician will complain, and (it must be confessed) sometimes with justice, of deficient rigour. But to this question there are two sides. For however important it may be to maintain a uniformly high standard in pure mathematics, the physicist may occasionally do well to rest content with arguments which are fairly satisfactory and conclusive from his point of view. To his mind, exercised in a different order of ideas, the more severe procedure of the pure mathematician may appear not more but less demonstrative.[3]

Characteristically, Rayleigh would first start out with the simplest possible mathematical representation of a physical situation (a one-dimensional model, for example), add complications one at a time, and then generalize his results. He examined each function for its limiting forms with large or small arguments; he investigated how many terms he needed to retain in a series function; and he developed powerful methods of approximation in which the complexities could be treated as perturbations. The Rayleigh-Ritz method, the Schrödinger-Rayleigh method, and the Wenzel-Kramer-Brillioun method are all later extensions by others of such mathematical techniques pioneered by Rayleigh.

During the period 1866-1871, while a fellow at Trinity, he also began his extensive correspondence with Maxwell and William Thomson. He had to resign the Trinity fellowship (which was for bachelors) when, in 1871, he married Evelyn Balfour, the sister of his college friend, Arthur Balfour. He had first met Miss Balfour

Plate 1. John William Strutt (circa 1870).

Plate 2. Evelyn Balfour, fiancee of John William Strutt (circa 1870).

when Arthur had taken him to a family dinner party. When John Strutt found that she was interested in music, he presented her with his copy of Helmholtz's "Tonempfindungen." Her reaction to this is, unfortunately, not recorded. With his new bride, John Strutt settled on the family estate at Terling, where he converted some of the rooms (the old stable and stable loft) to a private laboratory.

Soon after his marriage, he had a serious attack of rheumatic fever, which left him much weakened in health. He took an extended excursion to Egypt during his recuperation, accompanied by his wife and her sister, Eleanor Balfour. This included a long trip up the Nile in a house boat. During the trip he wrote a large portion of "The Theory of Sound," the first part of which was written with no access to a library. He polished this material extensively, however, between this time and its publication in 1877. Shortly after he returned to Terling, his father died (in 1873), and he succeeded to the title. He enlarged the laboratory, installed gas for a Bunsen burner, blowtorch, and lights, and commenced a series of experimental studies in optics and acoustics. Besides a large laboratory, a workshop, and a photographic darkroom, he had one room for experiments in optics and spectroscopy, the walls of which were painted black, reportedly with lampblack mixed in beer.

Plate 3. The second Baron Rayleigh, John James Strutt, father of John William Strutt (circa 1870).

Plate 4. John William Strutt, third Baron Rayleigh, at the time he was Cavendish Professor at Cambridge University (circa 1885).

Early Work in Optics

The earliest scientific interest of John Strutt was photography. The wet collodion process had been introduced only in 1851, and the photographer had to coat and sensitize the plate immediately before use. Strutt made his earliest picture (of a fern leaf) when he was fifteen. He became quite skilled in wet-plate photography (and later in the various dry processes). In the library at Terling there is a remarkable bound volume of detailed photographs of various ancient Egyptian monuments that he had made during his Nile trip of 1872-1873. His first scientific application of photography, begun in 1871, was in the copying of diffraction gratings. He wrote several papers on this subject. His original intention was to reduce a coarse grating photographically to obtain a finer ruling, but his first efforts were disappointing. He had almost immediate success, however, in copying glass gratings by contact printing (Papers 17, 18). (He also made collodion cast replicas of gratings (Paper 30) as early as 1873.) He even constructed circular zone plate gratings in 1871, four years before Soret.

Rayleigh subsequently made two other major contributions to photography: in 1887 (Paper 142), he described a technique for color photography that was later (in 1891) successfully carried out by G. Lippmann (and for which Lippmann received the Nobel prize in 1908). In 1891 (Paper 178), he presented the complete theory of pinhole photography, amplifying and consolidating the earlier work of Petzval in 1859.

In the paper of 1874 (Paper 30), he first showed that the resolving power of a grating is given by the product of the total number of ruled lines and the order of the spectrum. In a series of papers of 1879 and 1880 (Paper 62), he further considered the resolving power of gratings and introduced the well-known Rayleigh criterion: that two wavelengths can be considered resolved when the center of the diffraction image of the second wavelength falls on the first minimum of the diffraction pattern of the first wavelength. In this same series of papers he stated the Rayleigh Limit for aberrations in any optical instrument: "An optical system will give an image only slightly inferior to that produced by an absolutely perfect system if all the light arrives at the focus with differences of phase not exceeding one quarter of a wavelength, for then the resultant cannot differ much from the maximum."[4] He subsequently extended this concept in many papers on the aberrations of telescopes and microscopes (e.g., Papers 67, 126, 189, 289).

Another early subject that Strutt studied in the literature after completing his degree was the work of Maxwell on color perception. His notes on this are dated May 1865. In 1870 he commenced some color perception studies of his own (Paper 7). He found that if one combined a filter of an alkaline solution of litmus, which absorbs the yellow and orange (and looks blue in transmission), with a filter of potassium chromate, which removes the blue and bluish-green (and looks red in transmission), one obtains a sensation of yellow ("compound yellow") even though the spectral yellow has been filtered out. He then devised an instrument in which spectrally produced red light could be combined with green subjectively to match a spectrally produced yellow light (Paper 77). He found that, of twenty-three male observers, sixteen required about the same proportion of red and green light to match the yellow, but that five others (of whom three were his Balfour brothers-in-law Frank, Arthur and Gerald) required twice as much green as the others in order to match the yellow. (The other two required more red.) This was not color blindness in the ordinary (red-green) sense, as these subjects could distinguish red and green as well as the others. This sort of abnormal color vision is called anomalous trichromatism.

The Blue of the Sky: Rayleigh Scattering

In conducting his early experiments on color vision, Strutt had noticed that the color match was influenced by the blueness of the sky, and he was led to a study of the blue of the sky and the red of the sunset (Paper 8). From the time of Newton on, many physicists had ascribed the blue of the sky to reflection of sunlight from atmospheric particles in the form of thin plates (thin compared to the visible wavelengths), and the color to be blue of first order in Newton's scale. Clausius wrote a series of papers asserting that, if the blue of the sky is due to thin plates at all, these thin plates must be in the form of bubbles, presumably of water. He showed that, if the scattering agent were in the form of droplets instead of bubbles, a star, instead of appearing as a point, would be dilated into a disk. With bubbles, however, this does not occur, and a blue of first order in Newton's scale is produced. Critics of Clausius's bubble theory pointed out that the sky is bluer than Newton's first-order blue, that a mastic precipitated from an alcoholic suspension scatters light of a blue tint, and that the particles of this suspension are surely not bubbles. Tyndall made extensive measurements on the scattering of light from colloidal suspensions, and he found, in addition, that the blue light scattered at right angles from the incident beam was completely polarized.

In his 1871 paper, Strutt showed by a dimensional analysis that the intensity of sky light, if due to reflections from either thin plates or Clausius's bubbles, should vary with wavelength λ as λ^{-2} (i.e., the intensity of the blue light so reflected would be about four times that of red). If the scattered light were due to particles small compared to the wavelength, he showed from dimensional analysis, and then verified experimentally, that the intensity variation with wavelength was λ^{-4} (or the intensity of scattered blue light would be sixteen times that of red). He then proceeded to derive the quantitative relationship, including the polarization effects. In this first paper he used ether theory, with the scattering particles assumed to "load the ether so as to increase its inertia."[5] (He noted, however, that the formalism of the mathematics was independent of the assumption.) This paper is characteristic of Rayleigh's approach to a problem in assuming small particles, neglecting higher-order terms, and seeking limiting values of mathematical functions. Ten years later, in 1881, he rederived the relations in terms of Maxwell's theory (Paper 74). This time, he reconsidered some higher-order terms and solved the problem for spherical particles. In 1899 Rayleigh again returned to the problem of the blue of the sky (Paper 247), and showed that the atmospheric particle assumption was not necessary; the atmospheric molecules themselves could produce a scattering effect. The complete expression derived by Rayleigh for scattering by particles small compared to the wavelength of the incident radiation accounts for the variation of intensity and degree of polarization of the scattered light as a function of angle, wavelength, and refractive index of the particles (or of the gas itself). If the incident radiation is monochromatic, the wavelength is unchanged by scattering, and the Rayleigh formula then gives the angular scattering function: thus, in Raman spectroscopy, the scattered light of unchanged frequency is called the Rayleigh line, whereas the Stokes and anti-Stokes lines are shifted in frequency. Thomson scattering is an extension of Rayleigh's theory to very short wavelengths (wavelengths close to resonance) and accounts for the distribution of the X-ray continuum, or the scattering of free electrons.

In 1908 Gustav Mie, starting from Rayleigh's theory, and taking higher-order terms, solved the complete scattering problem for particles of size comparable to the wavelength.

The Cavendish Professorship

Until the second half of the nineteenth century, there was no teaching laboratory or course of instruction in "practical physics" where a student could obtain laboratory practice in experimental techniques. The great experimenters prior to this time—Newton, Cavendish, Young, Faraday, and others—had learned experimental techniques in private laboratories, or by helping an older master in his work.

In 1850, William Thomson cleaned out an old wine cellar and the adjoining coal cellar in the college basement at Glasgow in order to do laboratory studies in electricity. Here six or eight students helped Thomson in his research. There were no assistants and no workshop; if a student wanted a resistance coil he had to find some wire and wind it himself. But this was the beginning of academic experimental physics. Stokes had a room at Cambridge where he experimented, but he was unaided by students or assistants. In 1867, Professor R. B. Clifton at Oxford started a small class in practical physics, and in 1868 the Clarendon Laboratory was begun. In 1870, similar classes were begun in London at King's College and University College. The only similar teaching laboratory in Europe was that of Jamin at the Sorbonne, and in the United States that of Pickering at MIT. In 1869, a committee at Cambridge recommended that a special professorship be set up to teach and demonstrate experimental physics. In October 1870, the Chancellor of the University, the seventh Duke of Devonshire (William Cavendish, who had himself been a First Smith's Prizeman and Second Wrangler) offered to donate the funds (which ultimately amounted to £8500) for the construction of a suitable research laboratory. A month later the council of the University accepted his offer, named the laboratory the Cavendish Laboratory in his honor, and established the Cavendish Professorship.

Thomson, now Sir William, was invited to become the Cavendish Professor, but declined, as did Helmholtz. Maxwell was asked next, and (according to Kelvin) had he declined, the post would have been offered to Strutt. Strutt wrote to Maxwell (who, because of ill health, had retired from his professorship at King's College to his Scottish estate at Glenlair) urging him to accept the position: "What is wanted by most who know anything about it is not so much a lecturer as a mathematician who has actual experience in experimenting and who might direct the energies of the younger fellows and bachelors in a proper channel."[6] Maxwell accepted, and delivered his first lecture in October 1871. The laboratory building was not completed until 1874. Among early researchers at the Cavendish were R. T. Glazebrook in optics and Arthur Schuster in spectroscopy. Maxwell continued to give a series of rather elementary lectures, but spent a large part of his time editing the unpublished works of Henry Cavendish, and left the supervision of the laboratory courses to his demonstrator. Maxwell's health failed rapidly in 1879, and he died November 5, 1879.

Again Sir William Thomson was invited to become the Cavendish Professor, and again he declined. In addition to being a professor at Glasgow, he was now a very prosperous consulting electrical engineer and had a splendid 126-ton yacht berthed near where the Kelvin River flows into the Clyde. In December 1879 Lord Rayleigh was invited to become the Cavendish Professor; he accepted a five-year appointment. Although he was not in need, the agricultural depression of 1878-1879 had made life less pleasant at Terling. He began his duties early in 1880. Maxwell's demonstrator had resigned, and Rayleigh appointed as demonstrator R. T. Glazebrook, who was later to become the first director of the National Physical Laboratory.

In July 1879 the Meteorological Council initiated a request that the various types of hygrometers be compared and standardized. Stokes had arranged for this to be done at the Cavendish, and Maxwell picked William Napier Shaw, who was then working in Berlin with Helmholtz, to carry out this work. Maxwell died before Shaw arrived, but Rayleigh arranged for him to continue these meteorological studies and appointed him a second demonstrator. Rayleigh also appointed George Gordon to be in charge of the workshop. He had been a shipwright in Liverpool and was skillful and quick. His work was not pleasing to the eye, but it did what it was expected to do, which was all that Lord Rayleigh demanded.

The duties of the Cavendish Professor were not heavy: he was required to be in residence for eighteen weeks during the academic year and to deliver at least forty lectures during this period. The classes were not large: Rayleigh lectured on such topics as "the use of physical apparatus" and "Galvanic electricity and electromagnetism" to groups of sixteen or eighteen students, including one or two senior members of the University. The only texts that existed for the laboratory procedures were Kohlrausch's *Physical Measurements* and Pickering's *Elements of Physical Manipulation*, both published in 1873, until Glazebrook and Shaw organized the demonstration lecture notes into their well-known text, *Practical Physics*.

The total number of students at the Cavendish steadily rose from about twenty in 1877, to sixty-two in 1882, to ninety, with ten doing research, in 1885. Rayleigh's greatest contribution to the Cavendish, however, was his desire to stimulate the researchers into joint research projects: a Cavendish program, rather than the individual projects of each man. He chose as the basis for such a program the redetermination of the values of the practical electrical units. These studies have been described in more detail elsewhere.[7] He suggested a related problem to one of his young research students, J. J. Thomson: that he determine the ratio of the electrostatic unit to the electromagnetic unit. Weber, Maxwell, and William Thomson had all tried this in the past, with considerable variation in the results. Rayleigh himself designed the more important pieces of the apparatus. This was reported in one of J. J. Thomson's first papers[8] and was the beginning of a series of researches by Thomson that led ultimately to his discovery of the electron. Thomson later said, in describing Rayleigh's electrical researches at the Cavendish, that he changed chaos into order. Besides the electrical researches, Shaw began his meteorological measurements, Glazebrook began his optical studies on the reflectivity of crystals, Schuster pursued spectroscopic studies, Poynting developed the saccharimeter, and George and Horace Darwin began their studies of the tides. In this period Rayleigh himself was at a peak of productivity, writing some sixty papers in the five-year period: an average of one per month, and none of them trivial. At the Cavendish he continued acoustical researches, began his important studies on capillarity, and developed the Rayleigh test for color perception.

Two other Rayleigh innovations of the Cavendish period should be mentioned. In 1882 Rayleigh opened all classes and demonstrations to the women students of Girton and Newnham Colleges on the same basis as they were open to men. Rayleigh also introduced the practice of the common afternoon tea, in an effort to provide opportunity for informal discussion of scientific matters among the researchers.

At the end of December 1884, Rayleigh announced his intention to return to private studies at Terling, and he resigned the Cavendish Professorship. For a third time Sir William Thomson was asked to serve, but again he declined. To the surprise of many, the other senior candidates were passed over and the post was offered to twenty-eight-year-old J. J. Thomson. He continued and broadened Rayleigh's program of electrical studies, followed by studies of discharge phenomena in gases, X-rays, and radioactivity, making the Cavendish the foremost center of physics research of the late nineteenth and early twentieth century. A large number of Cavendish researchers have won the Nobel Prize, perhaps more than from any other laboratory, and the first of these was Rayleigh himself.

The Royal Society and the Royal Institution

At the end of December 1884, Rayleigh returned to Terling. He took with him as his assistant George Gordon, who had been in charge of the machine shop at the Cavendish. The scientists who visited Rayleigh at Terling all remarked on the simplicity and even crudeness of the laboratory apparatus and equipment. This was due partly to Rayleigh's dislike of superfluous elegance, and partly to his frugal nature and a reluctance to make any unnecessary expenditures. In any experiment the critical parts of the apparatus were constructed and calibrated with extreme care, but for the rest he made do with whatever was available. At Terling "sealing wax, string, rough unplaned woodwork, and glass tubes joined together by bulbous and unsightly joints met the eye in every direction."[9]

Rayleigh, however, had not withdrawn from active participation in contemporary science. In 1882, during his electrical measurements period, he had been president of the mathematical and physical section of the British Association for the Advancement of Science (B. A.), and in 1884 he was president of the B. A. That year the B. A. met at Montreal. After the meeting Rayleigh visited many laboratories in the United States: those of Newcomb and Michelson, Pickering, Rowland, and even of Edison.

There is a popular anecdote about Rayleigh concerning his contribution to the Encyclopedia Britannica. According to the anecdote, he was asked in 1884 to contribute the article on light, but it was not ready in time for the volume containing the letter "L." Very well, we can call it "Optics," said the editor, but again it was not ready in time. It finally appeared as "Wave Theory of Light." This anecdote is, however, apocryphal. The editor of the ninth edition of the Britannica had been a student of Professor Tait at Glasgow and had already asked Tait to contribute the article on Light (which he did). Rayleigh contributed a short article on Optics (Paper 119), which chiefly concerns geometrical optics, and a highly technical article on Wave Theory (Paper 148). A part of this latter paper had to be deleted in order to fit the space available in the last volume and appeared in *Nature* as "Aberration" (Paper 189). Taken together, these papers still constitute one of the most profound discussions of optics available. Many more recent books on the subject derive largely from these articles by Rayleigh.

In 1885 Stokes resigned as Secretary of the Royal Society; Rayleigh accepted the post, which he held until 1896. In this position, he had many of the functions of editor, as it involved the screening of communications from Fellows of the Royal Society to determine their suitability for inclusion in meetings in the proceedings. During his tenure of office the *Transactions* of the Royal Society were divided into separate series: A for the physical papers and B for the biological papers. (The corresponding change in the *Proceedings* of the Royal Society occurred in 1905.) In 1887 Rayleigh succeeded John Tyndall as Professor of Natural Philosophy at the Royal Institution, which post he held until 1905. The duties chiefly involved giving a series of six afternoon lectures and a Friday evening discourse in the season just before Easter. A three-room physical laboratory was also available. However, James Dewar, the Professor of Chemistry, had heavy machinery in the basement where he studied compressed gases and phenomena at low temperatures, and there was too much vibration in the building for precise studies. Rayleigh did not attempt to do serious research at the R. I. except during his argon studies, when he made use of the alternating current that was available there. At Terling it was necessary to run a gas engine continuously to obtain electricity, and even then the power was not enough.

Argon

To this period of his research belongs the study that brought him his greatest fame during his lifetime, although most non-British physicists today are not even aware that it was Rayleigh who first discovered argon. As Cavendish Professor, Rayleigh had been intrigued by Prout's hypothesis that the atomic weights should be integral numbers. Assuming hydrogen to be 1, oxygen was found to be not quite 16. Was the discrepancy real, or an experimental error? Rayleigh commenced research to determine the densities of these gases more precisely. In four successive determinations he obtained, as the ratio of the atomic weights of oxygen to hydrogen: 15.89, 15.882, 15.880, and 15.863. He next turned his attention to nitrogen. In a letter to *Nature* (September 29, 1892) he wrote: "I am much puzzled by some results on the density of nitrogen, and shall be obliged if any of your chemical readers can offer suggestions as to the cause. According to the methods of preparation I obtain two quite distinct values. The relative difference, amounting to about 1/1000 part, is small in itself, but it lies entirely outside the errors of experiment, and can only be attributed to a variation of the character of the gas."[10] His two sources of nitrogen had been ordinary air, with the oxygen removed by metallic copper, and a lighter nitrogen obtained by decomposition of ammonia. His letter to *Nature* failed to yield any suggestions. His neighbor Sir James Dewar said that it was obvious that some of the atmospheric N_2 was in an allotropic state, say N_3, just as some oxygen exists as ozone. Rayleigh thought about this, and spent two years preparing nitrogen by several techniques. Such nitrogen was always lighter in density than atmospheric nitrogen, even when it had been stored in a globe for eight months. One of his demonstration lectures at the Royal Institution was a repeat of some of Henry Cavendish's early studies on nitrogen: in a globe of ordinary air electrical sparking oxidized the nitrogen, and then the nitrous oxide was absorbed by potash. In this way all of the nitrogen was removed except (as Cavendish had noted) a very small residue. Rayleigh verified Cavendish's results, which had lain unnoticed in the literature for over a hundred years.

At this stage William Ramsay at the University of London joined the effort, and his technique was to remove the nitrogen by burning magnesium in a globe. Rayleigh used the sparking technique, removing most of the nitrogen at the Royal Institution, and taking the concentrate to Terling for final purification. For several months they wrote each other frequent letters on their progress. Hiebert has recently written a detailed description of the discovery and of the subsequent incredulity of the scientific world.[11] On August 4, 1894 Ramsay wrote Rayleigh: "I have isolated the gas. Its density is 19.075 and it is not absorbed by magnesium." Rayleigh replied on August 6: "I believe that I too have isolated the gas, though in miserably small quantities."[12] On August 13 they made a joint announcement to the British Association. Dewar again called it the allotropic form of nitrogen; another professor pointed out that the gas would have to lie in the platinum family of Mendeleeff's table. On January 31, 1895 Rayleigh and Ramsay presented their fifty-four-page joint paper giving the density, refractive index, solubility in water, ratio of specific heats, and atomic spectrum of the new gas, naming it argon (for *inert*; without work), and postulating a new zeroth column, for noble gases, in Mendeleeff's table. Some scientists argued that so heavy an element could not possibly be a gas. Rayleigh replied, "the result is, no doubt, very awkward. Indeed, I have seen some indications that the anomalous properties of argon are brought as a kind of accusation against us. But we had the very best intentions in the matter. The facts were too much for us, and all that we can do now is apologize for ourselves and for the gas."[13]

In the process of isolating argon, Rayleigh designed the refractometer (Papers 218 and 415) that bears his name, and the Rayleigh modification of the Huygens manometer. Kelvin hailed argon as undoubtedly the greatest scientific event of the year: "If anything could add to the interest which we must all feel in this startling discovery, it is the consideration of the way by which it was found . . . arduous work . . . commenced in 1882, has been continued for twelve years, by Rayleigh, with unremitting perseverance."[14] Rayleigh's and Ramsay's results were soon verified by others, and within the next few years Ramsay, with Travers and Soddy, isolated helium, neon, krypton, and xenon.

Blackbody Radiation: the Rayleigh-Jeans Law

From early times it had been known that substances sufficiently heated would begin to glow. Newton in his "Opticks" had asked, "do not all fix'd Bodies, when heated beyond a certain degree, emit light and shine; and is not this emission perform'd by the vibrating motions of their parts?'' In 1847 Draper had determined that all bodies began to emit red light when heated above $525°C$ (he heated his bodies in a crude blackbody enclosure). Wien, in 1876, arguing partly from thermodynamical considerations showed that, if λ_m is the wavelength of the maximum of the energy curve at absolute temperature T, then $\lambda_m T$ is a constant. By making some (not very plausible) assumptions concerning the radiating body, Wien obtained a formula for the intensity of radiation, μ_λ, between λ and $\lambda + \Delta\lambda$ in the form

$$\mu_\lambda = \frac{c_1}{\lambda^5} \, e^{-c_2/\lambda T},$$

which represented the observed data well at short wavelengths and reduced to the above relationship for λ_m. It did not fit the observed data of Lummer and Pringsheim for longer wavelengths, however.

In 1900 Rayleigh considered the problem of blackbody radiation (Paper 260). By assuming that all the ''standing waves'' that could possibly form inside an enclosure possessed the same quantity of energy, and by dividing the spectrum into intervals and counting how many waves had their periods in each interval, Rayleigh derived the formula

$$\mu_\lambda = \frac{c_1 T}{c_2 \lambda^4} \quad .$$

This appeared to be classically correct (save for a numerical factor in how to count the modes, which James Jeans pointed out to Rayleigh and published in 1905) and to agree with observed data at long wavelengths; but it was obviously incorrect as λ tended to zero, for then the intensity would tend to infinity. This disparity was later labeled the ''ultraviolet catastrophe.'' In 1900, in an effort to obtain a formula that would reduce to Wien's formula at short wavelengths and Rayleigh's formula at long wavelengths, Planck obtained—at first empirically—his formula, which agreed so well with observed data that he then (in 1901) put it on a theoretical basis by introducing his concept of the quantum of action. Like many other classical physicists, Rayleigh found it hard to conceive of energy being ''quantized.'' In a letter to Nernst in 1911 he wrote concerning his doubts about the quantum hypothesis: ''I must confess that I do not like this solution of the puzzle. Of course I have nothing to say against following out the consequences of the quantum theory—

a procedure which has already in the hands of able men led to some interesting results. But I have a difficulty in accepting it as a picture of what actually takes place."[15]

Final Years

The later years of Lord Rayleigh, from 1895 until his death in 1919, were years of honor and glory, affluence and influence. Through his marriage to Evelyn Balfour, Rayleigh had been brought close to high government circles: her uncle, the Marquess of Salisbury, had been Secretary for India in the Derby administration, and was to become Foreign Secretary under Disraeli and ultimately the successor of Disraeli as Conservative Leader and as Prime Minister. Rayleigh's brother-in-law, Arthur Balfour, later became his uncle's secretary and then, successively, a Cabinet member, Secretary for Ireland, First Lord of the Treasury, Prime Minister, First Lord of the Admiralty, and Foreign Secretary. Both Salisbury and Balfour sought Rayleigh's advice on many matters relative to scientific policies and appointments. Rayleigh is said to have persuaded Salisbury to recommend a baronetcy for George Gabriel Stokes in 1889, and the elevation of Sir William Thomson to the peerage as Baron Kelvin of Largs in 1892. Rayleigh was, however, a conservative man, and his scientific influence on the government was exercised with considerable prudence.

Rayleigh, in turn, served on many government committees, and was chairman of the committee that recommended the formation of the National Physical Laboratory. In 1909 he was appointed chairman of the Advisory Committee on Aeronautics. His interest in flying dated back to his Cavendish days. As early as 1883 he had published in *Nature* a paper on the dynamics of the soaring of birds.

In 1902, at the coronation of Edward VII, Rayleigh, Kelvin, and Huggins were the three scientists awarded the new Order of Merit. In 1904 Rayleigh was awarded the Nobel Prize in physics for his work on argon (Sir William Ramsay was awarded the Nobel Prize in chemistry the same year for his related work). Rayleigh donated the proceeds of his prize, £7000, to the Cavendish Laboratory for the construction of a new wing. In 1908 he succeeded the eighth Duke of Devonshire as Chancellor of Cambridge University (and broke somewhat with tradition: after the Public Orator had delivered a long eulogy in Latin, Rayleigh responded in English).

These committee and professional duties he performed ungrudgingly, although he preferred to remain at his physical studies in the laboratory at Terling. Here he continued to produce a steady output of publications. Between his first paper of 1869 and his last of 1919 he published 8 to 10 papers a year (a total of 446 articles, plus "The Theory of Sound") all of them interesting and useful. He spent most of his time at Terling except for the season just before Easter, when he stayed at the home of Balfour in London, attended the debates in the House of Lords, delivered his lectures at the Royal Institution, and participated on official committees. During the years his brother-in-law was Prime Minister, he stayed in London at No. 10 Downing Street. Through all this he remained unassuming; there is no evidence whatever of hauteur or condescension in his works. To him every honest, hard-working scientist was a respected equal. Even when he criticized, he tried to find mitigating circumstances. When young James Jeans wrote Lord Rayleigh that he thought the equipartition function should be corrected by a factor of 8 in Rayleigh's treatment of blackbody radiation, Rayleigh immediately corrected his "law" to the "Rayleigh-Jeans law."

Toward the revolutionary new ideas of physics, Rayleigh was somewhat aloof. In rapid succession Röntgen had discovered X-rays, Becquerel radioactivity, and J. J. Thomson the electron. These were all reasonably acceptable; in fact, J. J. Thomson had immediately extended Rayleigh scattering theory to X-ray scattering. Planck, in order to reconcile the Rayleigh treatment of blackbody radiation with the Wien treatment, introduced his quantum of action. Bohr was then able to explain the Rydberg and Balmer empirical observations of spectra in terms of stationary states. Einstein introduced relativity. Rayleigh followed all this with great interest, but said other younger workers would have to explain such matters: he was too old. In his last public address he said: "We live in times which are revolutionary in science as well as in politics. Perhaps some of those who accept 'relativity' views reducing time to merely one of the dimensions of a four-dimensional manifold, may regard the future as differing from the past no more than north differs from south. But here I am nearly out of my depth, and had better stop."[16]

Rayleigh's life, both public and private, was remarkably serene. There were no bitter struggles against adversity; his talent and ability were early recognized and never waned. He did encounter personal tragedy in the form of the premature deaths of two of his four sons, one at age six and the other at twenty-six. His eldest son, Robert (1875-1947), also became an eminent physicist. His son Arthur Charles (1878-1970) had a distinguished career in the Navy, becoming Admiral Beatty's Master of the Fleet at the Battle of

Jutland and afterward Director of Navigation at the Admiralty. Lady Rayleigh (1847-1934) was a talented artist and musician. For some twenty-five years before World War I she delighted to entertain both statesmen and men of science in weekend gatherings at Terling.

Rayleigh disliked quarrels, although he did not hesitate to express a contrary scientific view. He was very cautious in his judgment and did not like to have to give a quick opinion on anything. If he encountered an unexpected difficulty in his laboratory work he preferred to leave it and to work on something else while he thought about the difficulty for a day or so. He once confessed that he never understood someone else's experiment the first time it was explained to him. In his papers he scrupulously acknowledged assistance and sources of inspiration. He was embarrassed by some of the honors and awards he received. When at the height of his career he was asked to become President of the Royal Society he declined the offer, saying he would be just as good a president ten years later, when he might not be so good a researcher. (He was later president from 1905-1908.) When in 1914 he was awarded the Rumford Medal by the Royal Society for his work in optics, he wrote: "I am pleased that my optical work should be appreciated. It has been done perhaps more *con amore* than any other. But I hope I have not kept a good and younger man out."[17] Although his health deteriorated in early 1919, he continued to work on papers at Terling until a few days before his death on June 30, 1919.

Of Rayleigh's 446 papers in his collected works, nearly 200 concern optics; we have discussed only a small fraction of them here. By many, Rayleigh is considered to be mainly an acoustics man. His "The Theory of Sound" is still the primary reference in that field. Lindsay has given a detailed treatment of Rayleigh's impact on acoustics. He also made major contributions to hydrodynamics and to the theories of elastic solids, gas dynamics, capillarity, surface forces, and practically every subdiscipline of classical physics. His interests in physics were universal. In each field he left order where there had been disorder. He was the last of the great "sealing-wax and string" individual researchers whose interests spanned all of physics.

Springs of Creativity

In the mind of the average American, the most admirable formula for success is to start with little or nothing except a determination to make good, to fight hard (but fairly) against adversity, to overcome obstacles, and finally to achieve wealth, material comforts, and fame by dint of one's own labor and effort. Variants on this theme were recounted in the many popular success novels by Horatio Alger; one also thinks of Abraham Lincoln, born in a humble log cabin, working his way through school and rising to become President. Or Andrew Carnegie, the penniless young immigrant from Scotland who became a prosperous industrialist. Or Henry Ford, a bicycle repairman with a vision of a technological future. Or Thomas Edison, or George Eastman. Since most people are common people, there is something comforting and noble about achieving success by one's own labors, and rising above the common herd.

There is of course another kind of success: a few people start out rich and powerful and become even richer and more powerful. One can think of ruling families, such as Roosevelts or Rockefellers or Tafts, but somehow this route to success seems less admirable. We readily concede such slogans as "nothing succeeds like success" in areas such as business or politics; but in the realms of intellectual achievement, such as science or the fine arts, a rich man's son is seldom found among the greats. There is too little incentive among the rich to achieve further; it is necessity that is the mother of invention. One can think of Mendelssohn as a great composer who was also comfortably rich, or Prince Louis de Broglie as a rich physicist, but ordinarily man's spirit needs a battle with adversity in order to rise to higher heights.

Lord Rayleigh, the subject of our present discussion, is one of those rare exceptions. He was born into a wealthy family and lived a serene and comfortable life. He never had any need to work or to sweat; he could have occupied his life with social functions, business, or politics. But instead he chose to become a scientist—a very great scientist, as it turned out—principally because he enjoyed it: he found scientific endeavor intellectually satisfying. He had no objection to being wealthy—he recognized that many problems were simpler if one were rich—but he had no innate lust for power or more wealth as an aim for endeavor. He was quite content to apply his intellectual talents to scientific goals. Rayleigh possessed a very fortunate combination of natural curiosity, innate ability, sound technical training, and family wealth.

He was also lucky to be in the right place at the right time: for example, in his studies of electricity he was working in that period immediately following the experimental work of Faraday, the theoretical studies of Maxwell, and the practical inventions of Samuel F. B. Morse, Alexander Graham Bell, and Thomas Edison.

Of course there were other talented scientists of the British school of physics who were just as well trained and competent as Rayleigh—Stokes, Maxwell, or Kelvin, for example—but the researches of these scientists were largely tied to their teaching and academic activities.

Being comfortably wealthy made Rayleigh comfortably serene about material matters. William Thomson (Lord Kelvin) had become a prosperous electrical engineer by industry and hard work and by a careful eye to money matters. Although Kelvin published prodigiously on a wide variety of scientific topics, he was also very quick to patent and protect his rights on any practical inventions. Kelvin held the basic patent on the gyro-compass used on all of the modern ocean liners of his day, and he kept careful notes on the arrival and departure of every vessel (as reported in the London papers) to be sure his royalties were properly paid. Rayleigh, on the other hand, was completely indifferent to such matters. He made many practical improvements to the telephone, for example, and he also first developed the basic theory of parametric amplifiers, but he simply published his results and made no efforts to patent his ideas.

In matters of physics and scientific priority Rayleigh was also calm and gentlemanly. Kelvin could be irascible in "putting down" his fellow scientists; Rayleigh generally refrained from such tactics. In 1900 Samuel Pierpont Langley delivered a lecture at the Royal Institution on the possibilities of flight by manned aircraft. At the end of the lecture Kelvin strode to the blackboard to demolish the arguments of Langley and demonstrate that manned flight by a vehicle heavier than air would be physically impossible. Rayleigh, however, was more restrained, and opined that it was probably rather a matter of time and money.

Rayleigh was generous in acknowledging contributions of others. Perhaps the most dramatic example of this generosity occurred in 1891. In an article in the *Proceedings of the Royal Society* of June 1890 Rayleigh had published some results of experiments on the surface tension of pure and contaminated water.[18] A few months later he received a long letter in German from Miss Agnes Pockels. Her father and her brother were physicists, and she too was deeply interested in surface forces, even though there was at that time no mechanism for the formal university training of women. She had read Rayleigh's account of his experiments and wanted to tell him of some results she had already observed in a detailed series of experiments she had performed in the kitchen sink. She had divided the water in the sink into two areas, and had devised a means of skimming the surface of contaminants and of then measuring the surface forces. Rayleigh had the letter translated and saw at once that she had made several fundamental advances to the understanding of the physics involved, even beyond his previous paper. He then published her letter in Nature in 1891, with an introduction by Rayleigh commenting on the importance of her work.[19] This public recognition by the leading British scientist of the time (Rayleigh was at that time the Secretary of the Royal Society) brought instant recognition and fame to Agnes Pockels. She was subsequently even elected to the Hanover Academy of Sciences. (The American researcher Irving Langmuir adopted essentially her scheme for measuring surface forces and his subsequent efforts in surface physics won him a Nobel Prize in 1932. A detailed account of Agnes Pockels's contributions to surface chemistry has been published.)[20]

In his published papers Rayleigh often mentioned thoughts that occurred to him but that he did not pursue. He might remark as an aside that it would be interesting to investigate the effect of higher temperature, or pressure (or some similar parameter), on the phenomenon under consideration, but that he did not have the apparatus to pursue this at the moment. Remarks such as this proved to be gold mines for graduate students in physics and engineering. For years many graduate students' theses began with the sentence, "in 1887 (or some similar date from 1885 to 1915), Lord Rayleigh suggested that. . . ." and then proceeded to elaborate on the point suggested by Rayleigh. As an example of this sort of prescience by Rayleigh, we can observe his monumental paper of 1895 on argon (Paper 214, for which Rayleigh received the Nobel Prize in physics in 1904). After describing in detail the inertness of this noble gas, argon, to aqua regia, caustic soda, sodium peroxide, and almost every conceivable reagent, Rayleigh remarked: "It will be interesting to see if fluorine also is without action, but for the present that experiment must be postponed, on account of difficulties of manipulation."[21] For many years it was assumed that the noble gases could not be made to react, but in the middle 1960s a team of researchers at the Argonne National Laboratory found that fluorine reacted with xenon and argon to form hexafluorides (and at remarkably ordinary temperature and pressure). This astonishing result was almost anticipated in 1895 by Rayleigh.

In his lifetime Rayleigh won almost every honor to which a scientist could aspire: F.R.S., the Order of Merit, the Nobel Prize, President of the Royal Society. But he had not sought honors; the honors had sought him. When he retired as President of the Royal Society he wrote that if he had wanted a life of administration and functions he would never have given attention to science at all. When he received the Order of Merit he remarked that "the only merit of which he personally was conscious was that of having pleased himself by his studies, and any results that may have been due to his researches were owing to the fact that it had been a pleasure to him to become a physicist."[22]

A Short Rayleigh Bibliography

The only major work by Rayleigh that is not included in the *Scientific Papers* is his book *The Theory of Sound* (London, Vol. 1, 1877; Vol. 2, 1878. Second ed., London, Vol. 1, 1892; Vol. 2, 1896. First American ed., two volumes bound as one, Dover, New York, 1945). The Dover edition contains a historical introduction by R. Bruce Lindsay on the life of Rayleigh and a discussion of his work relating to acoustics.

Lindsay has also written a brief biography and source book: *Men of Physics: Lord Rayleigh — The Man and his Work* (Oxford and New York: Pergamon Press, 252 pp 1970), which contains selections from twenty-three of Rayleigh's papers.

Accounts of his activities as Cavendish Professor of Experimental Physics (1879-1885) are found in "A History of the Cavendish Laboratory, 1871-1910" (London: Longmans Green, 1910), in which R. T. Glazebrook wrote the chapter on the Rayleigh period. This period is summarized in "The Cavendish Laboratory" by Alexander Wood (Cambridge: Cambridge University Press, 1946). An interesting discussion of the archives of the Cavendish Laboratory is given by D. de Sola Price in Notes and Records of the Royal Society (London) 10 (1953), p. 142.

A popular account of the work by Rayleigh, with emphasis on his research leading to the discovery of argon, is given by Sir Oliver Lodge, *National Review* 32 (1898), p. 89. A more recent detailed discussion of the discovery of argon is the chapter of E. N. Hiebert in H. H. Hyman's "Noble-Gas Compounds" (Chicago: Univ. of Chicago Press, 1963). There is a chapter on Rayleigh in *Nobel Prize Winners in Physics, 1901-1950* by N. H. Heathcote (New York: H. Schuman, 1953).

Shortly after Rayleigh's death in 1919, there were several appraisals of his work in the various obituary notices. The most detailed is the fifty-page "Obituary Notice of Lord Rayleigh" by Sir Arthur Schuster, *Proceedings of the Royal Society* A98 (1921). Others include J. J. Thomson, *Nature* 103 (1919), p. 365; R. T. Glazebrook, *Nature* 103 (1919), p. 366; and Horace Lamb, *Nature* 103 (1919),

p. 368. Lamb also wrote a summary of Rayleigh's contributions to mathematics in *Proceedings of the London Mathematical Society* 20 (1922), p. xliii.

Considerable correspondence to and from Rayleigh is included in the Sylvanus Thompson *Life of Lord Kelvin* (London: Macmillan, 1910). *The Recollections and Reflections* of J. J. Thomson (London: G. Bell and Sons, 1936), contains many allusions to Rayleigh and his work.

Charles H. Giles has written in detail of Rayleigh's contributions to surface physics and his interaction with Agnes Pockels in *Chemical Industry* (London) *1971,* p. 42; *1971,* p. 324 and *1979,* p. 469.

The book by his son, Robert John Strutt, *Life of John William Strutt, 3rd Baron Rayleigh* (London: Edward Arnold and Co., 1924), is the most detailed biography of Rayleigh, particularly with respect to his personality and family life. This volume has been reprinted in an expanded version by the University of Wisconsin Press (1968).

Notes

1. Arthur Schuster, "Obituary Notice of Lord Rayleigh," *Proceedings of the Royal Society of London* A 98 (1921), pp. l-li.

2. R. B. Lindsay, Introduction to Rayleigh, *The Theory of Sound* (New York: Dover Publications, 1945).

3. Lord Rayleigh, *The Theory of Sound.*

4. Lord Rayleigh, *Scientific Papers* (Cambridge: Cambridge University Press, 1899-1920), 6 vols. Reprinted in 3 vols. (New York: Dover, 1964), Vol. I, p. 415.

5. Lord Rayleigh, *Scientific Papers,* Vol. I, p. 518.

6. Lord Rayleigh (R.J.S.), *Life of John William Strutt, Third Baron Rayleigh* (London: Arnold, 1924), p. 49.

7. J. N. Howard, 'Eleanor Mildred Sidgwick and the Rayleighs,' *Applied Optics* 3 (1964), pp. 1120-1122.

8. *Philosophical Transactions of the Royal Society* 174 (1883), p. 707.

9. J. J. Thomson, "Obituary Notice of Lord Rayleigh," *Nature* 103 (1919), p. 365.

10. Lord Rayleigh, *Scientific Papers,* Vol. IV, pp. 1, 2.

11. E. N. Hiebert in *Noble-Gas Compounds* by H. H. Hyman (Chicago: University of Chicago Press, 1963).

12. Lord Rayleigh, *Life of John William Strutt,* pp. 203, 204.

13. Ibid., p. 222.

14. Ibid., p. 214.

15. Lord Rayleigh, *Scientific Papers,* Vol. VI, p. 45.

16. Ibid., p. 653.

17. Lord Rayleigh, *Life of John William Strutt,* p. 333.

18. Lord Rayleigh, *Scientific Papers,* Vol. IV, p. 363.

19. A. Pockels, *Nature* 43 (1891), p. 437.

20. Charles H. Giles, "Pioneers of Surface Physics," *Chemical Industry,* 1971, pp. 42, 324; 1979, p. 469.

21. Lord Rayleigh, *Scientific Papers,* Vol. IV, pp. 176-179.

22. Lord Rayleigh, *Life of John William Strutt,* p. 312.

Chapter 7

Elmer Sperry and Adrian Leverkühn: A Comparison of Creative Styles

Thomas P. Hughes

To test the hypothesis that the study of creativity need not be restricted by disciplinary bounds, this essay compares Elmer Sperry (1860-1930), a hard-nosed American inventor known for his probity and common sense, and Adrian Leverkühn (1885-1940), a fictional German composer driven to insanity by syphilis. The comparison is facilitated by the availability of a detailed biography of Sperry[1] and by Thomas Mann's masterful novel, *Doctor Faustus,* which is about Leverkühn and creativity.[2]

Elsewhere I have attempted a disciplinary approach to the understanding of creativity by drawing generalizations from the case histories of several inventors other than Sperry.[3] In this essay, the effort is to gain insight by an unorthodox venture. Generalizations about creativity, formulated after my study of Sperry's inventive life, are tested by ascertaining their relevance to the life of the fictional composer, Leverkühn. Because Mann expressed his own views about creativity in his account of Leverkühn's, the comparison, in fact, is made between generalizations drawn from Sperry's life and Mann's insights into creativity based on his experience as a writer and his deep knowledge of creativity as found in classic works—especially German—of literature, philosophy, and musical composition. While writing *Dr. Faustus,* Mann was not only influenced by the work of Arnold Schönberg, but he had many discussions

I am indebted to Professor I. B. Holley, Jr. of Duke University for comments and suggestions for this essay.

Plate 1. Sperry holding the John Fritz medal, awarded in 1926 by the leading engineering societies of America.

as well about music with Theodor Adorno, the philosopher and music critic.[4]

Since Mann chose to offer his version of the Faust myth in his account of Leverkühn, I consider the relevance of the myth to Sperry's creativity. This is not as unconventional as it may first appear because a number of authors have used the myth as a general mode of explaining creativity, even among scientists, inventors, and engineers.[5] Goethe's version of the Faust myth, perhaps the most widely known and used, deeply influenced Mann, so this essay makes use of it directly, not always indirectly through Mann's account of Leverkühn.

Elmer Sperry was born on a small farm a few miles from the town of Cortland, New York. His mother, a school teacher, died giving him birth; his father worked for the local wagon works; his grandparents raised him on their farm until they moved into the town. He attended the local high school that was part of a normal school, or teachers' college. In 1880, on Christmas Eve, he astounded the citizenry by lighting the local Baptist Church with an arc light generator of his own design. These were the days of Edison: young men with inventive genius were nurtured by older men with money to invest; so local capitalists sent the young, upright, and achieving Sperry to make a fortune from his inventions in bustling Chicago. With the help of Chicago Baptists, who were also capitalists, he established at the age of twenty-one the Sperry Electric Light, Motor, and Car Brake Company. His arc lighting system was sold throughout the Midwest, but larger manufacturers stifled the enterprise, and Sperry got out of business management and committed himself to full-time invention. This he did by establishing a research and development company with a staff of one — Elmer Sperry. He proceeded to establish a number of companies based upon his patents and others' cash. Among successful companies based upon his patents were the Sperry Electric Mining Machine Company and Sperry Electric Railway Company. In 1907 he invented his first gyroscopic device, followed shortly by a series of applications. In 1910 he established the Sperry Gyroscope Company to develop and manufacture his gyrocompasses, ship stabilizer, and, later, his airplane stabilizer and automatic ship's pilot. He was fifty when he abandoned his resolve to avoid entanglement with companies because of his patents. He remained president and general manager of the Sperry Gyroscope Company until shortly before his death. As an old man he received many honors, including membership in the National Academy of Sciences, a rare distinction for an engineer and inventor; the presidency of the American Society of Mechanical Engineers; and the much-coveted John Fritz Medal awarded by the engineering societies. He was especially proud of his more than three hundred patented inventions.

Adrian Leverkühn was born on a more prosperous farm than Sperry and in East Germany rather than western New York. His parents sent him to neighboring Kaisersaschern to study music under the local choirmaster, Wendell Kretschmar, who not only taught him composition but instilled in him a thirst for philosophy, literature, and the arts. Kretschmar had known these in the universities and large German cities. Believing himself interested in advanced study in theology, Leverkühn studied the subject at the University of Halle, but the vulgar superstitions of his professor of theology changed his mind. Leverkühn then turned to his first love, composition, and pursued his interest as a student, first in Leipzig and then among the artists and their bourgeois patrons in Munich. In 1912, while working on an opera, "*Love's Labour's Lost*," in the Italian town of Palestrina, he encountered the devil. Mann leaves us to decide if the episode were a hallucination brought on by uncured syphilis contracted years earlier and untreated. With demonic creative powers, Leverkühn displayed impressive technical finesse and invented a radical atonal system. Oppressed by bourgeois conservatism in artistic matters, he deserted Munich and took quarters in a peasant farmhouse on the lovely Bavarian countryside. There he experienced the tragedy of Nepomuk, his strikingly beautiful five-year-old nephew who died in agony of cerebrospinal meningitis. Having vowed to the devil to purge himself of feelings of love, Leverkühn broke the pact because of his emotional reaction to the death of the child for whom he had felt great affection. Not long after, Leverkühn, his syphilis now in the late stage, lost his mind, the traumatic onslaught of mental illness coming with his collapse as he prepared to play his last and most radical composition, "The Lamentation of Dr. Faustus."

Leverkühn showed no interest in the technological transformation taking place around him in Germany, and Sperry's musical interest was limited to his wife's piano playing. They shared, nonetheless, many other experiences and attitudes. Sperry, we recall, was born on a farm. In early winter, even today, the site has a bleak aspect. For young Sperry, farm life was hard and unrewarding. There were few machines to save exhausting labor and few diversions for the long, cold, winter evenings. Nature, then, for him was hostile. More recent generations, backpacking among scenic splendors, find it difficult, if not impossible, to comprehend Sperry's attitude to the natural world. After moving to Cortland, he found highly stimulating the social life centered on the Baptist church and the intellectual opportunities provided by the Normal School and the library of the Young Mens' Christian Association. After leaving Cortland for Chicago and later Cleveland, Ohio, and Brooklyn, New York, he never evinced the slightest desire to return to the land or even to Cortland.

The manmade world proved far more supportive of Sperry than the natural one. He saw technology, the means of making a new world, as a way of eliminating backbreaking labor, excessive heat, freezing cold, and the other discomforts and hardships he associated with hostile nature. To a young man in late nineteenth-century America, technological invention was socially desirable and inventors heroes. It is not surprising that young Sperry rushed to the YMCA library in Cortland to read the latest issue of the *Patent Office Gazette* to learn who was inventing what. Nor is it surprising that, after visiting the celebration of technology and industry held in

Philadelphia in 1876, he decided to become an inventor and to create a new world.

Mann places young Leverkühn on the countryside, too, where he, like Sperry, reacted against it. Leverkühn, however, reacted not against its physical demands, but against the traditions and oppressive conservatism of rural culture in Germany. The beliefs and attitudes he encountered were medieval. While Sperry reacted by aspiring to make a new physical world, Leverkühn decided to leave the countryside to take part in creating a fresh culture, the kind of urban intellectual and social life suggested to him by his music teacher, Kretschmar. Leverkühn wanted a pluralistic, pliable environment with which he could interact spiritually and intellectually, making his mark upon it through such cultural creations as literature and music.

Dissatisfied with their situations, Sperry and Leverkühn both had alternatives. Ultimately they could have fantasized other places and thereby escaped; or they could have invented their living spaces, one a physical, the other a spiritual. They could have traveled physically and discovered other worlds; choosing the last alternative, they took the approach we call creative. Sperry invented machines and processes among which he felt at home, and Leverkühn invented a pure and orderly space filled with music.

What inspires creative persons like Sperry and Leverkühn to make new worlds? Many persons simply accept the world in which they find themselves. They do not imagine that other worlds can be made to exist for them. One source of inspiration for the creators is knowledge that other worlds exist and are being created. Sperry knew that a world outside the natural one of Cortland could be made because the technical magazines and books he read and the lecturers he heard told him about the world of artifacts that Americans were building. There was an evolving world populated by machines and processes, and he wanted to be in it and make some of it. This his letters and the recollections of those who knew him make clear.

For the young Leverkühn, the music teacher, Kretschmar, painted a picture of the culture of Leipzig, Dresden, and Munich. Mann tells us that Kretschmar conceived of culture as a single fabric woven by musicians, writers, painters, and others of creative genius. Leverkühn, inspired by this vision, longed to leave his family farm and the earthy sensuousness and unthinking acceptance of the natural order. He wanted to move to the manmade cities, the site of painting, sculpting, composing, building, and creative thinking.

Not only must the Sperrys and Leverkühns envisage themselves creating new worlds, but they must also find support from the old while creating the new. Often, therefore, they must find support from that which they would replace. For this reason, many creative persons wither for lack of nourishment. Both Sperry and Leverkühn, however, found modes for survival. They were able to draw from the old and still distance themselves from it. The distancing made less obvious their threat to the established order and also freed them from the close constraints that support often entails.

It was easier for Leverkühn than for Sperry. Mann grew up in a bourgeois society that tolerated second-generation wealth opting for Bohemia. Mann and his brother, Heinrich, stemmed from a Lübeck burgher family grown wealthy in trade. Supported by unearned income and encouraged by their mother, both left Lübeck to live as writers.[6] Mann, in his partly autobiographical novel about Leverkühn, never raises the question of how the composer supported himself as he labored for years on unpopular, radical compositions. Resigned fathers and culture-nurturing Wilhelmian mothers probably imposed fewer fetters upon creative expression than our own public foundations for funding the arts.

In distancing themselves from constraining organizational and social relationships, Sperry and Leverkühn showed the instincts of the radical creator. Sperry learned that organizations have a momentum generated by vested interests and that the inventor employed by them is constrained along the lines projected by organizational inertia. When he tried briefly to manage his first company, he found that routine stifled imagination. Sperry said he preferred inventions that changed existing situations ninety-five percent rather than those that improved them by five. Since the radical, ninety-five-percent type of inventions disquiet institutions that nurture them, this attitude is not well received by organizations settled in their ways. Similarly, Leverkühn left Munich, preferring isolation on the Bavarian countryside, after finding his circle of friends oppressively conventional in their attitudes toward music and art. Knowing this from first-hand experience, Mann has a masterful section in *Doctor Faustus* describing the Munich bourgeoisie that imposed its values and tastes on the arts and letters.[7]

Sperry knew that in foregoing organizational attachments, he was sacrificing security to obtain freedom. On several occasions, large corporations, General Electric among them, offered him generous terms to join their engineering and development staffs, but he chose the risky way of the independent inventor. Without an institutional base, Sperry and his family moved from Chicago to Cleveland, to Brooklyn, seeking those rare situations and places where a confluence of circumstances was appropriate for the development of his inventions. Leverkühn, too, was the outsider. Serenus Zeitbloom, his closest friend, tells us that this was a salient characteristic. As a theology student at Leipzig, he did not enter wholeheartedly into student life. Students treated the university years as a brief interval of carefree exploration of life and ideas before the inevitable day when they had to settle down to a bourgeois existence; Leverkühn, in contrast, embraced exploration and challenge of convention as an enduring way of life.

Refusing to accept the world in which they found themselves, believing that another could be created, distancing themselves from persons and organizations that might constrain their freedom to create, Sperry and Leverkühn also faced the problem of defining their creative aspirations. Precisely what kinds of problems did they choose and try to solve through invention and composition? Having arrived in Munich, where men and women were making a world of music, or in Chicago, where they were constructing a material one, on what kind of musical and technological problems did Sperry and Leverkühn concentrate their energies? Both Leverkühn and Sperry— and this may be true of most creative people—chose problems that, when solved, brought a new order. Leverkühn had found the countryside irrational and insensate to his aspirations, and then he discovered conventional music unacceptable. Sperry had found nature unpredictable and harsh in its effects, and then he found machines and processes imperfect. After moving to a manmade world, they both discovered that by their standards it was not rightly made or ordered.

Before considering their order-giving creations in some detail, we should seek the source of their ideals, or visions, of order that permitted them to identify disorder. If the concept of perfection is substituted for order, then a general explanation can be proffered. Since "order" can be defined as "a condition in which each thing is properly disposed with reference to other things and to its purpose," the equating of order with perfection is reasonable.

Both in the case of the composer and of the inventor, the visions of order were inspired, or at least reinforced, by the Judeo-Christian tradition from which they stemmed and which they knew intimately. Sperry tells us that Sundays in Cortland were filled with Sunday school, eleven-o'clock services, hymn singing for the imprisoned, sick, and elderly, and prayer meetings. Leverkühn studied theology at the university. Sperry and Leverkühn, then, had instilled in them a concept of the order and harmony of God's law and His heavenly realm. Christianity insisted that the world was disorderly and imperfect, and provided a vision of order and perfection permitting this judgment.

The history of science and technology provides many instances of the discoverers of natural law and the makers of the technological, or artificial, world assuming that there is a discoverable order in God's creations and an order imposable by men inspired by a God-given creative drive. In the Middle Ages, churchmen reminded Europeans that God gave them dominion over the earth and that they were destined to order it, insofar as possible, in accord with a vision of the perfection of the far universe where God's law prevailed.[8] The seven mechanical arts, according to medieval theologian Hugh of St. Victor, were technological activities with which men and women could invent and construct a man-made world more hospitable than the God-forsaken one they had inherited after the expulsion from Eden. Technology and invention had been unneeded there.[9] Copernicus used an elaborate train of epicycles and eccentrics to retain the perfection of circular motion for the heavenly bodies.[10] Orators and theologians told early nineteenth-century Americans that the harmony and grandeur of God's creation should be the model for the technological world they were building in the wilderness.[11] Einstein's assertion that God does not play dice with the world is a deep commitment to the order of natural law.[12] The essence of Goethe's Faust lies in the ultimate commitment of Faust to God-like creation of a physical world.[13]

Sperry and Leverkühn might have been satisfied with a part of the Christian equation: there is a perfection in God's law, the heavenly spheres, and heaven itself. They could then have retreated from the everyday world, nurtured a vision, and prepared for the divine perfection experienced by the saved soul. Like so many others of their culture, however, they were influenced by the other part of the equation, too: the world is redeemable, at least up to a point short of perfect order. They were willing to live with the tension, therefore, between the real and the ideal—until they could resolve it by invention. They had, in short, a deep discontent with the way things were and a Utopian vision of how they might be. This, too, is a salient characteristic of the creative person, inventor or composer.

The belief that the earthly realm can be brought to approximate the heavenly, or ideal, has often expressed itself in Utopian visions.[14] When Sperry embarked upon his inventive career, visions of unending progress toward an ideal world stimulated by, and involving, technology spread in the West. Sperry did not articulate visions of

Utopia, but he shared the belief widely held among Americans that technology and progress were synonymous. He also believed that his creations fed the stream of progress. Leverkühn did not share this faith in technology and progress, but he shared the Faustian vision portrayed by Goethe of the possibility of mortals achieving fulfillment of earthly desires through demonic powers. Among the desires Mephistopheles satisfied for Faust was that of knowing the perfect beauty of Helen of Troy.[15]

Neither Sperry nor Leverkühn aspired to create Utopias, but both did want to perfect a small part of the world. Sperry saw imperfection wherever he found inefficiency in things mechanical and deviation in things moving from the straight and narrow. He had a vision of the ideal machine that performed without friction, and a vision of the ideal vehicle that moved perfectly on course. Leverkühn envisaged a composition that was a rational system without one note or component not perfectly fulfilling its function within the system.[16]

Sperry's and Leverkühn's visions of order imply control. George Orwell has made clear the control implicit in many late nineteenth- and early twentieth-century Utopias. The Faustian legends, including Mann's, define a devil possessing impressive, even if ultimately limited, control of material circumstances and spiritual events on earth. To better understand Sperry's and Leverkühn's creativity, we should consider the order and control embodied in their inventions and compositions.

Sperry harnessed through controls, mostly feedback. Contemporary magazine articles and short biographical sketches portrayed him as an inventor of a bewildering variety of machines, processes, and technology. His admirers and the public relations people at his company said that he invented arc lights, generators, electric streetcars, automobiles, searchlights, gyrostabilizers, and gyrocompasses. After reading his 350 patents, I discovered that the lights, generators, streetcars, automobiles, and searchlights were not the inventions but, to use his metaphor, "brutes" needing control. His inventions were the controls for these things. For the arc light, he invented an automatic carbon feed; for the generator, an automatic output control; for the streetcar, the motorman's control; for an electric automobile, a speed control; and for the searchlight, an automatic focus. As a result, all functioned more efficiently. The automatic stabilizers kept level the airplanes and giant ships. His controls were feedback controls masterfully articulated decades before Norbert Wiener and others explicated and publicized the science of cybernetics. For feedback controls, he needed reliable references against which to measure errors, and his gyrocompass has proven to be one of the master references of modern technology, reliable anywhere on earth, in the air, and in space.

The creative drive of the fictional composer is notably similar to that of the inventor's. Leverkühn revealed his aspirations in discussing his first opera, *Love's Labour's Lost*. He had studied theology for two years at Halle, turned to his first love, music, and mastered the craft of composition in Leipzig under the tutelage of his boyhood teacher, Kretschmar. By the age of twenty-five, he had embarked on a life of musical composition. He told his only close friend, Zeitbloom, that "we need a system-master, a teacher of the objective and organization with enough genius to unite the old-established, the archaic, with the revolutionary."[17] We should carefully note Leverkühn's emphasis upon system and organization, and his desire to bring the revolutionary out of the archaic.

Mann anticipates Leverkühn's melancholy fate. The young composer tells his friend that a dialectical relationship exists between freedom and system. Freedom releases the productive powers, but then "some fine day" freedom "despairs of the possibility of being creative out of herself and seeks shelter and security in the objective." Freedom eventually realizes itself "in constraint, fulfills herself in the subordination to law, rule, coercion, system. . . ."[18] Leverkühn believes that he will freely create a music system and then forego his freedom in submission to his own creation. He anticipates that he will be ordered by the order he creates. We should ask, will he then be creative?

The musical system Leverkühn creates is the twelve tone. He outlined its character. The song "O lieb Mädel" in a Brentano cycle stimulated his invention of a fundamental figure. With it he determined interchangeable intervals and controlled the five notes (B, E, A, E, and E-flat) as well as the horizontal melody and the vertical harmony. "Not one [note] might appear which did not fulfill its function in the whole structure," Leverkühn insisted. There would no longer be a free note. The admiring Zeitbloom observed that composition would involve rational organization "through and through" and that the composer would gain an extraordinary "unity and congruity, a sort of astronomical regularity."[19] We should note again the reference by Leverkühn to system.

The day Leverkühn realized that he had, as anticipated, foregone his freedom, came as he sojourned in the picturesque hillside Italian village of Palestrina. Mann reminds us that Dante mentioned the village in the twenty-seventh canto of the *Inferno*. In Palestrina, the devil appeared to Leverkühn and told him that he had lost his soul years earlier in Leipzig. No longer suppressing irrational drives, Leverkühn there had visited a prostitute, Esmeralda. This was an act of surpassing symbolic importance because, until that incident, the composer believed he could live and create by pure reason and intellect. Through the experience with the prostitute, he not only symbolically acknowledged and gave in to irrational forces, but, more specifically, he contracted syphilis. Irrational forces at the disposal of the devil, not reason, would henceforth be the engine of Leverkühn's creativity; the syphilis, having reached an advanced state in Palestrina, can be taken, if the reader is so disposed, as an explanation for the Mephistophelian apparition.

For the twenty-four years following his intimacy with Esmeralda, demonic powers possessed the composer. Energies arising in Leverkühn brought him to compose "without a thought." The conventions of bourgeois music no longer constrained him. The devil explained to Leverkühn that "unparalysed by thought or by the mortal domination of reason" he has known and would know "shining, sparkling, vainglorious unreflectiveness." His inspiration caused shudders, tears, and raptures that did not come from God "who leaves to the understanding too much to do."[20] The devil added a final clause: Leverkühn could not know love. He was unconcerned, for years earlier he had renounced love for interest; the devil reminded him that the love of which the devil spoke was the love of humans. Leverkühn remained unimpressed and unconcerned.

Mann's insights into creativity lie embedded in Leverkühn's encounter with the devil at Palestrina. The insights are to be found on several levels. Mann obviously draws on his knowledge of Freudian psychology. Leverkühn unleashed the demonic and irrational powers of his Id through the episode of intercourse with the prostitute. This act released Leverkühn from bourgeois moral restraints. The energies so released, however, were unformed until Leverkühn imposed the method of composition he invented in the twelve-tone system. Leverkühn, we recall, longed for a system master. Driven by the libidinous energy, Leverkühn was satisfied to impose systematically the form of the twelve-tone system in order to compose. He did not realize that he had thereby lost his freedom and thus the power to create despite retaining his ability to compose. Leverkühn expected to sacrifice freedom to order, but he did not realize that this meant the loss of creativity. To understand his paradox, we must turn to Goethe's Faust—as Mann did—but first we return to Sperry.

And what about the engineer and inventor, Sperry? He made no pacts with the devil; I know of no Esmeraldas. The devil would not have been able to delude him about creativity as the devil deluded Leverkühn. If the devil had told Sperry that he would be unparalyzed by thought and know "shining, sparkling, vainglorious, unreflective" inspiration, Sperry would have known that the devil was offering excitement, but not creativity. Sperry created order and systems, but he had no illusion that he would master a method for creating them. He caught the essence of his own wisdom in a talk made late in his life:

Think as I may, I cannot discover any time in which I have felt in the course of my work that I was performing any of the acts usually attributed to the inventor. So far as I can see, I have come up against situations that seemed to me to call for assistance. I was not usually at all sure that I could aid in improving the state of affairs in any way, but was fascinated by the challenge. So I would study the matter over; I would have my assistants bring before me everything that had been published about it, including the patent literature dealing with attempts to better the situation. When I had the facts before me I simply did the obvious thing. I tried to discern the weakest point and strengthen it; often this involved alterations with many ramifications which immediately revealed the scope of the entire project. Almost never have I hit upon the right solution at first. I have brought up in my imagination one remedy after another and must confess that I have many times rejected them all not yet perceiving the one that looked simple, practical, and hard-headed. Sometimes it is days or even months later that I am brought face to face with something that suggests the simple solution that I am looking for. Then I go back and say to myself, now I am prepared to take the step. It is perfectly obvious that this is the way to do it and that the other ways all have their objections.[21]

Sperry offers to create technological systems, but no method, no system of creation; he says, "I have brought up in my imagination one remedy after another." In this we find his experience, and the wisdom drawn from it.

Goethe, I believe, would have recognized Sperry's wisdom even though Sperry's expression of it was unnuanced. Goethe also saw the paradox of creativity that Leverkühn did not. On the other hand, Leverkühn's creator, Mann, did. First Goethe's insight and, then, Mann's. Goethe in his *Faust* does not focus upon unleashing subconscious drives, but on hubris, or excessive pride. Today we might define it as a confusing of the earthly and the ideal, of man and God. Pride, however, is not the essence of Faust's pact with Mephistopheles; nor release of libidinal energy Leverkühn's undoing as a creative person.

In his pact with the devil, Goethe's Faust says to Mephistopheles:

If ever I lie down upon a bed of ease, let that be my final end! If you can cozen me with lies into a self-complacency, Or can beguile with pleasures you devise, Let that day be the last for me! This bet I offer!

He continues:

If I to any moment say: Linger on! You are so fair Put me in fetters straight-away, Then I can die for all I care![22]

Mephistopheles showed Faust pleasures corporeal, aesthetic, and intellectual without Faust's asking the moment to linger, until—and this is grist for the mill of the historian interested in technology—Faust became involved in land reclamation. This was his worldly pleasure of surpassing joy. Land reclamation is Godlike creation. Aided by the devil, Faust pushed back the water, established the land, and populated it with people who would endlessly strive to hold back the surrounding water and to live as a community of free persons. In this act, remarkably similar to *Genesis*, Faust aspired to the role of God but this pride was not his downfall. He lost the wager only when he asked that the moment linger. To ask the creative moment to linger was not only to lose the wager but to demand the impossible.

In asking the moment to linger, Faust was asking that the joy of creation be prolonged. Prolonging creating by repetition, systematically creating, and using a method to create, all are contradictions. The creative act is unique. After creation there is critical revision and systematization of the act. Even a dictionary definition makes this clear: "create—to cause to come into being, as something unique that would not naturally evolve or that is not made by ordinary process." Goethe's Faust nearly lost his soul for forgetting this; Mann's Leverkühn never knew this. He sought a method, a system of creation.

In *Faust* we encounter Goethe's belief that life—in contradistinction to death—is ceaseless striving. Mann also insisted that Goethe's Faust was no voluptuary, but an intellectual who recognized only one kind of slavery—inertia, or sloth. We should also recall that Dante, a seminal western conceptualizer of the devil and hell, describes the dwelling place of the devil as a cold, still, silent realm where activity is frozen. Mann, Goethe—and Sperry—recognized that life and creativity are Heraclitean. Leverkühn mistakenly believed that he, a mere mortal, could grasp an abiding principle or system according to which change and creativity take place. This would be the essence of pride.

We must turn to the final condition that the devil laid upon

Leverkühn: that he should not know human love. How does this fit into Mann's complex story of creativity? In *Doctor Faustus* and elsewhere in Mann's writing, he tells of the essential tension in his and others' creative lives.[23] The creative tension, he believes, can be sustained only by irony and love, the first for the short run, the second for the long run. Irony, we should recall, stresses the paradoxical nature of reality or the contrast between the real and the ideal. Mann believes love makes possible humans sustaining their ideals in the face of reality. Creativity is an act that brings the real nearer the ideal, at least for a time. To put it in terms that Sperry would have appreciated, irony and love make possible living with unsolved problems until imagination suggests the solution. The solution extinguishes the old problem and brings new ones, so the creative person knows no end to the tension and, thus, the opportunity for creation. "If ever I lie down upon a bed of ease, then let that be my final end!"

The lives of the inventor, the musician—and Goethe's scholar— suggest that the search for a method of creativity is destined to fail. The belief of some university and research laboratory administrators that an environment can be designed to eliminate the risks, the failures, the unpredictableness, and the elusiveness of creativity, is also mistaken. A far more realistic endeavor would be to foster an environment in which restless souls like Sperry and Leverkühn would be exposed to never-ending change and encouraged in their belief that from the chaos an order of their own design might be imposed—if only for the moment.

Notes

1. Thomas Parke Hughes, *Elmer Sperry: Inventor and Engineer* (Baltimore, Maryland: Johns Hopkins University Press, 1971).

2. Thomas Mann, *Doctor Faustus: The Life of the German Composer Adrian Leverkühn as Told by a Friend.* Translated from the German by H. T. Lowe-Porter (New York, N.Y.: Vintage, 1971). Originally published by Alfred A. Knopf, Inc. in 1948.

3. Thomas P. Hughes, "Inventors: The Problems They Choose, the Ideas They Have, and the Inventions They Make," in *Technological Innovation: A Critical Review of Current Knowledge,* ed. Patrick Kelly and Melvin Kranzberg (San Francisco California: San Francisco Press, 1978), pp. 166-82.

4. Thomas Mann, *The Story of a Novel: The Genesis of Doctor Faustus.* Translated from the German by Richard and Clara Winston (New York, N.Y.: Alfred A. Knopf, 1961), pp. 42-48, 72, 94-95, 150-155.

5. One of the most exotic uses of the Faust myth as metaphor is found in the first postwar issue of Germany's leading professional engineering journal in which Waldemar Hellmich, a former director of the *Verein Deutscher Ingenieure* (German Association of Engineers) interprets the behavior of German engineers during the Nazi period as Faustian.

W. Hellmich, "Der geistige Aufbruch der deutschen Ingenieure," *VDI-Zeitschrift,* XC (1948); Oswald Spengler in *The Decline of the West* (New York, N.Y.; Modern Library, 1965) terms the modern western civilization with its emphasis on engineering and science, the "Faustian." Essays by Thomas Mann on Goethe include "Goethe's Career as a Man of Letters" (1932); "Goethe and Tolstoy" (1922). Mann also wrote an essay on "Goethe's *Faust*" (1938). All three are reprinted in *Essays by Thomas Mann.* Translated from the German by H. T. Lowe-Porter (New York, N.Y.: Vintage, 1957).

    6. Nigel Hamilton, *The Brothers Mann: The Lives of Heinrich and Thomas Mann 1871-1950 and 1875-1955* (New Haven, Connecticut: Yale, 1979) provides a biography of the brothers and a criticism of their work.

    7. Mann, *Doctor Faustus,* pp. 324-335.

    8. Lynn White, Jr. "The Historical Roots of Our Ecologic Crisis," in *Machina Ex Deo* (Cambridge, Massachusetts: MIT, 1968), pp. 85-86.

    9. Friedrich Klemm, *A History of Western Technology* (Cambridge, Massachusetts: MIT, 1964), pp. 70-74. Klemm is quoting a selection from Hugo de Sancto Victore, *Didascalicon,* German version by Joseph Freundgen, Paderborn, 1896.

    10. Arthur Koestler, *The Act of Creation* (New York, N.Y.: Dell, 1973), p. 124.

    11. Perry Miller, *The Life of the Mind in America from the Revolution to the Civil War* (New York, N.Y.: Harcourt Brace and World, 1965), pp. 291-292, 300-304, 317, 319. Thomas Ewbank, "The World a Workshop," reprinted selection in T. P. Hughes, *Changing Attitudes Toward American Technology* (New York, N.Y.: Harper and Row, 1975), 213-218.

    12. Jeremy Bernstein, *Einstein* (New York, N.Y.: Penguin, 1979), p. 218.

    13. Johann Wolfgang von Goethe, *Faust.* Translated by George Madison Priest, Part II, Act V. Ronald Gray, "Goethe's *Faust,* Part II," *Cambridge Quarterly,* I (Winter 1965-1966), 355-379 sees Faust finding near fulfillment in the creation of a manmade world.

    14. Howard P. Segal, "American Visions of Technological Utopia," *Markham Review,* VII (Summer 1978), 65-76.

    15. Goethe, *Faust,* Part II, Act III.

    16. Elmer Sperry, p. 291; *Doctor Faustus,* p. 191; and Patrick Carnegy, *Faust as Musician: A Study of Thomas Mann's Novel Doctor Faustus* (New York, N.Y.: New Directions, 1975), p. 46. Carnegy compares and contrasts the twelve-tone method of Mann's Leverkühn with Arnold Schoenberg's.

    17. Mann, *Doctor Faustus,* p. 189.

    18. Ibid., p. 190.

    19. Ibid., p. 191.

    20. Ibid., p. 237. Carnegy in *Faust as Musician,* discusses the "Dialogue with the Devil," pp. 79-103.

    21. Hughes, *Elmer Sperry,* p. 293-294.

    22. Goethe, *Faust,* pp. 60-61.

    23. Mann, "Goethe's Career as a Man of Letters," p. 54.

Chapter 8

Walther Nernst and the Application of Physics to Chemistry

Erwin N. Hiebert

Walther Nernst was a physicist by training who early in his career turned his attention to the application of physical principles to the solution of chemical problems. He was a bold and resourceful theoretician and quick to latch on to new ideas, but he also possessed a keen and imaginative intuition for what was experimentally feasible and credible. In Göttingen and Berlin, over a period of four decades, Nernst and his colleagues and students managed substantially to illuminate those borderland areas where physics and chemistry converge.

Nernst established his reputation as a prominent physical chemist with his early work on electrolytic solution theory, but his greatest accomplishments were in the field of chemical thermodynamics. The third law of thermodynamics, or the "heat theorem" as Nernst first referred to it in 1906, was recognized at the time mainly as a practical method for computing chemical equilibria. For at least three decades Nernst and many other investigators not only sought to demonstrate the rigorous validity of the third law with experiments at ever lower temperatures, but attempted to find a more acceptable theoretical formulation than had been provided in 1906. From the documents that exist in the Nobel archives we know that for his contributions to electrochemistry and thermodynamics Nernst was recommended for the Nobel Prize in Chemistry or Physics every year for fourteen years before he received it in 1920

It is a pleasure to acknowledge National Science Foundation support for my research on Nernst.

for chemistry "in recognition of his work in thermochemistry." Such a delay does not stand out as too unusual when we recall that it took fourteen years in the case of Albert Einstein, twenty-eight for Max Born, and forty for J. H. Van Vleck.

Nernst died during the war in 1941 at the age of seventy-seven at his estate in Zibelle, which is now on the German-Polish border about ninety miles southeast of Berlin. He was pushed aside and ignored by the Nazis as early as the 1930s. Little information about his last years was available in those scientific circles that once had claimed him in their front ranks.[1] Thus Nernst's death was untimely, at least from the point of view of the brilliant constellation of physicists and chemists who had known him and his work most intimately, first in Leipzig, then in Göttingen, and finally in Berlin. I refer here to those who would have been able in the 1940s to provide a detailed, first-hand evaluation and analysis of his scientific creativity.

My aim in this paper is to give a broad picture of Nernst as a scientist, to explore some of the many facets of his career, and especially to stress his role in the generation of a school of thought and method whose legacy extends to our own time. This plump, bald-headed Prussian, endowed with a Pickwickian personality and sense of humor, was notable for his classy pince-nez spectacles, his artistically chiselled Burschenschaft scar from his Mensur duels, and his Cheshire cat grin. Always self-confident in intellectual matters, Nernst played many roles in science: teacher, experimentalist, theoretician, editor, organizer, administrator, amateur philosopher of science, and perhaps most important, creator of a school of scientific thought characterized by precisely thought-out research programs.

The sources of information for constructing an image of the whole man Nernst are, first and foremost, the corpus of his published scientific works. Other documents that are accessible and informative are the numerous discussions of the man and his contributions by both his contemporaries and more recent investigators. Then too we have, scattered here and there, Nernst's own comments about his work, accomplishments, beliefs, and methodological directives. Suffice it to say that one way to help seek out the self-image of a scientist like Nernst, and to discover the way in which he conceived of his own work and thought within the context of the scientific currents of his time, is to take seriously, but not uncritically, what he has to say as he reflects on these matters in so many of his essays and lectures. Besides, the historian can take advantage of Nernst, so to speak, by invading his more private life, to examine the uninhibited outpourings of his soul as revealed in the correspondence and informal interchanges with his most intimate friends and invisible opponents. While this invasion may not be quite fair to a man like Nernst, since he may not have intended to add these documents to the historical record, they in fact do help substantially to answer the kinds of questions that I have posed.

The eulogies and evaluative commentaries written about Nernst in the 1940s came out of a milieu in which virtually the entire scientific community that he had been a part of, had been shattered, humiliated, divided, and dispersed. In view of these historical wartime circumstances, it is in fact remarkable to discover how many persons from that once closely knit, and then completely fractured, community of experts ended up putting down on paper their earlier remembrances of this colorful, pugnacious, energetic, impulsive, and cagey impressario.

Nernst was a controversial figure. Evaluations of his scientific contributions and personality were many-sided during his lifetime and thereafter. His American students on the whole were critical of the man if not of his science. Irving Langmuir, who completed his doctorate under Nernst in Göttingen in 1906 and was awarded the Nobel Prize for chemistry in 1932, was asked to write an obituary notice for Nernst. He wrote to Ernst Solomon, who claimed to be the oldest then living student of Nernst from the Göttingen days: "Nernst was a very brilliant scientist and very stimulating to his students. We had great respect for his scientific abilities, but had less for his scientific honesty and very little for his personal characteristics. I do not care to publish anything in regard to Nernst's work. I think the same is probably true with the other American students of his."[2]

Another American who had done research in Nernst's laboratory in Göttingen, Robert A. Millikan, and who received the Nobel Prize in physics in 1923, wrote an obituary statement for the *Scientific Monthly*. His comments furnish important insights about how Nernst was launched into his early career in Göttingen:

In the spring of 1896 the new Institute of Physical Chemistry at Göttingen was dedicated with the thirty-year-old Walther Nernst as director. Arrhenius was the chief speaker and guest of honor. There were seventeen of us advanced students in that laboratory that spring, sixteen of whom called themselves physicists and one a chemist. Six of the seventeen were Americans. All of us 'sat in' on Nernst's general lectures which covered the material in his new book on 'physical chemistry' upon which his reputation at that early stage had largely been built. That book was notable in its grasp of the physics of the day with enough of chemistry to justify the title. The group in the laboratory regarded Nernst as essentially a physicist, well endowed with physical ingenuity and insight and a moderate knowledge of analytical procedures, who had the ability to get a new laboratory built for himself by capitalizing on the recent discoveries of Ostwald . . . of what physics had been doing throughout the nineteenth century. . . .

Nernst himself was a man of extremes. . . . He was a little fellow with a fish-like mouth and other well-marked idiosyncrasies. However, he was in the main popular in the laboratory, despite the fact that in the academic world he nearly always had a quarrel on with somebody. . . . Nernst's greatest strength was in physical insight rather than in theoretical analysis. . . .

At a later date in 1912, when he was in Berlin, "we were all trying to unravel the intricacies of the quantum theory, and specific heats showed us not only that equipartition had to break down, but just how it broke down. The third law of thermodynamics formulated at about this time is unquestionably the greatest monument to Nernst's scientific insight. . . ."

"[Nernst's] greatest weakness lay in his intense prejudices and the personal, rather than the objective, character of some of his judgments. . . . Politically Nernst remained a Prussian of the Prussians — a strange mixture of the virtues and vices of his race."[3]

A more charitable appraisal of Nernst was written by Albert Einstein, who had been in close contact with him for a period of almost two decades in Berlin beginning in 1914. In 1942 Einstein wrote:

[Walther Nernst] was one of the most distinctive and most interesting scholars with whom I have been closely connected during my life. He did not miss any of the physics colloquia in Berlin, and his brief remarks about the most varied subjects that were treated there, gave evidence of a truly staggering scientific instinct [einem wahrhaft verblueffenden wissenschaftlichen Instinkt] combined with a sovereign knowledge of an immense amount of factual material, that always was at his command, along with a rare mastery of experimental methods and tricks [Tricks] in which he excelled. And so it came about that we all not only sincerely admired him but also had for him a personal affection — this, in spite of the fact that we at times goodnaturedly laughed about his child-like vanity and self-love [kindliche Eitelkeit und Selbstliebe]. So long as his ego-centric weakness did not enter the picture, he exhibited an objectivity very rarely found, an infallible sense for the essential, and a genuine passion for the knowledge of the deep interrelations of nature. Without that passion his singularly creative productivity and his important influence on the scientific life of the first third of this century would not have been possible. . . .

He followed [the tradition of] Arrhenius, Ostwald and van't Hoff, as the last of the dynasty that based their investigations on thermodynamics, osmotic pressure and ionic theory. His activities to about 1905 in essence were restricted to this trend of thought [Gedankenkreis]. His theoretical equipment [Rüstzeug] was somewhat primitive but he mastered it with a rare dexterity. . . .

The beginnings of quantum theory were supported by the important results of his [high and low temperature] caloric investigations, and this in particular before Bohr's theory of the atom became the most important experimental domain for this theory. His work in theoretical chemistry offers both student and researcher a wealth of stimuli. It is theoretically elementary but spirited [geistreich], alive and fertile with suggestions about interrelationships of the most diverse kind. This again reflects his whole intellectual temperament.

Nernst was no one-sided man of learning. His healthy common sense successfully touched all areas of practical life, and every conversation with him brought something interesting to light. What distinguished him from almost all his fellow countrymen was a very far-reaching freedom from prejudices. He was neither nationalist nor militarist. He judged things and people almost exclusively by their direct success, and not according to any social or ethical idea. This, in fact, was the reverse side of his impartiality. At the same time he was interested in literature and exhibited a sense of wit and humor that is rare among persons who carry so heavy a work load. He was so original that I have never met anyone who resembled him in any essential way.[4]

So much for Einstein's 1942 remarks about Nernst.

Given these general evaluative comments by colleagues, it is appropriate to examine more directly Nernst's background and accomplishments. What were some of the environmental factors that helped to mould Nernst's make-up and motivate him to do what he did? What, in fact, did he accomplish? What significance did these accomplishments have? How were Nernst's ideas received by his contemporaries, and then by the scientists of succeeding generations?

In his youth at the Gymnasium Nernst's studies were focused on the classics, literature, and the natural sciences. He dreamed of becoming a poet, and although that aspiration dissolved he continued to nurture his love for literature and the theatre, especially for the plays of Shakespeare. Nernst's studies in physics began in 1883 with Heinrich Weber in Zurich and were continued through 1887 with Helmholtz in Berlin, Boltzmann and Albert von Ettingshausen in Graz, and Friedrich Kohlrausch in Würzburg. The circumstances surrounding Nernst's work with Kohlrausch on electrolytic solution theory undoubtedly provided the impulse and the point of departure for his interest in exploring the way in which physics might be applied to chemistry. In a letter of 1886 to Ostwald, Arrhenius wrote from Würzburg that there were very few students sufficiently advanced to carry out their own investigations, and that "the only one who is accomplishing something interesting is a very young man by the name of Nernst; he has discovered that the thermal conductivity of bismuth and air is markedly decreased with magnets."[5]

In September of 1887 Arrhenius, who had just presented his electrolytic theory of dissociation, introduced Nernst to Ostwald while on a visit to Boltzmann in Graz. Ostwald wrote to his wife that Nernst was planning to come to Riga to study with him there.[6] Before the end of 1887 Ostwald, together with van't Hoff, the author of the new theory for weak electrolytes, had published the first issue of the *Zeitschrift für physikalische Chemie,* and Ostwald had been appointed to a professorship in physical chemistry at the University of Leipzig with Nernst as his assistant. And thus it was that Nernst's career in physical chemistry was launched with Ostwald as the dominant figure in Leipzig and with strong support from two other intellectual European outposts where electrolytic solution chemistry, thermodynamics, and their correlation with the colligative properties of gases and liquids, were pursued with passion —van't Hoff in Amsterdam and Arrhenius in Stockholm.

Within the context of these *Ioner,* as they were called, Nernst published, within a year, his derivation of the law of diffusion of electrolytes in the limiting case of two kinds of ions in solution. This permitted him to evaluate the diffusion coefficient for infinitely dilute solutions and to demonstrate for concentration cells the connection between diffusion coefficient, ionic mobility, and electromotive force. Shortly thereafter, in 1890 and 1891, Nernst formulated his distribution law that gives the equilibrium concentrations of a solute distributed between two immiscible liquid phases at equilibrium. The Nernst distribution equation, for example, was used to demonstrate that ether tends to concentrate in brain and nerve tissues rather than in the acqueous blood phase.

By the time Nernst accepted an associate professorship in Göttingen in 1891, he had achieved an international reputation in electro- and solution chemistry.[7] In 1893 Nernst's views on how to correlate physics and chemistry at the theoretical level were published in his *Theoretische Chemie vom Standpunkt der Avogadroschen Regel und der Thermodynamik.* It is evident from an analysis of this text that Nernst conceived of the development of physical chemistry not so much as the shaping of a new discipline as the connection of hitherto rather independent sciences. Nernst's objective was to offer a synthesis of all of the relevant new investigations, or as he says:

"all that the physicist must know of chemistry and all that the chemist must know of physics unless both are content to be specialists in their own science."[8] The 15th edition of 1926 of Nernst's *Theoretische Chemie* was succeeded by the texts of Arnold Eucken and John Eggert, both of whom were trained under Nernst. The widespread adoption of Nernst's physical chemistry textbook can be attributed to a number of factors. It was designed to reach students at an intermediate theoretical level, and it covered a very wide range of interrelated phenomena with up-to-date illustrative examples and the description of experiments invented explicitly to facilitate an understanding of the theoretical principles.

When Boltzmann left his post in theoretical physics in Munich to return to Vienna in 1894, the position was offered to Nernst. He adroitly engineered the opportunity in order to secure in Göttingen a chair in physical chemistry and a new Institut für Physikalische Chemie und Elektrochemie—the only such position in Germany apart from Ostwald's in Leipzig. From then on Nernst was able to man a comprehensive experimental and theoretical team-oriented research program to investigate physicochemical problems that suited his fancy.

The design of new and innovative analytical instruments was one of Nernst's dominant interests, one that he pursued with his students in the construction of a microbalance and other special apparatus for the measurement of dielectric constants and the determination of molecular weights by freezing point depression in dilute solution and vapor density values at high temperatures. In the course of his studies on mass action and the synthesis of ammonia from its elements, Nernst constructed a reaction chamber that could withstand pressures of 75 atmospheres at temperatures of 1000°C. By comparison with Haber's yield of 0.01 percent ammonia at 1 atmosphere and 1000°C, Nernst and Jost by 1907 had achieved a 1.0 percent yield at 50 atmospheres and 685°C. It was just then that Nernst became too involved with his heat theorem to continue his ammonia studies, whereas Haber perfected the catalytic techniques that made the process for the synthesis of ammonia industrially attractive, and for which he received the Nobel Prize for chemistry in 1918.

Upon retirement of Hans Landolt in 1905, Nernst, with strong recommendations from Max Planck, accepted the chair for physical chemistry at the University of Berlin. Planck believed that Nernst was the only chemist who might be able to pull Berlin out of its chemical stagnation. In fact, Planck recognized that as a physicist, Nernst's interests would be focused more on the newly established physical chemistry than was to be expected from most chemists in Germany who so single-mindedly had channeled their best efforts into organic chemistry. In this evaluation, I would suggest, Planck was right, for Nernst at that time had a better and more comprehensive grasp of the domain of physical chemistry than Ostwald, Arrhenius, or even van't Hoff. In his 1906 Silliman lectures at Yale Nernst remarked that the customary separation of physics and chemistry was not altogether advantageous and was "especially embarrassing in exploring the boundary region where physicists and chemists need to work in concert."[9]

The University of Berlin, before the turn of the century, was one of the last bastions of opposition to the ionic theory of dissociation. Chemists there certainly had not understood the farreaching implications of recent advances in chemical thermodynamics. Helmholtz and Planck had made important theoretical contributions to the study of thermodynamics in relation to the problem of chemical equilibrium, and as early as 1890 had lent their support to the electrolytic theory of ionization and Nernst's electrochemical investigations. Van't Hoff, at the university and in his prestigious position in the Prussian Academy of Sciences, was no longer involved in scientific research. Helmholtz concluded at the time that the chemists in Berlin apparently were not capable of comprehending thermodynamics.

By 1905, when Nernst arrived in Berlin, the chemists were just beginning to tolerate the *Ioner* in an attempt to come to terms with the physical chemistry of Ostwald, van't Hoff, and Arrhenius. By then Nernst had adopted new priorities and perspectives—namely, the experimental verification and theoretical refinement of his heat theorem, and the exploration of problems connected with the rates of chemical processes. Thus until about the age of forty Nernst had worked primarily within the setting of physical chemistry that had been initiated in Leipzig, Amsterdam, and Stockholm. Thereafter, until World War I, Nernst pursued with resolution the question of the limits of applicability of chemical thermodynamics for chemical equilibrium, and the study of chemical kinetics.

Nernst drove from Göttingen to Berlin in his open automobile around Easter of 1905 and began to prepare for his new directorship of the chemical institute in the Bunsenstrasse. On December 23 he was back in Göttingen at the Academy of Sciences, where he delivered his classic *Wärme-Theorem* paper on the calculation of equilibria from thermal measurements.[10] The idea upon which this paper was based, and which subsequently was enunciated in the form of the third law of thermodynamics, undoubtedly had been essentially thought out while he still was in Göttingen. Nernst must have felt very confident about the scientific merits of his theorem because we know that he returned the page proofs to the editor with a note scribbled on the title page: "Bitte Revision! Im Ganzen 300 Separata!"[11]

We cannot begin here to lay out and analyze the arguments and the evidence that Nernst presented in his paper on his novel method for calculating chemical equilibrium exclusively from thermal data. Nor shall we be able to trace in detail the circumstances and deliberations that set the stage for the 1906 announcement as exhibited in the earlier work of Nernst, Arrhenius, van't Hoff, Haber, Le Chatelier, G. N. Lewis, and T. W. Richards. Much less will it be possible to follow year by year, over a period of some three decades through the 1930s, the experimental evidence, both critical and supportive, brought to bear on the question of the validity of the third law.[12]

The work of Boltzmann, Planck, Nernst, and Einstein lies at the root of twentieth-century advances in the thermodynamics of chemical processes; but the third law had its origin in chemistry and was conceived by Nernst in connection with the search for the mathematical criteria of chemical equilibrium and chemical spontaneity. For over a century chemists had struggled with the problem of explaining why certain chemical reactions take place while others do not; or more explicitly, how far a reaction will proceed before equilibrium prevails.[13]

By the end of the century the theoretical solution was seen, correctly, to turn on methods for evaluating the free energy for chemical processes. This could be accomplished, in principle, in three ways, all of which are relatively inaccessible from an experimental point of view. The Gibbs-Helmholtz equation, $\Delta F = \Delta H + T \left(\frac{\delta \Delta F}{\delta T} \right)_p$, relates the free energy ΔF to the heat content or enthalpy ΔH (readily determined calorimetrically) and the entropy change ΔS, the latter being expressed in the form of the thermal coefficient of free energy, since $\left(\frac{\delta \Delta F}{\delta T} \right)_p = -\Delta S$. Neither entropies nor thermal coefficients were readily available at that time by experimental means. It also was known that the free energy can be calculated from a knowledge of the equilibrium constant K, since $\Delta F = -RT\ln K$. Unfortunately, the ratio of products to reactants, and therefore the equilibrium constant, changes too markedly during chemical analysis to yield values for K in the case of most reactions. Physical methods for determining the concentrations of the constituents of a reaction—

for example, colorimetrically or from the rotation of plane polarized light — are ideal but had not yet been perfected at the turn of the century except for a very few special cases. Finally, free energies can be calculated from experimental data for reversible galvanic cells, since $\Delta F = -n\mathfrak{F}\mathcal{E}$; where $\mathfrak{F}$ is Faraday's constant and $\mathcal{E}$ is the electromotive force. Here too, only a few isolated cases were known for which a determination of the electromotive force of a chemical process was feasible.

Thus it was crystal clear to Nernst and to many of his contemporaries — Arrhenius, van't Hoff, Ostwald, Le Chatelier, Haber, Richards, and Lewis — that the Gibbs-Helmholtz equation in its integrated form was the theoretically sound point of departure for the solution to questions connected with chemical equilibrium and the feasibility of chemical processes. The integrated equation takes the form

$$\left(\frac{\delta\Delta F}{\delta T}\right)_p = -\alpha\ln T - \alpha - 2\beta T - \frac{3}{2}\gamma T^2 - \ldots + J,$$

where α, β, and γ are the calorimetrically determined heat capacity coefficients and J is the constant of integration. The constant J can be evaluated if the value of ΔF is known at some temperature. This, of course, in most cases, is just what was seen to be beyond experimental reach and therefore the root cause of the problem *ab initio*. It was here that the heat theorem came to the rescue, or so at least it seemed to Nernst.

Le Chatelier already in 1888, in a work devoted to analyzing the laws of chemical equilibrium, had suggested that the constant of integration was a determinate function of the physical properties of the reacting substances. He recognized that the ascertainment of this function would lead to a knowledge of the laws of chemical equilibrium and permit chemists to determine a priori the complete conditions for chemical spontaneity.[14] Fritz Haber in 1905 had referred to J as the "thermodynamically indeterminate constant."[15] Nernst suspected that the physical interpretation of the integrated Gibbs-Helmholtz equation was to be found in this hitherto inaccessible J. He conjectured furthermore that the clue to discovering a method for determining chemical affinities from thermal data alone was connected with what happens to the thermodynamic functions and the properties of matter at, and, more important, in the vicinity of absolute zero. That is, absolute zero, Nernst believed, would turn out to have a unique thermodynamic significance that is not embraced by the first and second laws of thermodynamics. And thus Nernst came to recognize that since chemical equilibria could not be computed within the existing thermodynamic framework, a supplementary hypothesis or theorem would be needed to describe the manner in which the free energy and heat content change, not at absolute zero (since there, as others had suggested, both ΔF and ΔH should be zero) but in the approach toward absolute zero. In fact, Nernst was right, since at equilibrium all of the properties of matter later were shown to vanish at that point.

In the considerations leading up to the 1906 paper Nernst simply ignored the theoretically vexatious issues connected with reactions involving gases. For gases the sum of the heat capacities of the reactants is not necessarily equal to that of the products, since their degrees of freedom may differ. Stoutheartedly and with characteristic insolence (call it sound physical intuition if you like)—a posture that would have been out of character for either Haber or Le Chatelier—Nernst restricted his focus to condensed phases where Kopp's law (the additivity of atomic heat capacities) was known to apply. He felt that extrapolation to absolute zero for solids was warranted, given that classical theory predicts that the molecular heats of compounds become equal to the sum of their atomic heats with decreasing temperatures. Nernst therefore reasoned that the free energy and heat content curves would come together asymptotically as $T \rightarrow 0$.

Referring to the integrated form of the Gibbs-Helmholtz equation (see above), Nernst postulated that $\lim_{T \rightarrow 0} \left(\frac{\delta \Delta F}{\delta T} \right)_p = 0$, and then $J = 0$, and $\alpha = \lim_{T \rightarrow 0} \Delta C_p = \lim_{T \rightarrow 0} \left(\frac{\delta \Delta H}{\delta T} \right)_p = 0$ where ΔC_p represents the heat capacity changes. Nernst stressed the fact that $\lim_{T \rightarrow 0} \left(\frac{\delta \Delta F}{\delta T} \right)_p = 0$ was a necessary and sufficient condition for a definitive solution to the problem of chemical affinity, whereas $\lim_{T \rightarrow 0} \left(\frac{\delta \Delta H}{\delta T} \right)_p = 0$ was a necessary but not sufficient condition.

In all of these deliberations Nernst was keenly aware of the need to demonstrate the experimental validity of his theorem at ever lower temperatures in order to ascertain whether it represented an approximate principle or an exact law. A reliable method for calculating the driving force for chemical reactivity—the original stimulus for Nernst's thrust into thermodynamics—henceforth became available to chemists. However, the theoretical status and implications of the heat theorem as a fundamental law of nature became the subject of critical discussions for another twenty years or more. In any case, Nernst lost no time in formulating an imposing research strategy that involved virtually the entire available facilities and manpower of the Institute for Physical Chemistry at the University of Berlin.

To achieve the goal of a rigorous test of the heat theorem turned out to be an enormously ambitious and experimentally challenging assignment. It entailed the construction of ingenious electrical and thermal equipment, a vacuum calorimeter, and a small hydrogen liquefier. Together Nernst and his team of assistants determined heats of reaction, and heat capacities and their temperature coefficients, for a great variety of chemical substances over the entire experimentally realizable range of temperatures down to liquid hydrogen temperatures and beyond.

At the time of Nernst's announcement of the heat theorem in 1906 he apparently was not aware of the idea that there might be any connection between his work on chemical thermodynamics and the quantum theory that Planck had begun to elaborate in 1900. In 1907 Einstein, in connection with his interest in Planck's radiation theory, concluded that quantum theory required the vanishing of the heat capacities of solids at the absolute zero of temperature. When Nernst visited Einstein in Zurich in March of 1910 the two men had an opportunity to discuss the extent of agreement between values calculated from the theory and the experiments then in process in Nernst's laboratory in Berlin.

Einstein clearly was pleased to discover that his conceptions were being supported by Nernst's experimental attack on the problem. Nernst unquestionably was delighted to have his heat theorem connected with Einstein's deductions for quantum theory. Einstein wrote to his good friend Michele Besso in May of 1911 that "the theory of specific heats had celebrated a true triumph," having been confirmed by the experiments of Nernst in Berlin.[16] A year after the Einstein-Nernst meeting, in 1911, Lindemann and Nernst demonstrated that there were some systematic deviations in the comparison of theory and data. Their revised equation did show better agreement than the Einstein derivation except at the very lowest temperature then attainable.

In a lecture in 1911 at the 83rd Naturforscherversammlung in Karlsruhe, Arnold Sommerfeld emphasized the importance of the Nernst heat theorem for the acceptance of the quantum theory. He pointed out that the experimental investigations on blackbody radiation at the Physikalisch-Technische Reichsanstalt in Berlin constituted one of the foundations of quantum theory, but that additional support now had come from quite another quarter: "Perhaps to be estimated as of equal merit is the work of the Nernst Institute which, in the systematic measurement of specific heats, has furnished a second no less powerful pillar to support the quantum theory."[17] This early support for the quantum theory must be seen within the context of the times prior to the endorsement inherent in the results derived from experimental spectroscopy and the 1913 Bohr theory of atomic structure.

At the first Solvay Congress in Brussels in 1911—attended by twenty-one leading scientists and organized on the initiative of Nernst—Einstein presented a paper on his quantum theory of specific heats as related to the Nernst-Lindemann empirical formula for the thermal energy of solids. Not long thereafter, in 1912, Max Born and Theodore von Kármán published a theoretically more convincing version of the Einstein and Nernst-Lindemann equations. About the same time, also in 1912, Peter Debye, working independently, and building on Einstein's conception, but proceeding from another point of view, announced in Bern at the Physikalische Gesellschaft, a theoretical solution essentially identical with the Born and von Kármán formulation. Debye had derived a proportionality relationship between atomic heats and the third power of the temperature that was in good agreement with the data at very low temperatures.

All of these accomplishments were interpreted by Nernst as contributing to a corroboration of his theorem. In 1914, in the face of considerable incredulity among his colleagues, Nernst offered some rather unconvincing reasons for postulating a state of degeneracy (Entartung) for gases at low temperatures. Later developments inherent in the application of Bose-Einstein and Fermi-Dirac statistics, and the demonstration that electrons in metals present a case of degeneracy at much higher temperatures, vindicated Nernst's concept if not the elementary rationale that he had invoked in formulating it.

The first world war brought Nernst's academically engineered research machinery in Berlin to a complete standstill. As in the case of most of his university associates he was drawn into military service, first as an administrator, then in connection with chemical warfare, and finally as an automobile chauffeur for the German army on the move from Belgium to France. We should mention here that Nernst had a great weakness for everything associated with automobiles and their functioning. During the second world war Nernst turned completely sour on the whole German war machinery under

Hitler. In fact, in part because two of his daughters had married men of non-Aryan origin, Nernst lived through difficult days in isolation with his family on his manorial estate in Zibelle.

Although Nernst's theorem had kept pace and gained in prominence with the successes of early quantum theory, by 1920 a number of experimental anomalies had come to light that could not so readily be squared with the third law. Over the next twenty years or so most of the bothersome details and so-called anomalies came to be resolved as genuine quantum effects associated with the liberation of energy that accompanies the degeneracy of internal degrees of freedom at the ever lower temperature being realized experimentally.

For the most part Nernst played the role of a nonparticipating bystander in regard to the intellectual skirmishes that surrounded the new low temperature studies that investigators, chiefly his own students, became involved in. Indeed he became rather bullheaded about insisting that his original formulation of the heat theorem should be applicable in an undisguised way along classical thermodynamic guidelines unencumbered by statistical modes of reasoning. Besides he was confident that this theorem would be confirmed experimentally on its own merits as a bona fide general law of nature on a par with the first and second laws. His posture became one of increasing self-preservation about his role in the discovery of the third law. To some extent this probably reflects the environmental circumstances associated with his reputation in Berlin. There, under the shadow of colossal scientific giants such as Planck and Einstein, Nernst, possessive as he was about his own contributions, must have developed those defenses that necessarily would preserve the self-image that he had constructed for himself. Following the successes of the quantum mechanical interpretations of specific heats by Einstein and Planck, Nernst adopted the position that the heat theorem was just as secure as the quantum theory from which it could be deduced. By taking this stand-offish position he of course remained aloof and even resentful toward a man like Francis Simon, who had received his doctorate in 1921 under Nernst on a study of specific heats down to liquid hydrogen, and then later during the 1920s and 1930s provided the definitive and convincing theoretical formulation of the third law that Nernst had so much wished for.

An anecdote about Nernst that varies somewhat from one version to another, but that I feel rather rings true in its fundamental message, goes something like this: Nernst in his lectures was accustomed to saying that the first law of thermodynamics had been discovered independently by three investigators (presumably Mayer, Joule, and

Helmholtz); the second law, by two independent investigators (Carnot and Clausius). Concerning the third law of thermodynamics Nernst would say, so the story goes: "Well, this I have just done by myself." According to another version of this anecdote, which also seems to suit Nernst's character, he added that it therefore should be obvious that there never could be a fourth law of thermodynamics.

After World War II, Friedrich Lindemann (later Lord Cherwell) and Franz (Sir Francis) Simon, both Nernst's students in Berlin, together with Kurt Mendelsohn, Nicholas Kurti, and others, continued this work at the Clarendon Laboratory in Oxford and achieved temperatures in the range of 10^{-5} degrees Kelvin. These explorations into the study of the low-temperature properties of matter put Nernst's third law on a far sounder experimental basis than in earlier days. Besides, these cryogenic investigations notably opened up new areas of study connected with solid state physics and chemistry phenomena, gas degeneracy, corresponding states, zero-point energies, λ-point phenomena, cooling by adiabatic demagnetization, electron and nuclear spins, superconductivity, and superfluidity.

After about 1920 Nernst no longer participated in these investigations. Instead he became completely preoccupied with other scientific problems: photochemistry, physicochemical astrophysics, the null-point energy of the ether, the thermodynamic synthesis of the observed stellar sequence, ideas on a steady-state universe, nuclear processes as the source of stellar energy, and other cosmological questions then in vogue. While others were immersed in third law discussions about low temperature specific heat anomalies, amorphous solids, frozen-in disorder, magnetic and isotopic effects, and electron and nuclear spin disorder, Nernst blithely continued to pursue his own new scientific interests.

This chapter in Nernst's career parallels the extraordinarily fertile years for physics and chemistry in Weimar Germany when seminars, colloquia, and laboratories in Berlin were buzzing with excitement and contagious, revolutionary ideas. Right up to the time when Hitler was appointed chancellor in 1933, scientists were moving full speed ahead on many fronts: Planck and Einstein on quantum theory, thermodynamics, and relativity; Max von Laue on crystal interference; Erwin Schrödinger and Fritz London on the applications of wave mechanics; Paschen and Ladenburg on spectroscopy; Otto Warburg on photochemistry; Otto Hahn on radiochemistry; Gustav Hertz on isotope separation by gaseous diffusion; Herbert Freundlich on capillary and colloid phenomena; and Michael Polanyi on chemical kinetics. Prominent in the Berlin scientific community, Nernst

Plate 1. Walther Nernst, Berlin 1922, the year he left the Physikalisches-Chemisches-Institut to take up the Presidency of the Physikalische-Technische-Reichsanstalt. Courtesy of the AIP Niels Bohr Library.

Plate 2. Walther and Emma (Lohmeyer) Nernst with the children, Kathrin and Dorothee, of Sir Francis and Lady (Charlotte) Simon in Oxford, 1938. Courtesy of Lady Simon.

Plate 3. Lord Cherwell (F. A. Lindemann) and Walther Nernst in 1938. Courtesy of Lady Simon.

Plate 4. Five Nobel Laureates in Physics and Chemistry in von Laue's study in Berlin, 1932: Nernst, Einstein, Planck, Millikan, and von Laue. Courtesy of the AIP Niels Bohr Library.

Plate 5. The Nernst family leaving Göttingen for Berlin, Easter 1905. Courtesy of the Archiv der Wissenschaften der Deutschen Demokratischen Republik, Berlin.

at one time or another came in contact with all of these investigators, and many others.

However one may view the whole sweep and outcome of third law history, it is apparent that a truly imposing cluster of fringe benefits were generated from within the Nernst school that began in Berlin and then extended its research program mainly at Oxford but also eventually spread to highly specialized cryogenic laboratories that sprang up in Cracow, Paris, London, Toronto, Leiden, Berkeley, and wherever research on the low temperature properties of matter was being pursued.

The wide spectrum of responses to the third law that characterized the 1930s is registered in the critical appraisal that was levelled against the theorem by R. H. Fowler and T. E. Sterne when they wrote:

We reach therefore the rather ruthless conclusion that *Nernst's Heat Theorem strictly applied may or may not be true, but is always irrelevant and useless — applied to 'ideal solid states' at the absolute zero which are physically useful concepts the theorem though often true is sometimes false, and failing in generality must be rejected altogether.* It is no disparagement to Nernst's great idea that it proves ultimately to be of limited generality. The part that it has played in stimulating a deeper understanding of all these constants, and its reaction on the development of the quantum theory itself cannot be overrated. But its usefulness is past and it should now be eliminated.[18]

By the end of the 1930s, just before the outbreak of World War II, and largely as a result of Simon's work in Berlin, and then after 1933 in Oxford, the third law was on the road toward widespread reception. It is true that by 1940 or so the third law had outworn the original purpose for which Nernst had suggested it because by then the entropies of substances no longer were seen to be dependent upon the exhaustive cataloguing of thermal data but, with the help of quantum considerations, could be calculated from the much more readily available spectroscopic information. And so it comes as no surprise that the claim was made that all of these developments inevitably would have fallen out of the logic and implications of quantum mechanics.

Simon recognized full well this situation, namely how the advancement of science often shifts priorities away from the original stimuli that constitute the motors of scientific discovery. In my opinion he responded to this sentiment with splendid historical insight. In his Guthrie lecture of 1956, the year in which he died, Simon wrote:

Of course, one could say the same of the Second Law, namely that statistical theory would have yielded all the information pronounced first by the empirical statements of Carnot and Clausius. The predictions of the Third Law would eventually have been produced by quantum theory, but I have to remind you only of the fact that we have so far no full quantum statistical explanation of the Third Law to show you that it would have come very much later. Also we must not forget that the Third Law was an extremely strong stimulus to the development of quantum theory and it is perhaps not quite idle to consider how the development would have taken place had Nernst's deliberations started ten years earlier as they might well have done. Perhaps the quantum of action would have been discovered as a consequence of the disappearing specific heats rather than from the ultra-violet catastrophe of the radiation laws.

Things do not always develop in the most direct or logical way; they depend on many chance observations, on personalities and sometimes even on economic needs. . . . I hope I have shown you how a great mind tackled a very obscure situation, at first only in order to elucidate some relatively narrow field, and how later, as the result of all the interaction and cross-fertilization with other fields, the Third Law emerged in all its generality, as we know it today.[19]

Nernst's writings, both scientific and extrascientific, to a notable degree, are devoid of any explicit, systematically worked out methodological or philosophical position. Nevertheless, he gives us ample evidence of deeply felt views, beliefs, suppositions, and preferred images of the mode of scientific endeavor that he patronized. He exhibited a taciturn, ever skeptical, attitude toward the utility of abstract and theoretical premises unnecessarily remote from experience. For example he judged the importance of Einstein's theory of Brownian motion above that of relativity theory on the merits of the former's tangible physical features. Generally speaking, he evaluated the role of hypotheses and theorems exclusively on the basis of their fertility for opening up significant new areas of scientific investigation. Clearly Nernst's compelling orientation was to stress experimental investigations that featured visualizable components. In his own experimental work his focus was directed so exclusively toward reliable results that he was not in the least distracted from his goal by having to use inelegant, makeshift instruments. He and his assistants often constructed their own equipment — transformers, pressure and temperature controlling devices, cooling apparatus, a microbalance, and everything else that was not readily on hand. Since Nernst was extraordinarily frugal, he looked with great disdain upon the misuse of energy and natural resources, and he saw to it that the equipment in his research laboratory was as small, simple, and economically constructed as possible.

The theoretical themes that Nernst pursued were related so directly to the enthusiastic tenacity with which he approached experimental and instrumental challenges, that pure and applied research just seem to have merged together in all of his inquiries. In keeping with this emphasis, Nernst exhibited a keen curiosity for the technological exploitation of physical and chemical principles. Nernst owned one of the first automobiles in Göttingen, experimented with various combustion fuels, wrote articles on the maximum efficiency of internal combustion engines, and demonstrated that a nitrous oxide injector could give his automobile the extra thrust that was necessary to go uphill with ease. In northern Italy on Monte Generoso, close to the Swiss border, Nernst experimented with an instrument designed to tap atmospheric electricity as an energy source.

Nernst's experiments on the electrolytic conduction of solids at high temperatures were put to use in 1904 in the invention of the so-called Nernst lamp. The trick was to construct filaments from a mixture of rare earth salts that would be less brittle at incandescence than the carbon filament lamps then in use. The Nernst lamp, although expensive to manufacture, was less fragile, more efficient, and did not require a vacuum. A short time after Nernst had sold the patent rights for his lamp for a handsome sum it became outdated by the invention of the tungsten lamp. In the early 1920s Nernst made some important contributions to the mechanism of ionic conduction in semiconductors. Sometimes Nernst's knack for technological innovation led to excessively rash ventures. A case in point was his attempt to reproduce the quality of a grand piano by furnishing small pianos with magnetically controlled loudspeaker amplification. The harmonics of Nernst's specially constructed Neo-Bechstein-flügel — the product of his *physique amusante*, as he referred to it — were scorned by musicians.

Max Bodenstein, who was closely associated with Nernst as student and colleague, and then succeeded him in the chair of physical chemistry at the University of Berlin, like Einstein has stressed Nernst's totally nonconformist personality. In his address of 1942 to the German Chemical Society in Berlin Bodenstein attributed Nernst's successes as a scientist to his clear, prosaic, mobile mind, unhampered by any fear of being shown to be wrong in his ideas. Bodenstein wrote: "Nernst possessed in a quite extraordinary way a feeling for what is scientifically possible. As a hunter he would forgive me for saying that he had an unusually fine nose for the true and, besides, a blissful phantasy that allowed him to represent graphically difficult matters to himself and to us." Bodenstein gave considerable weight to Nernst's fancy for imaginative and spirited aspirations [geistvolle Aperçus] and inventions thrown out liberally and spontaneously: "Sometimes [they were] explored more closely, sometimes conducive to further formulation, sometimes lighting up like meteors, and soon thereafter falling into oblivion."[20] His phantasies were easy-come-easy-go unless they turned out to reveal something novel and manageable.

Nernst was a firm-minded man, whose demands upon his students, as of himself, were severe—not with respect to examinations or book learning, but rather when it came to devotion to experimental research. In this regard his motto was: "Das Wissen ist der Tod der Forschung." He was remarkably free from false claims or concealment, generous to a fault, and liberal in sharing his knowledge and expertise with others. The external picture of Nernst that is given to us by those who knew him and worked with him most intimately is that he was sincere, innocent, and imbued with simple charms that were embellished to suit an occasion by a corrosive sense of humor and an unsolicited witty esprit. Students generally were not devoted to him as a person even when they admired his versatility and complete mastery of the many areas of scientific knowledge over which he ranged. His reputation as a classroom lecturer also was not exceptional, but students long remembered the anecdotes and witticisms that he would make from the podium whenever he wanted to illustrate a point. In his classroom lectures he frequently departed from the prescribed subject matter in order to talk about the most recent scientific advances, especially when they impinged upon his own work and interests. At such times it was so difficult to distinguish between his own contributions and those of others that it looked as if he and his colleagues had constructed most of the new physical chemistry.

Walther Nernst was a grand old Geheimrat of the old German school. Except for the World War II period, his good vintage years spanned half a century, from the late 1880s until the rise of Hitler. What, we may ask, were the springs of creativity that motivated and impelled him along the path of his unique scientific insights and perspectives, especially within those borderline domains where physics and chemistry overlap?

First, we may mention that he was singularly alert and open to what was happening around him in the scientific world. In truth, he was possessed by a naive, child-like curiosity that bordered on arrogance. He was convinced that there was nothing too difficult for him to handle. He missed nothing that transpired in the physics and chemistry colloquia. He was incessantly discussing and arguing the pros and cons of a given scientific idea—sometimes, in fact, rather hogging the conversation. Conspicuously poised in the front row, he was prepared to draw upon and impress his audience with his immense storehouse of factual information, ready to provide evidence for a specific point or line of interpretation.

Not unrelated to Nernst's naive openness and freedom from prejudice was his clearly discernible sense of wit and humor—his ability to recognize the wisdom of seeing that what nature chooses to teach scientists may not always coincide with the high-blown deductive schemes that they so proudly construct for themselves. As is well known, wit and humor, jokes for example, produce laughter and empathy within a given situation precisely because the outcome of the story that is told—the punchline—is so unexpected and so outrageous that the response can only be one of incredulity and a deep-down gut feeling that life, and science too, are full of surprise situations. They teach something about humility and an ultimate modesty in the face of natural phenomena. I would suggest that this sobering type of experience constitutes a significant component of all great creative discoveries. The topic of wit and humor as a springboard for exploring the history of science from a unique, if rather unconventional, perspective, appears to me, in fact, to be entirely worthy of serious attention by historians of science. Nernst would provide a paradigm case for such a study.

Second, Nernst had an uncanny ability to ferret out new relationships and to seize upon novel ideas no matter what their source. He was an expert at making quick and easy intuitive judgments without getting hung up on inherent contradictions generated by cross-currents from too many concepts and extra baggage. Einstein correctly stressed Nernst's breadth of learning and his basic antipathy to one-sided reconstructions. Apparently unlike Einstein, Nernst had little affinity for a unitary worldview. Not given over to grand systematics, Nernst rather was a pluralist and pragmatist; he chose to work on topics and problems that were intrinsically exciting yet manageable.

There is a snappy and enigmatic extant line fragment from the seventh century B. C. Greek lyric poet Archilochus that symbolizes the extremes I am trying to portray here. It goes like this: "The fox knows many things, but the hedgehog knows one big thing." Isaiah Berlin, in his *Essays on Tolstoy's View of History,* writes:

There exists a great chasm between those, on one side, who relate everything to a single central vision, one system less or more coherent or articulate, in terms of which they understand, think and feel—a single, universal, organizing principle in terms of which alone all that they are and say has significance—and, on the other side, those who pursue many ends, often unrelated and even contradictory, connected, if at all, only in some *de facto* way, for some psychological or physiological cause related by no moral or aesthetic principle; these last lead lives, perform acts, and entertain ideas that are centrifugal rather than centripetal, their thought is scattered or diffused, moving on many levels, seizing upon the essence of a vast variety of experiences and objects for what they are in themselves, without, consciously or unconsciously, seeking to fit them into, or exclude them from, any one unchanging, all-embracing, sometimes self-contradictory and incomplete, at times fanatical, unitary inner vision. The first kind of intellectual and artistic personality belongs to the hedgehogs, the second to the foxes."[21]

So for example, I suggest that Nernst was a fox while Einstein was a hedgehog. Nernst was not interested, as Einstein was, in building a worldview that would tie together the heterogeneous strands of twentieth-century physical thought. Nernst knew many things and was content to live in the many mansions built by science. His mode of working and reasoning featured thinking about, and moving back and forth among, topics and themes in a somewhat haphazard way. Contrary to public opinion, meandering mental pathways, even distractions, are not necessarily undesirable from the point of view of achieving creative insights. Interruptions and diversions, at least for some investigators, seem to enhance the ability to fabricate and test novel ideas and schemes.

My third point is that Nernst's own work reveals no essential tension between the roles of experiment and theory in science. He invariably conjoins them into one continuous give-and-take program in which experiment feeds theory and theory feeds experiment. This, we realize, is not our contemporary image of the scientist. Einstein, lovingly in fact, refers to Nernst's elementary, even primitive, theoretical equipment; but Einstein then has to admit that Nernst's deep passion for science, his originality, his uncanny intuitive grasp for the essentials, and his complete freedom from (theoretical) prejudice led him along the path toward singularly creative and productive consequences. "I have never met anyone," says Einstein, "who resembled him in any essential way."[22]

As Lewis and Randall wrote in their classic volume on chemical thermodynamics in 1923: "Nernst and his associates have made remarkable contributions both to theory and to practice. Some arithmetic and thermodynamic inaccuracy occasionally marring their work is far outweighed by brilliancy of imagination and originality of experimentation."[23] We may suggest that on the growing frontier of the unknown it may be asking too much to demand of an investigator the utmost in spontaneous, in-depth understanding in the field of action. Ideas can be presented in a clear way, but nevertheless be devoid of real content. Ideas also can be fuzzy and unclear, as Nernst's sometimes were, but implicitly fertile and rich in content. Clarity, if you will, comes mostly through hindsight. When something ends in a certain way, inevitably all will agree that it was bound to end that way.

I have tried to highlight those particulars in Nernst's career that seemed to me most illuminating in regard to his scientific creativity. Our most important insights into Nernst's innovative work, I have emphasized, can come only from careful analysis of his scientific papers, especially when correlated with an exploration of the work of others that he built on and extended. If I had undertaken this task with attention to the kind of historical and analytical detail and sophistication that is really convincing, it would have taken far more space and thought than this presentation will allow. I hope I have touched on the main outlines of Nernst's work sufficiently to convey some understanding for the choices he made, the parameters he focused on in his analyses, the kinds of questions that were high priority for him, the things he deliberately ignored, the expertise and finesse with which he combined the experimental and the theoretical elements in his approach, and so on. I also have chosen, here and there, to draw a caricature of Nernst's personality; and have intimated, without being very specific, that some more idiosyncratic and elusive factors inevitably entered into Nernst's work in science.

Speaking more generally, the topic of scientific creativity is fraught with intrinsic complexities. I should like to conclude with some remarks about this. First, the historical exploration of "creativity" immediately brings with it issues that are essentially philosophical, psychological, and contextual. In my view, "creativity analysis" is mainly an exercise in trying to illuminate the historical and contingent circumstances of scientific discovery rather than honing in, post facto, on the logical or reconstructive dimensions of what happens during acts of creative insight. In this connection let me quote from a paper of Carl Kordig's read at the Minnesota Center for Philosophy of Science in 1974:

Feigl, Popper, Reichenbach, and Braithwaite maintain that logic and philosophy do not analyze the very conceiving of new ideas. Popper writes 'the initial stage, the act of conceiving or inventing a theory, seems to me neither to call for logical analysis nor to be susceptible of it . . . there is no such thing as the logical method of having new ideas or a logical reconstruction of this process'. Reichenbach maintains that the philosophy of science cannot be concerned with reasons for suggesting hypotheses; it is concerned only with reasons for accepting hypotheses. Similarly Braithwaite claims that 'solution of . . . historical problems involves the individual psychology and the sociology of thought' which are not 'our business here'. The philosophy of science should analyze only completed arguments supporting already invented hypotheses. It evaluates reasons supporting hypotheses already proposed. Such is the standard account of discovery and justification. [24]

I only would want to add: History may not prove anything, but it reveals much.

When we therefore ask: What unambiguous guidelines for scientific discovery may one acknowledge? I suspect that the answer should be that there are none—at least not in the initial stages of creative perception. If Nernst had been asked how he made his discoveries he probably would have concurred with Newton, who, when asked that question, replied: "By always thinking unto them." Deciding how scientists reason, and why, must await the historical study of how individual scientists, in fact, have gone about their work. Unfortunately, the attendant circumstances of creativity in most case studies of discovery are not at all well understood.

The second point I want to make—and I think the case of Nernst provides an excellent example of this—is that creativity is often found to be related to the ability and the courage to break out of well established thinking patterns. The heart of a problem is often to be found in its outskirts. All of our normal thinking schemes are structured basically to preserve our acquired reasoning patterns. By contrast, a scientist might try to integrate all of the information thought to be relevant to the solution of a given problem, and to fit it into a new, even nonconformist, perspective. Actually, the history of science in its most revolutionary chapters is replete with examples in which on-hand ideas and newly acquired information are shifted around, reorganized, ignored, or exaggerated, thus to give birth to novelty that might otherwise be buried beneath mountains of information and an infinite storehouse of potentially fertile conceptual schemes. If our in-coming information, according to prescribed method, could be inserted readily into a partially completed scientific jig-saw puzzle, then undoubtedly most of us would have the key to winning Nobel Prizes. Obviously, the order of organization and the selection choices of the components of science hold one of the keys to creativity.

The very special organization that clicks into place in a new way is precisely what renders creativity so elusive and difficult to chart. I guess I am saying that creativity is somehow related to information processing. The psychologist Edward De Bono says it this way: "Scientific information trickles in slowly over time and does not arrive all at once, and yet, at each stage, the best use has to be made of available information for one cannot wait for what comes next. The actual sequence in which the information arrives sets up the pattern or the way in which we look at a situation. Because of the sequence effect, these patterns do not necessarily make the best use of available information. One may have to break out of these established patterns in order to look at things in a different way."[25] Creativity, I suggest, can be blocked by too much irrelevant information. Thus it is conceivable that the concepts we hold on to sometimes retard progress more than the ones that we do not have. Available and adequate ideas may, in fact, make it very difficult to come up with better ideas. Incidentally, wit and humor, manipulated by the mind, may often help an investigator to escape established ways of looking at things by stepping outside of existing experience.

My third point is an attempt to put into proper perspective the relative merits and pitfalls of invoking exclusively external factors to explain a given scientist's creativity—sociological, political, economic, ideological, religious, institutional, philosophical, and so on. Some sociologists of science have been trying desperately to demonstrate that circumstances external to science—the milieu, the Zeitgeist, the climate of opinion, the ideological and cultural context— have been the determinative factors responsible for structuring the internal, substantive content of scientific theories and concepts. On the whole, in my opinion, no convincing case of exclusively external causes, linked to internal developments, has yet been put forward. Having said this by no means implies, however, that such factors are unimportant. In fact, they are often more exciting and revealing about the way a scientist goes about his/her work than anything else that transpires. As John Hendry writes in a recent analysis of Paul Forman's paper that relates Weimar culture to quantum causality:

When internal considerations are taken into account as well, then it becomes immediately clear that no single set of influences—internal, social, philosophical, psychological, etc. — can be taken independently of the others, and that each physicist's reaction to a given problem will be determined by a complex of motivations, many of them immune to historical objectification. It may be that the development of scientific knowledge is ultimately anthropologically (sociologically or psychologically) determined, but if so the determination will probably operate at a level that is present beyond objectifiable demonstration through our very mode of thinking rather than through explicit conceptualizations. As the persistent failure of the advocates of a sociologically determined science to prove their case suggests, it will not be on the explicit level with which they . . . have been concerned."[26]

Precisely what scientists do when they are engaged in science is one of the most significant questions that can be posed by the historian of science. In whatever way this undertaking may be formulated, let us hope that the disjointed representation of the so-called internal and external dimensions of science is a thing of the past. It is rather pretentious to assume that historians could limit themselves to the evidence of the written word, without reference to the authors of the texts, or without recognizing the environmental circumstances in which the science of the texts evolved. To establish the way in which scientists go about their work, one must integrate all of the potentially illuminating historical components that are accessible and manageable: published and unpublished scientific contributions, personal reflections and methodological comments of the scientists, and, of course, the various contextual circumstances that surround scientific endeavor. The study of scientific creativity, in particular, is ill served by ignoring the incredibly rich, ongoing, spontaneous activity that lies hidden beneath the scientific inheritance that we all so much take for granted. The history of science is symbolized by time's unidirectional arrow, and it is the study of that irreversible process that promises to illuminate the springs of scientific creativity.

Notes

1. The most comprehensive and reliable sources of information about Nernst's life, work, and career include the following: Lord Cherwell (F. A. Lindemann) and F. Simon, "Walther Nernst, 1864-1941," in *Obituary Notices of the Fellows of the Royal Society of London* 4 (1942-1944), pp. 101-112; Max Bodenstein, "Walther Nernst, 25.6.1864-18.11.1941," *Berichte der Deutschen Chemischen Gesellschaft* 75 (1942), Abt. A (Vereinsnachrichten), pp. 79-104; K. F. Bonhoeffer, ed., "Dem Andenken an Walther Nernst," in *Naturwissenschaften* 31 (1943), pp. 257-275, 305-322, 397-415; Kurt Mendelssohn, *The World of Walther Nernst. The Rise and Fall of German Science 1864-1941* (Pittsburgh: Macmillan, 1973); Erwin Hiebert, "Herman Walther Nernst," *Dictionary of Scientific Biography* 15 (1978), pp. 432-453.

2. Einstein Collection, The Institute for Advanced Study, Princeton, N.J., Letters of Dr. Ernst Solomon of Santa Monica, California, to Einstein, dated 22 November 1941 and 4 February 1942.

3. Robert A. Millikan, "Walther Nernst, a Great Physicist, Passes," *Scientific Monthly* 54 (1942), pp. 85-86.

4. Translated by the author from what undoubtedly is the original German version of Einstein's "Nachruf Walther Nernst f. Scientific Monthly," 1942 that is in the Einstein Collection at the Institute for Advanced Study. It was published in English as "The Work and Personality of Walther Nernst," *Scientific Monthly* 54 (1942), pp. 195-196.

5. Hans-Günther Körber, ed., *Aus dem wissenschaftlichen Briefwechsel Wilhelm Ostwalds*, II. Teil (Berlin: Akademie-Verlag, 1869), p. 26.

6. Ibid., I. Teil, Berlin, 1861, p. 3.

7. Erwin Hiebert, "Nernst and Electrochemistry," Proceedings of the Symposium on Selected Topics in the History of Electrochemistry, *The Electrochemical Society, Proceedings* 78 (1978), pp. 180-200.

8. Walther Nernst, *Theoretische Chemie vom Standpunkt der Avogadroschen Regel und der Thermodynamik* (Göttingen: F. Encke, 1893), Vorwort.

9. Walther Nernst, *Experimental and Theoretical Applications of Thermodynamics to Chemistry*, London, 1907, p. 7.

10. W. Nernst, "Ueber die Berechnung chemischer Gleichgewichte aus thermischen Daten," *Nachrichten von der Gesellschaft der Wissenschaften zu Göttingen*, Mathematisch-physikalische Klasse, Berlin (1906), pp. 1-40.

11. Sir Francis Simon, "The Third Law of Thermodynamics. An Historical Survey," 40th Guthrie Lecture, *Year Book of the Physical Society* (1956), pp. 1-22. See esp. p. 1.

12. See Hiebert, "Hermann Walther Nernst," pp. 436-447.

13. Erwin Hiebert, "The Concept of Chemical Affinity in Thermodynamics," *Proceedings of the Xth International Congress of History of Science* (Ithaca, 1962), 2 (1964), pp. 871-873.

14. Henri Le Chatelier, "Recherches expérimentales et théoriques sur les équilibres chimiques," *Annales des Mines ou Recueil de Mémoires sur l'Exploitation des Mines . . .* 13 (1888), pp. 157-382. See chapter XI: Constante d'Integration.

15. Fritz Haber, *Thermodynamik technischer Gasreaktionen. Sieben Vorlesungen* (München: R. Oldenbourg, 1905). See p. 41ff. for a discussion of "Die thermodynamisch unbestimmte Konstante k."

16. *Albert Einstein—Michele Besso Correspondence, 1903-1955*, Paris, 1972, Einstein à Besso, Prag, 13.V.11, pp. 19-21.

17. Arnold Sommerfeld, "Das Plancksche Wirkungsquantum und seine allgemeine Bedeutung für die Molekülarphysik," *Physikalische Zeitschrift* 12 (1911), pp. 1057-1069. See p. 1060.

18. R. H. Fowler and T. E. Sterne, "Statistical Mechanics with Particular Reference to the Vapor Pressures and Entropies of Crystals," *Reviews of Modern Physics* 4 (1932), pp. 635-722. See p. 707.

19. Simon, "The Third Law," p. 21.

20. Bodenstein, "Walther Nernst," pp. 95-96.

21. Isaiah Berlin, *The Hedgehog and the Fox. An Essay on Tolstoy's View of History* (New York: New American Library, 1957), pp. 7-8.

22. Einstein, "Walther Nernst."

23. Gilbert Newton Lewis and Merle Randall, *Thermodynamics and the Free Energy of Chemical Substances* (New York and London: McGraw-Hill, 1923), p. 6.

24. Carl R. Kordig, "Discovery and Justification," *Philosophy of Science* 45 (1978), pp. 110-117. See p. 111. Kordig attempts to show in this paper that the distinction between

discovery and justification is ambiguous, and in what sense good reasons for discovery (but not necessarily initial acts of thinking) and good reasons for justification may be seen to be inextricably bound to particualr scientific theories. The point made is that a hypothesis needs good supporting reasons to be either plausible or acceptable, and that there is no *fundamental* difference between the reasons essential to plausibility and acceptability — only a difference of degree, acceptability requiring more than plausibility.

25. Edward De Bono, "Lateral Thinking and Creativity," *Proceedings of the Royal Institution of Great Britain* 45 (1972), pp. 283-298. See p. 291.

26. John Hendry, "Weimar Culture and Quantum Causality," *History of Science* 18 (1980), pp. 155-180. See p. 171.

Chapter 9

Albert Einstein and the Creative Act: The Case of Special Relativity

Stanley Goldberg

I

On December 31, 1978 a small notice tucked away on p. 17 of the first section of *The New York Times* announced that at the time of his death in 1955, Albert Einstein's brain had been removed from his body and entrusted for study to a team of experts headed by Dr. Thomas S. Harvey, the pathologist at Princeton Hospital, where Einstein died. At the time Harvey had said that although "it looks like any body else's [brain] ," clues to the source of Einstein's genius would be sought in the tissues and fluids that remained.

Now, twenty-three years later on the eve of the celebration of the centennial of Einstein's birth, Dr. Harvey had still not announced any results. The *Times* reporter speculated that this was perhaps due to the fact that even after careful study, Einstein's brain still looked like anyone else's.

When all is said and done, then, is it just an ordinary brain? "No," Dr. Harvey says. He had met Einstein, spoken with him, just before the great man's death. "No," he says again. "One thing we know is that it was not an ordinary brain."[1]

This is just one example, one of the more ghoulish and bizarre examples to be sure, of three types of approaches that have been used in recent times to understand what it is that makes someone like Albert Einstein a genius. In this case the assumption was made that genius is to be understood in terms of neural mechanisms within the brain or through other, more general biological processes. This view is related to the recent campaign to link intelligence, creativity,

Plate 1. Albert Einstein and H. A. Lorentz. Reproduced by permission of the AIP Niels Bohr Library.

and IQ scores to genetic factors.[2] A second approach, the one that has generated by far the most literature, is the attempt to objectify the concept of creativity by devising inventories and instruments closely related to IQ score tests for predicting creativity. Presumably, if one can predict with such an instrument who the creative individual will be, one can make some claim to understanding something about it. Such efforts have never had much success.[3] A third approach has been to obtain from those identified as creative geniuses, accounts of the conscious thought processes that led to the creative act. The most famous of these studies in which Einstein himself participated were Jacques Hadamard's *The Psychology of Invention in the Mathematical Field* and Max Wertheimer's *Productive Thinking.* The centennial of Einstein's birth motivated renewed attempts to understand Einstein's genius through examining his own anecdotal accounts.[4]

Creative thinking has always been a mystery. I think it must always remain so. Remember when people were encouraged to take Latin or geometry because these subjects "trained the mind"? How does the mind work, that Latin trains it? In Einstein's case, he reported that he was immediately taken with a book of Euclidean geometry given to him at the age of twelve and that even earlier, when told of the Pythagorean theorem, he had with much difficulty been able to prove it on the basis of the similarity of triangles. "It seemed evident," Einstein said, "that the relations of sides of the right angled triangle would have to be completely determined by one of the acute angles."[5] Given that Einstein solved this problem without studying geometry, and given that at twelve he was immediately comfortable with the structure of proof within Euclidean geometry, it is difficult to see how Einstein might be used as an example of "geometry training the mind."

Einstein's account of his early encounter with geometry was given in the context of his own musings on the nature of thinking. In reviewing that and other similar discussions that Einstein indulged in over the years, Gerald Holton concluded that Einstein did not think verbally at all but rather thought in terms of images.[6] In fact Holton went so far as to interpret the fact that Einstein did not talk until the age of three as evidence of his *resistance* to verbal language:

But long before he wrote scientific papers, Einstein was Einstein—already at the age of three, playing silently, resisting verbal language and refusing thereby to accept an externally imposed authority in names and rules by which many another child had to "civilize" and give up his own curiosity and imaginative play. It is a world that by its very definition we hardly know how to describe. But it is the world in which, from all the evidence we have, the play with geometric and other visual images, and hence the perception of such transformation properties of forms as symmetry and asymmetry, appear to have been basic for the development of successful thought itself.[7]

There are difficulties with this approach. One must take care not to confuse thought and language. If it is not possible to understand the relationship between training a person to think and a particular subject, it is just as difficult to label thinking as "geometrical," or "verbal," or "visual." It is not even possible to say what it means to "think critically" if by that one intends to describe a thinking *process* rather than a verbal interaction.

Einstein understood this. In 1936 he remarked:

It is a fact that the totality of sense experiences is so constituted as to permit putting them in order by means of thinking—a fact which can only leave us astonished, but which we shall never comprehend. One can say: The eternally incomprehensible thing about the world is its comprehensibility.[8]

Ten years later, in 1946, he wrote as follows:

For me it is not dubious that our thinking goes on for the most part without use of signs (words) and beyond that to a considerable degree unconsciously. For how, otherwise, should it happen that sometimes we "wonder" quite spontaneously about some experience?[9]

Thus our inner voice or inner pictures are probably more like *summaries* of thinking. By that time, the process, which occurs at some deep level, is completed. Even if we elucidated every chemical reaction in the brain and traced every neuron, and even if by artificial stimulation of individual neurons we were able to induce specific thoughts, thinking would remain an enigma. The somewhat popular analogy of the working brain to the operation of an electronic computer is not a good one; but a related analogy is much closer to the relationship that exists between the conscious weaving together of memories, sense experience, and insight to whatever the internal biological processes are. That analogy is, of course, the relationship between the language the programmer uses and the actual internal workings of the computer itself. The programmer need know nothing about transistors, capacitors, resistors, or inductors. He or she can be totally ignorant of the existence, let alone the nature, of integrated circuits or the method of their manufacture. He or she can even be totally ignorant of binary logic. As one sits at the terminal communicating with it in FORTRAN, or ALGOL or PASCAL, or APL, or COBOL, it doesn't even matter where the machine is. The programmer is totally unconscious of what the machine itself is doing. And although it is true that differences might exist in the conscious language individuals use, and although it is also true that different languages make certain concepts more easily accessible, there is no evidence at all that those differences are a significant variable in who becomes a creative scientist, let alone a creative person.

Einstein wasn't even consistent in describing the nature of his thought processes. Sometimes he referred to the signs of thought as images, sometimes as words.[10] In any event for Einstein to *tell* us how he thinks is like someone trying to describe the taste of pickled herring or the tactile sensation that one gets from touching a lizard. Yet the fact that it is futile to try to discover how a creative genius such as Einstein thinks does not mean that we can say nothing at all about the nature of the creative process in terms of the observable habits of individuals or in terms of the relationship of their epistemological credo to whatever they produce. In what follows I examine these relationships with respect to Einstein's creation of the special theory of relativity.

II

Einstein's genius can be characterized by three qualities: curiosity, intuition, and concentration. He had a childlike curiosity. It was almost as if he were wearing special glasses to make all that was irrelevant invisible. In 1905 theorists such as Max Abraham, H. A. Lorentz, and Henri Poincaré were all concentrating their energies on attempting to understand how ether might affect matter—in such a way, for example, as to change the dimensions of moving objects. As I shall explain later, at some point Einstein had realized that the heart of the problem lay not in any theory of matter, but rather in a theory of measurement. The central question of Einstein was "what does it mean to say that two events are simultaneous?"[11] The puzzle-solving analogy is a good one. All the pieces of the jigsaw puzzle had been laid out by others; but they were having a very difficult time seeing how to put the pieces together. Einstein came along and plopped the pieces in place in a manner that was totally at odds with what anyone thought possible. The analogy breaks down only because it was evident to almost no one else that Einstein had really solved the puzzle.

Second, Einstein had an unerring intuition for what the right question should be. He could be so sure of himself that in the face of seemingly contrary evidence, he could reject the results of experimental tests at variance with his own conclusions. In fact, he did this in at least two instances. The first time, shortly after publication of the special theory of relativity, a set of experiments on the trajectories of high-speed beta particles by Wilhelm Kaufmann (a man avowedly opposed to the concepts within the theory of relativity) led Kaufmann to the conclusion that the predictions of Einstein's theory were wrong and hence that the theory must be rejected in favor of another theory whose premises, as it turned out, were more to Kaufmann's liking. Kaufmann's results were used by many physicists concerned with the problems associated with the theory of relativity to reject any theory such as Einstein's. When Einstein finally commented on these results a year later, he said that he could see nothing wrong with the experiment; however, he confidently rejected the result on the grounds that only his own theory grew out of comprehensive considerations and applied quite generally. Later (as would almost always be the case in such instances involving Einstein's work), Kaufmann's experimental design, which at the time had seemed acceptable and faultless to almost everyone, proved to have contained subtle defects.[12]

Some twenty years later, when D. C. Miller reported that he had in fact detected the absolute motion of the earth, there were two immediate responses. Supporters of the theory of relativity simply laughed Miller down, while opponents to the theory defended the Miller work. Einstein apparently wrote Miller a private letter in which he pointed out that Miller's result might be explained by a subtle temperature variation of a tenth of a degree across the length of the experimental table. That result was, in fact, independently confirmed thirty years after the writing of that letter by someone totally ignorant of Einstein's suggestion.[13]

Third, Einstein could concentrate on a problem with uncommon zeal. Most people might give up for days or months or even years at a time. Not Einstein. After 1920, his commitment to developing a unified field theory, a single theory of explaining all physical inter-actions, was unshakable. Almost everyone else abandoned the attempt. A majority of the physics community was on record be-moaning the fact that as he got older, Einstein had run out of ideas. Hardly. Rather his ideas were no longer leading the mainstream as they had done for two decades. Not only did he not run out of ideas; they kept coming in a never-ending torrent. His concentration was such that even near death in 1955, his ever-present pad and pen were nearby so that he could continue working on his field equations.

This leads me to yet another point. The notion that after the publication of the general theory of relativity, Einstein no longer stayed in the mainstream of physics assumes that earlier he had been in the mainstream. But in fact, he was never *in* the mainstream. He had always followed an independent path that would invariably carry him ahead of the mainstream, where he would serve as a beacon for others. This was the case with special and general relativi-ty, with the quantization of light and the photoelectric equation, and now, it seems, with regard to unified field theory. The image of Einstein as a physicist is too confining. He was, it seems to me, a philosopher, in the classic sense of the word, who used physics to inform his philosophy. He never was, as his beloved idol, H. A. Lorentz (a physicist par excellence) was, part of the mainstream of physics.

III

Einstein has left a rich legacy of writings concerning his outlook on matters of epistemology, especially his views on the structure of scientific theories, the relationship of empirical evidence to theory, and the nature of reality. These have been reviewed in some detail over the last ten years, most extensively by Professor Gerald Holton.[14]

It has been argued[15] that early in his career, Einstein had been committed to Machian positivism and that later he had rejected such an empiricist position. But in fact, as Holton well documents, Einstein maintained an eclectic position throughout his life.[16] He never abandoned empiricist tenets when it came to the need to make clear what it was that measurement provided, and he never abandoned realist and idealist apriorism when it came to relating ideas to measurements. According to Einstein, no single epistemological system had the richness required to deal with the complexities presented by "the facts of experience." Thus, although Einstein never changed his mind about the fact that sensory experience is the only source of our knowledge about the world, he also maintained that it was an error to believe that theory is arrived at by induction from such sensory experience.[17]

The starting point for any theory is a set of postulates. Those postulates are then connected logically to a set of conclusions, and it is the conclusions that are compared to sensory experience. If we call the postulates A and the conclusions of the argument B, the form of any theoretical argument in science and its connection to sensory experience is as follows:

If A then B
I Observe B
Therefore A

Of course this is not a *logically* correct argument, since I have not shown, and cannot show, that there is only one set of postulates (A) that can be used to develop the conclusion (B). Einstein understood this well.[18] The role of logic in science is nothing more nor less than to connect the A's to the B's. It is the content of "then" in the above syllogism. The rules of logic are themselves human-made conventions, Einstein argued; without those rules, however, it would be impossible for people to communicate in any disciplined way about nature. Science would be impossible.[19]

Throughout his life Einstein was clear and insistent on the fact that not only are the postulates from which theoretical structures are developed not arrived at by some sort of induction from experience, neither are they arrived at by logic. Einstein often referred to these postulates as "concepts" or sometimes "laws." How does one arrive at them? In 1918 he said,

There is no logical path to these laws; only intuition resting on sympathetic understanding of experience can reach them.[20]

In 1933 he remarked that these concepts are

free inventions of the human intellect which cannot be justified either by the nature of that intellect or in any fashion *a priori*.[21]

These are just two examples of the countless times Einstein invoked the term "intuition" as the source of theoretical ideas in science.[22] They are summarized by the analogy he invoked in 1936: the relationship of observation to concept "is not analogous to that of soup to beef, but rather of check number to overcoat."[23]

Given that Einstein believed that the creation of scientific theories depended on the free play of concepts and the use of sensitive intuition, one might at first think that there would be no criteria that one could apply to select one theory as being superior to another. Indeed, although Einstein often referred to the need for external validation of theories — i.e., that the theories not be contradicted by experience[24] — there are an infinite number of sets of axioms (freely chosen on the basis of intuition) that can account for any sense experiences.

First of all it should be noted that Einstein was not speaking of a simple-minded notion of falsification when he insisted that theories not be contradicted by experience. As I have already pointed out, several times in his career he resisted abandoning theories because one experiment seemed to indicate that the predictions of the theory were not correct.[25]

A second criterion is required. Einstein referred to it as the "inner perfection" as opposed to the "external confirmation." This inner perfection is a function of "naturalness or logical simplicity of the premises" of a theory.[26] How does one decide which set to choose from the myriad of possible combinations of principles and concepts that are available? According to Einstein,

These fundamental concepts and postulates, which cannot be further reduced logically form the essential part of a theory, which reason cannot touch. It is the grand object of all theory to make these irreducible elements as simple and as few in number as possible without having to renounce the adequate representation of any empirical content whatever.[27]

One understands then why Einstein in 1905 might have been pleased with and confident about his solution to the problem of the photoelectric effect. He had satisfied all of his conditions for a good theory — the fewest possible number of postulates required to account for all of the facts. One can only stand in wonder and awe at Einstein's self-assurance at the age of twenty-six in the face of almost uniform rejection of the theory. In fact, eight years later, on the eve of its confirmation, which even took R. A. Millikan (the person doing the experiment) by surprise,[28] the fundamental postulate of the theory—the quantization of light—was dismissed by those recommending Einstein for the prestigious directorship of the Kaiser Wilhelm Institute for Physics. According to the letter of recommendation written by Max Planck and Walter Nernst, "That he [Einstein] may sometimes have missed the target in his speculations, as for example in his theory of light quanta, cannot really be held against him. For in the most exact of natural sciences every innovation entails risks."[29]

Einstein regarded his criterion for a good theory, a minimum number of axioms capable of accounting for all of the experimental evidence, as a developmental aspect of the progress of science. Such a criterion had not been very prominent in the eighteenth and nineteenth centuries. But he expressed the belief that it was steadily gaining ground.[30] In fact, according to Einstein, the special theory of relativity

is a fine example of the fundamental character of the modern development of theoretical science. The hypotheses with which it starts become steadily more abstract and remote from experience. On the other hand it gets nearer to the grand aim of all science which is to cover the greatest possible number of empirical facts by logical deduction from the smallest possible number of hypotheses and axioms.[31]

There seems to be a paradox in this. Whereas Einstein saw simplicity in hewing theoretical structures to the barest number of abstract postulates necessary to comprehend the matrix of experimental evidence which the theory is supposed to comprehend, others found his reasoning difficult, if not impossible, to understand. In fact in the first four or five years after publication of the theory of relativity, fewer than five physicists in Europe and America seemed to comprehend what it was that Einstein (as opposed to Lorentz or Minkowski) was talking about.[32] The problem that many of these physicists seemed to have with Einstein's special theory of relativity was precisely that which Einstein saw as its strength—it was too abstract, too removed from what they considered to be the realm of experience and therefore not physics.[33] On the other hand, the fact that the theory, as published in 1905, contains only two postulates— the principle of relativity and the invariance of the speed of light—

violated the criterion of others, for example Henri Poincaré, that a theory be flexible enough to be modified in the face of contrary instances. Einstein's theory did not have that feature. Lorentz's theory did. Poincaré supported the Lorentz theory.[34]

There is a serious puzzle here. Scholars in the history and philosophy of science concerned with the development of Einstein's special theory of relativity have concentrated a good deal of effort on trying to puzzle out the sources of Einstein's ideas. Much has been accomplished in identifying the probable influences on Einstein's early work.[35] It has been shown that the first paper on the theory of relativity does indeed conform to the tenets that Einstein himself espoused for good theories.[36] Thus, while experiment *suggests* that a principle of relativity might be operative, Einstein elevated the principle to a postulate, thereby removing it from the realm of experimental test. This aspect of the theory is quite comprehensible. While making the principle of relativity a postulate was a bold move, it was an act that fit well the model Einstein later espoused so often in his epistemological writings. It fit well with his notion of the importance of "the free play of concepts."[37]

The puzzle concerns the second postulate. That postulate states that the speed of light is an invariant. Not only does the speed of light have the same value in all directions in any inertial frame of reference; it has the same value in *all* such frames of reference.

Some commentators have tried to explain the source of the second postulate as strictly a matter of experiment.[38] Others have interpreted it as simply Einstein's recognition of a "law of physics." That law is contained within Maxwell's field equations where the velocity of light plays the role of a constant.[39] Still others see the source of the second postulate in musing Einstein did when at the age of sixteen he wondered how the propagation of electromagnetic energy would appear to someone moving at the speed of light.[40] And still others see in the second postulate a specific example of Einstein's "method for constructing theories," which, according to this view, "started . . . by postulating principles which were not intuitively obvious" and were even contradictory to intuitions.[41] Taking a cue from Einstein's own introductory remarks concerning the second postulate that it is only apparently irreconcilable with the Principle of Relativity,[42] some consider Einstein an epistemological magician who was able to show that the resolution was indeed the content of the special theory of relativity, in particular the Lorentz transformation equations.[43]

Not all of these views of how Einstein discovered the second postulate and what its epistemological content is can be right. In fact, in my view, none of them is right.

The second postulate is beyond the pale of experimental test. As we shall see, the heart of the problem is that it is impossible to make a one-way measurement of the speed of light. Nor can the invariance of the speed of light be a law of physics resulting from the role that light plays in Maxwell's equations, since the form that Maxwell's equations takes in different frames of reference is a *result* of the postulates of the special theory of relativity. A statement that is both a postulate and a result in the same theory is a circular statement. And although Einstein certainly speaks of hitting on a paradox at the age of sixteen with regard to the appearance of the propagation of electromagnetic radiation to an observer moving at the speed of light, he also says that this paradox contains "the *germ* of the special theory of relativity."[44]

The difficulty has been that most scholars have been captivated by what Einstein has had to *say* about the status of theories, the source of ideas, and the relationships between concepts and conclusions of theoretical arguments and how those in turn relate to experience. And when they do compare Einstein's epistemological writings or his private letters in which he muses about theory, with his work in relativity, they almost always restrict the comparison to one paper: Einstein's first paper on relativity theory, published in 1905. It is understandable that we should be so intrigued in looking for the clues to the meaning of the basis of the theory of relativity in Einstein's private and public writings on epistemology. But the correlation is not clearcut. In fact it is, I think, misleading and ambiguous enough to lead to the variety of mutually contradictory positions enumerated above. But even more serious is the fact that all of the interpretations we have reviewed lack that sense of physical intuition that everyone agrees is one of the keystones of Einstein's genius. The solution to the problem is not to be found in Einstein's writings about his beliefs, but in his substantive papers themselves. We ought to take more seriously Einstein's own dictum in these matters: "If you want to find out anything from the theoretical physicists about the methods they use, I advise you to stick closely to one principle: don't listen to their words, fix your attention on their deeds."[45]

IV

In the first twelve years of its existence, Einstein gave two different accounts of the basis of the theory of relativity. One of these accounts was for professional physicists familiar with the theoretical and physical problems associated with the theory, and the second account was for lay people within and without the physics community. The logic of the two accounts is different, although the conclusions (the Lorentz transformation equations, and all of the kinematical results) are the same. What I am saying is that Einstein used *two* different sets of postulates: one set for talking to professionals, one set for talking to nonprofessionals.

The structure of Einstein's first paper on relativity[46] is well known. He begins with two postulates: the principle of relativity and the invariance of the speed of light, which he himself says only seem to contradict each other. There is really no justification for the second postulate in this paper save that it gives proper results. It is abstract and unphysical. It is for that reason, I think, more than any other that so many physicists—including Max Planck, Wilhelm Wien, Arnold Sommerfeld, Max Born and Hermann Minkowski—interpreted Einstein's theory as a generalization of Lorentz's 1904 theory and Lorentz's point of view.

I hold that to see Einstein's theory as a generalization of Lorentz's is a serious confusion. In the Lorentz theory the principle of relativity is not explicit, the transformation equations that Einstein derives from first principles are stated as a priori postulates, and the invariance of the speed of light and the fact that the speed of light is the ultimate speed, are contingencies.[47]

In his theory, Einstein uses the two postulates to immediately deduce the fact that measurements of the simultaneity of distant events will be relative. There is, at best, only one inertial frame of reference that will judge two events not at the same place to be simultaneous. All other frames of reference will necessarily decide that one of the events preceeded the other. Subsequently, Einstein uses the postulates to derive the Lorentz transformation equations, the equations Lorentz postulated as a way of accounting for known experimental results.

Not only is the structure of this version of Einstein's theory not as physically intuitive as one might expect; it contains steps that are unnecessary, indeed irrelevant, to the development. These steps are precisely the ones that subsequent commentors have made so much of—the steps that show that given the two postulates, relativity of simultaneity ensues as one consequence.

There is no better testimony to the fact that the discussion of simultaneity in Einstein's first paper is not central to the *logical* development than a paper that Einstein published two years later. In that paper, a review of the field written at the request of Johannes

Stark and intended for other experts,[48] Einstein begins as before by stating the two postulates: the principle of relativity and the invariance of the speed of light. Einstein then goes on to remark that as he will show in what follows, two events not at the same place, which are judged to be simultaneous in one frame of reference, will be judged to be not simultaneous in other frames of reference. The interesting thing is that Einstein never does bother to show that, nor does it make any difference whatsoever to the structure of the argument.[49]

As I remarked earlier, the argument, though logically correct, is not very physical. I think the reason for this is that the first technical presentation that Einstein made of the special theory of relativity did not reflect the manner in which he originally thought through the theory. What it does reflect is the fact that even at the start of his career, Einstein was committed to the notion that the most important feature that theory could exhibit was the minimum number of postulates necessary to build a set of conclusions that accounts for all of the evidence. The price Einstein paid for this parsimony, which, let us recall, he said repeatedly was the "grand object of all theory," was high. It was the loss of a real sense of the physical meaning of the theory, in particular of the second postulate, the invariance of the speed of light. It is not too surprising, then, that most physicists committed to a more direct link between theory and experiment should have been puzzled by or resistant to Einstein's theory.

In the next few years, Einstein gave several accounts of the special theory of relativity to lay audiences. The structure of the basis of the theory in those presentations was decidedly different from the structure we have just discussed. On the one hand, these versions of the theory were not quite as parsimonious of postulates; on the other hand, the rationale for the postulates was much more physical and much more comprehensible.[50]

Einstein's account of the theory in such popularizations began, as his technical papers began, by discussing the experimental basis for the principle of relativity. In the eighteenth and early nineteenth centuries, Einstein said, as long as one had confidence in the possibility of a mechanical description of all phenomena, there seemed no reason to doubt the principle of relativity.

Unlike his early technical papers, here the principle of relativity did not stand alone: a concept elevated to a postulate by suggestive experimental results. It was immersed in a matrix of other postulates, which included concepts of the measurement of spatial and temporal coordinates and Newton's first axiom (the Law of Inertia). The consequences of these postulates were the Galilean transformation equations and the classical velocity addition law.

When one turned to optical and electromagnetic phenomena there were difficulties. A conflict appeared between the classical velocity addition law and the law of the propagation of light. Because of the motion of the earth through the presumably absolutely fixed ether, one expected to find that the speed of light in different directions was different. Even if it were not possible to measure the speed of light itself in any one direction, one should see manifestations of the difference by making use of so-called ether drift experimental apparati. This proved not to be the case. It is likely that it was this problem that the sixteen-year-old Einstein had in mind in his musing on how a light beam would appear to an observer moving at the speed of light. But the next step of Einstein's formulation of the special theory of relativity for lay audiences was not to postulate the invariance of the speed of light as he did for professional audiences; it was rather to ask the question "what does it mean to say that two events are simultaneous?"

My guess is that sometime in the early spring of 1905, Einstein had realized after ten years of thinking about these problems that judgments of simultaneity were central to both temporal and spatial measurements. For example, to say that an event occurs at 8:00 is really to say that the occurrence of the event is simultaneous with the arrival of the hands of some clock to a definite position. Furthermore, although judgments of simultaneity are not problematic when the events happen at the same place, there is a serious problem when the events are separated spatially. In order for it to be possible to determine whether or not two events are simultaneous, the information that the events occurred has to reach the person or instrument making the measurement. If the information arrives "at the same time," the temptation is to declare that the events occurred simultaneously. But such a declaration, Einstein explained to his lay audiences, assumed that the speed with which information of this sort is transported through space is the same in all directions. In other words, if the information is being transported by light signals, judgments of distant simultaneity assume that the speed of light is the same in different directions in the frame of reference in which the measurement is being made. (Fig. 1) Is that in fact the case? There is no way to tell. In order to make a one-way measurement of the speed of light, since nothing can keep up with it, two clocks would be required; and in order to determine the time elapsed

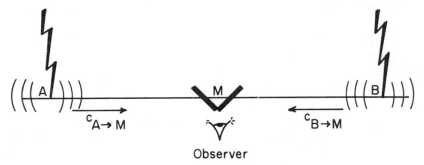

Observer

Figure 1. The puzzle presented by distant simultaneity. Adjacent to a straight railroad track, mirrors have been erected at M midway between points A and B allowing an observer at M to sight both A and B at the same time. The observer at M sees lightning strokes strike at A and B "at the same time." The observer's decision that the strokes, in fact, occurred simultaneously depends on the assumption that the speed of light in the direction A to M is the same as the speed of light in the direction B to M.

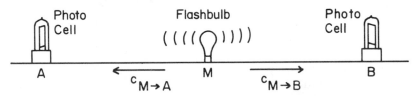

Figure 2. The puzzle of making a one-way measurement of the speed of light. To determine whether or not the speed of light is the same in the directions A to M and B to M (or vice versa), identical clocks have been placed at points A, B, and M. (As in Figure 1, the point M is midway between A and B.) The clocks at A and B are connected to identical photocell starters, and when the clock at M is started, a flashbulb is set off. The fact that the clocks at A and B start together does not mean that the speed of light is the same in all directions, since, as before, one must assume that the time required for light to travel from M to A is the same as the time for light to travel from M to B. But this is precisely what we are trying to determine. Einstein's solution to this dilemma was to stipulate that the speed of light in different directions in any inertial frame of reference has the same value. Given that stipulation, the observer in Figure 1 concludes that the strokes are simultaneous and the arrangement in Figure 2 provides a means for synchronizing clocks at different locations in any inertial frame of reference.

between the transmission and the arrival of the light signal, the clocks would have to be synchronized. But in order to synchronize them, I require comparative information about the speed of light in different directions. (Fig. 2) I am caught in a vicious circle.

It is at this point that Einstein's great physical intuition came into play. He realized that one had to *"stipulate"* that the speed of light

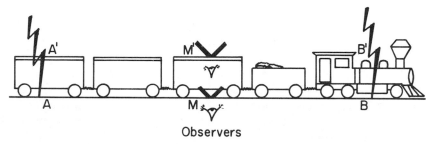

Observers

Figure 3. The relativity of simultaneity. The arrangement of mirrors on the embankment of Figure 1 (point M midway between A and B) is duplicated on a train (the mirrors are at point M' midway between A' and B'). When point M' is just opposite M, lightning strikes points A, A'B, and B'. As before, the observer at M concludes that the strokes occurred simultaneously. The observer at M' concludes that the strokes are not simultaneous. Since that observer is moving up toward the light spreading from the stroke at B and away from the light spreading from the stroke at A, he or she concludes that the stroke at B occurred before the stroke at A. Both observers are forced to stipulate that the speed of light is the same in all directions in their respective frames of reference.

was the same in all directions, and that is "a stipulation that I can make of my own free will in order to arrive at a definition of simultaneity."[51]

Later some philosophers of science quibbled with this stipulation on the grounds that in order to define distant simultaneity, one could use any signal speed one wanted — sound, for example, or the rate at which turtles move on the surface of the earth. And furthermore one need not stipulate that the signal speed be the same in all directions.[52] This is logically true; but, as Einstein himself pointed out so many times, doing science is not a matter of logic. With regard to the choice of light signals to define simultaneity, Einstein once remarked, "The only virture of axioms is to furnish fundamental propositions from which one can derive conclusions that fit the facts. . . . One could of course choose, say the velocity of sound instead of light. It would be reasonable, however, to select not the velocity of just 'any' process, but an 'outstanding' process. . . ."[53]

In order to decide on a meaningful criterion for measuring the simultaneity of distant events, Einstein stipulated that in one inertial frame of reference, the speed of light was the same in all directions. But if the principle of relativity is maintained, there is nothing special about one particular inertial frame of reference. In fact, the stipulation must hold for all inertial frames of reference. It follows immediately that two spatially separate events that are simultaneous in one inertial frame of reference, will not be simultaneous in any other inertial frame of reference. (Fig. 3) The relativity of simultaneity is a direct consequence of Einstein's realization that some stipulation had to be made about one signal speed. This may seem very simple today. It must have been very difficult for many of Einstein's colleagues to understand. For example, as late as 1927, even the great physicist H. A. Lorentz objected to Einstein's analysis on the grounds that "my notion of time is so definite that I clearly distinguish in my picture what is simultaneous and what is not."[54]

I am sure that Einstein would have replied there is no question about the fact that one observer can clearly distinguish what is simultaneous and what is not. This says nothing, of course, about whether different inertial observers will agree on the matter.

There is still a paradox to be resolved. There is a contradiction between the classical velocity addition law and the stipulation in every inertial frame of reference that speed of light is the same in all directions. Einstein realized that Newton had assumed implicitly, without even being aware of it, that it was possible to transmit information from one place to another instantaneously. It was that assumption, together with the principle of relativity, that stood behind the derivation of the classical velocity addition law. If one dropped the assumption of an infinite signal speed, the classical velocity addition law was no longer valid. Logically, one way all inertial observers can agree on the principle of relativity and also maintain that the speed of light is the same in all directions is to postulate that the speed of light is invariant—that it has the same value in all inertial frames of reference. The immediate consequence of the principle of relativity and the postulate of the invariance of the speed of light, as we have seen, is the Lorentz transformation equations. One of the deductions from those transformation equations is a new velocity addition law that would reduce to the classical law for an infinite signal speed and that contains within itself the second postulate.

Einstein's *physical* reasoning for the special theory of relativity may be summarized as follows: In developing his theory of measurement of spatial and temporal coordinates, Newton had assumed, besides the principle of relativity, the possibility of an infinite signal speed. If that assumption is dropped and replaced with the stipulation that speed of light is the same in all directions in any inertial frame of reference, simultaneity no longer has the absolute character previously ascribed to it, and the classical equations for comparing the spatial and temporal coordinates of events must be replaced by a new set of transformation equations.

In this sense the special theory of relativity is not a dynamical theory about matter or radiation or their interaction, as Lorentz's theory or Abraham's theory had been. Einstein's theory is a theory of measurement. When that theory of measurement is applied to dynamical theories—for example, when it is combined with Newton's laws of motion—interesting things emerge. Mass is no longer an invariant, and the energy content of a body is proportional to the body's mass. Such results say nothing about the nature of matter, of mass, of energy. In Einstein's hands, they are only manifestations of how we measure and of our need to objectify and operationalize the self-evident concept "simultaneity."

All of this physical thinking about the foundations of his theory of measurement was elaborated on by Einstein for lay audiences. What lay audiences seemed to find unacceptable was Einstein's brazen approach of unapologetically starting from principles that are only suggested by experiment rather than empirically deriving the results of all experiments and thereby arriving at some general principles.[55]

The physical reasoning behind the postulates was totally absent from papers Einstein presented to professionals. There, apparently supremely confident not only in his views about nature but also in his beliefs concerning the proper form that theories should take, he stripped the presentation down to the barest number of postulates necessary to do the job: the principle of relativity and the invariance of the speed of light. The trade-off was a fairly substantial one. The abstract nature and leanness of the underpinnings left almost everyone who read it adrift as to its meaning.

In the face of the ensuing furor, only once, as far as I know, did Einstein blink. In 1907, Paul Ehrenfest raised the issue of whether or not a deformable electron could move inertially. If it could not, then additional hypotheses would have to be introduced into the theory of relativity. Einstein's answer was immediate:

The principle of relativity or, more precisely, the principle of relativity together with the principle of the constancy of the velocity of light, is not to be interpreted as a "closed system," not really as a system at all, but rather merely as a heuristic principle which considered by itself, contains only statements about rigid bodies, clocks, and light signals. Anything beyond that that the theory of relativity supplies is in the connections it requires between laws that would otherwise appear to be independent of each other.[56]

Not many people have lived who could stand by so confidently while the rest of the world argued, debated, cloyed, taunted, insinuated, rejected, misinterpreted, and renounced. Along with Einstein, in modern times one thinks of Pasteur, Darwin, Marie Curie, Freud, Picasso, and a few others. Having such a tough hide is of course not sufficient to characterize creative genius. Not only must one be pigheadedly stubborn, one also has to be right. By being right I do not mean giving the right answers, but asking the right questions.

Notes

1. "Matter and Mind," *The Sunday New York Times* 127 (December 31, 1978), section 1, p. 17.

2. R. W. Gerard, "The Biological Basis of Imagination," in B. Ghiselin, ed., *The Creative Process* (New York: New American Library, 1952), pp. 226-251. R. Herrnstein, "IQ.," *The Atlantic* 114 (September 1971), pp. 43-64.

3. See F. Barron, *Creative Person and Creative Process* (New York: Holt, Rinehart and Winston, 1969) and the enormous literature cited therein. Cf. M. A. Wallach, *The Intelligence/Creativity Distinction* (Morristown: General Learning Press, 1971). M. A. Wallach, "Tests Tell Us Little About Talent," *American Scientist* 64 (1976), pp. 57-63. J. M. Blum, *Pseudoscience and Mental Ability* (New York: Monthly Review Press, 1978).

4. Jacques Hadamard, *The Psychology of Invention in the Mathematical Field* (New York: Dover Publications, 1954). Max Wertheimer, *Productive Thinking* (New York: Harper, 1945). Cf. G. Holton, "What Precisely is 'Thinking'? . . . Einstein's Answer," *The Physics Teacher* 17 (1979), pp. 157-164; hereafter referred to as "What Precisely is Thinking."

5. A. Einstein, "Autobiographical Notes," in P. A. Schillp, ed., *Albert Einstein: Philosopher-Scientist* (New York: Harper Torchbooks, 1958), pp. 9-11. Cf. G. Holton, "On Trying to Understand Scientific Genius," in G. Holton, *Thematic Origins of Scientific Thought* (Cambridge, Mass: Harvard University Press, 1973), p. 368; hereafter referred to as "On Trying to Understand."

6. Holton, "What Precisely is Thinking"; "On Trying to Understand."

7. Holton, "On Trying to Understand," p. 370.

8. A. Einstein, "Physics and Reality," in *Ideas and Opinions* (New York: Crown, 1954), pp. 290-323. Translation is by G. Holton in "What Precisely is Thinking," p. 163.

9. A. Einstein, "Autobiographical Notes," p. 9. Cf. Holton, "On Trying to Understand," p. 368.

10. Ibid.

11. For a discussion of the relationship between the work of Abraham, Poincaré, and Lorentz, see S. Goldberg, "The Abraham Theory of the Electron: The Symbiosis between Experiment and Theory," *Archives for the History of the Exact Sciences* 7 (1970), pp. 9-25; S. Goldberg, "Henri Poincaré and Einstein's Theory of Relativity," *American Journal of Physics* 35 (1967), pp. 934-944; S. Goldberg, "Poincaré's Silence and Einstein's Relativity," *British Journal for the History of Science* 5 (1970), pp. 73-84.

12. For details see S. Goldberg, "The Abraham Theory of the Electron" and S. Goldberg, "Max Planck's Philosophy of Nature and His Elaboration of the Special Theory of Relativity," *Historical Studies in the Physical Sciences* 7 (1976), pp. 125-160.

13. R. S. Shankland et al., "A New Analysis of the Interferometer Observations of Dayton C. Miller," *Reviews of Modern Physics* 27 (1955), pp. 167-178. Although there is no record of the letter Einstein wrote to Miller, Miller's response is in Einstein's papers at the Einstein archives in Princeton, N.J. Shankland published several papers recounting conversations that he had over the years with Einstein. In one of those he notes the following:

"When we finally found the cause of Miller's . . . [result] to be temperature gradients across the interferometer, Einstein was genuinely pleased and, wrote me a fine letter on the subject. I only learned after his death that he had written to [Paul] Ehrenfest after Miller's 1921 announcement suggesting that temperature effects might be responsible for the results; it is curious that he never mentioned this to me." R. S. Shankland, "Conversations with Albert Einstein II," *American Journal of Physics* 41 (1973), pp. 895-901. See p. 897.

14. In addition to the articles by Holton already cited, the reader is directed to the following articles collected in G. Holton, *Thematic Origins of Scientific Thought:* "Influences on Einstein's Early Work," pp. 197-218; "Mach, Einstein and the Search for Reality," pp. 219-260; "Einstein, Michelson and the 'Crucial Experiment,' " pp. 261-352. See also G. Holton, "Einstein's Model for Constructing a Scientific Theory," in P. C. Aichelburg and R. U. Sexl, eds., *Albert Einstein: His Influence on Physics, Philosophy and Politics* (Braunschweig: Vieweg, 1979). Holton has done a superb job in identifying the positions that Einstein maintained with regard to the relationship between theory, evidence, and belief. My own analysis owes much to Holton's pathbreaking efforts. Differences between us are largely a matter of emphasis.

15. For example, see R. W. Clark, *Einstein: The Life and Times* (New York: World Publishing Co., 1971), pp. 37-39.

16. See especially, Holton, "Mach, Einstein and the Search for Reality," and "What Precisely is Thinking."

17. A. Einstein, "Reply to Criticism," in P. A. Schillp, *Albert Einstein: Philosopher Scientist*, p. 684. Cf. Holton, "What Precisely is Thinking," p. 160.

18. See especially his essays "Physics and Reality" and "Geometry and Experience," in Einstein, *Ideas and Opinions.*

19. See especially, Einstein's essay "Theoretical Physics" in *Ideas and Opinions.* Holton has discussed this point in some detail in "What Precisely is Thinking," pp. 160-171 and "Einstein's Model for Constructing a Scientific Theory," p. 119.

20. A. Einstein, "Principles of Research," in *Ideas and Opinions.*

21. A. Einstein, "On the Method of Theoretical Physics," in *Ideas and Opinions.*

22. Holton has supplied a large range of quotations from Einstein's epistemological writings. See especially G. Holton, "What Precisely is Thinking" and "Einstein's Model for Constructing a Scientific Theory."

23. A. Einstein, "Physics and Reality," in *Ideas and Opinions.* Holton's description of this analogy as "marvelous" is quite apt. See Holton, "What Precisely is Thinking."

24. A. Einstein, "Autobiographical Notes," p. 21.

25. G. Holton, "Einstein's Model for Constructing a Scientific Theory," pp. 122-123. In Holton's opinion to reject a theory on the basis of a single experiment would be "extreme experimenticism not warranted by the delicate and difficult nature of experiments in modern science." Holton goes on to cite the danger of appealing to an experiment for the disconfirmation of one theory when that same experiment will be used in support of another theory that itself is less satisfactory on other grounds, for example on what Einstein would have referred to as the "inner perfection."

26. A. Einstein, "Autobiographical Notes," p. 23.

27. A. Einstein, "On the Method of Theoretical Physics," in *Ideas and Opinions.*

28. R. A. Millikan, "A Direct Determination of h," *Physical Review* 4 (1914), pp. 73-75. As late as 1917, Millikan not only thought Einstein's theory to be erroneous, he also thought Einstein had rejected it. On this point see Jeremy Bernstein, *Einstein* (New York: Viking Press, 1973), pp. 189-190.

29. Quoted in R. W. Clark, *Einstein: The Life and Times*, p. 169.

30. A. Einstein, "On the Method of Theoretical Physics," in *Ideas and Opinions.*

31. A. Einstein, "The Problem of Space, Ether and the Field in Physics," in *Ideas and Opinions.*

32. S. Goldberg, *Early Response to Einstein's Special Theory of Relativity, 1905-1912: A Case Study in National Differences* (Cambridge, Mass: Ph.D. Dissertation, 1968). This study is scheduled to be published by Tomash Publishers. Cf. S. Goldberg, *Understanding Relativity*, Part II Birkhäuser-Boston, (in press).

33. Ibid.

34. S. Goldberg, "Poincaré's Silence and Einstein's Relativity."

35. The most penetrating study is by Gerald Holton, "Influences on Einstein's Early Work."

36. Cf. Bernulf Kanitscheider, "Einstein's Treatment of Theoretical Concepts," and A. I. Miller, "On the History of the Special Theory of Relativity," in Aichelburg and Sexl, *Albert Einstein*, pp. 137-158 and 89-108.

37. G. Holton, "What Precisely is Thinking."

38. R. C. Tolman argued this position for years. Strains of it can still be found in American textbook accounts of the theory of relativity. S. Goldberg, *Understanding Relativity*, Chapter 10. Cf. R. Resnick, *Introduction to Special Relativity* (New York: Wiley, 1968), p. 36.

39. This is the implicit argument made by A. I. Miller, "On the History," pp. 99-102. Often one finds an eclectic blending of the view that the second postulate is dictated by experiment and Maxwell's equations. Cf. E. F. Taylor and J. A. Wheeler, *Spacetime Physics* (San Francisco: W. H. Freeman and Co., 1966), pp. 13-17.

40. Banesh Hoffman, "An Einstein Paradox," *Transactions of the New York Academy of Science* 36 (1974), pp. 730-737.

41. Kanitscheider, *Einstein's Treatment*, pp. 146-147.

42. A. Einstein, trans. W. Perrett and G. B. Jeffery, "On the Electrodynamics of Moving Bodies," in A. Einstein, H. A. Lorentz, H. Minkowski, and H. Weyl, *The Principle of Relativity* (New York: Dover Publications, n.d.), pp. 35-65.

43. A. P. French, *Special Relativity* (Cambridge, Mass.: MIT Press, 1966), pp. 65-68.

44. Einstein, "Autobiographical Notes," p. 53, emphasis added.

45. Einstein, "On the Method of Theoretical Physics."

46. Einstein, "On the Electrodynamics of Moving Bodies."

47. S. Goldberg, "Early Response," Chapters 1, 2, 5. Cf. A. I. Miller, "On the History," note 67. It should be pointed out that Miller does not place much significance in the confusion.

48. A. Einstein, Über das Relativitätsprinzip und die aus demselben gezogenen Folgerungen," *Jahrbuch der Radioaktivität und Elektronik* 4 (1907), pp. 411-462.

49. It is true that Einstein finally does discuss the problem of the relativity of simultaneity in this paper, but only in the very last sections when he is considering, not inertial frames of reference, but the problem of measurements made in frames of reference which are accelerating relative to each other. Ibid., pp. 454-458.

50. A. Einstein, "Die Relativitäts-Theorie," *Vierteljahresschrift der Naturforschenden Gesellschaft in Zürich* 56 (1911), pp. 1-14. "Diskussion," Ibid., pp. II-IX. A. Einstein, *Relativity: The Special, The General Theory* (New York: Crown 1956). This book was originally published in 1916.

51. A. Einstein, *Relativity: The Special, The General Theory*, p. 23.

52. A. Grünbaum, *Philosophical Problems of Space and Time*, (New York: Alfred A. Knopf, 1963), pp. 345-359.

53. Quoted by Wertheimer, *Productive Thinking*, p. 179.

54. H. A. Lorentz, *Problems of Modern Physics* (Boston: Ginn and Co., 1927), p. 221. Cf. S. Goldberg, *Understanding Relativity*, Chap. 3.

55. See in particular the discussion between Einstein and his audience in A. Einstein, "Relativitäts-Theorie."

56. This issue is discussed in M. Klein, *Paul Ehrenfest* (Amsterdam: North Holland Publishing Co., 1970). Klein does not give the exchange the same interpretation that I do. Cf. S. Goldberg, *Early Response* Chapter 2. S. Goldberg, *Understanding Relativity,* Chapter 3. The translation is by Klein.

Chapter 10

Erwin Schrödinger and the Descriptive Tradition

Linda Wessels

Erwin Schrödinger is best known for his contributions to quantum theory. He discovered the basic dynamic equation of the theory, the Schrödinger equation. He developed methods for applying that equation, methods that form the core of what we now call wave mechanics.[1] He was also one of the most persistent and eloquent critics of the standard interpretation of quantum mechanics, the "Copenhagen interpretation." His 1936 analysis of compound quantum systems made precise the interpretational challenge raised by Einstein, Podolsky, and Rosen in their famous 1935 paper on the completeness of quantum theory.[2] And even now, amidst the recent revival of interest in interpretational issues, the grin of Schrödinger's cat still haunts the new attempts to make sense of microphysics.[3] The focus of this paper will be on methodological aspects of Schrödinger's early work on wave mechanics. But before moving to that very specific topic, I want to mention some of the other ways in which Schrödinger's creative talents manifested themselves.

In the sciences, Schrödinger's activities went well beyond quantum theory. He worked throughout his career on statistical mechanics and on relativity and cosmology. His contributions in these areas ranged from technical research papers to lively introductory surveys.[4]

I am grateful to Schrödinger's daughter, Frau Ruth Braunizer, who lives in Nettingsdorf-Fabrik and Alpbach, Austria, for permission to reproduce the photographs from her private collection included here. I also thank the National Science Foundation for partial support of the research on which this paper is based.

During the late 1930s and the 1940s he struggled to develop a unified field theory; in the late 1940s he even thought for a while that he had succeeded.[5] Schrödinger also had a decisive influence on the biological sciences. In the 1940s his little book, *What is Life?*, alerted many physicists to the possibility of applying modern molecular and atomic theory to genetics and inspired a number of them to begin research in the field of molecular biology.[6]

Schrödinger's interests and abilities spilled over into nonscientific activities too. He had a gift for languages. In addition to his native German, he spoke English, French, and Spanish, and he read and wrote in all four of these languages plus two ancient ones, Greek and Latin.[7] He translated Greek and English poetry and also wrote poetry himself, in both English and German. In 1949 he published a volume of poetry containing some of his own creations, as well as some of his translations.[8] He also studied and wrote on philosophy. His private papers and some of his popular writings reveal his long-standing interest in issues of metaphysics, epistemology, and ethics. These papers also show that the holism of Eastern mysticism captured his philosophical imagination early and persisted as a strong theme in his writings until his death.[9] In matters of art, Schrödinger was primarily a spectator. Having been raised in fin de siècle Vienna, he was an avid theater-goer. Schrödinger's active artistic outlet was weaving. His mastery of that craft is evident in the pieces of his work still kept by his family.[10]

This brief summary gives but a glimpse of the complex personality that was Schrödinger's. A comprehensive analysis of the attitudes and methods that lay behind his various activities would surely reveal multiple connections among the forces that inspired and guided him, and would trace the springs of at least some of these forces to Schrödinger's boyhood and academic training in Vienna. Such a comprehensive analysis would require more space that I have available, however. My purpose in this paper is to provide only a small but, I think, crucial piece of that analysis. I shall attempt to delineate a methodological assumption that was central to Schrödinger's development of wave mechanics, to examine the role this assumption played at various stages in that development, and, finally, to consider the question why Schrödinger was committed to it. This analysis may give some insight both into Schrödinger's general approach to scientific activity, and into the sorts of methodological decisions that every scientist must face in the course of discovering and developing a new idea.

I.

Schrödinger began his career in physics in 1910, when he received his doctorate from the University of Vienna.[11] He stayed on in Vienna as assistant to Franz Exner in the Second Physical Institute until the outbreak of World War I. During the war he was an artillery officer on the southwest front. Then in 1920 and 1921 he advanced through a series of positions in Jena, Stuttgart, and Breslau, until in the fall of 1921 he accepted a position as full professor at the University of Zurich. By 1925 he was well known in the European physics community, recognized primarily for his work in statistical mechanics and for several articles on some narrowly defined issues in atomic theory. It was in late 1925 that Schrödinger discovered how to apply to atomic theory the wave equation that now bears his name.

Schrödinger has said in many places that the inspiration for wave mechanics was de Broglie's conjecture that matter does not consist merely of particles, but of particles paired with waves.[12] In his 1924 Ph.D. thesis de Broglie had suggested that each material particle is guided in its motion by a "phase wave," a wave that always remains in phase with a periodic process internal to the particle. According to this view the particle tends to move along a ray of the wave. The frequency of the wave is given by the energy of the particle divided by Planck's constant.[13] Work published by Schrödinger just before the discovery of wave mechanics and his private correspondence of that period give us a fairly detailed picture of the role that de Broglie's idea played.[14]

In the summer and fall of 1925 Schrödinger was working on quantum gas theory. Einstein had just developed an apparently fruitful approach to gas theory based on a new statistical method introduced the year before in connection with light quanta by S. N. Bose.[15] Most physicists, including Schrödinger, found the Bose-Einstein statistics quite mysterious. Schrödinger was attempting to gain some understanding of them by deriving Einstein's results for gases on the basis of some new physical assumptions plus the usual, intuitively acceptable, Maxwell-Boltzmann statistics.[16] In early 1925 Einstein had suggested in one of his papers on the new gas theory that de Broglie's wave-particle model of matter might be used to develop such a derivation.[17] In late October of 1925, Schrödinger obtained a copy of de Broglie's thesis and saw for himself what that model was and how it might be applied.[18]

The idea that matter might really be a wave phenomenon captured Schrödinger's imagination. First, he was intrigued by de Broglie's demonstration that the length given by Bohr's theory for an orbit of an atomic electron is exactly equal to a whole number of wavelengths of the phase wave that, according to de Broglie, accompanies the electron.[19] Schrödinger immediately set out to determine the shape of such a phase wave by constructing a wave that was sufficiently refracted about the nucleus to make its rays coincide with equal energy Bohr-Sommerfeld orbits, where the frequency of the wave was the energy of the orbits divided by Planck's constant, and the wavelength was some rational fraction of the lengths of each of the orbits. He could not get a satisfactory construction, however. The required ray curvature was so great that the wave fronts were ill-behaved.[20]

Schrödinger then tried another tack. He turned back to the problem of deriving Einstein's quantum gas theory, now taking the de Broglie particle-wave model as the physical assumption to be combined with classical statistics. Assuming that the gas is a superposition of the many phase waves associated with the gas molecules, and that, furthermore, this superposition is stationary when the gas is in equilibrium, Schrödinger calculated the characteristic wavelengths allowed by the boundary conditions set by the gas container. Each of these characteristic wavelengths was then identified as the wavelength of a molecular phase wave. Since de Broglie's theory gave the corresponding velocity of the phase wave, the phase wave frequency could be calculated, and from this using $E = h\nu$, the energy. This gave the energy spectrum of the gas molecules; standard Maxwell-Boltzmann statistics could then be applied to get the macroscopic properties of the gas. Schrödinger's results were identical with those obtained by Einstein using the new statistics.[21]

Schrödinger took this success as evidence for the physical assumption on which his derivation depended, the assumption that molecules can be treated as if they were waves. Perhaps, he speculated at the end of his paper, there are no material particles at all, but only waves. Matter might only appear to be made of particles, he suggested, because sometimes these waves form into packets, packets that move almost as if they were classical particles.[22]

Schrödinger took his speculation seriously. In late 1925 he once again set out to determine the shape and behavior of the waves around an atomic nucleus. This time he did not try to reproduce the old electron orbits, however, or even to construct appropriately contorted waves. Instead he adopted the more conventional strategy of finding a wave equation that, when restricted by suitable boundary conditions, gives as solutions the wave functions for the characteristic modes of vibration. We do not have a record of the steps and missteps that Schrödinger took to find the appropriate wave equation. We do know, however, that by late December of 1925 or early January of 1926 he had found an equation that worked, the so-called time-independent Schrödinger equation.[23] When applied to the hydrogen atom, the touchstone of any atomic theory, the equation yielded modes of oscillation with energy values that matched those of the hydrogen spectrum.

Thus Schrödinger's discovery of the wave equation for matter was the result of a series of attempts to elaborate de Broglie's notion of a phase wave by working out detailed applications of that notion in gas theory and atomic theory. Some perspective on Schrödinger's approach can be gained by comparing it with three other examples of theoretical discovery: the development of a law of electromagnetic induction by Ampère, the development of the laws of electricity and magnetism by Maxwell, and the discovery of energy quanta by Planck. As in Schrödinger's case, all of these discoveries came as the result of an attempt to solve a specific theoretical problem on the basis of some fundamental theoretical assumptions.[24] Ampére began with an assumption about the type of law he sought. Supposing that the inductive force acted along the line connecting two current elements, he used the results of ingeniously designed and carefully executed experiments to provide the details and parameters of the formal expression for that force.[25] Maxwell approached his task by using Faraday's notion of lines of force to construct an elaborate model of the ether, and then explored the behavior of that model on the assumption that it satisfied the laws of classical mechanics.[26] Planck's discovery came out of his attempt to use statistical techniques and the concept of entropy to set his new radiation law on the foundation of classical mechanics and electrodynamics.[27] We have seen that like Maxwell, Schrödinger assumed that a model, in his case a wave model of matter, was a reliable guide to theory construction. Like Ampère, Schrödinger was committed to finding an equation of a certain type, a partial differential wave equation; in Schrödinger's case the restriction on type was dictated by the model on which he had fastened.

There are other interesting similarities and differences among these four discovery processes—more than I can explore here. But one more comparison will help bring out an important aspect of Schrödinger's achievement. Ampère set out to construct an equation that correctly described electromagnetic induction and in addition satisfied a certain assumption. He succeeded. Planck, on the other hand, failed to find a theoretical foundation for his radiation law that satisfied the constraints with which he had begun. In fact, the subsequent battle with the quantum indicates that there is no foundation for Planck's radiation law consistent with the laws of both classical mechanics and electrodynamics. Schrödinger's "solution" of the problem he was working on, that of finding a wave equation for matter waves, was more like Planck's in this respect, than that of Ampère. For in Schrödinger's case too, the "solution" violated the constraints he originally took to define his problem. The functions satisfying the time-independent Schrödinger equation could not be taken to describe directly physical waves. In the case of n interacting particles, the solutions of the Schrödinger equation are functions of 3n spatial coordinates, corresponding to the n sets of 3 spatial coordinates for each interacting particle. Such solutions might be said to give the characteristics of a wave in an abstract 3n-dimensional mathematical space, but not of a wave in 3-dimensional physical space. The idea motivating Schrödinger's search for a wave equation had been, however, that each so-called particle actually was a wave, and that the equation he sought would determine the physical characteristics of that wave. A 3n-dimensional solution of his equation did not determine those characteristics directly, and more importantly, there was no way to determine uniquely from that solution a set of n 3-dimensional functions that might be taken as descriptions of the n physical waves corresponding to the n so-called "particles."

Schrödinger recognized immediately that the wave equation he had found was not of the sort he had expected to find. At that point he had to make a choice: either to reject the new equation and continue to look for a way to describe the assumed matter waves, or to give up his original plan of describing matter waves, and develop a theory of matter based on the new equation. Important to this decision was the fact that the equation worked. When he applied it to several of the touchstone problems of quantum theory, the harmonic oscillator, the simple rotator, the vibrational rotator, and the hydrogen atom (some of the same applications that had recently been used by Heisenberg, Born, Jordan and Pauli to check the new matrix mechanics), Schrödinger obtained precisely the energy spectra required. He even got the half-integer rather than zero energy ground state for the harmonic oscillator, a result that Heisenberg had proudly displayed several months before when he introduced his new quantum kinematics.[28] Schrödinger, therefore, chose to stick with the new equation.

II.

Schrödinger reported these results in two papers, completed in January and February of 1926.[29] But discovery of equations and preliminary applications are only the first steps in the development of a theory. In the next three months he went on to uncover the relation between matrix and wave mechanics, to determine from this the proper wave mechanical expressions for line intensities and polarizations, and to do a wave-mechanical calculation of the relative line intensities in the Stark effect.[30] He set a young visitor to Zurich, Erwin Fues, to work on the wave mechanics of diatomic molecules.[31] Schrödinger himself turned to the problem of treating nonisolated systems. By June of 1926 he had constructed the time-dependent wave equation, developed a perturbation method to go with it, and applied these to the notoriously troublesome phenomenon of dispersion.[32] Except perhaps for proportionality factors, he derived a result equivalent to Kramer's dispersion formula, the formula that had guided Heisenberg in his discovery of matrix mechanics.

For Schrödinger, however, an equation, or even a mathematically formulated theory encompassing rules and techniques for application, was not enough. It is true that in his first paper on wave mechanics, he presented his new equation in a very abstract way, as the result of an extremum problem that, in itself, was given no physically intuitive motivation. But Schrödinger's private correspondence, and even some passages toward the end of that first paper, show that he had already started the search for some physical model that would be an appropriate interpretation of the abstract theory he was beginning to shape.[33] He still thought that somehow a wave model could be used. In the case of the hydrogen electron, for example, each of the solutions to the time-independent wave equation, the ψ-functions, was correlated with one of the energy values of the old Bohr orbits. Thus each ψ-function could be assigned a specific wave frequency, using the by then standard equation, $E = h\nu$. Schrödinger suggested at the end of his first paper, therefore, that there is some sort of wave corresponding to the hydrogen electron. The nth solution of the wave equation represents the wave form corresponding to the old picture of an electron in the nth Bohr orbit. It is a stationary wave that oscillates with frequency E_n/h, but gives rise to no radiation. In classical wave theory, noted Schrödinger, superpositions of such characteristic stationary waves can arise. Perhaps at times the electron wave also takes the form of a sum of the characteristic ψ-functions. This might be thought of as the wave version of Bohr electron transitions, the process by which spectral radiation is produced. On Schrödinger's picture the spectral frequencies are just the differences between frequencies of pairs of the characteristic oscillations. Thus, Schrödinger suggested, radiation might be explained as a beat phenomenon produced when matter waves develop into a superposition of two or more of these characteristic forms.[34]

The shape of the matter wave in these various situations was left completely undetermined by this interpretation of the ψ-function. But at least some part of the underlying physical picture could be filled in. In his second paper on wave mechanics Schrödinger made the connection between his theory and the motion of matter waves more explicit by deriving the wave equation parameters on the basis of the formal analogy between Fermat's principle for geometrical optics and Maupertuis's extremum principle for classical particle mechanics.[35] In this paper he also made explicit his basic commitment to providing a more complete physical picture of the systems that were presumably the object of his theory: "[I]t has been doubted whether atomic events can even be described in the space-time form of thought. From the philosophical standpoint, I would consider a definitive decision of this sort to be equivalent to complete surrender. For we cannot really change our form of thought, and what we cannot comprehend within it we cannot understand at all."[36] It was a commitment that was diametrically opposed to the intuitions that had developed in people who had worked closely with the old Bohr theory, intuitions that then formed the basis for the construction and interpretation of matrix mechanics.[37] It was this commitment, however, that apparently had motivated Schrödinger in his attempts to apply the de Broglie idea, and had therefore brought him to the discovery of wave mechanics. It was also the commitment that would shape his subsequent work on the theory.

Schrödinger's goal was not, it must be noted, simply a return to the descriptions of classical physics. As he pointed out in a letter to Max Planck, written at about the same time his second paper on wave mechanics was completed, the space-time picture he sought could not be drawn in a purely classical way. "I obviously do not mean," he explained, ". . . that these ψ-oscillations are perhaps mass oscillations in the sense of the ordinary mechanics. On the contrary. They or something similar to them appear to lie at the basis of all mechanics and electrodynamics."[38]

The extent to which Schrödinger felt free to revise even the classical physical concepts in the construction of this picture is revealed by his reaction to the following problem, posed in a letter from H. A. Lorentz.[39] Consider an atom with E_1, E_2, and E_3 as the energies of its first three states. According to the Bohr theory, if the atom originally has energy E_1, it can be made to produce radiation of frequency $\frac{E_3 - E_2}{h}$ by providing it with enough energy to put it into the third state, i.e., by providing it with energy $E_3 - E_1$. A transition from the third to the second state will then yield the radiation in question. Experiments such as those conducted by Franck and Hertz confirm that the energy required is indeed $E_3 - E_1$. But according to Schrödinger's interpretation, radiation of frequency $\frac{E_3 - E_2}{h}$ is produced only when both the third and second characteristic oscillation modes are excited. This would seem to require an energy input of $E_3 + E_2 - E_1$, which exceeds the experimentally determined energy requirement by the amount E_2.

In his reply to Lorentz, Schrödinger explained that this was not a problem for his interpretation because in his view, the classical notion of energy is simply not applicable to the atomic oscillations:

In no case do I consider it correct to speak of the *energy of the individual proper oscillation*, measured perhaps by the *square of its amplitude* . . . The *only* property of the individual proper oscillation that has anything to do with energy is its *frequency*, I believe.

The question naturally arises: but why must I supply a quite definite energy to the atom in order just to excite a definite proper oscillation? Now, 'supply a definite amount of energy' really means here either 'bombard with electrons of definite velocity' or 'irradiate with light of definite frequency' . . . [A] physicist of the old days would have opened wide his eyes and his mouth if someone had said to him: to irradiate with light of definite frequency 'means' to supply a definite amount of energy. . . . The basis for the statement . . . which would be so hard to understand for the physicist of the old days, can be seen in the fact that light of a definite frequency is always capable of producing the same physical effects as electrons of a definite velocity. But, from the fact of this equivalence, the opposite conclusion can be drawn with the same inevitability: the electron moving with a definite velocity must be a wave phenomenon whose frequency is that of the light which is experimentally equivalent to it with regard to the excitation of resonance.[40]

By identifying frequency as the fundamental property of matter, Schrödinger was able to replace the problem of energy bookkeeping described by Lorentz with the problem of frequency bookkeeping. The latter involves not the simple addition and subtraction method required by energy conservation, but a more complicated entry system in which the frequencies of pairs of matter waves are matched with a simple frequency in the surrounding electromagnetic field. In making this identification, Schrödinger rejected the classical tenet that mechanical energy (kinetic and potential energy) is the measure of one material body's capacity to effect change in another. At the microlevel, according to Schrödinger, the frequency of oscillation is the "energetic property" of a material system, since it is the frequency that determines the extent to which that system can produce physical changes in another.

Schrödinger never completed patching together this wave interpretation, because in mid-March of 1926 he stumbled onto an even more promising way of understanding his new theory. For it was in mid-March that Schrödinger discovered the formal connection between wave and matrix mechanics, the translation between wave functions and matrices that is now found in every elementary text on quantum physics.[41] (Pauli and Carl Eckart also discovered this connection at about the same time.[42]) This discovery solved one of the major problems that had faced wave mechanics up to that time. One of the advantages of matrix mechanics was that it had the resources to determine not only spectral line frequencies, but also line intensities and polarizations. The intensity of radiation polarized in, say, the x-direction was said to be proportional to the square of a certain element in the matrix representing the x-spatial coordinate. Initially, Schrödinger had no idea how such information could be obtained from the wave equation and its solutions. Once the translation scheme relating matrix and wave mechanics was found, however, the answer fell right out. With this answer, there also fell out the suggestion of a new interpretation.

In matrix mechanics, it was assumed that intensities were proportional to the squares of elements in the coordinate matrices because according to the way Heisenberg developed the theory, these squares are proportional to the Einstein emission and absorbtion coefficients. But according to Bohr's correspondence principle, these coefficients are, in turn, related to the squares of classical dipole moment amplitudes. If one compares the expression for a classical dipole moment amplitude and the expression for the wave mechanical translation of the corresponding coordinate matrix element, a formal analogy leads naturally to the conclusion that the square of the ψ-function plays the same role in wave mechanics as the expression for charge density in classical electrodynamics. Thus Schrödinger was led to propose his electrodynamic interpretation of wave mechanics, in which the square of the ψ-function of a given system gives the charge density distribution of that system.[43]

I cannot go into the details of this argument from analogy here, nor can I even begin to list the various implications of this interpretation. Perhaps it is enough to point out that if one accepts Schrödinger's assumption that during the radiation process the atomic electrons are in a superposition of the characteristic ψ-functions, then the electrodynamic interpretation plus classical electrodynamics predict precisely in all cases the correct spectral frequencies and polarizations, and in almost all cases, the correct relative line intensities. Even with this second interpretation, however, Schrödinger did not return to a purely classical picture. The classical notion of energy still had no place in this scheme, and unlike the radiation process, the absorbtion of radiation by an atom did not seem to obey the usual laws of electrodynamics.[44]

More significant than the details of this second interpretation is the evidence that it and the first interpretation give us of a striking feature of Schrödinger's approach. I noted earlier a similarity between the methods employed by Maxwell and Schrödinger. Maxwell, like Schrödinger, attempted to develop a theoretical account of a certain type of phenomenon by using a model of the system thought to underlie the phenomenon. Both Maxwell's and Schrödinger's theories arose as a result of attempts to construct equations describing the behavior of the model. And like Schrödinger, Maxwell found that the resulting equations seemed to describe the observable phenomena correctly, but failed to really fit the model with which he began. At one point, then, Maxwell dropped the project of working out a mechanical model of the ether to fit his new equations and simply proceeded to develop a theory of electricity and magnetism on the basis of the equations alone. He did continue to believe that there was a mechanical ether that gave rise to the phenomena described by his theory; the electrical energy was identified as the kinetic energy of the underlying ether, the magnetic energy was the potential energy of the ether.[45] But once the equations of electricity and magnetism were determined, he no longer felt it was necessary to spell out the details of the ether model and its connection with the equations in order to complete the theory itself.

Schrödinger, on the other hand, thought that such models and connections between model and equations were necessary parts of a good theory. When the equations of wave mechanics could not be used to determine the structure of matter waves as he had envisioned, he began to search for a different way to connect the equations and a model. Initially he thought the wave picture might be saved. But when a new, more promising model presented itself in March of 1926, Schrödinger was willing to abandon his original wave conception and adopt the potentially more fruitful electrodynamic interpretation. His goal was not simply to find a wave interpretation as such, but to find some description of the spatio-temporal behavior of atomic processes that was consistent with the new theory.

In the end, neither Schrödinger's wave nor his electrodynamic interpretation were accepted. In mid-1926 Born offered a statistical interpretation of the ψ-function that was almost universally adopted within the year.[46] In early 1927 Heisenberg presented the uncertainty relations as proof that space-time pictures are impossible,[47] and in the fall of the same year Bohr doomed the notion of a space-time picture to the shadowy fate of a complementary concept.[48] In November, 1928, Schrödinger publicly abandoned his wave and electrodynamic interpretations, and adopted Heisenberg's view that the uncertainty relations imply that no space-time pictures of microprocesses can be constructed. "We took . . . as unobjectionable until now . . . the simple requirement that somehow the events [described in our picture of reality] must be completely determined and unambiguous down to the smallest space-time detail . . . ," he explained. But, he continued, "[i]n so far as the basic assumptions of quantum theory hold true, arbitrarily fine observations are impossible—[so] they do not need to be covered by our picture and perhaps cannot be. . . . This realization, which we owe to Heisenberg, strikes deep . . . into our physical world picture; it alters the conception of what should ever be understood as a physical world picture."[49]

Schrödinger would not, perhaps could not, continue to work on quantum theory without such a physical picture. While after 1928 he did publish sporadically on quantum mechanics, his subsequent work in physics focused primarily on statistical mechanics, general relativity and unified field theory. Then in 1952 Schrödinger launched a new campaign to unmask the prevailing Copenhagen interpretation, in which he again called for space-time pictures and argued for a new version of his old wave interpretation.[50] But unlike de Broglie, who at about that same time returned to the task of constructing a precise mathematical theory based on his old pilot wave interpretation,

Plate 1. Erwin Schrödinger around 1900, with his parents, Rudolf and Georgina Schrödinger, and the family poodle.

Plate 2. An early photograph of Schrödinger.

Plate 3. Schrödinger with his wife, Annemarie, December, 1926. They are about to leave for a lecture tour of the U.S.; Schrödinger's topic will be his new wave mechanics.

Plate 5. Schrödinger in 1946 with his mother's sister, Rhoda. This photo was taken in Dublin, which was Schrödinger's home from 1939 to 1956.

Plate 4. Schrödinger relaxing in Belgium, 1938, after fleeing occupied Austria.

Plate 6. Erwin and Annemarie after the war, in one of their favorite vacation spots, the Tyrolean village of Alpbach.

Plate 7. Schrödinger in his home in Vienna, shortly after his return to Austria in 1956.

Schrödinger did not attempt to work out his new wave picture in detail. Where in 1925 such an idea had been the starting point for the creation of a new physical theory, it now gave rise only to philosophical polemic.

III.

We have seen that in his work on wave mechanics, Schrödinger was guided by a specific vision of the scientific task. He believed that in addition to predicting correctly the results of experiment, a physical theory must include a spatio-temporal picture of the physical systems that give rise to these experimental results, and the mathematical laws of the theory must give an account of the behavior of these systems in space and time. In the first stage of his work Schrödinger had a model of the microsystems underlying atomic and molecular phenomena. His belief led him to search for a more detailed description of that model, and eventually, for the mathematical equation governing its behavior. The equation he found, the (time-independent) Schrödinger equation, did not provide a direct description of the underlying systems as he had hoped. But his search did end successfully in the sense that the equation was adequate to save the phenomena. In the second stage of his work on wave mechanics, Schrödinger tried to develop a theory based on his equation by seeking new ways to apply the equation, or a time-dependent extension of it, to the phenomena, and also, by finding a new way to relate his formal equations to a model of microsystems. Once again the search for spatio-temporal models failed to reach its intended goal; in this stage, however, it did not even yield a fruitful byproduct. Neither the wave interpretation nor the electrodynamic interpretation led to the discovery of new ways to apply the equations of wave mechanics. They were, in fact, products of such discoveries.

   This is not to say that in the second stage Schrödinger was wrong in his choice of research strategy. Such a value judgment can only be made by assessing the rational expectations of success and failure at the time the choice was made. But Schrödinger's strategy was clearly quite different from those of most others working on quantum theory, who were not interested in developing spatio-temporal descriptions of microsystems. Why was Schrödinger so committed to finding such intuitive and mathematical descriptions? A likely and perhaps generally accepted answer is that he was a scientific realist, one who believes that it is the task of science to describe the actual furniture of the world. But, in fact, Schrödinger's view on science were more complex than this. In order to understand them, we must look at his views on more general philosophical issues.

Schrödinger's writings on philosophy show the strong influence of Ernst Mach. Schrödinger had begun reading Mach's works even before he went to the university, probably under the guidance of his father, a successful Viennese businessman and respected botanist.[51] This interest was reinforced when he attended the University of Vienna, where Mach's intellectual influence was still strong.[52] Schrödinger adopted Mach's theory of neutral monism, which was based on the assumption that at bottom there exist neither physical things nor human minds, but only "neutral elements." We experience these neutral elements as sensations; out of them we build our material/physical world. Science, on this view, is simply a more sophisticated and systematic version of an activity in which all humans are constantly engaged, that of intellectually constructing an account of a fictional physical world, an account that imposes an organization on our past experiences of the neutral elements and allows us to predict our future experiences. The elements can be used, and indeed are used, to construct other types of accounts too. The idea that the world also contains minds, and the conception that each person has of his or her own mind, is just another way of finding patterns in the relations among the elements, another way to organize them into a coherent picture.[53]

But Schrödinger rejected Mach's contention that economy is the *sole* criterion to be imposed on this organization. Rather, he looked to the second of his intellectual heros, Ludwig Boltzmann, for an account of the aim of scientific theory making.[54] Boltzmann had argued, in conscious opposition to Mach, that in science one is not after merely convenient and efficient organization. In addition one must also construct "pictures," in Schrödinger's own words, "clear, almost naively clear, and detailed pictures,"[55] that specify the spatio-temporal properties of physical systems and their behavior in space and time.

This acceptance of Boltzmann's view of the task of science made Schrödinger look like a scientific realist, of course. In his last paper on wave mechanics, written in 1958, Schrödinger was still calling for a "realistic" interpretation of the ψ-function. "[A]s long as the state vector plays the role it does," he wrote, "it must be taken to represent 'the real world in space and time.'" But his belief in neutral monism rendered this merely an apparent realism. In the very same article from which I just quoted we also find this caution:

"Naturally our urge to form a picture in space and time . . . must not be framed ontologically, this would be rather naive science. . . . From Democritus to Bertrand Russell there have been thinkers who became aware of the obvious fact that our sensible, perceiving, feeling, thinking ego, and the so-called external world consist of the same elements, only comprehended in different arrangements."[56]

Our original question now looks even more puzzling. Why did Schrödinger think that physical theories had to be descriptive when on his own account even the most successful of such theories could not be understood as describing anything that actually exists? In a number of places Schrödinger tried to argue for his view of the aim of science. Frequently he appealed to the scientific tradition, "a particular mental attitude discovered by Greek thinkers and descended from them to us." A characteristic part of that attitude, he argued, is "the hope that nature can be understood"; therefore, "what matters to us is essentially the picture."[57] In a letter to Wien, he suggested that the source of that tradition is the connection between science and our everyday experience. "The purpose of atomic theory is to fit our experience relative to it with the rest of our thought. In so far as it has to do with the external world, the rest of our thought takes place in space and time."[58] In other places he emphasized the role of habit: "It has become a convenient habit to picture our constructs as a reality. In everyday life we all follow this habit. . . . Physics takes its start from everyday experience, which it continues by more subtle means."[59]

Schrödinger recognized that scientists are not irrevocably bound to tradition and habit, of course. Rather, tradition constrains the development and interpretation of new theories because it is the framework in which many of the problems addressed by new theories are both discovered and formulated. In his paper on the relation between matrix and wave mechanics, for example, Schrödinger explained: "The problems which . . . the development of atomic dynamics brings . . . are presented to us by experimental physics in an eminantly intuitive form; as for example, how two colliding atoms or molecules rebound from one another. . . . To me it seems extraordinarily difficult to tackle problems of the above kind as long as we feel obligated on philosophical grounds to repress intuition . . . and to operate only with such abstract ideas as transition probabilities and energy levels. . . ."[60]

A look at the way quantum mechanics is applied does confirm Schrödinger's claim. Most of the symbols of the theory are identified with spatio-temporal concepts, and the choice of the appropriate quantum mechanical equations for application to a given macroscopic phenomenon depends on using one or more spatio-temporal models of the underlying microprocesses. But the fact that Bohr could agree with all of the premises and steps of the argument that I have just pieced together from Schrödinger's writings, shows that the argument is not enough to justify Schrödinger's position on interpretational issues. Without some further assumption there is no reason to suppose that only a single coherent spatio-temporal model must suffice in all applications of a theory. The assumption of some sort of scientific realism might do the trick. The assumption of neutral monism clearly will not.

In the end, Schrödinger's commitment to finding a coherent description of microsystems is best explained not by looking at his attempts to give a rational argument for the role of tradition in science, but by considering the formative role of traditional science on Schrödinger himself. Schrödinger learned his physics in Boltzmann's Institute at Vienna. He entered the Institute the Fall after Boltzmann had committed suicide, but his teachers were physicists that Boltzmann had gathered together—men who shared Boltzmann's view of science, who in some cases had been Boltzmann's students. There Schrödinger was trained to develop and use realistic intuitive and mathematical descriptions of microsystems to explain macrophenomena, and to regard this as the proper approach to science—in explicit opposition to the approach urged by the other major influence in Vienna at that time, Ernst Mach. The text books and journal articles of the day reinforced this approach. The first of his own journal articles were written in this environment, under the influence of these same people and this same tradition. It was not until after the First World War that physicists would be weaned on the paradoxes of Bohr's theory of the atom. They would learn to use a model, even several models, without worrying about whether they had a complete picture, or even whether their models were entirely compatible with their theory or with each other. Schrödinger was unwilling, probably unable, to adapt to this new way of working.

Even at the time he invented and developed wave mechanics, Schrödinger's commitment to the descriptive tradition was becoming outmoded. Yet that commitment was essential to the creative act for which he is best known. It pushed him to search for a Boltzmannian underpinning of Bose-Einstein statistics; when de Broglie's waves promised to provide that underpinning and, at the same time, to replace the jumping electrons of Bohr's heretical theory of the atom, Schrödinger's descriptive approach called for a full spatio-temporal description of those waves and their behaviour; this call ultimately led to his search for a wave equation of matter. There is an obvious irony in Schrödinger's situation: his equation became the cornerstone of a new physics that rejected the descriptive tradition from which it sprang. Such ironies are not unusual in the history of science. The cases of Maxwell and Planck mentioned above provide two more examples: the ether models crucial to Maxwell's development of the electro-magnetic equations were soon discarded, even by Maxwell himself; the Maxwellian theory of continuous radiation that was basic to Planck's derivation of the black-body law was overthrown by quantum theory, a descendent of the novelty imbedded in that derivation, the quantum of energy. Such is often the nature of creative innovation in science.

A second irony of Schrödinger's situation is perhaps not so usual: it was Schrödinger himself who contributed unwillingly but significantly to the downfall of the assumptions on which his work had rested. For it was the failure of his persistent and imaginative search for a descriptive interpretation in the second stage of his work on wave mechanics that revealed, more clearly than anything that had come before, the challenge that microphysics poses to the descriptive tradition. Many physicists in Schrödinger's generation, and most in earlier generations, hoped that Schrödinger's attempt would be successful. When it wasn't, the way was paved for a general acceptance of the Copenhagen interpretation. The new way of working with models that Schrödinger could not adopt stood as the only available option once his own intuitive interpretations proved inadequate.

Notes

1. E. Schrödinger, "Quantisierung als Eigenwertproblem, Erste Mitteilung," *Annalen der Physik* 79 (1926), pp. 361-376 (sent for publication January 26, 1926); "Quantisierung, Zweite Mitteilung," ibid. 79, pp. 489-527 (sent February 22); "Über das Verhältnis der Heisenberg-Born-Jordanschen Quantenmechanik zu der Meinen," ibid. 79, pp. 734-756 (sent March 17); "Quantisierung, Dritte Mitteilung," ibid. 80, pp. 437-490 (sent May 6); "Quantisierung, Vierte Mitteilung," ibid. 81, pp. 109-139 (sent June 19). Reprinted in E. Schrödinger, *Abhandlungen Zur Wellenmechanik* (Leipzig: J. A. Barth, 1927); the translation of the second edition of *Abhandlungen* is *Collected Papers on Wave Mechanics*, trans. J. F. Shearer and W. M. Deans (London: Blackie, 1928).

2. E. Schrödinger, "Probability Relations Between Separated Systems," *Proceedings of the Cambridge Philosophical Society* 32 (1936), pp. 446-452. See also E. Schrödinger, "Discussion of Probability Relations Between Separated Systems," ibid. 31 (1935), pp. 555-563.

3. Schrödinger's cat is introduced in E. Schrödinger, "Die gegenwärtige Situation in der Quantenmechanik," *Die Naturwissenschaften* 23 (1935), pp. 807-812, 823-828, and 844-849.

4. See William T. Scott, *Erwin Schrödinger. An Introduction to His Writings* (Amherst: University of Massachusetts Press, 1967) for a comprehensive bibliography of Schrödinger's scientific and nonscientific writings. P. Hanle provides an analysis of Schrödinger's early work on statistical mechanics in his Ph.D. dissertation, "Erwin Schrödinger's Statistical Mechanics, 1912-1925," Yale University, 1975.

5. E. Schrödinger, "The General Unitary Theory of the Physical Fields," *Proceedings of the Royal Irish Academy* 49A (1943), pp. 43-58, and subsequent publications. See letters written by Schrödinger on January 1 and January 20, 1943 to unidentified correspondents in the Archive for the History of Modern Physics (hereafter AHQP), Library of the American Philosophical Society, Philadelphia, Reel 37, Section 1.

6. E. Schrödinger, *What is Life?* (Cambridge: Cambridge University Press, 1944).

7. Schrödinger wrote scientific papers in all four of the modern languages mentioned. His private papers are sprinkled with passages written in English, Spanish, and Latin. See AHQP Reels 39-44 and 46, and private papers held by Frau Ruth Braunizer, Alpbach, Austria. His private library contains large numbers of books in all four of the modern languages, and more than a few in the ancient ones. Hans Thirring recalls that Schrödinger translated Homer from the original into English ("Erwin Schrödinger zum 60. Geburtstag," *Acta Physica Austriaca* 1 (1947), p. 109).

8. E. Schrödinger, *Gedichte* (Godesberg (now Düseldorf): Verlag Helmut Küpper, 1949).

9. See Schrödinger's private notebooks, AHQP Reels 39 and 44, *Science, Theory and Man* (New York: Dover, 1957), *Mind and Matter* (Cambridge: Cambridge University Press, 1959) and *My View of the World* (Cambridge: Cambridge University Press, 1964).

10. These pieces are in the possession of Ruth Braunizer, Alpbach, Austria.

11. Biographical details are found in "Erwin Schrödinger," autobiographical sketch in *Nobel Lectures in Physics*, Vol. II, 1922-1941 (Amsterdam: Elsevier, 1965), pp. 317-319.

12. E. Schrödinger, "Quantisierung, Erste Mitteilung," *Collected Papers*, p. 9; "Quantisierung, Zweite Mitteilung," ibid. p. 20; "Der stetige Übergang von der Mikro-zur Makromechanik," ibid. p. 41; "Über der Verhältnis," ibid. p. 46; letter from Schrödinger to A. Einstein, April 23, 1926, in K. Przibram, ed., *Letters on Wave Mechanics,* trans. M. Klein, (New York: Philosophical Library, 1967), p. 26; letter from Schrödinger to W. Wien, June 18, 1926, AHQP.

13. L. de Broglie, "Recherches sur la théorie des quanta," *Annales de Physique* 3 (1925), pp. 22-128 (see p. 33).

14. For a more detailed account than is presented below, see M. Klein, "Einstein and the Wave-Particle Duality," *The Natural Philosopher* 3 (1964), pp. 3-49, and L. Wessels, "Schrödinger's Route to Wave Mechanics," *Studies in the History and Philosophy of Science* 10 (1977), pp. 311-340.

15. A. Einstein, "Quantentheorie des einatomigen idealen Gases," *Berlin Akademie der Wissenschaft Sitzungsberichte* 1924, pp. 261-267, and 1925, pp. 3-14.

16. E. Schrödinger, "Bemerkungen über die statistische Entropiedefinition beim idealen Gas," *Berlin Akademie der Wissenschaft Sitzungsberichte* 1925, pp. 434-441, and "Die Energiestufen des idealen einatomigen Gasmodelle," ibid. 1926, pp. 23-26. These and Schrödinger's other papers on quantum gas theory are analyzed in P. Hanle, "The Coming of Age of Erwin Schrödinger: His Quantum Statistics of Ideal Gases," *Archive for History of Exact Sciences* 17 (1977), pp. 165-192.

17. Einstein, "Quantentheorie des einatomigen idealen Gases," 1925.

18. P. Hanle, "Erwin Schrödinger's Reaction to Louis de Broglie's Thesis on the Quantum Theory," *Isis* 68 (1977), pp. 606-609, and "The Schrödinger-Einstein Correspondence and the Sources of Wave Mechanics," *American Journal of Physics* 47 (1979), pp. 644-648.

19. For an explanation of why this aspect of de Broglie's work captured Schrödinger's

attention see V. V. Raman and P. Forman, "Why Was it Schrödinger Who Developed de Broglie's Ideas?" *Historical Studies in the Physical Sciences* 1 (1969), pp. 291-314. Confirmation of Raman and Forman's thesis is provided in Hanle, "Erwin Schrödinger's Reaction" and "The Schrödinger-Einstein Correspondence," and in Schrödinger's letter to Max Born of January 6, 1938, AHQP Reel 37, Section 3.

20. Letter from Schrödinger to A. Landé, November 16, 1925, The Niels Bohr Library, American Institute of Physics, New York. The relevant portion of this letter is translated in Raman and Forman "Why Was it Schrödinger?" p. 313.

21. E. Schrödinger, "Zur Einsteinschen Gastheorie," *Physikalische Zeitschrift* 27 (1926), pp. 95-101.

22. Schrödinger, "Zur Einsteinschen Gastheorie," Section 5.

23. Initially Schrödinger's aim was a relativistic equation. In late 1925 he had fastened on what we now call the Klein-Gordon equation. But when he worked out the solutions to this equation for hydrogen, he found that it did not give the correct energy spectrum. Shortly after that, he discovered that the nonrelativistic version of that equation did give a correct account of (gross) spectral structure. See Schrödinger's letter to W. Wien, December 27, 1925, AHQP; Schrödinger's letter to W. Yourgrau, February 29, 1956, in W. Yourgrau and S. Mandelstam, *Variational Principles in Dynamics and Quantum Theory* (New York: Pitman, 2nd edition, 1968), p. 114; P. A. M. Dirac, "Professor Erwin Schrödinger— Obituary," *Nature* 189 (1961), pp. 355-356; and the interview with D. Dennison in AHQP, conducted by T. S. Kuhn.

24. T. Nickles argues that scientific discovery is in general a problem-solving activity, and he has begun to develop a detailed account of his view. See "What is a Problem that We May Solve It?" forthcoming in *Synthese* (1981). He has attempted to illustrate his contention in an analysis of Planck's discovery of energy quanta in "Planck's Changing Problem Situation and his Construction of the Quantum Theory," read at the meeting of the History of Science Society, Toronto, October 19, 1980.

25. A.-M. Ampere, "Théorie Mathématique des Phénomènes Électro-dynamiques," *Memoires de l'Academie Royale des Sciences,* vi (1825), p. 175.

26. J. C. Maxwell, "On Physical Lines of Force," *Philosophical Magazine* XXI (1861-1862), reprinted in W. D. Niven, ed., *The Scientific Papers of James Clark Maxwell,* Vol. I (New York: Dover, 1966), pp. 451-513.

27. M. Planck, "Zur Theorie des Gesetzes der Energieverteilung in Normalspektrum," *Verhandlungen der Deutsch Physikalisches Gesellschaft* 2 (1900), pp. 237-245, translated in D. ter Haar, *The Old Quantum Theory* (Oxford: Pergamon, 1967), and in H. Kangro, ed., *Original Papers in Quantum Physics,* trans. D. ter Haar and S. G. Brush (London: Taylor and Francis, 1972); and "Über das Gesetz der Energieverteilung in Normalspektrum," *Annalen der Physik* 4 (1901), pp. 553-563.

28. W. Heisenberg, "Über quantentheoretische Umdeutung kinematischer und mechanischer Beziehungen," *Zeitschrift für Physik* 33 (1925), pp. 879-893, translated in B. L. van der Waerden, ed., *Sources of Quantum Mechanics* (New York: Dover, 1968), pp. 261-276.

29. Schrödinger, "Quantisierung, Erste Mitteilung," and "Quantisierung, Zweite Mitteilung."

30. Schrödinger, " Über das Verhältnis," and "Quantisierung, Dritte Mitteilung."

31. Letter from E. Fues to T. S. Kuhn, May 26, 1963, AHQP, Reel 66. The result was Fues's "Das Eigenschwingungsspektrum zweiatomiger Moleküle in der Undulationsmechanik," *Annalen der Physik* 80 (1926), pp. 367-396, and "Zur Intensität der Bandenlinien und des Affinitätsspektrums Zweiatomiger Moleküle," ibid. 81 (1926), pp. 281-313.

32. Schrödinger, "Quantisierung, Vierte Mitteilung."

33. Schrödinger, "Quantisierung, Erste Mitteilung," Section 3; letter from Schrödinger to Wien, December 27, 1925; letter to M. Planck, February 26, 1926, AHQP, Reel 41;

letters to W. Wien, February 22, and May 6, 1926, AHQP; letter to H. A. Lorentz, June 6, 1926, in Przibram, 55-66.

34. Schrödinger, "Quantisierung, Erste Mitteilung," Section 3.

35. Schrödinger, "Quantisierung, Zweite Mitteilung," Section 1.

36. Ibid., pp. 26-27.

37. See E. MacKinnon, "Niels Bohr on the Unity of Science," in R. N. Giere and P. D. Asquith, eds., *PSA 1980*, Vol. 2 (East Lansing: Philosophy of Science Association, 1981), P. Forman, "The Doublet Riddle and Atomic Physics *circa* 1924," *Isis* 59 (1968), pp. 156-174; and D. Serwer, *"Unmechanischer Zwang:* Pauli, Heisenberg, and the Rejection of the Mechanical Atom, 1923-1925," *Historical Studies in the Physical Sciences* 8 (1977), pp. 189-256.

38. Schrödinger to Planck, February 26, 1926.

39. Letter from H. A. Lorentz to Schrödinger, May 27, 1926, in Przibram, pp. 43-54.

40. Schrödinger to Lorentz, June 6, 1926, Przibram, 60-61.

41. See for example, L. I. Schiff, *Quantum Mechanics* (New York: McGraw-Hill, 3rd edition, 1968), p. 155.

42. Letter from W. Pauli to P. Jordan, April 12, 1926, in B. L. van der Waerden, "From Matrix Mechanics to Unified Quantum Mechanics," pp. 289-293, in J. Mehra, ed., *The Physicist's Conception of Nature* (Dordrecht: Reidel, 1973), pp. 276-293. C. Eckart, "The Solution of the Problem of the Simple Oscillator by a Combination of the Schrödinger and the Lanczos Theories," *Proceedings of the National Academy of Science* 12 (1926), pp. 473-476, and "Operator Calculus and the Solution of the Equation of Quantum Dynamics," *Physical Review* 28 (1926), pp. 711-726.

43. A simple example will illustrate the suggestion inherent in the connection between matrix and wave mechanics. Consider the element x_{ij} of the matrix representing the x-coordinate of the hydrogen electron. The square of that element, $|x_{ij}|^2$, was assumed to be proportional to the Einstein coefficient of emission for radiation polarized in the x-direction, emitted in a spontaneous transition from the ith to the jth state of the atom. (See B. L. van der Waerden, "Introduction," *Sources of Quantum Mechanics*, pp. 30-33). According to Bohr's correspondence principle, for states of large principle quantum number, the emission coefficient is equal to the amplitude of the classical dipole moment of the moving electron, $\iiint x \cdot \rho(x, y, z) dx dy dz$, where $\rho(x, y, z)$ is the spatial density of the electron charge. On the other hand, the wave mechanical counterpart to the matrix element x_{ij} is the integral $\iiint x \cdot \Psi_i^*(x, y, z) \cdot \Psi_j(x, y, z) dx dy dz$, where Ψ_i and Ψ_j are the 'wave functions' representing the ith and j^{th} oscillation modes. According to Schrödinger's model, the radiation in question is given off when both of these modes are excited, that is when the electron wave is in the superposition $\overline{\Psi} = c_i\Psi_i(x, y, z) + c_j\Psi_j(x, y, z)$. The intensity, then, is proportional to the cross-term in the expression $\iiint x \cdot |\overline{\Psi}|^2 dx dy dz = |c_i|^2 \iiint x \cdot |\Psi_i|^2 dx dy dz + |c_j|^2 \iiint x \cdot |\Psi_j|^2 dx dy dz + (c_i^* c_j + c_i c_j^*) \iiint x \cdot \Psi_i^* \cdot \Psi_j dx dy dz$. When this expression is compared with that for the dipole moment amplitude related to it via matrix mechanics, the suggestion is obvious: the square of the wave function should be interpreted as charge density. This interpretation explains why the first two terms in the expansion of $\iiint x \cdot |\overline{\Psi}|^2 dx dy dz$ do not contribute to the radiation intensity. Each represents the dipole moment amplitude of the atom when only a single stationary state is excited, a situation in which it is assumed that no radiation is produced. This explanation is borne out by a calculation of one of those terms, which shows that a dipole with charge distribution $\rho(x, y, z) = |\Psi_i(x, y, z)|^2$ is one that, according to classical electrodynamics, produces no radiation (Schrödinger, Quantisierung, Vierte Mitteilung," *Collected Papers*, pp. 122-123).

44. Schrödinger, "Quantisierung, Vierte Mitteilung," *Collected Papers*, pp. 107-110, and pp. 120-123.

45. J. C. Maxwell, *Treatise on Electricity and Magnetism, Volume II*, Articles 568-577 (Oxford, 1873), pp. 196-206.

46. M. Born, "Zur Quantenmechanik der Stossvorgänge," *Zeitschrift für Physik* 37 (1926), pp. 863-867, reprinted in M. Born *Ausgewählte Abhandlungen*, Vol. 2 (Göttingen: Vandernhoek and Ruprecht, 1963), pp. 228-232; and "Quantenmechanik der Stössvorgänge," *Zeitschrift für Physik* 38 (1926), pp. 803-827, reprinted in *Ausgewählte Abhandlungen*, Vol. 2, pp. 233-257. The interpretation Born offered was not the one now commonly associated with this name. See L. Wessels, "What Was Max Born's Statistical Interpretation?" in R. Giere and P. Asquith.

47. W. Heisenberg, "Über den auschaulichen Inhalt der quantentheoretischen Kinematik und Mechanik," *Zeitschrift für Physik* 43 (1927), pp. 172-198.

48. Bohr first presented his interpretation in terms of complementarity at the Como Conference, held September 11-20, 1927, and then in an informal discussion at the Solvay Conference held October 24-29, 1927. His first published presentation was in N. Bohr, "The Quantum Postulate and the Recent Development of Atomic Theory," *Nature* 121 (1928), pp. 580-590, reprinted in N. Bohr, *Atomic Theory and the Description of Nature* (Cambridge: Cambridge University Press, 1934), pp. 52-91.

49. E. Schrödinger, "Neue Wege in der Physik," *Elektrotechnische Zeitschrift* 50 (1929), pp. 15-16. See also E. Schrödinger, "Der erkenntnistheoretische Wert physikalisches Modellvorstellungen," *Jahresbericht des physikalischen Vereins Frankfurt am Main* 1928/29, pp. 44-51, translated as "Conceptual Models in Physics and their Philosophical Value," in Schrödinger, *Science, Theory and Man*, pp. 148-165.

50. Letter from Schrödinger to N. Bohr, June 3, 1952, AHQP, Bohr Scientific Correspondence, Reel 33. Between 1952 and 1958 Schrödinger wrote eight papers challenging various aspects of the by then traditional Copenhagen interpretation and, in some of them, suggesting a wave alternative. See W. T. Scott, "Bibliography," for references to these papers.

51. In Schrödinger's library (Alpbach, Austria) can still be found a copy of Mach's *Analyse der Empfindung* purchased by his father in 1902.

52. Letter from Schrödinger to A. S. Eddington, March 22, 1940, AHQP, Reel 37.

53. E. Mach, *The Analysis of Sensations*, C. M. Williams, trans. (New York: Dover, 1959). For examples of Schrödinger's writings that show the influence of Mach, see: "Seek for the Road," written in 1925, published in *My View of the World* (Cambridge: Cambridge University Press, 1964); "On the Peculiarity of the Scientific World View," *Acta Physica Austriaca* 1 (1947), pp. 201-245, reprinted in *What is Life? and Other Scientific Essays* (Garden City, N.Y.: Doubleday Anchor, 1956); *Nature and the Greeks* (Cambridge: Cambridge University, 1954); "Mind and Matter," in *What is Life? and Mind and Matter* (Cambridge: Cambridge University Press, 1967); and "What is Real," completed in 1960, published in *My View of the World*.

54. L. Boltzmann, *Theoretical Physics and Philosophical Problems*, Volume 5 in the Vienna Circle Collection, B. McGuinnes, ed. (Dordrecht: Reidel, 1974). For Schrödinger's comments on Boltzmann, see Schrödinger's letter to Eddington, March 22, 1940, and "The Spirit of Science," in *What is Life? and Other Scientific Essays*, p. 237.

55. Schrödinger to Eddington, March 22, 1940.

56. E. Schrödinger, "Might Perhaps Energy be a Merely Statistical Concept?" *Il Nuovo Cimento* 9 (1958), pp. 162-170. The first quoted passage is on page 169, the second on page 168.

57. Schrödinger, "On the Peculiarity of the World View," *What is Life? and Other Scientific Essays*, pp. 182, 191.

58. Letter from Schrödinger to W. Wien, August 25, 1926, AHQP.

59. E. Schrödinger, "What is an Elementary Particle?, *Endeavor* 9 (1950), pp. 109-116, reprinted in *Science, Theory and Man*; the quotation is on pages 203-204 in the latter.

60. Schrödinger, " Über das Verhältnis," *Collected Papers*, p. 59.

Chapter 11

Michael Polanyi's Creativity in Chemistry

William T. Scott

Michael Polanyi is well known to physical chemists for his work in surface phenomena, strength of materials, and rates of chemical reactions, and to social scientists, philosophers, and theologians for his views of the knowing process and the relation of persons to the world. To the public, however, his reputation is not yet what this profound and sensitive genius deserves. This essay is an account of his scientific creativity along with some glimpses of his new way of looking at the world and at the position of ourselves in the world. Michael Polanyi offers us a new theory of society drawn from his participation in the community of science, a new way of looking at the personal and social process of acquiring knowledge drawn from his own research, and a profound conception of creativity in knowing and of creativity in the world itself.

Michael Polanyi was born in Budapest in 1891, into a lively intellectual and artistic family. His father Mihaly was a railroad engineer and later a railroad financier who cared deeply about the quality of education for his children and hired English and French governesses to teach them. He lost his money about the year 1900 after a flood washed out the rail lines, and he conscientiously paid off the stockholders before accepting anything for himself and family. Michael's mother, Cecile, was a strong, vital, intellectual woman who kept in close touch with the new movements of thought and art that flooded into Hungary in those prewar days. She held salons for the avant-garde in poetry, politics, and science, first in the Polanyis' large apartment, and after Mihaly died and the family fortune was lost, in rented gathering places. These stimulating evenings were an important formative influence for young Michael, as were the activities of his older sister Laura, who became a historian, and his older brothers, Adolf, a future engineer, and Karl, a future economist and social critic. Around the family dinner table there would be passionate intellectual discussion seasoned by a deep sense of loyalty and affection. The background was well laid for Michael's later intense sharing of ideas with scientific colleagues. The family managed to survive financial problems by using their cultural and intellectual training in a variety of creative ways. Michael early learned the art of making himself useful to industry, a practice that later helped him keep solvent as well as build constructive relations between industrial and academic chemistry. He became fluent in four languages, for besides Hungarian learned in school and English and French at home, he and his mother used German almost exclusively. In his early years, when he was ten or twelve, he read the scientific romances of H. G. Wells, as they appeared, *The Time Machine, The First Men on the Moon, A Modern Utopia,* and other works that extolled the power of science both as a way of knowing nature and as a road to the making of a better world.

Polanyi's schooling was at the famous Minta Gymnasium in Budapest, where he earned grades equivalent to straight A's in Hungarian, Latin, Greek, German, natural science, physics, mathematics, religion, philosophy, natural history, and descriptive geometry. He knew he was bright. At parties he would be the center of one group of people after another who listened intently to his opinions. A niece who was about ten at the time remembers him as "pontificating." Personal friends have told of his being quietly charming, but essentially a secret person, sometimes in a brooding mood when he had retreated into deep thought. Of all the many friends he had throughout his life, few got truly close to him.

During his formative years, Polanyi was immersed in the political milieu of the interaction and conflict between the liberal tradition of the 1848 revolutions, which had been deeply inspired by the English and American conceptions of liberty, and the Marxist tradition, arising from the same period, that called for a revolution based on dialectical materialism and on the power of the proletariat. But the tradition that moved him the most was that of science. He had a great passion to know what the world is like and a strong ambition to become a scientist. In his great work *Personal Knowledge,*[1] written after he had shifted his career from chemistry to philosophy, he was quite explicit in his view that science—and all ways of knowing—

Plate 1. Michael Polanyi as a medical officer in the Austro-Hungarian army about 1915.

Plate 2. Polanyi in 1931 as head of the section of reaction kinetics of the Kaiser-Wilhelm-Institut for Physical Chemistry and Electrochemistry and professor at the Technische Hochschule, Berlin.

Plate 3. Polanyi in 1965 at Wesleyan University, Middletown, Connecticut.

must be grounded in the intellectual passion to make contact with reality. Objectivity, he says, is not something free of value, but something we desire as the highest value in science.

Although devotion to science inspired Polanyi at an early stage, he was not sure enough of himself to matriculate in chemistry when he entered the University of Budapest. Furthermore, the likelihood of his making a living at science seemed much less than that of success in the available professions of engineering, law, and medicine; since his brothers were in the first two, he chose medicine. At the university he took the various basic science requirements, finding, according to his friend and fellow student the mathematician George Polya, that the physics lectures by Lorand Eötvös were by far the best and most interesting. From these lectures and from the great treatises by Nernst and Planck he got caught up with the marvelously logical and yet empirically grounded science of thermodynamics. As soon as he had completed most of his medical studies, he joined the group of Hungarian students at Karlsruhe, in Germany, where under the tutelage of professors Bredig and Fajans he took courses in physical chemistry and started right off in research.

Thermodynamics is a subject that combines remarkable theoretical deductions from the two great principles of the conservation of energy and of increasing entropy, with the many experimental applications concerned with the interactions of heat and mechanical work. Polanyi was curious about extensions of the theory as well as about its empirical consequences. His approach to the world was one of taking from the scientific tradition the best available view of a given circumstance and choosing a puzzling feature or a possible new coherence dimly seen as a problem to work on, reasoning theoretically under the guidance of a deep intuition of the reality of the situation as he sought a solution to the problem. He did not work alone, however—if colleagues were not available, he sought guidance through extensive correspondence with established scientists.

His first effort in thermodynamics[2] concerned the new heat theorem of Nernst, now called the third law. The law says that as the temperature of any object or system goes to absolute zero, the entropy also goes to zero. The quantum theory of Planck and Einstein was important, for it said that at very low temperatures there would not be enough energy for any quantum jumps to occur. It occurred to Polanyi that if the pressure got extremely large even at ordinary temperatures, the energy needed for the smallest quantum jump would go up, so that finally at infinite pressure the entropy would also go to zero. This idea illustrates the disciplined curiosity he exercised throughout his life, the type of curiosity that does not spread out all over the place but stays close to the bounds of the known parts of the subject matter, the valid tradition to which a person is centrally committed.

Polanyi wrote down his idea while back in Budapest and sent the paper to Professor Bredig, with a request that it be sent to Einstein for comments. Einstein read it with interest and reported to Bredig, "I like the paper of your Mr. Polanyi very much." As Polanyi wrote later about himself[3]: "Bang, I was created a scientist!" After he completed his medical degree, he returned to Karlsruhe to take more courses in physical chemistry and continue his research. The high-pressure entropy idea did not bear fruit. We never get to high enough pressures for Polanyi's idea to have any applications, but the low-temperature theorem is useful because in practical terms systems can operate close enough to absolute zero for experimental data to be correlated by this theorem. Hence Polanyi turned to seeking a derivation of Nernst's theorem that would satisfy his passion for a unification of deduction and physical insight. He sent his ideas to Einstein and to Nernst; the kindly letters from Einstein were a sort of fatherly guidance to the young man in getting his reasoning straightened out. It was unfortunate that this contact with Einstein never developed into a close friendship, for over the years they would have had much to share.

When World War I started in 1914 Michael Polanyi was called into service in the Austro-Hungarian army as a medical officer. He had several leaves of absence, partly due to his illness with diphtheria, and he managed to keep on with correspondence and with writing papers in physical chemistry. Polanyi found applications of thermodynamics to colloids, which led to problems of the adsorption of gases on the surfaces of colloidal droplets. A natural extension then was an effort to explain the adsorption isotherm, the relation of gas pressure to the volume of gas adsorbed at a given temperature. Following an idea of Eucken he attacked the problem by considering that the forces between the adsorbing solid and the atoms or molecules in several layers at the surface must simply cause a condensation without changing the equation of state of the oncoming gas. Figure 1, from his paper, sketches several layers of the region where adsorption occurs. His theory used a function representing the volume available at a given energy of the adsorbed molecules and derived the way the adsorption isotherm must vary with temperature. The paper, written in 1915 and 1916, was subsequently offered to the University of Budapest as a doctoral dissertation[4]; and in

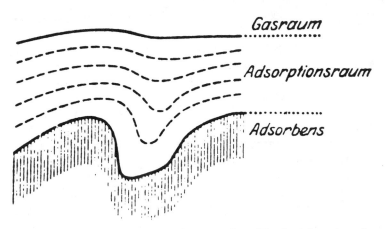

Figure 1. The multi-layered adsorption space, from "On the Adsorption of Gases on Solid Substances," *Festschrift Kaiser Wilhelm Gesellschaft Zehnjähriges Jubiläum,* (1921), p. 172.

1917 Michael Polanyi became a Ph.D. in physical chemistry. The adsorption theory had a curious history, for when he presented it to his colleagues in Berlin in 1921, Nernst and Einstein objected that the then-prevalent Bohr theory had no place in it for such long-range forces, so that Polanyi was undoubtedly wrong. He wrote years later that his career was almost ended at that meeting. Hermann Mark, who was there at the time, remarked that these objections were not important to the chemists, because the adsorption theory seemed to represent the chemical situation well while the Bohr theory was rather remote from their consideration. A series of later papers provided both experimental evidence and improved reasoning, but it was only after quantum mechanics was developed in the late twenties that Michael Polanyi got Fritz London to help him establish the theory on a sound quantum-mechanical foundation of superposable dispersion and exchange forces.[5]

Let me point briefly here to Polanyi's productivity in his three main fields of science. Figure 2 shows in bar-graph style the numbers of papers published each year in the fields of adsorption, of X-rays, fibers, and crystals, and of reaction kinetics. Each letter represents a paper, many of them written with collaborators. Adsorption occupied him considerably in 1920 but much less in later years, except for a spurt in 1925-1928. The chart shows his unusual ability to keep several projects going at a time, although it does not show his extensive consulting work involving electric lamp production, colloids, insulation, and hydrogen reduction.

year	adsorption	x-rays, fibers, crystals	reaction kinetics
1914	A A A		
1915			
1916	A		
1917	A A		
1918			
1919	A		
1920	A A A A A	X	R R R R R R
1921	A A	X X X X X X	
1922		X X X X X X	
1923		X X X X X X X	
1924	A	X X X X X	
1925		X X X X X X X X X	R F
1926		X X	F H H R
1927		X	R F R F
1928	A A A A	X X X X	H R F F F R R F F F
1929	A A	X	H
1930	A	X X X X	H F T R
1931		X	T T T R
1932	A		T F F F T R F R H
1933	A		R H R H R F R R R R H H R
1934		X	F R R F H R T R H H R H R R R R
1935	A		R R R R R R R R
1936			F R T H H T H
1937			T R R R R
1938		X	T R
1939			R R R
1940			R H H
1941			H T T
1942			T
1943			R T R
1944			
1945			R
1946			R R R
1947			R R R R R
1948			R
1949			R R

A adsorption
X x-rays, fibers, crystals
T transition theory
R reaction kinetics
H hydrogen exchange
F flame

Figure 2. Constructed by William T. Scott.

Polanyi's theory of adsorption was capable of handling the reaction between two molecular species in contact with a solid. The fields of heterogeneous catalysis and of basic reaction-rate theory were thus opened up to him. This aspect of research, in which one thing was always leading to another, continued throughout his life. Science is like that, and even more, so are we. Polanyi put it in terms of irreversibility—every idea, whether a discovery or mere observation, changes us, and opens up ways to further changes. We cannot go back to our state of ignorance. These new elements in our thought and belief that we come to accept as valid we take into ourselves, and we commit ourselves to them. This is the essence of the personal element in knowing that Polanyi experienced in his life and later wrote and lectured on extensively.

How were reaction rates to be investigated? The simplest cases should be taken up first. Polanyi found that Bodenstein and Lind[6] in 1906 had studied an important, simple reaction, the formation of hydrogen bromide from hydrogen and bromine in the gas phase where no problems of the liquid state were involved and the effects of wall reactions can presumably be minimized. The ordinary statistical theory of chemical reaction rates would have a formula like this for the concentrations, represented by quantities in brackets:

$$d[HBr]/dt = k[H_2]^{1/2}[Br_2]^{1/2}.$$

However, Bodenstein and Lind found

$$d[HBr]/dt = \frac{k[Br]^{1/2}[H_2]}{1 + k'[HBr]/[Br_2]}.$$

In considering how to explain this result in terms of collision probabilities and statistical assumptions about reaction rates, Polanyi found himself a new problem to work on, as he was in the rest of his career to generate and pursue to completion a huge number of fruitful scientific problems. While the people who worked with him learned by personal apprenticeship how he functioned, it was only in his philosophical period that he developed an explicit account of the nonexplicit process of sensing and committing oneself to a scientific problem. It was as his friend George Polya said for solving problems in mathematics: Look at the unknown! Paradoxical advice, for how can we look at something we do not know? And yet if we knew it, it would not be a problem. Polanyi's answer comes as an extension of how we look at anything, whether it is a thermometer or a logical deduction or the structure of a mechanism or a person we are talking to.[7] After all, science depends on proper seeing, both in observation and in conceptual reasoning. When we attend to something, we see in a subsidiary way all sorts of bits and clues that point us to the thing on which we are focussing, and we integrate these clues into the focal whole. I say "we" for although the integration usually happens in a quick, subconscious way, clearly no one or no thing other than our self does the job. Polanyi was later to call this subsidiary-to-focal process "tacit knowing." His own ability to see was extraordinary, as I myself once observed in his attention to an antique table in my home, or to the flowers in Berkeley in February, or to the detailed arrangement of a complex experiment.

A scientific problem has the character that many clues of known knowledge, of gaps in it, and of available resources, integrate in the scientist's consciousness into a partial coherence promising a fuller coherence yet to be found. It is necessarily vague yet clear enough to be a guide to action. In the case of chemical reactions and the hydrogen bromide data, Polanyi had his knowledge and skill in thermodynamics and his awareness of the ideas of statistical mechanics and the kinetic theory of collision probabilities, together with the evident situation that no mechanisms in terms of a series of exchanges and of quantum jumps were known for any chemical reaction, including this one. He also had in a deeper sense the basic traditions of physics and chemistry which had become part of his mental existence. All these and the puzzling formula came together for him in his effort to discuss the simplest stage of the reaction, $Br + H_2 \rightarrow HBr + H$. There was of course the previous stage in which bromine molecules, Br_2, become dissociated into Br atoms. Polanyi made the later widely adopted assumption that the concentrations of both the intermediate reaction radicals [Br] and [H] had a steady-state value during the process.

His paper[8] laid out the main aspects of the mechanism, as did two other papers[9] published at about the same time by Herzfeld and by Christiansen. Polanyi missed an important feature of the process, however, and as a result was led to publish four papers in a wild-goose chase for what he thought was going to be a great discovery. It was one of several cases he described later as failures caused by excessive ambition. He noted that ambition, like curiosity, is something a scientist should have neither too little nor too much of.

The wild-goose chase was based on a calculation of the rate at which the Br_2 molecules could dissociate by getting enough energy from thermal agitation. Polanyi showed that it was 300,000 times too slow for the observed rate for the reaction of atomic bromine with hydrogen. He wrote a paper[10] suggesting that chemical reactions like these were not mechanical in nature and must draw on an as yet undiscovered form of energy, probably directly out of the aether. Herzfeld[11] replied to this paper by pointing out, what was implicit in his earlier paper, that a chain reaction occurs. Some of the hydrogen atoms released in the reaction with bromine atoms will readily dissociate the bromine molecules. The chain mechanism as now understood is the following, where M represents a molecule involved only in the initiation and termination stages and not in the cyclic propagation stage. It could very well be another Br_2.

$$
\begin{aligned}
\text{Initiation:} \quad & Br_2 + M \rightarrow 2Br + M \\
\text{Propagation:} \quad & Br + H_2 \rightarrow HBr + H \\
& H + Br_2 \rightarrow HBr + Br \\
\text{Termination:} \quad & 2Br + M \rightarrow Br_2 + M
\end{aligned}
$$

One original self-dissociation of Br provides for several thousand steps of the chain. Whether Polanyi read the criticism of Herzfeld I have not yet discovered, but when he later returned to reaction kinetics, he took up chain reactions himself and worked out their theory in detail.[12] There was no extra energy from the aether and although his ambition to make a radical discovery was disappointed, he gave up the idea.

The work in reaction kinetics I have been describing was done in Budapest and after the war back in Karlsruhe while Polanyi was supporting himself by industrial consulting. In Karlsruhe he found a congenial atmosphere in which he could work, and a convivial group of Hungarian students. It was here that he met his future wife Magda, who was a chemistry student.

By the spring of 1920 he had established himself as a physical chemist and received an invitation to join the new Kaiser Wilhelm Institutes in Berlin, a group of research departments characterized by free scientific discussion and close relations among colleagues. He started work on October 1, 1920, but not in physical chemistry. The director, Fritz Haber, sent him to Herzog's Institute of Fiber Analysis. When he made his dutiful call on Haber, he was told,[13] "reaction velocity is a world problem. You should cook a piece of meat." That is, he should first become adept in a less demanding task. Training by apprenticeship is needed for any scientist to acquire both the tacit and explicit background as well as the discipline needed for success in research.

Polanyi's first assignment came about because Herzog and Scherrer[14] had independently made X-ray spot diagrams of cellulose that indicated the presence of a crystal structure. If the fibers were irradiated parallel to their long axes, the usual set of rings that one gets from randomly-oriented crystal powders appeared. When the rays were sent perpendicular to the fiber axes, however, an unusual and exciting set of 2-point and 4-point systems of spots was observed, as in Figure 3. Polanyi was asked to try to interpret these diagrams. He had to learn from scratch about X-ray diffraction because, as he later said, "owing to wars and revolutions and my exclusive interest in thermodynamics and kinetics,"[15] he had learned little of the subject. Very soon, by use of deductions from symmetry and his training in descriptive geometry, he solved the problem and showed how the diagrams could be used to provide information about the crystal arrangement.[16] He had cooked his piece of meat and had his second "bang"—he went from being just a new young fellow on the staff to one who was in command of the subject. Money for apparatus and for the hiring of new assistants was suddenly made available, and Hermann Mark, Erich Schmid, Ernst von Gomperz, and Karl Weissenberg became part of the group. Polanyi showed his extraordinary ability to sense how an experiment should be done and invented a new apparatus[17] involving the rotating-

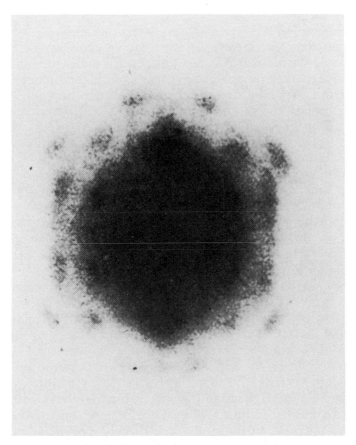

Figure 3. An early x-ray diffraction picture taken of cellulose fibers, from "Fibrous Structure by X-Ray Diffraction," *Naturwissenschaften 9* (1921), p. 87.

crystal method and the so-called layer-line diagrams, which became a standard in the field although he did almost no experimental work himself. His paper showing how to get 4-point diagrams from a group of crystals oriented at random but with one axis direction in common led to ways of deducing the spacing of the repeating crystal elements along the axis.[18] The ordinary Debye-Scherrer powder-pattern rings give only the distribution of interplanar spacings, but Polanyi's method allowed the determination of a second parameter as well, greatly improving the analysis of crystal structure.

Here Polanyi came close to what could have been a major feat. The X-ray results on cellulose showed that it was either a long chain of linked hexoses or merely an aggregate of four-glucose rings. He was not able to tell which it was; in fact, his colleagues were upset with the idea that two such different possibilities could be read from data. Polanyi later admitted that he had failed to take into account at the time that known chemical facts, including viscosity measurements, readily disposed of the aggregate idea. Not until Mark and Mayer[19] resolved the problem with more X-ray studies was the polymeric structure of cellulose established.

But different fruits came out of the fiber research. As Polanyi later said, one can characterize worthwhile research by its promise of fruitfulness.[20] In his view, however, fruitfulness in application for health or profit is not the right criterion. Astrology for most of us does not count as a fruitful research field, but its pay-off in the production of income is enormous. Alternatively, the fact that a project is in an area of possible social usefulness adds external importance to its intrinsic value and often justifies money being spent on it. But for an actual piece of scientific research, removed from technological development, it is fruitfulness in finding more truth about nature that we take into account in judging a person's work. In this case, the problem immediately presented itself of trying to duplicate the semi-ordered state of cellulose by putting some random crystals into order. The most likely possibility was to take a piece of metal made of disordered but tightly bound crystallites and to stretch it into a wire, thus lining up one of the crystal axes along the wire. In the study of such cold-worked wires, plastic flow was found, and the relation between strength and the slip of crystal planes established.[21]

Single-crystal wires were drawn from molten metals and needed to have their stress-strain properties studied, for which purpose Polanyi invented his widely used and beautifully designed "Dehnungsapparat", stretching apparatus,[22] shown in Figure 4.

Cold-working was found to lead to an increase in tensile strength. In fact, anything that upset the ideal crystal arrangement made the crystal stronger, in contradiction to what was generally thought at the time. Bending a crystal hardened it and bending it back brought about some recovery. Furthermore, the average actual strength was 3 or 4 orders of magnitude smaller than one might calculate from what was known at the time of interatomic forces. The basic idea for explaining these phenomena was developed by Polanyi in terms of a simple picture of a bent crystal. Figure 5 shows the upper or top compressed part of the bent crystal[23] and the lower or stretched part, and then the relief that occurs with a slip between two parts.

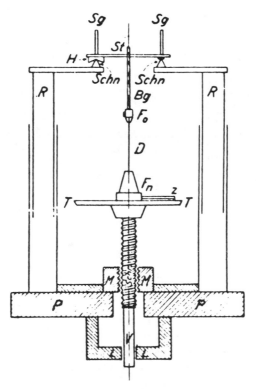

Figure 4. Polanyi's stretching apparatus ("Dehnungsapparat"), from "An Elongating Apparatus for Threads and Wires," *Zeitschrift für technische Physik* 6 (1925), p. 122.

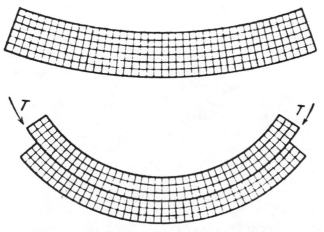

Figure 5. Diagram of a bent crystal and the relief produced by slip along a central initially plane surface, from "Deformation of Monocrystals," *Zeitschrift für Kristallographie* 61 (1925), p. 51.

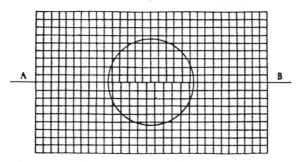

Figure 6. Polanyi's first published diagram of an edge dislocation, from "On a Form of Lattice Distortion That May Render a Crystal Plastic," *Zeitschrift für Physik* 89 (1934), p. 661.

Plastic flow involves slip, and slip in one direction means that the perpendicular planes no longer line up, transverse slipping is inhibited, and the crystal is strengthened.

Michael Polanyi left the Fiber Institute in 1923 when he was asked to head a department of reaction kinetics in the Kaiser Wilhelm Institute for Physical Chemistry and Electrochemistry under Haber's direction. He did not drop the subject of metals, however. With several colleagues he published twenty-three papers during his three years under Herzog, and another thirty papers during the next fifteen years. It was not until 1932 that Polanyi came upon the modern concept of dislocation for describing the strength of crystals. Figure 6 shows that by 1934[24] the bent crystal concept had shifted into a more general case of what we now call an edge dislocation. In a portion of a plane joining two parts of a crystal, n atoms of the lower side line up with n + 1 of the upper. As the planes slip by each other, a motion of only 1/n of an atomic separation shifts the dislocated line-up by one whole atom spacing overall. The result is a reduction of strength to 1/n of its theoretical value, thus accounting for the general weakness of crystals.

This idea of the dislocation was found and published simultaneously by G. I. Taylor[25] and also by E. Orovan.[26] The phenomenon of simultaneous discovery by special independent investigators has received some attention among historians of science. Polanyi describes any fruitful body of scientific work as taking place in an intellectual situation with intrinsic potentialities. Once knowledge and technique have developed sufficiently, there is a whole mass of properties of nature ready to be found, or to use a term borrowed from another discipline, revelation is ready to happen. Another metaphor that Polanyi used in his later writing[27] is that a community of scientists is a society of explorers. When a new piece of land is being explored, separate groups of individuals travel in different but overlapping places and report to each other, so that the topography gradually becomes evident to all and trustworthy maps can finally be made. In the case of metal properties, not only was a vast topography opened up for discovery, but a continuing discipline of study set up. Polanyi remarked in his retrospective account in 1962[28] that he and his co-workers were colonizing a terrain opened up by von Laue in 1912 when the first X-ray diffraction pictures were made.

In 1923, then, Polanyi went back to his favorite subject of physical chemistry and soon got into research in reaction kinetics. The fundamental piece of knowledge needed for this subject was information on the types of changes that occur when a single reacting molecule, atom, or ion strikes another. But one could not at that time do a direct-collision type of experiment. Slow gas reactions of the sort that take up energy had been studied by ordinary chemical means. The uninhibited exothermic reactions such as some of those in the hydrogen bromide chain must happen at every collision, however; and in ordinary circumstances, the molecules will react completely in much less than a millionth of a second. Ordinary chemical methods are far too slow.

Polanyi's brilliant idea for studying fast reactions was to let the two reacting gases, say sodium and chlorine, into opposite ends of a long narrow tube (Figure 7), at such low pressures that the mean free path was longer than the tube diameter. Alternatively, one gas was introduced by a jet at the center. As the gases met, they reacted within a narrow region near the center of the tube. The resulting sodium chloride molecules mainly stuck to the walls they could so easily reach. When the reaction was really fast, all the deposits on the walls were found near where the two bodies of gas met, but when it was slower, there was some interpenetration of the two original substances and the precipitates were spread out. A set of closely-fitting glass rings were placed inside the tube so that they could later be removed and the deposits on their inner sides analyzed. Another way of studying the reaction utilized the stage in which sodium atoms emit some of the released energy in the form of characteristic yellow light, forming the so-called highly dilute flame. The luminescence was photographed and its extent measured. The use of this light was so valuable that the entire set of researches was called the method of highly dilute flames.[29]

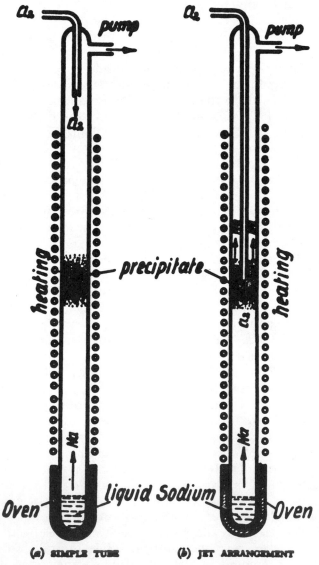

Figure 7. The original type of flame tube, and the modified version, from *Atomic Reactions* (London: Williams & Norgate, 1932, p. 35).

The simplest reactions to study were the so-called atomic reactions between a two-atom molecule and a single atom. The first experiments were done with sodium vapor and halogen gases, chlorine, bromine and iodine. The products NaCl, NaBr, and NaI were detected on the walls and the intensity of the yellow sodium light was found from the density of the photographs.

An immediate result of the first experiment was that the place of maximum precipitation was not the same as the place of maximum light, the latter being further along toward the sodium side. Thus these two occurrences must have been parts of two reactions, one that formed a sodium chloride molecule and a single chlorine atom, and another in which the chlorine atom reacted to form a vibrationally excited NaCl molecule, which before it precipitated could give its energy to the outer electron in a sodium atom, which in turn would emit light. The reactions are:

$$Na + Cl_2 \rightarrow NaCl + Cl$$
$$Cl + Na_2 \rightarrow NaCl^* + Na$$
$$NaCl^* + Na \rightarrow NaCl + Na^*.$$
$$\qquad \downarrow \qquad \downarrow$$
$$\text{precip.} \quad h\nu$$

A measure of the widths of the regions of precipitation and luminescence could be used along with the kinetic theory of collision rates to give a measure of the reaction rate constant. Figure 8 shows the distribution of the two substances, and their product, which measures the reaction rate. The width of the humped curve at half its maximum, in dimensionless units, was found to be about 3.0. By comparison with the experimental width in centimeters, the value of the reaction rate constant k can be determined. The experimental errors were obviously fairly large, but establishment of the otherwise unknown rate constant within a factor of two or even ten was a real success. Polanyi and about twenty-five co-workers studied more than a hundred reactions by this means and by later, improved arrangements. The letter F in Figure 2 shows the twenty flame papers bearing Polanyi's name. The alternative method of introducing the halogen or other reacting gas by means of a narrow tube (3 mm diameter) into the center of the main, 3 cm diameter, reaction tube was a major improvement. The reaction was more localized this way, and extraneous wall reactions minimized. Another improvement was that in place of looking for the chemiluminescent light produced by the reaction, the density of uncombined sodium atoms was observed by passing the yellow D light from a sodium lamp

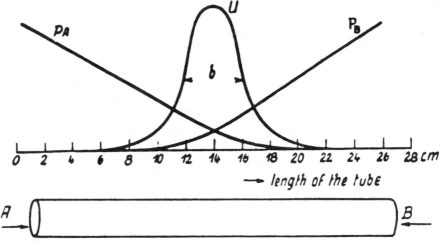

Figure 8. A schematic diagram of the variation of the pressures of the two reacting substances P_A and P_B, from *Atomic Reactions*, p. 33.

through the tube, and observing with a photocell the darkening caused by these sodium atoms absorbing their own natural frequency.

Christopher Baughan, a sympathetic but critical former co-worker, said that the flame method was *the* way to start the study of organic reactivity. Byers-Brown, who was a colleague of Polanyi toward the last years of his chemical work, told me that the flame experiments were the first method for getting at primitive reactions, and that the method was just achieving in the late 1970s the prominence it deserved. D. R. Herschbach,[30] reviewing in 1973 a Faraday Society discussion, begins by saying, "the happy saga of alkali reactions continues, with new episodes worthy of our heritage from Michael Polanyi," and finds no need to cite a reference.

The reaction mechanisms being unravelled by the method of highly dilute flames naturally called for theoretical explanation. Some preliminary steps were taken in two papers written with Polanyi's student Eugene Wigner,[31] later to win the Nobel Prize. After quantum mechanics was discovered in 1925 and 1926, Polanyi asked Max Born if this new development could provide a theory of reaction rates and activation energies. Born replied that the subject was too complicated, but Polanyi stuck to his belief that a simple theory could be found. When Fritz London in 1928[32] showed the way to a quantum mechanical theory of the chemical bond and then of the bonds among three atoms, Polanyi considered the idea of studying the energy of a system like H + HBr as the bromine comes

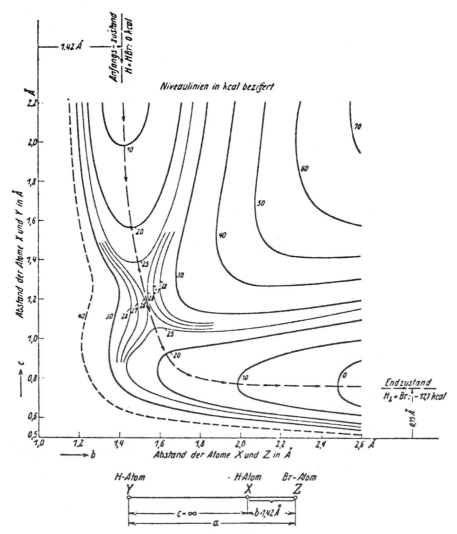

Figure 9. A contour diagram of the potential energy of the system H-H-Br, from
Polanyi & Eyring, "On Simple Gas Reactions," *Zeitschrift physikalische Chemie* B12
(1931), p. 292.

near one hydrogen and the other hydrogen recedes. To the simplicity
of the atomic reaction was added the feature that the reaction took
place most easily when all three atoms were in a straight line, as
shown on the bottom of Figure 9. If a contour map of energy was
made in terms of the Br-H and H-H distances, as in the figure, one
could imagine a ball rolling on the surface that describes the position
of all three atoms. When the ball rolls over the top of the pass, the
saddle point, the reaction becomes complete.

Polanyi suggested the rolling ball idea to Henry Eyring who had come to Berlin to work with him, and Eyring went right at a calculation of the graphs.[33] The actual rate at which the representative point goes over the hill depends on properties of the state of the system at the top of the pass. Polanyi and his close friend M. G. Evans[34] worked out the theory of this transition state, and Eyring and co-workers back at Princeton developed the idea of the activated complex in a parallel way. The letter T in Figure 2 shows the sixteen papers by Polanyi and co-workers on the transition state theory.

An important result from this work is that if homologous series of similar substances are used, the contours are similar enough that there is a useful linear relation between the heats of reaction ΔH and the energies of activation $E_{activation}$. As Evans and Polanyi wrote it,

$$E_{activation} = \alpha \Delta H + c.$$

Figure 10 shows some modern results.[35]

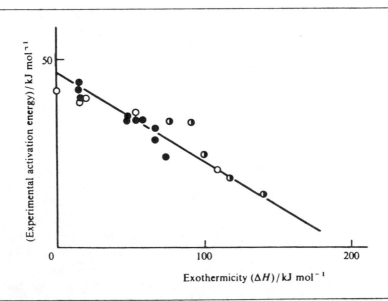

Figure 10. Taken from J Nicholas, *Chemical Kinetics,* (New York: John Wiley, 1976). Reproduced with permission of John Wiley.

While all this experimental and theoretical work was going on, happenings in England and Germany brought about a change in Michael Polanyi's career. In England, the University of Manchester started searching in 1928 for a new professor of physical chemistry to fill a vacated chair, and by 1932 had concluded with the help of W. L. Bragg that Michael Polanyi was the best man available. After considerable negotiation, he agreed to take the position. In an interview with the Manchester Faculty Senate he brilliantly discussed crystal structure, physical metallurgy, cellulose, contemporary French literature, and detective stories. In January of 1933, however, he withdrew, partly at least as a result of exposure on his trip to Manchester to its combination of fog and smog, and partly because of the poor state of the Manchester chemistry building and its facilities. But this was the period of Adolf Hitler's assumption of power in Germany. Although Polanyi was temporarily protected from the new racial laws by having fought in World War I, many of his close friends and collaborators found their jobs in danger. The Kaiser Wilhelm Gesellschaft's administration was law-abiding but also sympathetic to their staff, and did everything they could to postpone dismissals and make leaving easy. By April of 1933, Polanyi inquired of Manchester if he could re-apply, and they, having filled the chair with an organic chemist, made up a new chair for him. He accepted the appointment.

Polanyi's work in Berlin had been tremendously productive. The list in a report of the Institute included metallurgy, crystal physics, colloid chemistry, structural chemistry, luminescence, reaction kinetics, and catalysis. In spite of the break his creativity was not stifled. By the end of August 1933, when he finally left, he had had a large part of his own research equipment packed up for shipment and had arranged for two technicians to go with him. He brought to Manchester its first high vacuum mercury pumps, as well as a precision machine lathe.

Little time was lost in getting the reaction experiments and the theoretical work under way again, and the place rapidly became a beehive of activity. Polanyi kept track of the numerous experiments by daily visits through the laboratories and by holding group discussions both of the results obtained and of new speculative ideas. He was well aware of each piece of work; some he had thought out himself, and some were planned by trusted colleagues. But because he was a theorist who did not do experiments himself, his manipulative abilities left something to be desired. His laboratory workers reported that his temptation to turn stopcocks had to be resisted, for he could well ruin an experiment in his enthusiasm.

The discovery of deuterium by Harold Urey in 1932[36] reopened for Polanyi the field of heterogeneous catalysis, since deuterium made an excellent tracer for the reaction on a solid surface between hydrogen atoms and hydrogen molecules. Useful surfaces were those of platinum and nickel, sometimes in the form of cell electrodes. The main problem was the supply of deuterium and its detection in the reaction products. The attempt to separate heavy water from light by a series of diffusion tubes failed, so electrolytically separated heavy water was purchased commercially. For quantitative analysis Polanyi designed a micropycnometer[37] that could measure liquid densities to hundredths of a percent and better, and thus find the proportion of heavy water in a solution. Figure 11 shows a Cartesian diver with a glass bubble on top. The flat place makes the bubble easily compressible and the lower open-ended part allows a filling with water to make the diver just float in a given solution without deuterium. A small amount of deuterium in place of hydrogen will increase the density and require a small but measurable increase of external pressure to compress the bubble and keep the micropycnometer stationary.

Many experiments were carried out on catalyzed hydrogen exchange. Melvin Calvin, who had gotten his doctorate in 1935 in Minnesota and gone to Manchester on a post-doc, did some of the electrochemical work.[38] Figure 2 shows the resulting twenty hydrogen papers from the group, thirteen of which used deuterium. Some of the papers were theoretical, for transition rates are sensitive to the zero-point energies in the initial, activated, and final states, and the zero-point energy is considerably lower for deuterium than it is for hydrogen.

As work progressed on inorganic catalysts, Polanyi began to see a wide range of applications in biochemistry. Biological materials in general are too unstable for reliable physical-chemical experiments. But in 1936 Linstead reported the synthesis of phthalocyanine, a stable compound with interesting biochemical properties. Calvin was sent up to London to learn how to make it; he was then put to work on hydrogen exchange catalyzed by this material. This was the last experiment he did with Polanyi,[39] after which he went into porphyrins and then to chlorophyll. For his work on chlorophyll and photosynthesis Calvin won the Nobel Prize, becoming the second Polanyi associate to be thus honored.

As in Berlin, the variety of Polanyi's research areas in Manchester

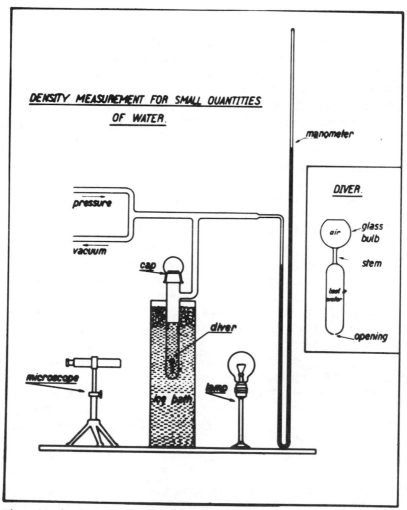

Figure 11. The Polanyi micropycnometer for measuring densities of water containing small amounts of deuterium. This diagram was kindly furnished to the author by Mr. A. R. Gilson, without restriction as to use.

was astoundingly rich. In addition to hydrogen exchange, the reaction kinetics work, both experimental and theoretical, was extended to ionic reactions in which an electron jump or electron switch occurs. Transition theory was extended to include steric hindrance and resonance among two or three possible alternate product structures. Pyrolysis, Friedel-Crafts reactions, and polymerization are terms descriptive of other phases of the work. The last-named branch led during World War II to some advances in the study of the polymerization of isobutene into synthetic rubber.

But I must turn now from an account of Polanyi's actual scientific creativity to the development of his philosophy of discovery and his conception of the knowing person in relation to the world. In his youth he was exposed to ideas about the use of science for human betterment, especially from the Marxist tradition, which he never espoused. After the Communist revolution, he became curious as to how the Soviets could claim to plan their economy when centralized planning and control did not seem possible. He helped organize a series of seminars in Berlin on economics, which included reports from the Soviet Union. This interest developed to the point that he published a little book in 1935 on USSR economics,[40] and ten years later a more extensive book, *Full Employment and Free Trade*.[41] One of his main points was that the number of economic decisions needed to be made daily in a large nation is far too great for any central authority to decide, no matter how moral this authority might be; he pointed out that the Soviets never did and never could control their economic system on rational principles. The information required could not be gathered, and sufficient communication could not be transmitted from the center to each person making decisions. Polanyi also became painfully aware of how the moral interest behind the communist movement became inverted into a totalitarian drive for power, especially when he experienced the disappearance of scientific friends in Russia and the sixteen-month imprisonment of his niece Eva as part of the Stalin purges.

When J. D. Bernal and J. G. Crowther in Britain proposed that science should be centrally planned for the good of society, Michael Polanyi responded[42] by demonstrating that no central authority in science could handle the huge number of daily decisions made by all the scientists of a nation in the pursuit of their research. Only the shared value of the search for truth could guide a group of independent researchers to coordinate their efforts in obtaining revelations from nature. The Marxist denial of truth as a value and power in itself was the philosophical fallacy in addition to the practical one that Polanyi saw as the grounds for rejecting what he called Bernalism.

These objections led Polanyi into an examination of how science actually functions and, further, into the whole process of knowing. In 1948 he exchanged his chair of physical chemistry for one in the Manchester faculty of economics and social studies, in which position he was able to devote full time to social and philosophical questions. I have told how scientific creativity for Polanyi involved the personal act of sensing a problem and pursuing its solution; and I have sketched a few examples of his own tremendous creative powers and well disciplined skills. I have indicated his reliance on the living scientific tradition and on the convivial sharing of thought whereby scientists coordinate with each other without centralized, authoritative control. Authority for him was neither a matter of decision making by superiors nor of general pronouncements about fact or method, but a matter of recognized weight of opinion on specific scientific results and theories.

The basic motive power for scientific research and discovery, according to Polanyi, is the questing imagination in search of new aspects of reality. The imaginative powers try out the visions that the intuition provides, developing them, reasoning with them, and designing experiments based on them, and they lead the investigator to decisions to adopt or modify a research program or just to take one more step in the hopes that the intuition will prove to be correct and a new contact with the real world will be made, where after all the final authority of science actually lies.

There are no rules for scientific discovery, as one can see in the first instance from the variety of paths that Michael Polanyi took, and in the second instance by putting together all the different kinds of creativity of the scientists represented in this series. The initial vagueness of a problem includes an indefiniteness in method, which generally is clarified by methodological improvements along with the advent of new knowledge. Only plausibility, not strict rules, can be the scientist's guide, and unsuccessful trials are to be expected—I have told of a few of Polanyi's. But, as he said, even the failures may contribute to our foreknowledge of hidden truth in redirecting our efforts and our intuitions.

How do we tell when we have found something? It has been popular to say that the context of discovery is different from the context of justification. But for Polanyi, discovery and justification utilize the same criteria—if the transition state idea did not clearly show a way to calculate a reaction rate, it would not have appealed to the imagination and the intuition, and would have been discarded. Following the initial sense of discovery, there is the time of detailed calculation and attention to possible sources of error in order to satisfy oneself that one is right. Next comes the rhetorical effort to convince colleagues who are knowledgeable enough to be critical in deciding whether something has indeed been found, and an irreversible addition to scientific knowledge has been made. Finally there are scientific reviews and textbooks that summarize established results and put them in context.

Much was found by Michael Polanyi and his many co-workers. Quite beyond all the specifics in adsorption, catalysis, X-rays, metals, reaction rates, and transition states, what kind of a world did Polanyi find the physical world to be? He rejected the old Newtonian-Laplacean conception of a deterministic world consisting of nothing but particles acted on by forces. In the first place, it denied the existence of persons and values and thus denied science itself. It was also intrinsically deficient. No aspect of the physical world has the exactitude claimed for the Newtonian theory, not only in the light of the probabilities of quantum mechanics but more widely in the inexactitude of all scientific theories and experiments and the inevitable tacit component of knowledge. More important, however, Polanyi found the Laplacean view useless as a model for science.[43] His successes in chemistry were mainly in terms of structures and mechanisms—where the adsorbed gases lie, what the crystal arrangements are, how dislocations explain plastic flow, what order of intermediate reactions occur in a sodium flame experiment. No amount of data about the coordinates of individual particles can tell us these things, because one would need in advance to label the particles as parts of the structures, and to change the labels as the particles move in and out.

More precisely, every organized system has its own laws of organization or order of operation, which control the boundary conditions for the underlying laws of physics, and so are not derivable from these laws. Hence the world, for Polanyi, is a hierarchy of many levels of complexity and organization, from elementary particles up to persons and to culture, each higher level being logically independent of the lower.[44] The laws of the lower levels, such as those of physics, are necessary to the higher levels, but are not sufficient since they are equally necessary to all types of existing or imaginary higher levels. The study of the world parallels these levels, for nature is capable of being grasped in successive stages, as Polanyi's work so well shows.

Among the laws of complex organization, one should be singled out for its special interest to Polanyi. That is the law of spontaneous ordering such as I have described for the community of scientists for coordinating with each other.[45] Another example is a community of buyers and sellers in a free market coordinating to develop a price structure.[46] And in the evolutionary span, survival efforts, curiosity in the exploration of new ecological niches, and chance mutations all coordinate into the release of the hidden potentialities of the ever-widening family tree of new species.[47]

Within an individual life, new ideas make creative changes, and in fact all of our conscious existence has an irreversible, growing character. Even the premises and methods of science undergo irreversible, creative changes with every act of discovery. We face an indefinite future, as the consequences of our efforts and our perceptions of the events around us will unfold in unforeseeable ways. Our security is not to be found in certainty but in faith, faith that we can make even more contact with reality and that we can together face problems, not only the scientific but the technical and especially the human, if we can utilize in community our powers of mind and perception.

The world of scientists and of all human beings, as well as the natural world in which we dwell is dynamic, creative, unpredictable, and with all its misery, full of enjoyment and hope. That is the message of the chemist and philosopher Michael Polanyi.

Notes

1. Michael Polanyi, *Personal Knowledge* (London: Routledge and Kegan Paul, 1958; Chicago: Chicago University Press, 1958; paperback 1974).

2. Michael Polanyi, "New Thermodynamic Consequences of the Quantum Hypothesis," *Zeitschrift für physikalische Chemie* 83 (1913), pp. 339-369.

3. Wakeman, John, ed. World Authors, 1950-1970. New York: H. W. Wilson, 1975, pp. 1151-1153, "Michael Polanyi".

4. Michael Polanyi, "Adsorption of Gases (Vapors) by a Solid Non-volatile Adsorbent," *Verhandlungen der Deutschen physikalischen Gesellschaft* 18 2/3 (1916), pp. 55-80.

5. Michael Polanyi and Fritz London, "The Theoretical Interpretation of Adsorption Forces," *Naturwissenschaften* 18 (1930), pp. 1099-1100.

6. Max Bodenstein, S. C. Lind, "The Rate of Formation of Hydrogen Bromide from its Elements," *Zeitschrift für physikalische Chemie* 57 (1906), pp. 168-192.

7. Michael Polanyi, "Tacit Knowing: Its Bearing on Some Problems of Philosophy," *Reviews of Modern Physics* 34 (October 1962), pp. 601-616.

8. Michael Polanyi, "Reaction Isochore and Reaction Velocity from the Standpoint of Statistics," *Zeitschrift für Elektrochemie* 26 (1920), pp. 49-54.

9. Karl F. Herzfeld, "Theory of the Speed of Reactions in Gases," *Annalen der Physik* 59 (1919), pp. 635-667.

J. A. Christiansen, "Reaction between Hydrogen and Bromine," *Det Kgl. Danske Videnskabernes Selskab* 14 (1919), pp. 1-19.

10. Michael Polanyi, "On the Nonmechanical Nature of Chemical Processes," *Zeitschrift für Physik* 1 (1920), pp. 337-344. This paper was important enough for Born to write to Einstein (November 1921), "I would like to know what you think of Polanyi's papers in rates of reactions; he maintains that these could not be explained without an as yet unknown kind of energy transmission. . . . Franck and I do not believe it." (Born-Einstein Letters, Walker, N.Y., 1971.) Einstein replied (30 December 1921) "Polanyi's ideas

make me shudder. But he has discovered difficulties for which I know no remedies as yet."

11. Karl F. Herzfeld, "Disruption Velocity of Molecules," *Zeitschrift für Physik* 8 (1921), pp. 132-136.

12. Michael Polanyi and S. v. Bogdandy, "Chemically Induced Chain Reactions in Mixtures of Halogens, Hydrogen and Methane," *Zeitschrift für Elektrochemie* 33 (1927), pp. 554-559.

13. Michael Polanyi, "My Time with X-Rays and Crystals," *Fifty Years of X-Ray Diffraction,* ed. P. P. Ewald. Utrecht, 1962. Chapter VII, Personal Reminiscences, p. 629.

14. R. O. Herzog and W. Jancke, "X-Ray Spectroscopic Investigations on Cellulose," *Zeitschrift für Physik* 3 (1920), pp. 196-198; P. Scherrer, in *Kolloidchemie* by R. Zsigmondy. Leipzig, O. Spamer.

15. Polanyi, "My Time with X-rays," p. 630.

16. Michael Polanyi, "The X-Ray Fibre Diagram," *Zeitschrift für Physik* 7 (1921), pp. 149-180.

17. Michael Polanyi, E. Schiebold, and K. Weissenberg, "On the Development of the Rotating Crystal Method," *Zeitschrift für Physik* 23 (1924), pp. 337-340.

18. Polanyi, "The X-Ray Fibre Diagram."

19. Kurt H. Meyer and H. Mark, "The Structure of the Crystallized Components of Cellulose." *Berichte der deutschen chemischen Gesellschaft* 61B, (1928), pp. 593-614.

20. Polanyi, *Personal Knowledge*, pp. 147-148, 169.

21. Michael Polanyi, "On Structural Changes in Metals through Cold Working," *Zeitschrift für Physik* 17 (1923), pp. 42-53.

22. Michael Polanyi, "An Elongating Apparatus for Threads and Wires," *Zeitschrift für technische Physik* 6 (1925), pp. 121-124.

23. Michael Polanyi, "Deformation of Monocrystals," *Zeitschrift für Kristallographie* 61 (1925), pp. 49-57.

24. Michael Polanyi, "On a Form of Lattice Distortion that May Render a Crystal Plastic," *Zeitschrift für Physik* 89 (1934), pp. 660-664.

25. G. I. Taylor, "Resistance to Shear in Metal Crystals," *Transactions of the Faraday Soc.* 24 (1928), pp. 121-125.

26. E. Orovan, "Plasticity of Crystals," *Zeitschrift für Physik* 89 (1934), pp. 605-659.

27. Michael Polanyi, *The Tacit Dimension: The Terry Lectures, Yale University, 1962* (London; Routledge and Kegan Paul, 1966; Garden City, New York: Doubleday and Company, 1966).

28. Polanyi, "My Time with X-Rays and Crystals," p. 97.

29. Michael Polanyi, H. Beutler, and S. v. Bogdandy, "On Luminescence of Highly Dilute Flames," *Naturwissenschaften* 14 (1926), p. 164.

Michael Polanyi and H. Beutler, "On Highly Dilute Flames: I," *Zeitschrift für physikalische Chemie* B1 (1928), pp. 3-20.

30. D. R. Herschbach, "Reactive Scattering," *Faraday Discussions of the Chemical Society* 55 (1973), pp. 234-251. See p. 234.

31. Michael Polanyi and E. Wigner, "Formation and Decomposition of Molecules," *Zeitschrift für Physik* 33 (1925), pp. 429-434.

Michael Polanyi and E. Wigner, "On the Interference of Characteristic Vibrations as the Cause of Energy Fluctuations and Chemical Changes," *Zeitschrift für physikalische Chemie* A139 (1928), pp. 439-452.

32. Fritz London, *Probleme der modernen Physik: Sommerfeld Festschrift*, ed. S. Hirzel, Leipzig, 1928, p. 104.

33. Michael Polanyi and H. Eyring, "On the Calculation of the Energy of Activation," *Naturwissenschaften* 18 (1930), pp. 914-915.

Michael Polanyi and H. Eyring, "On Simple Gas Reactions," *Zeitschrift für physikalische Chemie* B12 (1931), pp. 279-311.

34. Michael Polanyi and M. G. Evans, "Inertia and Driving Force of Chemical Reactions," *Transactions of the Faraday Soc.* 34 (1938), pp. 11-24.

35. John Nicholas, *Chemical Kinetics: A Modern Survey of Gas Reactions* (New York: John Wiley & Sons, 1976), p. 86.

36. Harold Urey, F. G. Brickwedde, and G. M. Murphy, "A Hydrogen Isotope of Mass 2," *Physical Review* 39 (1932), pp. 164-165.

37. Michael Polanyi and E. S. Gilfillan, "Micropycnometer for the Determination of Displacements of Iostopic Ratio in Water," *Zeitschrift für physikalische Chemie* A166 (1933), pp. 254-256.

38. Melvin Calvin, "The Platinum Electrode as a Catalyst for the Activation of Hydrogen," *Transactions of the Faraday Soc.* 32 (1936), pp. 1428-1436.

39. Michael Polanyi, M. Calvin, and E. G. Cockbain, "Activation of Hydrogen by Phthalocyanine and Copper Phthalocyanine," *Transactions of the Faraday Soc.* 32 (1936), pp. 1436-1443.

Michael Polanyi, M. Calvin and D. D. Eley, "Activation of Hydrogen by Phthalocyanine and Copper Phthalocyanine. II," *Transactions of the Faraday Soc.* 32 (1936), pp. 1443-1446.

40. Michael Polanyi, "U.S.S.R. Economics: Fundamental Data System and Spirit." *The Manchester School of Economics and Social Studies* 6 (1935), pp. 67-89. Separately printed as *U.S.S.R. Economics,* Manchester, Manchester University Press, 1935.

41. Michael Polanyi, *Full Employment and Free Trade* (Cambridge: Cambridge University Press, 1945), 2nd ed. 1948.

42. Michael Polanyi, "The Growth of Thought in Society," *Economica* 8 (1941), pp. 428-456.

43. Polanyi, *Personal Knowledge,* p. 139-142.

44. Michael Polanyi, "Life's Irreducible Structure," in *Knowing and Being: Essays by Michael Polanyi,* ed. Marjorie Grene (London: Routledge & Kegan Paul, 1969), pp. 225-239.

45. Michael Polanyi, "The Republic of Science: Its Political and Economic Theory," in *Knowing and Being,* pp. 49-73.

46. Ibid., p. 52.

47. Polanyi, *Personal Knowledge,* Chapter 13 "The Rise of Man," pp. 381-402.

Chapter 12

The Role of John von Neumann in the Computer Field

Herman H. Goldstine

John von Neumann was one of the world's great mathematicians. His virtuosity, originality, and profundity have seldom been equalled. He was moreover one of those whose natural interest spanned almost the entire spectrum of mathematics from formal logics at one end to applications to biology, economics, physics, and computers at the other. In what follows I am going to try to give some indications of how this great mathematical genius and warm, fun-loving human being contributed to one application: the computer field.

I delimit the field in this way since any attempt to depict von Neumann's entire scientific career would constitute a volume rather than a chapter and would make difficult reading for a general audience. I have therefore limited my field to one—in fact only to a part of one—of von Neumann's areas of interest. In doing this I can perhaps plead the world-wide relevance of his contribution to the computer field.

Jancsi, or Johnny, was born in Budapest on December 28, 1903 of a well-to-do Hungarian Jewish family at a time when the Austro-Hungarian Empire was still one of the four great empires of Europe. Budapest itself was at that time a great cultural center, and there were many important scientists, scholars, and artists in the Hungarian kingdom. The names of some still are familiar to us today. To mention just a few: Bela Schick and Albert Szent-Györgyi in biological sciences, Theodore von Kármán in engineering, John von Neumann in mathematics, Eugene Wigner in physics, George von Hevesy in chemistry, Bela Bartok, Zoltan Kodaly, Ernst von Dohnanyi in music, Andreas Alföldi, and Gyula Moravcsik in history.

John von Neumann, 1903-1957

Before carrying our discussion forward in time, I should say a few words about von Neumann as a man and as a scientist. This will help show how and why he was able to dominate the computer field as he did; it will also help explain some of his particular interests in that field. Von Neumann's father was a partner in one of Budapest's private banks and was undoubtedly a man of great intelligence and charm. That he was also very successful is attested to by the fact he was ennobled in 1913 by Emperor Franz Josef. This was the basis for the *von* in the family name. His mother, Margaret, was also an extraordinary woman with great perceptiveness and insight. She was endowed with enormous energy, which she expended freely on her children, John, Michael, and Nicholas.

As a child von Neumann showed his extraordinary abilities. He once told me that at age six he joked with his father in classical Greek. His ability to tell jokes and humorous stories was remarkable. He had the power of absolute recall and could bring back verbatim all manner of things—some important, others immaterial, including essentially every story that "tickled his fancy." He became a sort of walking encyclopedia for such tales; hardly a famous scientist or scholar visited him without bringing a verbal gift of some new stories. He could also recall verbatim papers he wrote at least twenty years before, and translate them from German to English as he spoke with absolutely no hesitation. I remember well such a performance at the Institute for Advanced Study when a number of visitors asked him to lecture on Hilbert-Space theory. He did, using exactly the same letters and symbols he had in his original papers.

Another quality he had to a very high degree was the ability to see through the details of extremely complex problems to their essences. He could do this in very diverse fields with lightning rapidity and extraordinary clarity. At the Institute students used to line up to ask his help on their researches, and he always responded with complete attentiveness and kindness, and with penetrating clarity. It was uncanny to watch him attending to visitor after visitor much like a professional man tending his clients or patients. These qualities are of course only the ones that seem of interest to us on this occasion. But we can sum him up as a man by quoting a line of Landor: "He warmed both hands before the fire of life."

As a young man von Neumann first studied chemical engineering in Berlin, where Fritz Haber tried to persuade him to pursue a career in chemistry. Fortunately for us he did not do so, but went instead to the Swiss Federal Institute of Technology in Zürich, where he came strongly under the influence of Hermann Weyl and George Polya. He received a degree in chemical engineering in 1925 and in the next year his Ph.D. in mathematics, with minors in chemistry and experimental physics, from Budapest.

This background was, I believe, fundamental to his career as it concerns us. Many mathematicians have been interested in the applications of mathematics. Few, however, have approached these applications as he did. His deep understanding of chemistry and physics enabled him to go to the very root of the matter and not be led astray by superficialities. It meant, for example, in discussions at Los Alamos that he was able to start from first principles and build up the appropriate mathematical tools to analyze a given situation. He was not wholly dependent on his physicist colleagues to do this. This is quite important since it meant he was not just a superb problem-solver but also a superb problem-formulator. This made him unique.

He had other qualities that were of enormous importance to him and to us. One was the absolutely unparalleled speed with which he could work. Another was his great ability and liking for numerical calculation. A third was his superb memory. These can be illustrated by several stories; I shall tell one that, though untrue, had wide circulation, and a second that I can vouch for.

It is said that one time in Zürich Weyl gave a long, complicated proof of a very profound and difficult theorem and emphasized why such a long proof was by the nature of the subject almost inevitable. The story goes that at the conclusion young von Neumann stood up and gave an extremely elegant and short proof based on a quite novel approach. Von Neumann assured me the story was not correct, but it does serve to illustrate perhaps what people recognized about the speed with which he thought.

The second story took place at the Aberdeen Proving Ground. A colleague of mine was trying to understand a theorem that depended on a function of the integers. After we tried unsuccessfully to understand what was going on, he decided to take home a desk calculator and do a few special cases. The next morning he came in looking very fatigued and told me he had spent most of the night calculating the first five cases. Just then von Neumann came in on a visit from Los Alamos and asked what was new. My colleague showed him the theorem, and von Neumann suggested we estimate the size of the function for a few cases. He did the first four cases in his head in a very few minutes and then the last case in just a few more.

His approach to his work was also quite different from that of many other great mathematicians I have been privileged to know. It was his wont to think about problems as he went to sleep and often he awoke in the middle of the night with an understanding of how to proceed. He would then get up and work for several hours before going back to sleep. He never seemed to wrestle with a difficulty as did some of his colleagues. Either it had to come elegantly and easily, or he put it aside until it suddenly did.

His ability to recall things or perhaps to do them de novo can be illustrated by what happened when three of us were working on a problem. Our colleague was lecturing to us on an approach to the problem when he got "stuck"; he stopped and said, "I'll run upstairs to get a book where I know the proof I need is given." Von Neumann replied, "Don't do that; I don't know the book, but I'll write out the proof for you."

In 1927 von Neumann became a Privatdozent in Berlin. In three years he established a world-wide reputation by his profound work on algebra, logics, and quantum mechanics.[1] From Berlin he often went to Göttingen, where he came under Hilbert's influence, which may have been what led him into both mathematical logic and quantum mechanics. It was the former interest that was to condition him to be profoundly interested in automata theory and later in the logical structure of computers. While at Göttingen he also became interested in a remarkable result of Courant, Friedrichs, and Lewy that was to have fundamental importance in the numerical solution of partial differential equations.[2] He stored up this result in his mind even though it seemed at the time to be no more than a curiosity. It bore rich fruit in von Neumann's hands at Los Alamos in the 1940s when it became absolutely essential and is today fittingly known as the Courant condition.

The modern electronic computer had its genesis in the United States during the Second World War. While a number of people — perhaps a dozen — played a substantial role in bringing the computer into being, it is certainly fair to attribute the main role to John von Neumann. In what follows I shall try to sort out the parts he played and show why his was the "lead" role in the epic story. I do not want anyone to feel I am depreciating or denigrating any other person; but I am convinced that von Neumann's participation in the development of the computer was qualitatively more essential, profound, and pervasive than that of anyone else. All participants were true pioneers and deserving of great praise and recognition. Von Neumann, however, was unique. Not only did he make fundamental contributions — perhaps we all did — he also integrated all these contributions into a coherent whole; he, probably alone, was able to persuade the scientific community of the importance of this new tool; and he showed that community how to use it and why it was so fundamental to their work. In doing these things he revolutionized applied mathematics. No one else, in my opinion, would have been able to do this at that time. Von Neumann's unique accomplishments, then, were his computer system and his revolution of the thinking of scientists.

Curiously, all the pioneering work on the modern electronic computer was done in ignorance of the long series of developments of computing instruments stretching back to the Thirty Years War in Germany. None of us was aware of our predecessors' efforts. The design of the modern machines constituted a discovery based not upon the work of a long chain of earlier people's work but rather upon two quite distinct trends: As is well known, World War II had spurred the development of electronic techniques and devices as well as the recognition of the need for very fast ways to perform scientific calculations. Von Neumann had no connection with or influence upon the initial design of the ENIAC—Electronic Numerical Integrator and Computer—, the first electronic computer, although he did redesign the machine some years later, as we shall see below. His great contribution came in the logical design of all subsequent computers. For this he was, I shall try to show, uniquely qualified by his great knowledge of formal logics.

In the succeeding pages I shall attempt to give a very brief (and over-simplified) account of von Neumann's background and interest in the subject of logics and its applications to automata and to computers. This story, as I shall tell it, reflects my personal prejudices, but it has the virtue of being first-hand, and of being documented. I should perhaps pause a moment to explain that in the United States there is considerable contention among some of the early contributors to the computer field as to where credit should go. No doubt there will be some challenge to my account of von Neumann's accomplishments. I might add, however, that such controversy will surely abate with the passage of enough time to allow historians to reach an impartial conclusion.

In order to explore von Neumann's role in the computer field, I shall first say a few more words about his early interest in mathematical logic, a subject on which he worked hard and produced several fundamental papers under Hilbert's influence. Already by 1925 he was writing on "Eine Axiomatisierung der Mengenlehre."[3] This work was motivated by the controversy that arose in the early part of this century when Russell, Weyl, and Brouwer each showed that the philosophical underpinnings of set theory were not completely sound.[4] To replace this unsound foundation Brouwer constructed his system of intuitionistic mathematics, which is such that the difficulties and antinomies do not arise. In doing this, however, much—perhaps half—of modern mathematics had to be jettisoned. Very few mathematicians were willing to accept, or at least practice, this new system of mathematics, and most kept on with "business as usual," hoping that someone else would straighten matters out.

It was Hilbert who first proposed trying to demonstrate, using intuitionistic methods, that the so-called classical mathematics was free of contradictions.[5] This great scheme of Hilbert's excited considerable interest among mathematicians in general and von Neumann in particular. His most important contribution to the subject perhaps was his paper "Zur Hilbertschen Beweistheorie," which appeared in 1927.[6] In this paper he defined a subsystem of classical analysis and showed rigorously by finitistic means that it is contradiction-free. He conjectured incorrectly that all analysis could be proved consistent by his methods.

In this connection he once told me that on two successive nights he dreamed how to make this proof and each night awakened and wrote out the proof, discovering each time a lacuna. He went on to say how fortunate it was for mathematics that he did not dream the third night how to complete the proof, since Gödel showed in 1931 that, in von Neumann's words, "its essential import however, was this: If a system of mathematics does not lead into contradiction, then this fact cannot be demonstrated with the procedures of that system. . . . My personal opinion, which is shared by many others, is, that Gödel has shown that Hilbert's program is essentially hopeless."[7]

An important consequence for von Neumann of all this interest in finitistic mathematics was its relation to numerical analysis. Algorithms for computers are, of course, finitistic in nature, and the computer because of its great speed makes it practically possible to carry out such algorithms. Von Neumann used to say the computer changed intuitionistic mathematics from theology to reality.

One of the most important of Hilbert's problems in mathematical logic is his so-called Entscheidungsproblem or Decision Problem. Hilbert asked if a procedure can be found so that one can decide whether or not any given "meaningful" proposition, expressed in the usual notations of symbolic logic, is provable. It was shown in 1936 both by Church and Turing that this is not possible.[8] (Parenthetically it should be remarked that this result is different from Gödel's theorem. What Gödel showed was that in the formalism of the *Principia* there are propositions such that neither such a proposition nor its contrary is provable.)

It is against this background that I want to examine von Neumann's interest in computers and computing; I shall do so after a short excursus on Alan Turing, an Englishman who wrote his doctoral dissertation at Princeton University, where he and von Neumann became acquainted. The latter thought so highly of Turing's work that he asked Turing to be his assistant for the academic year 1938-1939. Turing, however, decided it was more important that he return to England and take up a post at the Foreign Office to oppose the Nazi threat to the free world.

In any case Turing conceived of what he called "computable" numbers as those "real numbers whose expressions as a decimal are calculable by finite means." To investigate these numbers, or more generally computable functions, he developed the notion of an automaton or "computing machine" that could compute in a finite number of steps each computable number. It is not a priori clear that any one automaton can compute every computable number. Indeed it is perhaps Turing's greatest contribution to this field that he was able to show the existence of a universal automaton that can compute every computable number.

Turing's machine is of course a mathematical, not a physical, construct. It is a "black box," only some of whose attributes need discussion. The machine has only a finite number of states which can be numbered, say, from 1 to n. Thus at any instant the machine is in a state i where $1 \leqslant i \leqslant n$, and in the next instant it will change from this state to another state j. To understand how this change takes place, imagine a paper tape divided into squares, on each of which a datum may be recorded. The machine can "read" the tape a square at a time and act upon the information it finds on a given square. It can "read," "write," and "erase" the datum on a given square, which will always be a 0 or a 1. The machine operates on one square at a time, and can move the tape backwards or forwards a finite number of squares.

To make precise what is involved, suppose the machine is in state i and that the machine reads the number e (= 0, 1) on the tape. The specification of the new state j ($1 \leqslant j \leqslant n$), the number p of squares forward or backward the tape is to be moved, and the quantity f to be inscribed on the square reached by the tape after this move of p squares as functions of i and e, "is then the complete definition of the functioning of such an automaton."[9]

It is indeed remarkable that there can exist such a thing as the universal automaton mentioned earlier. Turing, however, noted, as we just saw, that the complete description of any conceivable automaton can be expressed finitistically, i.e., in a finite number of words. This description will "contain certain empty passages—those referring to the functions mentioned earlier (j, p, f in terms of i, e) which specify the actual functioning of the automaton. As long as they are left empty, this schema represents the general definition of the general automaton."[10] Von Neumann goes on to say "this automaton, which is constructed to read a description and to initiate the object described, is then the universal automaton in the sense of Turing. To make it duplicate any operation that any other automaton can perform, it suffices to furnish it with a description of the automaton in question and, in addition, with the instructions which that device would have required for the operation under consideration."

Let us now return to von Neumann. In the prewar period, the mathematicians of the Institute for Advanced Study were temporarily housed at Princeton University, and von Neumann's office was in the same university building as was Turing's. He followed Turing's work on automata theory closely. He was, therefore, completely conversant with all these ideas in the 1940s when he began to undertake ever more work for the United States in the war against the Axis powers. In 1943 he was invited by Oppenheimer to be a consultant to the group at Los Alamos. This was just at the time when one of the most remarkable assemblages of theoretical and experimental physicists the world had ever seen was forming. Ulam tells a very nice story illustrating the character of such a group.

When he [von Neumann] arrived, the Coordinating Council was just in session. Our Director, Oppenheimer, was reporting. . . . After he finished the speech he asked whether there were any questions or comments. The audience was impressed and no questions were asked. Then Oppenheimer suggested there might be questions on some other topics. After a second or two a deep voice (whose source has been lost to history) spoke, 'when shall we have a shoemaker on the hill?' Even though no scientific problem was discussed with Johnny at that time, he asserted that as of that moment he was fully familiar with the nature of Los Alamos.[11]

Very quickly von Neumann became a central figure in various activities that involved the solution of quite complex problems involving spherical shock waves. In fact, he was the leader in the effort to make a subcritical mass of material critical by compressing it with the help of a shock wave. This proved successful and led to the bomb used at Nagasaki. The study of such waves can be reduced to the solution of a nonlinear partial differential equation whose solution cannot be expressed by the usual analytical methods of classical mathematics. In working on the solutions of such equations von Neumann very quickly became an expert on numerical calculations and was constantly on the lookout for some way to effect such calculations in a practical way. Before the invention of the ENIAC it was essentially impossible to solve numerically any nonlinear partial differential equations because none of the then existent machines had the speed needed to carry out the very large numbers of calculations.

In the early spring of 1943 I was located at the University of Pennsylvania in charge of a substation of the Ballistic Research Laboratory of the U.S. Army's Ordnance Department. In this capacity I was approached by Professor J. G. Brainerd, who was in charge for the University of all matters relating to my substation. He told me that a faculty member, John W. Mauchly, had tentatively proposed the design and construction of an all-electronic digital computing machine. Brainerd felt that the idea was meritorious and that the University's Moore School of Electrical Engineering would be willing to undertake the development. This was a period when electronic techniques were just coming into being under the great stimulus of the war in general and in particular of the brilliant advances in radar and fire control. A few daring engineers and physicists such as John Atanasoff of the then Iowa State College were already trying to use electronic techniques to speed up digital computation. Mauchly had discussed with Atanasoff these ideas shortly before the Moore School proposal was made. Undoubtedly they influenced Mauchly's thinking.

In any case we accepted Brainerd's proposal virtually at once, and the so-called ENIAC project was underway before July 1, 1943 with J. Presper Eckert, Jr., a brilliant young graduate student, as chief engineer, Mauchly as his chief aide, Brainerd as the project supervisor, and myself as the officer in charge for the U.S. government and the person who headed the mathematical and programming side of the project.

The ENIAC development was a triumph for Eckert's engineering ability and tireless leadership. It was also a monument to Brainerd's quiet but firm administration and to Mauchly's idea. It was very fortunate for us that the technical staff—Arthur W. Burks, Joseph Chedaker, Chuan Chu, John H. Davis, Adele K. Goldstine, Harry Huskey, T. Kite Sharpless, and Robert Shaw, as well as a few others whose names I have forgotten—was composed of excellent engineers. The combined effort of the whole group, working essentially day and night, succeeded in seeing the machine to completion on February 15, 1946, when it was dedicated.

This machine was not a stored-program computer in the modern sense of the word, but it was not devoid of some programming capability. Let us see how Brainerd, Mauchly, and Eckert described the process in an appendix to their August 1942 proposal to me:

As already stated, the electronic computer utilizes the principle of counting to achieve its results. It is then, in every sense, the electric analogue of the mechanical adding, multiplying and dividing machines which are now manufactured for ordinary arithmetic purposes. However, the design of the electronic computer allows easy interconnection of a number of simple component devices and provides for a cycle of operations which will yield a step-by-step solution of any difference equation within its scope. The result of one calculation, such as a single multiplication, is immediately available for further operations in any way which is dictated by the equations governing the problem, and these numbers can be transferred from one component to another as required, without the necessity of copying them manually onto paper or from one component to another, as is the case when step-by-step solutions are performed with ordinary calculating machines. If one desires to visualize the mechanical analogy, he must conceive of a large number, say twenty or thirty, calculating machines, each capable of handling at least ten-digit numbers, and all interconnected by mechanical devices which see to it that the numerical result from an operation in one machine is properly transferred to some other machine, which is selected by a suitable program device; and one must further imagine that this program device is capable of arranging a cycle of different transfers and operations of this nature, with perhaps fifteen or twenty operations in each cycle. It may be said that even though such a mechanical device were constructed, and even though its speed of operation was considered satisfactory, the number of problems which it can solve within the lifetime which is determined by the wear of its parts would undoubtedly be very small. In stating that the electronic computer consists of components which are exactly analogous to the ordinary mechanical computing machine, it is intended that the analogy shall be interpreted rather completely. In particular, just as the ordinary computing machine utilizes the decimal system in performing its calculations, so may the electronic device. When a number, such as 1216, is to be injected into a particular register, it is not necessary for 1216 counts to be used. Instead, a total of 10 counts would be sufficient, one in the thousands register, two in the hundreds register, one in the tens register, and six in the units register. It is only in this way that almost unlimited accuracy can be obtained without unduly prolonging the time of operation. Electronic devices have been proposed for which this is not true, but such do not seem to merit consideration here."[12]

It was not until the middle of 1944 that I introduced von Neumann to the ENIAC project. He was already a consultant to the Ballistic Research Laboratory but was not yet aware of the ENIAC development. As soon as he learned about it the machine became a source of great delight to him, and it inspired all his interest in the field. This machine, even in its then incomplete form, was exactly what he needed to do the calculations he had been having carried out so laboriously at Los Alamos.

Here at last was a way to make the numerical solution of problems a reality. Von Neumann immediately realized this. For many years it was known in a number of important fields of physics exactly how to describe in precise mathematical forms the phenomena under study, but it was quite unknown how to solve the resulting mathematical formulas. Indeed since the earliest times the need to do this has formed the basis for many elegant advances, such as the discovery of trigonometry by Hipparchus and Ptolemy (150 B.C. and 150 A.D.), the discovery of logarithms by Napier and Briggs (1620s), and the invention of early digital calculators by Schickard, Pascal, and Leibniz.

The sort of phenomena von Neumann wished to study were usually describable by systems of nonlinear partial differential equations of so-called hyperbolic type and were generally intractable to known methods of mathematical analysis. It is therefore not surprising to realize that very few physicists or engineers tried to solve such systems. To the extent it was done at all, it was usually undertaken by a peculiar form of analog computation: physical experimentation. (There is of course a very valid use of experimentation: the measurement of physical or other fundamental constants.) For example, to study the flow of air over a wing, designers used—and still use—wind tunnels. This is mainly a form of analog computation for the solution of a system of nonlinear partial differential equations that can be written down without unreasonable difficulty.

This use of experimentation resulted in a situation in which virtually no physicist or engineer attempted to solve certain classes of physical problems by having recourse to mathematical equations and numerical procedures. In fact if anyone tried to solve such equations by digital means, he would probably get into serious numerical instabilities whereby a small error accidently introduced by the necessary rounding of numbers would grow unboundedly. The root of this matter was not got to until Courant, Friedrichs, and Lewy explicated the difficulty in a classic paper in 1927.[13] They discovered what was referred to above as the Courant condition; it is a condition that imposes certain restrictions on how a numerical grid can be laid down to guarantee a stable, step-by-step solution of various sorts of difference equations. Fortunately von Neumann was thoroughly conversant with this result and, perhaps more than anyone else, realized its crucial importance to the shock-wave calculations that needed to be carried out at Los Alamos and elsewhere.

It is therefore not surprising that von Neumann was unique among his contemporaries in being eager to undertake large-scale numerical calculations. In this respect he was like Gauss, who obviously deeply enjoyed computation for its own sake and who did what in his time were extensive calculations.[14] Von Neumann became extremely interested in the possibilities of using electronic digital means to solve his equations, and this opened up for him whole avenues into related fields. Von Neumann's abilities to do very extensive calculations with tremendous speed in his head were unbelievable. The story is told that once he was asked to solve the familiar problem of how far a fly travels who goes back and forth between two trains approaching each other. It is said he gave back the answer at once and the proposer remarked that von Neumann must have seen the trick immediately, to which von Neumann replied: "Trick? There is no trick, I merely summed the series."

During the period after the ENIAC was developed but not yet manufactured, there was a lull in intellectual activity; to keep busy, a number of us met frequently with von Neumann to discuss how a better computer could be built—the ENIAC's two chief defects were its huge size, about 20,000 vacuum tubes, and small memory, 20 ten-digit words or 40 five-digit ones. At first the discussions related to ways to overcome these defects, and a number of ingenious yet practical devices were proposed to this end. They included the so-called mercury delay lines or acoustic tanks, television-type tubes, and magnetic media such as tapes. The discussions soon changed to organizational and architectural problems, and here in particular von Neumann shone. This was his special métier; he had greater knowledge and insight than any of us.

There is controversy over exactly who discovered the stored-program concept in the course of these discussions involving principally Burks, Eckert, Adele Goldstine, Mauchly, von Neumann, and myself. To me it is clear that of all the group von Neumann was the one who best understood the concept and its importance, who first argued for its acceptance, and who constructed on paper a complete schematic of the machine and programmed this device to do a sort-merge. (I am convinced that his knowledge of Turing's ideas played a key role here in his thinking.) As von Neumann said:

There are certain items which are clearly one man's . . . the application of the acoustic tank to this problem was an idea we heard from Pres Eckert. There are other ideas where the situation was confused. So confused that the man who had originated the idea had himself talked out of it and changed his mind two or three times. Many times the man who had the idea first may not be the proponent of it. In these cases it would be practically impossible to settle its apostle.[15]

It is possible to date the discovery of the stored-program idea within narrow limits. On 21 August 1944 I wrote,

Von Neumann is displaying great interest in the ENIAC and is conferring with me weekly on the use of the machine. He is working on the aerodynamical problems of blast. . . . As I now see the future course of the ENIAC, there are two further directions in which we should pursue our researches. . . . I feel that the switches and controls of the ENIAC now arranged to be operated manually, can easily be positioned by mechanical relays and electromagnetic telephone switches which are instructed by a teletype tape. . . . In this manner tapes could be cut for many given problems and reused whenever needed. Thus we would not have to spend valuable minutes resetting switches when shifting from one phase of a problem to the next.

(The switches and controls referred to in that letter were the means for programming the ENIAC to do a particular problem.)

On 2 September 1944 I wrote the same man,

To illustrate the improvements I wish to realize, let me say that to solve a quite complex partial differential equation of von Neumann's . . . the new Harvard IBM will require about 80 hours as against ½ hour on ENIAC of which about 28 minutes will be spent just in card cutting and 2 minutes for computing. The card cutting is needed simply because the solution of partial differential equations requires the temporary storage of large amounts of data. We hope to build a cheap high-speed device for this purpose . . . . The second major improvement . . . can again be illustrated on the Harvard machine. To evaluate seven terms of a power series took 15 minutes on the Harvard device of which 3 minutes was set-up time, whereas it will take at least 15 minutes to set up ENIAC and about 1 second to do the computing. To remedy this disparity we propose a centralized programming device in which the program routine is stored in coded form in the same type storage devices suggested above. The other crucial advantage of central programming is that any routine, however complex, can be carried out whereas in the present ENIAC we are limited.[16]

Thus the stored-program concept was conceived some time during the fortnight between August 21, and September 2, 1944. This period must then be viewed in some sense as the most important in the early history of the modern computer. Soon after this the U.S. Ordnance Department gave the University a contract to start the development of a new computer, known as the EDVAC, whose design was indicated in a letter of September 13, 1944 from Brainerd to Col. P. N. Gillon, my superior, who had been solidly behind all the computer developments and continued to be. Brainerd's formal proposal read in part:

It is not feasible to increase the storage capacity of the ENIAC . . . to the extent necessary for handling non-linear partial differential equations. . . . The problem requires an entirely new approach. At the present time we know of two principles which might be used as a basis. One is the possible use of iconoscope tubes, concerning which Dr. von Neumann has talked to Dr. Zworykin of the RCA Research Laboratories, and another of which is the use of storage in a delay line, with which we have some experience. . . .

In the carrying out of the terms of this contract von Neumann wrote an elegant paper or report entitled "First Draft of a Report on the EDVAC" dated June 30, 1945 and circulated by the University. This paper contained a suggested organization for the machine, logical circuits for building the components, and the vocabulary or code of the computer. It was in this paper that von Neumann first made use of the neural analogy and drew circuits as if they were neural networks, drawing upon the ideas of Pitts and McCulloch.[17]

By this time the war was ending, and centrifugal forces sent the various members of the ENIAC/EDVAC group flying off to their peacetime activities. In particular von Neumann and I decided to set up at the Institute for Advanced Study a project to design and build a parallel, binary computer using for memory ideas based upon television tube techniques. This project was to complement the one at the University of Pennsylvania, which was concerned with a serial, binary computer using the delay line for its memory. The use of a parallel treatment for numbers led to a much faster machine than did the serial one, and the parallel machine rapidly took over the field.

The chief a priori advantage of the serial method was supposed to be a considerable saving of equipment, since only one digit at a time was processed. In fact, however, the chief use for vacuum tubes did not reside in the so-called arithmetic organ but rather in other parts such as the control, where the use of a serial system actually increased the equipment to the point where the parallel system was cheaper. It turned out in retrospect that a parallel machine using n digit numbers was at least n times faster than a comparable serial machine and that the former contained no more tubes than the latter.

It is perhaps not irrelevant to mention that at this time—around

1945-1950—the accepted thinking of many was that electronic devices were much less reliable than were electromechanical ones. There were many arguments and discussions on this point; not for some time did the general point of view and thinking change. At this time electronic devices had many shortcomings, but their speed was so great that overall there was no doubt they were incredibly faster than comparable electromechanical ones. The speed factor between the most primitive electronic machine, the ENIAC, and the most advanced electromechanical one was the order of 500! It was this factor that started the so-called Computer Revolution.

In this connection it should be remarked that inventions generally are revolutionary only if they enable us to do some important task at least one order of magnitude faster than it could previously be done. If the first computer had only been, say, five times faster than its electromechanical counterparts, five of these would have done the same task and would not have been impossibly large or expensive. Ten or a hundred machines is inconceivable.

The project at the Institute for Advanced Study was initiated in the spring of 1946 and was conceived of as being multi-faceted. There was a group concerned with what we called the logical design; this consisted at first of Burks, von Neumann, and me, and later just of von Neumann and me. There was an engineering group concerned with translating those designs into "hardware"; it was first headed by Julian Bigelow and later by James Pomerene. There was a numerical analysis group concerned with transforming that classical subject into the modern one we know today; it was led by von Neumann and me plus a number of excellent mathematicians who visited the Institute for varying periods of time. Finally there was a numerical meteorology group, which set as its task to transform meteorology from a qualitative and descriptive subject into a more quantitative one by solving the differential equations of a variety of models for the atmosphere; it was led by von Neumann and Jule Charney, a distinguished meteorologist, and consisted of a number of other meteorologists who visited the Institute from time to time. In all it was a very ambitious project that was highly successful.

The significance of the logical design work has been nicely summarized by Paul Armer in *Datamation*:

Who invented stored programming? Perhaps it doesn't matter much to anyone other than the principals involved just who gets the credit—we have the concept and it will surely stand as one of the great milestones in man's advance. . . . The leading contenders are the authors of the paper reprinted here [Burks, Goldstine, and von Neumann] and the group at the University of Pennsylvania led by J. Presper Eckert and John Mauchly. Others undoubtedly contributed, not the least of whom was Babbage. . . .

Nevertheless the paper reprinted here is the definitive paper in the computer field. Not only does it specify the design of a stored program computer, but it anticipates many knotty problems and suggests ingenious solutions. The machine described in the paper (variously known as the IAS, or Princeton, or von Neumann machine) was constructed and copied (never exactly), and the copies copied. . . .

At the time the paper was written, the principle of automatic calculation was well established (with Harvard's Mark I) as was the great advance gained by electronics (with ENIAC). The jump from that state-of-the-art to the detail of their paper is difficult to measure objectively today. . . .[18]

In fact the ideas made explicit in the papers we put out in this period were to be instrumental in shaping the course of the computer industry from the mid-1950s onward, and still today one hears frequently of the von Neumann architecture or machine.[19] The engineering group gave reality to these paper ideas, and the resulting machine is still to be seen on exhibit in the Smithsonian Institution's Museum of Science and Technology in Washington, D.C. The numerical analysis group produced a number of now classic papers on matrices and on the solution of partial differential equations. These papers served to initiate much continuing research on numerical techniques proper to the modern computer. Perhaps the single most important concept introduced was that of numerical stability, and the dominant theme was the development of stable algorithms. The numerical meteorology group succeeded so well that today the Weather Bureaus of most nations routinely calculate numerically their predictions by means that are derivative from the original ones developed at the Institute for Advanced Study.

In addition to his collaborative activities von Neumann also worked alone on automata theory and on some aspects of neurophysiology. In the former subject he made two major advances: he discovered what he descriptively named self-reproducing automata; and he also initiated work on automata constructed of unreliable components. In the case of self-reproducing automata he died before he had the opportunity to complete all the stages of the investigation; fortunately his notes were in reasonable shape, so that Burks was able to complete all proofs and publish the results.[20]

In this theory von Neumann looked into the fascinating question of how complex a machine must be so that its products are as complex as itself. Clearly most machines are not like this; usually an apparently highly sophisticated machine will be able to carry out at best a fairly simple function. What von Neumann asked and succeeded in discovering was how to design devices whose complexity was sufficiently great so that their products are exact copies of themselves.

This analysis was closely related to his interest in the human nervous system, which resulted in a volume on the relation of the computer to the brain.[21] Unhappily the writing of this book was undertaken after he became seriously ill, and he was simply unable to bring to it all the insights and perceptions that he surely would had he been in full health.

It is also a great pity that von Neumann did not live to see the discovery of the structures of DNA and RNA. He would have been delighted with this work and would in all likelihood have become immersed in some aspects of it himself. He certainly understood how close his ideas on automata theory were to genetics.[22]

Von Neumann's work on unreliable components was the other side of his studies in automata theory. He understood how important it would be to investigate the limits of complexity possible for a physical mechanism such as a computer and wanted to see if there were any such limits. He was able to show by the use of sufficient redundancy that arbitrarily reliable automata could be fabricated out of unreliable components. This subject was subsequently taken up by Winograd and Cowan in a very elegant book that von Neumann would have appreciated heartily.[23] In their work these men elegantly introduced the notion of entropy into the analysis and thus did what von Neumann always felt should be done. In fact he wrote: "Our present treatment of error is unsatisfactory and *ad hoc*. It is the author's conviction, voiced over many years, that error should be treated by thermodynamical methods, and be the subject of thermodynamical theory, as information has been, by the work of L. Szilard and C. E. Shannon."[24]

It would be a shame to close this paper without saying a few personal words about Jancsi, or Janscika, as he was called at home. He was not only a great mathematical virtuoso but also a great human being with a wonderful sense of humor and unsatiable appetites for food, jokes, and mainly for knowledge of all sorts that would relate in some way to his own interests, which were certainly catholic, ranging not only over virtually all mathematics but even over the history of Byzantium. He was constantly looking for new things to do, for new worlds to conquer, and it was tragic that just when he attained to high public office he became terminally ill.

One of the nicest things I know of President Eisenhower was the charming way he treated von Neumann, frequently having him to the White House for technical discussions. The President also saw to it that when Jancsi became so ill he needed to be in the hospital, he had the best suite of rooms in one of the best hospitals and next door to the presidential suite. It was in these rooms that von Neumann's final days were spent. Sadly also his mother, Gitus, died while he was there. She spent every day with him in the hospital and only stopped going when she could no longer live herself.

Sad as was his passing, life was nearly always enjoyable for him. He had a great zest and love of life that never completely left him. His books and his papers will long stand as a fitting memorial to a remarkable mathematician. It is my undoubted view that he did more than anyone else in our times to expand the boundaries of mathematics and to create what we now call the mathematical sciences.[25]

Notes

1. Cf. S. Ulam, "John von Neumann, 1903-1957," *Bulletin of the American Mathematical Society* 64 (1958), Number 3, part 2, pp. 1-49; S. Bochner, "John von Neumann," *National Academy of Sciences Biographical Memoirs* 32 (1958), pp. 438-457, or H. H. Goldstine and E. P. Wigner, "Scientific Work of J. von Neumann," *Science* 125 (1957), pp. 683-784.

2. R. Courant, K. Friedrichs and H. Lewy, Über die partiellen Differenzengleichungen der mathematischen Physik, *Mathematische Annalen* 100 (1928-1929), pp. 32-74.

3. John von Neumann, *Collected Works*, Vol. I, ed. A. H. Taub (New York: Pergamon Press, 1961), pps. 35-56.

4. A. N. Whitehead and B. Russell, *Principia Mathematica*, Cambridge, The University Press, 1910-1913; L. E. J. Brouwer, "Intuitionistische Mengenlehre," *Jahresbericht der deutschen Mathematiker Vereinung* 28 (1920), pp. 203-208; and H. Weyl, "Über die neue Grundlagenkrise der Mathematik," *Mathematische Zeitschrift* 10 (1921), pp. 39-79.

5. D. Hilbert, "Neubegründung der Mathematik, I, *Abhandlungen aus dem mathematischen Seminar der Universität Hamburg* I (1923), pp. 157-175, and "Die logischen Grundlagen der Mathematik," *Mathematische Annalen* 88 (1922), pp. 151-165.

6. John von Neumann, *Collected Works*, Vol. I, pp. 256-300.

7. Gödel's proof appears in K. Gödel, "Über formal unentscheidbare Sätze der Principia Mathematica und verwandter Systeme, I," *Monatshefte für Mathematik und Physik* 28 (1931), pp. 173-198.

8. A. Church, "A Note on the Entscheidungsproblem," *Journal of Symbolic Logic* I, (1936), pp. 40-41, 101-102. A. Turing, "On Computable Numbers, with an Application to the Entscheidungsproblem," *Proceedings of the London Mathematical Society*, Ser. 2, 42 (1937), pp. 230-265 and "Correction," 43 (1937), pp. 544-546.

9. John von Neumann, *Collected Works*, Vol. V, New York, 1963, pp. 288-328.

10. Ibid., pp. 314-315.

11. S. Ulam, "John von Neumann."

12. J. G. Brainerd, J. W. Mauchly, and J. P. Eckert, Jr., *The Use of High-Speed Vacuum Tube Devices for Calculating*, Private Memorandum, Moore School, Autust 1942. It appears

in *Computers and Their Role in the Physical Sciences,* ed. S. Fernbach and A. H. Taub. See H. H. Goldstine, *Early Electronic Computers* (Gordon & Breach Science Pubs., 1970), Chap 3.

13. R. Courant, K. Friedrichs and H. Lewy, "Über die partiellen Differenzengleichungen der Physik."

14. Gauss developed a whole theory and did an extensive calculation to relocate the newly discovered planetoid Ceres, which had disappeared from view during a spell of bad weather in Europe.

15. Remarks from Minutes of Conference held at the Moore School of Electrical Engineering on April 8, 1947 to discuss Patent Matters.

16. Letter, Goldstine to Gillon, September 2, 1944.

17. W. S. McCulloch and W. Pitts, "A Logical Calculus of the Ideas immanent in neuron Activity," *Bulletin of Mathematical Biophysics* 5 (1943), pp. 115-133.

18. *Datamation* reprinted parts of the Burks, Goldstine, and von Neumann paper entitled "Preliminary Discussion of the logical Design of an electronic digital computing Instrument. Part I," June 28, 1946 and 2d ed. September 2, 1947, in Vol. 8 (1962) with an introduction by Paul Armer, parts of which are quoted here.

19. Others were entitled *Planning and Coding of Problems for an electronic computing Instrument. Part II, Vols.* I, II, III, 1947-1948 and were written by von Neumann and myself.

20. John von Neumann, *Theory of Self-Reproducing Automata* (Urbana and London: Univ. of Illinois Press, 1966), ed. and compl. by A. W. Burks.

21. John von Neumann, *The Computer and the Brain* (New Haven: Yale University Press, 1958).

22. Cf., e.g., von Neumann, *Collected Works,* Vol. V, pp. 317-318. This is a paper entitled "The general and logical theory of automata" and was read in 1948.

23. S. Winograd and J. Cowan, *Reliable Computation in the Presence of Noise,* (Cambridge, Mass.: The M.I.T. Press, 1963).

24. John von Neumann, *Collected Works,* Vol. V, p. 329.

25. For more details on von Neumann see H. H. Goldstine, *The Computer from Pascal to von Neumann* (Princeton: Princeton Press, 1972).

Contributors

Donald S. L. Cardwell, Dept. of History of Science and Technology, University of Manchester Institute of Science and Technology, Manchester M60 1QD England

C. W. F. Everitt, W. W. Hansen Laboratories of Physics, Stanford University, Stanford, CA 94305

Stanley Goldberg, School of Natural Science, Hampshire College, Amherst, MA 01002

Herman H. Goldstine, The Institute for Advance Study, Princeton, NJ 08540

Erwin N. Hiebert, Dept. of the History of Science, Harvard University, Cambridge, MA 02138

John N. Howard, Air Force Geophysics Laboratory, Hanscom AFB, MA 01731

Thomas P. Hughes, Dept. of History and Sociology of Science, University of Pennsylvania, Philadelphia, PA 19174

Martin J. Klein, Dept. of History of Science, Yale University, New Haven, CT 06520

William T. Scott, Dept. of Physics, University of Nevada, Reno, NV 89557

Thomas B. Settle, Dept. of History of Science and Technology, Polytechnic Institute of New York, Brooklyn, NY 11201

Linda Wessels, Dept. of History and Philosophy of Science, Indiana University, Bloomington, IN 47401

Richard S. Westfall, Dept. of History and Philosophy of Science, Indiana University, Bloomington, IN 47401

Index

Index

Rutherford Aris is Regents' Professor in the department of chemical engineering and materials science at the University of Minnesota, and H. Ted Davis is professor and head of the same department. Roger H. Stuewer is professor of the history of science and technology at Minnesota. Aris's books include *Chemical Engineering in the University Context* and *The Mathematical Theory of Diffusion of Reaction in Permeable Catalysts*. He and Davis have both published extensively in journals of physics, chemistry, mathematics, and engineering. Stuewer is the author of *The Compton Effect: Turning Point in Physics* and editor of *Historical and Philosophical Perspectives of Science* and *Nuclear Physics in Retrospect*, both published by the University of Minnesota Press.